The Sound of Music FAQ

The Sound of Music FAQ

All That's Left to Know About Maria, the von Trapps, and Our Favorite Things

Barry Monush

APPLAUSE
THEATRE & CINEMA BOOKS

An Imprint of Hal Leonard Corporation

Published in 2015 by Applause Theatre & Cinema Books
An Imprint of Hal Leonard Corporation
7777 West Bluemound Road
Milwaukee, WI 53213

Trade Book Division Editorial Offices
33 Plymouth St., Montclair, NJ 07042

All photos are from the author's collection unless otherwise noted.

The FAQ series was conceived by Robert Rodriguez and developed with Stuart Shea.

Printed in the United States of America

Book design adapted by John J. Flannery

Library of Congress Cataloging-in-Publication Data

Monush, Barry.
    The Sound of music FAQ : all that's left to know about Maria, the von Trapps, and our favorite things / Barry Monush.
        pages cm
    Includes bibliographical references and index.
    ISBN 978-1-4803-6043-3 (pbk.)
1. Sound of music (Motion picture) I. Title. II. Title: Sound of music frequently asked questions.
    PN1997.S63373.M77 2015
    791.43'72–dc23
                            2014046379

www.applausebooks.com

In memory of Hilda Kelemen,
who first "took me to Salzburg" all those years ago,
with much gratitude

Contents

Acknowledgments

One of the unexpected pleasures of working on this book was the amount of help provided by librarians across the country and around the world. Better yet, these people not only were happy to do some research on my behalf, but occasionally shared some personal stories about having seen *The Sound of Music*.

A very special thanks to Christian Strasser ("My Man in Salzburg"), who was an absolute gentleman of infinite patience when it came to providing me with information on locations within and around the Austrian city. If everyone was as helpful and kind as Christian, every project would be a joy to work on.

Personal thanks to Benjamin Barrett for the Perth scoop; Brian Durnin, for getting me "Von Trapped" among other things; John Cerullo; Jim Howard, for the Oregonian touch; and James Sheridan, always knowledgeable, always helpful.

And so, for all those others who opened a window or two:

Roseann Agriesti, Duluth Public Library; Answer Squad at the LeRoy Collins Leon County Public Library; Barcelona Bibliotecari; Biblioteca Nacional de España; Brown County Central Library—Green Bay; Russ Butner, Margaret Herrick Library; Michael Coate, The DigiBits, for his invaluable information on exhibition; Tracey Codd-Lorenz, Expedia CruiseShipCenters; Dennis Copeland, Monterey Public Library; Kim Cowdrey, Onslow County Public Library; Marie Crilley; Jenny Cutting, Auckland Libraries; Jennifer Daugherty, New Hanover County Library; Arpita Deb, Melbourne Library Services; Françoise Devroe, Bibliothèque Charles Janssen; Christene Drewe, State Library of Queensland; Elizabeth Dunn, David M. Rubenstein Rare Book & Manuscript Library; David Elkouby, Hollywood Show; Sandra Enskat, St. Catherines Public Library; Peter Evans, Cardiff Libraries; Karen Falk, the Jim Henson Company Archives; Rosemarie Fischer, Morrin Centre; Jean Fisher, Tacoma Public Library; David Flegg, State Library of Victoria (*TSOM* in Melbourne); Gary Fleetwood; Roberto Gollo, Biblioteca Nazionale Braidense, Milano; Brian Guckian; Megan Halsband, Library of Congress, for *What's on in London?*; Stacey Harris, Port Chester-Rye Brook Public Library; Alex Hartmann, James V. Brown Library; Helsinki Library; Michelle Heng, National Library Singapore; Jeff Herberger; Barbara Heuberger, Managing Director, Salzburger Marionetttheater; Danièle Hoslet, Archives de la Ville de Bruxelles; Judy James, Akron-Summit County Public Library; Jane Jorgenson, Madison Public Library; Peter Kazmierczak, Bournemouth Libraries; Marybeth Keating; Molly Kinney, Mifflin Public Library; Dyron Knick, Roanoke Public Libraries; John and Betty Lowdermilk; Peggy Mainess, Hickory Library; Lyn Martin, Willard Library; Jackie McMillan, Dunedin Public Libraries; David J. McRae and Lucia M. Shannon, Brockton Public Library; Carol Merrill-Mirsky;

Rosanna Mojica, Beaumont Public Library System; Gary Morris; Nottingham Central Library—Local Studies Library; Shirley Nuell, Bristol Library; Roslyn Pachoca, Library of Congress; Rebecca Paller; Janelle Penney, Central Auckland Research Centre; Lora Peppers, Ouachita Parish Public Library; Pat Preblick, ABC; Jody Osicki, Equipe Quaestio Team; Katrin Perner, Panorama Tours; Laura Peters, The Muny; Christine Pu, Headquarters Library; Red Deer Public Library; Patti Renaud, Central Manchester Library—Christchurch; Jeremy Robichaud, Maynard Library; the Rodgers & Hammerstein Organization; Penny Rudkin, Southampton Central Library; Patrick Russ; Dan Sheahan, Fall River Main Library; Adrian Shindler, The British Library; Jane Simmons, Napier Library; Sarah Skrobis; Elaine Stefanko, Osterhout Free Library; Debbie Stewart and Kathryn Kulpa, Great Falls Library; Elisabeth Streit, The Austrian Film Museum; Bridget Summer, 5th Avenue Theatre in Seattle; Dale Taylor and David Govier, Manchester Central Library; Ola Törjas, Svenksa Filminstitutet; Kim Walsh, Sioux City Public Library; Philip Ward, City of Sydney Library Network; Wong Sze Wan, Hong Kong Leisure & Cultural Services; Stella Wentworth, Oxfordshire Libraries; Heather L. Wickert, Newport News Public Library System; Amanda Williams, Live Oak Public Libraries; Trent & Anne Wilson; Tom Wilson; Julie Woosley, Wayne Theatre Alliance; Sara, Sioux City Public Library; Rebecca, Akron-Summit County Public Library; and Paul, Historic Embassy Theatre.

Further thanks must go to all of those who endured my incessant mentioning of *The Sound of Music* in the period I worked on this project.

And of course the deepest gratitude of all to my life partner and fellow *Sound of Music* appreciator, Tom Lynch, for helping me ford various streams. Not sure what I did to deserve such support and companionship, but I'm tempted to say that somewhere in my youth or childhood I must have done something good.

Introduction
The Sound of . . . Asbury Park?

W hen I first saw *The Sound of Music*, I was six years old. And unlike pretty much any other movie I saw in my youth, I actually remember *when* I saw it.

The reason for attending the film was a celebration of my sister Michelle's birthday. Our cousin, Hilda Kelemen, took the two of us, along with our aunt, Olga Monush, to see the film on the Saturday afternoon leading up to my sister's birthday, which made the date October 16, 1965. The theatre was the Paramount, which was directly on the boardwalk in Asbury Park, New Jersey, a town my father would take us to sporadically throughout our childhoods so that we could go on rides (a Ferris wheel that went through the roof of a building!) and buy saltwater taffy. There were no further trips to the Paramount Theatre, however, during my so-called formative years, which was a shame.

I'm not sure when I agreed to see that October showing of *The Sound of Music*, but from my realization years later that this would have been a reserved-seat engagement, I assume Hilda bought four tickets in advance, with the belief that *somebody* in our family would be interested in filling that fourth seat. My mother was not available, because, as I recall, she was waiting for my sister's birthday gift, a piano, to show up at our house in Hazlet; my brother Bryan probably heard the title and instantly vetoed the idea; while my father basically never went to the movies, so that was that. At any rate, I'm sure that when *I* heard the title I was more than happy to be the fourth attendee, and certainly would have been easily swayed by the fact that the movie starred the very same lady who had just played *Mary Poppins*, a recent favorite of mine and of pretty much every other kid at that time.

I remember the Asbury Park theatre being quite full and that the four of us sat in the balcony, something unusual in itself because our local theatre, the Plaza, certainly did not have one, and most of our moviegoing of that era was confined to the Hazlet Drive-In. Therefore, it was clear, even to my six-year-old self, that *The Sound of Music* was something pretty special. How thrilling now to look back and realize that the spellbinding opening of the movie, which has become a part of motion picture folklore, was unfolding before my eyes for the very first time. I had no previous awareness of it whatsoever because it wasn't at that time the first and foremost "go-to" clip to represent the movie, nor had it been parodied *ad nauseam* as it would become in the decades since. Needless to say, the camera drifting dreamily over the Alps and finally zooming in on a woman spinning on a hilltop thoroughly plunged me into the story, which I was able to recall so much of for years after the fact, even though I hadn't the faintest idea in 1965 what Nazis were or what really was at stake for these characters.

Very clearly I remember a group of nuns singing "Maria"; the Trapp children marching downstairs and my surprise to see that the girl I was already watching each week on television play "Penny Robinson" on *Lost in Space* was one of the kids—the one who got swatted gently by her father with her book when she showed up late; the gathering in the bedroom during the rainstorm; a glass structure where a girl and boy sang—my first awareness of a gazebo; and Julie Andrews leaving quietly as the party was going on, which was followed by a first in my life—an intermission! This was yet another indication that I was witnessing something out of the ordinary.

During the break I recall sitting with my relatives in the upstairs lobby, and I assume we were all enjoying the movie and talked about the highlights, because we certainly returned for more. During the second half, one thing that stood out was the father yanking a flag down from the front of the house and tearing it. I had no idea that this was not just representative of the villains in *this* story but a symbol of universal evil that I would later learn about with disbelief and revulsion once all the details were spelled out. Several other "Act 2" moments were seared into my consciousness: the family standing on a strange-looking stage with arches surrounding them as they sang; the incredibly tense moment when they were forced to hide behind gravestones in order not to be caught; and that final image of them climbing over the mountain to safety. I wasn't a child given to crying or emotional outbursts at the movies, but I remember finding this incredibly uplifting and satisfying, or whatever words one might use at six years old.

Admittedly, there were few movies from my childhood that struck me as a waste of my time—I simply loved going to the theatre whenever we did; even those movies that probably weren't very good were still worth a squint. *The Sound of Music*, just like *Mary Poppins*, really stood out to me, however, beyond most of the others. It was so much higher on the pop culture scale that it didn't even show up on television within a scant few years of its release, on one of those many prime-time movie slots, as so many other theatrical features did. But it was always with me, not just in memory, but because that very same piano my mother had waited for on that October afternoon eventually had the songbook for the movie's score sitting on it, which meant that that famous poster image of Julie Andrews prancing on the hill with her carrying bag in one hand and her guitar in the other became an indelible one to me.

As I grew older and began to take a much greater interest in movies, I found out all sorts of things about *The Sound of Music* that confirmed my assumption that it was a cut above so many of the others. I remember looking at a copy of *The World Almanac* in our house that revealed two amazing things about the movie: that it had won the Academy Award for Best Picture of 1965 (in 1965 I had no idea what an Academy Award, or Oscar, was), and that it sat at the very top of the list of the biggest moneymaking movies of all time. Wow! Not bad as cinematic achievements go. Apparently this was the sort of film that was revered and cherished by absolutely *everyone*. Then I *really* started getting deeper and deeper into movies and began buying and receiving all kinds of books about them and reading several others in the library. Imagine my surprise when I started coming across an occasional cutting or snide remark about something I assumed was held sacred.

As the world (both the real one and that of the movies) got more uninhibited and, alas, less graceful in the 1970s, I started to wonder if this cherished part of my past was something that wasn't going to fit anymore in a society that preferred the "R"-rated edginess of *Dirty Harry* or *The Godfather* or *One Flew Over the Cuckoo's Nest* (outstanding movies, each of them, by the way—I am not the sort to draw battle lines between conflicting styles of movies), or other things that seemed tougher, more explicit, and often more bleak. There was also a tremendous negativity among many of my peers toward motion picture musicals, a genre that seemed to be losing its cultural importance during that era; as far as many of them were concerned, musicals were something you enjoyed when you were a child, if at all. While so many others dismissed them as square and irrelevant to what was dominating the airwaves, I couldn't get enough of them. I fervidly sought out anything in which someone sang or danced, be they Fred Astaire musicals or Peter O'Toole croaking his way through the remake of *Goodbye, Mr. Chips*. This genre spoke to me, and my love for it included everything about *The Sound of Music* that made me glad to have joined the caravan down to Asbury Park that day in 1965.

When next I got a chance to see *The Sound of Music*, I was sixteen (dare I say it?, going on seventeen), and it was making its much-heralded premiere on the *ABC Sunday Night Movie*, after staying a full eleven years away from the small screen. This time my mother finally got to see it, for it was only the two of us who watched, as I recall. (My brother hadn't altered his feelings toward musicals, and my sister was otherwise engaged). I was delighted that so much of the movie had stayed in my mind, and now I was fully aware of the Nazi menace. As far as I was concerned, this was still good stuff, despite the fact that the *TV Guide* critic, who had the widest reach of pretty much any film reviewer during that era, took great glee in mocking the hell out of the movie. In a further negative reaction, the only thing that sticks with me about the next day in school was overhearing one jerky guy telling someone that the minute the father came into the living room and started singing with his kids he'd had enough and stopped watching. Okay, so now I got it—*The Sound of Music* was, shall we say? . . . a polarizing movie.

Through the years I would encounter people of all persuasions—those who worshipped *The Sound of Music*, those who called it without hesitation their favorite movie, those who cringed or smirked at the very mention of its name, those who proudly trumpeted having seen it countless times, those who pretended to treat it like camp while knowing every scene and song by heart, and those who took pride in claiming they had avoided it altogether and never had any intention of seeing it. The response was passionate and direct; this was not something that people had to stop and think about as to which movie you were referring to. As with all genuine classics, it was indelible, monumental, and impactful; it was its own unique animal, so to speak.

Fortunately, I ended up in a partnership with someone who loved the movie as much I did. Rodgers and Hammerstein and Julie Andrews were magical names to Tom (who, for the record, had first seen *The Sound of Music* in its reserved-seat engagement at the Bellevue Theatre in Upper Montclair, New Jersey). I was thrilled that we got the opportunity to see it on the big screen together, in 70mm no less, when it was reissued for its twenty-fifth anniversary in August 1990 at the Gotham Theatre in New York. This time, I had matured to the point where the ending actually had me tearing up, as the Trapps made their ascent and "Climb Ev'ry Mountain" was sung chorally over that image. Contrary to what I'd been told and foolishly believed, all of us don't harden with cynicism as the years go by; some of us feel things even more deeply, depending on our experience. As the camera pulled back from that Alpine peak and then rose up to the skies, damn if I didn't feel inspired. For some, the unpredictability of human interaction, the unfairness of life, and the easier choice to go for pessimism over hope cause them to look down on naked displays of emotion on screen with a considerable dose of superiority and disdain. For me, I couldn't simply pretend that I didn't feel what I was feeling, and this movie made me feel.

So, here it was, more than twenty years from *that* date, and my publisher approached me about doing a book on *The Sound of Music*. Again, I based my response on my feelings, and my feelings were extremely positive. Sometimes you're forced to find angles in order to write about something, to dig deep to give something greater importance than it deserves. On the contrary, this was a movie that was *so* mighty a cultural touchstone that I felt the possibilities were endless. I was so excited at the prospect of researching, reading about, and getting even closer to *The Sound of Music* that I found myself working on the project before any contracts were even signed. I didn't mind. It would have been worth the effort regardless, just to find myself submerged in a lost world of 70mm musicals with intermissions, roadshow attractions with reserved-seat tickets, movies that were made first and foremost to attract people to see them *in a cinema* where their glorious presentation could not be duplicated elsewhere; of a film at the very top of the list of the most highly attended motion pictures released in my favorite decade of movies, the sixties.

I discovered that I never once got tired of listening to the Richard Rodgers and Oscar Hammerstein II songs just as I never stopped finding that opening flight over Austria a mesmerizing piece of filmmaking; that my admiration for Julie Andrews rose even higher than it already stood; that I got very good at determining exactly where each sequence in the movie was taking place in conjunction to the layout of Salzburg; and that my reaction to the movie itself was still a strong one.

In some cases when I mentioned working on this project, I was pleasantly surprised to hear certain people I assumed would dismiss it tell me how much they liked it, just as I was disappointed to hear people whom I hoped would champion it, trash it, or at the very least politely smile and keep their opinions to themselves. (This is a musical that all too often those who claim to adore the genre will use as an example of one they do *not* like; perhaps its staggering degree of popularity makes it so for those who prefer their club be more "exclusive").

I cannot help but be more amused than offended by some of the more vitriolic condemnations of the movie at the time, in light of the fact that *The Sound of Music* didn't just overcome those negative dismissals but did something precious few motion pictures have ever done, becoming a genuine phenomenon of worldwide proportions, a cultural touchstone, an instantly recognizable and formidable addition to mass entertainment, that kept speaking to generations to come. This impact has caused me to always question the easy, textbook summarization of the cinematic sixties as one where a lot of "dead wood" of more traditional, old world Hollywood filmmaking was cleared away by films like *Bonnie and Clyde* and *The Graduate,* in part because audiences were so keen to move on and reject them anyway. What a strange and whopping generalization that is. Where precisely does *The Sound of Music* fit into this assessment? We're not talking about something that cleaned up at the turnstiles quickly in 1965 and then faded from the heart and mind in light of the "new Hollywood" represented by the countercultural revolution of the time. No. *The Sound of Music* was kept in cinemas off and on for a staggering 4 ½ year period, which meant that it was playing alongside *Alice's Restaurant* and *Easy Rider* around the time it was withdrawn from circulation in the latter half of 1969. And still doing good business, I might add.

So, the question always arises: what were the elements that made *The Sound of Music* the most popular motion picture of its time and the most widely attended movie musical *ever?* As Tevye would say after much pondering, "I don't know." People have tossed their theories around about the glorious Rodgers and Hammerstein score, the breathtaking Austrian locations, the strong concentration on the importance of family, the magic of Julie Andrews. That's all very nice, and of course all of those things came together to weave a special spell. But I've spent my whole life seeing some absolutely wonderful movies that did middling to fair to awful business, and some pretty terrible ones that made a whole truckload of cash. Who can ever predict the pulse of so many people? I don't think it's possible to come up with the right answers or the right formula. Sometimes a movie just hits at the right time and conquers a wider demographic than anyone could predict. I'm inclined to quote Robert Wise, as he wrote in the introduction to Julia Hirsch's wonderful book on the making of the film: "What makes a motion picture a hit around the world? Specifically, what made *The Sound of Music* the most beloved film of its time? The answer to all these questions is simple—I don't know. I wish I did, because then I could repeat that success."

I do know that I am grateful for the day Mary Martin took a look at the German film of the Trapp Family story, which set the wheels in motion for the Broadway musical that begat this motion picture about which mine is certainly not the first book written. I'm thrilled that *The Sound of Music* was a part of my childhood and my *whole* life. I'm happy that it made movie musicals a desirable property in Hollywood for several years to come. Unlike fatalists who act as if it committed some terrible sin because it unleashed a whole crop of film musicals that couldn't hope to live up to its box office success, you can bet I'm delighted that Robert Morse sang to a mirror in *How to Succeed in Business*, that Julie Andrews and Mary Tyler Moore had to dance to make a hotel elevator run in *Thoroughly Modern Millie*, that Barbra Streisand got on that tugboat in *Funny Girl*, that the streets of London came alive with vendors to serenade Mark Lester in *Oliver!*, that Sammy Davis Jr. grooved with a garage full of hippies in *Sweet Charity*, that Streisand sustained that note as the parade marched on in *Hello, Dolly!*; that Topol stomped joyously while hay rained down in his barn in *Fiddler on the Roof*; and that Joel Grey and Liza Minnelli got orgiastic over currency in *Cabaret*. This is all great stuff I couldn't imagine a world without, iconic moments that have enriched my life as a devout lover of musicals.

You will find people asking whether certain movies are *great* movies; a curious question, as I've never been convinced that there is a general consensus on anything when it comes to assessing a motion picture's value for the ages. Certain films made important strides; opened new doors, advanced storytelling both in a literary sense and by addressing previously untapped subject matter and therefore deserved the high praise bestowed upon them. But there are lists compiled all the time of "great" movies that feature titles I don't imagine would mean a blessed thing to your average moviegoer, or perhaps no longer possess the power or significance that once allowed them to be dubbed important or groundbreaking. When you come right down to it, like anything, it's subjective. If you can't stand to sit through some of the titles on the "best" list you've consulted, then there's nothing says your opinion or feelings are negated by someone else's insistence or belief. Similarly, if you have spent your life watching select movies *over* and *over* again because they move you, fill you with intense pleasure, deeply affect you, or trigger some indescribable, positive reaction within you, then to hell with anyone who tells you this sacred title in your life is inconsequential or not everybody else's idea of great.

Often lists of the great movies or of the great musicals feature *The Sound of Music*, and I am certainly not going to argue with that. The tumultuous effect this movie had on the industry when it was first released; the unexpected amount of money it made; and its continued effect on so many people puts it in a special realm that few others have entered. But that makes it sound like monetary gain trumps quality. Of course it also happens to be a high-quality film made with an incredible degree of know-how in terms of giving audiences an emotional payoff. It has and continues to rankle many, but the number of people who have embraced it way beyond your average motion picture cannot be underestimated. Every time I see the film I find myself engaged and engrossed, thrilled that such a motion picture was not only made so superbly but that it genuinely took the world by storm, giving me the sort of faith in audiences that happens all too seldom these days.

Now I have been given the great opportunity to celebrate something that I believe will never cease being celebrated, and I hope I have done it proud.

The Basic "Do-Re-Mi's" of This Book

I've tried my best to approach this topic from as many different angles as possible, in hopes of avoiding repeating many of the same stories and facts that have been made available elsewhere over the years. A crazy goal, I know, because you can't be *this* famous a movie and not have tales of your creation and legacy be familiar to even the most casual of film fans. However, I'm hoping that I've been able to collect a substantial amount of ephemera and fun facts to keep this engrossing for both the intense *Sound of Music* worshippers and the casual fans.

In order to prevent repeating the title of the movie, *over and over* again, I have taken, on many occasions, to referring to it simply as *TSOM*. If you haven't figured out in a short while that this is the abbreviation of *The Sound of Music*, perhaps you shouldn't be tackling a book of *any* size.

The Sound of Music
FAQ

The Sound of Music Timeline

Key Events in the Trapp Lives, the Stage Musical, and the Motion Picture

1880: Georg Johannes Ritter von Trapp is born in Zara, an Austrian harbor on the Dalmatian Coast (now Zadar in Croatia), on April 4.

1889: Howard Lindsay (book writer of *TSOM*) is born in Waterford, New York, on March 29.

1892: Peggy Wood (Mother Abbess in the film of *TSOM*) is born Mary Margaret Wood in Brooklyn, New York, on February 9.

1893: Russel Crouse (book writer of *TSOM*) is born in Findlay, Ohio, on February 20.

1895: Oscar Greeley Clendenning Hammerstein (Oscar Hammerstein II) is born in New York City on July 12.

1898: Norma Varden (Frau Schmidt in the film of *TSOM*) is born in London on January 20.

1902: Richard Charles Rodgers is born in Queens, New York, on June 28.

1905: Maria Augusta Kutschera is born on a train traveling between Tirol and Vienna, Austria-Hungary, on January 26.
    Richard Haydn (the film's Max Detweiler) is born George Richard Haydon in London on March 10.

1910: Georg von Trapp is given command of the SM U-6 submarine, christened by Agathe Whitehead, the granddaughter of the inventor of the torpedo.

1911: On January 14, Georg Trapp marries Agathe Whitehead (born June 14, 1890) in Fiume at the Austrian Naval Academy Chapel.
    The first Trapp child, Rupert Georg, is born in Pola, Austria-Hungary, on November 11.

1912: *TSOM*'s associate producer and musical supervisor Saul Chaplin is born Saul Elias Kaplan in Brooklyn on February 19.

1913: Anna Lee (the film's Sister Margaretta) is born Joan Boniface Winnifrith in Ightham, Kent, England on January 2.
    The first Trapp daughter, Agathe Johanna Erwina Gobertina Trapp, is born in Pola on March 12.

Mary Martin (the original stage Maria) is born in Weatherford, Texas, on December 1.

1914: Robert Earle Wise (director and producer of the film of *TSOM*) is born in Winchester, Indiana, on September 14.

The third of the captain's children, Maria Franziska Gobertina Trapp, is born in Zell am See, Salzburg, Austria, on September 28.

1915: The captain is awarded the Knight's Cross of the Military Order of Maria Theresa, thereby becoming a baron.

Ben Wright (Herr Zeller in the film of *TSOM*) is born in London on May 5.

Ernest Paul Lehman (screenwriter of *TSOM*) is born in New York City on December 8.

Werner Ritter von Trapp, the fourth Trapp child, is born in Zell am See, Salzburg, Austria, on December 21.

1917: Hedwig Maria Adolphine Gobertina (Trapp child #5), is born in Zell am see, Salzburg, Austria on July 28.

1918: As the war ended, the Austro-Hungarian Empire was divided, with Hungary separating itself from Austria. The Austrian Navy ceased to exist, with Yugoslavia and Italy taking over their ships.

Georg von Trapp ends his military service.

1919: Johanna Karolina von Trapp (sixth child) is born in Zell am See, Salzburg, Austria, on September 7.

1920: Betty Mae (later Portia) Nelson (Sister Berthe in the film of *TSOM*) is born in Brigham City, Utah, on May 27.

1921: The seventh and final Trapp child from the marriage of Georg von Trapp and Agathe Whitehead, Martina, is born in Vienna, Austria, on February 17.

1922: Eleanor Jean Parker (The Baroness in the film of *TSOM*) is born on June 26, in Cederville, OH

Agathe Whitehead Trapp dies of scarlet fever on September 2.

1924: The widowed Captain von Trapp and his children move into a new villa in Aigen, north of Salzburg. This is the home depicted in the stage and movie versions of *The Sound of Music.*

Theodor Meir Bikel (the original Captain von Trapp on stage) is born in Vienna, Austria, on May 2.

1926: Maria Kutschera arrives from the Nonnberg Abbey to tutor the captain's third eldest child, Maria, who is ailing from grippe.

1927: Georg von Trapp (47) and Maria Kutschera (22) are married in the church at Nonnberg Abbey on November 26.

1929: The first of Maria's children with the captain and the eighth of the captain's offspring, Rosmarie, is born in Salzburg on February 8.

Arthur Christopher Orme Plummer (who will simplify his stage name to Christopher Plummer) is born in Toronto, Canada, on December 13.

1930: Margaret Nixon McEathron, who will perform under the name Marni Nixon (Sister Sophia in the film), is born in Altadena, California, on February 22.

1931: The second of Maria and the captain's children, Eleonore (nicknamed "Lorli"), is born in Salzburg on May 14.

1935: Georg von Trapp publishes his memoirs of serving in the Austrian Navy, *Bis zum letzten Flaggenschuss* (*To the Last Salute*), through Anton Pustet Publishing House in Salzburg.

Julia Elizabeth Wells (the future Julie Andrews) is born in Walton-on-Thames, Surrey, England, on October 1.

1936: The Trapp Family Singers begin performing professionally.

1937: The Trapp Family performs at the Mozarteum in Salzburg Music Festival, bringing them their greatest attention to date. They are billed as Chamber Choir Trapp.

1938: The Nazis invade Austria on March 11.

The Trapp Family leave Austria (by train), crossing into Italy. They then journey to England, where they take the ship *American Farmer* to America, departing Southampton on October 7.

1939: The last of the von Trapp offspring and the only one to be born in America, Johannes, arrives on January 17 in Philadelphia, Pennsylvania. This brings the total number of Trapp children up to ten.

The Trapps start their first American concert tour in Easton, Pennsylvania.

Because of the expiration of their visas, the Trapps are required to return to Europe. They begin touring there in Copenhagen, on March 12.

The Trapps return to America in September, taking up residence in Merion, Pennsylvania.

1941: The Trapps settle in Stowe, Vermont, eventually turning their farm into a lodge for guests.

1942: The film's Liesl, Charmian Carr, is born Charmian Anne Farnon in Chicago on December 27.

1943: The first stage musical collaboration of Richard Rodgers and Oscar Hammerstein II, *Oklahoma!*, opens on Broadway at the St. James Theatre on March 31. When it closes on May 29, 1948 after 2,212 performances, it is the longest-running Broadway musical up to that time.

Daniel Truhitte (Rolf Gruber in the film of *TSOM*) is born in Sacramento, California, on September 10.

1944: The first film to credit Robert Wise as director (sharing the billing with Gunther von Fritsch), *The Curse of the Cat People*, premieres in New York City, on March 3, 21 years before the debut of *The Sound of Music*.

1947: Georg von Trapp dies of lung cancer on May 30 in Stowe, Vermont.

1948: The Trapp Family officially becomes U.S. citizens.

1949: Maria von Trapp's account of her life and family, *The Story of the Trapp Family Singers*, is published by Lippincott.

Heather Menzies (Louisa in the film of *TSOM*) is born in Toronto, Canada, on December 3.

1950: Nicholas Hammond (Friedrich in the film of *TSOM*) is born in Washington, DC, on May 15.

Duane Chase (Kurt in the film of *TSOM*) is born in Los Angeles on December 12.

1952: Angela Margaret Cartwright (Brigitta in the film of *TSOM*) is born in Cheshire, England, on September 9.

Maria's second book, *Yesterday, Today and Forever: The Religious Life of a Remarkable Family*, is published by Lippincott.

1955: Maria's third book, *Around the Year with the Trapp Family*, is published by Pantheon.

1956: The Trapp Family Singers perform their last concert, in Concord, New Hampshire, on January 26.

Debbie (Debra) Turner (Marta in the film of *TSOM*) is born in Arcadia, California, on September 5.

The first movie based on the life of the Trapp Family, *Die Trapp-Familie*, starring Ruth Leuwirk as Maria and Hans Holt as Baron von Trapp, and directed by Wolfgang Liebeneiner, opens in West Germany on October 6.

1957: Mary Martin sees *Die Trapp-Familie* and thinks it could be turned into a play. Howard Lindsay and Russel Crouse agree to adapt the story for the stage, and Rodgers and Hammerstein will write songs once they have gotten their current show, *Flower Drum Song*, up and running.

1958: Christopher Plummer is seen in his first motion picture, *Stage Struck*, costarring Henry Fonda and Susan Strasberg, and directed by Sidney Lumet. It opens on April 22.

Kym Karath (Gretl in the film of *TSOM*), the youngest cast member, is born Anthea Kimberly Karath in Los Angeles on August 4.

The second movie based on the Trapp story, *Die Trapp-Familie in Amerika*, with Ruth Leuwirk and Hans Holt returning to their roles and Wolfgang Liebeneiner again directing, opens in West Germany on October 17.

1959: The new Rodgers & Hammerstein musical, starring Mary Martin, with Theodore Bikel, *The Sound of Music*, opens on Broadway at the Lunt-Fontanne Theatre on November 16, after five preview performances. The advance sales are tremendous, and it is an instant hit.

Maria Augusta Trapp publishes her fourth book (written with Ruth T. Murdoch), *A Family on Wheels: Further Adventures of the Trapp Family Singers*, through Lippincott.

1960: On Sunday, April 24, at the 14th Annual Tony Award ceremony held at the Astor Hotel Grand Ballroom in New York, *The Sound of Music* wins the Tony Award for Best Musical (in a tie with *Fiorello!*). Additional Tonys for *TSOM* are won by Mary Martin, Patricia Neway (as Mother Abbess), Scenic Designer Oliver Smith, and Conductor/Musical Director Frederick Dvonch. (The presenters for that evening's ceremony include the film version's Captain von Trapp, Christopher Plummer).

July: 20th Century-Fox purchases the movie rights to *TSOM* for a record $1,250,000, giving the Broadway show a 100 percent profit on its $400,000 investment. Rodgers and Hammerstein, Lindsay and Crouse, and Maria Trapp are entitled to the 60 percent author share, which after the deduction of 10 percent commissions, comes to $675,000. The production is to receive 10 percent of the gross in excess of $12,500,000. The property is also to return to the producers after twelve years, and the film is not to be released before 1964.

Oscar Hammerstein II dies at his home in Doylestown, Pennsylvania, on August 23. *TSOM* is his last show, and "Edelweiss" the last song he ever wrote.

1961: Having bought the rights to the two German films, 20th Century-Fox edits them into one English-dubbed feature and releases it as *The Trapp Family* in Los Angeles on March 22.

The Sound of Music premieres in the West End at the Palace Theatre on May 18. Jean Bayless stars as Maria and Roger Dann as the captain. This version proves even more popular than the Broadway production.

The Trapp Family is released in the New York metropolitan area on a double bill with the Elvis Presley film *Wild in the Country*, on August 30.

1962: *The Sound of Music* moves to the Mark Hellinger Theatre for its final seven months; starting November 6.

1963: *The Sound of Music* closes on Broadway on June 15. It has run 1,443 performances, making it, at the time, the eleventh-longest-running show in Broadway history and the fourth-longest-running musical.

Associate producer Saul Chaplin and writer Ernest Lehman begin scouting locations in Salzburg for the movie of *The Sound of Music.*

1964: *The Sound of Music* commences shooting under the direction of Robert Wise at 20th Century-Fox Studios in Los Angeles on Thursday, March 26.

The cast and crew of *TSOM* begin shooting exteriors in Salzburg, Austria, on April 23. They remain on location until July 3.

The company resumes shooting at the Fox Studios on July 6.

Principal photography on *TSOM* finishes at Fox on August 21.

Julie Andrews's first on-screen role, in Walt Disney's *Mary Poppins*, debuts on August 26 in Hollywood at Grauman's Chinese Theatre.

1965: The gala premiere of *The Sound of Music* takes place on March 2 at the Rivoli Theatre in New York. That same day the soundtrack album first appears in record stores. The following day the movie's official, reserved-seat engagement begins.

The Sound of Music has its gala West Coast premiere in Beverly Hills at the Fox Wilshire Theatre on March 10.

The Sound of Music has its first overseas, reserved-seat opening, at the Dominion Theatre in London on March 29th. It will run at this theatre longer than any of its other bookings, for 170 weeks (more than three years).

Julie Andrews wins the Academy Award for Best Actress of 1964 for her performance in *Mary Poppins*. The ceremony takes place on April 5.

TSOM soundtrack hits the top of the British LP charts for the first time, on June 5. It will remain there until August 7 and then return on several occasions over the next several years.

The soundtrack for *TSOM* becomes the #1 best-selling LP in America for two weeks in a row: November 13 and 20.

1966: The Academy Award nominations for 1965 are announced on February 21. *TSOM* receives ten nominations (tying with MGM's epic *Doctor Zhivago*): Picture, Actress (Julie Andrews), Supporting Actress (Peggy Wood), Director, Costume Design—Color, Cinematography—Color, Art Direction-Set Decoration—Color, Film Editing, Sound Recording, and Scoring of Music—Adaptation or Treatment.

The 38th Annual Academy Awards are held at the Santa Monica Civic Auditorium on Monday, April 18, 1966. *TSOM* ends up winning five out of the ten Oscars for which it was nominated: Best Sound, Best Scoring of Music, Best Film Editing, Best Director, and, most significantly, Best Picture of the Year.

As *TSOM* is wrapping up its road show engagements, the movie finally starts playing in reserved performances, which allow customers to buy tickets ahead to reserve an individual showing rather than individual seats. December 21.

1967: The West End run of *The Sound of Music* at the Palace Theatre ends on January 14, totaling 2,385 performances. At the time it held the record for the longest London run of an American musical.

On June 21, *TSOM* becomes a general admission attraction for the first time since its premiere, more than two years and three months earlier.

On November 15, *TSOM* is released into another batch of theatres under the general admission policy.

On December 20; *TSOM* receives a two-week-long holiday booking in many areas.

1968: On June 29, *TSOM* finally ends its 170-week run (totaling three years and three months) at the Dominion Theatre in London, the house to show the movie longer than any other venue.

On August 14, *TSOM* returns again for another series of general admission bookings.

1969: After four and a half years of bookings, *The Sound of Music* ends its run in movie theatres. It is officially withdrawn by 20th Century-Fox on December 8. It has become the highest-grossing motion picture in history.

1972: Maria von Trapp's fifth and final book about her life, *Maria*, is published.

1973: *TSOM* returns to movie theatres for the first time since 1969, premiering on the same days it originally debuted in 1965: March 2 in New York and March 10 in Los Angeles.

1976: ABC broadcasts *The Sound of Music* on television for the first time, on Sunday, February 29, in a three-hour, 25-minute time slot. It draws a total-household rating of 33.6 and a 49 share of the television audience.

1978: Peggy Wood ("Mother Abbess") dies in Stamford, Connecticut, on March 18.

1979: On Sunday, February 25, *The Sound of Music* makes the first of twenty appearances on NBC over the course of the next twenty-one years.

TSOM makes its home video debut in the VHS format on Magnetic Video in March.

Richard Rodgers dies at his home in New York City on December 30.

1985: Richard Haydn ("Max Detweiler") dies in Los Angeles on April 25.

1987: Maria von Trapp dies of heart failure at the age of eighty-two, in Morrisville, Vermont, on March 28. She is buried in the family cemetery on the property of their lodge.

1990: Twenty-fifth anniversary 70mm showings of *TSOM* take place in New York and Los Angeles starting on August 24, prior to the film's latest premiere on video.

1991: An animated television series, *Torappu ikka monogatari* (*The Trapp Family Story*), based on the lives of the Trapp Family, debuts on the Fuji Television Network on January 13.

1998: The American Film Institute announces its choice for the 100 Greatest American Movies of All Time. *TSOM* is ranked #55 on the list.

TSOM receives its first Broadway revival, opening at the Martin Beck Theatre on March 12, with Rebecca Luker and Michael Siberry in the leads. It will run for 533 performances, closing February 6, 1999.

The surviving Trapp children are awarded the Golden Decoration of Honor from Salzburg; the seven movie children are presented with the Mozart Medalon; December 2.

1999: The first "Sing-a-long-a" (called "Sing-a-long" in America) version of *TSOM* takes place in London starting on August 13.

2000: Charmian Carr publishes her memoir and calls it *Forever Liesl.*

2001: Portia Nelson ("Sister Berthe") dies in New York City on March 6.

2004: Anna Lee ("Sister Margaretta") dies in Beverly Hills on May 14.

2005: Screenwriter Ernest Lehman dies in Los Angeles on July 2.

Director Robert Wise dies of heart failure at the UCLA Medical Center in Los Angeles on September 14.

2006: The American Film Institute announces its choices for the 25 Greatest Movie Musicals of All Time. *TSOM* is ranked #4 on the list.

2010: Julie Andrews and Christopher Plummer, along with all seven of the actors who played the Trapp children, are reunited for a well-publicized episode of *The Oprah Winfrey Show*, on October 28.

2013: NBC presents *The Sound of Music Live!*, which, as the title states, is a live presentation of the Rodgers and Hammerstein stage musical; Carrie Underwood and Stephen Moyer are the stars. It airs to large ratings on December 5.

Eleanor Parker ("The Baroness") dies in Palm Springs, California, on December 9.

The Trapp Connection

How Maria's Autobiography Influenced the Musical

While there wouldn't have been *The Sound of Music* without the existence of Maria von Trapp and her family, what really opened their story up to the world and proved the catalyst for the subsequent screen, stage, and then (again) screen adaptations was Maria's first book, *The Story of the Trapp Family Singers*.

The 309-page bio was published by Lippincott of Philadelphia and released January 28, 1949. Although the 1956 German film, *Die Trapp-Familie*, and its follow-up, *Die Trapp-Familie in Amerika* (1958), borrowed much of their plotlines from this book, with the customary dramatic license applied here and there, it was not specifically credited on screen. Similarly, the Broadway playbill for *TSOM* bears no mention of the book, instead opting for "Based on the story of the Trapp Family Singers," while the movie gives special mention to George Hurdalek for the screenplay he wrote for *Die Trapp-Familie*.

Here is a chapter-by-chapter rundown of what Maria chose to include from her life story and which instances were dramatized on stage and screen.

Part One

Chapter 1: "Just Loaned"

The book commences with Maria summoned to see the Reverend Mother while teaching a class at the abbey. Although a similar schoolroom scene is included in the German film, the stage musical chose only to make a passing mention of the educator side of Maria's life, when she is told by the Trapp housekeeper that she will be instructing the children in a classroom setting. The film, however, eliminates all such references. The book explains that she had just finished attending the State Teacher's College for Progressive Education in Vienna and was required to get her master of education degree before she officially entered the novitiate of the Holy Order of St. Benedict.

Maria admits to being a handful at Nonnberg Abbey in Salzburg, mentioning inappropriate whistling, sliding down bannisters, and racing on staircases. Oscar Hammerstein's lyrics for "Maria" would incorporate the first ("and whistles on the stair"), while the German film would make room for the bannister sliding

The original Trapp lodge in Stowe, Vermont, as it appeared on a postcard.

and the musical movie would show Julie Andrews racing past her fellow nuns before realizing the error of her actions. (Andrews had already done her share of bannister sliding—albeit in the opposite direction—in *Mary Poppins*.)

The Mother Abbess explains that doctors believe Maria should be sent away to have normal exercise for an eight-month period, having developed headaches because of the abrupt change from mountain climbing to a cloistered existence. Needless to say, Maria's health was never made an issue in Howard Lindsay and Russel Crouse's book for the musical, or the film script.

Likewise, the reason she is assigned to the Trapp Family is not simply to act as governess for all seven children, but more specifically to tutor Captain von Trapp's second daughter, Maria. The real name of this particular child was reason enough for Lindsay and Crouse to come up with new names in the musical for *all* of the children; in order to dispense with the constant confusion of having *two* characters referred to by the same name on stage, this child becoming (approximately) Louisa.

Maria describes her bus trip to the Trapp villa in Aigen, twenty minutes from Salzburg, as well as leaving the abbey carrying all her possessions (mostly books) in a leather satchel and her guitar in hand. This is very much replicated in the 1965 film, during the "I Have Confidence" song, although no indication is ever given that Maria is loaded down with reading material.

The butler who answers the door and lets Maria into the Trapp house was named Hanz, although the German film saw fit to change it to "Franz," thereby prompting Lindsay and Crouse to follow suit. The red-white-red Austrian flag with the crest in the center as described in the book *does* hang inside the Trapp

An original ad for one of the Trapp Family Singers' concert tours of the early 1950s.

villa in the 1956 German film and has its place in the stage version, but is not in evidence in the 1965 movie musical when Maria first enters. (It does appear later, as a "statement" of sorts, at the party the captain throws for Elsa.)

The captain summoning his children by using a brass whistle was very much a reality, and not made up for the musical, although Maria describes the Trapp offspring as all being dressed in *blue* sailor suits at her first encounter with them, not the white ones seen on stage and in the '65 film. The intention was not so much a militaristic ritual as the whistle being convenient for getting the youngsters' attention when they were too far away for calling. Being ill with the grippe, Maria (the child) is the one missing from the initial Trapp children lineup in Maria's telling of the story, not the equivalent Brigitta, as in the musical.

Although Maria von Trapp does not focus too clearly on dates in her book, she points out that the captain's wife has been dead four years at the time of her arrival, a passage of time not specified in the musical, and that she was the twenty-sixth in a long line of nurses (the musical whittles this number down to twelve), governesses, and teachers (the names of just two of her predecessors are mentioned in passing in the '65 film script). The actual housekeeper had a title, being called Baroness Matilda, thereby prompting another change in the musical, which has stripped her of any suggestion of nobility and made her simply "Frau Schmidt."

Chapter 2: "Glories of the Past"

Maria mentions there being twenty people total in the Trapp household, including other servants mentioned by name (Resi, the chief cook; Mariandl, the kitchen maid; Poldi and Lisi, the housemaids; and Pepi, the gardener). Not surprisingly, these are all dispensed with in the musical, there being a bit part on stage only for a maid named Ursula, and no emphasis made of anyone other than Frau Schmidt, Franz, and an unnamed servant (presumably that same Ursula) on staff in the '65 movie.

Baroness Matilda gives Maria (and therefore the reader) the background on the captain: fighting at the Chinese Boxer Rebellion; taking command of one of the first submarines of the Austrian Navy; how the young lady who christened his sub was the daughter of the inventor of the torpedo, Robert Whitehead (Maria seems resistant to writing the name of Captain von Trapp's first wife; it was Agathe); and how the captain ended up marrying this girl. She further explains that the captain and Agathe's home was in Pola, site of the Austrian Navy Yard, overlooking the sea; how they were forced to evacuate because of the war (WWI); and how the captain's wife lived with her mother as her husband went off to serve his country. The captain's title of baron was an offshoot of him being awarded the Maria Theresa Cross (or Maria-Theresien-Thaler, if you will) for valor during the war, which automatically gave him the baronetcy honor. (The German Trapp films had him being referred to as "Baron," but the musical stuck with the less lofty-sounding "Captain"). Because Austria suffered defeat, the country was stripped of its seacoast, thereby rendering naval service no longer necessary and putting the captain out of a job. Scarlet fever eventually claimed his wife. Apart from the Mother Abbess explaining to Maria that her employer is a widower and a retired sea captain as well as mentioning the Maria Theresa medal, none of this other information was given in the musical. Lindsay and Crouse, and subsequently Ernest Lehman, left it up to audiences to figure out geographically and historically how someone had served in the navy for a country that, during the course of the events unfolding in the show, was landlocked.

Also mentioned is the fact that the family moved into the Trapp villa, at which Maria arrived and in which the musical took place, *after* the mother had passed away. Maria is also told in this chapter that the captain expects to marry Princess Yvonne. This character became Elsa Schraeder in *The Sound of Music* and is referred to in the film's credits as "the Baroness."

Chapter 3: "The Baron Doesn't Want It . . ."

It is here that the musical portion of the story begins, as teacher Maria allows the sickly child Maria to try playing the violin in place of the girl's desire to practice the piano, as she had done before getting ill. During a rainy afternoon, the children hear Maria playing her guitar, and she encourages them to sing with her. They don't know any songs except "Silent Night." In time, Maria has taught them enough that they have a repertory of eight old songs and six new ones. ("Silent Night/Stille Nacht, heilige Nacht" is performed by the children in the 1956 German film.)

The musical dispensed with the fact that the Trapp children became adept at playing musical instruments in addition to singing. (The German films *do* show them playing their instruments). The rainy weather, however, was retained for *TSOM*, being given the more dramatic status of a nighttime storm, allowing Maria to sing "The Lonely Goatherd" to her young charges on stage and "My Favorite Things" on screen.

Chapter 4: "An Austrian Christmas"

The captain comes in on Maria and the children singing "In Dulci Jubilo" and is so pleased with what he hears that he ends up accompanying them on his violin, which he had not played in years.

For the musical, the captain overheard his offspring harmonizing on "The Sound of Music," which he finished singing with them. For the film, he subsequently joined daughter Liesl on guitar for "Edelweiss," which had been saved for Act 2 in the show. Clearly it was a wise choice to change instruments for the musical, as enough critics complained that it felt like an old-fashioned operetta anyway. A guitar was something audiences of the 1960s could more easily relate to. If nothing else, the movie's Captain von Trapp (like Maria) now had something in common with three of the Beatles.

Chapter 5: "God's Will Hath No Why"

The concept of "the will of God" dictating the way was retained for the musical in several bits of dialogue. It was preached to Maria, not by the Mother Abbess, as was more dramatically convenient for the show, but by a priest. Princess Yvonne (whom the children refer to as "Aunt Yvonne") almost instantly upon meeting Maria tells her that it is quite clear that the captain is in love with his children's new governess, but that she intends to marry him nevertheless. In the stage musical, it is one of the children, Brigitta, who first brings this up to Maria. In the '65 script revisions, the revelation goes back again to the baroness/princess, but further on in the storyline. When the real-life Maria confronted the captain about her burgeoning feelings, she told him she would check with the Mistress of Novices back at Nonnberg to get her blessing (once again leaving the Mother Abbess out of the equation). She gives the date of their marriage as November 26, 1927, which, of course, predates the time chosen for the musical by more than a decade. (This is also the very first time that Maria von Trapp gives her readers any sort of exact date in which to place the events.)

It was the playscript's idea to jump the story ahead in time, having Maria come into the Trapps' lives on the eve of the Anschluss; this meant that many of the events that happened in the interim (between the years 1927 and 1938) would be removed from the musical adaptation. In the book, the princess simply fades away from the storyline, rather than being portrayed as putting up any kind of fight for the captain. The changed timeline for the stage musical meant that part of her reason for separating with the captain involved her complacency toward the threatening political situation (as stated in the song "No Way to Stop It"), something that was removed for the '65 film adaptation.

Chapter 6: "Feasts in a Family"

Mostly a chapter creating a feeling of life with the Trapps, with various holidays described, especially Easter. It is also brought up that the captain had only just joined the church a year before Maria arrived at the villa, but has become religious enough to insist that his children learn the scriptures. It is also specified here that the family worked on one new number every evening, with Maria singing tenor, the captain bass.

While it was important to show the religious world Maria came from, it was not deemed necessary to keep the theological emphasis throughout the musical, no doubt a wise choice in expanding its appeal. How the captain raised his children or how they felt about the Catholic Church was never addressed on stage or screen.

The entire Trapp family, along with their musical director, Father Wasner, pose before their touring bus in San Francisco in 1946.

Chapter 7: "A Festival Summer and a Baby"

Maria relates how hosting the captain's mooching relatives during the Salzburg Music Festival takes its toll on them all. In this chapter she gives birth to her first child with the captain, Rosmarie, born in 1929. This brings *die Kinder* count up to eight. Of course, Rosmarie and both subsequent children born to Maria and the captain, Eleonore and Johannes, were dropped from the musical's storyline. (Although the two girls were cut from the German films as well, one of their names was kept, substituting "Rosmarie" for the character pertaining to Johanna. The scripters kept the baby for reasons of cuteness.)

Chapter 8: "Uncle Peter and His Handbook"

The family takes a vacation at the town where the captain (and his first wife) once lived and was stationed, Pola, now part of Italy. There is also more background given here about the captain's early life, including how he was born in Zara, halfway down the Dalmatian Coast, the son of a naval officer.

Chapter 9: "An Operation, a Turtle, and a Long-Distance Call"

The second of the three children left out of the musical, Eleonore (nicknamed "Lorli"), is born two years after Rosmarie. Around this time, the Trapps found

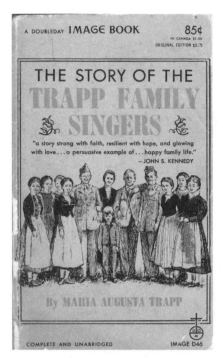

A DOUBLEDAY IMAGE BOOK   85¢
IN CANADA $1.00
ORIGINAL EDITION $3.75

THE STORY OF THE
TRAPP FAMILY
SINGERS

"a story strong with faith, resilient with hope, and glowing with love...a persuasive example of...happy family life."
—JOHN S. KENNEDY

By MARIA AUGUSTA TRAPP

COMPLETE AND UNABRIDGED   IMAGE D46

A 1955 Doubleday paperback of Maria Augusta Trapp's book.

out that the bank that held their money had collapsed and they were facing ruin.

Although their financial state played a key part in the Trapps' decision to sing professionally (and remained in the 1956 German film), there was enough drama in the Nazi invasion as far as the musical was concerned, and no mention was ever made of monetary woes.

Chapter 10: "Aren't We Lucky!"

Forced to dismiss six of the eight servants (pretty much bringing them down to the number in the musical), give up the car, and close parts of the house, the Trapps then come up with the idea of renting rooms to students of the Catholic University. The captain's office is converted to a chapel, with permission from the archbishop. Around this time their oldest child, Rupert (the Friedrich equivalent in the musical), went off to Innsbruck to study premed. During Easter of 1935, Father Wasner comes to say mass and hears the Trapps sing. He is so impressed he insists they take their music more seriously, hence the birth of the Trapp Family Singers.

The German film covered this part of the story, but there was no room in the musical to deal with how the Trapp villa became the Trapp Hotel. Also, a car would play an important part in their escape plan in the 1965 screenplay, so there was no way that the cinematic version of the family would be able to part with that.

This chapter first introduces the reader to the single most important aspect of the story that was eliminated altogether from *The Sound of Music*, Father Wasner. Wasner (whom Maria never refers to by his first name; it was Franz) was so crucial a part of the family's success that he would join them in America when they escaped from their homeland. His closest counterpart in the Lindsay-Crouse script is cynical impresario Max Detweiler, who serves as the family's manager and booker, but in no way instructs them on their musical selections, as did Father Wasner. This was no doubt another conscious decision to reduce the amount of religion in the musical.

Chapter 11: "Never Again"

Maria mentions having previously sung "in one of those mountain meadows overlooking the valley." This description perfectly fits the location used for the unforgettable opening in the 1965 musical film.

In August 1936, professional opera singer Lotte Lehmann, inquiring about renting the house, is enchanted by the Trapp voices and is the one who enters them in a music festival concert for group singing. Although the Trapps are certain they are bombing, they end up winning first prize. It is made clear here that the captain isn't pleased with the idea of his family being on stage, an objection carried over into the musical's script. (It is also noted that unlike the musical, Captain von Trapp does *not* at any point perform on stage with his family.) With no equivalent of Ms. Lehmann in the stage play, it is left up to Max to be the one to enter the Trapps in the singing competition.

Chapter 12: "From Hobby to Profession"

The Nonnberg Abbey again enters the picture, as Maria takes daughter Rosmarie there for schooling. The Trapps rise in fame as they sing on the radio, at an important state affair for foreign dignitaries, and at public concerts at the Kleinen Musikvereinssaal, on the same day Marian Anderson performs. With so many offers pouring in, the Trapps end up doing a concert tour of Europe.

This sort of notoriety and multiple performances are nowhere in evidence in the musical, which instead builds up to a single concert that the Trapps use to execute their escape from the Nazis. Because they flee directly after their performance, the musical gives the impression that the Trapps "sang and ran," so to speak, being heard in Austria on stage one time only.

Chapter 13: "And the Lord Said to Abram . . ."

On March 11, 1938, Austria is invaded by Germany. The musical has this happen while Maria and the captain are on their honeymoon, when, as noted, their marriage took place more than a decade prior.

As the Nazis marched into Salzburg to declare their new rule, the order was given for all the bells in the city to be rung. This incident was most effectively dramatized in the '65 film, by having the joyous sound of the Trapps' wedding bells meld into the somber pealing of a single bell as a line of storm troopers march into the Residenzplatz.

The Trapp butler, Hans, tells his employers that he has been "a member of the (Nazi) party" for some time. Although he stays on as their servant, the family no longer trusts him. In the 1956 German film, Franz/Hans shows a heroic side, despite his allegiance to the SS, lying to allow the family to make their escape. The stage musical has Liesl gasp at the realization that the family servant is now the enemy, although he remains in their employ. In the '65 film, there is a glimpse of Franz at the window, well aware of the captain and his family silently attempting to escape. Because Herr Zeller and his troops show up moments later, one is left to contemplate whether or not it was the Trapp servant who spilled the beans.

The Trapps are told that Adolf Hitler will be visiting and expects to see the Nazi flag flying on every house. The captain insists he cannot afford one, is given one by the authorities, but says he will *not* put it up. In the '65 film, the flag is placed in front of the Trapp villa against their wishes by the musical's chief villain, Herr Zeller, and his flunkies. In one of the movie's great rousing moments, the captain yanks it down and tears it apart.

The Trapp child Eleonore makes her own negative statement toward the Nazis when she creates a stir by refusing to sing their anthem in school. Although Liesl expresses revulsion toward Rolf's conversion to Nazism, the musical kept the Trapp kids pretty quiet where their political feelings were concerned and left that to the adults.

We are informed in this chapter that Maria has already lost two children since Eleonore's birth and is worried that she will do so with her latest pregnancy. The captain sensibly suggests an abortion, which would make perfect sense for a struggling family already feeding the mouths of nine children, but Maria is incensed, reminding him that they are Catholics. In the musical, eliminating the three Trapp kids borne by Maria herself meant there needn't be any thought of discussing just why a family with their share of hardships couldn't see fit to practice some degree of birth control, so this controversial issue remained in the background.

The captain receives an offer from Germany to take command of one of their new submarines and help establish naval bases in the Adriatic and Mediterranean seas. He is initially excited because of the advanced technology; but his conscience gets the better of him, and he realizes he must refuse. In the stage musical, his ambivalence toward this decision does arise, as he pleads with Maria to help him come to terms with what he must do. In the '65 screen version, the captain is much less torn, being dismissive of the offer and knowing instantly that the family must high-tail it out of Austria or face persecution.

It is mentioned that Rupert has graduated from medical school and has received his own offer, to work in a Vienna hospital. Because the musical has the Rupert equivalent Friedrich being all of thirteen years of age, this conflict played no part in the drama.

The Trapps are chosen to sing at Hitler's birthday party, and it is this particular offer that accelerates their flight from Austria. The musical saw fit to tie their departure to the Salzburg music festival, so that there would be some musical-related tension in the sequence.

Part 2

Chapter 1: "On the 'American Farmer'"

At this point, Maria's true-life account of her family and *The Sound of Music* pretty much part company, as the book now details the Trapp Family's life in America and their growing success as concert artists. This would be dramatized on screen in the 1958 German movie "sequel," *Die Trapp-Familie in Amerika.*

One point that does arise in this chapter in connection with the musical is the means by which the Trapps fled from Austria. Since there was a train station within walking distance of their villa, they merely boarded it and journeyed to Italy. Their timing was beyond lucky. The very next day, the border was closed and all citizens of Austria were forbidden to leave the country.

An escape over the mountains was simply too dramatically satisfying for Lindsay and Crouse to resist, so the suspense-free train ride was disposed of in favor of seeing the family begin their ascent on stage as "Climb Ev'ry Mountain" was sung by the chorus, and the even more effective sight of them climbing an actual mountain and venturing into neutral Switzerland to freedom in the '65 movie. To justify this exhausting trek, the musical had the border being closed *before* their planned escape.

Geographically, the musical was taking great dramatic license. The climb from the mountains near Salzburg would have taken the Trapps directly into the even greater dangers of Germany, *not* Switzerland. The family would have to have headed some 321 km southwest toward Bludenz in order to cross into Switzerland. In fact, the final shot in the '65 movie was done at Ahornbüchsenkopf in Bavaria, not far from Hitler's "Eagle's Nest" mountain retreat.

The Trapps were able to stay in Italy until the captain's back pay was available and they could journey to London to sail to the United States. In October 1938, they boarded the *American Farmer*, a small boat for seventy passengers, scheduled for an eleven-day journey. This happened some six weeks after they landed in South Tirol, Italy, following their flight from Austria. On board the boat to America, Maria started learning English.

Although the remainder of the book is not pertinent to the events in *TSOM*, it does offer answers to many questions fans of the musical might have had regarding the fate of the Trapps.

Chapter 2: "The First Ten Years Are the Hardest"

The Trapps actually had a reason to go to America and the help of someone in making sure they got there. Charlie Wagner offered them a contract for fourteen concerts in America starting in the autumn of 1938 through March 1939.

When the Trapp Family arrived in New York, they took up residence at the Hotel Wellington at 7th Avenue and 55th Street. This establishment was nine blocks up and one block east of the theatre (then the Globe, a cinema; later the Lunt-Fontanne), where *The Sound of Music* would debut on stage twenty-one years later, and five blocks north of the back of the Rivoli Theatre where the movie of *The Sound of Music* would open another twenty-six years down the line. The Wellington and the Lunt-Fontanne are still there; the Rivoli is not.

Chapter 3: "Getting Settled"

The Trapps gave their first U.S. concert at Lafayette College in Easton, Pennsylvania, in October 1938. Their first important Town Hall concert in Manhattan took place that year as well.

Chapter 4: "Barbara"

The tenth and final Trapp child, Johannes, is born in Philadelphia in January 1939.

Chapter 5: "What Next?"

When their visas expire, the Trapps are obliged to leave the United States by March 4, 1939. They sail to Europe on the *Normandie*, having been booked to perform in Copenhagen.

Chapter 6: "In Sight of the Statue of Liberty"

Despite the impression the musical gives that the Trapps had no intention of returning to Austria while the Nazis were in power, the women of the family did, in fact, drop by in July 1939, observing the many changes since they had left. When the war began in September 1939, their concerts were cancelled, prompting them to return again to America on visitors visas. Only their eldest son, Rupert, had an immigration visa.

Because of Maria's enthusiasm over returning to the States, a statement she made to immigration officials about her intention to *never* leave resulted in the family being detained for a considerable amount of time at Ellis Island. Their U.S. friends intervened, approaching their congressmen about clearing up the misunderstanding, allowing them to finally go. A version of this incident did become the dramatic climax of the original German film of the story.

This printing of Maria's book, with its tie-in movie cover, arrived late into the movie's theatrical run, first appearing in April 1968.

Chapter 7: "Learning New Ways"

In this chapter, Maria admits that they were not always successful in their U.S. engagements, often playing to poor attendance.

Chapter 8: "The Miracle"

Their new American booking agent, Frederick Schang, signs them up despite telling Maria that their act lacks "sex appeal," that he isn't crazy about their choice of music, or their demeanor or their staging. Other than that . . . apparently, he found *something* to like. (This became part of the plotline of the 1958 German movie sequel to their story).

Chapter 9: "Merion"

The Trapp Family takes up residence at 262 Merion Road in Merion, Pennsylvania. At this point they put together a handicraft exhibit to make further money.

Chapter 10: "The Fly"

The title of the chapter is a reference to how Maria won over an audience when a fly flew in her mouth during a performance, managing to milk a good degree of humor out of the incident, thereby adding some welcome levity to a customarily staid act.

Frederick Schang does get his wish to see the Trapps vary their act, adding American songs to the program including "Sweet Honey-Suckling Bees," "Early One Morning," and "Just as the Tide Is Flowing."

It is in this chapter that the basic format of the typical Trapp Family concert is described, consisting of five parts:

Later editions of Maria's book not only changed the title but made the name of the musical and its star more prominent than the author.

1. Sacred music from the sixteenth and seventeenth centuries
2. Music played on ancient instruments, including recorders, viola da gamba, and the spinet
3. Madrigals and ballads
4. Austrian folk songs and mountain calls
5. American folk songs

Chapter 11: "Stowe in Vermont"

The Trapp Family's interest in finding a summer home takes them to Stowe, Vermont, about twenty-five miles northwest of the state capitol of Montpelier. They decide against the initial property, a tourist house equipped for twenty people, opting instead for a farm identified as Luce Hill, with a shabby house and some crooked barns. The family selects this location because of its physical similarity to Austria. This property will eventually become the Trapp Lodge. (Finding the place and turning it into their home was a key sequence in the second German Trapp film.)

Chapter 12: "A New Chapter"

The Trapp sons, Rupert and Werner, receive their draft letters, which forces the group to learn pieces expressly for female voices.

Chapter 13: "The End of a Perfect Stay"

The Trapps make the move from Pennsylvania to Stowe, Vermont.

Chapter 14: "The New House"

Again looking for ways to supplement their income, the Trapps start making maple syrup, something they'd never even heard of before.

Chapter 15: "Concerts in Wartime"

In 1943, the Trapps embarked on their sixth American concert tour, receiving an extra boost of publicity by being profiled in *Life* magazine (specifically the November 8th issue, as "*Life* Visits the Trapp Family in Vermont").

Chapter 16: "Trapp Family Music Camp"

The Trapps buy a nearby abandoned army camp and its barracks, converting it to a summer music camp, which they opened in July 1944. Maria is nearly fined and jailed because authorities are convinced that she is disregarding wartime restrictions and using new lumber, thereby breaking the law. All is resolved.

Chapter 17: "Snapshots of the Camp."

Further details of the camp are related in this chapter.

Chapter 18: "Trapp Family Austrian Relief"

Following World War II, the Trapp Family establishes a relief fund to send to those in need back home in Austria.

Chapter 19: "A Letter"

In the form of a letter, Maria relates the sad details of the captain's death and his burial on the grounds of the Trapp Family lodge.

Chapter 20: "The Memorable Year"

Maria chronicles a year of mostly hardships, including Rosmarie running away from home, Lorli being struck by a pickup truck, and Maria herself being sick with a uremic condition.

Chapter 21: "Cor Unum"

The Trapps name their Vermont home "Cor Unum," from the Latin "Cor Unum et Anima Una" ("They were one heart and one soul").

When *the* Trapps Were *Die* Trapps

The First Cinematic Versions of the Trapp Story

Pretty much everyone who has worshipped the movie of *The Sound of Music* is well aware that it first came to life as a Broadway stage musical. Less known is the fact that there are not one but *two* previous movies that cover the story of Maria and the Trapp Family Singers. Although both pictures did good business in West Germany, where they were produced (in 1956 and 1958, respectively), there was no great rush or desire on the part of American distributors to release them over here. The first picture, *Die Trapp-Familie*, did, however, play a very important role in the development of *The Sound of Music*, as it was screened by Mary Martin and her husband, producer Richard Halliday, and gave them the idea of a possible stage show, albeit one they initially envisioned consisting of the actual traditional songs the Trapps had sung, and not a full-scale original score. It was not until they approached Richard Rodgers and Oscar Hammerstein II with the odd idea of the team perhaps contributing one new number that the more obvious idea came to fruition: why not have two of Broadway's greatest songwriters create their own full score for the story?

It was because of the eventual success on stage of *The Sound of Music* and 20th Century-Fox's purchase of the rights to turn it into a movie that finally allowed some version of the German Trapp films to see the light of day on American cinema screens. Fox did not, however, picture the two movies (*Die Trapp-Familie in Amerika* was the second one) as separate "art-house" entities showing in select venues with their original German language soundtrack, instead wanting to present them to a wider audience. To this end the studio took the drastic step of not only dubbing the films into English but trimming out a great deal of footage (mainly from the second installment) and piecing them together as one movie, *The Trapp Family*.

Here is the content of the two German movies and an idea of what was whittled down to make the dubbed version.

Ein Welterfolg kehrt wieder

The first cinematic version of the Trapp story, *Die Trapp-Familie*, opened in Germany in 1956.

Die Trapp-Familie

Gloria Film distribution; a Divina-Film production. Director: Wolfgang Liebeneiner. Producer: Ilse Kubaschewski. Screenplay: George Hurdalek. Dialogue: Herbert Reinecker. Photography: Werner Krien. Art Director: Robert Herlth. Costumes: Brigitte Scholz. Music: Franz Grothe. Editors: Margot von Schlieffen, Salvatore Billitteri. Eastmancolor. 106 minutes. West Germany release date: October 9, 1956.

CAST: Ruth Leuwerik (Maria), Hans Holt (Baron von Trapp), Maria Holst (Princess Yvonne), Josef Meinrad (Dr. Wasner), Friedrich Domin (Rudy Gruber), Hilde von Stolz (Baroness Mathilde), Michael Ande (Werner), Knut Mahlke (Rupert), Ursula Wolff (Agathe), Angelika Werth (Hedwig), Monika Wolf (Maria, child), Ursula Ettrich (Rosmarie), Monika Ettrich (Martina), Agnes Windeck (Äbtissin), Gretl Theimer (Köchin), Liesl Kartlstadt (Raphaela), Karl Ehmann (Diener), Hans Schumm (Petroff), Joseph Offenbach (Samish), Peter Capell (Ellis Island Officer)

As the other nuns at Nonnberg go about their daily rituals in solemnity, Maria disrupts matters by sliding down a bannister, as is her customary behavior. While teaching class, she is summoned to see the Reverend Mother, who informs Maria that it is best she spend some time away from the abbey. To this end the Reverend Mother has arranged for her to serve as governess for the widowed Baron von Trapp's large family. Although she is reluctant to leave, Maria is convinced that since this is God's will, she will do her best. Changing from her nun's garments to street clothes, she leaves the holy world behind.

At the Trapp villa she is awestruck by the grand Austrian flag hung inside the house foyer; Baron von Trapp explains to her that it belonged to the last flag-ship of the Austrian naval service, for which he once served as a captain. He then summons his offspring with his bosun's whistle and they arrive, marching in military fashion, to introduce themselves. They are Rupert, Agathe, Werner, Hedwig, Maria, Rosmarie, and Martina. At dinner Maria is once again struck by the rigid formality with which the children have been instructed to behave.

Figuring her new charges need the freedom to romp and have fun like most children, Maria makes them play clothes and allows them to let loose to their hearts' content, much to the shock of the Trapp housekeeper, Matilda, who informs the new governess that this is not in keeping with the baron's orders.

Matilda phones the baron, who is in Vienna visiting Princess Yvonne, to tell him of the chaos that has erupted at the villa. He plans to return as soon as he can. Yvonne suggests he send the children to a boarding school, but the baron, having gone to one himself when he was young, will not hear of it. Meanwhile, during a thunderstorm, Maria welcomes the frightened children into her room and calms them down by playing her guitar and instructing them to join her in the song. Again, Matilda expresses her displeasure, this time to the family butler, Franz.

The following day the children are once again having the time of their lives playing in the yard. Martina picks up the garden hose to spray them all with water and ends up accidentally soaking the baron, who has unexpectedly returned and is startled by what he sees. The baron brings this pandemonium to order by blowing his whistle and sends the children into the house. He is determined to confront Maria about this breach of conduct, but is surprised to suddenly hear singing. Inside the house, he finds his new governess playing the guitar while his children sing in beautiful harmony. He is enchanted by what he hears. After the children leave, Maria tries to explain the situation, telling her employer that he is running his house like a prison, that the children will grow up unhappy if things continue in this manner. Realizing she is right and grateful that she has brought music back into their lives, the baron agrees to be patient and less strict.

Christmas arrives, and it is clear that there is much more joy in the house and that Maria has entirely won over her new charges. For the entertainment of the guests, she accompanies the children as they sing "Silent Night" and has them act out a version of "Sleeping Beauty." During this presentation, Princess Yvonne sees all too clearly how comfortable the baron and Maria have become together, certain that they have fallen for one another. When Yvonne confronts Maria about this, Maria is so upset that she begins packing her things, knowing she must return to the abbey at once. When the children find out that she has chosen to go, they beg their father to convince her to change her mind. Learning from Maria that Yvonne has suggested the baron's employee is in love with him, he feels relieved that the ice has been broken. Although the idea was for the baron to marry Yvonne, he assures Maria that he cannot because there is now another woman in his life—her. Still nervous at this revelation, Maria tells him that she must first consult the Reverend Mother about the situation. Knowing that the two of them are in love, the Reverend Mother tells Maria that it is only right that she and the baron should marry. Returning to the villa with the news, Maria and the baron embrace; as they kiss, the children cheer. Maria and the baron are married at the abbey chapel.

Time has passed, and Maria and the baron have their first child together. Father Wasner shows up at the villa as Maria and the children are playing their instruments. Hoping to show off their other skills to the clergyman, Maria has the children sing Scarlatti's "Hallelujah." The priest is very impressed by what he hears and is invited by Maria to coach them. Wasner agrees. Meanwhile, the baron's friend Rudy confesses that he is on the verge of bankruptcy because of the world economic situation. He assures the baron that he has nothing to worry about as the Trapp fortune is held in an English bank. The baron wants to help Austria so he plans to have his money transferred to Rudy's bank. This plan backfires; the money is lost and, as a result of his now desperate situation, Rudy takes his own life. In order to solve the family's dilemma, Maria comes up with the idea of turning the villa into a hotel to make money. Although this proves helpful, Rupert and Werner see another opportunity to increase the family's finances when they spot a poster in town looking for singing groups to compete in the Salzburg Festival. The boys decide the family should enter, but know it is best to keep this from their father, who is not keen to have his children perform on stage.

When the Trapp Family arrive for their spot in the festival, the baron is dismayed when he learns they will be heard on the radio as well. Werner breaks down and admits he was responsible for entering their names in the contest and is so upset he is not even sure he can sing. But Maria is insistent that they persevere and explains to the audience that they do not consider themselves professionals, they simply like to sing and make music at home. The crowd, however, is enchanted, and the Trapps end up winning first prize. Backstage, an American agent offers to represent the act.

Hearing Hitler on the radio, the baron and Maria are worried about the change that is coming to Austria. To drive the point home, even their butler Franz has taken to wearing a Nazi pin. Following an angry confrontation with another representative of the SS, Maria suggests that they consider the offer from the agent to come to America. The family pack as if going on an outing and quietly leave the property; when the SS troops arrive, Franz covers for the Trapps, allowing them to escape.

In America, a misunderstanding causes the family to be detained on Ellis Island, where they try to convince the authorities that they are in their new country to perform. They sing for the other detainees, with Father Wasner conducting, and the crowd is deeply moved. The American agent who had met with them back in Austria shows up to intervene on the family's behalf, and all is cleared up. The Trapps are now able to perform on stage as originally planned and receive a warm response from the Americans.

Die Trapp-Familie in Amerika

Gloria Film distribution; a Divina-Film production. Director: Wolfgang Liebeneiner. Producers: Utz Utermann, Ilse Kubaschewski. Screenplay: Herbert Reinecker. Photography: Werner Krien. Costumes: Brigitte Scholz. Music: Franz Grothe. Editor: Margot von Schlieffen. Eastmancolor. 87 minutes. West Germany release date: October 17, 1958.

CAST: In addition to the same actors returning as Maria, the baron, Father Wasner, and the children, the cast included: Wolfgang Wahl (Patrick), Holger Hagen (Mr. Harris), Adrienne Gessner (Mrs. Hammerfield), Peter Esser (Mr. Hammerfield)

Having successfully escaped from the Nazi invasion of Austria, Maria, Baron von Trapp, their children, and their music instructor, Father Wasner, travel around America performing their concerts, with Patrick serving as their German-speaking driver. Although they've kept busy and have been given the opportunity to see so much of America, the baron is dismayed that they have once again shown up at a concert hall with so few people in the audience. They begin to wonder if perhaps they are not presenting the right sort of program to attract attention. Returning to New York City, they take up residence in a tiny apartment on Manhattan's Lower East Side. Despite their concert bookings, their small savings are clearly running out. Hoping to help their parents, Werner and Rupert try playing a slot machine at a nearby bar, but have better luck singing, which so impresses a drunken sailor he gives them money. When Maria and the baron return home, the entire tenement is enchanted as they listen to the Trapp children sing, showing their support for the struggling family.

Maria and her family go in search of the agent who had met them in Austria, Mr. Harris. When they arrive at his office, they are informed that Harris has left New York, but they can audition for his son. The Trapp act, however, doesn't appeal to him because they lack any kind of "sex appeal." Undaunted, Maria takes off for a local bookstore to do research on the topic, only to be told that such a thing cannot be learned in a book, as some of the ladies in the store demonstrate what sex appeal is all about. When Maria drops by Central Park to practice sashaying about, she is spotted by a construction worker who believes she is on the lookout for some company, only to be turned off when she informs him she is the mother of eight children. Back at Mr. Harris's office, the outspoken agent tells Maria she and her group have no entertainment value; that they are like "lama enten," lame ducks, which only makes Maria more incensed. Her anger suddenly appeals to Harris, who decides he'll manage the Trapps, after all, if they can raise $5,000 needed for publicity.

Mrs. Hammerfield, who had spotted the Trapps at the Harris office, invites the family to perform at a posh party at her apartment for a $300 fee. When Maria informs Mrs. Hammerfield of their need for $5,000, Mr. Hammerfield rejects the idea, saying he prefers Strauss waltzes to Bach. To appease him, Maria decides they will sing Strauss, despite Father Wasner's objections. The crowd is so overjoyed by the Trapp singing that Mr. Hammerfield rips up his initial check for $300 and writes them a new check for the $5,000 they need. With Hammerfield receiving 10 percent of their profits, the Trapps now go all out to publicize their act, with Maria even agreeing to pose for photographers in the nun's wimple she once wore.

Once again they are traveling the country singing, going to such locations as Houston, Miami, and Buffalo. Although they have been able to attract larger audiences, there is still a feeling that they are not reaching everyone, as they have noticed some people walking out during the concerts and too many of the spectators reacting politely rather than enthusiastically. In the lobby, a disgruntled patron complains that he can't enjoy what he can't understand.

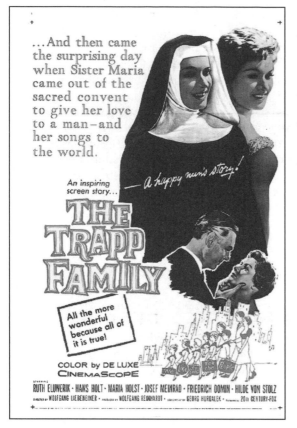

...And then came the surprising day when Sister Maria came out of the sacred convent to give her love to a man–and her songs to the world.

An inspiring screen story...

— a happy nun's story!

THE TRAPP FAMILY

All the more wonderful because all of it is true!

COLOR by DE LUXE CINEMASCOPE

RUTH LEUWERIK · HANS HOLT · MARIA HOLST · JOSEF MEINRAD · FRIEDRICH DOMIN · HILDE VON STOLZ
DIRECTED BY WOLFGANG LIEBENEINER · PRODUCED BY WOLFGANG REINHARDT · SCREENPLAY BY GEORG HURDALEK · RELEASED BY 20th CENTURY-FOX

In anticipation of their future musical film, 20th Century-Fox bought the two German Trapp movies, stitched them together, dubbed them, and gave them a typical bit of Hollywood advertising.

Although the Trapps are clearly disappointed, Maria is still certain that the United States is the country where they belong. She is further convinced when they stumble upon a dilapidated building in Vermont. Because the landscape so thoroughly reminds her of Austria, she knows that they must make it their new home.

Arriving late for their next concert, Maria tries to explain their situation in fractured English and ends up winning over the audience. The crowd is further charmed when baby Johannes starts crawling out on stage during the performance. The very unpretentious nature of the presentation loosens everyone up, and the response is encouraging. Knowing they are on the right track, the Trapps decide to add some more familiar tunes to their repertoire including "O Susanna." They are finally a hit and are able to repair the Vermont property and build their new home.

Just as they are certain all is well, the law shows up at their new farm informing them that their visitors permits have expired and that they will have to return to Europe. Seeking help, they turn to the Hammerfields. Mr. Hammerfield intervenes on their behalf and contacts the Immigration Office, settling the matter. The Trapps can now stay. To celebrate their good fortune, they begin to sing spontaneously at the office, once again attracting an appreciative crowd of listeners.

The Trapp Family

Distribution in the United States by 20th Century-Fox. Executive Producer: Heinz Abel. Book by George Hurdalek. Script by Hebert Reinecker. English Adaptation Written and Directed by Lee Kresel. Reedited print: 105 minutes.

The dubbed/combined print of *Die Trapp-Familie* and *Die Trapp-Familie in Amerika* opened in the Los Angeles area on March 22, 1961 and in the New York area on August 30, 1961 on a double bill with Elvis Presley's *Wild in the Country*. Songs include: "Hort Hier Hasen (See the Hare)," "Tales of the Vienna Woods," "Echo Song," "Yachlied," and "O Susanna."

The reedited and combined English-language version includes credits in English and a title card explaining that the year is 1936, which means this version has also jumped ahead in time for the sake of storytelling. Narration by Maria helps to clarify any holes in the storyline caused by the severe cuts.

The "new" version includes most of the scenes from *Die Trapp-Familie* until the family departs for America. Once Franz is seen closing the gate behind them, there is an extreme jump in the narrative of the two German movies; we next see the family arriving at the New York offices of the agent who had contacted them in Europe. This meant that the detainment scene on Ellis Island that had ended the first movie was eliminated altogether.

Similarly, the "drama" that had concluded *Die Trapp-Familie in Amerika*, when authorities explain to the family that they must return to Europe because of expired visitor permits, is now missing as well. Instead, the shortened movie ends with the upbeat musical number of the Trapps rebuilding their newfound home in Vermont.

Approximately one hour and fifteen minutes is given over to footage from *Die Trapp-Familie*; the concluding half hour comes from *Die Trapp-Familie in Amerika*.

In the United States, a soundtrack of *The Trapp Family* was released on 20th Fox Records (Fox 3044). Music. Frank Grothe. Choir Director: Rudolph Lamy. Orchestra Conductor: Kurt Graunke. The LP contained the following:

Side 1

Hort Hier Hasen (See the Hare—Treasure Hunt) (Dehmel) (2:24)
Wir Bauen uns ein Haus (We Are Building Ourselves a House) (Dehmel) (2:33)
La-La-La (1:45)
Echo Song (1:07)
Tales of the Vienna Woods (Johann Strauss) (3:20)
Am Bruenn vor dem Tore (At the Fountain by the Gate) (3:44)
Exultate Deo (Praise the Lord, Jehovah) (Antonio Scarlatti) (1:23)
Traveling On (Instrumental) (1:24)

Side 2

Oh, Susanna (Stephen Foster) (1:38)
Ich Wollt', Ich Hatt' eine Fiedel (I Wished I Had a Fiddle) (Dehmel) (2:40)
Wenn alle Brunnlein Fliessen (When the Little Fountain Flows) (2:01)
Kein Schoner Land (No Nicer Country Land) (2:19)
Wir Bauen uns ein Haus (Instrumental) (Dehmel) (2:00)
Old Black Joe (Stephen Foster) (2:56)
Acclamation (Instrumental Montage) (4:00)

The Sound of Music on Stage

The Theatrical History of the Musical

ORIGINAL BROADWAY PRODUCTION

The original Broadway Production of *The Sound of Music* opened on Thursday, November 18, 1959 at the Lunt-Fontanne Theatre at 205 West 46th Street in New York. It had played five previews (starting November 11) and posted record advance sales of $2,325,000.

Formerly the Globe Theatre when it opened in January 1910, this venue became a movie house starting in the 1930s and remained so until 1957. Renamed after one of the theatre's most distinguished acting couples, Alfred Lunt and Lynne Fontanne, it reopened for live theatre on May 5, 1958 with the Lunts starring in Friedrich Dürrenmatt's *The Visit*. Previous tenants in the Globe days had included *She's My Baby* (1928), with songs by Richard Rodgers and Lorenz Hart.

Following *The Visit*, the house opened its stage to the musical *Goldilocks*, the Les Ballets Africains; and John Gielgud in *Much Ado About Nothing*.

Prior to the Broadway opening, *TSOM* played out of town at:

- Shubert Theatre, 247 College Street, New Haven, CT (October 3–10, 1959; this version did not yet have "Edelweiss" added to the production)
- Shubert Theatre, 265 Tremont Street, Boston, MA (October 14, 1959– November 7, 1959); 28 performances

Variety reported the first week's gross at the Lunt-Fontanne as $75,000 for the 1,402-seat theatre, with tickets at a $9.90 top. This ticket price made *TSOM* the highest on Broadway at the time, followed by *Destry Rides Again*, *Fiorello!*, *Gypsy*, and *Take Me Along* all charging $9.40, and *Redhead* a bargain at $9.20.

TSOM moved to the Mark Hellinger Theatre on November 6, 1962 and ran there until June 15, 1963.

At the time *TSOM* closed with an $81,500 take for its 181st week, it was still charging $9.90. It reportedly had made an estimated $2,500,000 profit on a $500,000 investment.

The Original Cast

Mary Martin as Maria Rainer

Already something of a theatre legend, Mary Martin had once before created gold in collaboration with Rodgers and Hammerstein, playing Nurse Nellie Forbush in their 1949 Pulitzer Prize winner, *South Pacific*. It became one of the seminal musicals of the American theatre, brought her a Tony Award, and at the time of its closing was bested only by Rodgers and Hammerstein's *Oklahoma!* for longevity of a musical show.

Born in Wetherford, Texas, on December 1, 1913, Martin studied voice, violin, and dancing at an early age. She ended up married at the ripe old age of sixteen and two years later gave birth to a son, future actor Larry Hagman. To make a living, she opened the Mary Hagman School of Dance in her hometown. Figuring she needed to better study her chosen profession, she moved to Hollywood to attend the Fanchon and Marco School of Dance. For them she

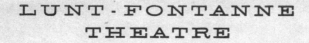

LUNT · FONTANNE
THEATRE

LELAND HAYWARD · RICHARD HALLIDAY
RICHARD RODGERS · OSCAR HAMMERSTEIN 2nd
present

MARY MARTIN
In A New Musical Play

THE SOUND OF MUSIC

Music by   Lyrics by
RICHARD RODGERS   OSCAR HAMMERSTEIN 2nd

Book by
HOWARD LINDSAY and RUSSEL CROUSE
Suggested by "The Trapp Family Singers" by Maria Augusta Trapp

THEODORE BIKEL
with
PATRICIA NEWAY   KURT KASZNAR   MARION MARLOWE
JOHN RANDOLPH   NAN McFARLAND   LAURI PETERS   BRIAN DAVIES
MARILYN ROGERS   MURIEL O'MALLEY   ELIZABETH HOWELL   KAREN SHEPARD

Entire Production Directed by
VINCENT J. DONEHUE

Musical Numbers Staged by **JOE LAYTON**
Scenic Production by **OLIVER SMITH**
Costumes by **LUCINDA BALLARD**
Mary Martin's clothes by **MAINBOCHER**
Lighting by **JEAN ROSENTHAL**

Musical Director   Orchestrations by   Choral Arrangements by
FREDERICK DVONCH   ROBERT RUSSELL BENNETT   TRUDE RITTMAN

The credit page on the original playbill for *The Sound of Music* on Broadway.

Columbia Records' heavy promotion worked wonders, turning the Broadway cast album into the longest-charting #1 hit of its kind.

sang "So Red the Rose" as part of their stage presentations both in San Francisco and Hollywood, and realized she was making a greater impression with her vocal talents than with her terpsichorean skills. To this end, she sang on radio on *Gateway to Hollywood* and did night-club gigs there at the Cinegrill and Casanova. It was her swing rendition of "Il Bacio" at the Trocadero that brought her to the attention of producer Lawrence Schwab, who offered her a role on Broadway in *Ring out the News.*

When that deal collapsed, Martin found herself searching for work in New York and scored an immediate success with her very first Broadway credit, Cole Porter's *Leave It to Me!* (1938), playing the secondary role of William Gaxton's girlfriend, Dolly Winslow. It was her rendition of "My Heart Belongs to Daddy" that caused a stir; stole attention from its stars, Victor Moore and Sophie Tucker; put her on the cover of the December 19, 1938 issue of *Life;* and had Hollywood calling. (Martin had already provided the singing voice to Gypsy Rose Lee for the song "Daughter of Mademoiselle" in the 20th Century-Fox comedy *Battle of Broadway* and for Margaret Sullavan's rendition of "Pack Up Your Troubles" in MGM's *The Shopworn Angel*). She signed a contract with Paramount Pictures and appeared for them in nine movies (from *The Great Victor Herbert* in 1939 to *True to Life* in 1943), but her heart really belonged to the stage. Her tenure at the studio, however, would allow her to star twice opposite Bing Crosby (*Rhythm on the River* and *Birth of the Blues*), and despite her own dismissal of her time in front of the cameras, she proved to be just about his most appealing leading lady of all. Mary married for the second time, in 1940, to Paramount story editor Richard Halliday, who eventually produced several properties for his wife. Once she left Paramount, she would be seen in only two more movies, in both instances playing herself: Warners' Cole Porter biopic, *Night and Day* (1946), in which she reprised "My Heart Belongs to Daddy," and *Main Street to Broadway* (1953), which gave her the opportunity to introduce a Rodgers and Hammerstein song, "There's Music in You."

Returning to the stage after her Hollywood venture, Martin scored another hit, as the department store mannequin brought to life in the Kurt Weill-Ogden Nash musical *One Touch of Venus* (1943), and then chalked up her shortest Broadway musical run (142 performances, February–June 1946) in *Lute Song* (music by Raymond Scott; lyrics: Bernard Hanighen). She bounced back by touring in Irving Berlin's *Annie Get Your Gun* and followed this with *South Pacific.*

Prior to these she had made her West End debut, playing four months in a Noël Coward musical, *Pacific 1860* (1948). Between two straight roles, in *Kind Sir* (1953) and a revival of *The Skin of Our Teeth* (1955), she soared to another height, literally, with the 1954 musical version of *Peter Pan*, with a score shared by no less than five contributing songwriters, Mark "Moose" Charlap, Carolyn Leigh, Jule Styne, Betty Comden, and Adolph Green. It brought her a second Tony and then rose even higher in popularity when the production was broadcast live on NBC on *Producers' Showcase* on March 5, 1955. Staged again in 1956 and then filmed for posterity in 1960, it brought her a whole new generation of fans and became another of her defining roles.

Shortly before appearing in *The Sound of Music*, she had solidified her stardom on the small screen starring in productions of *Born Yesterday* (1956) and *Annie Get Your Gun* (1957). The latter was directed by Vincent J. Donehue, who would also oversee her March 1959 special *Music with Mary Martin*, as well as *The Sound of Music*.

At the time she first played Maria, Mary Martin was forty-five years old, but the discrepancy between her age and that of the real Maria at the time she first entered the Trapp household (twenty-one) hardly mattered to the adoring audiences.

Theodore Bikel as Captain Georg von Trapp

Being not only authentically Austrian but accomplished at playing the guitar, Theodore Bikel (born in Vienna on May 2, 1924) proved ideal casting for Captain von Trapp. His own family had, in fact, faced a similar dilemma as the Trapps, having to flee Austria once the Nazis took power in 1938. In Bikel's case, however, being Jewish, the threat was even greater. Settling in Israel, he took an interest in dramatics, joining the Habima Theater in Tel Aviv and then journeying to London to attend the Royal Academy of Dramatic Arts. A role in a 1948 revival of *You Can't Take It with You* led to director Laurence Olivier casting him as one of Stanley and Mitch's poker-playing pals in the London debut (October 12, 1949) of Tennessee Williams's *A Streetcar Named Desire*, starring Olivier's wife, Vivien Leigh. This, in turn, brought him his first film, John Huston's Oscar-winning *The African Queen* (1951), popping up near the climax as a German sailor. That same year he returned to the West End to play a Russian in Peter Ustinov's comedy *The Love of Four Colonels*, which he would stay with for two years.

Continuing his run of supporting roles in movies, Bikel covered nearly every nationality possible, playing a Serbian king in the Oscar-nominated *Moulin Rouge* (1952); a Belgian opera director in *Melba* (1953; which featured Robert Morley playing Oscar Hammerstein II's father); a Dutch doctor living in Canada in *The Little Kidnappers* (1953); a German naval officer in *Above Us the Waves* (1955); and a French general in *The Pride and the Passion* (1956). During this time he made his Broadway debut (February 1955), playing an imposing French police inspector in the short-lived *Tonight in Samarkand*, followed later that year by the more successful *The Lark*, as a French captain pressured into helping Joan of Arc (Julie Harris). (The cast included Christopher Plummer, putting the two future Captain von Trapps in the same property for the only time). For playing a doctor in the drama *The Rope Dancers* (1957), Bikel earned his first Tony nomination. He finally appeared in an American-made movie when Stanley Kramer cast him as the sympathetic southern sheriff in *The Defiant Ones* (1958), which brought him an Oscar nomination for supporting actor. He was also seen in another of the year's top releases, as a psychiatrist offering assistance to condemned prisoner Susan Hayward in *I Want to Live!*, directed by Robert Wise.

After the head of Elektra Records, Jac Holzman, heard Bikel perform, he signed him to his label, launching his second career as a noted folk singer with a 1955 album, known alternately as *Theodore Bikel Sings Songs of Israel* and *Folksongs of Israel*. There followed *An Actor's Holiday* (1956) and *Songs of a Russian Gypsy* (1958), among others. He did not shut down this side of his career to concentrate exclusively on *TSOM*, however, appearing for two concerts at Town Hall on November 29, 1959, only two weeks after the musical's Broadway opening.

At the time *The Sound of Music* premiered on Broadway, Bikel was thirty-five, a decade and a year younger than the real Captain von Trapp was at the time he and Maria first crossed paths.

Patricia Neway as Mother Abbess

A noted soprano with the New York City Opera, Neway (born September 30, 1919 in New York) had studied voice privately and at the Mannes School of Music, leading up to her 1942 Broadway debut in the chorus of *La Vie Parisienne* and professional opera debut singing the role of Fiordiligi in Mozart's *Così fan tutte* with the Chautauqua Opera in 1946. She made her name four years later when she starred as Magda, a woman trying desperately to save her family from an oppressive dictatorship, in Gian Carlo Menotti's *The Consul*. Premiering on Broadway at the Ethel Barrymore Theatre in March 1950, it had a successful run of 269 performances and earned the Pulitzer Prize for music and the New York Drama Critics Award as Best Musical. (Neway would reprise the part for five New York City Opera revivals and record it for television in 1960, during her run in *The Sound of Music*.) She returned to Broadway and Menotti in 1958 for the five-performance *Maria Golovin*, which she also sang at City Opera and for *NBC Opera* in 1959.

Being forty years old at the time she first played the Mother Abbess, this actually made Neway five years younger than Mary Martin.

Kurt Kasznar as Max Detweiler

Like Theodore Bikel, Kurt Kasznar was Vienna born (on August 12, 1913) but had an even closer link to the real world of the Trapp Family, having made his professional stage debut at the Salzburg Festival, in the 1932 version of the annual presentation *Jedermann* (*Everyman*). Although he had already appeared while still a boy in a pair of quickly forgotten silent short subjects, his career proper didn't really take off until he became a member of Max Reinhardt's theatre company. With the terror of the Third Reich looming, Kasznar jumped at the chance to go to New York with Reinhardt's massive spectacle *The Eternal Road*, which debuted at the Manhattan Opera House in January 1937. He staged, produced, and contributed songs to a musical revue, *Crazy with the Heat*, which had two Broadway runs in 1941, and wrote and starred in a one-act, *First Cousins*, which ran during wartime as part of an all-military omnibus called *Army Play-by-Play*.

His biggest stage success to date came with *The Happy Time* (1950), playing drunken Uncle Louis, a performance good enough to earn him a contract with MGM and a chance to repeat the role in Columbia's 1952 movie adaptation. The play also put him on the inside track in getting the role of Max Detweiler, since *Happy Time* was produced by Richard Rodgers and Oscar Hammerstein II.

Much like Bikel, Kasznar was now called on to essay a number of thickly accented character parts on screen. He was a duped art dealer in *The Light Touch* (1952); the mysterious next-door neighbor Billy Gray is certain has poisoned his dog in *Talk About a Stranger* (1952); Mel Ferrer's carnival partner in *Lili* (1953); Mexican priests in both *Sombrero* and *Ride, Vaquero!* (1953); Kate's father, Baptista, in the production of "The Taming of the Shrew" being staged in *Kiss Me, Kate* (1953); a cuckolded army captain on a mission in Indo-China in *Jump into Hell* (1955), which actually gave him second billing; and a corrupt West African official in *Legend of the Lost* (1957). There were also opportunities to sing, cavorting around a piano with Bob Fosse and Gower Champion for "Nothing Is Impossible" in *Give a Girl a Break* (1953) and rounding out a quartet that also featured Betty Garrett, Janet Leigh, and Dick York for "I'm Great," in *My Sister Eileen* (1955).

Marion Marlowe as Elsa Schraeder

The St. Louis native (born March 7, 1929) was already singing on radio by the time she was five and, following school, modeled, entertained with the USO, and joined the Light Opera Guild of St. Louis. Spotted by a British producer while performing in a nightclub, she was invited to join the cast of the 1949 London revue *Sauce Tartare* (which included a pre-stardom Audrey Hepburn). Back on her home turf she was chosen by television host Arthur Godfrey to be a regular on his weekly CBS variety series *Arthur Godfrey and His Friends*, mostly paired up to sing with Frank Parker. This led to recordings, which included Rodgers & Hart's "Blue Moon" and Kern & Hammerstein's "I've Told Every Little Star," and enough fame that Marlowe landed on the December 11, 1954 cover of *TV Guide*. Within the year she was fired by the notoriously prickly Godfrey, but rebounded with several appearances on *The Ed Sullivan Show* and *The Jack Paar Tonight Show*, as well as countless nightclub bookings. Her single "The Man in the Raincoat" reached #14 on the *Billboard* charts in 1955. The same year she won the role of Elsa in *The Sound of Music*, she released a solo album on Design Records, *Dearly Beloved*, which *also* featured "I've Told Every Little Star."

John Randolph as Franz, the Butler

At the time he was cast as the Trapp butler, John Randolph (born Emanuel Kirsch Cohen in New York City on June 1, 1915) was on the Hollywood blacklist for having refused to testify before the House Un-American Activities Committee in 1955. This did not, however, affect his stage work, which had been his principal means of support since he made his Broadway bow in 1938, as a herald in *Coriolanus*. His very full resume in New York alone included *Command Decision; Come Back, Little Sheba*, as the milkman; *Peer Gynt; The Visit*; and the musicals *Paint Your Wagon*, as a miner, and *House of Flowers*, as a smuggler. Only months before being cast in *TSOM*, he was seen on Broadway in the playlet "Portrait of a Madonna," part of the Jessica Tandy-Hume Cronyn omnibus *Triple Play*.

Nan McFarland as Frau Schmidt, the Housekeeper

A product of Chicago's Goodman Theatre and Conservatory of Music, McFarland (born in Chicago on July 20, 1916) spent the first part of her Broadway career doing small roles in such classics as *Othello, Cyrano de Bergerac, The Alchemist,* and *Man and Superman,* and a more substantial one as the mother of an escaped con in Horton Foote's short-lived *The Chase*. She preceded her role in *The Sound of Music* by appearing in a trio of successes, *My 3 Angels*, as a gossip; *Auntie Mame*, as Beauregard's Southern aunt; and *The Diary of Anne Frank*, as the eternally distressed Mrs. Van Daan, which she also did on tour.

Lauri Peters as Liesl

A scholarship recipient of the American School of Ballet, Peters (who was born in Detroit on July 2, 1943) continued her dance studies at the School of Performing Arts and then performed with the New York City Ballet. This led to chorus work in the Jule Styne-Comden & Green musical *Say Darling* in 1958. She moved up to a larger part, playing one of the Bennett sisters in *First Impressions*, an attempt to put Jane Austen's *Pride and Prejudice* to music that opened in March 1959 but would only eke out eighty-four performances. It was, however, where she was spotted by Richard Rodgers, who suggested she audition for his new show. Peters actually *was* 16 (going on 17) at the time *TSOM* premiered.

Brian Davies as Rolf Gruber

Born in Rhondda Valey, Wales (on November 15, 1938), Davies and his family came to the United States when he was ten, settling in Indianapolis. His original involvement in the world of Richard Rodgers came when he was cast as Valentine in a revival of the Rodgers & Hart show *Babes in Arms*, which was rewritten by George Oppenheimer under Rodgers's supervision. This opened at the Royal Poinciana Playhouse in Palm Beach in March 1959 with a planned tour to follow. Once the show closed early, Davies was now available to take on the role of Rolf and make his Broadway debut in *The Sound of Music*.

Marilyn Rogers as Brigitta

The only one of the Trapp Kids outside of Lauri Peters to receive a separate bio in the playbill, Rogers (born in New York City on October 4, 1947) had recently vacated the role of Amaryllis in Meredith Willson's *The Music Man* and prior to that had debuted on Broadway in 1957 in the drama *Hide and Seek*, which boasted Basil Rathbone and Geraldine Fitzgerald in the cast, but closed after seven performances. According to the playbill she was twelve years old.

Muriel O'Malley as Sister Margaretta

O'Malley already had a Rodgers and Hammerstein credit on her resume, having appeared as "Grandma Taylor" in their 1947 musical *Allegro*. She was also in the 1951 revival of one of Hammerstein's collaborations with Jerome Kern, *Music in the Air*.

Elizabeth Howell as Sister Berthe

She had appeared as one of Shannon Bolin's buddies, "Doris," in the 1955 musical *Damn Yankees*.

Karen Shepard as Sister Sophia

Joining the company of *My Fair Lady* as a servant, Shepard was also given the job of understudying the role of "Eliza."

The remaining five Trapp children were combined into a shared paragraph in the playbill, in this order:

Kathy Dunn as Louisa

Another twelve-year-old cast member, according to her playbill entry, Dunn had already written the words to nine songs, two of which had been published. Her mother had been a singer with Jimmy Dorsey's band under the name Julie Short, and Dunn had made her Broadway debut in 1956 in the comedy *Uncle Willie*.

Evanna Lien as Gretl

Eight-year-old Lien had shown up on local children's television and did bit parts in three 1959 movies: *It Happened to Jane*, *The Best of Everything*, and *Happy Anniversary*.

Mary Susan Locke as Marta

Locke had already appeared on Broadway earlier in 1959 in the short-lived *A Desert Incident*, in support of Shepperd Strudwick and Cameron Prud'homme. The nine-year-old had studied with the Ballet Russe de Monte Carlo.

William Snowden as Friedrich

At thirteen, Snowden had no previous Broadway credits, but had sung in the children's chorus of several LPs.

Joseph Stewart as Kurt

Another newcomer to Broadway, twelve-year-old Stewart's playbill bio mentioned the boy having worked in summer theatre and off-Broadway without clarifying precisely what in.

Luce Ennis as Ursula

(replaced by Bernice Saunders, November 1961; and by Shirley Mendonca)

Stefan Gierasch as Herr Zeller

(replaced by Milton Luchan, November 1961)

Kirby Smith as Baron Elberfeld

(replaced by Webb Tilton, 1961)

Sue Yaeger as A Postulant

(replaced by Sara Letton, November 1961)

Michael Gorrin as Admiral Von Schreiber

(replaced by Jay Velie in September 1962)

The ensemble: Joanne Birks, Patricia Brooks, June Card, Dorothy Dallas, Ceil Delli, Luce Enis, Cleo Fry, Barbara George, Lucas Hoving, Patricia Kelly, Maria Kova, Shirley Mendonca, Kathy Miller, Lorna Nash, Keith Prentice, Nancy Reeves, Bernice Saunders, Connie Sharman, Gloria Stevens, Tatiana Troyanos, Mimi Vondra.

Sheppard Kerman played Herr Zeller in New Haven and then was demoted to "Herr Ullrich" in the Shubert Theatre tryout, but this character did not make it to the Broadway opening. Kerman stayed on as a "Max" understudy. Stefan Giersach became "Zeller" in Boston. Joey Heatherton was listed as an understudy to Liesl and Louisa.

On opening night, Rene Guerin (who had been "A Postulant" during the out-of-town tryout) was standby for Maria, Kenneth Harvey for the captain. Both would eventually play the roles in regional theatres.

Broadway Cast Replacements

Maria

Mary Martin would stay with the show until October 7, 1961, after which she was replaced by Martha Wright. Jeannie Carson took over for Wright starting on July 2, 1962 (Carson would then take the role in the bus-and-truck tour of the show that began that fall). Nancy Dussault took over for Carson on September 5, 1962.

Captain von Trapp

Donald Scott moved into the role as of October 1961. (He later played the part in London).

Mother Abbess

Elizabeth Howell (who had played Sister Berthe) took over the role starting the week of October 9, 1961.

Max

Kurt Kasznar's understudy, Sheppard Kerman, did get a chance to be listed in the playbill as Max in December 1961 while Kasznar was on break; Kasznar continued until Paul Lipson took over on July 2, 1962.

Liesl

Lauri Peters ended her run on October 14, 1961 and was succeeded that month by Marissa Mason, then by Imelda De Martin, as of July 2, 1962.

Broadway's fourth Maria, Nancy Dussault, recieved her own souvenir program cover.

Brigitta

Mary Susan Locke moved up to this role as of June 1961; the part was later played by Nita Novy, starting in August 1962.

Friedrich

Ronnie Tourso took over in May 1961; Richard Carafa, who had played Kurt during the national tour, came in to play Friedrich starting July 23, 1962.

Louisa

Patty Michael took over the role in November 1962, but Kathy Dunn would return to the part in 1963.

Kurt

Kenny Dore filled in for Joseph Stewart starting in December 1961; Stewart was officially followed by Tommy Leap (as of April 5, 1962), then Paul Mace, and finally Royston Thomas.

Marta

Evanna Lien moved up to this role (as of June 1961); it was later played by Christopher Norris, starting in August 1962.

Gretl

Valerie Lee took over the part as of June 1961; she was followed by Laura Michaels (as of April 1962) and then Leslie Smith in October 1962.

Rolf

Jon Voight began playing the part in September 1961; Peter Van Hattum then took over in June 1962. [*Note: Voight and Lauri Peters married in 1962 — after she had left the show — and remained wed until 1967.*]

Elsa

Lois Hunt (as of October 1961) and then Jen Nelson (as of July 2, 1962).

Sister Berthe

Played by Lizabeth Pritchett, starting the week of October 9, 1962.

Sister Margaretta

Played by Nadine Lewis, as of March 1962.

Franz

Jay Barney took over the part.

Zeller

Milton Luchan took on the role starting the week of May 29, 1961.

TONY AWARDS

14th Annual Awards for the 1959–60 Season
Presented on Sunday, April 24, 1960 at the Astor Hotel Grand Ballroom in New
     York City
Broadcast on WCBS-TV Channel 2 in NYC

Best Musical (Tie)

Winner: *The Sound of Music* by Howard Lindsay and Russel Crouse; Lyrics by
Oscar Hammerstein II; Music by Richard Rodgers; Produced by Leland Hayward,
Richard Halliday, Richard Rodgers, Oscar Hammerstein II.
Fiorello! by Jerome Weidman and George Abbott; Lyrics by Sheldon Harnick;
Music by Jerry Bock; Produced by Robert E. Griffith and Harold S. Prince.
Nominees: *Gypsy; Once Upon a Mattress; Take Me Along*

Best Actress in a Musical

Winner: Mary Martin, *The Sound of Music*
Nominees: Carol Burnett (*Once Upon a Mattress*); Dolores Gray (*Destry Rides Again*); Eileen Herlie (*Take Me Along*); Ethel Merman (*Gypsy*)

Best Supporting or Featured Actress in a Musical

Winner: Patricia Neway, *The Sound of Music*
Nominees: Sandra Church (*Gypsy*); Pert Kelton (*Greenwillow*); Lauri Peters and
the Children—Kathy Dunn, Evanna Lien, Mary Susan Locke, Marilyn Rogers,
William Snowden, Joseph Stewart (*The Sound of Music*) [*Certainly one of the more
curious nominations in Tony history, poor William Snowden and Joseph Stewart being
designated "actresses" by their inclusion here.*]

Best Scenic Designer

Winner: Oliver Smith, *The Sound of Music*
Nominees: Cecil Beaton, (*Saratoga*); William and Jean Eckart, (*Fiorello!*); Peter Larkin, (*Greenwillow*); Jo Mielziner, (*Gypsy*)

Best Conductor/Musical Director

Winner: Frederick Dvonch, *The Sound of Music*
Nominees: Abba Bogin (*Greenwillow*); Lehman Engel (*Take Me Along*); Hal Hastings (*Fiorello!*); Milton Rosenstock (*Gypsy*)

Supporting or Featured Actor in a Musical

Winner: Tom Bosley, *Fiorello!*
Nominees: Theodore Bikel, *The Sound of Music;* Kurt Kasznar, *The Sound of Music,* Howard Da Silva (*Fiorello!*); Jack Klugman (*Gypsy*)

Director of a Musical

Winner: George Abbott, *Fiorello!*
Nominees: Vincent J. Donehue, *The Sound of Music;* Peter Glenville (*Take Me Along*); Michael Kidd (*Destry Rides Again*); Jerome Robbins (*Gypsy*)

Additional Awards

Theatre World Award

Lauri Peters, Promising Newcomer

New York Drama Critics Awards

Female in a Musical: Mary Martin, *The Sound of Music*
Composer: Richard Rodgers, *The Sound of Music*

Longest Runs on Broadway

When *The Sound of Music* closed on June 15, 1963 at 1,443 performances, this put it at #11 on the list of the longest-running Broadway productions of all time; and as the fourth all-time long-running musical (two of the others being R&H titles). (M) indicates musical.

1. *Life with Father:* 3,224 performances (11/8/39–7/12/47)
2. *Tobacco Road:* 3,182 performances (12/4/33–5/31/41)
3. *My Fair Lady* (M): 2,717 performances (3/15/56–9/29/62)
4. *Abie's Irish Rose:* 2,328 performances (5/23/22–10/1/27)

5. *Oklahoma!* (M): 2,212 performances (3/31/43–5/29/48)
6. *South Pacific* (M): 1,925 performances (4/7/49–1/16/54)
7. *Harvey:* 1,775 performances (11/1/44–1/15/49)
8. *Born Yesterday:* 1,642 performances (2/4/46–12/31/49)
9. *The Voice of the Turtle:* 1,557 performances (12/8/43–1/3/48)
10. *Arsenic and Old Lace:* 1,444 performances (1/10/41–6/17/44)
11. **The Sound of Music (M): 1,443 performances (11/15/59–6/15/63)**
12. *Hellzapoppin':* 1,404 performances (9/22/38–12/17/41)

American Touring Company of Original Production

Started at: Riviera Theatre, Detroit, February 27, 1961
Ended at: O'Keefe Center, Toronto, November 23, 1963

CAST: Florence Henderson (Maria), John Myhers (Captain von Trapp), Beatrice Krebs (Mother Abbess), Lynn Brinker (Elsa), Jack Collins (Max), Imelda De Martin (Liesl), Peter Van Hattum (Rolf), Ricky Wayne (Friedrich), Melanie Dana (Louisa), Nita Novy (Brigitta), Linda Ross (Marta), Richard Carafa (Kurt), Christopher Norris (Gretl), Graziella Polacco (Sister Berthe), Karen Ford (Sister Margaretta), Grace Olsen (Sister Sophia), Shev Rogers (Franz), Jane Rose (Frau Schmidt), Larry Swanson (Herr Zeller), Kenneth Mars (Baron Elberfeld), Jay Velie (Admiral von Schreiber), Jyll Alexander (Postulant/Ensemble), Betsy Hepburn (Ursula/Ensemble), Adele Baker, Jeremy Brown, Alice Cannon, Alice Evans, Maxine Foster, Barbara Gregory, Grace Ann Hays, Evelyn Keller, Beverly Morrison, Barbara Newborn, Anna Nunnally, Gloria Shepherd, Sally Ann Sherrill (Ensemble)

February 27–April 1, 1961: Riviera Theatre, Detroit
April 4–22, 1961: O'Keefe Centre, Toronto
April 24–May 8, 1961: Hanna Theatre, Cleveland
May 23–27, 1961: KRNT Theatre, Des Moines
May 29–June 3, 1961: Paramount Theatre, Omaha
June 5–15, 1961: Music Hall, Kansas City
June 19–July 22, 1961: War Memorial Opera House, San Francisco
July 24–September 16, 1961: Los Angeles Civic Light Opera
September 18–23, 1961: Auditorium, Pasadena
September 26–30, 1961: Auditorium, Denver

For select playbills for the national tour of *The Sound of Music*, some theatres chose to present an out-of-character image of its star, Florence Henderson.

October 7–22, 1961: State Fair Music Hall, Dallas

October 25–November 11, 1961: American Theatre, St. Louis

November 14, 1961–November 10, 1962: Shubert Theatre, Chicago

[*During the Chicago run, Florence Henderson handed the role of Maria over to Barbara Meister on June 4, 1962. Meister would stay with the show for the rest of its run, as did John Myhers, who continued playing Captain von Trapp. Among the replacements were Marthe Erolle taking over Elsa from Lynn Brinker, Jane Zachary becoming Liesl, and Helen Noyes as the new Frau Schmidt. Grace Olsen had a brief run as Maria in March of 1961.*]

November 12–24, 1962: Orpheum, Minneapolis

November 26–December 1, 1962: Auditorium, St. Paul

December 3–22, 1962: New Pabst Theatre, Milwaukee

December 24–29, 1962: Brown Theatre, Louisville

December 31, 1962–January 5, 1963: Veterans War Memorial Theatre, Columbus

January 7–19, 1963: Shubert, Cincinnati

January 21–26, 1963: Murat, Indianapolis

January 28–February 3, 1963: Memorial Theatre, Dayton

February 4–17, 1963: Penn, Pittsburgh

February 19–24, 1963: Auditorium, Rochester

February 26–March 2, 1963: Bushnell, Hartford

March 4–16, 1963: Ford's Theatre, Baltimore

March 18–April 13. 1963: Colonial, Boston

April 15–20, 1963: Playhouse, Wilmington

April 22–June 15, 1963: Shubert, Philadelphia

June 17–August 24, 1963: National Theatre, Washington, DC

August 26–31, 1963: Shubert, New Haven

September 2–7, 1963: Bushnell, Hartford

September 9–21, 1963: Hanna, Cleveland

September 23–28, 1963: Shubert, Cincinnati

September 30–October 4, 1963: Nixon, Pittsburgh

October 6–November 9, 1963: Fisher, Detroit

November 11–23, 1963: O'Keefe Center, Toronto

The second national tour, encompassing thirty-five weeks and covering 125 cities, was launched at the Hershey Community Theatre on September 17, 1962, with Jeannie Carson and John Van Dreelen as the stars, under the direction of John Fearnley. It was presented by producer Henry Guettel (Richard Rodgers's son-in-law). Venues included the Paramount in Anderson, Indiana; the Stuart Theatre in Lincoln, Nebraska; the Mosque in Richmond, Virginia; and the Orpheum in Madison, Wisconsin.

Also in the company were:

Rosalind Hupp (Mother Abbess), Wally Griffin (Max), Marijane Maricle (Elsa), Ethelyne Dunfee and Mary Jane Ferguson (Liesl), Tommy Long (Friedrich), Sharon McCartin (Louisa), Paul Robertson (Kurt), Linda Wright (Brigitta),

Laurie Wright (Marta), Carla Wright (Gretl), Bill Galarno (Rolf), Harrison Fisher and Dick Alvo (Herr Zeller), Jessica Quinn (Sister Berthe), and Sandra Eames (Sister Margaretta).

Additional Notable U.S. Productions of *TSOM*

1964

Judith McCauley and Lawrence Brooks (Palm Beach & Cleveland Musicarnaval)

Ann Blyth and Webb Tilton; also Sandy Duncan (Liesl) and Danny Lockin (Rolf) (Tenthouse Theatre, Chicago; Dallas Summer Musicals)

Martha Wright and John Bargarey (Oakdale Musical Theatre, Wallingford, CT)

Janet Blair and John Myhers; also Werner Klemperer as Max (San Fernando Valley Music Theatre, Woodland Hills, CA; Valley Forge Music Fair, Valley Forge, PA; Painters Mill, Owings Mills, MD; Shady Grove, Gaithersburg, MD; Storrowton Music Fair, Springfield, MA; Camden County Music Fair, Hammonton, NJ)

Willi Burke and John Bargarey (Warwick Musical Theatre, RI)

Film star Ann Blyth (*Mildred Pierce, The Great Caruso*) got her chance to play Maria on more than one occasion; this engagement took place the year before the movie opened.

For the second leg of the first national tour, Barbara Meister took over the role of Maria, with John Myhers continuing in the role of Captain von Trapp.

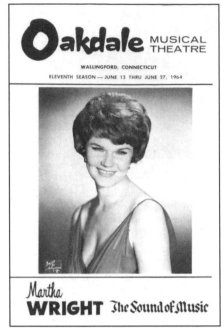

Mary Martin's immediate successor on Broadway, Martha Wright, continued to play Maria in regional productions of the show.

Gloria DeHaven (*Best Foot Forward, Three Little Words*) was one of the actresses who stepped into the Maria role in regional theatre shortly before the film took the world by storm.

Betty Ann Grove (Little Theatre on the Square, Sullivan, IL)

Gloria De Haven and Kenneth Harvey; also Nan McFarland as Frau Schmidt (Westbury Music Fair, New York); De Haven was also in Kenley Players (Warren, OH) second production of the show that year

Anita Bryant and Paul Richards (Kenley Players, Warren)

Nancy Dussault and Webb Tilton (Kansas City Starlight Theatre)

Shirley Jones and Stephen Elliott (Westbury Music Fair, and tour; incl. Camden County Music Fair, NJ)

Evelyn Wyckoff and Dean Norton; also Robert Prosky as Max (Ogunquit Playhouse, ME; Pocono Playhouse, Mountainhome, PA)

Wynne Miller and Shev Rodgers; also Claramae Turner as Mother Abbess; Richard Carafa, who had played Friedrich on Broadway, repeated the part here (The Muny, St. Louis) [*Miller took over the part from Barbara Cook, who was originally scheduled to play Maria*]

Renee Guerin and Erik Silyu; also Dick Latessa as Max (Cape Cod Melody Tent) [*Note: Guerin had been the standby for Mary Martin in the original Broadway production.*]

Mimi Turque and Lawrence Brooks (Northland Playhouse, Southfield, MI; production returned later that season w/Judith McCauley as Maria)

1965

Gisele MacKenzie and Stephen Elliott (Oakdale Musical Theatre, Wallingford, CT)

Marta Marquez and Raul Davila; and mostly Hispanic cast (Lincoln Center Out-of-Doors and Alliance of Latin Arts Inc.)

Bernadette Peters (as Liesl) (Mt. Gretna Playhouse, PA)

Willi Burke and Erik Silyu (Cape Cod Melody Tent)

1966

Shirley Jones and Stephen Elliott (Kenley Players and Westbury Music Fair)

1967

Constance Towers and Bob Wright; also Christopher Hewett as Max, Sandy Duncan as Liesl, Nadine Lewis (from Broadway production) returned as Sister Margaretta (New York City Center Light Opera; April 26–May 14)

Patrice Munsel and Reid Shelton (Starlight Theatre, Kansas City, MO)

Eileen Christy and Art Lund (Sacramento Light Opera Association)

Willi Burke and Erik Silyu (Casa Manana, Fort Worth, TX)

1968

Florence Henderson and Bob Wright; and Claramae Turner as Mother Abbess (The Muny)

Jane Powell and Webb Tilton; also Patricia Neway as Mother Abbess (Warwick Musical Theatre; Oakdale Music Theatre)

Dorothy Collins and Richard Eastham; also Werner Klemperer as Max (Melodyland Theatre, Anaheim, California; Little Theatre on the Square, et al.; Ronald Holgate would also play the captain during this tour)

Marilyn Savage and Irwin Denson (South Shore Music Circus, Cohasset, MA)

1970

Constance Towers and John Michael King; also Christopher Hewett as Max (Jones Beach Marine Theatre, Wantagh, NY)

Barbara Meister and Erik Silyu; also Taina Elg as Elsa; Director: Christopher Hewett (Paper Mill Playhouse, Millburn, NJ)

Barbara Eden and Reid Shelton; also Marvin Kaplan as Max and Laura Dean as Gretl (Shady Grove Music Fair)

1971

Carol Lawrence and Norwood Smith; also Lizabeth Pritchett (from the Broadway show) now playing Mother Abbess (tour, incl. Oakdale Musical Theatre; Cleveland Musicarnaval)

Leave it to the Kenley Players to deem genie headgear an acceptable substitute for a wimple, when Barbara Eden played Maria in their 1971 presentation of the show.

Sally Ann Howes (*Chitty Chitty Bang Bang*) strummed Maria's guitar for the Los Angeles Civic Light Opera presentation of *The Sound of Music* in 1972.

Constance Towers and John Michael King; also Christopher Hewett as Max
    (Jones Beach Marine Theatre, Wantagh, NY)
Barbara Eden and Terence Monk (Kenley Players)

1972

Sally Ann Howes and Bob Wright; also Werner Klemperer as Max, Patricia
    Morison as Elsa, Bill (William) Katt as Rolf (San Francisco Civic Light Opera;
    Los Angeles Civic Light Opera; Fisher Theatre, Detroit) [*Note: Dorothy Jeakins,
    who designed the costumes for the film also provided the costumes for this production.*]
Jane Powell and Joseph Campanella; also Cliff Norton as Max (The Muny)
Shirley Jones and H. M.Wynant; also Patrick Cassidy and Sarah Jessica Parker
    (Dallas State Fair Music Hall and tour)
Ann Blyth and Mitchell Gregg (Melody Top Music Tent, Milwaukee)

1974

Jeanne Shea and Roger Franklin (Thunderbird Dinner Theatre, Jacksonville FL)

1977

Shirley Jones; also with Patrick Cassidy and Sarah Jessica Parker (as well as her sib-
    lings Toby and Rachel Parker) (The Muny; Starlight Theatre, Kansas City, MO)

1978

Ann Blyth and Jean-Pierre Aumont (Cape Cod Melody Tent; Melody Fair, North Tonawanda, NY; Valley Forge Fair, Valley Forge, PA; Smithville Theatre, Smithville, NJ)

Florence Henderson and Edward Mulhare (Los Angeles Civic Light Opera; San Francisco Civic Light Opera)

Sally Ann Howes and Earl Wrightson (U.S. Military Academy at West Point; and tour)

Anna Maria Alberghetti and William Chapman (Sacramento Light Opera)

Suellen Estey and Jack Davison (Corning Glass Center, Corning, NY)

1979

Barbara Meister and Jean-Pierre Aumont (Paper Mill Playhouse)

Adrienne Doucette and Farley Granger (Coachlight Dinner Theatre, Nanuet, NY)

Marianne Tatum and David Barron (Equity Library Theatre, New York, September 20–October 14)

Judy O'Dea and David Cryer (Sebastian's Dinner Playhouse, San Clemente, CA)

1980

Constance Towers and Earl Wrightson (Jones Beach Theatre)

Carol Lawrence and Terence Monk (Kenley Players)

1982

Roberta Peters and Theodore Bikel; also Marni Nixon as Elsa (Valley Forge Music Fair; Westbury Music Fair)

Victoria Mallory and George Peppard (The Muny)

1983

Judy Kaye and George Peppard (Atlanta Theatre of the Stars; Cincinnati Opera)

1990

Debby Boone and Laurence Guittard; also Marianne Tatum as Elsa and Werner Klemperer as Max; Director: James Hammerstein (New York State Theatre, Lincoln Center—March 2–April 22)

1993

Christine Andreas and Ken Kercheval; also Marni Nixon as Mother Abbess (The Muny)

1993–95

Marie Osmond and Laurence Guittard (replacing Keir Dullea, who left the tour only a week into it); Director: James Hammerstein (Tour; starting at Lyric Opera House)

2003

Amanda Watkins and Robert Cuccioli; also Nick Jonas as Kurt (Paper Mill Playhouse)

2005

Kate Baldwin and Robert Westenberg (The Muny)
Paige Davis and Robert Cuccioli (Benedum Center, Pittsburgh)

2010

Ashley Brown and Tom Hewitt (The Muny)

2011

Jennifer Hope Wills and Robert Cuccioli (Benedum Center, Pittsburgh)
Sarah Pfisterer and Patrick Cassidy (Reagle Music Theatre—Boston)

2012

Laura Osnes and Tony Goldwyn; also Brooke Shields as Elsa; and (from the film): Daniel Truhitte (Baron Elberfeld), Nicholas Hammond, Kym Karath, and HeatherMenzies (Trio of the Saengerbund of Herwegen) (Concert: Carnegie Hall, April 24, 2012)
Melissa Errico and John Schneider; also Marni Nixon as Mother Abbess, Rachel York as Elsa, and Jeffrey Tambor as Max (Hollywood Bowl, July 28–30)
Elena Shadow and Ben Davis; with Edward Hibbert as Max (Paper Mill Playhouse)

One of several presentations of *The Sound of Music* at New Jersey's Paper Mill Playhouse, with an anonymous lady being passed off as the star of the show.

2014

Jenn Gambatese and Billy Zane; with Edward Hibbert as Max (Lyric Opera of Chicago)

1998 BROADWAY REVIVAL

PLAYBILL

MARTIN BECK THEATRE

Martin Beck Theatre
March 12, 1998–June 20, 1999; 533 performances; 38 previews, from February 6, 1998

CAST: Rebecca Luker (Maria), succeeded by Laura Benanti (originally part of the company as "A Postulant" and Ensemble); Michael Siberry (Captain von Trapp), succeeded by Richard Chamberlain; Patti Cohenour (Mother Abbess), Jan Maxwell (Baroness Schraeder), Fred Applegate (Max), Sara Zelle (Liesl), Dashiell Eaves (Rolf), Patricia Connolly (Frau Schmidt), Ryan Hopkins (Friedrich), Natalie Hall (Louisa), Matthew Ballinger (Kurt), Tracy Alison Walsh (Brigitta), Andrea Bowen (Marta), Ashley Rose Orr (Gretl), John Curless (Franz), Gina Ferrall (Sister Berthe), Jeanne Lehman (Sister Margaretta), Timothy Landfield (Zeller), Ann Brown (Sister Sophia), Martha Hawley (Baroness Elberfeld), Gannon McHale (Baron Elberfeld), Lynn C. Pinto (Ursual, Maid), Reno Roop (Admiral von Schreiber); Anne Allgood, Joan Barber, Kelly Cae Hogan, Siri Howard, Matt Loney, Patricia Phillips, Kristie Dale Sanders, Ben Sheaffer (Ensemble)

The Sound of Music returned at last to Broadway in 1998. *Courtesy of Playbill®*

Director: Susan H. Schulman.
Tony nominee: Revival of a Musical
Drama Desk nominee: Outstanding Orchestrations

When Richard Chamberlain took over role of Captain Georg von Trapp, he played it from March 10 to June 27, 1999. This version thereafter toured with Chamberlain to the following locations:

August 24–September 5, 1999: Orpheum Theatre, Minneapolis
September 7, 1999: Tivoli Theatre, Chattanooga
September 10–12, 1999: Gallard Auditorium, Charleston
September 14–19, 1999: Fox Theatre, Atlanta
September 21–26, 1999: Lyric Opera House, Baltimore
September 28–October 3, 1999: Oakdale Theatre, Wallingford, CT
October 5–10, 1999: T.P.A.C.'s Jackson Hall, Nashville
October 12–17, 1999: Clowes Hall, Indianapolis
October 19–November 7, 1999: Colonial Theatre, Boston
November 9–21, 1999: Palace Theatre, Cleveland
November 23–28, 1999: Palace Theatre, Columbus
November 30–December 5, 1999: Bob Carr, Orlando

December 8–19, 1999: Tampa Performing Arts Center, Tampa

December 21–26, 1999: Jones Hall, Houston

December 28, 1999–January 2, 2000: Peace Center, Greenville, SC

January 4–9, 2000: Kravis Center, West Palm Beach

January 11–23, 2000: Merriam Theatre, Philadelphia

January 25–30, 2000: War Memorial, Greensboro, NC

February 1–6, 2000: Fox Theatre, St. Louis

February 8–13, 2000: New Jersey Performing Arts Center, Newark

February 15–27, 2000: Shubert Theatre, Chicago

March 1–5, 2000: Pantages Theatre, Los Angeles

March 7–19, 2000: Civic Theatre, San Diego

March 14–19, 2000: Gammage Auditorium, Tempe, AZ

March 21–April 2, 2000: Orange County Performing Arts Center, Costa Mesa, CA

April 4–9, 2000: Civic Center, Portland, OR

April 11–23, 2000: Paramount Theatre, Seattle

April 25–30, 2000: Denver Center for Performing Arts, Denver

May 2–14, 2000: Golden Gate Theatre, San Francisco

May 16–21, 2000: Masonic Temple Theatre, Detroit

May 23–28, 2000: Memorial Auditorium, Raleigh

This production was worth noting not only for bringing *TSOM* back to Broadway for the first time since the original production, but for the number of changes in the script.

Although it does open with the abbey sequence and the "Preludium" choral pieces, the dialogue between the nuns about Maria's whereabouts actually precedes the songs.

The opening verse ("My day in the hills has come to an end, I know . . .") is cut here, so that the title song begins as it does in the movie ("The hills are alive . . .").

"My Favorite Things" is no longer a duet between the Mother Abbess and Maria, and is therefore removed from the scene in the former's office, as is the pertaining dialogue that introduces the song. Once the scene has ended, Maria is helped by her fellow nuns to change her abbey outfit to street clothing as she begins to sing "I Have Confidence," from the film. This means that the reprise of "My Favorite Things" sung by Maria in the abbey corridor (used as a scene change) is also gone.

For the scene where the children join Maria in her bedroom, "The Lonely Goatherd" has been removed and replaced by "My Favorite Things," to echo the same scene in the movie. Here, unlike the film, the children actually join Maria in singing the song.

Scene 8 from the original show, with the Trapp girls dropping off one by one as they react to the storm, had been used as another scene-change filler and was thereby excised from this version.

The captain is no longer present in the scene where Elsa and Max sing "How Can Love Survive?" (The lyrics "No little cold water flat have we/Warmed by a glow of insolvency/Up to your necks in security" were omitted)

At the end of Scene 9, Maria does not sing the "Do-Re-Mi" reprise.

Scene 10 of the Trapp children discussing the upcoming party was removed, although some of the lines were carried over into the party sequence itself.

In Act II, some additional lines were added for the captain in his argument with Max about the oncoming takeover by Germany. For example, Max's suggestion that Georg wait until it blows over prompts the captain to ask, "Can you guarantee it will all just blow over?" This line does not appear in the original playscript.

Because "An Ordinary Couple" has been replaced by "Something Good," there is new dialogue for the captain leading into the song.

Scene 3 of Act II, with Maria looking at herself in the mirror, is omitted.

For the reprise of "Sixteen Going on Seventeen," the lyric that over the years began to irk more and more women who felt it sounded demeaning, "And you belong *to* him," has been softened by the replacement of "to" with "with."

After the captain receives his telegram from Germany telling him he is to report back to naval duty, there is no longer any ambivalence suggested, since the line "I admit it would be exciting to have a ship under me again" has been cut. Maria's response to her husband begging for her help in the matter has been changed from the more passive "Georg, whatever you decide, will be my decision" to "You *know* what your decision must be."

So that the sequence between Admiral von Schreiber's arrival at the house and the concert can transition smoothly, Maria asks Liesl to run and get her guitar. This allows a spot for the displaced "The Lonely Goatherd," which is done here by Maria and the children at the festival. This relocation meant that the brief rendition of it with Max and the children at the top of the second act was no longer a reprise but the audience's first hearing of some of the tune. Putting the number here meant the reprise of "Do-Re-Mi" was no longer needed.

In the final scene at the abbey, Gretl's question about why God let the Nazis in was removed.

Orginal London Production

Palace Theatre
Cambridge Circus at Shaftesbury Avenue and Charing Cross Road
May 18, 1961–January 14, 1967
Opened as the Royal English Opera House in January 1891, this imposing red-brick structure soon after became the Palace Theatre of Varieties and then, in 1911, simply the Palace Theatre; 1,400 seats.

Richard Rodgers and Oscar Hammerstein II were as beloved and popular in the West End as they were back on Broadway. They had already won over London audiences in a big way with *Oklahoma!* (1,543 performances; 1947–50); *Carousel* (566 performances; 1950–51); *South Pacific* (802 performances; 1951–53); *The King and I* (926 performances; 1953–56); and *Flower Drum Song* (464 performances; 1960–61). The last had, in fact, just ended its run at the Palace

Theatre on April 29, 1961, only twenty days before *The Sound of Music* would have its official opening there, on May 18, 1961.

The Sound of Music ran at the Palace for 2,385 performances before closing on January 14, 1967, outrunning the Broadway original. Unlike Broadway, the West End stage production was still playing during the bulk of the *Sound of Music* movie's London engagement at the Dominion Theatre; and it broke the record at the time by being the longest-running Broadway show to play the West End.

Presented by Williamson Music, Ltd.

London Production Supervisor and Director: Jerome Whyte. Musical Numbers Staged by Joe Layton. Costumes: Lucinda Ballard. Scenic Production: Oliver Smith. Music Director: Robert Lowe. Orchestrations: Robert Russell Bennett. Choral Arrangement: Trude Rittman. Evenings: 7:30 p.m. Wednesday and Saturday matinees: 2:30 p.m.

Original London Cast Principals

Jean Bayless as Maria

Twenty-five years old at the time she auditioned for Richard Rodgers in New York, Bayless actually had a connection to the future Maria of the movie, Julie Andrews, having once lived with her and Millicent Martin for three months in Manhattan. Bayless was there to replace Andrews in her first Broadway stage hit, *The Boy Friend* (after New York, Bayless would tour in the show), while the latter went on to *My Fair Lady* and further fame. Previously in London, Bayless had danced alongside Audrey Hepburn and Marcel le Bon in the revue *Sauce Tartare* at the Cambridge Theatre in 1949. (Marion Marlowe, who played Elsa in the Broadway production of *TSOM*, was also in this show.) She was billed for a spell as Jo Ann Bayless, but returned to Jean by the time she got *TSOM*.

She was followed by Sonia Rees in the role of Maria.

Roger Dann as Captain von Trapp

Figuring a Gallic accent could pass for an Austrian one, Frenchman Roger Dann opened in *The Sound of Music* two days after his fiftieth birthday. Some of his Broadway credits connected him with several parties involved in *TSOM*. He had taken over from Claude Dauphin in the play *The Happy Time* (which was produced by Rodgers and Hammerstein and featured Kurt Kasznar, who would originate the role of Max in *TSOM*), and had appeared in the cast of the 1953–54 comedy *The Prescott Proposals*, which was written by *TSOM* book writers Howard Lindsay and Russel Crouse, while Leland Hayward was the producer. Dann had one notable American film credit around this time, portraying Anne Baxter's husband in the Alfred Hitchcock thriller *I Confess* (1953), which took place in French Quebec.

Constance Shacklock as Mother Abbess

From 1946 to 1956, Shacklock was a member of the Covent Garden Opera Company, performing such roles as Carmen, Octavian in *Der Rosenkavalier,* and Mrs. Sedley in *Peter Grimes.* She stayed with *TSOM* for its six-year run.

Eunice Gayson as Elsa Schrader

Gayson had appeared on stage in tours of *Born Yesterday* and *The Little Hut,* as well as the movies *Down Among the Z Men* (starring the Goons) and *Revenge of Frankenstein,* as Peter Cushing's lab assistant.

Harold Kasket as Max Detweiler

Kasket had appeared in *Caesar and Cleopatra* and *Antony and Cleopatra* with Laurence Olivier and Vivien Leigh, both in London and New York. The role he played in *The Bespoke Overcoat* at the Arts Theatre had been written expressly for him. He spent the 1955–56 season at the Old Vic, appeared in *Camino Real* at the Phoenix, and in *Mr. Fox of Venice* at the Piccadilly Theatre. Movies included *Moulin Rouge, Beau Brummell, The Man Who Knew Too Much, Bhowani Junction, The 7th Voyage of Sinbad, The Mouse That Roared,* and *S.O.S. Pacific.*

Additional Cast Members

Barbara Brown as Liesl
Nicholas Bennett as Rolf Gruber
John Coxall or Paul Ellison as Friedrich
Janet Ware or Janet Aust as Louisa
John Bosch or Robert Langley as Kurt
Susan Whitnell or Ann Dyer as Brigitta
Ann Dyer or Susan Marshall as Marta
Melanie Parr or Diane Cane as Gretl
Sylvia Beamish as Sister Berthe, Mistress of Novices
Olive Gilbert as Sister Margaretta, Mistress of Postulants
Lynn Kennington as Sister Sophia
Jay Denyer as Franz, the Butler
Diana Beaumont as Frau Schmidt, the Housekeeper
Betty Wood as Ursula
Peter Swanwick as Herr Zeller, the Gauleiter
Jack Lorenzo as Baron Elberfeld
Marilyn Dougan as A Postulant
Hilary Wontner as Admiral Von Schreiber

Neighbours of Captain von Trapp, nuns, novices, postulants, contestants in the Festival Concert: Patricia Brooke-Greene, Irene Cole, May Cunningham, Marilyn Dougan, Marie Fidock, Elaine Howells, Patricia Kilgarriff, Joan Lilley, Marie Lorraine, Alison McGuire, Georgina Pearce, Sonia Peters, Patricia Ridgway, Tina Ruta, Lita Tovey, Betty Wood, Christina Wren.

Other London Replacements include:

Maria: Paula Hendrix; *Captain:* Donald Scott (1963-67); *Max:* Ferdy Mayne, John Blythe; *Rolf Gruber:* Richard Loaring; *Liesl:* Susan Passmore; *Friedrich:* David McAlister; *Louisa:* Melanie Park; *Kurt:* Derek Lamden; *Brigitta:* Helen Worth, Diane Caine; *Marta:* Julie Booth, Diane Caine; *Gretl:* Diane Robillard; *Sister Berthe:* Marie Lorraine; *Franz:* Trevor Rachins; *Frau Schmidt:* Carolyn Gray; *Baron Elberfeld:* John Wynyard; *A Postulant:* Veronica Page; *Admiral Von Schreiber:* Nevil Whiting

[*Note: Cast members Barbara Brown (Liesl) and George Rutland (understudy for Rolf) were married on August 24, 1962, and were years later spotlighted in UK papers when they celebrated their fiftieth anniversary.*]

By the time it closed on January 14, 1967, *The Sound of Music* would enter the record books as the longest-running Broadway show to play London and find itself second only to *Oliver!* as the longest-running musical of any origin. All of these achievements would be overwhelmed in modern times by the mega-musical long runs of Andrew Lloyd Webber shows and others. (The five longest-running musicals in West End history as of 2014 are *Les Misérables, The Phantom of the Opera, Blood Brothers, Cats,* and *Starlight Express.*) *The Lion King* (1999), the 1997 revival of *Chicago, Wicked* (2005), *Jersey Boys* (2008)and the 1993 revival of *Grease* have since topped *TSOM* for long-running Broadway shows to play in London.

TSOM was followed on February 8, 1961 at the Palace Theatre by the American musical *110 in the Shade* with original Broadway cast members Stephen Douglas and Inga Swenson repeating their roles. It ran for 101 performances; alas, someone did not have the imagination to let it run another 9.

The 15 Longest-Running Shows in London West End History When *TSOM* Closed in 1967

1. *The Mousetrap* (Opened November 25, 1952—still running). It had been running over 8 ½ years when *The Sound* arrived.
2. *Aldwych Farces* (February 2, 1923–June 3, 1933 at the Aldwych). These are actually twelve different plays that ran a varying number of performances, almost one right after the other.
3. *Oliver!* (2,618 performances; opened June 30, 1960 at the New Theatre; closed September 1966 after six years). Lionel Bart's tuneful take on Charles Dickens was the longest-running West End musical up to that time and would hold this record for many years.
4. *The Sound of Music* (2,385 performances; Palace; 1961–67) USA
5. *Salad Days* (2,283 performances; opened August 5, 1954 at the Vaudeville Theatre) This musical starred Dorothy Reynolds, John Warner, Eleanor Drew; book and lyrics: Dorothy Reynolds and Julian Slade; music: Julian Slade. Ran 5 ½ years.
6. *My Fair Lady* (2,281 performances, at Theatre Royal Drury Lane; April 30, 1958–October 1963) USA

7. *Chu Chin Chow* (2,238 performances; Aug. 3, 1916–July 22, 1921 at His Majesty's); music: Frederic Norton; written by Oscar Asche; Asche was one of the stars too; also Courtice Pounds and Norman Williams; based on *Ali Baba and the 40 Thieves*.

8. *Beyond the Fringe* (2,200 total performances; opened May 10, 1961 at Fortune for 1,184 performances; transferred to the Mayfair, April 15, 1964, for 1,016 performances)

9. *The Boy Friend* (2,082 performances; opened at Wyndham's on January 14, 1954, following runs at the Players' Theatre Club and Embassy Theatre)

10. *Blithe Spirit* (1,997 performances; opened at the Piccadilly July 21, 1941); transferred to St. James and then Duchess.

11. *The Whitehall Follies* (1,920 performances; opened at the Whitehall on April 6, 1942; ran to 1947); first striptease show put on in the West End; Phyllis Dixey leased the theatre and the production remained there for five years.

12. *Worm's Eye View* (1,745 performances); revival of the 1945 show, which had played for 500 performances at the Whitehall starting December 18, 1945; it returned to play 1,745 at the Whitehall starting in 1947; written by R. F. Delderfield.

13. *Me and My Girl* (1,646 performances at the Victoria Palace; starting on December 16, 1937, starring Lupino Lane). A year after closing in 1940, it was back in the West End for another 208 performances.

14. *Together Again* (1,566 performances at the Victoria Palace, starting April 7, 1947); the Crazy Gang revue.

15. *Oklahoma!* (1,543 performances at the Theatre Royal Drury Lane; starting April 30, 1947, with Howard Keel and Betty Jane Watson) USA

LONDON REVIVALS

Apollo Victoria Theatre, August 18, 1981–September 18, 1982

CAST: Petula Clark (Maria), Michael Jayston (Captain von Trapp), Honor Blackman (Elsa Schraeder), June Bronhill (Mother Abbess), John Bennett (Max), Claire Parker (Liesl), Paul Shearstone (Rolf), Mary Dee (Sister Berthe), Patricia Conti (Sister Margaretta), Mercia Glossop (Frau Schmidt). Alternating Trapp children: David Graham, Leigh Pointer, Kevin Hueston (Friedrich), Lucy Jarvis, Helen Anker, Tracy Read (Louisa); Martina Grant, Karena Thomas, Amanda Fisher (Brigitta); Noel O'Connell, Simon Bowen, Dominic Gilvary (Kurt); Natasha Byrne, Vikki Woodman, Prudence Oliver (Marta); Leesa Cameron, Nicola Donohue, Annabel Walker (Gretl)

Director: John Fearnley.
Choreographer: Ronald Hynd.

The very first official West End revival was notable for a number of reasons. For one thing, it marked the long overdue legit stage debut of noted pop singer-actress Petula Clark. Clark had been reluctant to take on the role, knowing that at forty-eight years old, she risked criticism for inappropriate casting. Instead, the show brought her some of the best reviews of her career and proved a box office hit; the actress extending her initial six-month contract to thirteen. With the largest advance sale in British theatre history up to that time, *TSOM* broke another record for having the highest attendance figure for a single week (October 25–31). It was also the official reopening production that changed this venue from a cinema (located opposite the city's famed Victoria Station) to a legit theatre.

Another reason the production warranted notice was that it had so extensively restructured the piece to bear a closer resemblance to the movie, making room for both of Richard Rodgers's new songs. ("Something Good" took the place of "An Ordinary Couple" as it would in most future revivals). "My Favorite Things" was moved to Maria's bedroom to echo the film, thereby allowing the lead-in to the "Sixteen Going on Seventeen" reprise ("A Bell Is No Bell") to fill the vacated space in the Mother Abbess's office. "The Lonely Goatherd" was done as a puppet show albeit at a village fair, while Max, Elsa, and the captain's second-act number, "No Way to Stop It," was omitted.

Noteworthy in the cast was June Bronhill, who was the first actress to play Maria in Australia (1961), this time cast as the Mother Abbess. Captain von Trapp was played by Michael Jayston, best remembered by movie audiences for playing part of the title roles in *Nicholas and Alexandra* (1971), and Elsa was played by Honor Blackman, who had achieved immortality as the unforgettably named "Pussy Galore" in the 1964 James Bond adventure *Goldfinger*.

The show received a great boost of publicity when Maria von Trapp declared it "the best *Sound of Music* I have ever seen. The people in the show lived up to how they were in real life. I was in tears at the end."

Sadler's Wells, June 18–September 5, 1992

CAST: Liz Robertson (Maria), Christopher Cazenove (Captain von Trapp), Linda Hibberd (Mother Abbess), Jan Waters (Elsa), Robin Nedwell (Max), Lottie Mayor (Liesl), George Asprey (Rolf). Alternating Trapp children: Samuel Trounce, Philippe Reynolds, Nicholas Field (Friedrich), Heather Jones, Angela Forry, Louisa Cartwright Tucker (Louisa), Kevin Bishop, David Cooper, Christopher Johns (Kurt), Laura Penta, Ellie Beaven, Honour Tomkinson (Brigitta), Claire Slater, Suzannah Butcher, Summer Vaigncourt-Strallen (Marta), Cydney Uffindell-Phillips, Olivia Ferrer, Jessica Fox (Gretl).

Director/Choreographer: Wendy Toye.
Producers: Ronald S. Lee Ltd., Shochiku Company Ltd.
Musical Director: Nick Davies.

The following year, Liz Robertson reprised Maria, and Linda Hibberd the Mother Abbess on the Pickwick *Shows Collection* CD recording, with Denis Quilley as the captain.

London Palladium, November 15, 2006–February 21, 2009

Andrew Lloyd Webber held a TV talent competition to find "Maria" for this production. Connie Fisher won and played Maria von Trapp for a year. (See Chapter 15.)

CAST: Connie Fisher (Maria; alternates: Aoife Mulholland, Gemma Baird; Fisher succeeded by Summer Strallen, who had played Marta in the 1992 revival), Alexander Hanson (Captain; replacing Simon Shepherd, who withdrew from production following the first two public performances, on November 3 and 4; the understudy, Christopher Dickins, played the part until Hanson was ready; Hanson was succeed by Simon Burke, Simon MacCorkindale); Lesley Garrett (Mother Abbess; succeeded by Margaret Preece); Lauren Ward (Baroness Schraeder), Ian Gelber (Max Detweiler), Sophie Bould (Liesl; succeeded by Amy Lennox); Neil McDermott (Rolf)

Director: Jeremy Sams
Choreographer: Arlene Phillips.

TOUR:

CAST: Connie Fisher (Maria), Michael Praed (Captain von Trapp), Margaret Preece (Mother Abbess; succeeded by Marilyn Hill Smith and Lesley Garrett); Janica Mulcahy (Elsa), Martin Callaghan (Max), Claire Fishenden (Liesl), Jeremy Taylor (Rolf; succeeded by Chris Barton on June 29, 2010); Jenna Boyd (Frau Schmidt)

The production toured in:
September 2–26, 2009: Alhambra Theatre, Bradford
September 29–October 24, 2009: Mayflower Theater, Southampton
October 27–November 14, 2009: Milton Keynes Theatre, Milton Keynes
November 17–December 5, 2009: Empire, Sunderland
December 15, 2009–January 16, 2010: Palace Theatre, Manchester
January 19–February 20, 2010: Playhouse, Edinburgh, Scotland
February 24–March 20, 2010: Opera House, Belfast, Ireland
March 24–April 17, 2010: His Majesty's Theatre, Aberdeen, Scotland
(*The show took a three-week hiatus.*)
May 11–29, 2010: Venue Cymru Llandudno, Llandudno
June 1–19, 2010: Congress Theatre, Eastbourne
June 22–July 10, 2010: New Victoria Theatre, Woking
July 13–August 21, 2010: Hippodrome, Birmingham (*Praed all but the last week*)
(*Due to Fisher's hiatus to marry and honeymoon, Kirsty Malpass was Maria for the next two engagements.*)
August 24–September 18, 2010: Theatre Royal, Plymouth
September 22–October 9, 2010: Pavilion, Bournemouth
October 12–30, 2010: Liverpool Empire, Liverpool (*Connie Fisher returned*)

November 2–December 4, 2010: Hippodrome, Bristol

December 7, 2010–January 2, 2011: New Theatre, Oxford

(*Maria was now Verity Rushworth; the captain played by Jason Donovan; Philippa Buxton was the alternate Maria*)

January 29–February 12, 2011: New Theatre, Hull

February 15–March 5, 2011: Regent Theatre, Stoke-on-Trent

March 15–April 2, 2011: Millennium Forum, Derry

April 5–30, 2011: Canal Theatre, Dublin

May 10–June 4, 2011: King's Theatre, Glasgow,

June 7–25, 2011: Grand Theatre, Leeds

July 15–August 6, 2011: Theatre Royal, Nottingham (*Kieron Crook played the captain for this engagement.*)

August 9–20, 2011: Theatre Royal, Norwich

(*Fisher was supposed to return for these engagements but did not because of vocal problems.*)

August 23–September 3, 2011: Millennium Centre, Cardiff

September 5–17, 2011: Palace Theatre, Manchester (*Donovan left after this; Kieron Crook returned to play the captain.*)

September 20–October 8, 2011: Theatre Royal, Newcastle

October 11–22, 2011: New Wimbledon Theatre, Wimbledon

Regent's Park Open Air Theatre
July 25–September 14, 2013 (extended by a week from its original announced dates). Presented by arrangement with Josef Weinberger Limited on behalf of R&H Theatricals of New York.
Director: Rachel Kavanaugh.
Choreographer: Alistair David.
Orchestrations: Chris Walker.

CAST: Charlotte Wakefield (Maria), Michael Xavier (Captain von Trapp), Helen Hobson (Mother Abbess), Michael Matus (Max), Caroline Keiff (Elsa), Faye Bookes (Liesl), Joshua Tonks (Rolf Gruber). Alternating Trapp children: Finlay Banks, Matthew Muncey, Jaydon Vijn (Friedrich), Elise Bugeja, Lily Burgering, Mia Jenkins (Louisa), Alistair Blair, Oliver Breedon, Arthur Gledhill-Franks (Kurt), Isabelle Allen, Imogen Gurney, Ava Merson-O'Brien (Brigitta), Jaime Adler, Emily Carey, Amybeth McNulty (Marta), Gemma Fray, Sarah Huttlestone, Honor Kneafsey (Gretl)

ORIGINAL AUSTRALIAN COMPANY

Princess Theatre
163 Spring Street, Melbourne, Victoria, Australia.
    (This 1,488-seat venue opened in 1857).
October 20, 1961–September 22, 1962

CAST: June Bronhill (Maria), Peter Graves (Captain von Trapp), Rosina Raisbeck (Mother Abbess), Lola Brooks (Elsa), Eric Reiman (Max), Julie Day (Liesl), Tony Jenkins (Rolf), Lorna Forbes (Frau Schmidt), Lola Brooks (Elsa), Barry Balmer (Franz). Alternating Trapp children: William Hambly, John Sullivan (Friedrich), Yvonne Barrett, Patty McGrath (Louisa), Angela Kendall, Nancy Hawthorn (Brigitta), Robert Patterson, Roger Smeed, Paul Nolan (Kurt), Helen Robson, Jenny O'Connell, Ann Heales (Marta), Heather Charles, Gayle Kinzel, Fay Huggan (Gretl)

Touring company featured Vanessa Lee (Graves's wife as Maria), who had stepped in for Bronhill during illness in June 1962. When Bronhill left in January 1963 she was replaced by Renee Guerin, who had been Mary Martin's standby in the New York production.

This also played at the Tivoli in Sydney, starting September 28, 1962; Her Majesty's in Adelaide, starting June 19, 1963; Elizabethan in Sydney, December 28, 1963.

1999 Australian Revival

Lyric Theatre
Sydney, New South Wales
November 11, 1999–February 13, 2000

CAST: Lisa McCune (Maria), John Waters (Captain von Trapp), Eilene Hannan (Mother Abbess), Bert Newton (Max), Tim Draxl (Rolf), Rachel Marley (Marta), Pia Morley (Liesl)

(This was based on the 1998 Broadway revival.)

This production also toured until February 2001; in Melbourne (Princess Theatre, March 21–July 15, 2000), Brisbane (Lyric, QPAC, August 3–September 16, 2000), Perth (Burswood Entertainment Centre, October 7–November 12, 2000), and Adelaide (Festival Centre; January 6–February 11, 2001).

Rachael Beck took over as Maria for the Perth and Adelaide seasons, Rob Guest as Captain von Trapp in Perth.

Elsewhere:

San Juan

Tapia Theatre, September–October 1966
Camille Carrion (Maria), Raul Davilia (Captain)

Dublin

Gaiety Theatre, 1970
Kitty Sullivan (Maria), Ray McAnally (Captain)

Volksoper, Vienna

Starting February 26, 2005

The first major Austrian production of the stage version of *TSOM* (translated into German) opened in 2005 to mixed reviews. (There had been a minor version done in Innsbruck, and a satirical production in Vienna in 1993.) It was soon added to the company's repertoire and returned several times after that, scheduled for twelve to twenty performances each season: 2006, 2007, 2008, 2012. It was also done at the Oper Graz in 2009, 2010.

CAST: Sandra Pires (Maria; succeeded by Martina Dorak, Johanna Arrouas), Michael Kraus (Captain von Trapp; succeeded by Kurt Schreibermayer), Heidi Brunner (Mother Abbess; succeeded by Gabriele Sima and Ulrike Steinsky), Renate Pitschneider (Elsa), Peter Pikl (Max), Dagmar Bernhard (Liesl), Tina Lemperg (Gretl)

Director: Renaud Doucet.

Sample translated lyric: "The hills are alive with the sound of music" became "The most beautiful song is the song of the mountain." This production kept with the updated script, dropping "An Ordinary Couple" and replacing it with "Something Good."

Toronto

Princess of Wales Theatre, October 15, 2008–January 19, 2010

At 69 weeks and over 500 performances, it was the longest-running revival to play Toronto.

CAST: Elicia MacKenzie (Maria), Burke Moses (Captain von Trapp), Noella Huet (Mother Abbess), Brigitte Robinson (Frau Schmidt), Megan Nuttall (Liesl), Keith Dinicol (Max Detweiler)

Director: Jeremy Sams.

This was the North American premiere of the same production that had been revived in London starting in 2006; Elicia MacKenzie was chosen by TV viewers (on a series that ran in July and August 2008); her runner-up, Janna Polzin, played Maria at Wednesday and Saturday matinees.

Paris

Theatre du Chatelet
December 6, 2009–January 3, 2010

CAST: Sylvia Schwartz, Julie Fuchs, Christine Arand (Maria), Rod Gilfry (Captain von Trapp), Kim Criswell (Mother Abbess), Christine Arand (Elsa), Laurent Alvaro (Max), Carin Gilfry (Liesl), James McOran-Campbell (Rolf).

Presented in English under the direction of Emilio Sagi.

Salzburg

Salzburger Landestheater
Scwarzstraße 22
Premiere: October 23, 2011 (this ran each season until May 25, 2014)

ORIGINAL CAST: Wietske van Tongeren (Maria), Uwe Kroeger (Captain von Trapp), Frances Pappas and Marianne Larsen (Mother Abbess), Hanna Kastner (Liesl), Franziska Becker (Elsa), Hubert Wild and Simon Schnorr (Max), Sebastian Smulders (Rolf). Multiple actors alternated the roles of the other six Trapp children.

Directors: Andreas Gergen and Christian Struppeck.
Musical Director: Peter Ewaldt.
German Adaptation: Heiko Wohlgemuth and Kevin Schroeder.
Fifty-two years after its Broadway debut and forty-seven years after 20th Century-Fox arrived in the city to capture the sights and sounds of Salzburg on film, *The Sound of Music* finally had a production of the show performed (by live actors, not puppets) there.

Translated into German, this meant that there were liberties taken with the lyrics. For example "Doe, a deer, a female dear" became "Do, so wie der Donaustrom," which means "Do, like the Danube river" (!). Also, because of the geographical implausibility of it, the Trapps no longer escaped over the mountains into Switzerland, as the locals were all too aware that such a trip would lead you into Germany.

The youngest of Maria von Trapp's children, Johannes, was in attendance at the premiere.

From Stage to Screen

Changes in the Motion Picture from the Original Playscript

W hile many stage-to-screen transfers have been taken to task for the myriad changes made in an effort to present something a bit different in the motion picture version, *The Sound of Music* is often cited as a rare example of the many tweaks, edits, rewrites, revisions, shifted scenes and songs being considered for the most part an improvement over the original.

To give a clear example of how the Howard Lindsay and Russel Crouse book changed from Broadway to Hollywood, here is a breakdown of each scene as it happened on stage with the key revisions by Ernest Lehman that took place in the equivalent scenes in the 1965 movie.

ACT ONE

Scene 1: Nonnberg Abbey

For anyone familiar with *The Sound of Music* expressly through its film version, the very opening of the stage musical throws you a curve—it does *not* start with the title song. Having dispensed with an overture (a tradition Richard Rodgers claimed he was never too fond of anyway), the curtain rises on the nuns at Nonnberg singing the "Preludium," consisting of "Dixit Dominus," "Morning Hymn," and "Allelulia," all of which ended up in the movie in the scene that followed Julie Andrews's performance of "The Sound of Music" and the opening credits.

Once the musical portion of Scene 1 is finished in the play, multiple nun voices are heard inquiring about the whereabouts of Maria, revealed in the follow-up scene.

Scene 2: A mountainside near Nonnberg Abbey

In the theatre, Maria was actually first seen positioned in a tree (she, after all, according to the lyrics in "Maria," "climbs a tree and scrapes her knee . . ."), as she sang the opening verse to the title song "My days in the hills have come to an end, I know . . . ." This verse ended up being cut from the film, musical coordinator Saul Chaplin and company correctly theorizing that it was much more exciting to plunge right into the refrain, helping to make "The hills are

Elsa (Eleanor Parker) isn't quite getting through to her lover, Georg (Christopher Plummer), as a certain governess has clearly captured his heart.

alive with the sound of music" the signature line of the entire piece. There are, however, instrumental strains of the verse heard on the soundtrack as the camera drifts over the landscape before it approaches Julie Andrews on her hilltop. This song also contains the one instance of a "changed" or "alternate" lyric. The original line about laughing like a brook has it tripping and falling "Over stones *in* its way." In the movie, Julie Andrews sings "Over stones *on* its way."

Scene 3: The office of the Mother Abbess, the next morning

The discussion among the Reverend Mother and the Mistress of Novices and the Mistress of Postulants involves the eligibility of another postulant, named Irmagard, who is deemed too pretentiously pious to enter the abbey, before it leads to their concern over Maria. Irmagard was left out of the film script, and the dialogue is almost entirely new until the exchange between Mother Abbess and Sister Sophia, the latter answering about her feelings of Maria that "I love her dearly." The song "Maria" was sung by Mother Abbess, Sister Berthe, Sister Margaretta, and Sister Sophia on stage, whereas they are joined by two other nuns on screen, Sister Catherine and Sister Agatha. The number also changed location from the Mother Abbess's office to an interior courtyard of the abbey, with Maria seen racing by after the singing is concluded. She was not seen at the abbey in the play until she was led quietly into the Reverend Mother's office.

On stage the Mother Abbess mentions giving Maria permission to leave the abbey for the previous scene in the tree, while her hilltop rendezvous on screen seems to have been her own impulsive decision. Although Maria explains both on stage and screen that she was brought up on the mountain in question (Untersberg is used in the film, while the landmass remains anonymous in the play), only the theatre script allows the Reverend Mother to give us a tiny glimpse into *her* background, revealing that she too was brought up there.

The discussion of breaking the rules about singing in the abbey led on stage to the Mother Abbess asking Maria about a specific song she heard her singing in the garden. It turns out the Reverend Mother sang the same song as a child, allowing the two of them to share the tune, "My Favorite Things." Ernest Lehman's film script would drop the idea of any song being sung in this scene and move this particular number into the bedroom scene at the Trapp villa, to be shared by Maria with the children.

On Broadway some historical background was related by the Mother Abbess about Captain von Trapp, explaining to Maria that he was given the Maria Teresa Medal by the emperor for heroism in the Adriatic, which was indeed the case with the real-life captain. On screen he is merely referred to as "a retired officer of the Imperial Navy." Maria being told here that the captain's wife has died is in the screenplay only, this information not being said to her on stage at this point: One of Lehman's most noted (and quoted) lines spoken during this scene does *not* appear in the Lindsay-Crouse script: "When the Lord closes a door . . . somewhere He opens a window."

As a button on the scene on stage, Maria asks permission to sing one final line from "My Favorite Things," prompting a disapproving look from Sister Berthe.

Scene 4: A corridor in the abbey

As was a theatre tradition/necessity in the days before state-of-the-art revolving or quick-changing set designs, certain scenes were staged before a curtain with the idea of not only keeping the audience entertained but to cover a more substantial change of scenery going on for the next scene. At this point on stage, Maria sings a reprise of "My Favorite Things" in hopes of elevating her spirits. As she leaves, Sister Margaretta punctuates the scene with one final line from "Maria."

For the film, Richard Rodgers was asked to contribute a new song that would show Maria exiting the abbey and going from trepidation to a willful confidence. Hence, "I Have Confidence," which received uncredited contributions from musical director Saul Chaplin and screenwriter Ernest Lehman. (Rodgers seemed to have trouble grasping Chaplin's concept for the first portion of the song, so Chaplin and Lehman came up with it.) This song would also allow the filmmakers to do a superb visual transition from the abbey to the Trapp villa, showing Maria singing through the streets of Salzburg, taking the bus to Aigen, and making her way up to the front door of her new employer's house.

Later stage productions would use the new script that substituted "I Have Confidence" for the "My Favorite Things" reprise.

Scene 5: The living room of the Trapp villa, that afternoon

On stage, Captain von Trapp was first introduced trying to summon his house-keeper, Frau Schmidt, with his bosun's whistle, leading to a conversation with the villa's butler, Franz. Exposition that would show up during the pinecone/dinner scene in the movie is given here, about the captain's romantic interest in Frau Schrader (Elsa), his need to leave the next day to be with her, and how he will be returning in a month with both Elsa and impresario Max Detweiler in tow. In the play, mention of a telegram not being delivered leads Frau Schmidt to call the delivery boy "scatterbrained" and for Franz to assure her that should Germany take over Austria they would bring efficiency. She warns him not to let the captain hear such talk. All of this was eliminated for the film, with no discussion of telegraph boy Rolf Gruber before he first appeared on screen. There is also dialogue between Schmidt and Franz about how humiliating the latter feels being summoned by a whistle. The line about the whistle being "humiliating" would be given on screen to Maria and spoken directly to the captain, following his introduction of his children.

For the playscript, Maria was first spotted in the living room by the captain after she had dropped to her knees to pray about her new job and its prospects. Lehman decided to make their initial meeting more confrontational, having the captain suddenly appear in the doorway of the villa's ballroom, admonishing the new governess for letting herself in there, explaining that "certain rooms are not to be disturbed." On Broadway, Maria and the captain introduced themselves by name (Maria was given the last name of "Rainer," while none was spoken of in the movie), but there were no such pleasantries exchanged on screen. (The real-life Maria's last name was *not* Rainer but Kutschera. Lindsay and Crouse chose to use her mother's maiden name in place of the true one.)

The actual number of pre-Maria governesses in the real Trapp story, twenty-six, was paired down for the musical to twelve, at least according to the captain's recollection. During this scene on stage, he made no mention of his wife's passing, as he does here in the film. (It was left up to Frau Schmidt to finally make mention to Maria of the captain's wife's death in the original play, in the scene in Maria's bedroom.) The dialogue on Broadway during this exchange also suggested that Maria would actually be instructing her new charges in a classroom setting, while any indication of her teaching skills (which the real Maria possessed) was cut from the motion picture adaptation.

Only those *very* familiar with the real Trapp story might have noticed the renaming for the musical of the housekeeper (originally Baroness Matilda) and the butler Hans became Franz; it is far more noticeable that dramatic license has been taken completely with the Trapp children, each one assigned a new name, when they show up and introduce themselves in order of age. The real-life Rupert, the captain's eldest, has swapped places with sister Agathe, so that the Agathe-equivalent, Liesl, could be the focus of a subplot involving her coming of age and being interested in romance. (This romance between a Trapp daughter and an aspiring Nazi had no basis in reality.)

After the captain departs and leaves Maria to take care of her new charges, the playscript brought up the topic of music, leading to the children confessing that they don't know any songs, nor do they know how to sing. It is at this moment that Maria takes up the guitar she has brought with her and gives them a simple instruction, to the tune of "Do-Re-Mi." For the movie, Lehman's script put this song on the back burner to be used later on, more effectively, after the ice has been broken, so to speak, between Maria and the children. In the interim came the bedroom scene, allowing Maria to show her comforting nature by singing with the children ("The Lonely Goatherd" on stage, "My Favorite Things" on film). For the movie this was followed by a day's outing montage leading up to the travelogue-style presentation of "Do-Re-Mi," which became one of the most memorable sequences of all.

Scene 6: Outside the Trapp villa, that afternoon

Liesl has her clandestine meeting with Rolf, the telegraph boy, having no need to excuse herself from the dinner table in the Broadway show, as the eating sequence was present only in the film. The ominous exchange about Rolf having "a way of knowing things" when he tells Liesl he's aware that her father is home was not included in the movie script, nor was Rolf accidentally mentioning the appearance from Berlin of a Colonel Schneider staying with the Gauleiter (Herr Zeller), which suggested that Rolf was consciously keeping information about the oncoming Anschluss secret from Captain von Trapp. Lehman opted for playful dialogue about a fake telegram read by Rolf in order to amuse Liesl. While Liesl boasts of her father having been decorated for "bravery" in the playscript, the movie was more specific in citing the emperor as having performed the decorating task.

The scene leads up to and concludes with "Sixteen Going on Seventeen," much as in the film.

Scene 7: Maria's bedroom, later that evening

As Maria and Frau Schmidt discuss getting extra material so that the former can make clothing for the children, the stage script includes some revelatory dialogue from Schmidt on how her employer comes home each time a new governess is hired, and her theory of how the children "get rid of their governesses just because they want to see their father." This was not included in the film script. On Broadway there was also mention made here of musical evenings at the house when the captain's wife would sing and he himself would play either the violin or guitar. Any musical skills the wife possessed went unmentioned in the movie, while any suggestion of the captain playing the violin was dropped in favor of emphasizing a far less "highfalutin'" instrument, the guitar.

When Liesl tells Maria how easy it is to climb to the upper windows, the original script has her mention her sister Louisa being able to do so with "a toad in her hand." Since a frog had actually received an on-camera moment earlier in the movie, when Maria found it in her pocket, the revised line tossed out the amphibian and made it the creepier "jar of spiders."

Once all seven children are present in this scene in the play, the cue for Maria chirping "The Lonely Goatherd" was the line "Maybe if we all sing loud enough we won't hear the thunder." Since the song was replaced with "My Favorite Things" for the movie, the dialogue needed to be changed to have Marta say that the thunder "makes me want to cry." Maria thereby offered her remedy for unhappiness, by thinking of "nice things," which, in turn, paved the way for the replacement song. With the children now on hand during this song, each was given a chance to toss in *their* "favorite things," as spoken dialogue. These included pussy willows, Christmas, and pillow fights. Obviously, since this was Maria and Mother Abbess's song on stage, the willows and the pillows were not necessary.

The lights came down on stage as soon as the song ended, whereas the film had a disapproving captain show up, cutting the number short as he admonished the new governess for her lack of discipline. This allowed Lehman to include an exchange in which Maria covered for Liesl's meeting with Rolf, thereby giving the teen further reason to trust her. Not wanting to deprive the song of a big finish, the film script did have Maria resume singing "My Favorite Things" once everyone else had cleared the room, leading to her coming up with the idea of using the drapes for clothing.

Scene 8: A hallway in the Trapp villa

This was another scene written for the stage expressly to cover a change of scenery. As the thunderstorm continues from the previous scene, Gretl enters with a candle, followed by Marta, Brigitta, and Louisa. In an effort to stay brave, Gretl tries some yodeling, only to discover that her older sisters have abandoned her. At the sound of another thunderclap, Gretl retreats as well. There was clearly no need for any of this in the movie.

Scene 9: The terrace of the Trapp villa, six weeks later

The baroness, Elsa Schrader (there was no such title given the character on stage), and Max Detweiler are introduced in the play on the Trapp villa terrace; for the film they are first seen in the captain's car as they drive toward the house. The screenplay allowed for two extra bits of business, neither possible in the confines of a theatre; first, having the Trapp children playing in the trees above the captain and his party as they drive by, unaware of who these "urchins" are, and then, most notably, Maria and her charges rowing a boat, tipping it over and falling in the lake as they express their excitement over the captain's long-awaited return.

Lunt-Fontanne Theatre

PLAYBILL

a weekly magazine for theatregoers

THE SOUND OF MUSIC

The original playbill cover of *The Sound of Music* during Mary Martin's two-year run in the show. *Courtesy of Playbill*®

The exchanges between the captain and Elsa, establishing their relationship, are quite different between stage and screen. In the Broadway script, Elsa talks about the need for the captain to spend some time in Vienna should they be wed, because she must still handle her late husband's estate, being the actual president of a corporation. No such status of the baroness is discussed on screen. Instead, the captain dismisses the thought of spending time in Vienna, criticizing Elsa's lavish and pretentious lifestyle, "gossiping gaily with bores I detest." In the theatre, Max and Elsa's conversation about coaxing the captain into marrying her led directly to their comical song about how doomed the couple will be because they are *not* poor and suffering, "How Can Love Survive." Since it was decided that neither Max nor Elsa would be joining in the singing on screen, this song was excised. Instead, an instrumental version was heard later playing in the Trapp ballroom as their guests waltzed.

The play also threw in some dialogue about a nearby neighbor, Baron Elberfeld, who would later show up at the party to argue politics with Herr Zeller. While the baron and his wife were retained for the party scene on screen, their names remained unspoken. (Only the Baroness E is listed in the end credits.) Lindsay and Crouse opted to have Max scouting talent for the "Kaltzberg Festival," while Lehman's script stuck with the authentic Salzburg Folk Festival. In contrast, whereas the play had him inquiring about whether the Nonnberg Abbey had a choir, the film had him overhear singing from the fictitious Klopmann Monastery. The arrival of Rolf to deliver a telegraph to Max included the teen giving a "heil" salute in both versions, but the captain's angry response that he "will not be heiled!" was omitted for the movie. Max's passive reaction to the imminent political takeover suggested by Rolf's behavior brought a rather jokey response from the captain on stage, "It's a good thing you haven't any character, because if you had I'm convinced I'd hate you." The film script chose to make it more angry; after Max blithely declares he has no political convictions, the captain snaps at him, "You can help it. You *must* help it"; certainly a stronger pay off.

Following the singing by the children of "The Sound of Music" and the captain melting his icy manner in order to join in, the stage version gave Maria a short reprise of "Do-Re-Mi," followed by a conversation between her and Elsa, who wants to make certain that the woman she now senses might be her rival will not be sticking around. The screenplay instead jumped from the "Sound of Music" scene to Maria and the children performing "The Lonely Goatherd" as a puppet show, a newly invented sequence to justify using the song that had been booted out of the bedroom scene.

Scene 10: A hallway in the Trapp villa, one week later

This was another scene inserted into the original stage show in order to change to a different set. The children speak with Frau Schmidt, who tells them there used to be many parties at the Trapp villa, prompting Louisa to remember, wistfully, a certain lady who was at those parties all the time—clearly a reference to her mother. The scene ends with the children dancing together, something that was retained in the film to take place on the terrace, outside the house.

Scene 11: The living room, the same evening

The party at the Trapp villa begins with the hint of a heated exchange over the Anchluss between Herr Zeller and guest Baron Elberfeld. In the play Elsa has made herself absent from the festivities at first, complaining of a headache—no such faux ailment was mention on screen. Brigitta gets more to do on stage, blurting out that it is quite obvious Elsa wasn't really ill; discussing with her father how tense the guests seem; and, most importantly, being the one who tells Maria that it is all too clear that her father is in love with the governess. The film script had Elsa make this revelation. (Because of her extended part, the original playbill gave the actress playing Brigitta a separate bio entry; the other five younger children were grouped together.) Lehman's screenplay gave viewers a one-line explanation of what exactly the "Laendler" was, something not mentioned in the play.

Curiously, the stage show had Elsa make the announcement that the children were going to say goodnight to the guests in a special way, as if she is the one responsible for their rendition of "So Long, Farewell." Wisely, the movie had Maria do this. On Broadway, their song followed both Maria's awkward awareness that her feelings for the captain are obvious, and the captain insisting she join them at the dinner table. The latter moment had prompted a rather snobby reaction from Max, who feels uncomfortable that they would be sharing their meal with "a nursemaid." Not wanting Max to appear so pretentious, the film script made him the one who insisted Maria be included at dinner, *after* he has been enchanted by the children's song. Because it was up to Elsa to confront Maria about the growing attraction between the governess and her employer, a new scene in the film took place in Maria's room, where she and Elsa have gone to pick out an appropriate dress for the party.

The scene ended in the Lindsay-Crouse version with Maria exiting the house, but without leaving any sort of note about her decision to go. The film added the note and also used this as the point to insert the intermission. The Broadway show had two more scenes to go before the break.

Scene 12: A corridor in the abbey

Yet another crossover moment to cover a scene change, as Sister Sophia leads a new postulant to Mother Abbess's office, and the nuns are again heard singing the "Morning Hymn" portion of the "Preludium." The film inserted not only the equivalent of "Scene 1 from Act 2" prior to taking us back to the abbey, but also included a whole new scene of the children trekking there in hopes of speaking with their AWOL governess.

Scene 13: The office of the Mother Abbess, three days later

Maria's revelation to the Mother Abbess that she has left the Trapp family because of her confusion over her feelings for the captain, played pretty similarly on stage and screen, leading up to the Reverend Mother's stirring rendition of "Climb Ev'ry Mountain."

ACT TWO

Scene 1: The terrace, the same day

Despite moving "Climb Ev'ry Mountain" *after* the intermission for the movie, both play and film pretty much begin their second halves with the same intention, with the children trying to carry on after Maria has left. The stage version has them playing blind man's bluff with Max as they reprise "The Lonely Goatherd"; the movie opts to show them halfheartedly bouncing a ball between themselves and Elsa. Here again is a distinct improvement in the screen transfer, as the new scene more clearly gives one the impression that this effort and levity are forced, with Elsa placed in the hopeless position of trying to be the Trapp children's "mother." Playing and singing with Max suggests more fun than they should be having at this point, considering their feeling of despair over losing their beloved governess.

To give Elsa a bit more edge and less sympathy, Lehman's screenplay has her conspiratorially hint to Max that after she has wed Georg she intends to send his offspring to boarding school. In contrast, the captain's reaction to whether

Maria is going to be coming back or not receives a more blunt and dismissive "we are not to mention Fraulein Maria" on stage, while the film makes the captain pretend to be more cavalier about her abrupt departure, trying to convince himself that he doesn't care.

While the original Lindsay & Crouse script had this scene lead pretty quickly to the children's rendition of "My Favorite Things" being interrupted by the return of Maria, the screenplay inserted the newly created scene of the children visiting the abbey in hopes of speaking to their governess, which, in turn led to "Climb Ev'ry Mountain." Back on the terrace of the Trapp villa, yet another new dialogue sequence was created for the movie, with the captain questioning his children about where they have gone and the seven of them making up a none-too-convincing story about picking berries. This exchange preceded Maria's return to the Trapps.

The original sheet music for the title song, as published by Williamson Music, Inc.

At this point in the Broadway show, the political situation in Austria arose, causing Max to admit to his lack of convictions and the necessity to straddle the fence and make sure you stay on the side of those in power. This led to Elsa and Max trying to persuade the captain to their line of thinking and the song "No Way to Stop It." This number brought a very political slant to the relationship between the captain and Elsa, and became an important reason why they both come to the conclusion that they cannot be wed. This was probably the most unfortunate omission from Lehman's script, since it was decided from the get-go that Max and Elsa would not have singing roles. For the movie, the captain and Elsa have a conversation in which they admit that their getting married would be all wrong, but it stems exclusively from the fact that they know all too well that Maria has stolen the captain's heart.

The screenplay contained a stronger exchange between Maria and the captain, in which the latter confessed his true feelings for her, making their growing romantic feelings less abrupt than they seemed on stage. The stage show had followed this declaration of love between them with the song "An Ordinary Couple," which Richard Rodgers later admitted was not the satisfying number he hoped it would be. Because neither Robert Wise nor Ernest Lehman wanted to keep this song in the picture, they asked Rodgers to come up with a substitute, hence the replacement, "Something Good." This became so clearly the preferred number that future stage productions would use it instead of "An Ordinary Couple," which basically faded from memory, familiar principally to those who owned the original cast album.

Scene 2: A corridor in the abbey, two weeks later

Another moment written to allow for a scene change on stage, this merely showed the nuns having a silent encounter in the corridor with three young postulants, and then Sisters Margaretta and Berthe putting the Mother Abbess's cape upon her for the upcoming ceremony. Naturally, none of this showed up on film.

Scene 3: The office of the Mother Abbess, immediately following

Maria is dressing for her wedding and asks the Reverend Mother for permission to look at herself in a mirror, which the Mother Abbess allows on this occasion. Although the film showed Maria putting on her veil in the abbey corridor and then walking with the nuns through the courtyard to the church, there was no dialogue about a mirror or talk of any kind needed.

Scene 4: A cloister overlooking the chapel

The wedding of the captain and Maria is bracketed on stage by more hymnal music from the sisters at the abbey. The film chooses to include only the choral version of "Maria." Because Maria is led directly from the Nonnberg Abbey to the church, where the nuns watch her wedding from behind the gated doorway, the movie wants to give us the impression that the cathedral is part of the abbey property, but contradicts this by cutting to a shot of the outside of the church as the bells ring in celebration. This makes it clear that this is *not* the Nonnberg Abbey as we've seen in previous establishing shots, but another church altogether (one in Mondsee, in fact).

This scene on film allows for a potent shot showing the Residenzplatz in Salzburg draped with Nazi flags, indicating that the Anchluss has happened. This turn of events had been mentioned on stage, after the fact.

Scene 5: The living room, one month later

Max rehearses the children for the festival while their father and new mother are on their honeymoon. Rather than have this take place at the Trapp house, the film relocated the scene to the actual stage of the Festival Hall, at the Rock Riding School. Herr Zeller's exchange with Max on stage had him reminding him to fly the Nazi flag at the Trapp villa, or else. On screen, Zeller instead indicates that he and his goons have taken the liberty to rectify the error themselves. This gave the captain the opportunity to pull the offending banner down from the front of the house and tear it in half in the movie, a high point for film audiences.

The moment of Rolf delivering the telegram to be given to Captain von Trapp had taken place at the house in the Broadway version, coming *after* the captain and Maria have returned from their honeymoon, and *after* Maria and Liesl had reprised "Sixteen Going on Seventeen." Rolf had rudely refused to hand the missive to either Liesl or Maria, instead making sure the Trapp butler, Franz, himself now a full Nazi party supporter, gets it. (The playscript has Maria and Liesl reacting with shock that the family butler is in league with the new regime; no such reaction was included in the film script.) The movie had Rolf arriving with the telegram outside the Festival Hall, following rehearsal, and despite his abrupt manner toward the girl he once loved, he had no objections to handing the message to Liesl.

On stage, after the captain has dismissed Max's intentions to have the children sing at the festival, Liesl had spoken with her new mother about Maria's love for Liesl's father, while the film expanded upon their discussion to have it reflect the teen's troubled feelings about the man *she* loves, given the previous exchange with Rolf. On Broadway, the reprise of "Sixteen Going on Seventeen" included an introductory verse that had at one point been intended to start "Climb Ev'ry Mountain." Starting with the phrase "A bell is no bell till you ring it," this portion of the song ended up not being used in the movie version.

In the original script, the captain's reaction to the telegram ordering him to resume his naval commission caused him to admit to being excited by the prospect of once again commanding his own ship, followed by a helpless plea of "Please, Maria, help me!" The movie omitted any suggestion of torn feelings over the matter and had the captain express in no uncertain terms that the family would be leaving the country, ASAP. On stage, this dialogue was followed by the arrival at the Trapp villa of Admiral von Schrieber (spoken of but unseen in the movie), with Maria covering their actual intentions by informing Schrieber and Zeller that the family would be performing in the festival, thereby buying them some time to plan their escape. The equivalent of this scene on screen was reset before the Trapp villa as the captain and his family try to escape quietly by pushing their car through the front gates until Zeller catches them and offers to escort them to keep an eye on them.

Scene 6: The concert hall, three days later

On Broadway it was only in this scene, on the stage of the Festival Hall, where the audience *first* heard "Edelweiss," which had already popped up in the first half of the movie, during a sequence in which the captain plays it in the parlor on his guitar and duets with Liesl. The concert scene on screen sticks pretty closely to the events from the stage original, although the two runners-up in the contest have swapped places, with one of them now becoming the Toby Reiser Quinent instead of the "Trio of the *saengerbund* of Herwegen."

Scene 7: The garden of Nonnberg Abbey, that night

As the Trapps take refuge at the Nonnberg Abbey, they are sheltered in the garden, with the explanation that the Nazis never search outside, perhaps a stretch in credibility for a team of storm troopers who would be so brazen as to tread on holy ground in the first place. Knowing this moment required more suspense, Lehman had the Trapps hide behind tombstones with a gated and locked cemetery at the abbey. This led to perhaps the most glaring change in behavior from stage to screen; whereas Rolf had allowed the Trapps to escape in the Broadway original, no such generosity prevailed on screen, where he blows the whistle after being questioned about his loyalty to the Nazis by the captain. Therefore, it was up to Sisters Margaretta and Berthe to slow things up for the enemy, removing engine parts in order to make sure Zeller and his goons could not follow the Trapps as they sped away in a car borrowed from the abbey caretaker.

The Trapps would make their dramatic departure from Austria up the mountain path, which, of course, was enhanced on screen by seeing them heading to the peak of the real thing.

Although "Climb Ev'ry Mountain" was heard on the soundtrack for the movie climax, there was no reason to retain the Mother Abbess's dramatic introduction to the song, quoting lines from Isaiah 55:12.

From Hollywood to Austria and Back Again

The Sound of Music Filming Schedule

T he interior shooting was done at the 20th Century-Fox Studios at 10201 West Pico Boulevard in Los Angeles, California.

Although much of the back-lot and the standing sets that had made this the largest of all studio facilities had been sold off for redevelopment and for the construction of Century City to compensate for the financial losses on *Cleopatra* (1963), among other productions, the section housing the soundstages was much the same as it had been since the studio's heyday at the time *TSOM* was shot there.

Los Angeles (Fox Studios)

Principal Photography began on:

Thursday, March 26, 1964. 20th Century-Fox Studios, Stage 15

Interior: Maria's bedroom at the villa

Maria is shown her room by Frau Schmidt, who mentions the captain's status as a widower.

Measuring 207' x 130' and 40' in height, Stage 15 was among the six largest soundstages at Fox, located at the southern end of the property, close to West Pico Boulevard, on the Fox lot's First Street, between Stages 16 and 14; it was where the bulk of interior filming on *TSOM* would take place, since all rooms at the Trapp villa were constructed there. At the start of production, only Maria's room and the second-floor balcony were completed; the rest of the villa was erected while the company was filming in Austria.

Friday, March 27, 1964. Stage 15

Interior: Maria's bedroom

Liesl enters the bedroom wet, while Maria prays; the remaining Trapp children show up because they are afraid of the storm. [*While these scenes were being shot, rehearsals continued with the nuns and Captain von Trapp on Stage 12.*]

The Nonnberg Abbey in Salzburg, the exterior of which was seen following the opening credits of *The Sound of Music*.

Monday, March 30, 1964. Stage 15

Interior: Maria's bedroom
Captain von Trapp enters to find his children cavorting with Maria to "My Favorite Things" and scolds her.

Wednesday, April 1, 1964. Stage 15

Interior: Maria's bedroom
Once she is left alone, Maria reprises "My Favorite Thing" and comes up with the idea for utilizing the drapes that are being replaced.

Thursday, April 2–Tuesday, April 7, 1964. Stage 16

(Faux) Exterior: Abbey courtyard
The nuns are seen going about their business at the abbey; Mother Abbess and Sisters Berthe, Margaretta, and Sophia converge to discuss Maria's behavior, leading to the song "Maria." [*Stage 16, located west of Stage 15, housed the largest of the abbey interiors, the courtyard, as well as a corridor off this room.*]

Wednesday, April 8, 1964. Stage 16

(Faux) Exterior: Abbey courtyard

Further along in the story, Maria is paraded through the courtyard in her wedding gown on her way to marry Captain von Trapp, with the nuns following.

[*Note: This sequence suggested that Maria was being married at the chapel at the Nonnberg Abbey, since the continuity gives one the impression that she is being led directly there within the cloistered walls. Once we get to the wedding at the cathedral in Mondsee, we are asked to suspend disbelief, especially once the camera pulls away from the church to the sound of pealing bells, the location clearly being different than that of Nonnberg.*]

This day also includes shooting the scene of Herr Zeller and his goons running through the courtyard searching for the Trapps.

Interior: Room off abbey cloister

The nuns help Maria dress for her wedding.

Thursday, April 9, 1964. Stage 16

Interior: Room off abbey cloister

Nuns prepare Maria for her wedding.

(Faux) Exterior: Abbey corridor

The Trapps await the inevitable arrival of Herr Zeller; Sister Berthe is summoned to the front gate; Sister Berthe and Sister Margaretta reveal their automotive "sin" to Mother Abbess.

So identified did *The Sound of Music* become with Salzburg that postcards have popped up over the years, specifically highlighting the movie locations.

Friday, April 10, 1964. Stage 5

Interior: Maria's room at the abbey
Maria is summoned to speak with Mother Abbess

Interior: Abbey corridor
Maria walks with Mother Abbess

(Faux) Exterior: Abbey graveyard and crypts
The Trapps hide from Herr Zeller and his men.
[*The second largest of all the soundstages at 20th Century-Fox, at 210' x 133' and a height of 40', Stage 5 is located further north on the Fox lot, at Eighth Street, closer to West Olympic Boulevard.*]
At this time, choreographers Marc Breaux and Dee Dee Wood flew with Associate Producer Saul Chaplin to Salzburg to map out the choreography for "Do-Re-Mi" and "I Have Confidence" with the prerecorded tracks.

Monday, April 13–Friday, April 17, 1964. Stage 5

(Faux) Exterior: Abbey graveyard and crypts
The Trapps hiding behind the gravestones, their confrontation with Rolf ("you'll never be one of them"), and their eventual escape (getting into the nearby automobile) are filmed during this week.
On Saturday, April 18, the cast principals are flown on Pam Am Flight #120 from Los Angeles to London, en route to Austria; the following day, Robert Wise and the crew fly out of LA on American Airlines Flight #2.

Austria

TSOM cast and crew were placed in the following Salzburg hotels for the intended eight-week shoot (which became eleven weeks).
Österreichischer Hof (presently Hotel Sacher), at Schwartzstraße, 5-7, near the Salzach River, hosted cast members Julie Andrews, Christopher Plummer, and Eleanor Parker (who would arrive at a later date); director Robert Wise, choreographers Marc Breaux and Dee Dee Wood, cinematographer Ted McCord, and associate producer Saul Chaplin.
Hotel Bristol, at Makartzplatz 4, not a block away from the Österreichischer Hof, was the temporary quarters of cast members Richard Haydn, Peggy Wood, Ben Wright, Portia Nelson, and Anna Lee.
Hotel Mirabell, further up the Salzach at Elisabethkai 58-60, paid host to the seven actors playing the Trapp children and the bulk of the camera crew.
The remaining technical crew members were at the Winkler.
Anticipating uncooperative weather, Boris Leven had the set for the Mother Abbess's office constructed at Dürer Studios at Kreuzbergpromenade in the Parsch section of Salzburg, east of the center of the city. This small facility was established in 1948 by the ÖFA (Österreichische Filmatelier-Gesellschaft) and

operated under them until 1962 when it was purchased by Otto Dürer, who renamed it Dürer Studios. The "lot" consisted of two smaller studio spaces built into an existing farm building, and a larger hall, where *TSOM* scenes were to be shot. Dürer Studios would also serve as the home base for the production while it was stationed in Austria, where such tasks as casting local actors for smaller parts were accomplished.

Wednesday, April 22–Thursday, April 23, 1964. Church of St. Michael, Mondsee

Interior: Cathedral

For the wedding of Maria and Captain von Trapp, a former Benedictine monastery-turned-cathedral was selected in the town of Mondsee, about twenty-six kms east of the center of Salzburg. The processional, with Maria marching down the aisle while the nuns' chorus reprises her theme song, "Maria," was the first chance the cast and crew got to experience the less-than-mild temperatures of Austria, as the building was quite frigid. (The aerial shot of the camera pulling away from the church's exterior as the bells rang was done by the second-unit crew.)

Friday, April 24, 1964. St. Margarethen Chapel (Margarethen Kappelle), Salzburg

Interior: Abbey chapel

This church within the grounds of St. Peter's Cemetery, west of Kapitelplatz, was the first "cover set" the company was required to shoot at because of rain. This featured the scenes of the nuns singing vespers in the opening "Preludium."

The cemetery at this chapel was the inspiration for the one built on the Fox stages for the movie's climax; as a result, the real one has often been inadvertently passed off as a "film location" to those who assume the sequence was shot in Salzburg.

Saturday, April 25, 1964. Dürer Studios, Salzburg

Interior: Mother Abbess's office

Because the rains continued to come, Maria's first scene speaking with the Reverend Mother in her office was shot at the local studio.

Residenzplatz, Salzburg

Exterior: Residenzplatz

When the rain let up, Robert Wise was able to shoot the most uncomfortable scene for the locals, the dramatic representation of the Anschluss, as the Germans march into the square amid Nazi flags draped from the Residenz Palace. When the studio received some resistance about the scene being staged, they had a backup plan they knew would come off as even more incendiary: allow the actual footage of the takeover to be seen instead. This would show the Austrians cheering and welcoming the conquest, whereas the scene as scripted for the film would be staged solemnly, with a bell tolling ominously in the foreground. The Salzburg officials happily opted for the Hollywood interpretation of history.

Monday, April 27–Tuesday, May 5, 1964. Rock Riding School (Felsenreitschule), Salzburg

Exterior (night). Festival stage

For the scene of the Trapp Family participating in the Salzburg Festival, one of the actual sites used for the real festival was chosen, providing one of the most striking visual backdrops in the film.

Built in 1693 to be used by the Archbishop Johann Ernst von Thun as his summer riding school, the structure featured multiple arches hovering over the stage area, each of them requiring special lighting by the movie crew to give the required mood.

This scene of Liesl (Charmian Carr) introducing Maria (Julie Andrews) to Rolf (Daniel Truhitte) was meant to appear during the Salzburg montage prior to the "Do-Re-Mi" number, but ended up on the cutting-room floor.

The building is one of a grouping of three festival halls, located below the Monchsberg Terrace on Hofstallgrasse.

The Trapps were heard singing a portion of "Do-Re-Mi," as well as "Edelweiss," joined by the audience (a chorus of seventy-five voices was required for the soundtrack); and their "escape" number, a reprise of "So Long, Farewell." There were also glimpses of the other participants in the festival, and the scowling face of Herr Zeller. The night shooting gave the cast and crew some of their chilliest temperatures of all, while rain once again put a halt to things on the evenings of April 28 and May 4. (May 1st, or May Day, a national holiday in Austria, meant that all shooting was put on hold for the day; Robert Wise and many others from the company spent the day visiting Vienna.)

Monday, May 4, 1964. Dürer Studios, Salzburg

Interior: Mother Abbess's office
Once again the sequences of Maria and the Mother Abbess in the latter's office were done while the inclement weather quashed the possibility of outdoor filming.

Wednesday, May 6, 1964. Rock Riding School (Felsenreitschule), Salzburg

Exterior: (day) Festival stage
Max is seen rehearsing the children on stage when Herr Zeller shows up offering an ominous "heil" salute.

Thursday, May 7, 1964. Toscaninihof outside Rock Riding School, Salzburg

Exterior: Outside the Festival Hall
In the area outside the Riding School, Zeller and his men are seen arriving by car; the children and Max are seen leaving by car, but not before Liesl has had a moment to speak with the now fully converted junior Nazi Rolf.

Thursday, May 8–Friday, May 9, 1964. Nonnberg Abbey, Salzburg

Exterior: Nonnberg Abbey
Although it was expressly forbidden for Hollywood to film any footage *inside* Nonnberg Abbey, the real Mother Abbess in charge permitted exterior shooting, including the outer courtyard leading to the front gate.

The seven Trapp children come to the front gate, hoping to see Maria, only to be told by Sister Margaretta that she cannot be summoned (filmed May 8).

Maria is seen here singing the opening to "I Have Confidence" as she nervously begins her journey to the Trapp villa and her new life. The sequence of Sister Berthe answering Herr Zeller's ring and unlocking the gate for him and his storm troopers was also done at this time (May 9).

The abbey was indeed the actual one the real Maria von Trapp had been cloistered at, being located on the hill overlooking Nonnberggasse. It had also been glimpsed in the previous movie about Maria von Trapp, *Die Trapp-Familie* (1956).

Monday, May 11, 1964. Mönchsberg Terrace, Salzburg

Exterior: Nonnberg Abbey

Although the scene of Maria continuing her opening lines of "I Have Confidence" appears to be taking place directly outside the abbey gate, this moment required a "cheat" shot to give it a more striking visual. Therefore, the scene was actually done at Mönchsberg, a panoramic terrace overlooking the city, with the Fraziskanerkirche (Franciscan Church) (to the left) and the Salzburg Cathedral (on the right) the most prominent buildings in Maria's view.

Tuesday, May 12, 1964. Mirabell Gardens, outside Mirabell Palace, Salzburg

Exterior: Mirabell Gardens

For many *TSOM* fans not willing to go searching for meadows in mountains, this is the most desirable location spot to visit, as the final and most easily replicated portion of the exhilarating "Do-Re-Mi" sequence takes place here.

The Baroque Mirabell Palace (which houses the offices of the Salzburg mayor and town council), the version that now stands, was redesigned from the original 1606 structure by Lukas von Hildebrandt and constructed between

Perhaps the most desirable destination of all *Sound of Music* fans is Salzburg's Mirabell Gardens, site of the climax of the "Do-Re-Mi" number.

Julie Andrews and the children give their impressions of the Borghese Fencer statues at Salzburg's Mirabell Gardens during the exhilarating "Do-Re-Mi" number.

1721 and 1727. It can be seen to the left at the close of the song. The gardens as seen today are from Franz Anton Danreiter's remodeling of the original, which took place around 1730.

In order of how each location within the gardens appears in the film, Maria and her charges were seen cavorting around:

The Pegasus Fountain, around which the family traipses, is located in the section of the park known as the Small Parterre, directly in front of the palace, and can again be glimpsed in the background as Maria and the children jump on the steps. Designed by Kaspar Gras, the statue at the fountain's center was originally part of the well on the Kapitelplatz way back in 1661, but ended up being installed on the Mirabell grounds in 1913.

The Hedge Arcade, the canopied tunnel of foliage through which the children race, is located on the western side of the Small Parterre.

The Borghese Fencers or Gladiator statues with the thrusting arms between which Maria and the children imitate their poses are located at the southern entrance to the gardens and were sculpted by Bernhard Michael Mandl. Glimpsed in the background are a similar pair sculpted by Mandl's father-in-law, Andreas Götzinger.

Große Fontäne, or **Central Fountain**, which the children pass as they do their intersecting movements, is located in the center of the Grand Parterre section of the grounds.

Dwarf Garden (**Zwergelgarten**) features the statue the Trapp children take turns tapping on the head. Although these sculptures were created in 1715, they were absent from the grounds for years, until they were recovered and restored in 1921. There are nine dwarves remaining from the original twenty-eight.

The steps at the north entrance of the Small Parterre are where choreographers Marc Breaux and Dee Dee Wood came up with the idea of having the Trapp children leap forward and backward depending on what notes of "Do-Re-Mi" they were emphasizing; it was Julie Andrews's idea to go for the high note at the song's climax, as she stands at the top of the steps. This is one of many shots in the movie where the Hohensalzburg Castle (High Salzburg Fortress), which looms high over the city, can be seen in the distance, making for a very stunning backdrop to Mirabell.

Wednesday, May 13, 1964. Winkler's Terrace, Salzburg

Exterior: Terrace

For the middle portion of "Do-Re-Mi," which picks up in the center of Salzburg after opening at a field in Werfen, Maria explains to her pupils how to put the random notes together to form a song. For this sequence the crew used Winkler's Terrace, which also places Hohensalzburg Castle very firmly and prominently in the background.

Thursday, May 14–Friday, May 15, 1964. Dürer Studios, Salzburg

Interior: Mother Abbess's office

Once again the rains came, sending the company back to Dürer, where the "Climb Ev'ry Mountain" number was shot.

Saturday, May 16, 1964. Salzburg

As part of the pre-"Do-Re-Mi" montage to be underscored with an instrumental version of "My Favorite Things," three locations were used this day.

Exterior: Mozartsteg (Mozart Bridge)

Maria and the children are seen racing across the bridge, excitedly pointing to nothing in particular while wearing their curtain-made outfits. This art *nouveau* pedestrian bridge over the Salzach River, linking Mozartplatz and Steingasse, was built in 1903.

Exterior: Salzach River

Another portion of the "My Favorite Things" montage shows Maria and the children gleefully skipping along the banks of the Salzach, which cuts through the center of Salzburg. (Poor Kym Karath falls during the scene, but it looked "cute" enough, rather than harmful, so it was kept in the film rather than reshot.)

Exterior: Kajetanerplatz

For the scene where Maria juggles a tomato for the children, a marketplace was set up with the yellow-colored Kajetaner Church visible in the background.

Starting the week of May 18, 1964, the second-unit crew began shooting under the supervision of Maurice Zuberano. This involved the use of an Alouette Helicopter (from Paris) with an MCS Camera and Helivision Mount for aerial scenes. Most

Maria and the children cross over the Mozart Bridge during the "My Favorite Things" montage.

crucial among these were the stunning collection of shots that opened the film and led up to Maria spinning on her hilltop singing the title song.

This sequence included glimpses of the Bavarian Alps and dizzying overhead shots of Konigsee and Obersee Lakes in Berchtesgadener Land; Sparber Mountaintop near Wolfgangsee looking toward St. Gilgen; Drachenwand (Dragon Wall) cliffs near Lake Mondsee: the picturesque town of St. Gilen on Wolfgangsee; Kloster Hoglworth, Anger, Berchtesgadener Land; and Schloss Anif, Salzburg. The last, a lovely castle sitting on a lake, would be captured on film that same year for a sequence in *The Great Race*, providing the setting for where Jack Lemmon is held prisoner, requiring Tony Curtis (or his double) to swim the lake to rescue him. That film was directed by Julie Andrews's future husband, Blake Edwards.

There were also shots taken of various churches in the area to be shown over the opening credits. These included: Filialkirche at Kirchberg in Eugendorf; Kuchl Church; Church of Mariahilf; (Nikolaikirche) Pilgrimage Church of St. Nicholas in Golling an der Salzach; Kirche Elsbethen, Salzburg; and Maria Plain Church in Salzburg.

Also shot for use as an insert during the scene in which the captain drives Elsa and Max to his house was the Kapuzinerkloster to stand in for what is referred to in the movie as "The Kloppman Monastery." This Capuchin monastery was transformed from the original Trompeterschlossl fortification in 1594 and sits high above Salzburg on the Kapuzinberg near the northern bank of the Salzach and southeast of the Mirabell Gardens. At 636 meters, it is the highest elevation in the city.

The Pentecostal holiday and steady rain for two days kept the company from filming for a four-day stretch.

Thursday, May 21, 1964. Siegmundplatz (since renamed Karajanplatz) Horse Pond, Salzburg

Exterior: Siegmundplatz

The Horse Pond provided the backdrop for one brief scene with Maria leading the children past it on their way to their "Do-Re-Mi" outing. This structure originally created to provide drinking water and to wash horses was built by Johann Bernard Fischer von Erlach and then rebuilt by Prince Archbishop Firmian in 1732, when the frescoes were added. The centerpiece is a horse statue named "Der Rossebändige," which translates approximately into "The Horse Tamer."

This scene was meant to be longer, providing another moment for Rolf to show up and speak with Liesl, who invited him to join them on their picnic and then introduced him to Maria. Since this was Rolf in his increasingly antisocial, burgeoning Nazi phase, he not only rebuked Liesl's invite, but chided her for wearing clothing he considered childish. Nor was he particularly polite to Maria. Robert Wise concluded (wisely) that this held up the flow of the "My Favorite Things" montage, not to mention adding unnecessary minutes onto the film, and had it cut

Friday, May 22, 1964. Salzburg

Exterior: Kapitelplatz

As part of the "I Have Confidence" sequence, Maria is seen walking through this square as the Hohensalzburg Castle once again looms large behind her.

Exterior: Residenzplatz
Exterior: Domplatz

The main attraction here is the Residenzbrunnen Fountain, referred to as the largest Baroque fountain in Central Europe. It was built between 1656 and 1661 by Tomasso di Garona and Antonio Dario from marble taken from Mount Untersberg (the mountain Maria refers to in the script as "my mountain"). Maria is seen splashing some water at one of the four horse statues on display.

Also filmed was Maria walking under the archway that connects Residenzplatz with Domplatz. This scene is of note because it was here that the real-life Maria von Trapp was permitted by director Robert Wise to make her first and last motion picture appearance. Because she had dropped by the set, it seemed courteous (not

This image has appeared in many a book as an example of an anachronism in the movie because the orange crate near Julie Andrews' feet says it is from "Israel," which had not been established at the time the story was taking place. All very well; but the scene as it appears in the final print is shot from the vegetable display upward, and the crate is not even visible on screen.

to mention press-worthy) to find a benign place to stick her in the background. Dressed in traditional Tyrolean garb, she, along with daughter Rosmarie, was asked to walk across the square far off in the distance behind Julie Andrews. Even on the 70mm screen it took the keenest of eyes to spot her, and her presence only became known in subsequent years because it was mentioned on several documentaries and DVD extras. She does *not* receive billing in the credits.

Saturday, May 23–Wednesday, June 3, 1964. Bertelsmann, Salzburg

Exterior: Trapp villa grounds

Needing a lakefront property, *TSOM* location scouts found their lake, Leopoldskron (or Leopoldskroner Weiher), but encountered some resistance from the occupants of the property they desired, Schloss Leopoldskron (Leopoldskron Palace), which was now the site of the Salzburg Global Seminar. Not wishing to disturb the seminary residents, the crew moved the location over to the next property (then called Bertelsmann), where the back patio that led down to the very distinctive horse gates (from Leopoldskron) was recreated.

Several scenes were shot there over a week and a half period including the Trapp children playing a very forced game of ball with the equally unenthusiastic Elsa; the captain questioning his offspring about their claim to have gone berry picking; Max and Elsa conversing over lemonade; the captain walking with Elsa; Maria's return from the abbey; and the famous boat tipping moment. On Thursday, May 28, the ever-present rain caused the crew to improvise, filming the children's halfhearted rendition of "The Sound of Music" underneath a protective tarp.

Spotted in the distance during the captain and Elsa's lakeside walk is a gazebo. Although this structure, since relocated to the gardens at Hellbrunn Palace, remains a tourist destination for *TSOM* fans visiting Austria, it is its studio replication that could lay claim to housing both "Sixteen Going on Seventeen" and "Something Good." Being able to shoot within a structure with movable glass panels allowed much more flexibility and the ability to control the nighttime ambiance required for both songs (not to mention the rain needed for "Sixteen"), so the Trapp grounds were recreated back at 20th Century-Fox Studios.

Thursday, June 4, 1964. Melweg, Marktschellenberg, Bavaria

Exterior: Melweg, Bavaria

This is the day when the single most famous image in *TSOM* was shot—Maria's spin in the hilltop field, as a helicopter swooped toward her.

Julie Andrews would later recount, frequently, for a press and public eager to hear anything about the shooting of the movie, how the downdraft from the helicopter continually knocked her over once the shot was completed and the craft circled back around for another take. Julie's immortal spin was supposedly devised to make the blowing from the helicopter less noticeable.

Although Fox asked the farmer on whose field this scene was filmed to keep the grass tall for when the crew would return later in the month for remaining shots, this request fell on deaf ears.

Exterior: Ahornbüchsenkopf, Bavaria

Surprisingly, on the very same day the famous opening was shot, the closing scene was accomplished as well, as the crew hopped south from here to a mountaintop off Rossfeld Panorama Road directly on the border of Germany and Austria, not far from Adolf Hitler's mountainside retreat, Obersalzburg (The Eagle's Nest). The captain is seen leading his family up and across the border to what is supposed to be Switzerland as the chorus sings "Climb Ev'ry Mountain" and the camera pans up to the sky for the stirring finale.

Although the youngest cast member, Kym Karath, would play her part for the initial close shot, the following long shot had her replaced by a lighter stand-in who was easier for Christopher Plummer to tote on his back.

Friday, June 5–Sunday, June 7, 1964. Bertelsmann, Salzburg

Exterior: Trapp villa

To capture some sequences taking place on the grounds of the Trapp villa at night, the crew returned for three days. Liesl going to the terrace to meet Rolf was done in the earlier hours, cinematographer Ted McCord using the traditional "day-for-night" lighting to make it appear later.

Also filmed were Maria walking by the lake at night, a sequence of Captain von Trapp looking toward Maria's window from the porch (subsequently cut), and Maria on the porch.

Monday, June 8, 1964. Frohnburg Palace, Salzburg

Exterior: Trapp villa

Wanting the right lake and the right house proved problematic for the filmmakers, so, through the magic of editing, the Trapp villa was created by combining two different locations together (Bertelsmann and Frohnburg), often requiring actors to speak lines before one backdrop while addressing someone whose reaction needed to be filmed at the other site.

Built by Prince Archbishop Max Gandolph over a twenty-year period (1660–80) and located at Hellbrunner Allee 53, south of the city center, Frohnburg Palace was purchased by the Republic of Austria in 1957 in order to serve as the residence for students of the Mozarteum music conservatory.

On this day, Maria was seen speaking to the captain with the back of Frohnburg visible behind them.

Tuesday, June 9, 1964. Frohnburg Palace, Salzburg

Exterior: Trapp villa

Needing to keep the press happy and informed, 20th Century-Fox arranged to fly journalists to the European locations of their three prestigious productions that were intended for reserved-seat engagements in 1965: *Those Magnificent Men in Their Flying Machines*, being shot in England; *The Agony and the Ecstasy*, in Italy; and *TSOM*. On this day reporters got to see Maria cavorting down the road (Hellbrunner Allee) leading up to the yellow wall surrounding the grounds of Frohnburg Palace, while singing "I Have Confidence."

Wednesday, June 10–Saturday, June 13, 1964. Frohnburg Palace, Salzburg

Exterior: Trapp villa

On these four days, the crew worked at night to film the Trapps' attempted escape, pushing their car quietly down the driveway and out the gate; Herr Zeller's confrontation with them; and Rolf dropping a telegram off to Franz the butler, prior to his scene with Liesl at the gazebo. On the 13th, none of the cast principals was required, as this day consisted of filming the various cars and carriages arriving at the house for the Trapp party.

Monday, June 15–Friday, June 19, 1964. Frohnburg Palace, Salzburg

Exterior: Trapp villa
For this week, filming concentrated on daytime scenes at the Villa, including a wet Maria arguing with the captain following the boat tipping; Rolf being dismissed by the captain after he delivers a telegram; the captain tearing down the Nazi flag from the front of his home; Max arriving by car with the children; Maria getting off the bus as she nears her destination; and Maria arriving at the villa as she finishes "I Have Confidence."

Saturday, June 20, 1964. Salzburg

Exterior: Nonntaler Haupstraße
During the "Do-Re-Mi" number, Maria continues to teach the children how to sing the correct notes at they are driven through town on a horse-drawn carriage, or fiacre. Because the original actor selected for the role did not show up for the day's shoot, the film's assistant director, Ridgeway Callow, filled in for him, playing the fiacre driver.

Exterior: Nonnberg Abbey, outer courtyard
Maria is seen leaving the abbey in solemnity as she begins "I Have Confidence."

Monday, June 22–Tuesday, June 23, 1964. Mondsee

Exterior: Bicycle Road, Dachsbrucke, near Mondsee
Maria and the children do their bicycle formation as they sing "Do-Re-Mi," a choreographed movement that had already been practiced back on the Fox lot.

Tuesday, June 23, 1964. Kreuzstein-near-Mondsee

Exterior: Tree-lined road leading to Trapp villa
A car driven by the captain with his guests Elsa and Max makes its way along a tree-lined road where, unbeknownst to the captain, his own children, along with Maria, are the "urchins" cavorting in the trees above.

For safety purposes, and because it wasn't necessary to catch their faces, stand-ins were used for the Trapp children. Similarly, for the long shots, doubles were used for the captain, Elsa, and Max.

Wednesday, June 24–Friday, June 26, 1964. Werfen

On a field majestically surrounded by mountains and with Hohenwerfen Castle visible in the background, Maria and her charges enjoy their picnic, leading up to her starting "Do-Re-Mi." Over the course of three days this sequence was frequently put on hold because of the ever-present rain. The final image of the "My Favorite Things" montage, of Maria and the children running through the meadow, was also filmed during this time.

At this time, Christopher Plummer, Eleanor Parker, and Richard Haydn left for their trip back to the States, by way of London, as they were not needed for any further shots in Austria.

(Film fans know Hohenwerfen Castle best as the stand-in for "Schloss Adler" in the 1969 adventure *Where Eagles Dare.*)

Sunday, June 28–Friday, July 3, 1964. Melweg, Marktschellenberg, Bavaria

Exterior: Maria's mountain

Having captured the famous spinning sequence weeks earlier, the crew returns with Julie Andrews to the same Melweg location to shoot the rest of the title song, only to face constant opposition from the rain. Fake trees and a brook (tripping and falling) were created on the site for Maria to cavort around them, although the owner of the property caused further tension when he punctured holes in the lining used for the latter, angry that his field has been temporarily altered by Hollywood.

While all this waiting and stopping and starting are going on, the second unit did retakes of Liesl and Rolf's eventually cut scene at the Horse Fountain, while Maurice Zuberano shot (Monday, June 29) Julie Andrew's stand-in, Larri Thomas, with the children at the Schaftberg railway at St. Wolfgang Scharbergbahn mountain valley for the "Favorite Things" (instrumental) montage. Once this scene was in the can, the children were finished with the location shoot and able to return to the U.S.

There are also process plates for the car and bus scenes shot; the rear view of the mountains from Bertelsmann was used for the reflection in the bus windows, as Maria journeys to the villa.

The title song was finally filmed on Friday, July 3, after the sun mercifully

20th Century-Fox proudly trumpeted the on-location-filming of its current slate of releases: *Those Magnificent Men in Their Flying Machine, The Sound of Music, Zorba the Greek,* and *Von Ryan's Express.* All were box office successes.

broke through, and Robert Wise and his team were finally ready to pack it in and return to the safety of the covered soundstages of Los Angeles.

At this point the movie was twenty-three days behind schedule.

Los Angeles (Fox Studios)

Monday, July 6–Wednesday, July 8, 1964. 20th Century-Fox Studios, Stage 15

Interior: Trapp villa dining room

During the Austrian shoot, Boris Leven and his crew constructed the rest of the interior of the Trapp villa on Stage 15 (only Maria's bedroom had been finished and used previously). This consisted of the great hall, ballroom, courtyard (for the "Laendler" scene), terrace, dining room, and parlor, all built connected as they would have been in an actual house.

Shooting began with the dining room scene, as the captain and his offspring await Maria's arrival at the table, resulting in the pinecone prank and the children crying. Also shot was a close-up of butler Franz opening the door.

Thursday, July 9–Friday, July 10, 1964, Stage 15

Interior: Great hall/ballroom

Maria first arrives, overwhelmed by the size of the house; she then checks out the ballroom and is startled by the captain.

Monday, July 13–Wednesday, July 15, 1964, Stage 15

Interior: Great hall

One of the movie's most famous scenes, the summoning of the children by the captain with his bosun's whistle and their introduction to Maria, was shot on these days; as was Maria's unexpected encounter with a frog.

Thursday, July 16, 1964, Stage 15

Interior: Great hall.

During the party sequence, the captain confronts his unfriendly guest, Herr Zeller.

Friday, July 17, 1964, Stage 15

Interior: Great hall

The Trapp children sing "So Long, Farewell" for the benefit of the party guests.

(Around this point, the second-unit crew finished with their shots in Austria.)

Monday, July 20–Tuesday, July 21, 1964, Stage 15

Interior: Ballroom
(Faux) Exterior: Courtyard
While the adults are engaged in their party in the ballroom, the Trapp children look on with curiosity from the courtyard and do some dancing of their own.

Wednesday, July 22, 1964, Stage 15

Exterior: Courtyard
It is on this day that the "Laendler" is filmed, the sequence in which Maria's feelings for the captain, and vice versa, become more than obvious not only to them but to Elsa.

Thursday, July 23, 1964, Stage 15

Exterior: Courtyard
Interior: Great hall
Continuation of "Laendler" and "So Long, Farewell" scenes.

Friday, July 24, 1964, Stage 15

Interior: Great hall
The captain and Maria return from their honeymoon.

Monday, July 27, 1964, Stage 15

(Faux) Exterior: Terrace
The captain and Elsa come to the realization that she is *not* the woman he should be marrying and part, amicably.

Tuesday, July 28, 1964, Stage 15

Interior: Parlor
Having returned from her honeymoon, Maria is now Liesl's new mother, and the two of them discuss the latter's torn feelings over Rolf, leading into a reprise of "Sixteen Going on Seventeen."

Wednesday, July 29, 1964, Stage 15

Interior: Maria's bedroom
Hoping her revelation will have the outcome she seeks, Elsa tells Maria that it is all too obvious that the captain is in love with his new governess. Shocked

at the news and fully aware of her own feelings, Elsa's ploy works and Maria begins packing her bags.

Thursday, July 30, 1964, Stage 15

Interior: Parlor/Great hall
Having received the fateful telegram instructing him to report to Bremerhaven to resume his naval career, this time for Germany, the captain informs his new wife that they must leave Austria at once.

Thursday, July 30–Monday August 3, 1964, Stage 15

Interior: Ballroom
The children and Maria perform "The Lonely Goatherd" as a puppet show, for the amusement of their father, Max, and Elsa.

Tuesday, August 4, 1964, Stage 15

Interior: Ballroom/Great hall
The scene following the puppet show has Max and the captain engaged in a discussion/argument over entering the family in the festival contest.

(Meanwhile, over at Stage 3 on the Fox lot, the close-ups of the puppets from "The Lonely Goatherd" number are filmed while Bil Baird and his team pull the strings.)

Wednesday, August 5, 1964, Stage 15

Interior: Parlor
The captain and Liesl sing "Edelweiss."

Thursday, August 6, 1964, Stage 15

Interior: Parlor
This day the captain is filmed entering the parlor as his children sing "The Sound of Music." There is also dialogue between the captain, Elsa, and Max, following the musical presentation, after which the captain, lost in thought about the future of Austria and his feelings for his new employee, wanders to the terrace. This latter portion ended up being chopped from the release print of the film.

Friday, August 7, 1964, Stage 15

Interior: Parlor
The children perform "The Sound of Music" as a wet Maria looks on.

Monday, August 10, 1964, Stage 15

Interior: Great hall
Close-ups on the children for the "So Long, Farewell" number are filmed, as is the scene of Maria silently departing the villa as the party continues, leaving behind a note explaining her absence.

Interior: Parlor
Close-ups of the children singing "The Sound of Music" and of their attentive audience are filmed.

Tuesday, August 11–Wednesday, August 12, 1964, Stage 8.

The company moves to yet another soundstage, over at the northern end of the lot, between 9th and 10th Streets. Here the exterior of the Trapp villa and, most importantly, the gazebo/pavilion, are recreated as an interior set for scenes taking place at night.

(Faux) Exterior: Gazebo/pavilion
Maria is seen walking around the grounds, lost in thought, joined by the captain, who reveals his feelings about her.

Thursday, August 13, 1964, Stage 8

Interior: Gazebo/pavilion
In one of the most frequently retold stories about the making of the movie, the intimacy of Maria and the captain trying to sing "Something Good" was constantly interrupted by a discordant noise being made by the light filters. This, along with the challenge of singing directly into one another's faces in close-up, caused Plummer and Andrews to give in to the giggles. Ultimately, Robert Wise came up with the idea to relight the scene and have them sing it in silhouette, and therefore one of the most romantic of all movie moments came to be. So the story goes.

Friday, August 14–Tuesday, August 18, 1964, Stage 8

Interior: Pavilion
While Julie Andrews and Christopher Plummer's problems shooting in the gazebo were merely harmless, Charmian Carr was not so lucky. While filming her dance with Rolf (Daniel Truhitte), the poor girl misjudged her distance and put her foot through the glass on the structure, requiring bandaging and further delays. The injury was not so damaging that "Sixteen Going on Seventeen" could not be completed in a few days' time, giving many movie audiences their lasting impression of what goes on, or at least *should* go on, in a gazebo.

Thursday, August 20–Friday, August 21, 1964, Stage 6

Exterior: Trapp car

The company moves over to yet another soundstage on the lot, one directly across 9th Street from Stage 8. This one is used to film the captain, Max, and Elsa in the car before a process screen on which the action filmed in Austria will be projected, allowing it to appear that they are driving under the trees in which the Trapp children are waving to them.

(Because the background projection was not precisely in sync, this sequence had to be refilmed at a later date.)

Stage 15

Interior: Great hall

Gretl is seen creeping along the upper balcony to Maria's room while the storm rages outside; this brief scene is ultimately deemed unnecessary and not used in the final movie.

There is also an insert needed of the frog crawling on the floor after being dropped by Maria (the legs in the shot were done by a stand-in). One can only assume that the frog was not kept on salary during the entire length of the shoot, as it has now concluded after 114 days.

Interior: Dining room

Insert of the pinecone on which Maria has just sat unexpectedly, prior to eating her dinner.

During late August–early September, the cast does looping of whatever dialogue has come off as inaudible or unclear; they also pose for character portraits to be used for the movie's publicity.

The reshoot of the car scene is done on September 1, 1964. This officially finishes all shooting on the movie.

Behind the Credits

The Cast and Crew and Their Contributions to the Film

Just who were some of those folks who worked on *The Sound of Music*? There were certainly a great many unsung craftspeople and behind-the-scenes persons who made the movie the special one that it is. Listed here are each of the credits in the opening titles (screen by screen) and a bit of information behind who was doing what.

20th Century-Fox

Unlike most of the Fox output, *The Sound of Music* opens *without* the famous thumping fanfare composed in 1933 by Alfred Newman, choosing to have the marquee with the swaying drum-lights appear in silence, making it that much more effective to segue into the eerily hypnotic fade-in on the cloud-shrouded, snow-capped Alps with the wind blowing softly on the soundtrack.

The curiously named motion picture studio began life as two different companies, Fox Films (named after founder William Fox, not the animal) and Twentieth Century Pictures, until they merged in 1935, forming one of the top companies in Hollywood.

Director Robert Wise at work.

A Robert Wise production

The Sound of Music's director, Robert Wise, had first turned to producing in 1953 with the Gary Cooper film *Return to Paradise*, helping his longtime friend Mark Robson, who was serving as that movie's director. Wise began producing his own directorial efforts with the 1959 Harry Belafonte-Robert Ryan crime melodrama *Odds Against Tomorrow*, and would do so with the three movies that came between that one and *TSOM*: *West Side Story* (thereby earning Wise the Academy Award when this won the Best Picture Oscar of 1961), *Two for the Seesaw* (1962), and *The Haunting* (1963). This credit precludes Wise having a separate one as "Producer."

Of Rodgers and Hammerstein's

So well known were the songwriting team of Richard Rodgers and Oscar Hammerstein II that there was no need to even include their first names upfront. It was not only contractual to have their names before the title, it was a selling point:

Starring Julie Andrews   Christopher Plummer

Despite this being Julie's movie first and foremost, her status as a relative motion picture novice meant she was obliged to share her opening credit screen with Christopher Plummer, who had only one more appearance before the movie camera to her two at the time they were cast in *TSOM*.

Co-starring Richard Haydn

Having a movie career dating back to 1941 meant that Haydn (Max Detweiler) was given a respectful solo screen credit, one of only two actors in the movie to rate this. (Eleanor Parker was the other.)

With Peggy Wood
and
Anna Lee
Portia Nelson
Ben Wright
Daniel Truhitte

Veteran Peggy Wood (the Mother Abbess) quite deservedly gets her name in larger type over her two "flanking nuns," Anna Lee (Sister Margaretta, the Mistress of

Postulants) and Portia Nelson (Sister Berthe, the Mistress of Novices), while Ben Wright, being the chief Nazi villain of the piece, Herr Zeller, understandably finds himself a notch above the story's less-certain SS member, Daniel Truhitte, who, as telegraph boy Rolf, was, after all, a newcomer to the movie scene.

In the final credit roll, Peggy Wood is billed as "Mother Abbess," as has been the case for the actress playing this character in all stage productions of *TSOM*, although she is never referred to on screen this way, instead being addressed as "Reverend Mother." For her substantial role, Wood was included on the movie's poster and select ads that could accommodate more names.

Norma Varden
Marni Nixon
Gil Stuart
Evadne Baker
Doris Lloyd

Varden portrayed the Trapp housekeeper, Frau Schmidt, and was certainly the most familiar face in this group, even for those uncertain of the actress's name. She was also the only one in the cast who could lay claim to appearing in another movie with songs by Richard Rodgers, *Evergreen* (1935; lyrics by Lorenz Hart), in which she was glimpsed as a barmaid.

For Marni Nixon (portraying Sister Sophia, the nun who loves Maria "dearly," while recognizing she "always seems to be in trouble") this was a red-letter credit, being the first time she was listed on screen despite having ghost-sung in three of the most popular movie musicals of all time (*The King and I*, for Deborah Kerr; *West Side Story*, for Natalie Wood, and *My Fair Lady*, for Audrey Hepburn).

Gil Stuart, as the Trapps' somewhat sinister butler, Franz, had actually done Nazi duty for Robert Wise before, in the 1953 war adventure *The Desert Rats*.

Evadne Baker had the distinction of speaking the movie's very first post-credits line (specifically "Reverend Mother"), as Sister Bernice, the nun unaware of Maria's whereabouts. No doubt being under contract to 20th Century-Fox helped earn her an upfront credit.

Having had all-purpose British roles of all shapes and sizes since silent movies, Doris Lloyd justified getting billing, although her character is never referred to on screen by name. Credited at the end as "Baroness Elberfeld," she greets Captain von Trapp during his dinner party, with a man one can only assume is Baron Elberfeld. The character was given more to say in the play, but had only a single line in the screen transfer.

The Children
Charmian Carr
Nicholas Hammond
Heather Menzies
Duane Chase
Angela Cartwright
Debbie Turner
Kym Karath

Fittingly, the seven Trapp children were billed according to their screen ages and frequent, military-like positioning: Carr (Liesl), Hammond (Friedrich), Menzies (Louisa), Chase (Kurt), Cartwright (Brigitta), Turner (Marta), and Karath (Gretl). Having the most substantial role among the youngsters, Carr's name was the only one of the seven to be featured on the movie poster and the bulk of the ads (billed after Peggy Wood and directly before "The Bil Baird Marionettes").

And Eleanor Parker as "The Baroness"

While she couldn't match what Julie Andrews and Christopher Plummer would achieve throughout the remainder of their careers, Eleanor Parker was, in truth, the biggest "name" movie-wise at the time of her casting, with three Oscar nominations on her resume (*Caged*, 1950; *Detective Story*, 1951; and *Interrupted Melody*, 1955) and top billing on countless films. (Her credits included one previous collaboration with *Sound of Music* director Robert Wise, the Warner Bros. melodrama *Three Secrets*, in 1950). She therefore got what is known in the business as "ink," a special listing to round out the cast principals. Along with Richard Haydn, she was the only cast member to get a separate title card on screen, and the only one to have her character mentioned up front. This billing would appear this way on the movie poster and all full ads for the picture.

[*Note: As was the custom during this period, movie credits did not list every actor who had something to say on screen (or those who were sometimes silent but essential to the action), a rather curious and uncharitable habit that was rectified when the 1970s came along. Because of this, a few key players remained unidentified to those watching TSOM.*]

Chief among these were two of the ladies who chimed in on "Maria," Ada Beth Lee, who was Sister Catherine, and Doreen Trydon (Sister Agatha). Others uncredited included the driver of the fiacre during "Do-Re-Mi," played by assistant director Ridgeway Callow; and the Nazi who informs the anticipatory audience at the music festival that "They're gone!" when the Trapps cannot be found. (This last role was filled by the assistant director's son, Alan Callow.)

Music by Richard Rodgers
Lyrics by Oscar Hammerstein II
Additional Words and Music by Richard Rodgers

Many fans who knew the movie first probably paid little attention to the fact that there were additional songs that were *not* in the Broadway show, "I Have Confidence" and "Something Good." Insomuch as Hammerstein had passed away in 1960, these tunes required Rodgers to provide the lyrics as well as the music. While Saul Chaplin and Ernest Lehman ended up working on the former song, it was understood that this credit for "Additional Words and Music by" was to single out Rodgers and Rodgers only.

Music Supervised, Arranged and Conducted by Irwin Kostal

Kostal was a very obvious choice to join the *TSOM* team, having worked in this same capacity on Julie Andrews's previous screen musical, *Mary Poppins* (1964); as the musical director and orchestrator on her 1961 special with Carol Burnett, *Julie and Carol at Carnegie Hall* (at Andrews's request); and as the supervisor and orchestrator on Robert Wise's *West Side Story*. Although Saul Chaplin was important in making so many of the musical decisions on the picture, he decided he would not take any such billing since he was already receiving an associate producer credit. Kostal later served as the conductor on Julie's immediate post-*TSOM* special, *The Julie Andrews Show* (1965), and as the orchestrator on Richard Rodgers's short-lived Henry VIII musical *Rex* (1976).

Production Designed by Boris Leven

It was Leven who made all the decisions about the look of the film, nearly all the exteriors being already established locations in Salzburg and the surrounding areas. The principal "outdoor" setting that ended up being done on a soundstage was both sequences involving the gazebo at night. Leven created all the interiors of the Trapp home and the Nonnberg Abbey on the soundstages of the 20th Century-Fox studios in Los Angeles. (Because of inclement weather, one set from the abbey, Reverend Mother's office, was built at the Dürer Studio in Salzburg.)

Leven was another Oscar-winning member of the *West Side Story* team to work on *TSOM* as well. He was considered important enough that his name was included among the few behind-the-scenes contributors on the full poster for *TSOM*.

In this wardrobe test, Julie Andrews models her "escape" outfit for the final scenes of *The Sound of Music*.

Director of Photography, Ted McCord, A.S.C.

The man responsible for capturing *TSOM*'s visuals on film had already received an Oscar nomination for his black-and-white photography for one of Robert Wise's previous movies, *Two for the Seesaw* (1962). His other Oscar nomination was for *Johnny Belinda* (1948), which he shot during his long tenure at Warner Bros.

The familiar initials, found after the names of most in this field, stand for the American Society of Cinematographers.

Choreography by Marc Breaux and Dee Dee Wood

Like Irwin Kostal, the married team of Breaux and Wood were very much favored by Julie Andrews, the two having taught her the dance steps for *Mary Poppins*. Because *TSOM* was "smaller" in terms of dancing (there would be no large ensemble numbers, for example), their work consisted of the movement for the Trapp children during "So Long, Farewell"; Julie scampering down the lane before reaching the Trapp villa; the bits of business for "Do-Re-Mi" (striking a tea-drinking pose, jumping the steps at the Mirabell Gardens, et al.); the "Laendler" dances between Charmian Carr and Nicholas Hammond, Duane Chase and Julie Andrews, and then Andrews with Christopher Plummer; and, most elaborately, the gazebo dance by Carr and Daniel Truhitte.

Costumes Designed by Dorothy Jeakins
Puppeteers, Bil Baird and Cora Baird

The winner of two Academy Awards (for *Joan of Arc* in 1948, thereby making her the first person to win in this category, and for *Samson and Delilah*, two years later), with another to come (for 1964's *The Night of the Iguana*), Dorothy Jeakins already had one Rodgers and Hammerstein movie musical on her resume, *South Pacific* (1958).

Bil and Cora Baird provided the marionettes and pulled the strings off screen for "The Lonely Goatherd" sequence. Baird's creations were a familiar sight on television since the early 1950s, when they appeared in the all-puppet serial *Life of Snarky Parker*. (This show, coincidentally, was directed by Yul Brynner, shortly before he would get his breakthrough role in Rodgers and Hammerstein's *The King and I*). Interestingly, the Baird puppets were given more prominence in the movie's print advertising, as "The Bil Baird Marionettes," being listed among the *cast* after Peggy Wood and Charmian Carr.

Second Unit Supervision, Maurice Zuberano
Vocal Supervision, Robert Tucker

The job of the second unit is to capture visuals that would not necessarily require cast principals or the guiding hand of the director. In the case of *TSOM*, Zuberano's contribution is inestimable, since he designed the unforgettable opening sequence, guiding the camera down from the frigid Alps over the Austrian lake district and above the field where Julie Andrews was captured singing the title song. His previous such contribution to *West Side Story* was similar and equally memorable, the aerial views of Manhattan that launched that film.

Another *West Side Story* alumnus, Robert Tucker, was engaged by Saul Chaplin, who had worked extensively with him during his tenure at MGM. It was Tucker's task to coach the cast on their singing.

Film Editor, William Reynolds, A.C.E.
Additional Photography, Paul Beeson, B.S.C.
Sound by Murray Spivack and Bernard Freericks

Although Robert Wise had previously been one of the most highly regarded editors in Hollywood, he required someone who did this sort of duty full-time to work on the movies he directed. During his long tenure cutting for Fox, Reynolds chalked up a previous collaboration with Wise, his sci-fi classic *The Day the Earth Stood Still* (1951), and would be called on again for *The Sand Pebbles* (1966), *Star!* (1968), *Two People* (1973), and *Rooftops* (1989). The initials following his name stand for American Cinema Editors.

Given the task of photographing second-unit material was Paul Beeson, who, as the initials following his name indicate, was a member of the British Society of Cinematographers, one of several UK crew members on the shoot.

The men responsible for making sure *Sound* had the right "sound," balancing the elements correctly, were *West Side Story* alumnus Murray Spivack and 20th Century-Fox's sound department veteran Bernard Freericks.

Unit Production Manager, Saul Wurtzel
Assistant Director, Ridgeway Callow
Dialogue Coach, Pamela Danova
Music Editor, Robert Mayer
Set Decorations, Walter M. Scott, Ruby Levitt

Basically the one in charge of administration and budgetary considerations, Saul Wurtzel had been a part of the 20th Century-Fox company since the 1930s. (As Robert Wise's next two films, *The Sand Pebbles* and *Star!*, were for Fox, Wurtzel worked in this capacity on those productions as well.)

Arranging the logistics of the shoot and the production schedule, Ridgeway Callow had done this job for Robert Wise already, on his 1957 film *Until They Sail*. He also had the distinction of appearing *before* the cameras as well, playing the (silent) fiacre driver during the "Do-Re-Mi" number.

Primarily an acting coach who focused on helping the performers sound authentic and consistent when speaking their dialogue, Pamela Danova was, at the time, married to actor Cesare Danova. (As Pamela Matthews, she herself had started out as an actor.)

Robert Mayer was responsible for the technical aspects of the soundtrack, mixing and dubbing the music. He held this position on the films of two other Rodgers and Hammerstein musicals, *The King and I* and *South Pacific*.

Walter M. Scott was part of the 20th Century-Fox set decoration unit since the 1940s, bringing home Oscars for *The Robe* (1953), *The King and I* (1956), *The Diary of Anne Frank* (1959), and *Cleopatra* (1963).

Ruby Levitt had spent the bulk of her career decorating sets for Universal Pictures (earning an Oscar nomination there for *Pillow Talk*, 1959).

Special Photographic Effects, L.B. Abbott, A.S.C., Emil Kosa, Jr.
Sound Recording Supervised by Fred Hynes and James Corcoran
Makeup by Ben Nye
Hair Styles by Margaret Donovan
Aerial Views Photographed with an MCS-70 Camera

Abbott and Kosa were employees of the 20th Century-Fox Studios whose job it was to provide whatever process work was needed for trick shots. Because *TSOM* was not a "special effects" movie by any stretch of the imagination, the one sequence that required any degree of obvious "trickery" was the rear projection shot of Christopher Plummer, Eleanor Parker, and Richard Haydn driving in their car toward the Trapp villa, noticing the "urchins" calling to them from the trees they have climbed.

Called on to record the action were Fred Hynes (from Todd-AO) and James Corcoran (from Fox); the former had collected Oscars for *Oklahoma!* (1955), *South*

Pacific (1958), and *West Side Story* (1961). It was these two who were in the running for the Oscar in the sound category.

The head of the Fox makeup department, Ben Nye, was not asked to do anything out of the ordinary for *TSOM*, none of the principals required to look facially odd or to age in any peculiar way.

The hair styles, however, were another deal, as several cast members who were *not* naturally golden-haired were required to look *very* blond, most notably Daniel Truhitte, as Rolf, and Nicholas Hammond, as the older of the Trapp boys, Friedrich. Eleanor Parker was given a striking platinum blonde look and Julie Andrews a rather unflattering bob suitable for someone who has spent time in an abbey wearing a wimple. Margaret Donovan was part of the Fox team at the time.

MCS-70 referred to the 70mm camera developed by Modern Cinema Systems in Munich.

Produced in Todd-AO
Developed by the American Optical Company and Magna

As an easier solution to the three-film Cinerama format, this single-camera process was co-developed in the early 1950s by producer Mike Todd (Magna Theatre Corporation) and the Buffalo, New York–based American Optical Company. The idea was to provide a widescreen image of greater clarity and depth than any of the others, to be projected on a slightly curved screen. The first movie to be shown in this process was the 1955 adaptation of Rodgers and Hammerstein's *Oklahoma!*

Color by DeLuxe
Copyright © MCMLXV by Argyle Enterprises, Inc. Twentieth Century-Fox Film Corporation
All Rights Reserved

DeLuxe was the preferred process used on all 20th Century-Fox productions starting in 1954.

Following the standard copyright year (in Roman numerals) of 1965 is the name of Robert Wise's production company, Argyle Enterprises, Inc., which also shows up at the end of the film.

With the Partial Use of Ideas by Georg Hurdalek

This is the most cryptic credit to appear in the opening because it does not share the screen with the other names responsible for the writing. Hurdalek was the script writer responsible for turning Maria von Trapp's 1949 memoir into the screenplay for *Die Trapp-Familie* (1956). Because enough elements of his structure and storytelling remained in both the stage and film adaptations, he is given a nod here. (He was not mentioned in the playbill for the show).

It is worth noting that although the Broadway original contained the credit "Suggested by 'The Trapp Family Singers' by Maria Augusta Trapp," there is no mention of Maria, the Trapps, the previous movies, or Maria's memoir, *The Story of the Trapp Family Singers,* in the film credits.

From the Stage Musical with Music and Lyrics by Richard Rodgers and Oscar Hammerstein II
Book by Howard Lindsay and Russel Crouse
Originally Produced on the Stage by Leland Hayward, Richard Halliday, Richard Rodgers and Oscar Hammerstein II

As was often the tradition when stage musicals were adapted to the screen, the songwriters would receive a second mention in the credits in the section citing those responsible for the source, the Broadway original. This brought the mention in the opening credits up to five for Richard Rodgers.

Screenplay by Ernest Lehman

As the one person who believed in the piece from the first time he saw it on stage, inestimable credit must be given to Lehman for making the movie the success it would turn out to be. This marked his fourth collaboration with director Robert Wise (following *Executive Suite* (1954), *Somebody Up There Likes Me* (1956), and *West Side Story*), and his second adaptation of a Rodgers and Hammerstein show (as he had done in 1956 for *The King and I*).

Associate Producer, Saul Chaplin

Insomuch as he was considered so crucial to overseeing the production and Robert Wise would be taking no separate producer credit, it was only fitting that Saul Chaplin received the spot usually reserved on most films for the chief producer. Unlike his previous Wise collaboration, *West Side Story*, Chaplin took no separate "Music Supervisor" credit here.

Directed by Robert Wise

This was Wise's twenty-ninth solo directorial credit (his first, *The Curse of the Cat People*, in 1944, and *West Side Story* were shared) and his seventh assignment for 20th Century-Fox (with two more to come).

Meet the Cast of
The Sound of Music

What the Principals Did
Before the Movie

Julie Andrews as Maria

When Julie Andrews stepped before the cameras on March 26, 1964 to shoot her first scene from *The Sound of Music*, she had not yet been seen on motion picture screens, despite the fact that she had been working in the entertainment industry professionally for nearly twenty years. Within a year of that March date, she would become, arguably, the most famous and instantly recognizable woman in all of show business. During those first two decades in the spotlight, she'd advanced to different levels of fame and recognition, but the double punch of *Mary Poppins* and *The Sound of Music* would elevate her into the pantheon of motion picture luminaries.

Born Julia Elizabeth Wells in Walton-on-Thames, UK, on October 1, 1935, she had a fringe show business connection, since her mother, outside of giving lessons, would play the piano professionally in theatre gigs. It was this life that brought Mrs. Wells into contact with a tenor named Ted Andrews, with whom she fell in love, thereby causing her to divorce Julie's father. Although Julie was none too happy with this upheaval in her life, it was her stepfather who was instrumental in discovering her astounding singing capabilities, giving her lessons starting when she was nine years old and coming to the realization that the girl was good enough to train professionally. In no time she was joining her mother and stepfather on stage to sing, becoming the undisputed highlight of the act.

This led to her London debut, on October 23, 1947, in a revue entitled *Starlight Roof* at the Hippodrome, sharing the stage with such other performers as Pat Kirkwood, Michael Bentine (future member of the Goons), and American comedian Wally Boag. It was Julie (now taking her stepfather's last name for her professional one) who again captured most of the audience attention, singing the Polonaise from *Mignon* and "I am Titania." She would stay in the show for a year, leading a highly unconventional life for a twelve-year-old, commuting by herself by train from her suburban home to the city.

CONGRATULATIONS JULIE!

We are proud to add your hand and foot prints to the honored collection in the forecourt of Grauman's Chinese Theatre.

Eugene V. Klein

Eugene V. Klein
President,
NATIONAL GENERAL CORPORATION

GRAUMAN'S
Chinese

20
Century-Fox presents
THE SOUND of MUSIC
NOW FOX WILSHIRE

On March 26, 1966, while *The Sound of Music* was still packing them in at the Fox Wilshire in Beverly Hills, Julie Andrews joined the ranks of the honored luminaries asked to place their handprints in the forecourt of the fabled Grauman's Chinese Theatre. (For the record, the film playing Grauman's at the time was not one of Julie's but the latest James Bond adventure, *Thunderball.*)

Thanks to her astonishing, very adult, four-octave vocal range, there was great demand for the youngster, who sang both in concerts and on the radio before taking the title role in the pantomime *Humpty Dumpty*, which ran at the London Casino from Christmas 1948 to March of the following year. In 1950, she joined the cast of a radio series, *Educating Archie*, Archie being a ventriloquist dummy, operated by Peter Brough. That same year she sang in the *Music for Millions* concerts and did another panto, *Red Riding Hood,* at the Royal Theatre Nottingham. Back at the London Casino, she was in a third of this ilk, *Aladdin,* for Christmas of 1951, and then toured the following spring in the revue *Look In.* By this point she had already been tested and rejected for possible motion picture work, although she did get a chance to put her voice on film, dubbing the role of the heroine in a 1949 Italian animated feature, *La rosa di Bagdad.* Released in the UK in 1952 as *The Rose of Baghdad*, it very quietly marked Andrews's actual "debut" in films, although it would not show up in the American market for another fifteen years, once the actress had become famous, retitled *The Singing Princess.*

It was back to panto again, this time for Christmas of 1952, doing *Jack and the Beanstalk* at Coventry Hippodrome; another revue, *Caps and Belles*, which toured the provinces during 1953; and then a return to London for her fourth and final pantomime, a prescient title, and one that would be crucial in her breakthrough, *Cinderella.* Running between Christmas 1953 and March 1954, it brought Julie her customary favorable notices and an offer from director Cy Feuer to audition for the role of the innocent ingénue, Polly, in the Broadway transfer of the London stage smash *The Boy Friend*. Despite her trepidation about picking up and moving to America, Andrews realized she was being given an incredible opportunity to expand her audience. Before embarking on the trip, she took a gamble on doing what was basically a straight play with music (she had three songs), *Mountain Fire*. In what amounted to the most bizarre bit of miscasting in her entire career, she played a teen from the Ozarks, an experience she looked back upon with much misgiving. Luckily, after some summer playdates, the show folded without reaching London. Andrews had better things to look forward to anyway. Having agreed to do *The Boy Friend* for no more than one year, she opened in the show at the Royale Theatre in New York on September 30, 1954, one day before her nineteenth birthday, and received rapturous notices. Chiming in on the title song, "I Could Be Happy with You," "A Room in Bloomsbury," and "Poor Little Pierrette," Andrews was hailed as an exciting new addition to the Broadway theatre, few Americans having had any previous knowledge of her on this side of the pond. She was given a 1955 Theatre World Award for Promising Newcomer.

As luck would have it, her insistence on signing with *The Boy Friend* for only a year made her available when Alan Jay Lerner came looking for the right woman to hold her own against Rex Harrison in Lerner and Frederick Loewe's musical adaptation of Bernard Shaw's *Pygmalion*. While the show was being prepared, Andrews made her first venture to Hollywood when Bing Crosby requested her to be one of his co-stars in the original television musical *High Tor* (Julie received a "Presenting" credit up front). Filmed in color for *Ford Star Jubilee*, with songs by Maxwell Anderson (lyrics) and Arthur Schwartz (music), the production found Andrews playing the spirit of a Dutch settler in the Hudson Valley and allowed her one solo, "Sad Is the Life of a Sailor's Wife," a portion of "When You're in Love," and a duet with Crosby, "Once Upon a Long Ago." It aired on CBS on March 10, 1956, only five days before the Lerner and Loewe show, *My Fair Lady*, opened on Broadway at the Mark Hellinger Theatre. *Fair Lady* became one of only a handful of musicals to receive the closest thing to unanimous raves as it was championed as the smartest and must luscious show to come along in years. Overnight, Andrews was hailed as nothing less than Broadway royalty for her performance, which gave her six unforgettable songs to perform in her peerless manner: "Wouldn't It Be Loverly?," "Just You Wait," "The Rain in Spain," "I Could Have Danced All Night," "Show Me," and "Without You." Although *Lady* won six Tony Awards, including that for Best Musical, Andrews had to be content with a Best Actress nomination, losing to Judy Holliday (for *Bells Are Ringing*).

If the movies didn't come knocking, television was certainly interested, as Julie was invited to perform on several variety programs, including *The Ed Sullivan Show* (singing "I Could Have Danced All Night" on July 15, 1956, and March 19, 1961), *The Dinah Shore Chevy Show* (1958), *The Jack Benny Hour* (1959), and *The Bell Telephone Hour* (1960). Most significant of all was a live telecast of the first and only Richard Rodgers and Oscar Hammerstein II musical to be written expressly for the medium, *Cinderella*. In the central role, Andrews created yet another indelible character for the ages, singing "In My Own Little Corner," "Impossible/ It's Possible" (with Edie Adams), "Ten Minutes Ago" (with Jon Cypher), "Do I Love You Because You're Beautiful?" (with Cypher), and "When You're Driving Through the Moonlight/A Lovely Night" (with Kaye Ballard, Alice Ghostley, and Ilka Chase). Also on hand, playing the king, was playwright-actor Howard Lindsay, who would, two years later, collaborate on the book for *The Sound of Music.*

Unlike the softly received *High Tor, Rodgers & Hammerstein's Cinderella* was not only treated as a major "event" but became perhaps the most beloved of all original musicals done for the small screen. Its initial March 31, 1957 CBS telecast was one of the most widely viewed of the decade and was one more pivotal highlight that advanced Andrews's career. Julie rated an Emmy nomination (the only member of the cast to be recognized) for Best Single Performance—Lead or Support, but the trophy went to Polly Bergen for playing *Helen Morgan* on *Playhouse 90.*

After staying with *My Fair Lady* in New York for nearly two years (leaving on February 1, 1958), she, Harrison, and Stanley Holloway (who played her father, Alfred Doolittle) brought the show to London, where it opened at the Theatre Royal, Drury Lane on April 30, 1958 for another batch of rave notices and unprecedented demand for tickets. Julie left the show on August 8, 1959 and, despite being so closely identified with the property, would be famously passed over for the movie version in favor of Audrey Hepburn (while Harrison and Holloway *did* get the chance to recreate their roles). The New York engagement of *My Fair Lady* ran a total of 2,717 performances (closing September 29, 1962), making it, at the time, the longest-running musical in Broadway history. In London, it chalked up 2,281 performances before closing in October 1963 as the second-longest-running musical in West End history (after *Salad Days*) and the longest-running American musical to play there, until *The Sound of Music* broke that record.

Because of the huge interest in Andrews's vocal abilities, she was heard not only on the cast albums of *The Boy Friend* and *My Fair Lady* and the soundtracks for *High Tor* and *Cinderella,* but on her own solo recordings: *Tell It Again: Songs of Sense and Nonsense* (Angel, 1957), a collection of children's tunes, performed with Martyn Green; *The Lass with the Delicate Air* (RCA Victor, 1957); *Julie Andrews Sings* (RCA Victor, 1958), which included Rodgers and Hammerstein's "It Might as Well Be Spring" from *State Fair* and Rodgers and Hart's "Falling in Love with Love" from *The Boys from Syracuse; Rose-Marie* (RCA Victor, 1959), a new recording of the stage score by Herbert Stothart and Oscar Hammerstein II, featuring Giorgio Tozzi; *Broadway's Fair Julie* (Columbia, 1961), where the tracks included Rodgers and Hammerstein's "A Fellow Needs a Girl" from *Allegro,* and Rodgers and Hart's "I Didn't Know What Time It Was" from *Too Many Girls;* and *Don't Go in the Lion's Cage Tonight* (Columbia, 1962).

Andrews solidified her reputation as a Broadway treasure with a second Lerner and Loewe musical, *Camelot,* playing Queen Guenevere opposite Richard Burton as King Arthur. Despite a troubled rehearsal period and mixed notices, this eventually became a celebrated favorite and a long-running success, with 873 performances to its name. Andrews sang "The Simple Joys of Maidenhood," "The Lusty Month of May" (with the ensemble), "Then You May Take Me to the Fair" (with John Cullum, James Gannon, and Bruce Yarnell), "The Jousts" (with Burton and the Ensemble), "Before I Gaze at You Again," "What Do the Simple Folk Do?" (with Burton), and "I Loved You Once in Silence." Although the show would win four Tony Awards (including one for Burton), Andrews again went home empty-handed.

It was back to television for multiple appearances on *The Garry Moore Show*, which would prove instrumental in bonding her with series regular Carol Burnett, with whom she performed Frank Loesser's "Big D" (from *The Most Happy Fella*) in a segment (from the May 2, 1961 episode) that went over so well that plans were soon underway to pair up the two women in their own television special. *Julie and Carol at Carnegie Hall* (taped: March 5, 1962; aired on CBS on June 11, 1962) was yet another credit that came to be cherished by admirers of both ladies as well as aficionados of what became, with the passing decades, the lost art of prime-time musical comedy specials. In one of the great prescient bits of satire in the history of the genre, Andrews and Burnett poked fun at *The Sound of Music* in a segment called "The Pratt Family Singers."

By this point somebody with great power in Hollywood had caught Andrews's performance in *Camelot* and finally decided that if no one else in the movie industry was going to capture her unique talents on film, he would do so. That powerful man was Walt Disney, who had tossed aside his initial instinct of possibly casting (ironically) Mary Martin as the magical nanny Mary Poppins in his proposed musical adaptation of P. L. Travers's famed series of children's books. Not certain what to expect from a studio head whose empire had been founded on animation, an initially skeptical Andrews was ultimately wooed and won over by the obvious loving care that Disney intended to put into the production, which, to sweeten the pot, would now include Julie's husband, Tony Walton (they had married on May 10, 1959), to serve as "Costume and Design Consultant." Principal photography on the project took place entirely at the Disney Studios in Burbank between early May and late August 1963.

With nearly a year needed to fine-tune *Mary Poppins*'s many special effects following principal photography, Andrews went off to do a second film, in a role that took her far away from music, fantasy, or anything else that she'd already been pigeonholed in. In MGM's *The Americanization of Emily* (her only movie to be filmed in black and white), she was cast as World War II WREN Emily Barham, who, despite reservations about getting involved with an irresponsible and cowardly American lieutenant (James Garner), ends up falling into bed and eventually in love with him. This was clearly adult fare, boasting a very sharp and often savage screenplay by Paddy Chayefsky, and it was another smart career choice on Andrews's part. Because of having essayed so different a role, she found it easier to accept the follow-up offer, to play another governess assigned to take care of some children who are receiving no love from their father. (The official press announcement of her casting in *The Sound of Music* appeared in the November 20, 1963, issue of *Variety.*)

Her movie career had at last taken off, and she was on a roll. By the time she returned from filming *The Sound of Music* in Austria, *Mary Poppins* was ready to launch in cinemas, and with it, Julie Andrews instantly joined the front ranks of great movie stars.

Casting Possibilities and Suggestions

Although Richard Rodgers assumed that Hollywood would go for the most obvious choice for Maria, their biggest singing star/box office attraction of the early 1960s, **Doris Day**, this was never really taken into consideration. Ernest Lehman wanted Julie Andrews from the start, and both producer-director Robert Wise and associate producer Saul Chaplin concurred.

When William Wyler was involved in the project, **Audrey Hepburn's** name arose, insomuch as Paramount had initially purchased the German Trapp films back in the 1950s with the idea of turning them into a vehicle for her. This was mere talk, as was Wise's list to placate Fox, which consisted of such ladies as **Leslie Caron**, **Anne Bancroft**, and **Angie Dickinson**. As **Mary Martin** would have turned fifty by the time the movie went into production, there was no real consideration of using her.

Christopher Plummer as Captain von Trapp

To understand the lowly opinion Christopher Plummer professed to have for the movie for which the majority of the world would know him best, one need only look at his resume leading up to *TSOM.* So associated was he with classical theatre, with lofty roles and serious drama, that he himself admitted that he was something of a snob about his position in the world of entertainment. How much credibility would someone who'd tackled Hamlet and Cyrano have, after all, if he picked up a guitar and sang a "sentimental" show tune to a gaggle of sweet children? Of course, it was his very casting that helped elevate the role of Captain von Trapp to something more than it had ever been on the stage.

Born Arthur Christopher Orme Plummer in Toronto, Canada, on December 13, 1929, his great-grandfather, John Abbott, had been the country's prime minister in the 1890s, while a distant cousin was the cinema's best-remembered interpreter of Dr. Watson, Nigel Bruce (whom Plummer would never actually meet, face to face). It seemed at first that if he was going to excel at anything in the arts, it would be as a pianist, studying the instrument as a child, until his casting in a high school production of *Pride and Prejudice* changed his mind entirely; he was fervidly committed to becoming a professional actor from that point on. And unlike so many, he didn't have to wait for long, nor did he officially study at a drama school. One of his teachers, it so happened, ran the Montreal Repertory Theatre, and Plummer debuted for them, at age sixteen, in a play called *Asmodée* (*The Intruder*). Two years later, for the same company, he was Oedipus in Jean Cocteau's *The Infernal Machine*. Around this time he was hired as a go-fer and bit actor for Stage Society, which soon after changed its name to the Canadian Repertory Company. For them he was seen in *The Rivals* and the light comedy *John Loves Mary*, before going south to join the Bermuda Rep Theatre. This out-of-the-way group cast him as Old Mahon in *The Playboy of the Western World*; Ben in *The Little Foxes*; Duke Mantee (the role made famous by Humphrey Bogart, although one pictures Plummer more suitably cast as the poetic Alan Squier, originally done by Leslie Howard) in *The Petrified Forest*; and Anthony Cavendish (a send-up of John Barrymore, whom he would later play for real) in *The Royal Family* (all 1952.) He toured with Edward Everett Horton in a farce, *Nina,* in 1952, and was building up enough of a reputation that he was invited to make his television debut, as Montano, the governor vacating his position to Othello (Lorne Greene), in a CBC broadcast of the Shakespeare tragedy, aired in 1953. Later that year he made his first American television appearance (given an "introducing" credit up front), on a presentation of *Westinghouse Studio One Summer Theatre* of "The Gathering Night," which was Rudyard Kipling's *The Light That Failed,* given a new name because Westinghouse didn't like the sound of that title following their credit. On *Broadway Television Theatre* he played yet another role previously done by Humphrey Bogart, the Irish stable-hand pining for his selfish employer, in *Dark Victory* (1953), only this time his was the better casting.

The following year he finally made it to Broadway, although for one so instantly associated with the stage, his initial efforts in New York were rocky at best. *The Starcross Story,* involving the film industry, found him sharing the stage with the likes of Eva LaGallienne and Mary Astor, but due to both dismissive reviews and a pending plagiarism lawsuit, the play opened and closed on the same night (January 13, 1954). By year's end he was back in New York for *Home Is the Hero,* as an Irish thug; that fared marginally better, running nearly a month. Supporting Tyrone Power and Katharine Cornell, he was a Hungarian nobleman in *The Dark Is Light Enough,* a comedy set in Austria that increased Plummer's Broadway longevity to two months and earned him a Theatre World Award. What really made him a significant name in theatre was his Mark Antony in *Julius Caesar,* which launched the new Stratford Theatre in Connecticut in the summer of 1955. (He alternated it with playing Ferdinand in *The Tempest*; scenes from both were captured on tape for an episode of *The Ed Sullivan Show.*)

From there it was back to television to play Christian, in support of José Ferrer, in *Cyrano de Bergerac,* after which Plummer finally scored a hit on Broadway, with *The Lark* (1955), Lillian Hellman's adaptation of Jean Anouilh's drama about Joan of Arc. As the cynical Earl of Warwick, eager to see Joan executed, he was in the company of Julie Harris, Boris Karloff, and another actor who would one day pick up Captain von Trapp's guitar, Theodore Bikel. When the play was restaged for television's *Hallmark Hall of Fame,* Plummer was not invited to repeat his role (Denholm Elliott played it), although he would soon become very closely associated with the prestigious specials presented by this company. For them he was memorably reteamed with Harris for *Little Moon of Alban* (1958; as a wounded Irish soldier, earning his first Emmy nomination); *Johnny Belinda* (1958; as the sympathetic doctor, playing the part with a French accent); and *A Doll's House* (1959; as Nora's unfeeling husband). Without Harris, *Hallmark* put him in *Captain Brassbound's Conversion* (1960), opposite Greer Garson; *Time Remembered* (1961), as Prince Albert, co-starring with Edith Evans; and *Cyrano de Bergerac* (1962), this time in the lead. The last was a particular favorite role of Plummer's; he had played it that same year at the Stratford Shakespeare Festival, along with Macbeth (in a production that received a satellite telecast).

During this time Plummer married (1956) and divorced (1960) his first wife, actress Tammy Grimes, with whom he had his only child, future actress Amanda Plummer (b. 1957). He also solidified his position as one of the finest of all classical actors with a run of great roles (1956–62) at the Stratford Shakespeare Festival, back home in Toronto: *Hamlet*; Sir Andrew Aguecheek in *Twelfth Night*; Leontes in *The Winter's Tale*; Mercutio in *Romeo and Juliet*; and *Macbeth*; and with the Royal Shakespeare Company (1961) in the UK: Benedick in *Much Ado About Nothing* and *Richard III*.

Another quick flop on Broadway, *Night of the Auk* (December 1956), brought him into contact with director Sidney Lumet, who offered a compensation of sorts, one of the leads in a theatrical feature he was about to direct, *Stage Struck* (RKO, 1958), a remake of Katharine Hepburn's first Oscar winner, *Morning Glory* (1933). As playwright Joe Sheridan (played in the original film by Douglas Fairbanks Jr.), Plummer received a special "introducing" credit, and did, in fact, have just as large a role as top-billed Henry Fonda; this was no secondary part, but one essential to the story, giving the actor plenty of screen time. Both he and Fonda were faced with the task of making it plausible that they could both instantly flip over the insufferable character played at high decibel by Susan Strasberg, and both somehow pulled it off. Despite this being a rather superficial glimpse into the New York theatrical world, Plummer looked sharp and handsome on screen, had presence, and charm. *Stage Struck* proved a successful screen test, of sorts, even if the movie made little impact, being an inferior resurrection of a better movie and one of the last features made by the slowly expiring RKO Pictures, their shaky financial state requiring the actual distribution to be handled by Buena Vista.

No sooner had he done one movie than Plummer was offered his next, *Wind Across the Everglades*, promised him by its screenwriter, Budd Schulberg, who had also dangled the stage version of his novel *The Disenchanted* as a potential come-on as well. The play went to Plummer's friend Jason Robards (who won a Tony for it), while Plummer ended up filming in the swamps of Florida, with a barely functional Nicholas Ray as director, an erratic script, and an oddball supporting cast that included an Israeli leading lady (Chana Eden); Ringling Brothers clown Emmett Kelly; stripper Gypsy Rose Lee; Pulitzer Prize–winning author MacKinlay Kantor; and wrestler Tony Galento. Burl Ives took top billing; Peter Falk was making his motion picture debut; and Plummer really carried the bulk of the film, as a teacher crusading for bird conservation. With Ray eventually sent packing and Schulberg taking over the directorial reins, Plummer was disenchanted (pun intended) with the whole affair, the well-meaning subject matter of which didn't appeal to the public at all. Schulberg would never again write a movie script, and Plummer did not appear again on motion picture screens for another six years.

In the meantime, he was back on Broadway for his longest run yet (364 performances), in *J.B.* (1958), which earned a Pulitzer Prize for author Archibald MacLeish. Plummer was the Devil. When Peter O'Toole proved unavailable because of the elongated shooting schedule for *Lawrence of Arabia*, Plummer got his chance to make his West End debut (1961), as the petulant King Henry II in *Becket*, a performance good enough to win him the Evening Standard Award. He was evil for his next New York credit, portraying an allegorical version of Adolf Hitler in Bertolt Brecht's *Arturo Ui* (1963), which folded after a mere five performances but would rise in reputation over the years. For *DuPont Show of the Month*, he took on James Stewart's old role of the reporter in *The Philadelphia Story* (1959), and for the BBC, Plummer played the dual roles of Rudolf Rassendyll and King Rudolf in *The Prisoner of Zenda* (1964). Most acclaimed of all was *Hamlet at Elsinore* (1964), shot in Denmark on locations approximating those in the play. Plummer received a second Emmy nomination for it.

Prior to that, his motion picture career proper started, when Richard Harris dropped out of the epic *The Fall of the Roman Empire* (1964) and producer Samuel Bronston went searching for Plummer to replace him. As the increasingly unhinged Emperor Commodous, the actor went for unexpected levels of over-the-top camp in a film that turned out to be a decidedly hit or miss affair. As far as the critics were concerned, the misses outweighed the hits, most of them trashing the $19,000,000 production, which lost a small fortune. Its failure gave it a sullied reputation, although it was, in truth, the most entertaining of the three movies Plummer had made so far.

Perhaps it was his lack of success on the big screen that made him so quickly reject the first offer to appear in *The Sound of Music*. After further convincing by director Robert Wise, and Ernest Lehman's promise to incorporate some of the actor's ideas into the script for making Captain von Trapp edgier and more interesting, Plummer agreed to come aboard. A central factor was his own wish to someday see *Cyrano de Bergerac* turned into a stage musical; he looked upon *TSOM* as an opportunity to flex his muscles in this genre. This did not quite come to be, as his inadequate vocals in the pre-recordings made associate producer Saul Chaplin more than certain that somebody else would do the captain's singing. While Plummer nearly backed out on hearing this news, he begrudgingly stayed on; one of the wisest decisions of his entire career. *The Sound of Music* would elevate him, for all time, to a movie-star level even the greatest of all classical roles could not.

Casting possibilities and suggestions

According to the casting notice in the December 13, 1963 issue of *Backstage*: "The co-star role with Julie Andrews, should be late 30s or early 40s, attractive, strong, personable, romantic. Must be a very good actor."

The initial casting ideas for the captain were all over the place.

The stage Von Trapp, **Theodore Bikel**, was looked upon strictly as character material where the movie industry was concerned, so he was hardly a consideration.

Those that were actually tested included **Edward Mulhare**, who had succeeded Rex Harrison as Henry Higgins in the original production of *My Fair Lady* and stayed with that show for three years. He would get his chance to play the captain thirteen years down the line when he starred opposite Florence Henderson in *TSOM* at the Los Angeles and San Francisco Light Opera companies.

Oskar Werner, an actual Austrian—although his most famous role at this point was taking one of the leads in a French film, *Jules and Jim* (1962)—was also tested, but Robert Wise was not crazy about the idea of the captain having a pronounced accent, preferring that the Trapps sounded English, rather than Germanic. Werner ended up doing *Ship of Fools* instead and earned himself an Oscar nomination for it.

Yul Brynner was extremely interested in taking on the captain's part and did have the benefit of being closely associated with another Rodgers and Hammerstein property, *The King and I* (1956). Once again the accent put him out of the running as far as Wise was concerned.

More curious than any of these was the serious consideration of **Walter Matthau** for the part. Certainly a fine actor and an outstanding comedic one, he was, however, hardly anyone's ideal matinee idol image of the captain, nor had he graduated at this point to steady leads as he would by the end of the decade. He was also put on the list of possible "Max's" but would have to wait until 1969 to co-star in a big 20th Century-Fox musical, when he played Horace Vandergelder in *Hello, Dolly!*

Peter Finch, who had recently impressed in such films as *The Nun's Story* (1959) and *No Love for Johnnie* (1961), was another strong contender but was tied up with other projects. Other names that came to mind included **Sean Connery**, who had such heat from the splash he made in the first James Bond epic, *Dr. No* (1963 in U.S.), that he was under consideration for pretty much *everything* at this period in time; **Bing Crosby**, who was certainly a movie and singing legend, but would have been more than thirty years Julie Andrews's senior (he had co-starred with Julie on television in the musical special *High Tor*); **Richard Burton**, who had already paired up with Andrews on Broadway in *Camelot*; **Rex Harrison**, which would have given Andrews the motion picture opportunity she missed when she didn't get to repeat her stage role in *My Fair Lady* opposite him in the 1964 film version; and **David Niven**, who, like Matthau, was also taken into consideration to play Max.

Wise was dead set on Plummer, however, and made it his goal to get him.

Eleanor Parker as the Baroness (Elsa Schrader)

If it was her misfortune to play a character some fans of *TSOM* would hiss, Eleanor Parker had the compensation of being treated at the time of filming as the closest thing in the cast to a genuine movie star. Even her special "and" billing verified this. She had twenty-two years of movie experience behind her at the time *TSOM* began filming, after all, not to mention three Oscar nominations in the leading category.

Born an only child in Cedarsville, Ohio, on June 26, 1922, Parker's family moved to Cleveland when she was a teen, and it was there that her interest in acting began, participating in a small theatre group. Encouraged by her parents, she joined a stock company at the Rice School of the Spoken Word on Martha's Vineyard when she was fifteen. Four years later she found herself in Southern California, as a member of the prestigious Pasadena Playhouse. Conflicting reports have her being discovered by a Warner Bros. talent scout either while on stage or merely while sitting watching her fellow thespians perform. She was certainly beautiful, and Warners banked on her having something to offer in the acting department as well, although it wasn't too encouraging that her first role, in the Errol Flynn General Custer biopic *They Died with Their Boots On* (1941), ended up on the cutting-room floor. She therefore was first seen on screen (in glorious Technicolor) in a national defense two-reeler about the Medical Corps, *Soldiers in White* (1942). While she was taking acting classes on the Warners lot, the studio decided to try her out for real with a "B" picture, *Buses Roar*, as one of said vehicle's endangered passengers.

Moving up to "A" products, she was Ambassador Walter Huston's daughter in *Mission to Moscow* (1943), which ran into a bit of controversy later on in the McCarthy era because of its favorable portrait of Russian-American relations, and she was asked to play dead (as were the rest of her co-stars) in *Between Two Worlds* (1944), a remake of *Outward Bound*, as a suicide realizing she is now in the afterworld. She was a factory worker who falls for soldier Dennis Morgan in *The Very Thought of You* (1944), her first main-feature lead, and was considered known enough by movie audiences to be one of the many guest stars in the flag-waving *Hollywood Canteen* (1944). Playing the devoted girl back home to blinded soldier John Garfield in *Pride of the Marines* (1945) was a major step forward and one of her best-liked performances of the time, but nobody was impressed by her efforts to follow in the footsteps of Bette Davis in the sorry remake of *Of Human Bondage* (1946), as the slatternly and thoughtless waitress who keeps Paul Henreid ensnared.

It was a triumph of sorts to go from being cut out of one of his movies to twice being Errol Flynn's leading lady, but *Never Say Goodbye* (1946) and *Escape Me Never* (1947) were among that actor's weakest vehicles of this era. Parker did fare very nicely, however, as the naïve girl entertaining soldier Ronald Reagan in a good adaptation of the long-running stage comedy *The Voice of the Turtle* (1947), probably her most satisfying work to date. *The Woman in White* (1948) gave her the opportunity to play a dual role, and *Chain Lightning* (1950) allowed

Richard Haydn as Max Detweiler and Eleanor Parker as the Baroness.

her to star opposite Humphrey Bogart, but she got the best of all her roles at the studio just as her contract was expiring, in *Caged* (1950), as the timid girl sent to a women's prison who ends up as hardened as the rest of the incarcerated ladies, a surprisingly grim melodrama for its time. For her efforts she earned the first of her Oscar nominations. That same year she finished off her tenure at Warners with *Three Secrets*, as one of the women who believes it might be her offspring who has survived a plane crash. It was important in her snagging the role of the baroness in *TSOM* since the director was Robert Wise, who was impressed with her talents and was very happy working with her.

There was no honor in being connected with one of the most poorly regarded of all biopics, *Valentino* (1951), as a fictitious silent movie actress, but she bounced back, playing Kirk Douglas's neglected wife in *Detective Story* (1951), and despite this being a glorified supporting role, found herself up for an Oscar again, in the leading category. MGM was interested in adding her to its stable of stars, and she began there on a high note, sparring with Stewart Granger in a superior swashbuckler, *Scaramouche* (1952). She then did the loyal wife bit (to Robert Taylor) in *Above and Beyond* (1952), about the air force pilot chosen to drop the atomic bomb. She was the shady lady out to spring her lover John Forsythe from prison in *Escape from Fort Bravo* (1953); was upstaged by the climactic ant attack in *The Naked Jungle* (1954), on loan to Paramount; and dabbled in some broad acting for some broad comedy, as a backwoods hellion in *Many Rivers to Cross* (1955). This was followed by one of her cinematic triumphs, playing real-life opera singer Marjorie Lawrence, who is crippled by polio, in *Interrupted Melody* (1955), the sort of lush melodrama that was very much in vogue at the time. In addition to being a box office success, it brought her a third Oscar nomination and became Parker's own favorite of her movies. Within months she was back in a wheelchair for *The Man with the Golden Arm* (1955), only this time it wasn't on the level, playing Frank Sinatra's manipulative wife who has faked her paralysis, an example of the actress at her most undisciplined. She went schizo playing a woman with *two* additional personalities in *Lizzie* (1957), but timed it badly, because Joanne Woodward was getting all the acclaim that same year for the similar *The Three Faces of Eve*.

Back with Sinatra, she was the nice widower who gives his life a lift in *A Hole in the Head* (1959); Robert Mitchum's frigid wife in the epic *Home from the Hill* (1960); and made her dramatic television debut, playing a nun, in "The Gambler, the Nun and the Radio," on *Buick-Electra Playhouse* (1960). She continued to make appearances in episodic dramatic series while showing up in the movies, in the woeful sequel, *Return to Peyton Place* (1961), reprising the part Lana Turner had done the first time out; *Madison Avenue* (1962), where she went from frump to chic business executive; and *Panic Button* (1964), which was given a token theatrical release around the time she was summoned at the last minute by Robert Wise to play the baroness Elsa Schraeder, after several other possible candidates proved unsuitable.

Casting possibilities and suggestions

Looking for ladies who could project beauty and a cool elegance, some smart choices were considered: **Dana Wynter**, who, in fact, was born in Germany, although she grew up in England; **Dina Merrill**, **Arlene Dahl**, **Rhonda Fleming**, and **Vera Miles**. Wynter was the only one of this group who was actually *younger* than Christopher Plummer.

Richard Haydn as Max Detweiler

Although poor Max Detweiler had both his original stage songs taken away from him for the movie version of *The Sound of Music*, the man who played him, Richard Haydn, would have been right at home contributing to the musical portion of the story. Haydn had, after all, studied dancing when young, figuring it would be a way to enter the profession that so intrigued him. The London-born (March 10, 1905) George Richard Haydn landed his first theatre-related position working as the personal secretary to James White, manager of London's Gaiety Theatre. Once White passed on, Haydn finally got his chance to be seen on stage, joining the chorus of *Betty in Mayfair* (1925) and then understudying future *Frankenstein* director James Whale (as Medvedenko) in a West End revival of *The Seagull*. There followed the 1927 revue *One Dam Thing After Another* (which contained the Rodgers and Hart song "My Heart Stood Still" before it popped up in *A Connecticut Yankee*); a minuscule part, along with the job of understudying lead Sonnie Hale, in Noël Coward's songfest *This Year of Grace* (when it traveled to America in 1928, Haydn turned down his chance to cross the Atlantic with the show); a Parisian production of the musical *Hit the Deck*; rep work in Edinburgh; and a drag turn as an aged soprano in an act he himself wrote, "The Jubilee Duettists," which played the Windmill Theatre (and was actually captured on film for a short subject in 1933).

During a lull in employment, Haydn ended up in Jamaica, working as an overseer at a banana plantation, of all things, until a traveling British stock company swept him up and took him back where he belonged, on the stage. Frustrated that he wasn't making much of an impact, Haydn devised an outrageous character, Edwin Carp, a ninny with a nasal voice whose lectures were highlighted by his imitations of fish. Trying out the act at the Gate Theatre, he caught the eye of Noël Coward, who had no recollection of the actor having worked for him previously. Now high on Haydn, Coward insisted he come to America at last when the Master dusted off a previous revue, *Words and Music*, to open on Broadway in January 1939, as *Set to Music*. Although Haydn appeared in several sketches, it was the reprise of the adenoidal Carp, complete with dullard makeup and droopy mustache, that won him all the attention. A year later he was back reprising the character, this time giving his tips on cooking, in another revue, John Murray Anderson's *Two for the Show*. Haydn also provided material for another sketch in the show, "The Age of Innocence," playing an aging scout. Hollywood was very anxious to have him by this point, but Haydn was insistent that he not make his movie debut merely reprising Edwin Carp, wanting to be seen as an actor capable of a wider range.

Finally, he accepted an offer from 20th Century-Fox (starting off at the studio where he would make *TSOM* twenty-three years later) to play undergraduate Charley Wyckham, the nephew of the title character impersonated by Jack Benny in *Charley's Aunt* (1941), which basically required him to play it straight while Benny got the laughs. (He certainly gave the part more authenticity than Benny and the other actor playing his roommate, James Ellison, neither of whose American accents gave one the feeling of being at Oxford.) Edwin Carp was not far off from Haydn's follow-up character, mousy botany expert Professor Oddly, in the Samuel Goldwyn comedy *Ball of Fire*, convincingly playing an elderly gent among genuinely older actors. Having roles in two of the year's top comedies was nothing to "carp" about, and Haydn had effectively launched his career as one of the most sought-after character players in Hollywood, making it his home from that point on and never appearing in an actual UK-produced film.

He was a snooty composer who helps save the day for Claudette Colbert in *No Time for Love* (1943); the nervous servant who becomes an early victim in the Agatha Christie classic *And Then There Were None* (1945); the village headmaster who tries to help Tom Drake get a scholarship in *The Green Years* (1946); the pompous, mother-dominated chemist who changes his mind about marrying Jennifer Jones in *Cluny Brown* (1946); one of the scientists working to develop the atom bomb in *The Beginning or the End* (1947); and the earl who foolishly marries wanton Linda Darnell in *Forever Amber* (1947), essaying one of his most atypical and unsympathetic characters, and ending up in flames as a result. In 1948, he had two of his very best roles, as the prissy and nosy next-door neighbor who meets his match in acerbic Clifton Webb in *Sitting Pretty*, and the emperor

Franz-Josef in Billy Wilder's *The Emperor Waltz*, hidden under tons of makeup, once again pulling off enacting a man older than his years, and playing most of the film with a head cold. The latter film's producer/co-writer, Charles Brackett, gave Haydn the opportunity to direct on three occasions at Paramount, with the farce *Miss Tatlock's Millions* (1948; Haydn also gave himself a supporting part, billed as "Richard Rancyd"); *Dear Wife* (1949; and cameoing under the name "Stanley Stayle"); and the Bing Crosby musical *Mr. Music* (1950; this time as "Claude Curdl"). Disney hired him for one of the most "Carp"-influenced of all his screen roles, providing the very languid voice of the Caterpillar in *Alice in Wonderland* (1951), where his reading of "Who-o-o ar-r-r-e *you?*" became the line most readily associated with him.

Back to human roles, he was a British jockey in a Martin & Lewis comedy, *Money from Home* (1953); teamed with Clark Gable to smuggle their women out of Russia in the anti-Red drama *Never Let Me Go* (1953); taunted Ernest Truex for his religious beliefs in the soap opera *Twilight of the Gods* (1957); and deceived Doris Day into staging her own husband's play in *Please Don't Eat the Daisies* (1960). Over on television, he was back doing *Charley's Aunt* (1957), this time as the guardian after Auntie's fortune, relinquishing his old role to Tom Tryon, and the *Twilight Zone* episode "A Thing About Machines" (1960), as a cranky critic whose machinery extracts revenge for all the abuse he has heaped upon them. It was off to Irwin Allen's world of fantasy for *The Lost World* (1960) and *Five Weeks in a Balloon* (1962), and to the South Pacific as the botanist who joins the mutineers in the remake of *Mutiny on the Bounty* (1962), where his part was bigger in the expanded television print.

As for his star-making creation, he published a humorous novel in 1954, *The Journals of Edwin Carp*, punctuated by illustrations by Ronald Searle, and brought the old boor out of mothballs for an episode of *The Dick Van Dyke Show*, appropriately entitled "The Return of Edwin Carp," shot shortly before he embarked upon his role in *The Sound of Music*.

Casting possibilities and suggestions

This was the only role for which anyone connected with the Broadway original was actually given some consideration—**Kurt Kasznar**, who had more than proven himself in character parts in Hollywood for a decade.

Thanks to his success in *What Ever Happened to Baby Jane?*, jumbo-sized **Victor Buono** was one of the top contenders, but he didn't feel the role was challenging enough and asked that the part be expanded, something screenwriter Ernest Lehman didn't think was warranted.

Another possibility, an authentic Viennese, was **Walter Slezak**, who could actually sing, had they bothered to leave Max's songs in. Englishmen **Robert Morley** and **Noël Coward** were certainly tempting suggestions, since they excelled at spitting out acidic remarks with such dexterity. Certainly these all made more sense than television comedian **Louis Nye**, another name on the list.

Peggy Wood as Mother Abbess

When the Mother Abbess turned her back to begin "Climb Ev'ry Mountain," there were presumably varied reactions. To those who knew Peggy Wood exclusively from her long-running TV series *Mama*, there might have been some surprise that the lady could sing so well. Those who'd been following her career long before the tube came into our homes, however, were well acquainted with the fact that Wood had trilled in both New York and London in various musicals and operettas. As for those *very* familiar with the sound of Peggy's voice, there was instant awareness that the vibrations coming from her mouth were *not* hers at all (they belonged to Margery MacKay). Realizing she could no longer wow them as she had so many years back, Wood agreed to let someone else sing for her. If the movie role for which generations to come would know her best was compromised, it hardly mattered, for her career had had its share of musical peaks.

Born in Brooklyn on February 9, 1892, it was decided when she was eight that Margaret Wood would study voice in hopes of a career in opera, at one point being instructed by Emma Calvé, who had sung the lead in *Carmen*. It was operetta and musical comedy that became her forte, Wood first scoring a role in the chorus of the original 1910 Broadway run of Victor Herbert's *Naughty Marietta*, at the age of eighteen. She was seldom in need of work over the next several years, singing in such musicals as Herbert's *The Madcap Duchess* (1913); the George M. Cohan revue *Hello, Broadway!* (1914), where she rated some solo bits; and Jerome Kern's *Love o' Mike* (1917), where her big song in the second act was "A Lonesome Little Tune." Having proven herself, she was awarded the leading role in the original production of the Sigmund Romberg/Rida Johnson Young operetta *Maytime*. It opened at the Shubert Theatre on August 16, 1917 and became one of the top hits of its era, running a very impressive 492 performances and making Wood a Broadway star. In it, she introduced the enduring "Will You Remember?"

As a result of her success, she was invited to be Will Rogers's co-star in his second movie vehicle, *Almost a Husband* (1919), as the Southern bride he is tricked into marrying. Wood would not return to films for another ten years. In the interim, she was back on Broadway, singing in *Marjolaine* (1922) and *The Clinging Vine* (1922), until expanding her range by doing comedy with *The Bride* (1924) and Shaw's *Candida* (1925), and then Shakespeare with *King Henry IV, Part I* (1927), as Lady Percy, and *The Merchant of Venice* (1928), as Portia, in support of George Arliss.

MGM asked her to play Lewis Stone's wife in a part-talkie, *Wonder of Women* (1929), a melodrama that earned an Oscar nomination in the writing category. Wood had already concluded that she preferred live theatre and jumped at the chance when Noël Coward offered her the starring role(s) in his three-act operetta *Bitter-Sweet* (he wrote it with her in mind), bringing her to London in 1929. This was her second smash musical, running 967 performances and

Singing nuns. Left to right, Anna Lee, Peggy Wood, and Portia Nelson.

allowing her to be the first to sing another standard, "I'll See You Again." She stayed abroad to appear in the 1932 West End debut of Jerome Kern's *The Cat and the Fiddle* (which played the Palace Theatre, where *The Sound of Music* would have its London opening twenty-nine years later). Back in America, she hopped between theatre and film assignments. In the latter, Will Rogers asked her back again to play his wife, this time a social climber, in *Handy Andy* (1934), which she did expressly out of loyalty to the star, having no great fondness for the piece. She dropped into support for *The Right to Live* (1935), as Colin Clive's dedicated nurse; *Jalna* (1935), as a member of a Canadian dynasty having her share of romantic woes; and *A Star Is Born* (1937), as the central casting secretary offering advice to Janet Gaynor, certainly her best-known movie until *TSOM*. Around this same time she published a show business novel, *Star-Wagon* (1936).

She returned to Broadway in 1937 with a play she co-wrote with Ward Morehouse, *Miss Quis*, but its run was short. Wood had much better luck with another Noël Coward collaboration, appearing in the original Broadway production of his most popular comedy, *Blithe Spirit* (1941), as Clifton Webb's second wife, Ruth, and staying with the show for the year and a half-plus it ran there. (She would perform it again, overseas, for the troops, during World War II.) Hollywood came calling yet again, but they weren't interested in spotlighting a woman over fifty, so Wood was given mother roles in negligible productions like *Magnificent Doll* (1946; sire to Ginger Rogers's Dolly Madison) and *Dream Girl* (1948; Betty Hutton was her offspring).

If she was put off by the tedium of filming, television presented a more appealing option. CBS was preparing a weekly series based on Kathryn Forbes's memoir *Mama's Bank Account*, which had already been turned into the successful stage play *I Remember Mama* (1944), which had been written by John Van Druten and produced by Richard Rodgers and Oscar Hammerstein II. There was an equally popular 1948 movie adaptation starring Irene Dunne, in an Oscar-nominated performance. The following year Peggy Wood became the latest Mama, the level-headed but loving Norwegian immigrant struggling to take care of her brood in turn-of-the-century San Francisco, in the newly christened *Mama*. Presented live from New York's Grand Central CBS Studio 41, the show became one of the new medium's first sizable hits, a Friday night staple for the next seven years. Peggy Wood was suddenly better known than ever before. She received Emmy nominations in 1952 (simply for Best Actress, with no program designation) and 1957, by which time the series was being taped. It would end its days on the late Sunday afternoon schedule.

During the show's run, Wood returned to Broadway for two brief revivals, *Getting Married* (1951) and *Charley's Aunt* (1953), in the title role. Around this same time she showed up as one of the many cameo stars in her only fifties movie credit, *Main Street to Broadway* (1953), which also included appearances by Rodgers and Hammerstein. There was a vocal guest spot, singing on the New York stage for the last time, in the opera *The Transposed Heads* (1958); a comedy with Imogene Coca, *The Girls in 509* (1958); a short-lived farce that found her playing Hera to John Emery's Zeus, *Rape of the Belt* (1960); and her off-Broadway debut, playing an alcoholic actress about to make a comeback, in the playlet *Opening Night* (1963). Back on screen, she was the mother-in-law of the title character in the biblical spectacle *The Story of Ruth* (1960), and was serving as the president of the American National Theater and Academy (ANTA) at the time she was selected to play the Mother Abbess.

Casting possibilities and suggestions

This part brought up two of the most intriguing names mentioned in all the casting: **Irene Dunne** and **Jeanette MacDonald**. Although neither had appeared in a movie in more than a decade, they had been genuine stars in their day and could both sing. MacDonald had even trilled her share of Richard Rodgers songs on screen, having starred in *Love Me Tonight* and *I Married an Angel*; while both women had Hammerstein credits, with *Show Boat* (Dunne) and *Rose-Marie* and *New Moon* (MacDonald). Nothing went beyond the stage of mere talk where either lady was concerned.

Among the others tested were the very first recipient of the Oscar for Supporting actress, **Gale Sondergaard**, and **Barbara O'Neil**, whose greatest claim to cinematic fame was playing Vivien Leigh's mother in *Gone with the Wind*.

Charmian Carr as Liesl

In an ironic twist, Charmian Carr came from a show business family and ended up outdistancing all of them in fame, despite the fact that she initially held no ambitions in this direction and spent far less time plying her trade than they did. Her father was a big band conductor who spent more time on the road than he did at home; her mother had been singing and dancing in vaudeville since she was a child. Under her maiden name of Rita Oehmen, mom had enjoyed enough success in clubs that Hollywood came calling, with RKO trying her out as George O'Brien's leading lady in the low-budget western *Gun Law* (1938). There were other appearances in short subjects and a passing role in a Lucille Ball comedy, *Go Chase Yourself* (1938), by which time interest had dried up. Despite this, she could still lay claim to having starred in more movies than would Charmian.

Born Charmian Farnnon on December 27, 1942 in Chicago, her older sister Sharon took up acting under her real name, while her younger sibling, Darleen, would borrow the new last name Charmian was given by 20th Century-Fox, when she herself began landing roles on television. Although Charmian had studied ballet since she was four years old, she had no intention of using this skill in a professional capacity and was working as a doctor's assistant at the time her mother was informed by her friend, casting agent Marian Gardner, that Fox was looking for someone age sixteen or thereabouts to play Liesl in their movie of *The Sound of Music*. Utterly unfamiliar with the material, but game to give it a try, Carr's lack of experience gave her just the right sweet, unpretentious quality director Robert Wise was looking for, and she got the part.

Carr was the last of the seven Trapp children to be hired, entering rehearsals late in the game. Fox had great plans for her, deciding that she would be the "face of *The Sound of Music*," signing her to a seven-year contract and sending her around the country and overseas to publicize the finished project, off and on, over a two-year period. Although she made no effort to hide the fact that she was twenty-one at the time she was hired, the Fox publicity department didn't want to spoil the illusion of someone who was, after all, about to become famous for singing "Sixteen Going on Seventeen." They therefore kept her age vague, or in that same range.

Nicholas Hammond as Friedrich

Although Nicholas Hammond had acting in his genes, his mother had already left that world behind by the time her son was born in Washington, D.C., on May 15, 1950. As Eileen Bennett, she had been seen on screen as comedian George Formby's love interest in *Much Too Shy* (1942) and as Sally Ann Howes's older sister in *Thursday's Child* (1943); as well as nabbing the ingénue part in the original West End production of *Arsenic and Old Lace* (1942). During its long run, she had fallen for an American army colonel, married him before the play's 1945 closing, and then opted for a life of globetrotting required of a military man's wife, Nicholas's older brother being born in Paris. Following his birth, Nicholas's family lived in both France and England before settling in Arlington, Virginia.

Knowing her son was keen on trying out acting, Nicholas's mother spotted an item in a Washington paper looking for English youngsters about her boy's age, or those who could pass for British, for Peter Brooks's film adaptation of William

The Trapp kids model their sailor suits for this wardrobe test; left to right: Julie Andrews, Charmian Carr, Nicholas Hammond (before his blond dye job), Heather Menzies, Duane Chase, Angela Cartwright, Debbie Turner, Kym Karath, and Christopher Plummer.

Golding's much-read novel *Lord of the Flies*. Hammond got the assignment, along with several other raw and previously unseen boys, many of whom would never again appear on screen. Young Nicholas was a member of Jack's (Tom Chapin) choir, first seen marching along the beach singing "Kyrie Eleison," who later becomes one of his "hunters." He introduced himself on screen as "Robert," but basically stayed a background figure for the rest of the movie. No sooner had the picture finished shooting on the island of Vieques, near Puerto Rico, than Hammond was cast as Michael Redgrave's son in *The Complaisant Lover*, which ran in New York, starting November 1, 1961, for 101 performances. Written by Graham Greene, the play boasted a cast that also consisted of Googie Withers, Richard Johnson, Sandy Dennis, and Gene Wilder, in his Broadway debut. Hammond next appeared on an episode of *The Defenders* (1962), as the son of a man (Arthur Hill) who has strangled his business partner after discovering he has only six months to live. Hammond's big scene required him to be called to the witness stand to speak on his father's behalf.

After winning acclaim and receiving a Palme d'Or nomination at the Cannes Film Festival, *Lord of the Flies* finally made its long overdue appearance in American cinemas in the summer of 1963 (it would not see the light of day in England until the following year). Within a few months, Hammond won the role of Friedrich in *TSOM*, requiring him to dye his hair a very Austrian-looking but often physically painful blond.

Heather Menzies as Louisa

As the Trapp child who flitted and floated during the "So Long, Farewell" number, it should come as no surprise that Heather Menzies's earliest training was as a dancer. Born to Scottish parents in Toronto, Canada, on December 3, 1949, she found herself, five years later, living in Florida. When she was ten, her family uprooted yet again, this time to Southern California, where Heather's father had accepted a position as a commercial artist. First a student at the Falcon Studios in Hollywood, Heather then advanced to the Hollywood Children's Theatre in Santa Monica, where she continued to train not only in movement but in acting and singing. Spotted by an agent in a play, she got an audition for the ABC sitcom *My Three Sons* and made her debut before the cameras in an episode entitled "The Ballad of Lissa Stratemeyer," a spoof of *Lysistrata*, in which she was paired up with guest star Bobby Diamond. By the time it aired, on April 30, 1964, Heather was over in Austria, filming scenes of the Salzburg Festival at the Rock Riding School.

Duane Chase as Kurt

Yet another member of the *Sound of Music* company to have no official dramatic acting credits on film or television prior to casting, Chase was born in Los Angeles on December 12, 1950, making him thirteen years old during filming. Coming from a family that had dabbled in acting (his aunt, Susan Brown, had several professional credits, appearing on episodes of *Alfred Hitchcock Presents* and in the Fox film *The Stripper*), Chase managed to land some appearances on television commercials and in print ads. Having trained in acting, singing, and dancing, he was able to present himself impressively enough to win the role of Kurt.

Angela Cartwright as Brigitta

If there was one member of the cinematic Trapp children most likely to be recognized by those attending the movie in 1965, it was Angela Cartwright. She had, after all, just come off seven seasons on the hit television sitcom *The Danny Thomas Show* (1957–64) portraying his stepdaughter, Linda. During that time, she graced many a magazine cover and even released her own album, *Angela Cartwright . . . Sings* (Star Bright Records, 1959). Because of her very American television image, many were surprised to realize she hailed from the UK, being born on September 9, 1952 in Altrincham, Cheshire. Her family immigrated first to Canada, before settling in El Segundo, California.

Both she and her older sister, Veronica, began winning roles when they were very young, Angela showing up on some commercials before being cast, by Robert Wise, as Paul Newman's daughter in the biopic *Somebody Up There Likes Me* (1956). There followed a small part in *Something of Value* (1957), where she was required to be stabbed by Sidney Poitier. While her TV series was still running,

Warner Bros. gave her a pivotal role in a children's film, *Lad: A Dog* (1962), as the crippled girl who befriends the title collie. (Her sister, meanwhile, nabbed standout roles in *The Children's Hour* and *The Birds*.) Not long after finishing her work on *The Sound of Music*, Cartwright found herself back on the Fox lot to play Penny Robinson in the sci-fi series *Lost in Space*, which would run its entire three seasons while *TSOM* was having its amazing long life in movie theaters.

Debbie Turner as Marta

So similar were Turner's show business experiences to those of celluloid sibling Duane Chase that they were combined in the movie's production notes, which said they "had done some commercial modeling before being signed for *The Sound of Music*." Turner, who was born in Arcadia, California, on September 5, 1956, was already showing up in commercials while a baby, following the lead of her older siblings, Patricia and Michelle. She not only had no dramatic film or TV work prior to *TSOM* but, like co-stars Charmian Carr and Daniel Truhitte, would not be returning to movies after her role in the mightiest movie musical of them all.

Kym Karath as Gretl

She may have been a mere five years old when the cameras started rolling on *The Sound of Music* (she would turn six during shooting), but Kym Karath could boast of already having three movie credits to her name by then. Born Anthea Kimberly Karath in Los Angeles on August 4, 1958, she was yet another *TSOM* cast member for whom it was a natural inclination to enter show business because others in her family had already done so, her mother having sung opera in New York, her siblings having acted on television and film (her sister Frances was one of the "Hollywood Blondes" in the 1962 film of *Gypsy*).

It was thanks to the location of her father's restaurant, Albert Allen's in Hollywood, across from Desilu Studios, that she was spotted by some producers who were looking for children to fill out Henry Fonda and Maureen O'Hara's vast brood in the Warner Bros. drama *Spencer's Mountain*. Cast as the youngest, Patti-Cake Spencer, this meant one of her on-screen siblings was her future *TSOM* co-star, Angela Cartwright's sister, Veronica. That film opened in May 1963, and in very quick succession that summer, audiences could also see Karath playing one of Doris Day and James Garner's kids in *The Thrill of It All* and the offspring of Jack Lemmon and Dorothy Provine in *Good Neighbor Sam*.

The *Back Stage* announcement stated the following requirements for casting of the Trapp children: "Germanic or Nordic or Anglo-Saxon in appearance (no Latin types at all). Must have stage diction or English or Continental speech—no New York or Brooklyn or Bronx speech patterns or accents are acceptable. A good singing voice would be a great asset but it is not essential; however, some musical training would be of value."

Debbie Turner, Angela Cartwright, and Kym Karath in a wardrobe test photo for the parlor scene where they listen to their father play the guitar and sing the title song with Liesl.

Potential children casting

Pretty much every youngster in Hollywood was either put on the "maybe" list or actually auditioned, whether they were real singers/dancers or not.

Among those tested were **Kurt Russell**, who would end up starring in his own TV series around that time, *The Travels of Jaimie McPheeters*; **Veronica Cartwright** (for Louisa), fresh off her role in Hitchcock's *The Birds*, and the older sister of the girl who *did* get to play Brigitta, **Angela Cartwright**; **Jay North**, who had just finished his four-year stint as the title character of TV's *Dennis the Menace*; thirteen-year-old **Victoria Tennant**, years before she appeared as an adult in *The Winds of War* and *L.A. Story*; **Mia Farrow**, who instead got a key role in Fox's nighttime soap *Peyton Place*; fourteen-year-old **Brooke Adams**, who would later take leading roles in such movies as *Days of Heaven* and *Invasion of the Body Snatchers*; **Lesley Ann Warren**, whose casting would have been memorable, insomuch as she would reprise Julie Andrews's role in the 1965 TV revision of *Cinderella* and then co-star with Andrews, seventeen years in the future, in *Victor Victoria*; future Oscar winner **Richard Dreyfuss**; **Darlene Farnon**, Charmian Carr's younger sister, who did not get the part of Louisa but ended up helping provide additional vocal support to the Trapp children; **Kim Darby**, who capped the decade starring in *True Grit*; and members of the **Osmond Brothers**, who were coming to prominence at the time on *The Andy Williams Show*.

Anna Lee as Sister Margaretta

Of all the cinematic nuns cloistered at Nonnberg, Anna Lee was clearly the most at home, having grown up in a rectory at St. Peter's Church in Ightham, Kent, England, where her father was the clergyman. Lee had been born in that town on January 2, 1913 as Joan Boniface Winnifrith, and had an early brush with fame when, according to her memoir, as a small child she sat upon the lap of a visitor to the rectory, Sir Arthur Conan Doyle.

Inspired by having seen Tallulah Bankhead in a production of *Her Cardboard Lover*, Lee decided to become an actress, using her mother's contact with Sybil Thorndike to get an audition with Elsie Fogerty, the head of the Central School of Speech and Drama. Accepted there at the age of sixteen, she chalked up two years of studies until she went in search of extra work at Elstree Studios and was dismissed by the institution as a result. After understudying in a tour of the mystery *The Last Hour*, she joined the London Repertory Company at St. Regent's Theatre, earning roles in *The Constant Nymph*, *The Barretts of Wimpole Street*, and a version of *Jane Eyre* (her future husband would direct the best-known film adaptation of the story). Still seeking whatever work she could find in movies, she racked up credits in some "quota quickies" and finally got a substantial part in *Rolling in Money* (1934), as the daughter of a duke, and agreed to sign a contract with Fox-British in hopes that this would allow her to work for the Fox Studios in Hollywood. Nothing came of this, however.

After playing an aviatrix in *The Camels Are Coming* (1934) for Gaumont-British, Lee was signed to a contact, turned from a brunette to a blonde, and officially received her new "stage name," Anna Lee. It was on that film that she also met rising director Robert Stevenson, whom she would marry in 1936. Prior to that she was seen supporting Jessie Mathews in the cross-dressing comedy *First a Girl* (1935), which was notable for being based on the very same German film that would inspire *Victor Victoria* (1982), starring future *TSOM* cast member Julie Andrews.

In collaboration with Stevenson, Lee would do *King Solomon's Mines* (1937), perhaps her most famous British credit from this period, as the Irish girl looking for her dad in Africa (Deborah Kerr would do the role in the even better-known 1950 American remake); *Non-Stop New York* (1937), as a chorus girl trying to save an innocent man from being executed; and *Return to Yesterday* (1940), as an actress in love with her leading man. When Stevenson received an offer from producer David O. Selznick to come to Hollywood and direct, he jumped at the chance, knowing that the war was cutting back on filmmaking in his home country. Of course, Lee came along, scoring a supporting role in the John Wayne starrer *Seven Sinners* (1940) as his fiancée, losing him, according to billing, to Marlene Dietrich. That same year she was cast opposite Ronald Colman in a slight comedy, *My Life with Caroline*, as his frivolous wife, and made quite an impression. Although she would get to participate in some notable films, Hollywood never quite saw her as a top-tier attraction.

A pivotal credit at this point in her career was Fox's prestigious *How Green Was My Valley* (1941), as the girl who marries the oldest of the Morgan brothers

(Patric Knowles), only to lose him in a mining accident and have the man's young brother (Roddy McDowall) develop a crush on her. While hers was hardly the stand-out performance in a strong ensemble, she certainly pleased director John Ford, who would cast her on six more occasions over the years (*Fort Apache, Gideon of Scotland Yard, The Last Hurrah, The Horse Soldiers, Two Rode to Together,* and *7 Women*). *Valley* earned the Academy Award for Best Picture of the Year, giving Lee the distinction of appearing in two movies to achieve this honor (*TSOM* being the other, of course).

She was a resistance fighter in the wartime propaganda *Commandos Strike a Dawn* (1942); joined the expatriate cast of Brits in the omnibus *Forever and a Day* (1943), where it is worth noting that she did *not* rate being included among the eight top-billed stars, but was featured alphabetically in the "and" list (as was future *TSOM* cast member Richard Haydn); and helped hide Czech patriot Brian Donlevy from the Nazis in *Hangmen Also Die* (1943). For producer Val Lewton and RKO, she had perhaps her best-remembered movie role (and her own personal favorite), as the lady determined to put an end to the disgraceful conditions at London's notorious insane asylum, in *Bedlam* (1944). It was directed by Mark Robson, the good friend of her future *TSOM* director Robert Wise, who was also working at RKO at the time.

Fluctuating between leads and support, she had an example of the former, as a mountain climber, in the Monogram "B," *High Conquest* (1947), and then the latter, as the wife of George Sanders, in Fox's *The Ghost and Mrs. Muir* (1947). Having divorced Stevenson in 1944, she moved away from Hollywood to Texas and then later to Connecticut with husband number two. When she returned before the cameras in the early 1950s, it was mainly for television, being the commercial spokesperson for General Foods for their 1954 Rodgers and Hammerstein special; playing the mom on the series version of *A Date with Judy* (1951–52); and a panelist on the game show *It's News to Me* (1952). She nearly had an earlier chance to participate in a Rodgers and Hammerstein musical when the former spotted her on a *Robert Montgomery Presents* episode and asked if she would audition for the lead in the London production of *The King and I.* Although she was thought suitable in the acting department, Lee simply was not a strong enough singer and relinquished the role of Ann Leonowens to Valerie Hobson.

Apart from a rare behind-the-scenes credit, penning the script for an episode of *The Loretta Young Show* entitled "Faraway Island" (1958), she could be seen playing a nun on an episode of *Peter Gunn* (1958); Rock Hudson's bedridden mom in *This Earth Is Mine* (1959); essaying an atypical tough-lady part as a cigar-chomping alcoholic artist in *The Crimson Kimono* (1959); acting in two movies that featured her daughter, Venetia Stevenson (although they shared no scenes), *Jet over the Atlantic* (1959) and *The Big Night* (1960); and playing the well-meaning but nosy neighbor to the Hudson Sisters in the cult favorite *What Ever Happened to Baby Jane?* (1962). On television (again, under Ford's direction), she was a doctor's wife on an episode of *Wagon Train* (1960), which had the distinction of being not only the most-watched installment of this show but one of the all-time Nielsen record holders for any weekly series. Shortly before she was signed to do *TSOM*, she was hitting the bottle again, as the wife of a fading Hollywood mogul (Rod Steiger), on an episode of *Bob Hope Chrysler Theatre* (1964), "A Slow Fade to Black," which actually rated a theatrical showing (with additional footage), four years later, as *The Movie Maker*.

Although no mention would be made of it, Anna Lee's singing in *The Sound of Music* was assisted by Marie Vernon (formerly Marie Greene).

Portia Nelson as Sister Berthe

Perhaps it was her Mormon upbringing that made people picture Portia Nelson in a nun's habit; not only did she make her motion picture debut in *The Sound of Music* wearing such attire, but she did so in her follow-up movie, *The Trouble with Angels* (1966), and for her guest role on a 1967 episode of *The Big Valley*. She did not, however, come from a holy order, but the world of nightclubs and live performing. Born Betty Mae Nelson in Brigham City, Utah, on May 27, 1920, she got her stage name from a radio serial that was a favorite of hers, *Portia Faces Life*. Following some odd jobs that included working for film director Andre De Toth, she began her professional singing career at Nick Arden's nightclub in Sherman Oaks, California. An engagement at Café Gala on the Sunset Strip brought her to the attention of Herbert Jacoby, who invited her to do her act at his popular New York nightspot, the Blue Angel. Starting in 1950, Nelson would sing there off and on over a nine-year period. In addition to covering the standards, she wrote some of her own music and material, also concocting cabaret shows for Julius Monk and his Upstairs at the Downstairs club. Among her better-known compositions was "Angel Cake and Wine," recorded by Glenn Yarbrough in 1964.

During the 1950s, she continued to be a cabaret favorite, performing in such clubs as the Bon Soir and Café Society, as well as appearing on the legit stage in *The Golden Apple* (1954), a modern update on Homer that was so acclaimed off-Broadway it transferred to Broadway weeks later, for a briefer run than anticipated. As an eccentric scientist named Minerva, she did the Charleston and had the lead on the number "Doomed, Doomed, Doomed." The following year, she provided songs for the musical revue *Almost Crazy*, directed by Christopher Hewitt, who would later play Max Detweiler in several stage versions of *The Sound of Music*. Briefly, in 1959, Nelson could be heard on her own radio show, *Sunday in New York*.

Portia also released the solo albums *Love Songs for a Late Evening* (1953), which included Rodgers and Hart's "The Gentleman Is a Dope"; *Let Me Love You: Portia Nelson Sings the Songs of Bart Howard* (1956), which made her one of the first singers to record his classic "In Other Words/Fly Me to the Moon"; and *Autumn Leaves* (1956), with the Norman Paris Trio. Columbia Records producer/president Godard Lieberson hired her to participate in five studio recordings of notable musicals:

Rodgers and Hammerstein's *Oklahoma!* (1952), as Aunt Eller; Rodgers and Hart's *On Your Toes* (1952), where she got to sing "There's a Small Hotel" and "Glad to Be Unhappy," among others; Kern and Harbach's *Roberta* (1952), offering her rendition of "Yesterdays"; Rodgers and Hart's *The Boys from Syracuse* (1953), joining in on "Sing for Your Supper"; and Noël Coward's *Bittersweet*, the release of which was blocked by the composer. On it, Nelson sang the very same three roles originally created on stage by the woman she would later share the screen with in *The Sound of Music*, Peggy Wood.

Ben Wright as Herr Zeller

As *TSOM*'s most despicable character, the self-satisfied Herr Zeller, who is so unimpressed by the Trapp Family's musical performance that he sits impatiently at the Salzburg Festival like a theatre critic about to draw blood in his next day's review, Ben Wright was the sort of busy, under-the-radar character actor who was seldom in need of jobs but never knew for sure if he'd get a substantial role or a bit part, billing or none.

Born in London (his father was American) on May 5, 1915, he was accepted at the Royal Academy of Dramatic Arts at the age of sixteen. He made his West End debut in a quick flop, *Farewell Performance* (1936), at the Lyric Theatre, and then was back at the very same venue only weeks later for another short run, a revival of Patrick Hamilton's *Rope*, as one of the arrogant killers. Work continued steadily on the London stage, with further appearances in *Retreat from Folly* (1937); *Ladies & Gentlemen* (1937); *Idiot's Delight* (1938), the most successful of the lot; *Tony Draws a Horse* (1939); *Drake* (1939), which expired after a single performance; and *The Gentle People* (1939). Following service in the Royal Rifle Corps during World War II, a wedding brought him to America, and like fellow *TSOM* cast member Norma Varden, Wright realized he was more interested in plying his trade in Southern California than in the chillier climate of England and settled in Hollywood.

Priding himself on his ability to pull off a number of accents, he became a staple of radio, where he was able to fool listeners into believing he was the Green Lama's Turkish servant, Tulku (1949), and the Asian hotel worker Heyboy on *Have Gun, Will Travel* (1958–60). In addition, he got to play Sherlock Holmes for a season on ABC (1949–50), and also carried the detective mystery *Pursuit* (1951–52), as Inspector Peter Black.

In cinemas, he was an Australian soldier who barely conceals his contempt for commander Richard Burton in the war adventure *The Desert Rats* (1952), which gave him the opportunity to work under Robert Wise's direction for the first time. Again for Wise, he was the defense attorney in *Until They Sail* (1957), where his key moment was grilling Paul Newman on the witness stand about Piper Laurie's promiscuous behavior. Also in the courtroom, he read the charges against Tyrone Power in *Witness for the Prosecution* (1957); then was Charlton Heston's salvage partner who with him discovers the titular abandoned vessel in *The Wreck of the*

Mary Deare (1959); James Mason's incompetent assistant in *Journey to the Center of the Earth* (1959); Spencer Tracy's housekeeper in *Judgment at Nuremberg* (1961); the voice of Roger Radcliffe, the owner of *101 Dalmatians* (1961), for Disney; and the opening narrator for Fox's costly epic *Cleopatra* (1963).

Although he was nothing more than a glorified extra, appearing as a footman at the Embassy Ball in *My Fair Lady* (1964), this gave him the distinction of therefore appearing in back-to-back Oscar winners for Best Picture, *The Sound of Music*, of course, being the other.

Daniel Truhitte as Rolf Gruber

He sings, he dances; he's a convincing Nazi! Daniel Truhitte was given the unenviable task of playing a role made even less likable than his stage counterpart, Rolf now making the choice to blow the whistle on the hiding Trapps.

Born in Sacramento, California, on September 10, 1943, he first studied dancing at age six, voice starting when he was ten. Following high school he received a scholarship to Pasadena Playhouse and also took classes at Ambassador College. He did chorus work in productions of *Bells Are Ringing* (starring Celeste Holm) and *The Unsinkable Molly Brown* (Bruce Yarnell was Leadville Johnny Brown), and was given a showy spot at a Chevrolet industrial show in New York in 1963, dancing on the back of an El Camino. *TSOM* had already begun filming when he scored the role of Rolf, which required him to dye his brown hair a very ominous Aryan blond.

Norma Varden as Frau Schmidt

An unforgettable voice and face, if not an instantly recognizable name, Norma Varden was tall, nearly cartoonish in demeanor, and possessed plummy vocal tones that made her perfect for playing ladies both haughty and eccentric. She was born in London, on January 20, 1898. Initially, her parents thought her future lay in music, so she trained in Europe as a pianist until (much as would Christopher Plummer under similar circumstances) she decided she'd be more at home acting. To this end, she studied at the Guildhall School of Music, and made her London stage debut in 1920 in *The Wandering Jew*. She was also part of a notable modern dress production of *Hamlet* (1925), as the Player Queen; journeyed to the United States to appear in *When in Rome*, only to have it close in Atlantic City before reaching New York (she would never appear on Broadway); and then joined the West End's long-running *Aldwych Farces*, in *A Night Like This* (1930) and *Turkey Time* (1931), in both teamed incongruously for maximum laughs with Robertson Hare. When both plays were quickly filmed (1932, and 1933, respectively), she made her talking picture debut in them. One of her bit roles around this time, as a barmaid in the movie of *Evergreen*, was worth noting because it featured a score by Richard Rodgers and Lorenz Hart, thereby making her the only cast member of the film of *TSOM* to have previously appeared in a motion picture with songs by Rodgers. Becoming a favorite foil for some of Britain's notable comedians, she did three screen appearances opposite Will Hay, all of which were directed by American William Beaudine. It was visiting Beaudine that brought her to Southern California, just as England was entering the war, and Varden very quickly decided she'd prefer to make this her place of residence.

Starting in 1940, she was seldom out of work, although her roles ranged in size from stand-out supporting ones to tinier bits that didn't even rate up-front billing. She was one of bootlegger Robert Montgomery's British relatives in *The Earl of Chicago* (1940; her U.S. debut); the spinster chaperone traveling with a group of young ladies through the Caribbean in *Flying with Music* (1942), a forty-six-minute cheapie for Hal Roach Studios; philandering Robert Benchley's wife in *The Major and the Minor* (1942); the tourist whose husband is pickpocketed in the opening moments of *Casablanca* (1942); the cook Charles Coburn is trying to replace in *My Kingdom for a Cook* (1943); the village schoolteacher in *National Velvet* (1944); and the snooty coach passenger who snubs Simone Simon until she wants food from her in *Mademoiselle Fifi* (1944). Although the last was a minor credit, she was highlighted in a drunk scene, and it marked her first association with director Robert Wise. Over on radio she piped in on a few episodes of Jack Benny's show, as his mother (despite being four years younger than him) and as Mrs. Hudson to Basil Rathbone's Sherlock Holmes.

Back in cinemas she was the dress shop owner who cheats Linda Darnell in *Forever Amber* (1947); a hat shop customer mistaking Bob Hope for a mannequin in *Where There's Life* (1947); a bogus countess hired to impress Lucille Ball in *Fancy Pants* (1950); the party guest Robert Walker nearly strangles in *Strangers on a Train* (1951); Ann Blyth's guard in *Thunder on the Hill* (1951); and a congresswoman in *Something for the Birds* (1952), a second credit under Robert Wise's direction.

On television she was the neighbor the Ricardos switch apartments with in *I Love Lucy* (1953); a governess hired to take charge of Danny Thomas's kids on *Make Room for Daddy*, aired *before* future *TSOM* cast member Angela Cartwright joined the show; and the bubble-headed neighbor, Mrs. Johnson, on *Hazel*, a recurring role (1961–64) that was intended to be spun off into a separate series, a proposal that never came to be.

Meanwhile, back on the big screen, she patiently endured husband Charles Coburn's flirtatious eye in *Gentleman Prefer Blondes* (1953) and had one of her pivotal roles, as the wealthy lady who makes the mistake of befriending Tyrone Power and pays for it with her life, in *Witness for the Prosecution* (1957).

As far as Varden was concerned, it was the role of the Mother Abbess *she* felt best suited her in *TSOM*, but she settled for the smaller part of the housekeeper, Frau Schmidt. This meant she was needed for all of two days (her two scheduled shooting days—which included the very first scene shot on the movie, helping Julie Andrews to settle down in her room at the villa—separated by more than three months!) and did not get the chance to journey to Salzburg as she so fervently desired.

Marni Nixon as Sister Sophia

Probably the best known of all "ghost singers" in motion picture history, Marni Nixon had three of the best loved and most popular of all film musicals on her resume, vocalizing for Deborah Kerr in *The King and I* (1956), Natalie Wood in *West Side Story* (1961), and Audrey Hepburn in *My Fair Lady* (1964). It was Kerr who helped bring attention to Nixon, when she casually let it slip that she herself was *not* doing her own singing in the film, and had made it clear from the start that she was not going to be able to handle the vocal demands of the part and needed help. Although Nixon was contractually not allowed to be mentioned in the movie's publicity or opening credits, this was a breakthrough in citing these "unsung" (for lack of a better term) heroes of the genre.

As Margaret Nixon McEathron of Altadena, California (where she was born on February 22, 1930), Marni had originally envisioned herself as a classical violinist until realizing she was far more adept at singing. While quite young she had her first on-screen role, in a budget-conscious Lum and Abner comedy for RKO, *The Bashful Bachelor*, in 1942, and then joined the Roger Wagner Chorale. This meant she was featured on the soundtrack of the epic *Joan of Arc* (1948), as the heavenly choir heard by star Ingrid Bergman. Taking a messenger job on the MGM lot brought her into contact with composer Bronislau Kaper, who hired her to dub Margaret O'Brien, singing a Hindu number, in *The Secret Garden* (1949), neither meeting the actress nor seeing the clip before she made the recording. During the early 1950s, television audiences not only got to hear but see her when she made several appearances on Arthur Godfrey's popular weekly series. Back behind the microphone, she was required to hit some unreachable notes for Marilyn Monroe in the famous "Diamonds Are a Girl's Best Friend" number from *Gentlemen Prefer Blondes* (1953), and made her legit Broadway debut as a chorus member of *The Girl in the Pink Tights* (1954).

She found her contributions to *West Side Story* and *My Fair Lady* a bit less welcomed by the actresses she was dubbing, since both Wood and Hepburn were under the mistaken impression that they'd be doing their own chirping. Nixon's participation in the former (where she even provided a few notes for another of the movie's cast members, Rita Moreno) was especially beneficial, as the soundtrack album was so popular that the score's composer, Leonard Bernstein, generously relinquished one quarter of a percent of his own royalties to her. It also brought her into contact with musical director Saul Chaplin and director Robert Wise, who saw no reason not to have her be seen on screen when they needed some "backup" nuns for the "Maria" number in *The Sound of Music.*

The Dubbers

Margery MacKay (as the singing voice of Peggy Wood)

Because Peggy Wood was well aware that her once estimable singing skills were no longer up to par, she had no objections to Saul Chaplin finding someone else to provide her vocals for her contributions to "Maria" and, more importantly, the Mother Abbess's big solo, "Climb Ev'ry Mountain." The lady who did the singing was mezzo-soprano Margery MacKay.

Born Margery Knapp in 1925, the daughter of a minister, she was raised in Nashua, New Hampshire, and first attended Syracuse University before switching to USC where her opera training began. She sang with the Guild Opera Company for three seasons and performed in various productions for the Euterpe Opera Reading Club. In 1951 she first appeared as a soloist in Los Angeles' long-running concert series *Evenings on the Roof.* As part of the Los Angeles Civic Light Opera Association, she toured the West Coast in such shows as *The Merry Widow* and *Song of Norway*, and was part of the original cast of the Broadway-bound musical *Three Wishes for Jamie* (she was no longer part of the company when it came to New York a year later).

She made her New York City Opera debut in 1955 as Mercedes in *Carmen*, also performing there in productions of *Madama Butterfly, La Traviata, The Marriage of Figaro, The Bartered Bride,* and *Tosca,* among others. There were also appearances with the San Francisco Cosmopolitan Opera Company (*Rigoletto* in 1959), the Laguna Beach Festival of Opera (1963), and the Lyric Opera of Chicago. She was heard on such recordings as *The Robert Linn Music Collection, Vocal Music, Part 1* (1958), singing children's songs; Boulez's *Le Marteau sans Maitre* (*The Hammer Without a Master*) (1958); and the Chicago Lyric Opera's presentation of *Lucia di Lammermoor* (1961); and frequently performed in recitals with her husband, pianist Harper MacKay. She also had a film credit with one of *The Sound of Music*'s other players, Eleanor Parker, singing the role of Suzuki in the segment of *Madama Butterfly* seen in the 1955 Marjorie Lawrence biopic *Interrupted Melody.*

Initially, MacKay recorded "Climb Ev'ry Mountain" for Peggy Wood to lip-synch while shooting the scene in Austria. Wood, however, wasn't pleased with that particular rendition, finding it too operatic. Wood was, therefore, filmed singing with her own voice, which MacKay was then required to re-record in order to match Wood's lip movements.

Bill Lee (as the singing voice of Christopher Plummer)

As happened with many a star before him, Christopher Plummer agreed to do a movie musical with the assumption that he was going to be heard doing his own singing on screen. And, as was the case with such others as Natalie Wood and Audrey Hepburn, it became all too obvious that his efforts simply did not measure up when compared with genuine singers. Musical director/associate producer Saul Chaplin and director Robert Wise agreed to placate the actor up front, knowing that the singing was part of the bargaining chip used to get him to play Captain von Trapp in the first place. Chaplin, however, was convinced from the word "go" that Plummer was never going to make the grade, no matter how hard he rehearsed. Wise felt he owed it to his leading man to let him make his own decision after hearing how he sounded on the pre-recorded tracks. Humility won out, and Plummer had to admit that his adequate but underwhelming singing would come off as a detriment to his performance and okayed Chaplin finding a dubber.

The man chosen, baritone Bill Lee, was an old hand at this sort of thing, and had a long and varied career as a vocalist on television, on records, and singing on screen, both as a "ghost" and once in a while actually showing up on camera. Born in Johnson, Nebraska, on August 21, 1916, he first gained recognition in Hollywood in 1948, when he joined a newly formed quartet called the Mellomen (also known as the Mellomen Quartet and other variations), a group that also consisted of Thurl Ravenscroft, Bob Hamlin, and Max Smith (the members would vary over the years). They soon were in demand as backup singers both on radio and recordings for a wide variety of artists, including Rosemary Clooney, Doris Day, Bing Crosby, Spike Jones, and Elvis Presley (the Mellomen were seen as the Bible Singers in Presley's 1969 film *The Trouble with Girls*); as well as contributing to the Norman Luboff Choir. They also released their own separate recordings, including some radio transcription discs for Capitol and tracks like "My Buick, My Love, and I" (Capitol), "The Laura Lee/ Three Chimes of Silver" (Coral), and "I Walked into the Garden" (Decca). They could also be heard disguising themselves under a variety of aliases, from Big John & the Buzzards to the Crackerjacks.

On his own, Lee received a choice assignment that marked his first motion picture association with Richard Rodgers, the 1948 MGM biopic *Word and Music*, providing the vocals on "Manhattan" and "With a Song in My Heart" for Tom Drake, who was playing Rodgers in this fictionalized musical. For director Fritz Lang he sang the theme to the 1950 western *Rancho Notorious*, "Legend of Chuck-a-Luck," in this instance getting billing, as "William Lee."

Hired by Walt Disney to sing "Painting the Roses Red" in his 1951 animated version of *Alice in Wonderland*, this opened a whole new world for Lee, who became a regular contributor to songs in both Disney features and television programs, as well as one of the dependable names called upon to sing for his Disneyland Records unit. Lee also was heard on countless commercial jingles; released a solo album under his own name, *My Port of Call* (the track on the album called "Maria" was neither the one from *TSOM* nor *West Side Story*); and was the lead vocalist on Gordon Jenkins's original musical created for LP, *Seven Seas* (1953).

Elsewhere, he was the singing voice of Matt Mattox on "Lonesome Polecat" in the MGM hit *Seven Brides for Seven Brothers* (1954); was seen with his fellow Mellomen in cowboy gear performing "Bidin' My Time," in a production of *Girl Crazy* in the Universal biopic *The Glenn Miller Story* (1954); dubbed the Cole Porter tunes for actor Joseph Buloff in *Silk Stockings* (1957); and had his first experience filling in for an actor who wasn't strong enough to sing Rodgers and Hammerstein songs when John Kerr required dubbing on "Younger Than Springtime," "My Girl Back Home," and "You've Got to Be Taught" in the 1958 adaptation of *South Pacific*.

In another rare screen appearance, Lee and Mellomen partner Thurl Ravenscroft wore Hawaiian garb to grunt on a radio commercial with Danny Kaye in *The Five Pennies* (1959); while his animated credits include singing "Cruela De Vil" in *101 Dalmatians* (1961), which meant he was sharing the voice of the character of "Roger" with one of the future cast members of *The Sound of Music*, Ben Wright; backing up Paul Frees on "The Money Cat" in *Gay Purr-ee* (1962); singing for the ursine star himself in *Hey, There, It's Yogi Bear* (1964); and piping in on "Jolly Holiday," as a ram (with a cockney accent, starting off the barnyard serenade to Julie Andrews), in *Mary Poppins* (1964). (Lee also sang the roles of Bert the Chimney Sweep and Mr. Banks on Disney's budget-conscious studio LP of the movie score.)

Following his *TSOM* chores, he was invited back for more Rodgers and Hammerstein, showing up in the 1965 redo of their television musical *Cinderella*; while his voice was sharing the screen again with Julie Andrews, when he sang John Gavin's voice-over rendition of "Ah! Sweet Mystery of Life" in *Thoroughly Modern Millie* (1967). Visitors to both Disneyland and Walt Disney World continued to hear him for decades as a contributing vocalist to the Enchanted Tiki Room, Pirates of the Caribbean, the Haunted Mansion, and the Country Bear Jamboree.

Lee died on November 15, 1980.

Marie Vernon/Marie Greene (dubbed some notes for Anna Lee)

Although Anna Lee would do most of her own singing on "Maria," it was decided that a tiny bit of vocal tweaking was necessary. The 20th Century-Fox reports on the recordings made after shooting was completed on *TSOM* credited Marie Vernon (Marie Greene's married name after wedding sound engineer Vinton Vernon) as contributing all of "three notes" for Ms. Lee.

As Marie Green, she was known as a radio and band singer, mainly fronting for "Her Merry Men." That group was even showcased in their own 1941 short, *Marie Green and Her Merry Men,* at Warner Bros., the same year Universal gave them a specialty, singing their take on Strauss's "On the Beautiful Blue Danube" in an hour-long cheapie called *Ma! He's Making Eyes at Me.* The group released various V-Discs, including "I Know That You Know" and "Penthouse Serenade," while Greene (now with a third "e") recorded solo such songs as "Bill" (by Jerome Kern, P. G. Wodehouse, and Oscar Hammerstein II), "Carnations," "Intermezzo," and "September Song." She also sang with the Ray Bloch Four and on Garry Moore's 1942–43 radio show. Like fellow *TSOM* dubber Bill Lee, she could be heard in *Seven Brides for Seven Brothers* (1954), covering for Nancy Kilgas (as Alice) on "June Bride."

She already had two Rodgers and Hammerstein dubbing assignments on her resume at the time she was hired for her simple task on *TSOM*. In *Carousel* (1956), she gave the character of Louise (Susan Luckey) a voice for the "You'll Never Walk Alone" finale, and went even younger, singing "Dites Moi" as Rossano Brazzi's daughter Ngana (Candace Lee), in *South Pacific* (1958).

The Children

Although none of the seven actors chosen to play the Trapp children needed their entire vocal contributions covered by a professional singer, they were helped on each of the numbers to give their songs a stronger sound. (Their only musical moment not to call on additional singers was the "sad" version of "The Sound of Music" they attempt to sing once Maria has gone back to the abbey.) Those contributing to the additional vocals were Randy Perkins, Diane Burt, Sue McBain, and Charmian Carr's younger sister, Darlene Farnon (who would follow her sibling's lead and change her professional name to Darlene Carr). Darlene's most notable assist came when she hit the high note on "goodbye" for Duane Chase (as Kurt) at the end of his portion of "So Long, Farewell."

Darlene Carr would sing "My Own Home" at the end of Disney's *The Jungle Book* (1967) and play the daughters of David Niven (in the 1968 comedy *The Impossible Years*) and Henry Fonda (on the 1971 series *The Smith Family*) among her many other future jobs.

Roadshow

The Sound of Music and Its Exclusive Engagements in Cinemas

For audiences only aware of movie exhibition from the 1970s onward, it might be hard to fathom the concept of *waiting* to see a movie, or that particular movie being in circulation for months or perhaps a year or more in order to actually give cinemagoers a chance to attend an attraction at their leisure. When the modern norm is to open a new film on a Friday on *thousands* of screens across the country for fast and maximum payback at the turnstiles, it probably seems downright quaint that during the 1960s, it was more desirable (and expected) for movies to roll out slowly.

It was, in truth, a better system, one that gave motion picture exhibition more resonance and importance than it has today. Beyond the playing of pictures at cinemas for as long as people might want to see them, building word of mouth, and keeping them around so that they genuinely *registered* as part of the pop cultural zeitgeist, there were select movies that received even better handling than that.

Treated like Broadway shows, they were booked into some of the finest and largest theatres in the country for prestigious presentations, with reserved-seat tickets, intermissions, and souvenir booklets on sale in the lobby. Often an overture and entr'acte were played over closed, velvet curtains; ushers were in attendance; and the daily schedule was restricted to two showings, one in the afternoon, the other in the evening. "Roadshow engagements" was the Hollywood term, and they were quite an event, requiring in most instances the advance commitment of purchasing tickets and journeying to a (usually) downtown venue at a time when seeing movies in an urban setting was at the end of its heyday, but not considered unthinkable.

As was the case with most of the major musicals of the era, *The Sound of Music* was treated as a "hard ticket" event, one of 20th Century-Fox's three big roadshow attractions for 1965 (the other two were *Those Magnificent Men in Their Flying Machines* and *The Agony and the Ecstasy*). Its "rollout" in the United States found it in an increasing number of reserved-seat venues over a two-year period.

Just for the record, two advance sneak previews were held prior to these bookings that included three brief sequences ultimately cut from the release prInterior: These sneaks took place, with director Robert Wise in attendance, on

Friday, January 15, 1965 at the Mann Theatre in Minneapolis, Minnesota, and Saturday, January 16, 1965 at the Brook Theatre in Tulsa, Oklahoma.

According to preview cards filled out by the audience, the movie received 223 "excellent" votes, 3 "good," and no "fair" in Minneapolis; 137 "excellent," 2 "good" and no "fair" in Tulsa.

Both of these theatres would eventually host reserved-seat showings of the film, the Mann starting March 24, 1965; the Brook on April 6, 1965.

Here, thanks immeasurably to information from Michael Choate and from Patrick Crowley and Ross Melnick's peerless Cinema Treasures site, are the American (and some Canadian and overseas, mainly the UK) locations where *TSOM* had its prestigious first-run showings.

It all began in Manhattan . . .

UNITED STATES

1965

Tuesday, March 2, 1965

New York, NY

Rivoli Theatre, 1620 Broadway, 1,545 seats. Ticket Prices: Evenings (Mon thru Thurs): Orchestra: $3.25; Loge: $3.75; Balcony: $2.50 and $2.00; Evenings (Fri, Sat, Sun & Holidays): Orchestra: $3.75; Loge: $4.25; Balcony: $3.00 and $2.50; Matinees (Wed): Orchestra: $2.50; Loge: $3.00; Balcony: $2.25 and $1.75; Matinees (Sat, Sun, Holidays): Orchestra: $3.25; Loge: $3.75; Balcony: $2.50 & $2.00. (There were additional holiday matinees April 15 thru 23). Daily at 2:30 p.m. and 8:30 p.m.

The official public unveiling of *The Sound of Music* came, not in Hollywood, but in New York at the Rivoli, one of the city's prime "event" venues, located on Broadway between 49th and 50th streets. Opened in 1917 for the grand unveiling of the Douglas Fairbanks adventure *A Modern Musketeer*, the Rivoli had been converted to 70mm Todd-AO exhibition for the October 1955 premiere of Rodgers and Hammerstein's *Oklahoma!* (This was the very first motion picture made in this format, thereby making the Rivoli the first theater to show a movie this way.)

Robert Wise's previous musical triumph, *West Side Story* (1961), had enjoyed a seventy-seven-week run there, while, appropriately, the *other* Julie Andrews smash of the era, *Mary Poppins*, immediately preceded *TSOM*'s opening, having transferred there on February 3, 1965. Ten days after *Music* finished its run on December 11, 1966, Robert Wise's follow-up feature, *The Sand Pebbles*, moved in.

TSOM would enjoy a 93-week run at this location, landing it in second place for longest 70mm run in Manhattan exhibition history (*Around the World in Eighty Days*, which also played the Rivoli starting in 1956, was #1, with 103 weeks; *This Is Cinerama*, from 1952, was the all-time New York record holder with 123 weeks, but this was shown not in 70mm but in Cinerama, of course).

20th Century-Fox invites you to
The Happiest Sound In All The World

An invitation to the first official New York press screening of *The Sound of Music*, held at the Manhattan theatre where the movie would have its reserved-seat engagement, the Rivoli.

Prior to the March 2nd opening, advance sales of tickets for *TSOM* in Manhattan reached $350,000, surpassed at the same house only by *Cleopatra*, which had charged higher prices. ($75,000 worth of tickets were sold for *TSOM*'s premiere showing). Salim M. Hassenein, the executive vice president of UA Theaters, owner of the Rivoli, reported, however, that *TSOM* was "the biggest grossing film, week by week, to ever play the theater." Indeed, in October 1966, two months before it exited this venue, the *New York Times* reported that the musical had taken in $1,470,000 at this location alone. This contradicted an ad that ran in *Motion Picture Exhibitor* on March 9, 1966 celebrating the first-year anniversary for theatres that had debuted the movie in March of the previous year. According to this report, the Rivoli could already lay claim to having taken in $2,250,000 in *TSOM* box office receipts.

Among those attending *TSOM*'s opening night gala premiere on March 2nd to benefit the Mary MacArthur Memorial Fund-March of Dimes were Robert Wise, Julie Andrews, Richard Rodgers; the musical's original book writers Howard Lindsay and Russel Crouse; Adlai Stevenson, Bette Davis, Harry Belafonte, Gower Champion, Samuel Goldwyn, Cy Feuer, Kitty Carlisle, Helen Hayes, Eva Gabor, Goddard Lieberson, Jean-Pierre Aumont, Dorothy Fields, Leonard Bernstein; the star of the stage musical's first touring production, Florence Henderson; Beatrice Lillie; and future mayor John Lindsay.

Variety reported a 1st-week gross of $45,118; 2nd week, $44,000; 21st week of July 28, 1965, $52,000; 25th week of August 25, 1965, $58,000. On the year anniversary, March 2, 1966, the week's gross was $39,000, a clear indication that public interest continued to be strong. Shortly after *The Sand Pebbles* settled into

The gala March 2, 1965 opening night of the film at its first reserved-seat venue, the Rivoli Theatre on Broadway in Manhattan.

the Rivoli (for its thirty-five-week run), the theatre dedicated a bronze plaque to Robert Wise for his "great motion picture achievements." The theatre was grateful for the monetary rewards brought in not only by *The Sound of Music* but by *West Side Story*'s lengthy, 77-week stay (1961–63). Down the line the venue would also play host to Wise's reunion with Julie Andrews, *Star!* (1968; twenty-three weeks).

The Rivoli would lose its luster throughout the seventies as the Times Square area no longer became the desirable location for film premieres, being twinned in December 1981 and finally shutting its doors for good in June 1987. An office building now stands on the spot.

Wednesday, March 10, 1965

Beverly Hills, CA

Fox Wilshire Theatre, 844 Wilshire Boulevard, 1,990 seats. Ticket Prices: Evenings (Sun thru Thurs & Sun Matinee & Holidays): Orchestra: $3.00; Loge: $3.50; Balcony Loge: $3.50; Balcony: $3.00; Evenings (Fri, Sat & Holiday): Orchestra: $3.50; Loge: $4.00; Balcony Loge: $4.00; Balcony: $3.50; Matinees (Wed & Sat): Orchestra: $2.50; Loge: $3.00; Balcony Loge: $3.00; Balcony: $2.50. Twice daily at 2:00 p.m. and 8:30 p.m.

TSOM's Southern California booking was not in Hollywood proper, but at the Fox Wilshire in Beverly Hills.

Opened in 1930, this art deco venue underwent a major renovation in 1960, equipping it for 70mm presentations (with a curved screen and six-track stereophonic sound) and making the seating roomier, thereby cutting the original capacity by about 200. The building was noted for its fifty-foot rotating "FOX" sign that sat atop the six-story tower of apartments located above the theatre.

Just before *TSOM* opened here, Sophia Loren and Marcello Mastroianni's *Marriage—Italian Style* was finishing up its eleven-week run.

In attendance for *TSOM*'s opening night gala, a benefit for the American Cancer Society, were, from the film: Robert Wise, Julie Andrews, Christopher Plummer, all seven of the children (who arrived in a horse-drawn fiacre, like the one used in the "Do-Re-Mi" sequence), Eleanor Parker, Daniel Truhitte, Anna Lee, Marni Nixon, and Ben Wright. Lorne Greene served as master of ceremonies, while an ad in the *Los Angeles Times* promised the following additional celebrities in attendance: Fred Astaire, James Coburn, Chuck Connors, Richard Crenna, Doris Day, Julie Andrews's future husband Blake Edwards, Mia Farrow (who had auditioned for the role of Liesl), Anne Francis, Zsa Zsa Gabor, James Garner, Charlton Heston, Glynis Johns, Jerry Lewis, Fred MacMurray, Agnes Moorehead, Hugh O'Brian, Ryan O'Neal, Gregory Peck, Suzanne Pleshette, Lee Remick, Edward G. Robinson, Cesar Romero, Phil Silvers, Frank Sinatra, Jill St. John, Robert Stack, Rod Taylor, and Russ Tamblyn (who, briefly, in the 1950s, was the son-in-law of *TSOM* player Anna Lee, having married her daughter, Venetia Stevenson).

TSOM cast members Duane Chase, Debbie Turner, and Kym Karath all hailed from Southern California.

After *TSOM*'s March 10th opening, the following week's *Variety* reported capacity attendance and a $42,200 gross. In its May 10th issue, *Boxoffice* reported that the film had topped the Fox Wilshire's previous all-time attendance record, once held by Otto Preminger's 1960 film of *Exodus*.

A day short of the year anniversary, *Motion Picture Exhibitor* ran an ad claiming *TSOM* had made $1,750,000 at this theatre alone.

TSOM would better its East Coast roadshow run by a single week, playing for a ninety-four-week stretch. As with the Rivoli in New York, *TSOM*'s run was followed here by the reserved-seat engagement of *The Sand Pebbles*. Because there was still tremendous demand for *TSOM* tickets, this exclusive engagement was picked up to continue at the Carthay Circle (a seven-mile drive west from this location), starting on December 25, 1966.

TSOM ended up back here in 1969 for a return engagement run.

After its closing in 1977, the Fox Wilshire was later renovated for live theatre attractions, eventually changing its name to the Saban.

Wednesday, March 17, 1965

Boston, MA
Gary Theatre, 131 Stuart Street; 1,277 seats; $2.00-$3.30 tickets (83 weeks).

Opened in 1911 as the Plymouth, remodeled (including Todd-AO installation and a new, five-story marquee) in 1957, it was renamed the Gary (after owner Ben Sack's son). Robert Wise's previous musical Oscar winner, *West Side Story*, had its reserved-seat run here; while *Mary Poppins* preceded *TSOM* as the attraction, though not as a roadshow event.

Following *TSOM*'s run, *Hawaii* was the next film booked here. This meant that between October 22, 1964 and May 8, 1967, this venue exclusively showed films starring Julie Andrews. (It was not the last Andrews booking of the decade either, as her reunion with director Robert Wise, *Star!*, opened here in November 1968.)

Variety reported a $32,000 take for *TSOM*'s first week of exhibition at the Gary.

Maria von Trapp and members of her family were in attendance at the opening here, as were Senator Edward Kennedy and his wife.

The building was demolished in 1978.

Chicago, IL

Michael Todd Theatre, 180-190 N. Dearborn Street; 1,000 seats; $1.75–$3.00 (93 weeks).

Originally the Harris Theatre (opened in 1922 for legit presentations); showman Michael Todd took over the space in the 1950s and installed the Todd-AO process.

Motion Picture Exhibitor ran an ad on March 9, 1966 stating that *TSOM* had grossed $1,500,000 at this theatre alone; the theatre itself reported 700,000 persons having seen the movie during this period.

Although the interior was eventually demolished, the building façade later became part of the Goodman Theatre complex.

Chicago was *TSOM* cast member Charmian Carr's birthplace.

Detroit, MI

Madison Theatre, 20 Witherell Street (at Grand Circus Park); 1,408 seats; $1.50–$3.00 (98 weeks).

Opened in 1917 as part of a five-story office building, the Madison was renovated for 70mm exhibition in 1961, losing its neoclassical façade in the process. It closed in 1984.

Miami Beach, FL

Colony Theatre, 1040 Lincoln Road (at Lennox); 894 seats; $2.00–$3.50 (82 weeks).

This art deco house opened in 1935, in the heart of the South Beach section of the city. It became a performing arts venue in 1976.

TSOM premiere offered $10 tickets sponsored by the Greater Miami Philharmonic Society. The tremendous success of the picture at this location meant it passed on booking *Doctor Zhivago* as its winter '66 attraction, preferring to hold on to *TSOM*.

Philadelphia, PA

Midtown Theatre, 1412 Chestnut Street; 1,200 seats; $2.00–$2.75 (93 weeks).

The city's go-to house for reserved-seat attractions had previously hosted the long runs of the Rodgers and Hammerstein musicals *Oklahoma!* and *South Pacific*, not to mention Robert Wise's *West Side Story*. *Mary Poppins* was the attraction just before *TSOM* opened here.

This particular venue made show business headlines when 20th Century-Fox actually sued to keep them from ending *TSOM*'s run on November 15, 1966. According to the studio, the theatre owner could only stop showing the film if the gross receipts were lower than $7,615 during three consecutive weeks. Since the lowest figure posted was $8,223 (on October 11, the 82nd week), this meant there was no justification for the decision to cease screening the picture. Fox was clearly worried about not cashing in on the lucrative holiday season box office and was in a panic that other theatres might follow suit. The Midtown did end up holding onto the picture until the end of December.

Later twinned, the Midtown closed as a movie theatre in 1995 and subsequently became the Prince Music Theater (named for Broadway director-producer Harold Prince, son-in-law of *TSOM*'s associate producer, Saul Chaplin).

Washington, DC
Ontario Theatre, 1700 Columbia Road NW; 1,240 seats; $1.75-$3.00 (97 weeks).

Located northwest of central DC in the Adams Morgan section of the nation's capital, this 1,400-seat house opened in 1951. *Mary Poppins* had played here for sixteen weeks prior to *TSOM*'s premiere; it was followed by Robert Wise's *The Sand Pebbles*. This, in turn, was followed by Julie Andrews in *Thoroughly Modern Millie*.

The theater closed in 1986.

Washington, D.C. was the birthplace of *TSOM* cast member Nicholas Hammond.

Thursday, March 18, 1965

San Francisco, CA
United Artists Theatre, 1077 Market Street; 1,148 seats; $1.75–$3.75 (93 weeks).

Originally Grauman's Imperial, this theatre opened in 1912, was renamed the Premiere, and finally the United Artists in 1931. The building was placed on the National Register of Historic Places in 1986 and closed in 2013. In its later days of operation, it had ceased showing movies and opted for "adult" live performances.

Wednesday, March 24, 1965

Atlanta, GA
Martin Cinerama, 583 Peachtree Street; 858 seats (90 weeks).

Starting life as a live playhouse in 1926, this theatre (which previously went under the names the Erlanger and the Tower) installed a curved screen for exhibition of Cinerama features in the 1950s, the remodeling reducing the seating from 1,790 seats to 858. Following the Cinerama era, it was refitted for 70mm exhibition.

When *TSOM* ended its run here, it had broken all records, grossing more than $900,000, with sold-out shows each of the six weekends leading up to the closing. Other sixties attractions at the Martin included Julie Andrews's *Mary Poppins, Hawaii,* and *Thoroughly Modern Millie.*

Later taken over by a church and then demolished in 1995.

Baltimore, MD

New Theatre, 210 W. Lexington Street; 1,800 seats; $1.50-$2.00 (91 weeks)

Opened in 1910, it was renovated substantially in the late 1940s to increase its seating capacity to 1,800. It closed its doors in 1986.

Cleveland, OH

Ohio Theatre, 1511 Euclid Avenue; 1,020 seats; $1.50–$2.00 (91 weeks).

A Renaissance Revival palace originally boasting 2,153 seats, the Ohio had gone through various stages since its 1921 opening, providing space for legit theatre and a casino, before turning to movies in the 1930s. Previous roadshow tenants here included Rodgers and Hammerstein's *South Pacific* and Robert Wise's *West Side Story.*

Closed only four years after *TSOM* opened there, it was restored after extensive damage, being added to the National Register of Historic Places in 1978.

Dallas, TX

Inwood Theatre, 5458 W. Lovers Lane (92 weeks).

Opened in 1947 at a cost of $200,000, with an art moderne décor, this venue is located about six miles north on the Dallas North Tollway from Dealey Plaza, where the city had gained notoriety sixteen months earlier because of the Kennedy assassination.

On the eve of the first-year anniversary of showing *TSOM*, March 23, 1966, the film's Liesl, Charmian Carr, was invited to cut the first slice of a celebratory cake as part of a red carpet event. In August 1966, Chuck Seabough became the 300,000th person to see *TSOM* at the Inwood and as a reward was given a copy of the soundtrack, a season pass for two at Interstate Theatres, and a paid-for night on the town that included dinner at the Statler Stake House.

This run was followed by another Julie Andrews picture shown on a reserved-seat basis, *Hawaii.*

Despite fire damage in the 1980s and multiplexing, the theatre continues to show movies. Its tower sign was designated a Dallas landmark in 1988.

Denver, CO

Aladdin Theatre, 2000 E. Colfax Avenue; 900 seats; $1.25–$2.50 (112 weeks).

As its name suggests, the Aladdin resembled an Arabian palace with dome and mock minarets. It opened to great fanfare in 1926. (Soon after, it became the first theatre in the area and reportedly the second in the entire United States to offer sound.) In the mid-1950s, it was updated for 70mm and 6-track stereo.

Years after the roadshow movie era came to an end, the Aladdin tried offering live theatre before shuttering in 1984.

Milwaukee, WI

Strand Theatre, 510 W. Wisconsin Avenue; $1.75–$3.00 (97 weeks).

While boasting some 2,000 seats, the Strand was one of the roadshow venues that was built (in 1914) without a mezzanine. A year into its run, the management reported that 301,283 patrons had seen *TSOM* during its 595 performances here.

The theatre closed in 1978 and was razed two years later.

Minneapolis, MN

Mann Theatre, 708 Hennepin Avenue; 1,000 seats; $1.55-$2.75 (95 weeks).

A former vaudeville house called the Pantages, this 1916 structure was bought and updated for 70mm exhibition by Ted Mann in 1961, hence its new name. A week after *TSOM* debuted, *Variety* reported a $20,000 take, despite sub-zero temperatures!

The Mann was closed in 1984 and was later restored for live theatre shows.

Warwick, RI

Warwick Cinema, 780 Post Road; 1,000 seats (86 weeks).

Rather than being booked in one of nearby Providence's downtown theatres, *TSOM* landed its roadshow engagement for the area in this suburb south of the capital city, at Warwick's first-ever cinema, which had only just opened in March 1964.

Since demolished.

Salt Lake City, UT

Utah Theatre, 148 S. Main Street; 1,444 seats (95 weeks).

This venue, a former vaudeville palace from 1920 (built at a reported cost of $2,250,000), was located in the capital city of Utah, approximately ninety miles south of Brigham City, where *TSOM* cast member Portia Nelson was born. In January 1966, it was reported that 309,000 people had seen the film here in the forty weeks tabulated, while Salt Lake City's total population was only 199,300.

Movie exhibition ceased here in 1988.

Wednesday, March 31, 1965

Buffalo, NY

Teck Theatre, 760 Main Street; 1,200 seats; $1.75–$2.75 (79 weeks).

Dating all the way back to 1887, this once-live venue (the Music Hall) became the Shea's Teck in 1900 and went through hard times when the Depression hit, remaining vacant between 1933 and 1945. It reopened for movies in 1945, once again called Shea's Teck, and then received a total overhaul to make way for Cinerama in 1953. Following the Cinerama boom, it began showing reserved-seat attractions in flat 70mm. It was one of many downtown sites hurt by the city's gradual economic decline, inevitably facing the wrecking ball in 1992.

Charlotte, NC

Carolina Theatre, 226 N. Tryon Street (79 weeks).

An opulent Mediterranean-style theater, the Carolina opened in 1927, was revamped for widescreen in 1953, and was a frequent venue for live stage acts as well as films. The 20th Century-Fox biblical epic *The Story of Ruth* premiered here in 1960, with one of its stars (and future Mother Abbess of *TSOM*), Peggy Wood, in attendance. The auditorium was renovated yet again in 1961 for Cinerama exhibition.

This theatre (along with the Utah in Salt Lake City) became one of the first to host more ticket buyers for *TSOM* than the city's population! According to the January 26, 1966 issue of *Motion Picture Exhibitor*, 240,000 people had seen the film in thirty-two weeks, while Charlotte had a population of only 225,000.

The cinema closed in 1978, was added to the Registry of Historical Places ten years later, and continued to wait for years for restoration to take place.

Cincinnati, OH

International 70, 16 E. Sixth Street; 1,502 seats; $1.75–$3.00 (79 weeks).

The former Palace Theatre hosted vaudeville between 1919 and 1928, then switched to films. It was torn down in 1982.

Honolulu, HI

Kuhio Theatre, 2095 Kuhio Avenue; $1.50–$2.50 (81 weeks).

TSOM played in the U.S. off the mainland for the first time at this theatre, which opened in the Waikiki section of the city in 1946 and was later renovated for occasional roadshow exhibition. (Prior to *TSOM*, the last such film at this house was 1959's *Ben-Hur*.) In October 1965, *Variety* reported that *TSOM* had made more money than any other film ever shown in Hawaii, topping the record *My Fair Lady* had recently achieved during its thirty-one-week run at the Cinerama.

Fittingly, Julie Andrews's follow-up movie, *Hawaii*, later had its premiere here.

The Kuhio was demolished in 1996 to make way for a shopping center.

Houston, TX

Alabama Theatre, 2922 S. Shepherd Drive (90 weeks).

This showing of *TSOM* took place not in downtown Houston but in a suburban area known as the Upper Kirby district. The art deco-moderne theatre opened in 1939 and closed in 1983, after which it became a bookstore that kept the theatre murals and balconies as part of its décor.

In August 1966, the theatre announced that *TSOM* had been seen there by nearly a million people, a city record.

Indianapolis, IN

Lyric Theatre, 135 N. Illinois Street (94 weeks).

Built in 1912 on the site of a smaller theatre of the same name, this former vaudeville house was given a costly renovation in 1956 in order to accommodate the Todd-AO 70mm presentation of Rodgers and Hammerstein's *Oklahoma!* After a decade of reserved-seat attractions, it closed in 1969.

Indiana was the home state of *TSOM* director Robert Wise, who was born in Winchester (eighty-five miles northeast of Indianapolis) and raised in Connersville (sixty-two miles east).

Phoenix, AZ

Vista Theatre, 215 N. Central Avenue; 730 seats (115 weeks).

Built in 1944, this served as a roadshow house throughout the 1960s, but was torn down in 1970 to make way for the Valley National Bank Building.

Richmond, VA

Willow Lawn Theater, 1601 Willow Lawn Drive; 811 seats (86 weeks).

This theater opened in 1956 for 70mm, roadshow presentations as part of the Willow Lawn Shopping Center. It closed in 1981.

This is one of several cinemas where *TSOM* cast member Charmian Carr was present at the opening.

St. Louis, MO

St. Louis Theatre, 718 N. Grand Avenue; $1.75–$3.00 (83 weeks).

This opulent palace stood out as being the theatre showing *TSOM* to boast the greatest number of seats, a whopping 3,800, according to *Variety*. *Sound* was the venue's last hurrah, in fact, at least as a roadshow movie house. Once the picture had run its course, the St. Louis closed after forty-two years of operation, and was renovated to accommodate the St. Louis Symphony Orchestra. A second renovation in 1995 brought about its current name, Powell Hall.

San Diego, CA

Loma Theatre, 3150 Rosecrans Street; 985 seats (133 weeks).

Opened in 1945, this house was modernized in 1960 for roadshow productions. Showing *TSOM* over a two-and-a-half-year period (finishing up in October 1967) meant that this particular locale ran the picture longer than any other theatre in the United States.

For the two-year anniversary, some of the kids from the film were invited to a celebration at the theatre. The follow-up Julie Andrews/Robert Wise collaboration, *Star!*, played here for a twelve-week run starting at Christmastime 1968. *TSOM* returned here for its 1973 reissue beginning in August 1973, playing for five weeks.

In later years, the building remained intact (with marquee and Loma tower) but gave the space over to a bookstore and a fitness center.

Seattle, WA

5th Avenue Theatre, 1308 Fifth Avenue; 2,115 seats (117 weeks).

Built in 1926 with a Chinese-style décor, this palace was considered one of the great roadshow theatres. It ceased operations in 1978, but was later restored to its full grandeur and now presents live theatre. (It has also hosted the *Sing-a-long Sound of Music*.)

Tuesday, April 6, 1965

Tulsa, OK

Brook Theater, 3307 S. Peoria Avenue; 700 seats (79 weeks).

Opened in 1949, this house also hosted an extensive run of the film of Rodgers and Hammerstein's *South Pacific*. It ceased showing movies in 1978. Retaining its sign and name, it now operates as a restaurant.

Wednesday, April 7, 1965

Columbus, OH

Northland Cinema, 1865 Morse Road; 978 seats; $2.00–$3.00 (84 weeks).

Central Ohio's first mall cinema, opened in 1964; it became a reserved-seat venue with the launching of *TSOM*. It was preceded by *Mary Poppins*, and would eventually play *Thoroughly Modern Millie*. The theatre closed in 1985.

Dayton, OH

Dabel Theater, 1920 S. Smithville Road; 742 seats (105 weeks).

This booking brought *TSOM* closest to the birthplace of cast member Eleanor Parker, who hailed from nearby Cedarville. Opened in 1947, the cinema was converted into a Cinerama house in 1963, giving it a large, curved screen but reducing the seating capacity from 950 to 742. It closed in 1992.

Des Moines, IA

Capri Theatre, 4115 University Avenue; 700 seats (113 weeks).

Originally opened in 1935 as the Uptown; remodeled for roadshow attractions in 1960.

In December 1965, *Variety* reported *TSOM* as having taken in over $100,000 at this site, more than the combined business on their three previous long-runs, *Ben-Hur, Cleopatra*, and *My Fair Lady*.

Jacksonville, FL

5 Points Theatre, 1028 Park Street (31 weeks).

Originally the Riverside, this was one of Florida's first movie theatres equipped to show talkies. Its roller-coaster life involved several closings and renovations, including making it available for Cinerama features; and times spent as clubs and a live theater venue. Miraculously, it came back to life as a single-screen cinema in 2008 and was renamed the Sun-Ray.

Louisville, KY

Rialto Theatre, 616 S. Fourth Street; 3,500 seats (64 weeks).

A 1921 theatre converted to roadshow screenings in the 1960s, until its closing in 1968. (When *TSOM* finished its run here, it transferred over to the

Penthouse on June 29, 1966 for another fifteen weeks, bringing the total weeks up to seventy-nine in Louisville.) The Rialto was one of the largest of all U.S. theatres to host *TSOM* and claimed to have sold tickets to some 300,000 patrons during its run.

Memphis, TN
Paramount Theater, 827 S. White Station Road; 858 seats (79 weeks).

One of the newer theaters to host the reserved-seat run of *TSOM*, this had just opened in November 1964 as part of the Eastgate Shopping Center. By September 1965, *TSOM* broke all prior city records with a $500,000 gross at this one house, passing previous champions *Goldfinger, My Fair Lady, Cleopatra,* and *West Side Story.*

This venue was demolished in 1990.

Norfolk, VA
Riverview Theatre, 3910 Granby Street; 685 seats (115 weeks).

Although it has been reported on many websites as the theatre with the longest run of *TSOM* in the United States, it was in fact bested by several other venues, including that in Omaha, two entries below this one. The theatre has since shuttered.

Oklahoma City, OK
Tower Theater, 425 NW 23rd Street; 1,500 seats (82 weeks)

Fittingly, for its name, this theatre was known for its towering sign and was renovated in the early 1960s to serve as a roadshow house. It was targeted for a new renovation and rebirth starting in 2013.

Omaha, NE
Dundee Theatre, 4952 Dodge Street; 475 seats (118 weeks).

Mainly catering to art house and independent films for most of its existence, the Dundee made room for the reserved-seat engagement of *TSOM* and played the film for so long (wrapping up in July 1967) that it ended up second only to the Loma in San Diego (which had nearly double the number of seats) for record number of weeks run in the United States.

Pittsburgh, PA
Nixon Theatre, 956 Liberty Avenue; 1,797 seats; $1.50–$3.00 (106 weeks).

A former legit house (which went under various names including the Senator until taking the Nixon name from another demolished theatre), in 1956 this switched to roadshow movie attractions, which alternated with live theatre (which, presciently, included the tour of *The Sound of Music,* which came here in September–October 1963). The Nixon was razed in 1975.

Portland, OR
Fox Theatre, 837 SW Broadway (at Taylor Street); 1,536 seats; $1.75–$3.00 (116 weeks).

Built in 1910 as the Heilig for live theatre, this venue switched over to movies in 1929 when it became the Hippodrome. Not satisfied with this name either, it went through another three—the Rialto, Music Box, and Mayfair—before Fox spent $1,000,000 converting it to widescreen and state-of-the-art sound in August 1954. According to *Boxoffice* magazine, the 1,536-seat Fox Theatre boasted of having the second-largest screen in the nation at the time (the Roxy in New York being the largest). The theatre also received some attention in the papers at the time, because a resident from nearby Milwaukie sat down and reproduced the script for *TSOM* from memory after only ten viewings, with only a single error in it.

The Fox was demolished in 1997 to make way for an office building that, ironically, kept the theatre's name, calling itself the Fox Tower.

San Antonio, TX

North Star Cinema 1 & 11, 600 North Star Mall (82 weeks).

TSOM received its first "multiplex" mall booking at this twin cinema that had only just opened on Christmas Day, 1964. Cinema 1 had 958 seats, while Cinema II had a smaller 526 capacity. As an example of *TSOM*'s tremendous dominance of the movie scene, this venue was so loath to see the run end that they bumped the scheduled booking of Fox's second-biggest attraction of 1965, *Those Magnificent Men in Their Flying Machines*, in order to keep playing the Julie Andrews musical.

Although the mall itself continues to thrive, the cinema was closed in 1982.

Tampa, FL

Palace Theatre, 700 Tampa Street; 750 seats; $1.25–$2.00 (77 weeks).

Following a stint as a successful destination for Cinerama features, the Palace installed 70mm projectors and became a reserved-seat house for most of the sixties, its longest run being *TSOM*. It closed in 1978.

Thursday, April 15, 1965

Orlando, FL

Beacham Theatre, 46 N. Orange Avenue; 1,135 seats (60 weeks).

Opened in 1921 to host both vaudeville and movies, it converted to Cinerama use the year before *TSOM* was booked here. In January 1966, the Beacham reported 105,171 *TSOM* admissions during a thirty-five-week period, versus the entire Orlando population of 88,135.

The theatre stopped showing films in 1975.

Rochester, NY

Monroe Theatre, 585 Monroe Avenue; 1,180 seats (85 weeks).

This 1927 house had its last gasp of glory during the 1960s when it hosted roadshow films like *TSOM*, but stopped mainstream exhibition in 1970. Afterwards, it showed porn before shuttering in the 1990s.

The April 21, 1965 issue of Variety reported *TSOM* having already taken in $2,625,852 in domestic release, counting the U.S. and Canada.

Thursday, May 27, 1965

Atlantic City, NJ

Virginia Theatre, Boardwalk and Virginia Avenue; 1,000 seats (79 weeks).

Located right on the boardwalk at New Jersey's famed ocean resort, near the Steel Pier, this theater specialized in 70mm roadshow attractions until its closing in 1973. One of the films to play there in its final year of operations was the reissue of *TSOM*.

Following its initial run here, *TSOM* moved over to the Shore Theatre to continue generating profits.

Fort Worth, TX

Palace Theatre, 113 E. 7th Street, Fort Worth, TX (21 weeks).

With a booking that took it up to mid-October 1965, this was the shortest exclusive engagement run of *TSOM* to date. (Perhaps the locals resented Mary Martin not getting to repeat her stage role? Fort Worth was, after all, located only twenty-nine miles west of Martin's birthplace of Weatherford.) This 1920 theatre was built to host live acts and seated 1,468, was revamped for 70mm roadshow attractions in the 1950s, and closed in 1976.

To herald it winning the magazine's Blue Ribbon Award, *Boxoffice* featured *The Sound of Music* on its cover, two months after its premiere.

Friday, May 28, 1965

DeWitt, NY

Shoppingtown Theatre, Eric Boulevard East; 1,009 seats (76 weeks).

Built in 1957 behind a shopping center in this suburb of Syracuse, it was the only Todd-AO-equipped theatre between New York and Buffalo at the time, launched with an encore presentation of *Oklahoma!* The debut here of *TSOM* meant that the cinema was continuing its celebration of Julie Andrews, as *Mary Poppins* had been the previous attraction here for months. The follow-up feature was the next Robert Wise production, *The Sand Pebbles*. During the run of *TSOM*, Maria von Trapp made an appearance at nearby Syracuse University to a packed house to talk about her story.

This site was replaced by upstate New York's first twin theatre in 1968.

The movie's reserved-seat engagement in Upper Montclair, New Jersey, offered its own playbill to its patrons.

Sunday, June 20, 1965

Albany, NY

Hellman Theatre, 1365 Washington Avenue; 1,060 seats; $2.00–$2.50 (31 weeks).

This theatre was built in 1960 at a cost of half a million dollars, across from SUNY, and showed Cinerama attractions until 1963. In January 1966, Albany became one of five cities in the United States to have more people see *TSOM* (176,536 admissions in twenty-seven weeks) than the city's total population (156,000). The Hellman was demolished in 1999.

Wednesday, June 23, 1965

Upper Montclair, NJ

Bellevue Theatre, 260 Bellevue Avenue (100 weeks).

Located approximately eighteen miles west of Times Square, New York, this Tudor décor theatre became the closest booking to the venue where *TSOM* was first launched in March. Formerly a horse stable, it opened as a movie house in 1923 and despite its reputation for roadshow bookings had the noisy disadvantage of being too closely located to the adjacent commuter railway line. A much-renovated, multiplexed version of the building still shows films.

Fairlawn, OH

Village Theatre, 55 N. Miller Road (at West Market); $1.50–$2.50 (91 weeks).

Newly opened in 1964, this cinema closed its doors in 1998.

Asbury Park, NJ

Paramount Theatre, 1300 Ocean Avenue; 1,995 seats; $2.00–$4.00 (76 weeks).

As with its Atlantic City booking, this theater was located directly on the boardwalk, and therefore in very close proximity to the Atlantic Ocean. It now hosts live attractions.

An example of the ads that ran in *TSOM*'s final weeks there: "Now really—After 71 Weeks in Asbury Park—You Wouldn't Want to Be One of the Few Who Missed This Picture, Would You?"

It is where the author of this book first saw the film, in October 1965.

Hamden, CT
Cinemart Theatre, 2300 Dixwell Avenue; 1,150 seats (73 weeks).

Opened in 1964 with the Connecticut premiere of the thriller *Charade*, this theatre was located in the Hamden Shopping Mart in a suburb of New Haven. It later went through the expected twinning before closing in the early 1990s.

Nashville, TN
Belle Meade Theatre, 4301 Harding Pike; 800 seats (69 weeks).

Once the most prestigious of the Music City's theatres, its lobby even included marble slabs on which celebrities had signed their names. It closed in 1991 after fifty-one years of service. Its ball-topped tower sign and remnants of its marquee were incorporated into the retail complex it became.

Scranton, PA
West Side Theater, 214 N. Main Avenue; 1,975 seats (53 weeks).

The theatre's projectionist, Tony Bianco, received a special nod in the July 5, 1966 *Variety* for having nursed the print of *TSOM* through 550 showings and making sure it unspooled each time in the best possible way. The building was demolished in 1989.

Shrewsbury, MA
White City Theatre, 50 Boston Turnpike (53 weeks).

This theatre was part of the White City Shopping Center, built on the site of what had been the former White City Amusement Park (1905–60). It opened in 1964 with *Mary Poppins* and closed in 2001.

Syosset, NY
Syosset Theatre, 565 Jericho Turnpike; 1,500 seats (78 weeks).

TSOM's Long Island booking became the New York State venue nearest to the site where it first debuted in Manhattan. This theatre opened in 1956 equipped with Todd-AO for an engagement of *Oklahoma!* After being tripled in 1983, it was closed in 1996 and eventually demolished.

Toledo, OH
Princess 70, 316 N. St. Clair Street; 940 seats (91 weeks).

This theatre had a fifty-three-year lifespan, opening in 1916 and closing in 1969.

West Hartford, CT
Elm Theater, 924 Quaker Lane South; 902 seats (77 weeks).

Opened in 1947, this cinema would last until 2002.

Youngstown, OH
State Theatre, 213 Federal Plaza West (51 weeks).

The success of *TSOM* at this house (proclaimed the "greatest film attraction in Youngstown history, in length of run, box office gross and number of persons seeing it" according to *Boxoffice* magazine), required the much-anticipated debut of the new James Bond epic, *Thunderball*, to relocate to the Newport Theatre instead.

The State later became a nightclub and was demolished in 2008.

Wednesday, July 7, 1965

Columbia, SC
Carolina Theatre, 224 Main Street (22 weeks)

Wednesday, July 14, 1965

Harrisburg, PA
Eric Theatre, 4400 Derry Street; 1,350 seats (67 weeks).
The Eric opened in 1963 for the exhibition of 70mm roadshow films.

Kansas City, MO
Midland Theatre, 1228 Main Street; 1,292 seats; $1.00–$3.00 (75 weeks).

Between its life as a 1927 movie palace and its refurbishing only months before *TSOM* opened here, the Midland spent time as a bowling alley and then a dual venue, the main auditorium known as the Saxon, with a miniature Studio Theatre carved underneath within a lounge. The Studio (eventually renamed the Screening Room) continued offering films during *TSOM*'s run and was touted as the "world's smallest theatre" by *Boxoffice*.

Toward the end of *TSOM*'s run, ads ran alerting potential customers that "Time is running out!!! See this wonderful motion picture as it should be seen! In 70mm film reproduction—6-track stereo sound and in the grandeur of the Midland Theatre."

Friday, July 16, 1965

Chattanooga, TN
Brainerd Cinerama, 3603 Brainerd Road; $1.50–$2.00 (31 weeks).
"Winning the Heart of Chattanooga!" proclaimed the local ads.

At this point, four and a half months into its run, Fox reported a gross of $12,710,956, representing the cumulative business for *TSOM* at seventy-one U.S. and Canadian theatres.

Boxoffice magazine reported that the Gary in Boston, the Michael Todd in Chicago, and the Madison in Detroit could all boast of *TSOM* having higher grosses over the subsequent weeks' run than it had for the opening week; something that was not the norm and clearly a testament to the favorable word-of-mouth.

Wednesday, July 21, 1965

Savannah, GA

Savannah Theatre, 222 Bull Street; 997 seats (12 weeks).

Although fire intervened, thereby not making it the original structure, there has been a theatre on this site since 1818, making it the oldest "location" where *TSOM* played. Although it spent (and now spends) most of its existence as a live theatre, the establishment did cater to motion picture exhibition for years, including 1965, which was not only the year *TSOM* was booked there, but the year it was designated Savannah's first National Historic landmark.

Clearly, this theatre had inflexible bookings, as attendance figures indicated they needn't have stopped exhibiting *TSOM* after three months. "Held Over Again!," said the October 1st ad. "It's the most phenomenal success in the history of the Savannah Theatre . . . Running twice as long as any other picture has ever run in Savannah. 35,000 have seen it."

Westbrook, ME

Cinema 1 & II, Riverside Street and Main Street at Westbrook Plaza (68 weeks).

Wichita, KS

Boulevard Theatre, 900 George Washington Boulevard; 972 seats (49 weeks).

Thursday, July 22, 1965

Birmingham, AL

Eastwood Mall, Crestwood Boulevard and US-78 (or Montevallo & Montclair) (17 weeks).

This venue opened at Christmas 1964, as part of the Eastwood Mall, which could lay claim, at the time, to being the first enclosed shopping center in the Southeast. The cinema *and* the mall are now memories.

Grand Rapids, MI

Midtown Theater, 123 Pearl Street (71 weeks).

Tuesday, August 3, 1965

El Paso, TX

Pershing Theater, 2905 Pershing Drive; 634 seats (17 weeks).

Wednesday, August 4, 1965

Albuquerque, NM

Sunshine Theater, 120 Central Avenue SW (16 weeks)

Sioux City, IA

Cinema, 1961 South Saint Aubin Street; 417 seats (47 weeks)

Friday, August 6, 1965

Cedar Rapids, IA
New Times 70 Theatre, 1415 First Avenue SE; 525 seats (65 weeks)
The "70" in its name did indeed refer to 70mm, which this theatre (simply the Times, when it opened in 1941) converted to in time for *TSOM*'s run there.

Lexington, KY
Kentucky Theatre, 214 E. Main Street; 1,276 seats (16 weeks)
A rare downtown movie house that hosted the reserved-seat run of *TSOM* that can actually boast of not only still showing movies, but doing so on a single screen. Built in 1922, it was restored in 1989.

Wednesday, August 11, 1965

Greenville, SC
Carolina Theatre, 310 N. Main Street (15 weeks)

Raleigh, NC
Ambassador Theatre, 115 Fayetteville Street; 1,477 seats (61 weeks)
This theatre became the second one in the state of North Carolina to lay claim to having hosted more ticket-buying customers (approximately 117,000) than the city's entire population (about 110,000).
North Carolina's only theatre able to screen Cinerama presentations, this became *the* go-to house for reserved-seat attractions during the 1960s.

Winston-Salem, NC
Winston Theatre, 64-643 W. Fourth Street (44 weeks)

Friday, August 13, 1965

Columbus, GA
Beverly Theater, 3100 Macon Road (13 weeks)

Wednesday, August 18, 1965

Erie, PA
Plaza Cinema, 800 W. Erie Plaza (21 weeks)

Variety ran an ad that stated "On March 12, 1965 *Life Magazine* predicted: "*The Sound of Music* is destined to be one of the biggest hits ever! . . . AND IT IS!" It then crossed out previous figures to bring them up-to-date, pointing out that "It has thrilled 16,454,709 people in 18 countries around the world." (Those locations, listed on a globe behind the familiar Julie Andrews image, included Canada, Manila, Rio de Janeiro, Lima, Johannesburg, Tokyo, London, Auckland, Hong Kong, Bangkok, Sydney, Port of Spain, and Buenos Aires).

Thursday, September 22, 1965

Sacramento, CA
Crest Theatre, 1013 K Street; 975 seats (59 weeks)

Spokane, WA
State Theater, 901 W. Sprague Street (54 weeks)

Knoxville, TN
Park Theatre, 2301 Magnolia Avenue East; 800 seats (40 weeks)

Eugene, OR
Fox Theatre, 996 Willamette Street (26 weeks)
    Originally called the Rex when it opened in 1910, this theatre received a widescreen renovation in 1955 and became the Fox. Since closing, it now houses a fitness center.

Little Rock, AR
Capitol Theatre, 324 W. Capitol Avenue (13 weeks)

Corpus Christi, TX
Tower Theater, 1647 S. Alameda Street (12 weeks)

Thursday, September 23, 1965

Augusta, GA
Daniel Village Theatre, 2803 Wrightsboro Road (19 weeks)

Beaumont, TX
Liberty Theatre, 347 Pearl Street; $1.50–$2.50 (12 weeks)
    Following the gala Golden Triangle (referring to the area between Beaumont, Port Arthur, and Orange) premiere of *TSOM*, local papers heralded it as "the gayest theatrical event ever filmed," back when the word had a different meaning to most of the public.

A reserved-seat ticket for *The Sound of Music*'s showing at the Durfee Theatre in Fall River, Massachusetts.

Macon, GA
Grand Theater, 651 Mulberry Street (14 weeks)

Wednesday, September 29, 1965

Tucson, AZ
Catalina Theatre, 2320 North Campbell Avenue (45 weeks)

Wednesday, October 6, 1965

Fall River, MA
Durfee Theatre, 30 N. Main Street (37 weeks)

West Springfield, MA
Showcase Cinemas, 864 Riverdale Road (36 weeks)

Thursday, October 14, 1965

Las Vegas, NV
Fox Theatre, 1800 E. Charleston Boulevard; 864 seats (24 weeks)
This venue had just opened earlier in the year, as part of the Charleston Plaza Shopping Center. It was equipped for 70mm and Todd-AO exhibition. The shopping center eventually became a mall, and the theatre is no more.

Wednesday, October 20, 1965

Moorhead, MN
Moorhead Theatre, 412 Center Avenue; 671 seats (53 weeks)
Not everyone was enchanted with the opportunity to see *TSOM* for an entire year's time at the same theatre. Located across the river from Fargo, North Dakota, this booking prompted a somewhat tongue-in-cheek protest by a group of local college students (from nearby Moorhead State College) calling themselves POOIE (People's Organization of Intelligent Educatees). The rallied mob carried picket signs with such slogans as "POOIE on Julie" and "49 Weeks of Schmaltz is Enough," and jokingly worried that children attending the film would come away negatively comparing their own mothers to Julie Andrews. They were no doubt relieved when the change in booking came within a month. One can only speculate on how many of the protestors had actually seen the movie.

New Orleans, LA
Saenger Orleans Theatre, 143 N. Rampart Street (56 weeks)
Opened in 1927 at a cost of $2,500,000, this vast theatre had its balcony turned into a separate cinema in 1964.

Wednesday, October 27, 1965

Springfield, IL
Lincoln Theatre, 329 S. Fifth Street
(23 weeks)

Thursday, October 28, 1965

Charleston, SC
Riviera Theater, 225 King Street;
$1.50–$2.00 (13 weeks)
    Opened in 1939, this art deco
theatre is listed on the National
Registry of Historic Places and now
operates as a conference center.

Fort Wayne, IN
Jefferson Theatre, 116 W. Jefferson
Boulevard (55 weeks)

Friday, October 29, 1965

Evansville, IN
Washington Theatre, 967 Washington
Avenue; 605 seats (33 weeks)

Wednesday, November 3, 1965

Fitchburg, MA
Saxon Theatre, 729 Main Street (16
weeks)

Thursday, November 10, 1965

Davenport, IA
Coronet Theatre, 1411 Harrison Street; 490 seats (74 weeks)
    "For the perfect show . . . take the entire family to see . . ." said the local ads.

Thursday, December 23, 1965

Colorado Springs, CO
Cooper 70, 17 S. Nevada Avenue (40 weeks)
    Another theatre named for the 70mm style of exhibition, this one opened
in November 1963.

The local playbill for *The Sound of Music*'s "road show" run in Boston.

Friday, December 24, 1965

Austin, TX
Varsity Theater, 2402 Guadalupe Street (22 weeks)

Saturday, December 25, 1965

Allentown, PA
Boyd Theatre, 28 N. Ninth Street (45 weeks)

Binghamton, NY
Capri Theatre, 236 Washington Street; 1,200 seats (27 weeks)
    Now a performing arts center known as the Forum.

Boise, ID
Ada Theatre, 700 W. Main Street (11 weeks)

Canton, OH
Palace Theatre, 605 Mark Avenue North (42 weeks)

Champaign, IL
Co-Ed Twin Theater, 614-616 E. Green Street (26 weeks)

Fresno, CA
Warners Theatre, 1400 Fulton Street at Tuolumne Street; 2,169 seats (33 weeks)
    Once the Pantages, this theatre dominated a block in downtown Fresno.
Oddly, with a single letter change, it now goes under the name Warnors, presenting mostly live shows.

Green Bay, WI
West Theatre, 405 W. Walnut Street; 791 seats (39 weeks)

Jacksonville, NC
Iwo Jima Theatre, 500 New Bridge Street; 599 seats; $1.75 (12 weeks)

Lubbock, TX
Village Theatre, 34th Street (41 weeks)

Lynchburg, VA
Warner Theatre, 1102 Main Street; 1,102 seats; $1.50–$2.00 (19 weeks)

Manchester, NH
Strand Theatre, 20 Hanover Street; $1.75–$3.00 (27 weeks)

Montgomery, AL
Empire Theater, 214 Montgomery Street; 776 seats; $1.50–$2.00 (18 weeks)
    It was in front of this theatre (which heralded itself as "Where friends, happiness, and entertainment meet") that Rosa Parks was arrested after refusing to vacate her bus seat to a white passenger in December 1955, thereby launching the citywide bus boycott and the civil rights movement. The Rosa Parks Memorial Library now stands on the site.

Newport News, VA
Newmarket Theatre, 688 79th Street (41 weeks)
   Virginia's first "rocking chair" theatre had only opened three months before *TSOM* played here.

Reno, NV
Crest Theater, 35 W. Second Street (19 weeks)

Roanoke, VA
Grandin Theatre, 1310 Grandin Road (39 weeks)

Shreveport, LA
Broadmoor Theater, 4026 Youree Drive; 840 seats (35 weeks)

Sioux Falls, SD
Cinema, 134 N. Phillips Avenue (44 weeks)

Utica, NY
Uptown Theatre, 2014 Genesee Street (26 weeks)

Williamsport, PA
Rialto Theatre, 470 Pine Street (26 weeks)

As 1965 came to a close, *TSOM* was playing in 122 theaters in the United States. At this point the film was available in forty-three states as a reserved-seat attraction; West Virginia, Mississippi, Montana, North Dakota, Alaska, and Delaware were shortly to follow.

During the Christmas season, for the weeks December 22, 1965 through January 4, 1966, *TSOM* grossed $3,000,000 in the U.S. alone.

In the worldwide market, all previous box office records were shattered in Brussels, Copenhagen, Malaysia, Tokyo, Perth and Sydney, Brazil, South Africa, New Zealand, Philippine Republic, Singapore, and Trinidad. In Puerto Rico, *TSOM* became the first movie to ever exceed 100,000 admissions.

For the fifty-two-week period ending December 25, 1965, 20th Century-Fox reported a gross of $162,626,000, a net profit of $11,726,000. *TSOM* was responsible for more than two-thirds of that figure. Others given their due were *Those Magnificent Men in Their Flying Machines*, *Von Ryan's Express*, *Zorba the Greek*, and *Hush. . . Hush, Sweet Charlotte*.

1966

Wednesday, January 19, 1966

Madison, WI
Hilldale Theatre, Hilldale Shopping Center, 702 N. Midvale Boulevard (39 weeks)
   This was Madison's first new indoor theatre since 1929.

Friday, January 21, 1966

Palm Beach, FL
Paramount Theatre, 145 N. Country Road; $1.75–$2.75 (20 weeks)

Wednesday, January 26, 1966

Mobile, AL
Loop Theatre, 2050 Government Street (25 weeks)

Friday, January 28, 1966

Bristol, TN
Paramount Theatre, 518 State Street (17 weeks)

After ten months, *TSOM* had officially become the largest-grossing motion picture in the history of cinema exhibition in Great Britain, with an estimated 35 million people throughout the country having seen it in its seventeen theatres and figures expected to exceed £6,500,000.

The film clearly provoked the sort of very positive response that caused repeat business, as was proven by a Nottingham, UK resident who had seen it 102 times; a Los Angeles woman who racked up 58 admissions; a sailor in Puerto Rico who had gone to 77 showings; not to mention Guinness Book of World Records champion Myra Franklin (see UK: April 18, 1965, Capitol Cinema).

Also noted were a minister in Shreveport, Louisiana, who had taken teen groups to see the film on twelve different occasions; and a group in Boston that bought out the entire Gary Theatre for two separate showings (one in the spring, one in the fall).

Wednesday, February 2, 1966

Cocoa (Beach), FL
Fine Arts Cinema, 300 Brevard Avenue (29 weeks)
This 1924 venue (which opened as the Aladdin Theatre) became the Historic Cocoa Village Playhouse, being listed on the National Register of Historic Places in 1991.

Reading, PA
Fox Theatre, 825 Berkshire Boulevard (41 weeks)

Tallahassee, FL
State Theatre, East College Avenue; $1.50–$2.00 (8 weeks)

Friday, February 4, 1966

Daytona Beach, FL
Beach Theatre, 510 Main Street (16 weeks)

Friday, February 11, 1966

Wheeling, WV
Victoria Theater, 1228 Market St. (20 weeks)
This 1904 theatre continues to operate as a live venue.

Wednesday, February 16, 1966

Lawrence, MA
Showcase Cinemas, 141 Winthrop Avenue (36 weeks)

Friday, February 18, 1966

Tuscaloosa, AL
Capri Theatre, 610 Greensboro Avenue (15 weeks)

Wednesday, February 23, 1966

Charleston, WV
Capitol Theatre, 123 Summers Street (17 weeks)
    Since restored and renamed the Capitol Center.

Huntington, WV
Orpheum Theatre, 1021 Fourth Avenue (18 weeks)

On the eve of its one-year anniversary, *TSOM* was reported by Motion Picture Exhibitor as being not only the top-grossing movie of 1965, but on its way to becoming the biggest box office success of all time. As of February 24, 1966, it had grossed $42,832,919 domestic at U.S. roadshow houses and $14,056,808 foreign at 354 venues, for a total of $56,889,727 worldwide.

It was also reported that of the *TSOM* roadshow houses, 65 of them had never before shown a movie with this reserved-seat policy; while several of the theatres had shattered all previous records including those in Baltimore, Boston, Cleveland, Cedar Rapids, Des Moines, Detroit, Indianapolis, Los Angeles, Oklahoma City, Raleigh, San Diego, and Seattle.

Thursday, March 3, 1966

These three Michigan theatres were getting *TSOM* one year and a day after its New York premiere.

Flint, MI
Palace Theatre, 205 East Kearsley Street (17 weeks)

Kalamazoo, MI
Capitol Theatre, 138 E. South Street (16 weeks)

Lansing, MI
Gladmer Theatre, 223 N. Washington Avenue (16 weeks)

For its March 9, 1966 issue, Motion Picture Exhibitor ran a first-anniversary ad congratulating *TSOM* on its unprecedented grosses at all the theatres where it had opened the previous March.

According to their figures, $2,250,000 in box office receipts were reported for the Rivoli in New York; $2,000,000 for the Dominion in London (presumably adjusted for U.S. rates); $1,750,000 at the Wilshire in L.A.; $1,500,000 at the Michael Todd in Chicago. In the $1,000,000 category were theatres in Boston, Detroit, Philadelphia, San Francisco, and Toronto; $750,000 was reported for Minneapolis, St. Louis, Salt Lake City, Seattle, and Washington D.C.; $500,000 for Atlanta, Baltimore, Buffalo, Charlotte, Cincinnati, Cleveland, Dallas, Denver, Honolulu, Houston, Indianapolis, Miami Beach, Milwaukee, Montreal, Phoenix, Providence, Richmond, San Diego, and Vancouver.

Wednesday, March 23, 1966

Billings, MT
Babcock Theatre, 2812 2nd Avenue North (27 weeks)

Jackson, MS
Paramount Theater, 115 E. Capitol Street (12 weeks)

Thursday, March 24, 1966

Amarillo, TX
Esquire Theatre, 1808 S. Washington Street (17 weeks)

Harlingen, TX
Rialto Theater, 103 W. Jackson Street (12 weeks)

Tyler, TX
Arcadia Theatre, 121 N. Spring Avenue (14 weeks)

Wednesday, March 30, 1966

New London, CT
Capitol Theatre, 43 Bank Street; $1.50–$2.50 (14 weeks)

Topeka, KS
Grand Theater, 615 SW Jackson Street (13 weeks)

St. Joseph, MO
Fox East Hills Theatre, East Hills Mall (13 weeks)

Springfield, MO
Gillioz Theatre, 325 Park Central East (13 weeks)

This 1926 movie palace (which stopped showing films on a regular basis in 1979) lives on as a performing arts center.

Great Falls, MT
Civic Center Theater, 2 Park Drive South (13 weeks)

This later became the Mansfield Theater.

State College, PA
Nittany Theater, 114 South Allen Street (10 weeks)

Thursday, March 31, 1966

Waco, TX
25th Street Theatre, 1006 N. 25th Street (13 weeks)

Wednesday, April 6, 1966

Charlottesville, VA
University Theatre, "The Corner" Main Street West (16 weeks)

Yakima, WA
Yakima Theatre, 11 South Second Street (19 weeks)

Thursday, April 7, 1966

Baton Rouge, LA
Paramount Theatre, 215 Third Street; $1.50–$2.00 (22 weeks)

The rebuilt Robert Morton Theatre Pipe Organ was played for the first time after more than thirty years for the opening of TSOM. This is one of the venues that went from reserved-seat to general admission policy during its run.

Monroe, LA
Eastgate Cinema, 201 N. Stanley Avenue (16 weeks)

Quincy, IL
State Theatre, 434 South Eighth Street (10 weeks)

Spartanburg, SC
Palmetto Theatre, 172 E. Main Street (14 weeks)

Friday, April 8, 1966

Rockford, IL
Times Theatre, 226 N. Main Street (25 weeks)

Thursday, April 14, 1966

Wichita Falls, TX
State Theatre, 817 Scott Street (10 weeks)

Thursday, April 21, 1966

Abilene, TX
Queen Theater, 1096 North 2nd Street (14 weeks)

Wednesday, May 25, 1966

Albany, NY
Hellman Theatre, 1365 Washington Avenue (9 weeks)
    A stunning example of the incredible popularity of *TSOM*; it had already played this theatre starting in June 1965. After its thirty-week run, the Hellman wanted it back, and so it got for another nine weeks.

Wildwood, NJ
Ocean Theatre, 2700 Boardwalk (at Poplar Ave) (19 weeks)
    This boardwalk location had just opened the year before, as a reserved-seat house.

Friday, May 27, 1966

Myrtle Beach, SC
Gloria Theatre, 210 9th Avenue North (17 weeks)

Wednesday, June 15, 1966

Duluth, MN
Duluth Theatre, 317 N. Central Avenue; $1.75–$2.25 (23 weeks)

Grand Forks, ND
Fox Theatre, 11 N. Fourth Street; $1.75–$2.25 (24 weeks)
    According to an October 1966 ad, "It has thrilled over 20,000 people in the Grand Forks area!"

Wednesday, June 22, 1966

Columbia, MO
Cinema Theatre, 1729 W. Broadway; 837 seats (15 weeks)
    A brand new cinema, this had just opened earlier that month, with a booking of The Glass Bottom Boat. It closed in 1999.

Lancaster, PA
Fulton Opera House, 12 North Prince Street; $1.50–$2.50 (20 weeks)
   This venue has the distinction of being listed on the National Historic Landmark register, being in service since 1852, as Fulton Hall. It was during a brief period in the sixties, when it showed films, that TSOM was booked here.

Thursday, June 23, 1966

Dubuque, IA
Strand Theatre, 1198 Main Street; $1.25–$2.25 (23 weeks)

Wednesday, June 29, 1966

Brockton, MA
Westgate Mall Cinema 1 & 11, 200 Westgate Drive (39 weeks)
   This twin cinema had opened the year prior with *Mary Poppins* and *Zorba the Greek. TSOM* debuted in Cinema II (*The Russians are Coming* was on the other screen) and was followed in this engagement by *Doctor Zhivago*. After the inevitable plexings over the years, it was closed in 2004.

Hyannis, MA
Center Theatre, 339 Main Street (14 weeks)

Louisville, KY
Penthouse Theatre, 625 S. Fourth Street (continuing from the Rialto, 15 weeks for a total of 79 weeks)
   This was the converted balcony of the United Artists Theatre (formerly the Palace).

Friday, July 1, 1966

Peoria, IL
Beverly Theater, 2515 N. Knoxville Avenue (23 weeks)

Tuesday, July 12, 1966

San Jose, CA
Century 22, 3162 Olsen Drive; 950 seats (67 weeks)
   With most of *TSOM*'s bookings during 1966, the theatres wound up running the film for shorter periods than those screening it the previous year. This domed venue was an exception, showing the movie for a year and three months. Also, unlike many of the selected locations for its roadshow run that were palaces dating back decades, the Century 22 had opened in March that same year, designed especially for Super 70mm attractions. It was joining the

nearby Century 21, which opened for Cinerama Films in 1964, and was joined across the highway in 1968 by Century 24. In later years, two smaller-domed auditoriums were built next to Century 22. The theaters closed in 2014.

Wednesday, July 27, 1966

Altoona, PA
Capitol Theatre, 1400 11th Avenue (12 weeks)

South Bend, IN
River Park Theater, 2929 Mishawaka Avenue; 592 seats (27 weeks)

> The August 31, 1966 Variety reported a worldwide rental of $60,044,000 for *TSOM* so far. The film became the fifth 20th Century-Fox release since 1952 to top world rentals of $25,000,000, the others being *The Robe* (1953), *South Pacific* (1958), *The Longest Day* (1962), and *Cleopatra*.

Wednesday, August 31, 1966

Fairless Hills, PA
Eric Cinema, Country Club Shopping Center, US Route 1 (28 weeks)

Wednesday, September 21, 1966

Anchorage, AK
Fireweed Theatre, 661 E. Fireweed Lane; 1,500 seats (12 weeks)

Oakland, CA
Roxie Theatre, 517 17th Street (35 weeks)

Stockton, CA
Ritz Theater, 426 E. Main Street, 926 seats (18 weeks)

Wednesday, October 5, 1966

Monterey, CA
Steinbeck Theater, 714 Cannery Row (26 weeks)
    Created from a former cannery and named after author John Steinbeck, this theatre had opened in 1959.

Wilmington, DE
Cinema 141, 1301 Centerville Road (41 weeks)

Wednesday, October 12, 1966

Burlington, VT
State Theatre, 156 Bank Street, 680 seats; $1.50–$2.50 (20 weeks)

"Unprecedented acclaim in the history of film runs in Vermont," said an enthusiastic local ad for *TSOM*.

The theatre burned down in 1975.

Edwardsville, PA
Gateway Cinema, Highway 11; $1.50–$2.25 (19 weeks)

This 1964 cinema was located outside Wilkes-Barre.

> By this point, industry statistics estimated that some 16 million people had seen the film and that approximately 3 percent was repeat business.

Wednesday, October 26, 1966

Boston, MA
Paris Cinema, 841 Boylston Street, 600 seats (13 weeks)

As soon as *TSOM* finished its reserved-seat run at the Gary Theatre, it resumed as an exclusive engagement attraction at this nearby venue.

Chelmsford, MA
Route 3 Cinema I & II, Eastgate Shopping Center, Chelmsford Street (11 weeks)

Maynard, MA
Fine Arts Theatre, 19 Summer Street (10 weeks)

Wednesday, November 2, 1966

Ellisville, MO (outside St. Louis)
Ellisville Theatre, 1185 Manchester Road, 1,100 seats (16 weeks)

This and the following theatre were the area bookings for *TSOM* after it had completed its 83-week run at the St. Louis Theatre.

Moline Acres, MO (outside St. Louis)
Lewis & Clark Theatre, Chambers Road at Lewis & Clark Boulevard, 1,042 seats (12 weeks)

Wednesday, December 21, 1966

Fredericksburg, VA
Victoria Theater, 1014 Caroline Street, 1,100 seats (11 weeks)

Harrisburg, PA
Eric Theater, 4400 Derry Street, 1,350 seats (8 weeks)

This was a return engagement to the very same theatre where *TSOM* had already played for twenty-two weeks.

Lebanon, PA
Colonial Theatre, 840 Cumberland Street (8 weeks)

Lewiston, PA
Embassy Theatre, 6 South Main Street (13 weeks)
    Despite initial efforts to replace *TSOM* with another attraction in January and then in February, public demand kept the movie at the Embassy for a three-month run.
    Although this 1927 venue stopped showing films in 1981, it was later restored and reopened as a performing arts center.

Petersburg, VA
(New) Bluebird Theatre, 143 N. Sycamore Street (6 weeks)

Trumbull, CT
United Artists, 5065 Main Street (26 weeks)
    This theatre had just opened the year prior. Later triplexed, it closed in 1998.

Waynesboro, VA
    Wayne Cinema, 521 W. Main Street, 450 seats (10 weeks)

Friday, December 23, 1966

Gainesville, FL
Florida Theater, 235 West University Avenue; $1.50–$2.00 (8 weeks)
    Although it was treated as a "Special Selective Engagement," there were no reserved seats required at this particular venue. The initial ad suggested "The Perfect Christmas Gift for Everyone—Tickets to 'The Sound of Music.'"
    This 1928 building continues to operate as a music and concert center.

Hickory, NC
Carolina Theater, 222 First Avenue NW; $1.00–$2.00 (9 weeks)
    A 1935 theater, this is still in operation, albeit with two screens.

Tacoma, WA
Temple Theatre, 47 St. Helens Avenue, 1,800 seats (23 weeks)
    Built in 1926, this venue now goes under the name Landmark Convention Center.

Sunday, December 25, 1966

Los Angeles, CA
Carthay Circle Theatre, 6316 San Vicente Boulevard (continuation from Fox Wilshire; 23 weeks; bringing total to 117)
    Two years after *TSOM* finished its run here, this famed LA theatre was razed.

1967

Friday, January 13, 1967

Durham, NC
Lakewood Center Theatre, 2000 Chapel Hill Road, 800 seats (14 weeks)
This venue had just opened in November 1966, with state-of-the-art sound and widescreen, not to mention rocking chair seating.

Wilmington, NC
Manor Theatre, 208 Market Street (10 weeks)

Thursday, February 2, 1967

Greensboro, NC
Terrace Theatre, 3120 Northline Avenue, 750 seats; $1.50–$2.00 (18 weeks)

CANADA

Wednesday, March 10, 1965

Toronto, Ontario, Canada
Eglinton Theatre, 400 Eglinton Avenue W., 802 seats; $2.00–$3.00
The first run of *TSOM* outside of the United States (in the birth city of cast members Christopher Plummer and Heather Menzies) began on the very same date as its Southern California opening. This showing would prove another smashing success, surpassing not only the film's New York and Los Angeles Area runs but all others in North America, playing for an amazing 146 weeks. (This means the film ran until the end of December 1967.)
Shortly after its 1936 opening, the Eglinton won the Royal Architecture Institute of Canada's Bronze Medal for its stunning art deco décor and became one of the top venues for movie exhibition in the city. Closed in 2002, it was afterwards designated a landmark and renamed the Eglinton Grand to be used for live presentations.

Wednesday, March 17, 1965

Vancouver, British Columbia, Canada
Ridge, 3131 Arbutus Street, 844 seats (99 weeks)
Opening in April 1950, the theatre would eventually close after sixty-three years of operation.

Thursday, March 18, 1965

Montreal, Quebec, Canada

Seville Theatre, 1255 Rue Sainte Catherine Ouest (98 weeks)

The 1,114-seat venue opened in 1929. The management of the theatre ran an ad confessing that they "tingled all over when our patrons emerge from every showing bubbling with pleasure and glowing with praise." They also mentioned that in the twenty-seven weeks *TSOM* had run thus far it had been seen by 157,984 patrons.

Although it ceased operations as a movie house in 1984, the building was not demolished until 2010.

Wednesday, March 31, 1965

Calgary, Alberta, Canada

Odeon Theatre, 612 Eighth Avenue SW; 653 seats (72 weeks)

Constructed within the Barron Building, in the late art moderne style, the Uptown Theatre opened in 1951. In 1965 it was purchased by the Odeon chain, who renovated the site for $100,000, then put their name on the venue. It was later twinned and then restored in 1993.

Edmonton, Alberta, Canada

Varscona, 10907 Whyte Avenue NW; 499 seats; $1.50–$2.50 (114 weeks)

Built in 1944, this relatively small venue for *TSOM* closed in1986 and was later demolished.

Thursday, April 1, 1965

Winnipeg, Manitoba, Canada

Kings Theatre, 1769 Portage Avenue; 720 seats (88 weeks)

Wednesday, October 27, 1965

Hamilton, Ontario, Canada

Century Theatre, 12 Mary Street (38 weeks)

Wednesday, February 9, 1966

Quebec, Canada

Cinema Sainte-Foy Salle Alouette (43 weeks)

Friday, February 18, 1966

Halifax, Nova Scotia

Paramount Theatre, 1577 Barrington Street (19 weeks)

Thursday, February 24, 1966

Kingston, Ontario
Hyland Theatre, 390 Princess Street; 690 seats (13 weeks)

Friday, March 18, 1966

Victoria, British Columbia
Odeon, 780 Yates Street (24 weeks)

Thursday, April 7, 1966

Waterloo, Ontario
Waterloo Theatre, 24 King Street North (22 weeks)

Thursday, June 30, 1966

Lethbridge, Alberta
Paramount Theatre, 723 4th Avenue (11 weeks)

Fort William (Thunder Bay), Ontario
Capitol Theatre, Brodie Street (11 weeks)

London, Ontario
Hyland Cinema, 240 Wharncliffe Road South; 514 seats (73 weeks)

Ottawa, Ontario
Nelson Theatre, 325 Rideau Street; 790 seats (55 weeks)

Sudbury, Ontario
Century Theatre, 16 Lisgar Street (14 weeks)

Wednesday, September 21, 1966

Brandon, Manitoba
Strand Theatre, 131 Tenth Street (4 weeks)

Regina, Saskatchewan
Capitol Theatre, 2035 12th Avenue at Scarth Street (16 weeks)

Thursday, September 22, 1966

Belleville, Ontario
Belle Theatre, 347 Front Street (7 weeks)

Brantford, Ontario
Odeon Brantford, 50 Market Street (6 weeks)

Moncton, New Brunswick
Paramount Theatre, 800 Main Street (6 weeks)

North Bay, Ontario
Capitol Theatre, 150 Main Street; 1,435 seats (5 weeks)

Peterborough, Ontario
Paramount Theatre, 286 George St. North (10 weeks)

Prince George, British Columbia
Parkwood Theatre, 1600 15th Avenue (4 weeks)

Sarnia, Ontario
Odeon Theatre, 192 Lochiel Street (10 weeks)

Sault Ste. Marie, Ontario
Algoma Theatre, 664 Queen Street East (5 weeks)

Thursday, October 13, 1966

Cornwall, Ontario
Capitol Theatre, 29 Second Street West (4 weeks)

Thursday, October 20, 1966

Brockville, Ontario
Capitol Theatre, 131 King Street West (5 weeks)

Timmins, Ontario
Victory Theatre, Cedar Street (4 weeks)

Windsor, Ontario
Park Theatre, 1377 Ottawa Street (22 weeks)

Friday, December 23, 1966

Guelph, Ontario
Palace Theatre, 106 Macdonell Street (4 weeks)

Niagara Falls, Ontario
Seneca Theater, 464 Queen Street (7 weeks)

Pointe-Claire, Quebec
Fairview Twin (16 weeks)

St. Catharines, Ontario
Pen Centre Cinemas, Cinema 2, Glendale Ave at Highway 406 (15 weeks)

Saskatoon, Saskatchewan
Paramount Theatre, 136 Second Avenue South (18 weeks)

Wednesday, December 28, 1966

St. John's, Newfoundland
Capitol Theatre, 25 Henry Street; 848 seats (7 weeks)

Thursday, December 29, 1966

Red Deer, Alberta
Paramount Theatre, 4717 Fiftieth Street (4 weeks before moving over to the Lux)

Thursday, January 12, 1967

Oshawa, Ontario
Regent Theatre, 44 King Street East (8 weeks)

Wednesday, January 18, 1967

Kamloops, British Columbia
Paramount Theatre, 503 Victoria Avenue (6 weeks)

Thursday, January 26, 1967

Lacombe (Red Deer), Alberta
Lux Theatre, Fiftieth Street (4 weeks, continuing from Paramount in Red Deer, for total of 8 weeks)

Wednesday, February 1, 1967

Montreal, Quebec
York Theatre, Rue Sainte-Catherine Ouest and Rue MacKay (7 weeks; continuation from Seville; adding up to 105 weeks)

Wednesday, February 8, 1967

West Vancouver, British Columbia
Park Royal Twin Cinema, 1086 Park Royal South (11 weeks; continuing from the Ridge for total of 110 weeks)

Thursday, March 23, 1967

Montreal, Quebec
Versailles, 7265 Sherbrooke East (7 weeks; continuing from the York for a total of 112 weeks)

UNITED KINGDOM

Monday, March 29, 1965

London, England

Dominion Theatre, 268 Tottenham Court Rd; 1,712 seats; tickets, U.S. equivalent of $1.45–$4.20 (170 weeks)

TSOM began its first overseas engagement in London, where it would end up having an incredible three-year, three-month run (this meant it finally wrapped up its stay on June 29, 1968). That made this particular booking the longest continuous run of *TSOM* of any theatre in the world.

Although this venue opened in 1930 with a live show, it converted expressly to movie exhibition two years later when it was bought by Gaumont British Theatres. In 1958, it was renovated for 70mm roadshow engagements (installing a forty-fix-foot-wide screen and stereophonic sound) and presented the movie of Rodgers & Hammerstein's *South Pacific* (starting on April 21), which became an unprecedented sensation, playing here for a staggering four-year, twenty-two-week run (!), finally closing on September 30, 1962. Because of the conversion to roadshow exhibition, the upper circle was closed off and several rows were removed near the front of the auditorium, thereby diminishing the original seating capacity by more than a thousand.

The UK premiere of *TSOM* was held to benefit the Variety Club Heart Fund and Dockland Settlements; among those in attendance were Princess Margaret and director Robert Wise. *Variety* reported a first-week gross of $36,500 with all shows sold to capacity. As of March 9, 1966, *Motion Picture Exhibitor* claimed that the movie had taken in $2,000,000 at this venue alone. By year end it broke the all-time house record.

Julie Andrews and Robert Wise's follow-up collaboration, *Star!*, had its world premiere here on July 18, 1968.

Starting in 1981, the Dominion returned to live shows and was lovingly restored in the early 1990s to continue in this capacity. Most successful of all the legit shows to play there was the Queen jukebox musical *We Will Rock You*, which opened in 2002 and remained there for twelve years.

Thursday, April 15, 1965

Bournemouth, England

Odeon Cinema, Lansdowne House, Christchurch Road; 1,978 seats (82 weeks)

The entrance to this 1937 venue was incorporated into the surrounding apartment buildings; the cinema later ended up a bingo hall.

Brighton, England

Regent Cinema, 133 Queen's Road (62 weeks)

This 1921 house was renovated in 1962 for 70mm exhibition; it ceased showing movies in 1973 and was demolished the following year.

London's Dominion Theatre held onto *The Sound of Music* longer than any other movie theatre in the world.

Manchester, England
Gaumont, 44-50 Oxford Street; 2,300 seats (128 weeks)

The city's grandest cinema opened in 1935. The day after *TSOM* ended its two-year, six-month run, the theatre brought back their previous long-run tenant, *South Pacific.*

Less than seven years after *TSOM* closed here, the cinema ceased showing movies and became a nightclub. It was demolished in 1990.

Friday, April 16, 1965

Glasgow, Scotland
Gaumont Glasgow, 140 Sauchiehall Street (140 weeks)

This theatre dated back to 1910 when it opened as the Picture House. Fifty years later it went through a modernization to host roadshow attractions. When it finished its run here, *TSOM* had been seen by over 2,000,000 patrons. One of those patrons, sixty-five-year-old widow Helen Macfarlane, made it a ritual to see the picture twice a week, on Tuesday and Saturday evenings. She took the same seat each time in the back stalls, the box office workers having her ticket ready for her before she would enter the theatre. "Yes, I know nearly every word of the story and every line of the songs by heart," she said. "I'll never forget this picture." For her reward she won a trip to London, sponsored by the cinema.

When *TSOM* ended its lengthy run just before Christmas 1967, it was immediately followed by another Julie Andrews film, *Thoroughly Modern Millie*.

Although the façade remains, the interior was demolished in 1972.

Sunday, April 18, 1965

Birmingham, England
Gaumont Cinema, Colmore Circus, Steelhouse Lane; 1,212 seats (168 weeks)

This cinema opened in 1931 and underwent a refurbishing some thirty years later to show 70mm films. It boasted of having the largest screen (84' x 33') in Europe (as its marquee proudly heralded) at the time *TSOM* played there. This amazing three-year, three-month run (closing July 6, 1968) put this cinema second only to the Dominion in London for the number of weeks the movie ran continuously at the same site.

Reportedly, Alice Jackson saw the film there so many times (figures run between 121 and 600!) that she was eventually granted free admission.

The Gaumont closed in 1983.

Blackpool, England
Palladium Cinema, Waterloo Road; 1,450 seats (46 weeks)

Ending its forty-eight-year run as a cinema, this became a bingo hall in 1976. That, in turn, has since shuttered.

Bristol, England, UK
Odeon, Union Street (95 weeks)

Opened in 1938 with a seating capacity of 1,945, this was yet another cinema where the public couldn't get enough of *TSOM*.

Said the *Bristol Evening* post on the movie's first anniversary, "*The Sound of Music* opened in Bristol a year ago today, and has so far delighted more than 600,000 West Country folks. Officially, it's supposed to end on May 14. But four previous closure dates have already passed. It is likely that *The Sound of Music* will be sounding next year." The film did indeed stick around until mid-February 1967 for another record-breaking run. (The cinema's previous record holder had been *South Pacific* at a mere 22 weeks.)

While multiplexed, this cinema still operates today.

Leeds, England
Majestic Cinema, Quebec and Wellington Streets; 2,392 seats (128 weeks)

This 1922 hall converted to 70mm three decades later and welcomed the 1958 movie of *South Pacific* for a forty-week run; *TSOM* tripled that record. Julie

Andrews's *Star!* would play here in 1968. The Majestic ceased showing movies in 1969, going from bingo hall to nightclub to merely vacant to an uncertain future.

Newcastle upon Tyne, England
Queen's Cinerama Theatre, Northumberland Place (140 weeks)
This 1913 building went over to 70mm attractions in 1958 for the area screening of *South Pacific*, and then became a Cinerama theatre five years later. It was demolished in 1983.

Southampton, England
Odeon Cinema, Above Bar St.; 2,700 seats (34 weeks)
Originally the Regal (opened in 1934), this became the Odeon in 1945. It was demolished in 1993.

Cardiff, Wales
Capitol Cinema, 116-118 Queen Street (82 weeks)
Opened in 1921, this was run by the Rank Organisation at the time *TSOM* played here. In *Music* lore, this is the theatre where arguably the movie's most ardent fan, widow Myra Franklin (forty-six at the time she attended opening night), entered the record books for seeing the movie at each of its twice-a-day showings. As of January 1966, she had seen *TSOM* 371 times; by April of that year, the figure had risen to 500. After her fifty-fifth appearance at the theatre, the management very generously decided to present Myra with a weekly pass in appreciation of her constant patronage. "I'm never bored," she was quoted as saying, "I see something new in it each time—and my ambition is to see it a thousand times." Whether Ms. Franklin ever went to any *other* movies during this period was not reported. Not surprisingly, she found her place in the *Guinness Book of World Records*, which reported that Ms. Franklin's total viewings topped off at 940 (!) times, putting her a mere 60 viewings short of her goal.
The Capitol had gone over to "X"-rated fare by the time it closed in January 1978.

Edinburgh, Scotland
Odeon Cinema Edinburgh, 7 Clerk Street (95 weeks)
What had opened in 1930 as the art deco New Victoria Cinema received its new name in the 1960s, after a renovation that allowed for widescreen exhibition. After multiplexing, it was no longer operating by 2004.

Sunday, June 6, 1965

Liverpool, England
Odeon, London Road and Pudsey Street (99 weeks)
Originally the Paramount Cinema, this venue was the largest in Liverpool at the time of its opening in 1934. It received its 70mm revamp in 1958 to show *South Pacific*. Only a year after *TSOM*'s 1967 closing, it was twinned, then tripled, and then quadrupled before being demolished in 2012.

Monday, July 12, 1965

Nottingham, England
Odeon, 9 Angel Row; 924 seats (112 weeks)

Anticipating the unfortunate multiplexing trend of the future, this was a rare instance of *The Sound of Music* having its roadshow engagement at a building that contained another screen. It had, in fact, been one of the premier attractions when this, the former Ritz Cinema, reopened as the very first UK theatre to be twinned. (Making it a Julie Andrews lovefest, the other film, fittingly, was *Mary Poppins*.) Although the upper auditorium was created to host the reserved-seat attractions, it contained 924 seats, versus the lower one, which was for regular attractions and had 1,450 seats.

This venue also boasted of being the world's first automated cinema, "The Cinema That Thinks for Itself," with forty-eight operations carried out by an electronic brain in the projection room.

Sunday, October 3, 1965

Sheffield, England
Oden Cinema, Flat Street; (71 weeks)

Opened (after a long delay caused by the war) in July 1956, this cinema boasted a very impressive 2,319 seats and was equipped to show 70mm attractions, but only lasted as a venue for motion pictures for a fifteen-year stretch. (It became a bingo hall.) This record run of *TSOM* was preceded by a ten-week run of Fox's second roadshow attraction of 1965, *Those Magnificent Men in Their Flying Machines*.

Sunday, December 26, 1965

Oxford, England
ABC Cinemas, George Street (57 weeks)

The former Ritz was revamped in 1959 to accommodate 70mm Todd-AO films, starting with *South Pacific*. After becoming the ABC Cinemas, it suffered a setback when a fire damaged it, but reopened in October 1964. It was triplexed in 1975.

Sunday, July 3, 1966

Norwich, England
Gaumont Cinema, All Saints Green (32 weeks)

The former Carlton inherited the name after the previous Gaumont Cinema closed in 1959. Like too many cinemas in the UK, it became a bingo hall before shutting down altogether in 2011.

TSOM was also booked as a reserved-seat attraction at the Odeon Cinema in Leicester, UK, starting on September 26, 1965.

AUSTRALIA/NEW ZEALAND

Friday, April 9, 1965

Auckland, New Zealand

Plaza Cinema, Queen Street (77 weeks)

This 1913 cinema (the former Princess) was modernized for 70mm and Todd-AO in 1958. Nine hundred patrons attended the final showing of *TSOM* on September 29, 1966, further proof that even the cinemas that held the film forever had fans clamoring for one last glimpse. "This is the last time I will come to the movies," said one extreme and devoted patron who was seeing the movie for the thirtieth time. "There can never be a picture to match this." Said the theatre's projectionist, N. Beriech, "It's like saying goodbye to an old friend."

This seventy-seven-week showing made the record books as the longest run of any film in New Zealand history.

Thursday, April 15, 1965

Christchurch, New Zealand

State Cinema, 730 Colombo Street (69 weeks)

Said the local ads: "After 69 Wonderful Weeks, it is farewell to the film loved by everyone!"

Saturday, April 17, 1965

Melbourne, Australia

Paris Theatre, 243 Bourke Street (139 weeks)

Opened as the Paramount, this theatre had the curious distinction of being temporarily called the Cleopatra when that Fox blockbuster played there in 1963. It became the Paris in time for *TSOM*, but was gone by the start of the next decade. Following its engagement here, *TSOM* moved over to the Esquire, on December 21, 1967, on the same street, at number 238.

Saturday, April 17, 1965

Sydney, Australia

Mayfair Theatre, 75 Castlereagh Street (140 weeks)

This theatre, which was refitted for Todd–AO exhibition, had hosted a three-year-plus run of *South Pacific*, then later welcomed *West Side Story*. It closed in 1979.

Following this run, *TSOM* moved over to the Hoyts Paris on Liverpool Street, where it would play until late September 1968; from there it was on to the Astra in the suburb of Parramatta. The film finally wrapped up its Australian bookings in the area on September 11, 1969.

Thursday, July 29, 1965

Brisbane, Australia
Paris Cinema, 176 Albert Street (72 weeks)

The former Empire (opened 1911) and then St. James Theatre was renovated and reopened in 1965 for exclusive cinema exhibition. It was demolished in 1986.

Friday, August 6, 1965

Dunedin, New Zealand
Octagon Theatre at the Octagon (30 weeks)

This was one more location where *TSOM* broke all existing attendance records, its thirty-week run besting the previous city record holder, *Ben-Hur*. More than 130,000 people had paid to see the movie here, more than the city's population. "The amazing thing was that we could have kept going for another month," said theatre manager O. R. Kenny. "Attendances did not drop below an economic figure and we did not have to keep it on for prestige purposes." The venue was obliged to clear the way for the next 20th Century-Fox roadshow attraction, *Those Magnificent Men in Their Flying Machines*.

This was another theatre that had a frequent attendee who became a momentary newsmaker in the community; this unidentified woman saw *TSOM* thirty-three times during its Dunedin run, receiving a complimentary pass after the thirteenth occasion.

Said the ads: "Recommended as Especially Suitable for Family Entertainment."

Wednesday, August 18, 1965

Perth, Australia
Paris Theatre, Plaza Arcade; Hay Street Mall (70 weeks)

Originally the Plaza, this venue had been extensively refurbished from its original 1937 design (built on the site of a previous theatre, the Majestic) in time for the roadshow engagement of *South Pacific*. It became the Paris for the premiere of *The Sound of Music*. The theatre closed in 1984 and served time as a disco, before being converted into shops.

Friday, November 5, 1965

Napier, New Zealand
State Theatre, 110 Dickens Street (6 weeks)

Friday, December 17, 1965

Wellington, New Zealand
King's Theatre, Dixon Street (41 weeks)

Thursday, February 17, 1966

Adelaide, Australia
Paris Theatre, Arcade Lane; 735 seats (119 weeks)
This theatre had only just changed its name from the Plaza to the Paris when *TSOM* debuted here. In late 1968, the same year the film wrapped up its long run (May), it was demolished.

TSOM was also booked at the State Cinema in Hastings, New Zealand, beginning in November 1965.

A Sampling of Exclusive Engagements Elsewhere in the World

Friday, May 20, 1966

Dublin, Ireland
Cinerama Theatre, Talbot Street (91 weeks)
This run of *TSOM* became the longest of any film to play in Ireland up to that time, finally closing on February 15, 1968. According to local advertising, "Over half a million people have seen it again and again!" The former New Electric Theatre converted to Cinerama starting in 1963, until it made way for *TSOM*, following a run of such movies as *How the West Was Won* and *It's a Mad Mad Mad Mad World*.
It closed in 1974.

Thursday, May 20, 1965

Buenos Aires, Argentina
Cine Ambassador, Lavalle 777 (96 weeks)

Wednesday, May 26, 1965

San Juan, Puerto Rico
Cine Metropolitan, Ponce de Leon Avenue; 920 seats (44 weeks)

Friday, June 11, 1965

Tokyo, Japan
Piccadilly Theatre (20 weeks)

Wednesday, June 16, 1965

Nairobi, Kenya
20th Century Cinema, Government Road (3 weeks)
The short run at this cinema made this the first venue at which Fox pulled out and called it quits while *TSOM* continued to astound most everywhere else.

A Japanese souvenir program for *The Sound of Music*.

Saturday, June 26, 1965

Tokyo, Japan
Piccadilly (20 weeks)

June 1965

Johannesburg, South Africa
Fine Arts, Kotze Street, Hillbrow;
760 seats (69 weeks)

The former Curzon Cinema was refurbished for 70mm exhibition and reopened with *TSOM*, which again broke records, running here longer than any other film in South African history. At the time of the film's first anniversary at the theatre, Nurse Veronica Wissekerk made the local news for having seen the film over 300 times.

Tuesday, July 6, 1965

Rio de Janeiro, Brazil
Cine Palacio, Rua do Passeio 38-40; 1, 900 seats (44 weeks)

Monday, July 12, 1965

Sao Paulo, Brazil
Cine Rivoli, Ramos de Azevedo Square (39 weeks)

Wednesday, July 14, 1965

Manila, Philippines
Ever Theatre, Rizal Avenue; 1, 300 seats (37 weeks)

Wednesday, July 21, 1965

Singapore
Orchard Theatre, Grange Road; $1.50–$4.00 (15 weeks)

Unlike the customary American reserved-seat showings, this theatre offered three shows a day. The cinema was demolished in 1994 and eventually replaced by a multiplex.

Thursday, August 12, 1965

Kampala, Uganda
Norman (2 weeks)

Friday, September 3, 1965

Tel Aviv, Israel
Peer (Fox Theatre) (25 weeks)

Tuesday, September 7, 1965

Santiago, Chile
Ducal (40 weeks)

Thursday, September 9, 1965

Caracas, Venezuela
Florida (48 weeks)

Friday, October 29, 1965

Bangkok, Thailand
Krung Kasem Theatre (20 weeks)

Thursday, November 18, 1965

Mexico City, Mexico
Cine Manacar, Insurgentes and Mixcoac (65 weeks)

Opened earlier that year, this 70mm house was where *TSOM* broke records for having the longest run of any movie in the city. The cinema was damaged by an earthquake in 1985 and demolished in 2013.

Thursday, December 9, 1965

Stockholm, Sweden
Biografen Riviera, Sveavageb 52 (145 weeks)

One of the most impressive of all overseas runs for *TSOM* took place at this 1920 venue, two months and two weeks shy of three years. It finally exited in order to clear the way for the next Julie Andrews–Robert Wise collaboration, *Star!* The theatre had been refurbished for 70mm exhibition in 1964. It closed in 2003.

Initially, the Swedish Government Censorship Board banned the film for children under the age of eleven, citing the final scenes involving the escape from the Nazis as being too intense. After an appeal, the ban had been lifted by the forty-sixth week of its run here.

The Spanish poster for *The Sound of Music* has given the movie the rather banal title of *Smiles and Tears*.

Friday, December 17, 1965

Zurich, Switzerland
Corso (6 weeks)

Monday, December 20, 1965

Barcelona, Spain
Aribau Cinema, Carrer d'Aribau 5; 1,174 seats (14 weeks)

Copenhagen, Denmark
Imperial Theatre, Ved Vesterport 4; 1,102 seats (24 weeks)

Madrid, Spain
Amaya, Paseo Martinez Campos, 9 (52 weeks)

Thursday, December 23, 1965

Antwerp, Belgium
Cine Rubens, Carnotstraat 13; 1,070 seats (12 weeks)

Bombay (Mumbai), India
Regal Cinema, Kala Ghoda, Colaba Causeway (47 weeks)
    Amazingly, this art deco, 1,178-seat cinema, which opened in 1933, is still operating as a single-screen theatre.

Brussels, Belgium
Varieties Theater, Rue de Malines 25 (12 weeks)

Saturday, December 25, 1965

Tokyo, Japan
Marunouchi Shochiku (8 weeks)

Yokohama, Japan
Piccadilly (8 weeks)

Frankfurt, West Germany
Metro (3 weeks)

West Berlin, West Germany
Royal (4 weeks)

What was so awesome about the success of *The Sound of Music* was its universal appeal; it was not simply an American phenomenon but was able to cross over into various countries and cultures that might not have been the customary audience for the musical genre. This appeal, however, had its limitations, as Fox discovered when it booked the film in Germany. The Germans were, after all, the villains of the piece. What's more, they had already made their version of the story, twice, with *Die Trapp-Familie* and *Die Trapp-Familie in Amerika*. Things got off to a bad start when Fox's German sales director, Wolfgang Wolf, took it upon himself to excise footage he worried would rub the locals the wrong way. When word got back to 20th in America, Wolf was fired and the footage reinstated. Either way, the German populace couldn't work up sufficient interest.

TSOM played some seventy-one theatres in Germany, bringing in $22,000 to the distributors, $8,000 less than was spent to advertise it there. It would spend four weeks playing in West Berlin, Munich, and Dusseldorf, and three weeks in Frankfurt and Hamburg. Disenchanted and figuring there was no reason to keep pouring money into a losing proposition, Fox ended up cancelling some 229 scheduled playdates.

Thursday, December 30, 1965

Milan, Italy
Cinema Cavour, Piazza Cavour 3; 650 seats (1 week)
Clearly the citizens of Milan were not as enamored of *TSOM* as much of the globe was as it vacated this prime spot after a single week's run.

Monday, January 10, 1966

Lisbon, Portugal
Tivoli (44 weeks)

Friday, February 18, 1966

Paris, France
Cameo (8 weeks)
Ermitage (8 weeks)

Tel Aviv, Israel
Ramat Gan (11 weeks)

Friday, March 11, 1966

Jerusalem, Israel
Orion (10 weeks)

Liesl and Rolf get most of the attention on the Italian movie poster for *The Sound of Music*.

Monday, July 11, 1966

Alexandria, Egypt
Amir (15 weeks)

Monday, October 24, 1966

Cairo, Egypt
Cairo Palace (23 weeks)

November 1966

Madras, India
Safire (20 weeks)

Thursday, December 22, 1966

Delhi, India
Odeon (17 weeks)

Thursday, March 17, 1966

Hong Kong, China
Queen's Theatre, 31 Queen's Road Central; 1,200 seats (12 weeks)
Royal Theatre, Nathan Road; 1,374 seats (12 weeks)
State Theatre, King's Road (10 weeks)

Thursday, April 7, 1966

Oslo, Norway
Colosseum Kino, Fridtjof Nansens vie 6, Majorstua; 1,158 seats

This domed cinema originally opened in 1928 and was renovated in1960 to accommodate 70mm projection. Only three years later it had to be rebuilt after a freak fire broke out during the premiere engagement of MGM's remake of *Mutiny on the Bounty*. Supposedly more than half a million people saw *TSOM* during its run here, a greater number than the entire population of the city.

Post–Roadshow Engagements—New York area

As the roadshow engagements for *TSOM* were ending or wrapping up in the New York metropolitan area, it was now time to take the film to the next level of availability, engagements that allowed for general admission, rather than specific seats being held.

Wednesday, December 21, 1966

Reserved performances (each individual showing could be booked in advance, but the choice of seats was no longer part of the deal):

New York: **Manhattan**—Cinema Rendezvous (25 weeks); **Bronx**—Valentine (19 weeks); **Brooklyn**—Marine (25 weeks); **Queens**—Lefrak City (42 weeks); **Staten Island**—Island Theatre (19 weeks); *Long Island:* **Huntington**—Whitman (25 weeks); **Lynbrook**—Lynbrook (25 weeks); *Rockland County:* **New City**—Cinema (25 weeks); *Dutchess County:* **Poughkeepsie**—Bardavon (14 weeks); *Westchester County:* **Scarsdale**—Scarsdale Plaza (15 weeks)

The next wide release in the NY area brought the film to regular, general admission at last, more than two years and three months after its debut. Said one of the ad lines, "The more you see it—the more it becomes one of your favorite things!"

Wednesday, June, 21, 1967

New York: **Manhattan**—Academy of Music (8 weeks), Riverside (8 weeks); **Bronx**—Interboro (14 weeks), Surrey (9 weeks), Wakefield (11 weeks); **Brooklyn**—Beverly (16 weeks), Nostrand (8 weeks), Oceana (8 weeks); **Queens**—Bayside (9 weeks), Community (8 weeks)

Long Island: **Bay Shore**—Regent (10 weeks), Franklin Square—Franklin (9 weeks); **Glen Cove**—Cove (8 weeks); **Massapequa**—Pequa (12 weeks); **Patchogue**—Rialto (8 weeks)

Upstate NY: **Newburgh**—Mid Valley (8 weeks); **Ossining**—Victoria (9 weeks); **Suffern**—Lafayette (9 weeks)

New Jersey: **Fairview**—Fairview (14 weeks); **Hackensack**—Fox (14 weeks); **Irvington**—Sanford (14 weeks); **Morristown**—Park (14 weeks); **Red Bank**—Carlton (10 weeks); **Westfield**—Rialto (14 weeks)

Friday, June 23, 1967

Rutherford, NJ—Rivoli (12 weeks)

Another batch of theatres in time for Thanksgiving: said the ad line: "See it at Regular Popular Prices!"

Wednesday, November 15, 1967

New York: **Manhattan**—68th St. Playhouse (4 weeks); Academy of Music (3 weeks); Riverside (3 weeks); **Bronx**—Palace (4 weeks); Valentine (3 weeks); **Brooklyn**—Albemarle (4 weeks); Duffield (3 weeks); Marboro (4 weeks); Ridgewood (4 weeks); **Queens**—Astoria (4 weeks); Jackson (4 weeks); Midway (3 weeks); *Long Island:* **Great Neck**—Squire (3 weeks); **Hempstead**—Calderone (3 weeks); **Hicksville**—Twin South (3 weeks); **Lynbrook**—Lynbrook (3 weeks); **Oyster Bay**—Pine Hollow (3 weeks); **Wantagh**—Wantagh (4 weeks)

Upstate NY: **Bedford Village**—Bedford Playhouse (3 weeks); **Bronxville**—Bronxville (3 weeks); **Port Chester**—Rye Ridge (4 weeks); **Yonkers**—Park Hill (4 weeks)

November 29, 1967

Yorktown Heights, NY—Triangle (1 week)

"Everywhere for the Holidays!" was the ad line used for this next seasonal release:

Wednesday, December 20, 1967

(Each of these bookings on this date ran for two weeks.)

New York: **Manhattan**—Alpine; **Bronx**—Allerton; Bainbridge; Dale; Melba; Ward; **Brooklyn**—Avenue U; Benson; Biltmore; Boro Park; Canarsie; Carroll; Cobble Hill; Commodore; Embassy; Fortway; Graham; Harbor; Kent; Meserole; Oasis; Sanders; **Queens**—Boulevard; Cambria; Center; Crossbay; De Luxe; Drake; Laurelton; Lefferts; Park; Parsons; Rochdale; Roosevelt; Town; Utopia; **Staten Island**—Lane; *Long Island:* **Baldwin**—Grand Ave.; **Deer Park**—Deer Park; **East Islip**—East Islip; **East Northport**—Larkfield; **East Rockaway**—Criterion; **Herricks**—Herricks; **Oceanside**—Oceanside; **Port Washington**—Sands Point; **Mamaroneck**—Playhouse; **Millerton**—Millerton; *Upstate NY:* **Brewster**—Cameo; **Dobbs Ferry**—Pickwick; **Dover Plains**—Dover; **Rosendale**—Rosendale; **Warwick**—Oakland; **West Haverstraw**—Plaza; **Yonkers**—Kent, Kimball; *New Jersey:* **Arlington**—Lincoln; **Bayonne**—Dewitt; **Bergenfield**—Palace; **Bloomfield**—Center; **Bound Brook**—Brook; **Caldwell**—Park; **Clifton**—Clifton; **Dunellen**—Dunellen; **Freehold**—Freehold; **Denville**—Denville; **Hillside**—Mayfair; **Keyport**—Strand; **Metuchen**—Forum; **Newark**—Elwood; **Nutley**—Franklin; **Ridgefield Park**—Rialto; **South River**—Capitol; **Tenafly**—Bergen; **Union City**—Cinema; **Woodbridge**—State.

Saturday, December 23, 1967

Rahway, NJ—Rahway (2 weeks); **Roselle Park, NJ**—Park (2 weeks)

Sunday, December 24, 1967

Bernardsville, NJ—Liberty (2 weeks)

Monday, December 25, 1967

Red Hook, NY—Lyceum (1 week)

Tuesday, December 26, 1967

(1 week each)
Highland, NY—Marionella; **Bronx, NY**—City Island; **Tarrytown, NY**—Music Hall

Wednesday, December 27, 1967

(1 week each)
Bellmore, NY—Bellmore; **Flemington, NJ**—Hunterdon; **Brooklyn, NY**—Tilyou

The Biggest Motion Picture Hit of All Time! See it NOW at a Theatre Near You! (ad line)

The prices at most of these theatres were $1.00 for adults; 50 cents for children under 12.

Wednesday, August 14, 1968

Long Island: **Bay Shore**—5th Avenue Drive-In (2 weeks); **Bellmore**—Playhouse (2 weeks); **Coram**– Coram Drive-In (2 weeks); **Fire Island**—Community (1 week); **Islip**—Islip (1 week); **Kings Park**—Kings Park (2 non-consecutive weeks); **Levittown**—Levittown (2 weeks); **Long Beach**—Nautilus (2 weeks); **Massapequa**—Pequa (1 week); **North Babylon**—North Babylon (1 week); **Oakdale**—Oakdale (2 non-consecutive weeks); **South Farmingdale**—Amity (1 week); **Westbury**—Westbury (1week); *New Jersey:* **Hawthorne**—Hawthorne (2 weeks); **Irvington**—Castle (2 weeks); **Keansburg**—Casino (1 week); **Morris Plains**—Morris Plains Drive-In (1 week); **Perth Amboy**—Majestic (1 week); **Spring Lake**—Ritz (1 week); *New York:* **Manhattan** (2 weeks each)—Embassy 72nd Street, Jade; **Bronx** (1 week each)—Beach, Laconia, Palace; **Brooklyn**—46th Street (1 week), Granada (2 weeks), Highway (2 weeks), Kameo (1 week); **Queens**—Colony (1 week); Haven (2 weeks); *Westchester, NY:* **Pelham**—Pelham (3 weeks); **Port Chester**—Embassy (2 weeks)

Wednesday, August 21, 1968

(These were all 1-week engagements)
New Jersey: **Bay Head**—Lorraine; **Elizabeth**—Elmora; **Manasquan**—Algonquin; **Verona**—Verona; *Long Island:* **Hicksville**—Hicksville

Wednesday, August 28, 1968

(1-week engagements)
Bronx—Devon, Surrey; **Queens**—Casino, Cinemart

Wednesday, September 4, 1968

Far Rockaway, NY—Town (1 week)

Friday, September 6, 1968

Manhattan—86th St. East (1 week)

Wednesday, September 11, 1968

Brooklyn—Pennway (1 week)

The final New York area engagement during the initial run of *TSOM* ran the following ad lines: "Last Chance! Because *The Sound of Music* is being taken out of circulation at the conclusion of this engagement. One Week Only! Don't miss the most popular motion picture ever made. *The Sound of Music* will not be shown again anywhere till 1973."

Wednesday, August 27, 1969

(Each of these engagements ran a week)
New York: **Manhattan**—Academy of Music, Anco 42nd St., Riverside; **Bronx**—Interboro, Valentine; **Brooklyn**—Albemarle, Duffield, Harbor, Marboro, Ridgewood; **Queens**—Astoria, Bayside, Crossbay, Jackson, Midway; **Staten Island**—Fox Plaza; *Long Island:* **Amityville**—Amityville; **Babylon**—Babylon; **Bay Shore**—Regent; **Glen Cove**—Cove; **Great Neck**—Playhouse; **Hempstead**—Calderone; **Hicksville**—Twin North; **Huntington**—Whitman; **Patchogue**—Rialto; **Riverhead**—Suffolk; **Rocky Point**—Rocky Point Drive-In; **Shirley**—Shirley Drive-In; **Valley Stream**—Valley Stream; **Wantagh**—Wantagh; **Westbury**—Westbury Drive-In; *Upstate NY:* **Bedford Village**—Bedford Playhouse; **Bronxville**—Bronxville; **New Rochelle**—Town; **Yonkers**—Park Hill.

In the Los Angeles area, *The Sound of Music* returned one more time (in its 70mm and six-track stereophonic sound version) to the theatre where it initially played for ninety-three weeks, the Fox Wilshire, starting on August 13, 1969. It played there this time for a single week.

Variety Box Office Report

1966

According to the January 5, 1966 issue of *Variety*, the rental figures for 1965 resulted in these being the top features to play during that time.

(Rental is only a portion of the receipts; the gross on a film customarily being approximately double or more of the rental figure.)

1.	*Mary Poppins* ('64 release)	$28,500,000
2.	**The Sound of Music**	**$20,000,000**
3.	*Goldfinger* ('64 release)	$19,700,000
4.	*My Fair Lady* ('64 release)	$19,000,000
5.	*What's New Pussycat*	$9,410,000

This already put *TSOM* in the Top 10 of the all-time box office rentals list, before it had opened in most of its potential markets. In the same 1966 issue of *Variety*, this was how the list of the all-time Top 10 moneymaking movies in the United States stood (rental figures):

1.	*Gone with the Wind*	$41,200,000
2.	*Ben-Hur*	$38,000,000
3.	*The Ten Commandments*	$34,200,000
4.	*Mary Poppins*	$28,500,000
5.	*Cleopatra*	$23,500,000
6.	*How the West Was Won*	$23,000,000
7.	*Around the World in Eighty Days*	$22,000,000
8.	**The Sound of Music**	**$20,000,000**
9.	*Goldfinger*	$19,700,000
10.	*West Side Story*	$19,000,000

1967

The January 4, 1967 *Variety* reported that *The Sound of Music* had already zoomed up to the very top of the all-time rental list, with plenty of playdates yet to come. During 1966 it was still mainly available in limited, reserved-seat showings. Thanks to a 1966 reissue, *The Ten Commandments* was able to change places with the other Charlton Heston biblical epic, *Ben-Hur*, and thereby stay in third place.

1.	**The Sound of Music**	**$42,500,000**
2.	*Gone with the Wind*	$41,200,000
3.	*The Ten Commandments*	$40,000,000
4.	*Ben-Hur*	$38,000,000
5.	*Mary Poppins*	$31,000,000
6.	*My Fair Lady*	$30,000,000
7.	*Thunderball*	$26,000,000

8.	*Cleopatra*	$23,500,000
9.	*How the West Was Won*	$23,000,000
	Around the World in Eighty Days	
	West Side Story	
10.	*Goldfinger*	$22,000,000

1968

For the January 3, 1968 *Variety* rundown of the all-time top rentals, *The Sound of Music* retained its crown, despite a much-heralded reissue of *Gone with the Wind*, which hoped to take back its long-held #1 spot. *TSOM* was now joined in the Top Five by its chief 1965 competitor, *Doctor Zhivago*.

1.	**The Sound of Music**	**$66,000,000**
2.	*Gone with the Wind*	$47,000,000
3.	*The Ten Commandments*	$40,000,000
4.	*Ben-Hur*	$38,000,000
5.	*Doctor Zhivago*	$34,500,000
6.	*Mary Poppins*	$31,000,000
7.	*My Fair Lady*	$30,000,000
	Cleopatra	
8.	*Thunderball*	$26,000,000
9.	*How the West Was Won*	$23,000,000
	Around the World in Eighty Days	
	West Side Story	
10.	*Goldfinger*	$22,000,000

1969

As of the January 8, 1969 *Variety* report on the all-time rental figures, *TSOM* held on to #1, despite very close competition from *Gone with the Wind*.

1.	**The Sound of Music**	**$72,000,000**
2.	*Gone with the Wind*	$70,400,000
3.	*The Ten Commandments*	$40,000,000
4.	*The Graduate*	$39,000,000
5.	*Ben-Hur*	$38,000,000
6.	*Doctor Zhivago*	$37,500,000
7.	*Mary Poppins*	$31,000,000
8.	*My Fair Lady*	$30,000,000
9.	*Thunderball*	$27,000,000
10.	*Cleopatra*	$26,000,000

1970

As the 1960s came to a close, the January 7, 1970 issue of *Variety* presented the list of the top rental films of all-time. *TSOM* reigned supreme.

1. ***The Sound of Music* (20th, 1965)**
   Rental: $72,000,000   (Gross: $153,571,000)
2. *Gone with the Wind* (Selznick-MGM, 1939)
   $71,105,300   ($156,110,000)
3. *The Graduate* (Avco Embassy, 1967)
   $43,100,000   ($104,901,839)
4. *The Ten Commandments* (Paramount, 1956)
   $40,000,000   ($65,000,000)
5. *Ben-Hur* (MGM, 1959)
   $39,105,033   ($74,000,000)
6. *Doctor Zhivago* (MGM, 1965)
   $38,243,000   ($90,486,000)
7. *Mary Poppins* (Disney-BV, 1964)
   $31,000,000   ($76,272,000)
8. *My Fair Lady* (Warner Bros., 1964)
   $30,000,000   ($72,000,000)
9. *Thunderball* (United Artists, 1965)
   $27,000,000   ($65,595,658)
10. *Cleopatra* (20th, 1963)
    $26,000,000   ($57,777,778)
11. *Guess Who's Coming to Dinner* (Col, 1967)
    $25,500,000   ($56,666,667)
12. *West Side Story* (United Artists, 1961)
    $25,000,000   ($43,656,822)
13. *Around the World in Eighty Days* (UA, 1956)
    $23,000,000   ($42,003,000)
14. *How the West Was Won* (MGM, 1963)
    $23,000,000   ($46,000,853)
15. *Goldfinger* (United Artists, 1964)
    $22,500,000   ($51,081,062)
16. *Bonnie and Clyde* (Warner Bros-7 Arts, 1967)
    $20,250,000   ($50,700,000)
17. *Valley of the Dolls* (20th, 1967)
    $20,000,000   ($44,432,255)
18. *The Odd Couple* (Paramount, 1968)
    $20,000,000   ($44,527,570)
19. *The Dirty Dozen* (MGM, 1967)
    $19,900,000   ($45,300,686)
20. *It's a Mad Mad Mad Mad World* (UA, 1963)
    $19,300,000   ($46,332,858)

Bring Back *The Sound*

1970

70mm showing at the Ziegfeld Theatre, 54th Street, New York, NY
    (as part of a series called *4 for the Ziegfeld*)

March 11—17, 1970

This was part of a four-package screening series (that began on February 18, 1970) also consisting of *Gone with the Wind, Doctor Zhivago,* and *The Bible. TSOM* was the last of the four to play. This series of films was the follow-up to the movie that opened the theatre, *Marooned,* after its nine-week engagement, which had started on December 18, 1969.

Official 1973 Reissue

"The wait is over! Now, you can thrill again to the happiest sound in the world."

Todd-AO showing in New York on the eighth anniversary: This actually opened on the very same day as the original premiere: March 2, 1973 (now a Friday).

In the New York area, the film's return was heralded with a full-page Gimbels Department Store ad in the *New York Times* that featured the familiar artwork of Julie Andrews and her guitar. "Gimbels . . . The store with all your favorite things hails America's 'Favorite Things' movie, *Sound of Music.* Returning to delight millions once again." This was a tie-in for the store, which was presenting the Bil Baird Puppeteers performing for free at both their Lexington Avenue branch and their Valley Stream, Long Island, location. As a further incentive, free tickets for the film were given to all children attending the Manhattan show on March 10th. The puppeteers presented the story of "Schnitzel, the Yodeling Goat," billed as the character from the movie, thereby giving the puppet a name that was not designated on screen. "The Lonely Goatherd" and "My Favorite Things" were part of the presentation.

New York engagements:

National Theatre, 1500 Broadway, Times Square, NYC

The return engagement was booked at this newly opened (at Christmas 1972) Times Square venue (the first one to open there in thirty years), where it would run for nine weeks.

During that time it was also booked for seven-week runs at:

Plainview Century, 227A South Oyster Bay, Plainview, Long Island, NY
UA Bellevue in Upper Montclair, NJ

The latter was one of the theatres where the 1965 roadshow engagement had originally played. According to *Boxoffice, TSOM* went into its third weekend of release there on a non-reserved-seat basis with most weekend performances sold out. To show how much times had changed in eight years, *TSOM* was soon replaced at this venue by a reserved-seat engagement of the controversial, X-rated *Last Tango in Paris*.

During the first few weeks of its reissue, *The Sound of Music* was booked into several other theatres where it had originally run as a roadshow engagement in 1965:

Akron (Village), Birmingham (Eastwood Mall), Dallas (Inwood), Des Moines (Capri), Evansville (where the Washington had now become the Cinema 35), Las Vegas (Fox), Memphis (Paramount), Milwaukee (Strand), Montreal (Seville), New Orleans (Saenger Orleans), Portland, OR (Fox), Providence/Warwick (Warwick Cinema), Seattle (5th Avenue), Syracuse (Shoppingtown), Tampa (Palace), Toronto (Eglinton), and Vancouver (Ridge).

On May 25, 1973, *TSOM* expanded in the New York area to the following theatres:

Manhattan—UA East, 85th Street & 1st Avenue (11 weeks); **Queens**—UA Quartet 1 & IV, Flushing (11 weeks); **Bronx**—UA Capri (8 weeks); **Brooklyn**—Century's Brook (8 weeks); **Nassau**—UA Playhouse, Great Neck (9 weeks); **Suffolk**—UA Brentwood, Bay Shore (8 weeks); **Rockland**—Carroll's Mall Cinema, Nanuet (7 weeks); **Staten Island**—UA Island, Springville (7 weeks); **Westchester**- UA Larchmont, Larchmont (11 weeks); **New Jersey**—UA Cinema 1&2, Hazlet (7 weeks); UA Cinema #2, South Plainfield (11 weeks); UA Teaneck, Teaneck (11 weeks).

On August 10th, the film branched out to several new locations in the New York metropolitan area with the ad line "Today—The happiest sound in all the world is at selected Flagship theatres!" It was not until the following week, on August 14th, that it would find its next Manhattan booking, at the Guild 50th. Another theatre, 72nd Street East, was added for a few days starting on August 31. Both engagements ended on September 4.

The Todd-AO showing in Beverly Hills was on the eighth anniversary of premiere there: March 15, 1973, this time at the Pacific Beverly Hills Theatre

There was a re-premiere on March 14 with cast principals from the film in attendance.

Expanded Southern California release went to:

Newport Beach on March 30, 1973
Additional 70mm engagements:
  Cinedome, Orange (June 27)
  Egyptian, Hollywood (July 20)
  Hastings, Pasadena (July 20)
  Doheny Plaza, Beverly Hills (August 22)
  4 Star, Miracle Mile, LA (August 22)
  United Artists, Pasadena (August 22)

This reissue engagement of *TSOM* opened right on top of Robert Wise's newest film, *Two People*, which debuted in New York City on March 18, 1973.

The success of the *TSOM* reissue can be measured in the film's place on *Variety*'s January 9, 1974 ranking of the Top 10 box office rental pictures that played during 1973.

1.	*The Poseidon Adventure* ('72 release)	$40,000,000
2.	*Deliverance* ('72 release)	$18,000,000
3.	*The Getaway* ('72 release)	$17,500,000
4.	*Live and Let Die*	$15,500,000
5.	*Paper Moon*	$13,000,000
6.	*Last Tango in Paris*	$12,625,000
7.	**The Sound of Music**	**$11,000,000**
8.	*Jesus Christ Superstar*	$10,800,000
9.	*The World's Greatest Athlete*	$10,600,000
10.	*American Graffiti*	$10,300,000

This meant that *TSOM* was still obliged to stay in the second-place spot where it had dropped in 1972 because of the tremendous success of Paramount's *The Godfather*. As of January 9, 1974, the All-Time Box Office Rental list stood as such:

1.	*The Godfather* (Paramount, 1972)	$85,000,000
2.	**The Sound of Music (20th, 1965)**	**$83,000,000**
3.	*Gone with the Wind* (Selznick-MGM, 1939)	$77,900,000
4.	*Love Story* (Paramount, 1970)	$50,000,000
5.	*The Graduate* (Avco Embassy, 1967)	$49,978,000

Because it still had some playdates in 1974, *TSOM* added another $891,000 in rental figures, which meant it stayed at #2 the following year.

Other Theatrical Playdates:

1975

In 70mm, "The 'Hall' is Alive with *The Sound of Music*" said the ads.

A Radio City Music Hall showing began on Thursday, August 28, 1975 and was scheduled for a three-week run (ending September 17, 1975); it was included with Peter Gennaro's "Star Spangled Rhythm" stage show.

This became the first reissued movie booked at the Radio City Music Hall that had *not* opened there on its original run. Earlier in 1973, *Mary Poppins* had become the first reissue to play at the Hall, but was returning to the establishment, having made its New York debut at Radio City in September 1964.

1978

August 25th, Todd-AO showings:

Century Plaza 2, Century City, CA
Egyptian 1, Hollywood, CA

(There had also been reissues in Salt Lake City, Denver, and Toronto that summer)

1990

"The Hills are alive . . . again!"
August 24, 1990
A 70mm print of *TSOM* was shown in Los Angeles at the Century Plaza in Century City (Cineplex Odeon at the time). This was preceded by a 25th Anniversary Re-Premiere the evening before.

A 70mm print of *TSOM* was shown in New York at the Trans-Lux Gotham.

2003

February 3, 2003
Restoration print, Todd-AO; 70mm print with DTS digital sound; this was a one-time showing of MP Academy Series: "Facets of the Diamond: 75 Years of Best Picture Winners."

It played at the Samuel Goldwyn, Beverly Hills.

Additional Screenings

Egyptian, Hollywood (March 20, 2003; part of a Robert Wise retrospective)
Aero, Santa Monica (June 25, 2006—70mm festival)
Egyptian, Hollywood (December 1, 2006—70mm festival)
Ziegfeld, New York (March 15–16, 18, 20, 2008)
Aero, Santa Monica (Nov. 30, 2008—Family Matinees)
Ziegfeld, New York (December 15-21, 2010; 45th anniversary with brand new 35mm print)
Egyptian, Hollywood (May 13, 2012, Mother's Day matinee)
Samuel Goldwyn, Beverly Hills (July 30, 2012—"The Last 70mm Film Festival")
Film Society of Lincoln Center, NY (December 23–25, 2012; 70mm festival)
Museum of the Moving Image, Queens, NY (January 26, 2014; as part of *See It Big!* Musicals festival)

All-Time Highest Grossing Motion Pictures in the U.S., Adjusted for Inflation

1. *Gone with the Wind* (Selznick/MGM; 1939)
   Adjusted Gross: $1,646,633,700   Unadjusted Gross: $198,676,459
2. *Star Wars* (20th; 1977)
   Adjusted Gross: $1,451,674,000   Unadjusted Gross: $460,998,007

3. *The Sound of Music* **(20th; 1965)**
   Adjusted Gross: $1,160,685,000   **Unadjusted Gross: $158,671,368**
4. *E.T.: The Extra-Terrestrial* (Universal; 1982)
   Adjusted Gross: $1,156,112,800   Unadjusted Gross: $435,110,554
5. *Titanic* (Paramount; 1997)
   Adjusted Gross: $1,104,116,900   Unadjusted Gross: $658,672,302
6. *The Ten Commandments* (Paramount; 1956)
   Adjusted Gross: $1,067,650,000   Unadjusted Gross: $65,500,000
7. *Jaws* (Universal; 1975)
   Adjusted Gross: $1,043,842,400   Unadjusted Gross: $260,000,000
8. *Doctor Zhivago* (MGM; 1965)
   Adjusted Gross: $1,011,704,000   Unadjusted Gross: $184,925,486
9. *The Exorcist* (Warner Bros.; 1973)
   Adjusted Gross: $901,383,200   Unadjusted Gross: $232,906,145
10. *Snow White and the Seven Dwarfs* (Disney; 1937)
    Adjusted Gross: $888,350,000   Unadjusted Gross: $760,507,625

Sound Thoughts

What Reviewers and Others Said About *The Sound of Music*

Julie Andrews (center) teaches the seven Trapp children the basic "Do-Re-Mi's" of singing.

S ome have rewritten history to give the impression that *The Sound of Music* was a triumph over a stream of bad reviews and negative comments. Although there were indeed those who had little love for the movie (take a look below and experience some of them), a deeper look into critical and industry comments at the time gives a more complex view of the situation. There were certainly plenty who championed the movie; if it had been blasted as thoroughly as legend has it, it is doubtful its box office would have swelled so tremendously or that Hollywood would have rewarded the film its highest honor of Best Picture of the Year.

Here, from 1965, are critics' comments, along with some industry feedback from both back then and over the years.

REVIEWERS

Baltimore Sun

"It would be hard to imagine a film-version of a Rodgers and Hammerstein hit that would not, on the whole, be entertaining, and *The Sound of Music* . . . is certainly no exception . . . The lyrical score . . . is as effective as ever in the stereophonic soundtrack, and its vocalization by Miss Andrews and the seven children leaves nothing to be desired."

—R. H. Gardner (March 26, 1965)

Boston Globe

"Julie Andrews is not only the leading candidate for this year's 'best actress of the year' award, but she is also a vital, radiant and delightful heroine in *The Sound of Music* . . . Now that the cinema has been taken up by the intellectually elite it is getting fashionable to be hard-boiled . . . But there's still an overwhelming audience which likes its love stories sentimental; its music of the Rodgers and Hammerstein quality; its humor gay, lively and innocuous. . . . One bit of advice—take all the children, as they will love every minute of the 174-minute long show . . ."

—Marjorie Adams (March 18, 1965)

Boxoffice

"Robert Wise's picturization filmed in Todd-AO and DeLuxe Color . . . will delight moviegoers of all ages and become one of filmdom's all-time blockbusters. It's ideal entertainment for the family, equally suited for adults and the youngsters . . . Christopher Plummer . . . is handsome, dignified and thoroughly believable as Captain von Trapp . . . The seven children deserve a separate paragraph for their refreshing naturalness, free from any touch of saccharinity . . . *The Sound of Music*, with its memorable Rodgers and Hammerstein score, its scenic backgrounds and, especially, Julie Andrews to give her utmost in song, is motion picture-making at its finest."

—Frank Leyendecker (March 8, 1965)

British Film Institute Monthly Film Bulletin

"To say that this version of the stage success contains everything one would expect, should serve as sufficient warning to those allergic to singing nuns and sweetly innocent children. It is, in fact, an exceedingly sugary experience (though some would say less so than the original) . . . Even these ingredients might have been bearable if the songs had been better; alas, this is one of Rodgers and Hammerstein's less memorable scores . . . there is little to suggest that Wise will ever become a great musical director—the most one can say is that his handling is tactful and efficiently smooth . . . ."

—J. G. (April, 1965)

Chicago Tribune

"*The Sound of Music* is not recommended fare for those on a schmaltz-free diet
. . . For everyone else, the film version of Rodgers and Hammerstein's stage
musical should prove a delightful mélange of Austria and Andrews, with the
emphasis on the latter . . . Miss Andrews is so brilliant in the role . . . that when
she's off-camera *The Sound of Music* seems tone-deaf . . . The children are suitably
rambunctious and talented .. But the kids seem to be 'on' all the time, and one
often longs for less juvenility and more Julie."

—Clifford Terry (March 18, 1965)

Christian Science Monitor

"It has come back as a musical to fill the big Todd-AO screen with its zest and its
love . . . Everything about it is more freshly attractive than ever . . . Thanks are
due everyone for this, including Miss Andrews' slightly angular buoyancy, Mr.
Plummer's deft acting, Mr. Wise's sympathetic direction, and the picturesque-
ness of Salzburg . . ."

—Louis Chapin (March 20, 1965)

Cleveland Plain Dealer

"After all that has been said and written about *The Sound of Music*, it is still
incredibly beauteous and wondrous on the big screen . . . The film's greatest
charm—and what virtue should take precedence over another?—seems to me to
be its utter un-affectedness and simplicity . . . As everyone knows the great charm
is the creation of the Rodgers and Hammerstein music and lyrics. Assuredly the
screen has never had a lovelier, more enchanting romantic musical than this
one which properly depends on the ages for its final virtues—beautiful music
and tender love."

—W. Ward Marsh (March 25, 1965)

Cosmopolitan

"The original Rodgers and Hammerstein score is lovely fun . . .
Choreographers Marc Breaux and Dee Dee Wood and director Robert Wise
have combined talents to make the entire film seem like a choreography . . .
Julie Andrews is a complete natural, and the children are charming. Richard
Haydn and Peggy Wood give fine supporting performances, Christopher
Plummer . . . makes his musical debut and he doesn't seem completely at
home in the milieu. But when he stands . . . looking back to his beloved land
of the edelweiss, it's easy to empathize. The audience, too, has a hard time
allowing the movie to end."

—Elizabeth Carter (April, 1965)

Cue

"If Julie Andrews were just turned loose to romp through Austria for three hours of film, that in itself would be worthy entertainment. But in addition to the utterly delightful Miss Andrews, co-starring with some breathtaking Austrian settings, we are being served a most appealing screen version of the Rodgers-Hammerstein musical about the Von Trapp family . . . But the total still adds up to a wonderful production job by director Robert Wise and associates—handsome, in beautiful color, life-like, melodic and an object lesson in how to make a film that a family can enjoy seeing together."

—William Wolf (March 6, 1965)

Dallas Morning News

"Robert Wise's screen version is both Rodgers and Hammerstein and Hollywood with debatable features by both. But if we may do some guessing, we would say this won't make the slightest difference. *The Sound of Music* may not be as good a movie as was *The King and I* but it could outstrip in film records such bigger efforts as *Oklahoma!* and *South Pacific* . . . Julie Andrews sings, hops and skips with intoxicating zest . . . If you like *Sound of Music* on stage, there's no reason not to cheer the Todd-AO version."

—John Rosenfield (March 24, 1965)

[*Note: In the full review, Rosenfield errs in presuming that cast member Marni Nixon ghosted the vocals for Peggy Wood.*]

Detroit News

"Hollywood has a bell ringer here. No doubt about it. Which is to say that 20th Century-Fox's version of the Broadway stage hit . . . will be around for a long while, delighting young and old and filling the box office coffers to overflowing. The glittering Todd-AO version of the Rodgers and Hammerstein classic . . . is like the original—big, beautiful, colorful, and schmaltzy, with probably one of the most appealing musical scores written . . . The studio has additionally cast the effervescent Julie Andrews in the leading role."

—John Finlayson (March 18, 1965)

Film Daily

"A charming Broadway musical hit is brought to the screen beautifully . . . There is a sweet, idyllic quality to this story of the singing Von Trapp family who face adventure and danger with courage and dignity. Enriching the pleasing quality and the warm sentimental flow of events is the Rodgers and Hammerstein music . . . This Robert Wise production shines with bright, total-family appeal . . . The picture is a memorable experience, alive with the sounds of felicity."

—Mandel Herbstman (March 3, 1965)

Glasgow Herald

"Never has the whole range of sentimental clichés been put on the screen with more confidence than in *The Sound of Music*, the latest and rather glorious version of the fortunes of the Von Trapp family. . . . Being descended from the stage musical—it does have a lavish supply of Rodgers and Hammerstein songs, and, even more, it does have Miss A[ndrews]. . . Her wholesome British charm injects a tang into the piece, which otherwise might have submerged in its own syrup . . . To be frank, Christopher Plummer as Von Trapp is rather a stick."

—Molly Plowright (April 19, 1965)

Life

"The happy news is that *Music* is a warm and beautiful experience—that increasingly rare film these days a family can go to see without being embarrassed. . . One of the treasures is the Rodgers and Hammerstein score. But its chief gem is Julie Andrews. Julie's radiance floods the screen, warms the heart and brings back the golden age of the Hollywood musical with a film destined to be one of the biggest hits ever."

(March 12, 1965)

Look

"Christopher Plummer . . . does a bracingly, biting widower. And Miss Andrews shows why she has a rich future in Hollywood. From the moment the camera finds her singing the title song in a meadow, she displays a quality more important than her shining face and silvery voice: an ability to define the difference between schmaltz and true human warmth."

—John Poppy (January 26, 1965)

Los Angeles Times

"They have taken this sweet, sometimes saccharine and structurally slight story of the Von Trapp Family Singers and transformed it into close to three hours of visual and vocal brilliance, all in the universal terms of cinema. They have invested it with new delights and even a sense of depth in human relationships—not to mention the swooning beauty of Salzburg and the Austrian Alps, which the stage, of course, could only suggest. . . . Its sound will ring out for a long time to come."

—Philip K. Scheuer (March 7, 1965)

Miami Herald

"*Sound of Music* is a great film—but more important than its greatness is that it is also great entertainment without stooping to excesses of any sort . . . Producer-director Robert Wise has wisely allowed the original vehicle to make its own political points. He has not imposed the additive of piped-up movie melodrama to emphasize the Nazi threat . . . In the words of one of its songs, climb every mountain, ford every stream, if you must, to see *Sound of Music*. It is a sound worth hearing. And seeing."

—George Bourke (March 18, 1965)

Miami News

"Suddenly the music soars through the theater and Julie Andrews is running and looking upward and she sings . . . And with that, start almost three hours of beauty and enchantment because Rodgers and Hammerstein's *Sound of Music* is underway. These are glorious hours that hold you through the last minute . . . This is a motion picture that'll be around for a long time. It has warmth and romance, charm and laughter, wholesomeness without being square . . . *The Sound of Music* is lovely to the ears and a delight to the eyes."

—Herb Kelly (March 18, 1965)

Milwaukee Sentinel

"*The Sound of Music* is not the best musical that Rodgers and Hammerstein wrote, but it may well be the most beautiful picture ever filmed, and the stars, Julie Andrews and Christopher Plummer, are captivating . . . Miss Andrews, in a short cropped blond hairdo, and Plummer in a series of miraculously well tailored costumes, make the Trapps seem completely winning. The children are charming enough to make one wish for seven youngsters of one's own."

—Joe Boyd (March 24, 1965)

Motion Picture Exhibitor

"Estimate: Highly entertaining and charming film version of stage musical . . . The story, a familiar one to many, holds interest pretty much on high throughout though a bit of editing and reduction in the running time might have served to improve it more. The performances are capable, with Julie Andrews brightening each and every scene that she is in. She receives fine support. The direction and production are superior, and the show, as a whole, looks as though it should be more successful with the majority of audiences."

—March 3, 1965 (no reviewer credited)

[*Note: Two weeks later, the same magazine decided to write a criticism of two of the film's harsher critics and their failure to connect with the public on this particular movie.*]

"Now we don't say every critic must agree. But when they are so far apart in their opinions, the public can't help but be confused. Miss [*New York Herald Tribune's* Judith] Crist and Mr. [*New York Times'* Bosley] Crowther can't stand what everybody seems to love. Generally, they seem to reserve highest praise for the murky foreign films that garner a handful of playdates and then disappear forever. Happily the public seems to agree with those critics who themselves were delighted with *The Sound of Music.* Business is booming; advance sales are soaring . . ."

—March 17, 1965 (again, no writer credited)

Motion Picture Herald

"It is precisely this fragile quality of magic and enchantment that producer-director Robert Wise has brilliantly captured in the handsome film version of the musical . . . On screen—even more so than on the stage—it comes over as a fable of goodness triumphant, a true "fairy tale" as it were, that will delight audiences of all ages . . . All of the actors contribute to the mood of enchantment that *The Sound of Music* creates . . . The music seems to have improved over the years . . . Everybody but the ultra-cynical should be enchanted with *The Sound of Music.*"

—Richard Gertner (March 17, 1965)

The New Republic

"Is there a special heaven for film critics? I feel confident of it after enduring all of *The Sound of Music.* At that, heaven is small enough compensation for sitting through this Rodgers and Hammerstein atrocity . . . Miss Andrews is rapidly becoming the most revoltingly refreshing actress in films. Christopher Plummer looked almost as bored as I felt . . . The songs are sickening and the picture manages to turn the Alps into sugar loaves."

—Stanley Kauffmann (March 20, 1965)

New York Daily News

"Robert Wise has transformed the delightful Rodgers and Hammerstein musical stage production of *The Sound of Music* into a magical film in which Julie Andrews gives an endearing performance in the role of Maria . . . Appealing to the whole family and giving Julie Andrews a chance to sing and perform charmingly, it presents Christopher Plummer as Captain Von Trapp, a role that is sure enhance the popularity of this fine actor . . . Robert Wise's direction is excellent, as he keeps his cast on the move throughout the slightly less than three-hour entertainment"

—Kate Cameron (March 3, 1965)

New York Herald Tribune

"One star and much scenery do not a two-hour-and-fifty-minutes-plus intermission entertainment make . . . This last, most remunerative and least inspired, let alone

sophisticated, of the Rodgers and Hammerstein collaborations is square and solid sugar. Calorie-counters, diabetics, and grown-ups from eight to eighty best beware."
—Judith Crist (March 3, 1965)

[*Note: Imagine the horror of album buyers when they opened the booklet included in* The Sound of Music *soundtrack to see that someone who hated the work on both stage and screen, Crist, was asked to write the appraisal. Talk about taking an assignment for "blood money!*]

New York Observer

"The film lasts three hour. I was mostly bored but intermittently, unexpectedly touched. The greens and blues of the landscape, as well as the baroque splendors of Salzburg itself, are thrillingly caught by Ted McCord's free-ranging camera; but it is Julie Andrews of the soaring voice and thrice-scrubbed innocence who makes me, even in guarded moments, catch my breath. The director is Robert Wise: given a task so inherently limiting, I cannot see how he can be faulted."
—Kenneth Tynan (March 28, 1965)

New York Post

"*The Sound of Music* . . . has the incomparable Julie Andrews, the actual location in beautiful mountainous Austrian Salzburg, and a marvelous, indestructibly appealing story no matter how much it is reorganized to 'musical' dimensions . . . It is not a picture that can fail of popularity. Anyway if any of the basic ingredients were found in short supply one could concentrate on Julie Andrews and her wholesome, rural-healthy being coupled with that excellent singing style. She brightens every scene she appears in and she's in almost all of them. Those who saw the stage-play say the movie's better."
—Archer Winsten (March 3, 1965)

New York Times

"Miss Andrews, with her air of radiant vigor, her appearance of plain-Jane wholesomeness and her ability to make her dialogue as vivid and appealing as she makes her songs, brings a nice sort of Mary Poppins logic and authority to the role, which is always in peril of collapsing under its weight of romantic nonsense and sentiment. Despite the hopeless pretense of reality with which she and the others have to contend . . . Miss Andrews treats the whole thing with the same air of serenely controlled self-confidence that she has when we first come upon her trilling the title song."
—Bosley Crowther (March 3, 1965)

"*The Sound of Music* is a pleasant, sugary romance, with a pretty musical score, a nice performance by Julie Andrews and some handsome scenery. There is a place for it in our culture. Nobody's squawking about it being made. But it can't hold a candle to *Darling* as a forceful, contemporary film."

—from Bosley Crowther's article on the Academy Awards, April 24, 1966

New York World-Telegram and Sun

"The film's charm grows and sentiment becomes unabashed and naively sweet but never cloying. The romantic doings remain hearty and sincere, extending a pretty little invitation to share their rosy happiness. Director Robert Wise has insisted on keeping his people substantial and credible with none of the coy tricks that are likely to creep into an idyllic rhapsody such as this, particularly when children are involved . . . The dominant force of Julie's [Andrews] presence certainly is demonstrated in this picture . . . Charmian Carr is a startling find, a beauty with poise and perceptive instinct for developing character . . ."

—Alton Cook (March 3, 1965)

New Yorker

"A huge, tasteless blowup of the celebrated Rodgers and Hammerstein musical . . . even the handful of authentic location shots have a hokey studio sheen . . . What a lack of imagination it requires to use the horror of that time as a device for furthering the plot of a silly musical about a family who, however attractive they may have been in real life, on the evidence shown here went rushing about incessantly whinnying, squealing, sulking, and singing tinkly songs!"

—Brendan Gill (March 6, 1965)

Newark Evening News

"The best thing the man behind the filmed *West Side Story* did for this redoing was to transport the whole enterprise to its natural locale . . . What makes the 20th Century-Fox picture a visual delight are those views of the Salzburg area in moist, muted colors . . . the movie is generally a superb achievement for [Robert] Wise and his colleagues . . . Miss Andrews is a sunny joy, with the sweetest singing voice this side of Paradise . . . Christopher Plummer is a handsome and impressive Capt. Trapp . . . Peggy Wood is touching as the Mother Abbess . . . ."

—Edward Southern Hipp (March 3, 1965)

[*Note: Hipp was one of a several critics who were under the impression that Plummer and Wood did their own singing.*]

The Oregonian

"What you ask of a musical . . . is that it be pretty and that the goo be confection, an exaggeration of possible goodness, rather than smothering falseness. In *The Sound of Music* the goo does get sticky—those kids work so strenuously at being adorable—but the movie is visually more than pretty, it's gorgeous . . . Any inclusion of Nazi Germany into a musical is a serious mistake . . . And the notion that bliss is the exclusive property of wealth and station . . . should be put on the shelf with Cinderella. But all in all, unless you're curdled beyond dreaming by the harsh realities, *The Sound of Music* will prove a prolonged delight to the eye."

—Jack Berry (April 8, 1965)

Philadelphia Inquirer

"Where *The Sound of Music* is concerned, nearly everything is 'loverly' in the innocent mind of this reviewer . . . But within the boundaries imposed by the long-running Rodgers and Hammerstein stage hit, Ernest Lehman has wrought a film translation that should please any audience which will check its ultra-sophistication for three melodious hours. The assets are many. Julie Andrews is grand, the Alps are grand, the R&H melodies are grand, and while the score and story are faithful to the original . . . the physical production has been greatly expanded."

—Henry T. Murdock (March 18, 1965)

Pittsburgh Post-Gazette

"I regard *Sound of Music* as something of a film phenomenon because its many and obvious faults don't destroy its ingratiating effect. If there's a parallel in musical motion pictures, I don't know about it . . . The film version has some, not much, of the over-sweetness, and a strong storyline-exaggeration, also known as schmaltz, in the second part particularly, but, still, the film is delightful . . . Like the stage play, it will be a tremendous and popular hit. . . . Miss Andrews easily outranks everybody else with her acting, her singing and her radiant talent."

—Lee McInerney (April 9, 1965)

San Francisco Chronicle

"*The Sound of Music* . . . is far better on screen than it was on stage. It is still too sweet for comfort, most of those it pictures are revealed as a flock of ninnies, and it lacks wit and suspense. But being photographed in the Austrian Alps and in Salzburg has brought to its somewhat silly drama a visual magnificence . . . It's a long, bland picture, often interestingly staged by [Robert] Wise but including some incredibly mawkish love scenes. However, it is pretty, and Miss Andrews handles an almost impossible assignment skillfully."

—Paine Knickerbocker (March 19, 1965)

Saturday Review

"If the film fails, it was not for want of trying. On the contrary, it might have been a matter of trying too hard, providing an excess of material that cried aloud for a little roughness and earthiness to make it a bit less cloying and its people a lot more believable . . . But of one thing I am certain: My own apathy to *The Sound of Music* is based on its knowing manipulation of shopworn but sure-fire materials. And I shall be very surprised if this careful calculation does not make it one of the outstanding commercial successes of 1965."

—Arthur Knight (March 20, 1965)

Time

"*The Sound of Music* satisfies nearly all the requirements for what moviemakers tout as wholesome family entertainment. It is tuneful, cheerful, and colorful . . . Though Robert Wise has made capital of the show's virtues, he can do little to disguise its faults . . . Viewers who want a movie to swell around them in big warm blobs will find *Sound of Music* easy to take. Sterner types may resist at the outset, but are apt to loosen up after a buoyant, heels-in-the-air song or two by Julie Andrews [who] turns every number into a bell ringer . . ."

(March 5, 1965)

Times of London

"Sheer professional knowhow can do wonders, and that is what we get here all along the line. The film version (which was nearly three hours but, mercifully and surprisingly, does not feel anything like as long) has been opened out to make maximum use of some dazzling Austrian locations, and directed with just the right amount of easy obviousness by Mr. Robert Wise: Much to please and nothing to disturb . . . It is a sweet mixture, and you need a strong stomach to appreciate it to the full. But those with a sweet tooth will happily gobble it all down."

—Our Film Critic (March 25, 1965)

Variety

"Superb. . . One of the top musicals to reach the screen. The production is pulsating, captivating drama set to the most imaginative use of lilting Rodgers and Hammerstein tunes, magnificently mounted with a brilliant cast . . . Miss Andrews endows her role with fine feeling and a sense of balance which assures continued star stature. Plummer also is particularly forceful . . . The seven children are ably portrayed, topped by Charmian Carr, who displays a nice voice . . . Every technical credit is top-flight and impressive."

—Whit. (1965)

Washington Post

"*The Sound of Music* probably will be the best loved picture of 1965. Gone is that sense of being buried alive in Hallmark Cards which accompanied the stage production. It is Miss Andrews, however, who makes the critical difference. Who else could possibly make you accept a silvery soprano singing to itself as she clicks her heels in joy racing down a country lane . . . Whatever Miss Andrews does becomes true, watchful and infectious .. It would be misleading not to admit that this is finely spun sugar indeed."

—Richard L. Coe (March 18, 1965)

INDUSTRY AND OTHERS

Asked in a July 6, 1970 interview on *The David Frost Show* which part she has played is most like herself, Julie Andrews replied "When all is said and done, *The Sound of Music*, I suppose."
Elsewhere:

"I was pigeonholed by it. But I will never put that part down, because it does seem to have pleased an awful lot of people."

"The music appeals to every generation. It was the last of the really old Hollywood musicals."

"It feels like a fresh breeze every time you see it. It's about joy, and I think everybody senses it. . . I don't think any of us who were involved in its creation could have anticipated its remarkable success."

—Julie Andrews (Maria in *TSOM*)

"The first act was good, but the second act might have been written by different people—say, Irving Hammerstein and Fred Rodgers . . . It has everything: children, religion, high society, royalty, Nazi Germany and Julie Andrews as the fairy on top of the Christmas tree. It's helped our film (*Doctor Dolittle*), because I can't believe that any studio that didn't have *The Sound of Music* behind it would get involved with such a brave, expensive project."

—Leslie Bricusse (1966; script and songwriter for Fox's *Doctor Dolittle*)

"I attended the first preview of *The Sound of Music* in Minneapolis and dubbed it 'The Sound of Money." I was correct."
    "No report you have received on the previews of *Sound of Music* can possibly do justice to the actual thrill of having actually been in the audience and witnessing the reaction. I was present at the Minneapolis preview at Dick's [Zanuck] invitation and I have never before observed such unanimous enthusiasm and love for a motion picture. The reaction is entirely deserved because the

production has everything going for it—a marvelously conceived and produced film, infinitely superior to the stage version."

—David Brown, Fox story editor
(the latter quote, from a telegram to Darryl Zanuck)

"I wouldn't understand for months. It was just a movie, after all. Not until I'd traveled around the world and witnessed the outpouring of emotion and enthusiasm in dozens of countries would I begin to comprehend the impact *The Sound of Music* was having on audiences around the globe . . . "

"*The Sound of Music* has been—and continues to be—a strong thread running throughout my entire adult life. There have been times when I was frustrated that a character I played when I was twenty-one would define me for the rest of my days. I have long known that nothing I ever do professionally will eclipse my role as Liesl. But I began to realize that, rather than being a burden, the 'identity' was a gift. It gave me a special family that has always supported me through my good times—and bad . . ."

—Charmian Carr (Liesl in *TSOM*)

"Even though it had a bad rap and is supposed to be all syrupy, with kids and music and stuff, it's really held up . . . Julie Andrews is just so good, so pure, you just root for her the way she turns those kids around. She's totally endearing."

—Angela Cartwright (Brigitta in *TSOM*)

"I was never so happy reading a script in my life. It was wonderful. Ernie (Lehman) had retained the elements that made *Sound of Music* such an enormous hit, but by changes and additions, he had improved it immeasurably. The characters were more clearly defined, it was more charming, and he had invented a truly exciting and suspenseful finish. Also, it read as if it had been written originally for the screen instead of being an adaptation of a stage play."

—Saul Chaplin (*TSOM* associate producer)

"In spite of its naiveté, you find yourself caught up; there's a tug at the heart. My principal emotion is jealousy . . . No, I don't wish I'd done it."

—George Cukor, director (*My Fair Lady*)

"Dick Zanuck begged me to direct *The Sound of Music,* and *Hello, Dolly!* too . . . But when I was reading the script to *The Sound of Music* and got to the point where they were yodeling with a goatherd, I said 'This isn't for me.'"

—Stanley Donen, director (*Singin' in the Rain, Funny Face*)

"I'll have to drag out all those old superlatives about Hollywood. It's as close to perfection as any movie musical I've ever seen . . . I know Oscar would have loved it. And there I go with the superlatives again."

—Dorothy Hammerstein (Oscar's widow)

"I've heard so many stories of *The Sound of Music* taking residence in theatres around the world and just running and running. In fact, there's a great story from a town in the States where the local student community actually started a protest . . . because *TSOM* was the only movie that had ever run in their local cinema. It just kept running! And now of course, it's a beloved classic, and I'm just so proud to have been a part of it. For me it really was one of the happiest times of my life."

—Nicholas Hammond (Friedrich in *TSOM*)

"Everything in it is nice and honey and bread-and-butter simple. I think the people who go back to see it time and again are going back for another dose of reassurance . . . (Julie) she's incredibly wholesome; she's everybody's wife, mother, daughter. It wouldn't have been the same picture with, say, Susan Hayward."

—Richard Haydn ("Max Detweiler," *TSOM*)

"I liked motion pictures better when you walked out with an uplift. Some said *Sound of Music* was corny. I love it."

—Susan Hayward (actress; July 1967)

"20th will hear nothing but the Sound of Money for years to come."

—Hedda Hopper, columnist

"One of the loveliest films with which I was ever associated . . ."

—Anna Lee ("Sister Margaretta, *TSOM*)

"It wasn't as sticky sweet as it might have been, though there are those who will disagree with that. But the very things we were on guard against are the things that appeal to so many people . . . A fantasy about a world that no longer exists, where everything comes out right in the end."

—Ernest Lehman, *TSOM* screenwriter

"The fantastic success of the picture of *The Sound of Music* must be credited to Robert Wise, producer and director, and scriptwriter Ernest Lehman. It was a success in the theatre but it could easily have been made into a failure as a motion picture . . . Much has been written about the success of *The Sound of Music* play and motion picture. Is it immodest of me to point out, because no one else *ever* does, that Russel Crouse and I had a hand in it?"

—Howard Lindsay (co-author of the stage version of *TSOM*)

"My kids . . . when they saw *The Sound of Music,* they couldn't believe it was Mommy up there. We had a screening . . . in Century City for its 25th Anniversary, on the big screen. All the people [involved] were invited, and my son and daughter came. My son wanted to see the Arnold Schwarzenegger movie playing next door! He was actually surprised that he liked *The Sound of Music*; he said 'This is a pretty good movie, Mom.' I replied, 'Well, yeah!'"

—Heather Menzies (Louisa in *TSOM*)

"My role as Sister Sophia wasn't a very large one, but I was happy to be visible on the screen for once . . . I adored the film and felt proud to be part of such a crowd-pleaser . . . This marked the third time I had been involved with an Oscar winning film."

[Nixon had provided the vocals for Natalie Wood in *West Side Story* and Audrey Hepburn in *My Fair Lady*, both Academy Award winners for Best Picture.]

—Marni Nixon (Sister Sophia in *TSOM*)

"Ludicrous though it may seem, I still harboured the old-fashioned stage actor's snobbism toward moviemaking. The moment we arrive in Austria to shoot the exteriors I was determined to present myself as a victim of circumstance—that I was doing the picture under duress, that it had been forced upon me and that I certainly deserved better. My behavior was unconscionable."

"The critics generally pooh-poohed the enterprise and it's always been my opinion they were too ashamed to admit they liked it lest their cynical, hard-boiled comrades of the press might call them sissies and banish them to the nearest convent."

"I went to a children's Easter party. They were going to show "S&M" [Plummer's jokey name for TSOM] as an after-lunch treat. Oh, my God, I thought, how am I going to escape? My friends, the hosts, pleaded with me to stay . . . Well, I stayed. I had not seen the movie for years and the more I watched, the more I realized what a terrific movie it is. The very best of its genre—warm, touching, joyous and absolutely timeless. I suddenly could see why it had brought such pleasure to so many people. Here I was, cynical old sod that I am, being totally seduced by the damned thing—and what's more, I felt a sudden surge of pride that I'd been part of it."

—Christopher Plummer
(from his autobiography *In Spite of Myself*)

"It's irresistible if you like people and children . . . I'm delighted with it—who wouldn't be?"

"It's the most successful picture that's ever been made and that's very pleasurable. It isn't just a question of money. What I enjoy particularly is what it has done for the unselfconscious people of the world—the self-conscious ones sneer a little at it. It *is* sentimental, but I don't see anything particularly wrong with that. I think people have been given a great deal of hope by that picture."

—Richard Rodgers (*TSOM* composer)

"We knew we had a great movie; we didn't know it was going to have the endurance for 50 years and play 3 times a year, and it's been a great experience; a big part of my life . . . If you're ever going to get a chance to make one movie—what better than *The Sound of Music?*"

—Daniel Truhitte (Rolf in *TSOM*)

"If our name had not been involved, I would have loved the movie, as all the other people did. But because our name was used and our life was portrayed inaccurately, I could not bear the thought of seeing the play and the movie more than once. I would not let them take away my memories."

"The shift in my feelings actually came from those who saw *The Sound of Music*, loved it, and connected it with our name and family. Little by little, I met people on many occasions who recognized me by my last name and connected me with the musical. Their faces lit up, and I felt a wave of friendliness coming toward me. I did not expect this result from the musical. Warmth and goodwill cannot be bought with millions of dollars. This is a matter of the heart."

—Agathe von Trapp (eldest of the Trapp daughters)

"Dear Robert Wise . . . You are a much greater artist than I could ever have thought. You have no idea how . . . indescribably happy I am now after reliving that portion of my life which you have so masterfully recreated. In the name of my family and myself I thank you."

—Maria von Trapp (in a letter to director Robert Wise)

"I have very little business sense and I have not made a lot of money . . . The great good that the film and the play are doing to individual lives is far beyond money . . . There seems to be so much despair in the world but so many people write about how much the film has helped them in restoring their confidence in God . . . I was happily surprised that Hollywood didn't change the real story too much."

—Maria von Trapp (September 1967 *The New York Times* article
in which she admitted to having seen the movie five times)

"I think that, by and large, in *Music*, we came close to the mark. To our mark. The play was very, very saccharine, and obviously we haven't eliminated that for all people. But we tried to tone it down . . . I think I'm satisfied with it."

"Obviously, one has to be very pleased and warmed by the spontaneous reactions that come up so often, in so many places around the world. That's most rewarding. The only slightly perverse thing about it is that it tends to make people forget and overlook some of the other films I've done that I'm very proud of, such as *The Body Snatcher, The Set-Up, The Day the Earth Stood Still, Executive Suite, The Haunting, Somebody Up There likes Me, I Want to Live!*, and *The Sand Pebbles*. The film buffs know all those, of course, but the average viewers don't know the directors and their films. *The Sound of Music* tends to engulf some of the other equally good work I did. It doesn't overpower *West Side Story* so much, but I get many more comments about *The Sound of Music* than I do about *West Side Story*. The subject matter and the nature of *The Sound of Music* were more universally popular. "

—Robert Wise, *TSOM* director

"I'm delighted that *The Sound of Music* is doing so well. Of course, it's an infallible piece of material. Even when second- and third- rate companies were doing the play, they did enormous business . . ."

—William Wyler (director who backed out of doing
The Sound of Music, opting for *The Collector*)

"It deals with good, wholesome subject matter—kids, nuns—and it entertains in a charming, romantic way."

—Richard Zanuck, head of production, 20th Century Fox

ALSO

"In all my years in the theatre business, I've never seen anything like it. Showing the film is like a ritual with me. It would almost be a sacrilege to have to stop it or spoil a scene."

—Lawrence Brock, projectionist at the
Ambassador Theatre in Raleigh, NC. (*Boxoffice,* January 10, 1966)

"Such a stellar family film has priced itself out of the market for many families . . . When a family night at the cinema costs 15 bucks, it's small wonder that families pass up the opportunity. It's a shame, too."

—Anonymous writer (*Boxoffice,* May 10, 1965),
regarding high price of reserved-seat tickets for *TSOM*

"*The Sound of Music* is a film of unrestrained happiness for all ages. The delightful children, excellent cast, handsome Christopher Plummer and the incomparable Julie, encompassed by breathless settings, combine to make a film never forgotten. This simple, unaffected story was a joy to behold after some of the more questionable themes of recent months."

—Mrs. Irvin J. Haus, 1st Vice President,
Federation of Motion Picture Councils, Milwaukee

"The biggest box office hit of recent years has been *The Sound of Music,* a film designed specifically to please family audiences. Its blend of color, music, children, romance, a smattering of religion, and an actress who exuded wholesomeness was a combination that theoretically was possible to duplicate. And yet its many imitators have met with public indifference if not scorn."

—Catholic Film Newspaper (September 5, 1968)

"This film has everything. Appeal to young and old, male and female, lovely songs, lively music, and effervescent performances by all its principals."

—Alex Greig, manager of the Gaumont Theatre in Glasgow
(December 1967)

The *Sound* Track (and the Cast Albums)

The Chart Success of *The Sound of Music* LPs

The RCA Victor soundtrack recording of *The Sound of Music* debuted in stores on the very same day the film was holding its New York premiere, Tuesday, March 2, 1965. It was made available in four different formats: long-play phonograph record, audio cassette, 8-track cartridge, and on ¼-inch reel-to-reel. That week's *Billboard* magazine carried an article about RCA's $100,000 publicity campaign for the LP, which would include the first-time use of full-color advertisements in newspapers. Such ads were seen in the *Los Angeles Times* (March 10), and the *Chicago Tribune* (March 17), while the *New York Times* carried a full-page black-and-white advertisement on March 2. It followed this with a four-color full-page ad in the *New York Times* magazine, on Sunday, March 14. (That same issue also featured an ad for Jumping-Jack shoes, letting you know that their "spring styles rate high with the youthful stars of *The Sound of Music*." Additional full-page ads showed up in *Esquire, Cue, New Yorker, Show,* and that most un-nun-like of publications, *Playboy,* not to mention several record-industry trade journals.)

The New York World's Fair (launching its second and final season) made room for a promotional display as part of its RCA pavilion, with listening rooms where fairgoers could hear the *Sound* soundtrack. The RCA Exhibition Hall (on 49th Street in Rockefeller Center) in Manhattan was given over to a display of the album, and the record label offered a special "open-end" interview album of Richard Rodgers to radio stations throughout the country.

It all appeared to be a good investment, as RCA reported a healthy, advance-distribution order of 250,000 albums.

In their review of the LP (February 24, 1965), *Variety,* calling it "a topflight musical package," raved that "Julie Andrews lights up the set with the glow of her lucid, high-flying pipes . . . ," but wrongly presumed one of her co-stars as well as her leading man were doing their own vocalizing when they wrote "Peggy Wood handles 'Climb Ev'ry Mountain' in excellent style. Christopher Plummer . . . is very effective in his duos with Miss Andrews . . ."

Other new RCA releases during this period include three *TSOM*-related LPs:

This booklet containing photos and information about the musical was included in the original RCA issue of the soundtrack album.

The Groovy Sound of Music by Gary Burton; *The Two Piano Sound of Derek and Ray Playing The Sound of Music and Other Richard Rodgers Hits* (Derek and Ray were Derek Gleeson and Don Ray); and *Music from "The Sound of Music"* by the Living Strings (on the RCA Camden label)

The Sound of Music

RCA Records
An Original Soundtrack Recording, LSOD-2005
Vocal Supervision by Robert Tucker; Produced for Records by Neely Plumb
Film Recording Engineers: Murray Spivak and Douglas Williams

RCA Victor Recording Engineer: John Norman
Film Music Editor: Robert Mayer

Side 1

1. Prelude and The Sound of Music (Maria) (2:33)
2. Overture and Preludium (Dixit Dominus) (Orchestra and Nuns Chorus) (3:12)
3. Morning Hymn and Alleluia (Nuns Chorus) (2:00)
4. Maria (Nuns Chorus) (3:15)
5. I Have Confidence (Maria) (3:21)
6. Sixteen Going on Seventeen (Rolf and Liesl) (3:13)
7. My Favorite Things (Maria) (2:16)
8. Climb Ev'ry Mountain (Mother Abbess) (2:13)

Side 2

1. The Lonely Goatherd (Maria and the Children) (3:08)
2. The Sound of Music (The Children and the Captain) (2:09)
3. Do-Re-Mi (Maria and the Children) (5:30)
4. Something Good (Maria and the Captain) (3:15)
5. Processional and Maria (Organ, Orchestra and Nuns Chorus) (2:25)
6. Edelweiss (The Captain, Maria, the Children and Chorus) (1:48)
7. So Long, Farewell (The Children) (2:52)
8. Climb Ev'ry Mountain (Reprise) (Chorus and Orchestra) (1:18)

US CHARTS

1965
March 20, 1965

In its third week on the market, *TSOM* soundtrack debuts on the *Billboard* charts at #109. Things bode well for the movie LP, as the charts that week are topped by two other soundtracks: *Goldfinger*, the third James Bond epic, scored by John Barry and featuring Shirley Bassey's classic rendition of the title song (at #1); and *Mary Poppins* (at #2), which, of course, featured Julie Andrews on many of the tracks.

The original Broadway cast album of *TSOM* was still on the charts at this time, at #139.

March 27, 1965

Entering the Top 100, *TSOM* jumps to #90 (directly below *The Beatles' Second Album* and one notch above the *West Side Story* soundtrack, the champion LP chart holder of the decade).

April 3, 1965

TSOM is now at #63, between Jerry Vale's *Have You Looked into Your Heart* and *The Jim Reeves Way*.

TSOM cast album clearly benefited from the movie and its soundtrack having such prominence in 1965 pop culture, as it has now risen to #127.

April 10, 1965

After a little more than a month of availability, *TSOM* soundtrack is awarded the RIAA (Recording Industry Associate of America) Gold Record Award, indicating sales of $1,000,000. Not surprisingly, the initial pressing of 250,000 albums was quickly exhausted.

TSOM LP makes a massive jump from #63 to #21 this week, ending up directly above Barbra Streisand's *People*. At this point the #1 and #2 positions have been reversed, with *Goldfinger* dropping to 2, while *Mary Poppins* takes the #1 spot, putting Julie Andrews on the highest-selling LP in America at the time.

April 17, 1965

Finding itself in the Top 20 for the first time, *TSOM* is #15, below the late Nat King Cole's *Ramblin' Rose* and directly above the soundtrack for the Hank Williams biopic *Your Cheatin' Heart*.

An ad heralding the coming of what would turn out to be one of the biggest-selling albums of the 1960s.

April 24, 1965

TSOM lands at #11, below *The Beach Boys Today!* and above the Supremes' *Where Did Our Love Go*.

May 1, 1965

Reaching #6, *TSOM* hits the Top 10 for the first time, two months after its debut. It will manage to stay comfortably positioned inside the Top 10 until August 1966. Its current position means that it is one of four soundtracks in the Top 10, the others being *Mary Poppins* (still holding at #1), *Goldfinger* (#3), and *My Fair Lady* (#9).

May 8, 1965

TSOM is #3, thereby hitting the Top 5, where it will remain at various positions for an entire year. Because *Mary Poppins* is still in the #1 spot, this means Julie Andrews is featured on two records in the Top 5. Between them is *Introducing Herman's Hermits*.

RCA ran this ad promoting the soundtrack in time for the Christmas season, when album sales were customarily at their highest.

May 22, 1965

With *TSOM* moving into the #2 slot and *Mary Poppins* still the reigning champ, Julie Andrews is now the principal vocalist on both of the top-charting LPs.

June 19, 1965

After four weeks, *TSOM* relinquishes its second-place position to *My Name Is Barbra* (Streisand).

This week, *TSOM* Broadway cast album is at #90, having hit #82 the week prior. #82 is the highest it will reach in this return to the charts.

July 10, 1965

TSOM dips to #5 and *Poppins* to #3 (after a thirteen-week reign at the top), as *Beatles VI* captures the top spot after only three weeks on the chart; *Herman's Hermits on Tour* is #2.

July 31, 1965

For the first time, *TSOM* LP leaps over *Mary Poppins*, taking the #3 spot, while *Mary* moves to #4.

August 14, 1965

The arrival of *Out of Our Heads* (Rolling Stones, at #3 in its second week on the charts) and *Summer Days (And Summer Nights!!)* (Beach Boys, at #4); pushes *TSOM* down to #5 (where it will remain for the next three weeks).

During the next two months, *TSOM* will continue to bounce between #3, 4, and 5, while the soundtrack for the Beatles' *Help!* takes the #1 spot for a nine-week stretch.

November 13, 1965

TSOM soundtrack finally hits the #1 spot on the *Billboard* charts, in its thirty-fifth week. *Help!* drops to #2.

November 20, 1965

TSOM spends its second (and last) week at the #1 position; the #2 record, Herb Alpert & the Tijuana Brass's *Whipped Cream & Other Delights* (boasting not only the hit single "Taste of Honey" but one of the era's most unforgettable and iconic album covers, a naked woman covered in whipped cream), will be *Sound of Music*'s chief challenger for the top spot, keeping it from the potential domination it might have maintained otherwise.

While this is taking place, *TSOM* cast album falls out of the Top 150 chart for the first time.

November 27, 1965

TSOM drops to #3, as *Whipped Cream* not unexpectedly moves to #1, where it will remain for the rest of the calendar year. *My Name Is Barbra, Two . . .* is #2.

December 18, 1965

Certainly an LP plenty of folks are purchasing with the Christmas season in mind, *TSOM* is up to #2 again; one notch over the satirical album *Welcome to the LBJ Ranch!*

December 25, 1965

As *TSOM* spends a second week at #2, RCA needn't feel glum about its inability to hit #1 again; a *Billboard* cover story reports that the soundtrack is moving at such a "hot clip" that since its March release, it is running 500 percent ahead of the staggering sales tallies racked up back in 1958 by the *South Pacific* soundtrack during *its* first nine months. *TSOM* is clearly expected to pass the two-million mark by year's end, selling at a rate of 400,000 copies a month (domestic figures). It is also the #1 seller in the UK at this point.

All of this is impressive to note, because, as the year comes to a close, the movie is only playing in 2 percent of the potential market.

Between this date and April 30, 1966, *TSOM* soundtrack will continue to bounce around in the Top 5, sharing the numbers not only with the mighty *Whipped Cream & Other Delights* but with newcomers like *Rubber Soul* (Beatles); another Herb Alpert album (*!!Going Places!!*); Frank Sinatra's *September of My Years*; one for the pro-war supporters, *Ballads of the Green Berets* (SSgt. Barry Sadler); *Boots* (Nancy Sinatra); *Just like Us!* (Paul Revere & the Raiders); *Color Me Barbra* (Streisand); and the Rolling Stones' *Big Hits (High Tide and Green Grass)*.

1966

May 7, 1966

TSOM falls out of the Top 5 for the first time in a year; landing at #6, below *Ballads of the Green Berets*. Herb Alpert is the *Billboard* king at the time, with *!!Going Places!!* #1 and *Whipped Cream* #2.

May 28, 1966

TSOM is not the sort of album to gently slip away after spending time at the top, as is the custom with most LPs, even the biggest hits among them. Here it is back in the Top 5 (at #5); under *Color Me Barbra*. In the meantime, another Herb Alpert album reaches #1: *What Now My Love*, followed by the Mamas and the Papas' debut *If You Can Believe Your Eyes and Ears* and the Rolling Stones' *Big Hits*.

June 25, 1966

TSOM is #5, topped for the first time by the soundtrack of its strongest opposition at this past April's Oscars, *Doctor Zhivago*, which is #4. *What Now My Love* and *If You Can Believe . . .* maintain the #1 and 2 spots; *Whipped Cream* #3.

August 6, 1966

For the first time since May 1965, *TSOM* drops from the Top 10, hitting #12. The Beatles' *Yesterday and Today* is the #1 LP for the week; Frank Sinatra's *Strangers in the Night* is #2.

August 13, 1966

Still resilient, *TSOM* jumps up to #10. *Yesterday and Today* is #1; *Zhivago* is #5; *Aftermath* by the Stones is #2.

Sept. 10, 1966

TSOM is back at #5, an incredible rebound under any circumstances. It falls directly under *Somewhere My Love* (Ray Conniff Singers), which not only contains the famous love theme from *Doctor Zhivago* (this week's #2 LP) indicated in the title, but has renditions of two *TSOM* numbers, "Edelweiss" and "So Long, Farewell"; the Beatles' newest, *Revolver*, is presently at #1.

　　TSOM will remain in the Top 5 until October 15, 1966 (when it will dip to #7), and leave the Top 10 on October 29, 1966 (when it will move into the #13 slot).

November 19, 1966

While *TSOM* manages yet another return to the Top 10, the debut album by the Monkees reaches #1, thereby trading places with the previous week's #1, the *Doctor Zhivago* soundtrack.

　　[*Note:* Variety *reported LP sales of* TSOM *had already reached 3,000,000 copies and was selling at a rate of 100,000 a week.*]

December 10, 1966

Once again, holidays sales are no doubt instrumental in bringing *TSOM* back into the Top 5, at #4! *The Monkees* (#1); *Zhivago* (#2).

　　TSOM will stick around in the top 5 again, until February 4, 1967, drop out for a week, and return there again on February 18th.

　　Billboard lists it as the #2 Top LP of 1966, behind *Whipped Cream & Other Delights.*

1967

February 25, 1967

TSOM is #7; the pop group of the moment, The Monkees, still dominates at both #1 & 2 (*More of the Monkees* and *The Monkees*); Frank Sinatra's *That's Life* moves above *TSOM* into #6.

　　From this date until June 3rd, *TSOM* will stubbornly retain a spot in the Top 10. June 3rd also marks the highest chart position for the latest Julie Andrews musical soundtrack, *Thoroughly Modern Millie*, which will only climb as high as #16 before beginning its descent.

June 10–September 30, 1967

TSOM retains some position between 12 and 20 during this time on the chart, most of which is dominated by the Beatles' *Sgt. Pepper's Lonely Hearts Club Band* becoming #1 starting on July 1, 1967.

October 7, 1967

TSOM hits its lowest position since April 3, 1965, landing at #29, while *Sgt. Pepper* continues to hold at #1.

October 28, 1967

TSOM bounds back into the Top 20 again, specifically hitting the #19 position. At the time, *Diana Ross and the Supremes Greatest Hits* is #1, *Sgt. Pepper* #2.

And things are going to get even better eight weeks down the line!

December 16, 1967

For the third year in a row, *TSOM* benefits from the holiday shopping sales, making another return to the Top 10, landing at #8. The Monkees' fourth album, *Pisces, Capricorn, Aquarius & Jones, Ltd.* is the #1 record, with *Supremes Greatest Hits* #2.

December 23, 1967

TSOM reaches the #7 spot, two years, nine months, and twenty-one days after it first hit stores, and will remain there for another four weeks. After that it will finally begin to drop out of the high numbers and continue to descend, albeit slowly. The Monkees and the Supremes stay in their leading positions.

According to *Billboard*'s annual figures, *TSOM* soundtrack is ranked as the fourth top LP of 1967, following *More of the Monkees, The Monkees,* and *Doctor Zhivago.*

1968

January 20, 1968

TSOM drops to #19, directly below the soundtrack for *Camelot* (another show Julie Andrews had done on stage and yet was passed over for the film adaptation).

After another three weeks, *TSOM* will finally bid goodbye to the Top 20.

March 2, 1968

This marks exactly three years since the release of the movie and the soundtrack. *TSOM* celebrates this anniversary by ranking at #21 on the *Billboard* charts. This week *Paul Mauriat and His Orchestra—Blooming Hits* (containing the hit single "Love Is Blue") is #1 and Bob Dylan's *John Wesley Harding* is #2.

At this point, the *TSOM* LP has spent 155 weeks on the charts. (As Herb Alpert's *Whipped Cream & Other Delights* is currently ranked at #44, and therefore under the coveted Top 40, this means that no other record in the Top 40 comes close to *Sound of Music*'s longevity.)

May 11, 1968

TSOM leaves the Top 40 for the first time in more than three years, dipping to #41. The soundtrack for *The Graduate* is currently the country's #1 LP. By the end of that movie's run it will take second place after *The Sound of Music* as the most popular motion picture of the 1960s.

December 14, 1968
This week's ranking of #86 is the lowest for *TSOM* during this year.

December 28, 1968
As 1968 comes to a close, *TSOM* is ranked at #65.

1969

May 17, 1969
After spending the first four months of 1969 dropping to various numbers between 100 and 200, *TSOM* finally disappears off the *Billboard* Top 200 chart, four years and two months after its debut there.

Top-Selling Soundtracks

According to *Variety*, the top-selling soundtrack LPs for the following years were:

1965
1. *Mary Poppins*
2. **The Sound of Music**
3. *My Fair Lady*
4. *Goldfinger*
5. *West Side Story*

1966
1. **The Sound of Music**
2. *Doctor Zhivago*
3. *Mary Poppins*
4. *My Fair Lady*
5. *Zorba the Greek*

1967
1. *Doctor Zhivago*
2. **The Sound of Music**
3. *A Man and a Woman*
4. *The Wild Angels*
5. *Thoroughly Modern Millie*

1968
1. *The Graduate*
2. **The Sound of Music**
3. *Camelot*
4. *The Good, the Bad and the Ugly*
5. *The Jungle Book*

Note

In the fall of 1972, after Ode Records (a subsidiary of A&M) claimed that Carole King's *Tapestry* had become the biggest-selling LP in history with 5,600,000 copies sold, RCA disputed this claim. As far as they were concerned, US sales for *The Sound of Music* soundtrack stood at that time at 6,000,000 copies. Internationally, they were approaching 13,000,000 copies.

The first TV showing of *The Sound of Music*, in February 1976, resulted in another 500,000 copies of the soundtrack being sold. RCA claimed at that point a worldwide total of 15,500,000 albums sold to date since its debut in March 1965 (according to *Variety*, May 5, 1976).

UK CHARTS

If the success of the soundtrack for *The Sound of Music* was a further verification of the movie's place in 1960s pop cultural history in America, the LP was even more phenomenal on the UK charts. Two weeks after the film's March 29, 1965 London opening, the album made its first appearance on their charts and would remain a staple in the Top 40 for a stunning span of time, finally bidding farewell in February 1973, by which time the entire film and music industry had gone through a head-spinning transition in terms of look, sound, audience demographics, thematic approach to material, and cultural impact. Despite all this, *TSOM* remained beloved and highly desirable for record buyers.

April 10, 1965
The Sound of Music LP reaches the UK Top 20 for the first time on April 10, 1965, landing at #17, one position above *Another Side of Bob Dylan*, three below the *Mary Poppins* soundtrack, and three notches above the *My Fair Lady* soundtrack. The #1 record at the time was *The Rolling Stones Vol. 2*; the second position was held by *Beatles for Sale*.

April 17, 1965
TSOM makes its first appearance in the Top 10, at #9, one position over *Mary Poppins*. Top of the charts is *The Freewheelin' Bob Dylan*.

May 8, 1965
TSOM ends up in the Top 5 for the first time, hitting #4. From this point until April 27, 1968, just short of three years by a week, *Sound of Music* will stay at some position or another in the Top 5. When it first appeared here, *Beatles for Sale* was #1.

June 5, 1965–August 7, 1965
Less than two months after its first UK chart appearance, *TSOM* becomes the #1 album in the country. It will continue to hold the top spot through August 7, 1965.

August 14, 1965
Starting on this date, *TSOM* relinquished the top spot to the Beatles' *Help!* for several weeks, but it was not down yet.

For the next two months, starting on August 21, all of the top three positions are held by movie-related LPs, with *TSOM* at #2 and *Mary Poppins* #3.

October 16, 1965–December 18, 1965
TSOM returns to #1 for this two-month stretch.

February 19, 1966–April 23, 1966
July 2, 1966–August 6, 1966
October 1, 1966–January 28, 1967
March 25, 1967–May 6, 1967
During each of these periods, *TSOM* was the UK's #1 album. On all other weeks during this time it could be found in the #2 position.

May 20, 1967
June 3, 1967
Back at #1 for these two separate weeks. The week between *TSOM* was #2 (when *More of the Monkees* was #1).

June 10, 1967
For the first time in more than two years, *TSOM* was neither in the #1 or 2 positions, dropping to #3, under the Beatles' *Sgt. Pepper's Lonely Hearts Club Band* (#1) and Jimi Hendrix's *Are You Experienced* (#2)

November 18, 1967
After five months fluctuating between 2 and 3, *TSOM* is back at #1; *Sgt. Pepper's* is #2.

December 2, 1967–December 16, 1967
For another three-week stretch, *TSOM* is #1 again.

January 27, 1968
For what will be the last time for some months, *TSOM* reaches the #1 position on the UK album charts. It will stay at some position in the Top 5 through April 20, 1968.

April 27, 1968
TSOM drops out of the Top 5, landing at #6. From now until August 10, 1968, it will stay at various positions in the Top 10.

August 17, 1968
While this date marks the first time *TSOM* leaves the Top 10 in three years and four months, it does not stay at #11 for long, bouncing up to #8 the following week. From this point through November 16, 1968, it will mainly be a Top 10 staple, with occasional dips to #11.

November 23, 1968
Amazingly and unexpectedly, *TSOM* finds itself right back in the #1 position, ten months after it had last appeared there. Although this might lead one to believe that it is unbeatable, it will mark the last time it appears in the leading spot. That this has happened three years and `
seven months after its chart debut cannot be underestimated in its accomplishment.

November 30, 1968—February 1, 1969

TSOM never leaves the Top 5 during this period.

February 15, 1969
March 1, 1969
March 8, 1969

TSOM reaches #2 for these three weeks.

March 29, 1969

Exactly four years to the day that *TSOM* opened in London, the soundtrack can boast of *still* being in the Top 10 of the UK album charts, holding position #6. The soundtrack of another popular musical has joined *TSOM* in the Top 10 during this period, *Oliver!*, which this week is directly below *Sound*, at #7.

April 5, 1969–April 25, 1970

Over the course of the next year, *TSOM* will remain in the Top 20, including its highest peak during this period, January 10, 1970, when it reaches #5.

May 2, 1970
December 26, 1970
January 2, 1971

TSOM hits its lowest position since entering the charts more than five years ago, being at #23. This dip is not permanent, as the album once again proves resilient in ways other records can't even hope to emulate. After spending months moving up and down between positions in the Top 20 and those in the Top 40, it rebounds sensationally at the holiday season, ending 1970 (December 26) and beginning 1971 (January 2) in the #5 spot.

January 8, 1972

Throughout 1971 and 1972, *TSOM* remains pretty consistently on the Top 40 chart, spending certain weeks off the chart only to jump back on it. Its last high position is reaching #16 on January 8, 1972.

February 3, 1973

TSOM appears at #39 on this week and then finally falls off the Top 40 chart for good. It winds up spending nearly eight full years as a chart regular in the UK. Its success is so tremendous that it is listed as the second best-selling album in the UK during the 1960s; the top position going to *Sgt. Pepper's Lonely Hearts Club Band*. Beatles albums also hold the #3 and 4 positions, *With the Beatles* and *Abbey Road*.

REISSUE

The 1994 CD reissue of the soundtrack included cuts that were not available on the original LP, put the songs back in the correct order in which they were performed in the movie, and contained the following tracks (those not credited to characters singing are instrumental):

1. Twentieth Century Fox Fanfare with CinemaScope Extension (Alfred Newman, 1954) (0:21)
2. Prelude and The Sound of Music (Maria) (3:28)
3. Main Title (2:40)
4. Preludium - (Dixit Dominus) – Morning Hymn –Alleluia (Nuns Chorus) (3:07)
5. Maria (Nuns Chorus) (3:13)
6. I Have Confidence (Maria) (3:41)
7. Sixteen Going on Seventeen (Rolf and Liesl) (4:53)
8. My Favorite Things (Maria) (2:30)
9. Salzburg Montage (1:53)
10. Do-Re-Mi (Maria and the Children) (5:32)
11. The Sound of Music (reprise) (The Children and the Captain) (2:10)
12. The Lonely Goatherd (Maria and the Children) (3:22)
13. Edelweiss (The Captain and Liesl) (2:17)
14. Grand Waltz (2:19)
15. Laendler (2:34)
16. So Long, Farewell (The Children) (2:58)
17. Processional Waltz (1:19)
18. Goodbye Maria/How Can Love Survive? (1:17)
19. Edelweiss Waltz (Act 1 Finale) (1:05)
20. Entr'acte (2:07)
21. Climb Ev'ry Mountain (Mother Abbess) (2:37)
22. Something Good (Maria and the Captain) (3:51)
23. Processional and Maria (Organ Intro with Nuns Chorus) (2:46)
24. Sixteen Going on Seventeen (reprise) (Maria and Liesl) (3:04)
25. Do-Re-Mi (reprise) (Maria, The Captain and the Children) (0:56)
26. Edelweiss (reprise) (The Captain, Maria, the Children and Chorus) (2:01)
27. Nuns and Nazis (2:39)
28. Escape/Climb Ev'ry Mountain (reprise/finale) (Chorus) (2:08)
29. End Title (0:38)

(Despite the effort to present a more complete representation of the movie's soundtrack, this CD still leaves out the Salzburg festival reprises of "My Favorite Things" and "So Long, Farewell.")

Richard Rodgers listens happily as Mary Martin, Theodore Bikel, and the children record the cast album for *The Sound of Music.*

ORIGINAL BROADWAY CAST ALBUM

The enthusiastic public response to both the movie of *The Sound of Music* and its soundtrack album certainly owes a debt of gratitude to not only the original Broadway show but its cast album, which proved one of the all-time highest-selling in this area.

The Sound of Music Original Broadway Cast

Columbia Masterworks
Produced for records by Goddard Lieberson; Engineers: Fred Plaut, Bud Graham.
Theodore Bikel appears courtesy of Elektra Records
Recorded at Columbia 30th Street Studios, November 22, 1959. (Previously the Adams-Parkhurst Memorial Presbyterian Church, this building, located at 207 East 30th Street in New York City, had been a recording studio since 1949.)

Side 1
1. Preludium (Orchestra, Nuns) (2:19)
2. The Sound of Music (Mary Martin) (2:43)
3. Maria (Patricia Neway, Muriel O'Malley, Elizabeth Howell, Karen Shepard) (3:24)
4. My Favorite Things (Mary Martin, Patricia Neway) (2:50)
5. Do-Re-Mi (Mary Martin, Children) (5:56)

6. Sixteen Going on Seventeen (Lauri Peters, Brian Davies) (3:52)
7. The Lonely Goatherd (Mary Martin, Children) (3:23)
8. How Can Love Survive (Marion Marlowe, Kurt Kasznar) (3:04)

Side 2
1. The Sound of Music (reprise) (Mary Martin, Children, Theodore Bikel) (3:15)
2. Laendler (Orchestra) (2:26)
3. So Long, Farewell (Children) (2:53)
4. Climb Ev'ry Mountain (Patricia Neway) (3:33)
5. No Way to Stop It (Theodore Bikel, Kurt Kasznar, Marion Marlowe) (3:07)
6. An Ordinary Couple (Mary Martin, Theodore Bikel) (3:38)
7. Processional (Nuns) (3:51)
8. Sixteen Going on Seventeen (reprise) (Mary Martin, Lauri Peters) (2:19)
9. Edelweiss (Theodore Bikel) (2:08)
10. Climb Ev'ry Mountain (Company) (1:40)

December 21, 1959
A little more than a month after its Broadway opening, *TSOM* cast album entered the Billboard Top 50 mono charts on this date, reaching #40. This certainly could not have been unexpected as Rodgers and Hammerstein were *well* represented there already, with the *South Pacific* soundtrack #4, the *Oklahoma!* soundtrack #33, the *South Pacific* cast album #41, and *The King and I* soundtrack #44. Only recently there had been appearances on the charts by the *Flower Drum Song* cast album and Richard Rodgers' music for the television series *Victory at Sea* (Volume 2), as well.

At the time of the *SOM* cast album debut, *Here We Go Again!* by the Kingston Trio was #1.

January 4, 1960
TSOM cracks the Top 10 on the mono charts for the first time, landing at #9.

January 11, 1960
TSOM is #7 on the mono charts but arrives on the stereo charts for the first time with an even more impressive positioning, #4.

Week ending January 29, 1960
TSOM becomes the #1 album on the stereo charts, while reaching #3 in mono.

February 12, 1960——
week ending April 22, 1960
Despite the fact that *TSOM* has been seen by only those with access to New York and lucky enough to get tickets during the show's very well-attended first three months, the cast album becomes the #1 record in the United States on both the mono and stereo charts. It will stay in this position on both charts through April 22, 1960.

April 29, 1960
This marks the final time *TSOM* cast album was ranked at #1 on the mono charts.

May 6, 1960
May 13, 1960

These two dates mark the last time *TSOM* cast album will be #1 on the stereo charts.

- At sixteen weeks, *TSOM* became the longest-charting #1 album of 1960; it also entered the record books as the Broadway cast album to stay longest in the top spot.
- The September 20, 1961 *Variety* announced that the cast album had hit the 1,000,000 sales mark, making this the third Rodgers and Hammerstein cast album to do so, following Decca's *Oklahoma!* and Columbia's *South Pacific*. (The soundtracks for *South Pacific* on RCA and *Oklahoma!* on Capitol had also passed 1,000,000 in sales.)
- The 1961 Columbia Masterworks compilation *This Is Broadway's Best,* a two-record set of great show-stoppers (B2W 1), included Mary Martin's recording of "The Lonely Goatherd" among its tracks. The cover of the album featured Al Hirschfeld caricatures, including one of Martin, Theodore Bikel, and Patricia Neway in *The Sound of Music,* but also featured an illustration of Martin in *South Pacific,* despite the fact that the track chosen from that show for this LP was "Some Enchanted Evening," sung by Ezio Pinza.

UK CAST ALBUM

Recorded May 28, 1961
His Master's Voice CSD 1365; His Master's Voice CLP 1453; EMI Regal/Star Line SRS 5003; Musical Director: Robert Lowe; Producer: Norman Newell

CAST: Jean Bayless (Maria), Roger Dann (Captain), Constance Shacklock (Mother

This ad for the Columbia Masterworks recording of *The Sound of Music* Broadway cast album could be found in many a playbill in 1960.

This EP of the original London cast album featured four of the numbers from the full cast LP: "The Sound of Music," "Sixteen Going on Seventeen," "Climb Ev'ry Mountain," and "The Lonely Goatherd."

The Australian cast album of the show slipped up when it came to spelling the name of one of its authors, Russel Crouse having only one "L" in his first name.

Abbess), Eunice Gayson (Elsa), Harold Kasket (Max), Barbara Brown (Liesl), Nicholas Bennett (Rolf)

There was also a 45 EP (7EG 8733) released with four songs from this recording:
Side 1: "The Sound of Music" and "You Are Sixteen"
Side 2: "Climb Ev'ry Mountain" and "The Lonely Goatherd"

AUSTRALIAN CAST ALBUM

The Sound of Music, Garnet H. Carroll presents June Bronhill and the original Australian cast

The Australian cast album marked the first time an LP had been made by the Australian cast of a Broadway musical. It was recorded three days after the opening of the show live on the stage of the Princess Theatre in Melbourne.
Musical Director: Eric Clapham.
Entire Production Directed by Charles Hickman
His Master's Voice/OCSD 7580 (Stereo) OCLP 7580 (Mono)
Released: November 16, 1961
    This was released on CD with June Bronhill's studio recordings of several of the songs, as well as separate recordings made by various artists.

Additional Cast Recordings:

1965

The Sound of Music Original Dutch Cast

Philips 625 821 QL
Johan Heesters, Mieke Bos, Teddy Scholten, Maria Ballings, Guus Verstraete
Conductor: Co van der Heide Wijma
Translated by Louis Dussee, Alfred Pleiter

1976

Música original de: La Novicia Rebelde (Mexican Cast Album)

Orfeón LP-13-2226
Lupita D'Alessio (Maria), Enrique Alvarez Felix (Captain von Trapp), Marta Felix (Mother Abbess)

1981

The Sound of Music

London revival cast recording
Epic EPC 70212

CAST: Petula Clark (Maria), Michael Jayston (Captain von Trapp), June Bronhill (Mother Abbess), Honor Blackman (Elsa), John Bennett (Max), Clare Parker (Liesl), Paul Shearstone (Rolf

This became the first *TSOM* cast album to include the two songs from the movie, "I Have Confidence" and "Something Good," the latter replacing "An Ordinary Couple." Rather than sing "My Favorite Things" in the Mother Abbess's office, as in the original show, "A Bell Is No Bell" was inserted here.

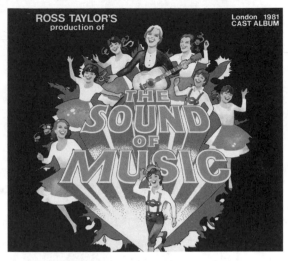

The original London cast album for the highly successful 1981 West End revival, starring Petula Clark.

1983

The Sound of Music

Australian Cast Recording
His Master's Voice OCSD 7580

CAST: Julie Anthony (Maria), Peter Bishop (Rolf), Pat Pitney (Liesl), Bartholomew John (Captain von Trapp), Anthea Moller (Mother Abbess), David Ravenswood (Max), Penelope Richards (Elsa), Judy Glenn, Isabel Townsend, Wendy de Beyer (Nuns)

EMI EMX-123
For this second Australian cast album, the script now allows for the two movie songs ("Something Good" replacing "An Ordinary Couple") and keeping two of the songs dropped from the film.

This version played for a season in Sydney and then toured major and regional centers.

1998

The Sound of Music: The New Broadway Cast Recording

RCA Victor CD

CAST: Rebecca Luker (Maria), Michael Sibbery (Captain von Trapp), Patti Cohenour (Mother Abbess), Fred Applegate (Max), Jan Maxwell (Elsa), Sara

Zelle (Liesl), Dashiell Eaves (Rolfe), Matthew Ballinger (Kurt), Andrea Bowen (Marta), Natalie Hall (Louisa), Ryan Hopkins (Friedrich), Ashley Rose Orr (Gretl),Tracy Allison Walsh (Brigitta)

"Something Good" replaces "An Ordinary Couple."

1999

The Sound of Music

Live Australian Cast Recording
BMG Intl.

CAST: Lisa McCune (Maria), John Waters (Captain von Trapp), Tim Draxl (Rolf), Eilene Hannan (Mother Abbess), Bert Newton (Max), Pia Morley (Liesl)

There was a 1999–2000 tour production starting in Sydney at the Lyric Theatre in November 1999 through February 2000; this was based on the 1998 Broadway revival. Tour continued at: Princess Theatre in Melbourne, March 21–July 5, 2000; Brisbane (9 weeks), and Perth (August 3, 2000, 6 weeks), Adelaide.

Listen to *The Sound*

The Sound of Music-Related Recordings

I t seemed for a period throughout the sixties that record stores were simply filled with *The Sound of Music*, in some form or another. Apart from the 1959 Columbia cast album and the 1965 RCA soundtrack (not to mention the British and Australian cast albums), here is a wide sampling of albums offering selections from the Rodgers and Hammerstein score, as well as LPs (and singles) by certain artists who saw fit to include a song (or two) from *TSOM* among their playlist.

1959

Alfred Newman Conducts Selections from Fiorello/The Sound of Music

Orchestrations: Ken Darby, Alfred Newman.
Capitol ST 1343
Side 2: "The Sound of Music"/"Do-Re-Mi"/"My Favorite Things"/"Climb Ev'ry Mountain"/"Sixteen Going on Seventeen"/"Maria"

In an unexpected tie, both of these shows ended up the winner of the Tony Award for Best Musical, so it is fitting they got to share an album.
Between 1940 and 1960 Newman served as the music director for 20th Century-Fox Studios. He received a record 9 Academy Awards in the scoring categories.

Hits from The Sound of Music

Various Artists
Phillips 435 165BE, BBE 12437 UK
"Sixteen Going on Seventeen," Leslie Uggams (Orchestra conducted by Frank De Vol)

Originally released as a 45: Columbia, 4-41531, w/"My Favorite Things." Uggams was indeed sixteen at the time she recorded this tune. She would sing it on the January 27, 1961 debut episode of *Sing Along with Mitch*, on which she was a regular.

"Climb Ev'ry Mountain," Tony Bennett (w/Frank De Vol conducting the orchestra and chorus) Originally released as a 45 "B" side: Columbia 4-415201, w/"Ask Anyone in Love" and later featured on the 1962 Bennett album *Mr. Broadway: Tony's Greatest Broadway Hits.*

"Do-Re-Mi," Mitch Miller (and the kids from *The Sound of Music* and the Sing-a-long chorus) Originally released as a 45: Columbia 4-41499)

"The Sound of Music," Doris Day (conductor: Frank De Vol) Originally released as a 45: Columbia 4-41542; w/"Heart Full of Love")

This EP threw together four separate Columbia recordings of songs from *TSOM.* Most interesting is Doris Day being one of the first vocalists to record the title song. When Fox purchased the rights to the show, Richard Rodgers assumed that Day would be the front-runner to play Maria in the movie version.

Music from Rodgers and Hammerstein's The Sound of Music

Norman Paris Quartet
Harmony Records HL-7235
    Side 1: "The Sound of Music"/"Maria"/"Sixteen Going on Seventeen"/"How Can Love Survive"/"My Favorite Things"
    Side 2: "Do-Re-Mi"/"So Long, Farewell"/"An Ordinary Couple"/"No Way to Stop It"/"Climb Ev'ry Mountain"
    Paris and his musicians later contributed to the live-action/film attraction "Wonderful World of Chemistry" at the New York World's Fair (1964–65).

The New Rodgers and Hammerstein Musical: The Sound of Music

Manny Klein and His Sextet
w/Manny Klein (trumpet); Bobby Hammack (piano), Morty Corb (bass), Robert Gibbons, Al Hendricks (guitars), Ronnie Lang (saxophone), Irving Cottler (drums), Frank Flynn (xylophone, bongos); Heinie Beau and Bobby Hammack, arrangers
Imperial Records 12038
    Side 1: "How Can Love Survive"/"Maria"/"An Ordinary Couple"/"Do-Re-Mi"/"The Lonely Goatherd"
    Side 2: "My Favorite Things"/"The Sound of Music"/"No Way to Stop It"/"Climb Ev'ry Mountain"/"Sixteen Going on Seventeen"
    This album was recorded on October 22–23, 1959, *before* the Broadway opening.
    Arriving five years before the celebrated John Coltrane track, this was the first released jazz recording of "My Favorite Things."
    Manny Klein had ghosted Montgomery Clift's bugle playing in the 1953 Oscar-winning film *From Here to Eternity.*

The Pete King Chorale Sings the Songs from the Rodgers & Hammerstein Musical The Sound of Music

Kapp Records KL-1175

Side 1: "The Sound of Music"/"My Favorite Things"/"The Lonely Goatherd"/"Sixteen Going on Seventeen"/"No Way to Stop It"/"Climb Ev'ry Mountain"

Side 2: "Do-Re-Mi"/"Maria"/"Edelweiss"/"How Can Love Survive"/"An Ordinary Couple"/"Climb Ev'ry Mountain" (reprise)

Arranger-conductor King released "My Favorite Things" as a Christmas 45 (K360-X) backed by "Little Shepherd Boy" in November 1960. It seemed that King was prescient in adapting this song as a holiday standard, as many future artists would do. This record received a Grammy nomination for Best Performance by a Chorus.

Rodgers and Hammerstein's New Musical The Sound of Music

"With a Great Broadway Vocal Cast"
Orchestra and Chorus conducted by William Carlisle
TOPS Records L1626 (Later issued on Mayfair Records 9626S-A)

Side 1: Overture/"Climb Ev'ry Mountain" (Alice Knight)/"The Lonely Goatherd" (Karen Leslie and the Children's Chorus)/"Sixteen Going on Seventeen" (Gerald Mann, Leslie)/"So Long, Farewell" (Children's Chorus)/"My Favorite Things" (Leslie, Babette George)

Side 2: "The Sound of Music" (Leslie)/"Maria" (George, Knight)/"How Can Love Survive" (Steve Morton, George)/"Do-Re-Mi" (Leslie, Children's Chorus)/"An Ordinary Couple" (Morton, George)

This studio recording does not assign specific roles to its singers; therefore Karen Leslie ends up singing Maria's part on the title song and "Lonely Goatherd," and yet also does Liesl's vocals on "Sixteen . . . ." Similarly, Babette George can be heard taking on the Mother Abbess part on "My Favorite Things," as well as playing Maria on "An Ordinary Couple."

According to the back of the LP, "TOPS presentation of *The Sound of Music* represents the unmistakable quality of lasting listening pleasure." This Los Angeles–based record label specialized

One of the cheaper *Sound of Music* LP knock-offs, this was made available principally in supermarkets.

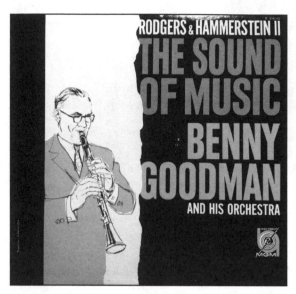

One of the very first albums to feature renditions of the Rodgers and Hammerstein score was recorded by the "King of Swing," Benny Goodman.

in releasing cheaper priced recordings to grocery stores, five-and-dimes, and other such places.

The Sound of Music: Benny Goodman and His Orchestra

MGM E3810

Side 1: "No Way to Stop It"/"Sixteen Going on Seventeen"/"So Long, Farewell"/ "Climb Ev'ry Mountain"

Side 2: "The Sound of Music"/"My Favorite Things"/"An Ordinary Couple"/"Maria"/"Do-Re-Mi"

Recorded November 20, 1959 in New York, only days after the Broadway show's opening.

The Sounds of a Thousand Strings Play Rodgers & Hammerstein's The Sound of Music

Conductor: Robert Kent
Performers: Janice Bryant, John Paige, Robert Kent Chorus
Crown Records CLP 5135

Side 1: Overture/"The Sound of Music"/"The Lonely Goat Herd"/"My Favorite Things"/"An Ordinary Couple"

Side 2: "16 Going on 17"/"How Can Love Survive?"/"Climb Every Mountain"/"Maria"/"So Long, Farewell" (listed as "Hello Farewell")/"Do-Re-Mi"

Not to be confused with 101 Strings, this was a studio orchestra that released records for Crown between 1958 and 1964.

Broadway Playbill: The Sound of Music/Gypsy/Fiorello

The Hi-Lo's
Performers: Clark Burroughs, Bob Morse, Gene Puerling, Don Shelton
Conductor: Warren Barker
Columbia CS 8213

Side 2: "My Favorite Things"/"The Sound of Music"/"Climb Ev'ry Mountain" (Side 2 is sharing with thee *Fiorello* songs)

The famous a cappella quartet formed in 1953 had just replaced original member and baritone Bob Strasen with Don Shelton.

1960

The Best from the Broadway Productions Fiorello! and The Sound of Music

Florence Henderson with Sid Bass, His Orchestra and Chorus
Camden CAL-599

Side 2: "The Sound of Music"/"Do-Re-Mi"/"The Lonely Goatherd"/"My Favorite Things"/"Climb Ev'ry Mountain"

Henderson played Maria in the first touring company of *TSOM* starting in February 1961. This meant that she recorded highlights from the score before she played the role.

This recording was later released on CD as *Florence Henderson Sings Songs of Broadway,* a combo of this LP and the LP *Songs from Gypsy and Flower Drum Song.*

Edmundo Ros and His Orchestra: Rodgers & Hammerstein's The Sound of Music (a.k.a. "The Ros Sound of Music")

Decca KL 4391; London Records PS 198

Side 1: "The Sound of Music" (cha-cha-cha)/"An Ordinary Couple" (mambo)/"Maria" (schottish)/"Edelweiss" (merengue)/"So Long, Farewell" (bolero)/"Do Re Mi" (paso-doble)

Side 2: "My Favorite Things" (Vals Creole)/"Sixteen Going on Seventeen" (baion)/"No Way to Stop It" (samba-batuque)/"Climb Ev'ry Mountain" (bolero mambo)/"The Lonely Goatherd" (baion)/"How Can Love Survive" (marcha)

This adaptation of *TSOM* is done in Latin tempos for dancing. *The Sound of Music*'s sweep was so wide that one could even hear a cha-cha-cha version of the title song!

June Bronhill Sings The Sound of Music

(with The Williams Singers and Michael Collins and His Orchestra)
His Master's Voice HMV 7EGO 8695

Side A: "Do-Re-Mi"/"The Sound of Music"

Side B: "My Favourite Things"/"Climb Ev'ry Mountain"

This 7" EP was released prior to Bronhill playing Maria in the 1961 Australian production of *TSOM*. The back of the EP says, "We feel privileged to be able to release June's vital but unaffected interpretation of these enchanting songs."

These tracks were later featured on the CD issue of the LP *June Bronhill: The Magic of the Musical.*

The London Theater Company Presents Music and Lyrics from Rodgers & Hammerstein's The Sound of Music

Full Cast Stage Production by the London Theater Company
Richmond B20079

Side 1: "The Sound of Music"/"My Favorite Things"/"Maria"/"Do-Re-Mi"/ "The Sound of Music"

Side 2: "Climb Ev'ry Mountain"/"Sixteen Going on Seventeen"/"No Way to Stop It"/"Edelweiss"/"Climb Ev'ry Mountain"

Members of The Trapp Family Singers and Chorus Arranged and Conducted by Franz Wasner Sing and Play the Songs from the Broadway Musical Inspired by Their Life Story. Rodgers and Hammerstein's The Sound of Music

RCA Victor LSP 2277

Side 1:

Preludium/"The Sound of Music"/"Maria"/"My Favorite Things"/"Sixteen Going on Seventeen"/"The Lonely Goatherd"/ "Climb Ev'ry Mountain"

Side 2: "Do-Re-Mi"/"Laendler"/"An Ordinary Couple"/Processional and Wedding March/"Edelweiss"/"So Long, Farewell"/"Climb Ev'ry Mountain" (reprise)

(On label: Selected by the Editors of Readers Digest Music Guide)

The back of the album states: "With Father Wasner as musical director and arranger, the Trapp Family Singers were reconvened in New York in December 1959, for the recording session . . . Some came with Mrs. Trapp and Father Wasner from Stowe; others traveled from Ohio . . . ."

Despite the fact that the Trapp Family Singers made it clear that *The Sound of Music* was *not* the real story of their lives, they had no objections to recording most of its songs. Not surprisingly, the most satirical numbers, "How Can Love Survive" and "No Way to Stop It," did not fit the more serious Trapp style and were not included.

As to be expected, nearly all of the numbers are performed chorally, with the exception of "Sixteen Going on Seventeen," in which

Despite their insistence that *The Sound of Music* was *not* an accurate telling of their story, the Trapp Family Singers had no qualms about recording their version of the Rodgers and Hammerstein score.

Rolf's role is done by a solo male vocalist, while the responding Liesl part is done by *two* women. In "So Long, Farewell," each exiting child is soloed by one of the Trapps. In the "Processional and Wedding March," there is no singing of "Maria," but part of "Preludium" is revised instead. To show off their prowess with their musical instruments as well, there is an instrumental track of the "Laendler."

This was later reissued on Warner Bros. Records to coincide with the 1965 movie release.

Variety: "The Trapp Family gives this music a superb rendition, enchanting in the lilt and polish of their choral arrangements."

Music from Rodgers & Hammerstein's The Sound of Music

Percy Faith and His Orchestra
Columbia CS 8215 (Reissued in 1966 as Columbia CS 8214)

Side 1: "The Sound of Music"/ "Maria"/ "My Favorite Things"/"Do-Re-Mi"/"No Way to Stop It"/"Climb Ev'ry Mountain"

Side 2: "So Long, Farewell"/"An Ordinary Couple"/"The Lonely Goatherd"/"Sixteen Going on Seventeen"/"How Can Love Survive"/"The Sound of Music" (Reprise)

A name synonymous with "easy listening," Percy Faith could boast the same year of this album's release of having the longest-charting single of 1960, "Theme from *A Summer Place*."

A compilation of Faith music from the later LP *The Sound of Music and Other Great Songs* has the title song along with

One of the stalwarts of the "easy listening" sound, Percy Faith, presents his version of the Rodgers and Hammerstein songs.

"Feelin' Groovy," "Aquarius," "Georgy Girl" "Midnight Cowboy" etc. It also was issued on a reel-to-reel w/Faith's *Camelot* album. A later album on Harmony Records, HS 11348: *Percy Faith: The Sounds of Music*, contains "The Sound of Music" and "Climb Ev'ry Mountain."

The Music from Rodgers & Hammerstein's The Sound of Music

The Paul Smith Quartet
Verve MGV 2128 (also issued on Verve MGVS 6128)

Side 1: "My Favorite Things"/"Climb Ev'ry Mountain"/ "Maria"/"The Lonely Goatherd"/"How Can Love Survive"/"The Sound of Music"

Side 2: "Edelweiss"/"So Long, Farewell"/"No Way to Stop It"/"An Ordinary Couple"/"Do-Re-Mi"

Paul Smith was a West Coast bop pianist.

Rodgers & Hammerstein's Music and Lyrics from The Sound of Music

Bob Sharples, His Orchestra and Complete Vocal Cast
Arranged and directed by Bob Sharples
Performers: Joyce Blair, Janet Waters, Roy Castle; with Bryan Johnson
Ace of Clubs ACL-1068 (This label was a UK subsidiary of Decca).

Side 1: "The Sound of Music" (Sharples Orchestra and chorus)/"My Favourite Things" (Blair)/"Maria" (chorus)/"Do-Re-Mi" (Blair & Children)/"Sixteen Going on Seventeen" (Orchestra)/"How Can Love Survive?" (Blair & Johnson)/"The Sound of Music" (Blair, Johnson, Chorus)

Side 2: "Climb Ev'ry Mountain" (chorus)/"Sixteen Going on Seventeen" (Waters, Castle)/"No Way to Stop It" (Johnson)/"The Lonely Goatherd" (Blair & Children)/"An Ordinary Couple" (Blair & Johnson)/"Edelweiss" (Johnson)/"Climb Ev'ry Mountain" (Waters & Chorus)

This was also released on London Records, LL 3179, and reissued in 1969 on Decca Eclipse.

The CD version offers additional cuts from the PYE Records release of 1961: "My Favourite Things" by Petula Clark; "Climb Ev'ry Mountain" by Dickie Valentine, "Do-Re-Mi" by Joan Regan, "The Sound of Music" by Edmund Hockridge, plus two from Decca's *Top Six Songs . . .* "Sixteen Going on Seventeen" by Mark Wynter, and "An Ordinary Couple" by Ken Dodd.

Selections from the New Broadway Musical
The Sound of Music by Rodgers and Hammerstein

Eddie Maynard and His Orchestra
Vocals: Patricia Roselle, Rosemary Hayes, Leonard Rogers
Spin-O-Rama MK-3078

Side 1: "The Sound of Music" (Roselle)/"Maria" (Rose Block, Ana Green, Babs Colon)/"Do-Re-Mi" (Roselle, Child Chorus)/"You are Sixteen" [title mistakenly listed as such] (Rogers & Green)/"My Favorite Things" (Roselle, Hayes)

Side 2: Entr'Acte (Orchestra)/"Climb Ev'ry Mountain" (Hayes)/"The Lonely Goatherd" (Roselle, Child Chorus)/"Ordinary Couple" (Walter Stiller & Roselle)/Finaletto (Orchestra)

Selections from The Sound of Music by Rodgers & Hammerstein

Dale Davis and His Orchestra
Vocals: Janet Anderson, Marion Garvey
Diplomat DS 2344

Side 1: "The Sound of Music"/"Climb Every Mountain" (spelled as such on the LP)/"My Favorite Things"/"Do-Re-Mi"

Side 2: "Sixteen Going on Seventeen"/"An Ordinary Couple"/"The Lonely Goat Herd"/"Maria"

The Sound of Music: Music Richard Rodgers, Lyrics Oscar Hammerstein II

John Senati and His Orchestra featuring Bill Jacob (piano)
Bravo Pops Symphony Orchestra
Bravo K 139 (also issued on Grand Prix KS 139)
    Side A: "The Sound of Music"/"Maria"/"My Favorite Things"/"Do-Re-Mi"
    Side B: "Sixteen Going on Seventeen"/"How Can Love Survive"/"So Long, Farewell"/"An Ordinary Couple"/"Climb Ev'ry Mountain"

The Sound of Music—Richard Hayman & His Orchestra

Mercury Wing SRW 16228 (also issued as Fontana, SFL 13009)
    Side 1: "The Sound of Music"/"Maria"/"My Favorite Things"/"Do-Re-Mi"/"Sixteen Going on Seventeen"
    Side 2: "Climb Ev'ry Mountain"/"An Ordinary Couple"/"No Way to Stop It"/"Edelweiss"/"So Long, Farewell"
    According to the liner notes, "Richard Hayman saw a dress rehearsal early in November, shortly before the opening. Hayman was so impressed by the entire production that he established a goal of trying to emulate instrumentally all the emotion and finesse which each of the cast imparted to their respective roles."
    The back of the album actually has descriptions of how each of the songs was performed in the show, including mention of which actors were playing the key roles on stage. Therefore, it is a bit misleading, making one believe Mary Martin and Theodore Bikel might be on the record.

The Songs from Rodgers and Hammerstein's The Sound of Music: The Complete Album

Soloists, Chorus, and Orchestra Directed by Russ Case
Performed by Gigi Durston and others
Rondo-lette Records SA 156
    Side 1: Overture/"The Sound of Music"/"Maria"/"My Favorite Things"/"Do-Re-Mi"/"Sixteen Going on Seventeen" (billed on label as being performcd by Teen Agers)/"The Lonely Goatherd"
    Side 2: "How Can Love Survive"/"So Long Farewell"/"Climb Ev'ry Mountain"/"No Way to Stop It"/"An Ordinary Couple"/"Edelweiss"/Finale
    Nightclub singer Gigi Durston had been a regular on an early CBS series, *The Sonny Kendis Show.*

The Sound of Music, Rodgers & Hammerstein, a Jazz Version Starring the Mitchell-Ruff Duo

(pianist) Dwike Mitchell, (bassist) Willie Ruff
Roulette R-52037

Side 1: "The Sound of Music"/"Climb Ev'ry Mountain"/"My Favorite Things"
Side 2: "Do-Re-Mi"/"The Lonely Goat Herd"/"Sixteen Going on Seventeen"/"An Ordinary Couple"

This duo was noted for defying Russian taboos, performing an unofficial, impromptu jazz concert at the Tchaikovsky Conservatory in Moscow in 1959.

1961

Dance to "The Sound of Music" and to the Other "Sound of Music" by Richard Rodgers

Tommy Kinsman and His Orchestra
Arranged by Bernard Ebbinghouse
Fontana 680 948, TL STFL 5139 UK

Side 1 is devoted to *TSOM*, with three medleys: two for quicksteps and one for foxtrots (only the title song is used in each).

Edmund Hockridge, Petula Clark, Dickie Valentine, Joan Regan (and the Children) Sing Hit Songs from The Sound of Music

The Peter Knight Orchestra and Chorus
PYE NEP 24138

EP w/Side 1: "The Sound of Music" (Hockridge)/"My Favourite Things" (Clark)
Side 2: "Climb Ev'ry Mountain" (Valentine)/"Do-Re-Mi" (Regan)

Petula Clark would get her chance to sing "My Favourite Things" in the context of the show when she played Maria in the 1981 London stage revival of *TSOM*.

The Six Top Songs from The Sound of Music

Performers: Eve Boswell, Ken Dodd, David Hughes, Bryan Johnson, Diane Todd, Mark Wynter
Conductor: Roland Shaw.
Decca DFE 6676 (45 single)

Side A: "The Sound of Music" (Hughes)/"My Favorite Things" (Todd)/"Sixteen Going on Seventeen" (Wynter & Todd)
Side B: "Do-Re-Mi" (Boswell)/"An Ordinary Couple" (Dodd)/"Climb Ev'ry Mountain" (Johnson)

These tracks were later featured on CD collections.

Songs from the Musical The Sound of Music; Music by Richard Rodgers; Lyrics by Oscar Hammerstein 2nd

Conductor: John Gregory
Artists: Andy Cole, Paul Rich, Iris Villiers

Embassy WEP 1060 (UK EP)

Side 1: "The Sound of Music" (Villiers)/"Sixteen Going on Seventeen" (Rich)/"My Favorite Things" (Villiers)

Side 2: "Climb Ev'ry Mountain" (Cole)/"Edelweiss" (Rich)/"Do-Re-Mi" (Villiers)

These tracks were later included on *Vocal Gems from Four Great Musicals, Album 2.*

The Sound of Music/Flower Drum Song

Senator Singers, Chorus and Orchestra

Senator Records WSR 822

Side 1: "The Sound of Music"/"Sixteen Going on Seventeen"/"My Favourite Things"/"Climb Ev'ry Mountain"/"Edelweiss"/"Do-Re-Mi"

Side 2: Eight songs from *Flower Drum Song*

1962

Rodgers & Hammerstein's Sound of Music

Ensemble and Orchestra of the Broadway Light Opera Society

Conductor: Frank Y. Bennett; performers: Jean Cook Robert Kerns, Glade Peterson

Concert Hall Records CM-2255

Side A: Overture/"The Sound of Music"/"Do-Re-Mi"/"Sixteen Going on Seventeen"

Side B: "How Can Love Survive"/"Climb Ev'ry Mountain"/"No Way to Stop It"/"An Ordinary Couple"/"My Favourite Things"

These three singers had done a studio cast recording of *Oklahoma!* as well.

The Sound of Music

Various

World Record Club LM 93 (also issued as World Record Club ST-89) (UK)

Side 1: Prelude and "The Sound of Music" (Adele Leigh and girl chorus)/"Maria" (Patricia Johnson, Barbara Elsy, Pauline Stevens and girl chorus)/"My Favourite Things" (Leigh, Johnson)/"Do-Re-Mi" (Leigh and the Aida Foster Children)/"Sixteen Going on Seventeen" (Peter Gilmore and Patricia Lynn)/"The Lonely Goatherd" (Leigh and girl chorus)

Side 2: "How Can Love Survive" (Maggie Fitzgibbon, William Dickie)/"Climb Ev'ry Mountain" (Johnson and chorus)/"No Way to Stop It" (Ian Wallace, Dickie, Fitzgibbon)/"An Ordinary Couple" (Leigh, Wallace)/"Edelweiss" (Wallace)/Finale (chorus)

Al Goodman conducted this Design Records LP of *The Sound of Music* score under the pseudonym Dean Franconi.

The Sound of Music

Dean Franconi, Conductor, The Sound Stage Orchestra
Performers: Bill Heyer, Jane A. Johnston
Design DLP-135
José Benard Directing the Children's Chorus
(Also released on: International Award Series KIA-1019; and Stereo Spectrum Records SDLP-135-A)

Side 1: "The Sound of Music" (Johnston)/"Maria" (Heyer)/"My Favorite Things" (Johnston)/"Do-Re-Mi" (Johnston & Children's Chorus)/"Sixteen Going on Seventeen" (Johnston & Heyer)

Side 2: "How Can Love Survive?" (Johnston, Heyer)/"So Long, Farewell" (Children's Chorus)/"An Ordinary Couple" (Johnston, Heyer)/"Climb Ev'ry Mountain" (Johnston, Heyer)/Finale

The back of the record says, "Here is your Christmas present for this year, and a great one it is. *The Sound of Music* is a charming, and what's most important, a great musical show."

Unlike most other *TSOM* records, this one does not bother to assign multiple singers to the different characters; Johnston covers all the women, Maria, Liesl, and Elsa; while Heyer takes the parts of the captain, Max, and Rolf. Since Heyer sings "Climb Ev'ry Mountain" with Johnston, he is presumably filling in for the Mother Abbess as well (!).

Franconi was a pseudonym for Al Goodman, who conducted many such LPs in this vein, covering everything from *Oklahoma!* and *The King and I* to *West Side Story* and *Born Free.*

The Sound of Music

Music Director: Jimmy Warren, conducting the New York Revue Orchestra
Performers: Steve Jackson, Carole Martin, with supporting soloists
Fidelio TLA-9080 (also issued as Summit TLA 9080 and Fidelio ATL 4080)

Side 1: Overture/"The Sound of Music"/"My Favorite Things"/"An Ordinary Couple"/"Do-Re-Mi"

Side 2: "Maria"/"Sixteen Going on Seventeen"/" Can Love Survive"/"Climb Every Mountain"/"So Long, Farewell"

Warren directed similar albums of *The King and I, Oklahoma!*, and *South Pacific* among others.

1963

Rodgers & Hammerstein: The Sound of Music

Complete Studio Production with Frances Boyd, Ann Gordon, Jan de Silva, Rudy Cartier, Louis Mencken, Paul Mason and the Broadway Theatre Orchestra and Chorus; Fritz Wallberg, music director
GM 129 EP
  Side 1: "The Sound of Music"/"Maria"/"The Lonely Goatherd"
  Side 2: "My Favourite Things"/"An Ordinary Couple"/"Climb Ev'ry Mountain"
  This was record 5 of the series *Library of Great Music* that included *Oklahoma!*
  Later issued in 1965 with additional tracks as an LP, with the "My Favorite Things" scene from the movie on the cover.
  Society SOC 945
  Side 1: Overture/"The Sound of Music"/"Maria"/"My Favourite Things"/"Do-Re-Mi"
  Side 2: "Sixteen Going on Seventeen"/"The Lonely Goatherd"/"So Long, Farewell"/"Climb Ev'ry Mountain"/Finale

1964

The Sound of Music International Pop Orchestra

110 Musicians with the Cheltenham Chorus
Wyncote SW 9076
  Side 1: "The Sound of Music"/"My Favorite Things"
  Side 2: "Do-Re-Mi"/"Climb Ev'ry Mountain"

Rodgers & Hammerstein's The Sound of Music

Dimitri's Hollywood Orchestra & Chorus
Clarion Records SD 602
[Note: Titles are as listed on the back of the album.]
  Side 1: Overture/"The Sound of Music"/"Goat Herd"/"My Favorite Things"/"Ordinary People" [this error inadvertently references Robert Redford's future directorial debut]/"16 Going on 17"
  Side 2: "How Can Love Survive"/"Climb Every Mountain"/"Maria"/"Hello Farewell"/"Do Re Mi"
  Dimitri refers to Dimitri Tiomkin, the Oscar-winning composer of such film scores as *High Noon, The High and the Mighty,* and *The Old Man and the Sea.*

1965

The Groovy Sound of Music

Gary Burton
RCA Victor LSP-3360
    Side A: "Climb Ev'ry Mountain"/"Maria"/"An Ordinary Couple"/"My Favorite Things"
    Side B: "Sixteen Going on Seventeen"/"Do-Re-Mi"/"Edelweiss"/"The Sound of Music"
    Who says the sisters of Nonnberg Abbey can't be groovy? A jazz record arranged by Gary Burton and Gary McFarland, this was released by the same label as the movie's soundtrack, RCA.

The orchestral sounds of the Living Strings tackled many musical scores, including *The Sound of Music*.

Music from The Sound of Music

Living Strings
Orchestrator: Johnny Douglas
    RCA Camden CAS-869 (Stereo), CAS-869 (Mono)
Side 1: Overture/"Maria"/"My Favorite Things"/"Do-Re-Mi"/"Climb Ev'ry Mountain"
    Side 2: "The Sound of Music"/"Sixteen Going on Seventeen"/"Something Good"/"Edelweiss"/"I Have Confidence"
    The back of the album informs you that the overture blends "The Sound of Music" with "Do-Re-Mi," "An Ordinary Couple," "Lonely," "Laendler" *more* "Sound of Music," and "Climb Ev'ry Mountain." This appears to be the first *TSOM*-related album to feature "I Have Confidence."
    Said *Variety* of the R&H score, "It seems to be tailor-made for the Living Strings' sound and it emerges as a memorable listening experience."

Music from Rodgers & Hammerstein's New Musical Play The Sound of Music

The Stratford Strings
Recorded in Europe
Decca/Vocalion DL 78975
    Side 1: "Sound of Music"/"Maria"/"My Favourite Things"/"Sixteen Going on Seventeen"/"Do-Re-Mi"/"Lonely Goatherd"
    Side 2: "How Can Our Love Survive" [mistakenly listed as such, with the additional "Our" thrown in]/"So Long, Farewell"/"Edelweiss"/"No Way to Stop It"/"Ordinary Couple"/"Climb Every Mountain"

Phase 4 Stereo Spectacular: Rodgers and Hammerstein's The Sound of Music

Ted Heath and His Music
Arranged by Roland Shaw (UK)
Decca PFS 4065 (also a version on London Records SP 44063)

Side 1: "Do-Re-Mi"/"The Sound of Music"/"Sixteen Going on Seventeen"/
"Preludium" (spelled "Praeludium" on back cover, but correctly on the label on
the London records version)/"How Can Love Survive?"/"The Lonely Goatherd"

Side 2: "My Favourite Things"/"Climb Ev'ry Mountain"/"An Ordinary
Couple"/"Something Good"/Finale

This LP makes room for both "An Ordinary Couple" and the song that
replaced it in the movie, "Something Good." There is no rendition of "I Have
Confidence," however.

Said *Variety* of the big band interpretation of the score, "This is a standout
stereo instrumental display on the R&H score . . ."

The Sound of Music

Happy Time Children's Chorus
Happy Time HT- 1035

Side 1: "The Sound of Music"/"Maria"/"My Favorite Things"/"Do-Re-Mi"/
"Sixteen Going on Seventeen"

Side 2: "How Can Love Survive"/"So Long, Farewell"/"An Ordinary
Couple"/"Climb Ev'ry Mountain"/Finale

For this LP aimed at the very young, there is no mention on the cover of
the two men responsible for the score; nor is there any indication of who is
singing what. Curiously, "An Ordinary Couple" and "How Can Love Survive"
are retained for the youngsters to sing.

The Sound of Music

Mike Sammes Singers
MFP Records MFP 1007
Singers: Maureen Hartley, Shirley Chapman, Richard Loaring, Heather Bishop,
Charles West; Conductor: Sam Fonteyn

Side 1: Preludium and "The Sound of Music" "Maria" (Hartley, Singers)/"Do-
Re-Mi" (Hartley, Children)/"My Favourite Things" (Hartley, Chapman)/"Sixteen
Going on Seventeen" (Loaring, Bishop)

Side 2: "The Lonely Goatherd" (Hartley, Children)/"Climb Ev'ry Mountain"
(Chapman)/"An Ordinary Couple" (Hartley, West)/"Edelweiss" (West)/Finish:
"Climb Ev'ry Mountain" (Chapman, Children)

This LP by British vocal session arranger Mike Sammes was of interest
because it featured Richard Loaring singing the role of Rolf, which he had first
played during the original West End run of *TSOM*. (also issued as Regal (EMI)
SREG 1003 UK and Capitol DT-91034)

Another helping of *The Sound of Music* score, this time by jazz pianist Eddie Cano.

The Sound of Music and the Sound of Cano

Music Director and Performer: Eddie Cano w/Eddie Cano (piano), Tony Reyes (bass), Fred Aguirre (drums and tymps), Eddie Talamantes (congas), Manuel Lopez (maracas), Carlos Mejia (bongos)
Reprise RS 6145
    Side 1: "The Sound of Music"/ "Do-Re-Mi"/"An Ordinary Couple"/"Maria"/ "Sixteen Going on Seventeen"/ "No Way to Stop It"
    Side 2: "My Favorite Things"/ "Climb Ev'ry Mountain"/"The Lonely Goatherd"/"Something Good"/"Edelweiss"/ "How Can Love Survive"

Cano was an Afro-Cuban Latin jazz pianist. Another LP that has both "An Ordinary Couple" and the song that replaced it in the movie, "Something Good."

The Sound of Music

The Parris Mitchell Strings Orchestra & Voices
Allegro ALL-777 (UK)
    Side 1: "The Sound of Music"/"Maria"/"My Favorite Things"/"Do-Re-Mi"/ "Sixteen Going on Seventeen"
    Side 2: "The Lonely Goatherd"/"How Can Love Survive"/"So Long, Farewell"/"Climb Ev'ry Mountain"/"No Way to Stop It"
    Highlights were also released as the EP *Do-Re-Mi Song from "TSOM"* with a rather garish Julie Andrews–looking illustration on the cover; this had: Side A: "Do-Re-Me"/"So Long, Farewell"; Side B: "The Lonely Goatherd"/"My Favourite Things" (Pickwick MP9005).
    This is also a Bravo! EP; BR348 in UK (1965) w/Side A: "The Sound of Music"/"My Favourite Things"; Side B: "Do-Re-Mi"/"Climb Ev'ry Mountain."

The Two Piano Sound of Derek and Ray Playing The Sound of Music and Other Richard Rodgers Hits

Derek Smith and Ray Cohen
Arranged and Conducted by Marty Gold
RCA Victor LSP-3353
    Side 1: "The Sound of Music"/"My Favorite Things"/"Do-Re-Mi"/"Climb Ev'ry Mountain"/"Edelweiss"/"Sixteen Going on Seventeen"

1966

Favorite Songs from The Sound of Music

The Sound Stage Chorus
Somerset Records SF- 23300

Side 1: "The Sound of Music"/"Do-Re-Mi"/"My Favorite Things"/"Sixteen Going on Seventeen"/"Climb Ev'ry Mountain"

Side 2 contains "songs of the Great American West and Favorites of the Deep South"

This was also released on Alshire records w/*Mary Poppins* songs on the flip side. That time the singers were billed as the Hollywood Soundstage Chorus. It was also released on Oscar Records (OS-112).

Mary Martin Tells the Story and Sings the Songs of Rodgers and Hammerstein's The Sound of Music

Robert Lowe and His Orchestra
Producer: Tutti Camarata
Disneyland ST 3936

(Also released as *Mary Martin Songs from The Sound of Music*, STER 1296, and as *Mary Martin Sings The Sound of Music, Rodgers and Hammerstein*, DQ 1296).

Side 1: "The Sound of Music"/"A Bell Is No Bell"/"My Favorite Things"/"Do-Re-Mi"/"The Sound of Music" (reprise; by the Children with Captain von Trapp)

Side 2: "The Lonely Goatherd"/ "So Long, Farewell"/ "Edelweiss"/"A Bell Is No Bell" (finale)

This was originally released with cover and booklet illustrations by Harry Wysocki; it was also released with two additional covers: one with just the title, and a contemporary illustration of kids on hilltop, with a fortress in the background.

Back of LP says: "Book by Howard Lindsay and Russell (misspelled with an extra "L") Crouse; and that "Because of Mary Martin's current stage commitments as the lead in *Hello, Dolly!* this recording was made in London." The text erroneously states that since the Broadway show's original run, Mary Martin has starred on not only radio and television but "screen" as well. (Following *Main Street to Broadway*

To cash in on the success of the movie, Disney hired *The Sound of Music*'s original Maria, Mary Martin, to both sing the score and tell the story for young listeners.

Disneyland Records offered this more adult-friendly version of Mary Martin's second recording of the show, concentrating on the songs.

A British recording of the score starred Anne Rogers as Maria and Patricia Routledge as the Mother Abbess.

in 1952, Martin would never again appear in a motion picture.)

Of interest is the inclusion of the introduction to the reprise of "Sixteen Going on Seventeen," treated like its own song, "A Bell Is No Bell," and sung twice. This verse meant a great deal to Martin, as she was handed the lyrics by Oscar Hammerstein privately during the rehearsals of *TSOM* and took the message to heart, singing it whenever possible.

The Sound of Music

Conductor: Alyn Ainsworth; Producer: Norman Newell.
Performers: Anne Rogers and Patricia Routledge.
Fanfare SIT 60008 (UK)
    Side 1: "The Sound of Music" (Rogers)/ "Maria" (Routledge, Lorraine Smith, Gloria Farndell, Janette Gail)/"I Have Confidence" (Rogers)/"Sixteen Going on Seventeen" (Ray Cornell, Kay Frazer)/"My Favourite Things" (Rogers)/"Climb Ev'ry Mountain" (Routledge)
    Side 2: "The Lonely Goatherd" (Rogers and Children's Chorus)/"Something Good" (Rogers, Gordon Traynor)/ "Do-Re-Mi" (Rogers & Children's Chorus)/"Edelweiss" (Traynor, Rogers, Children)/"So Long, Farewell" (Children)/"Climb Ev'ry Mountain" (reprise) (Routledge, Smith, Farndell, Gail)
    Ainsworth also released records of *West Side Story, My Fair Lady,* and *The Green Berets.* He was the conductor/arranger for several West End Shows, including *Gentlemen Prefer Blondes, A Funny Thing Happened . . . ,* and *Hello, Dolly!,* and orchestrated *The Roar of the Greasepaint.*
    This was also issued on Woman Privilege Records (AZ1): *Anne Rogers in Rodgers & Hammerstein's Sound of Music with Patricia Routledge,* and on the Music for Pleasure label, MFP 1255.

The Sound of Music

John Wakeford, Anita Sinclair, Diana Hope and Ann Drummond with the Times Square Theatre Chorus and Orchestra; Conductor: Hans Flynn
Saga ERO-8105 (UK)
   Side 1: Overture/"The Sound of Music"/"The Lonely Goat Herd" [accidentally listed as two words]/"My Favourite Things"/"An Ordinary Couple"/"Sixteen Going on Seventeen"
   Side 2: "How Can Love Survive"/"Climb Ev'ry Mountain"/"Maria"/"Farewell" [Note: listed as such on the LP]/"Do-Re-Mi"/"Maria"/"Climb Ev'ry Mountain Finale"
   Insomuch as it features an actual photo from the movie on the cover, it is curious that this album chooses to include two songs *not* heard on screen.

The Sound Stage Chorus and the Cinema Stage Orchestra Present Favourite Songs & Music from The Sound of Music and Doctor Zhivago

Marble Arch MAL 697 (Australia)
(also issued as *Favourite Songs and Music from "TSOM" and "Doctor Zhivago"* on Astor GGS 801)
Recorded under the direction of D. L. Miller
   Side A: "The Sound of Music"/"Do-Re-Mi"/"My Favourite Things"/"Sixteen Going on Seventeen"/"Climb Ev'ry Mountain"

1967

Dance to the Sound of Music with Phil Tate & His Orchestra

CBS EP6335 (UK EP)
Side 1: "The Sound of Music" (Foxtrot)/"Climb Ev'ry Mountain" (Foxtrot)
Side 2: "Do-Re-Mi" (Quickstep)/"Edelweiss" (Waltz)
Phil Tate was a British bandleader and composer.

The Denver Opera Foundation, Helen G. Bonflia, President, Presents Wynne Miller and Bob Wright in The Sound of Music

Denver Opera Foundation CM7205
Music Director: Max Di Julio

CAST: Wynne Miller (Maria), Bob Wright (Captain), Caroline Hobson (Mother Abbess), Loretta Curry (Elsa Schraeder), Anthony Del Signore (Max Detweiler), Kathy Savio (Liesl), Richard Hanson (Rolf)

   Side 1: Preludium (Dixit Dominus) and "The Sound of Music"/"Maria"/"My Favorite Things"/"Do-Re-Mi"/"Sixteen Going on Seventeen"/"Lonely Goatherd"

Side 2: Laendler/"How Can Love Survive"/"The Sound of Music" (reprise)/"Climb Ev'ry Mountain"/"No Way to Stop It"/"An Ordinary Couple"/Procession/"Sixteen Going on Seventeen" (reprise)/"Edelweiss"/Finale—"Climb Ev'ry Mountain"

Recorded on July 16, 1967 in Denver's Cheesman Park.

Roy Budd Is . . . The Sound of Music

PYE Records NPL-18195 (UK)
Music Director: Johnny Harris

Side 1: "The Sound of Music"/"Maria"/"Sixteen Going on Seventeen"/"My Favorite Things"/"Edelweiss"/"The Sound of Music" (reprise)

Side 2: "I Have Confidence"/"Something Good"/"Do-Re-Mi"/"The Lonely Goatherd"/"So Long, Farewell"/"Climb Ev'ry Mountain."

Budd was a British Jazz pianist and composer.

1968

Symphonic Pictures of Lerner & Loewe's My Fair Lady and Rodgers & Hammerstein's The Sound of Music

William Steinberg and the Pittsburgh Symphony Orchestra
Orchestrated by Robert Russell Bennett
Command Records/Command Classics/ABC 11041 SD

Side 1 contains *My Fair Lady.*

Side 2: "The Sound of Music"/"Climb Ev'ry Mountain"/"My Favorite Things"/"Edelweiss"

1969

The Sound of Music à GoGo

The Jack First Band
Arranged by Jacques Ysaye
Studio 33 Records 11001 (UK Release: Avenue Records AVE 11002)

Side 1: "No Way to Stop It"/"Edelweiss"/"The Sound of Music"/"My Favourite Things"/"An Ordinary Couple"/"Sixteen Going on Seventeen"

Side 2: "How Can Love Survive?"/"Climb Ev'ry Mountain"/"Do-Re-Mi"/"Something Good"/"The Lonely Goatherd"/"Maria"

This Dutch jazz album arrived late in the run of *TSOM* knock-offs.

1987

The Sound of Music

Studio Cast Recording
Erich Kunzel and the Cincinnati Pops Orchestra
The movie's Rolf, Dan Truhitte, is included on the chorus of this recording
Telarc CD 80162

CAST: Frederica von Stade (Maria), Eileen Farrell (Mother Abbess), Hakan Hagegard (Captain von Trapp), Barbara Daniels (Elsa), Lewis Dahle von Schlanbusch (Max Detweiler), Jeanne Menke (Liesl), Neil Jones (Rolf), Devon Biere (Friedrich), Michelle Kear (Louisa), Vincent Lee (Kurt), Heather McFadden (Brigitta), Heather Harpenau (Marta), Lauren Frederick (Gretl), Kimberly Barber (Sister Sophia), Sandra Graham (Sister Margaretta), Janet Stubbs (Sister Berthe)

This is a full recording of all the music from the show and the film.

Nature Music, "The Sound of Music"; 2) The Abbey Bells; 3) Mono Chant; 4) Morning Hymns; 5) Angelus Bells; 6) "Alleluia"; 7) "Maria"; 8) "My Favorite Things"; 9) "I Have Confidence"; 10) "Do-Re-Mi"; 11) "Sixteen Going on Seventeen"; 12) "The Lonely Goatherd"; 13) "How Can Love Survive?"; 14) "The Sound of Music"; 15) Party Scene: The Grand Waltz; "Laendler"; 16) "So Long, Farewell"; 17) "Climb Ev'ry Mountain"; 18) "No Way to Stop It"; 19) "An Ordinary Couple"; 20) "Something Good"; 21) Processional/ Confitemini Domino/"Alleluia"; 22) "Sixteen Going on Seventeen" (Reprise); 23) "Do-Re-Mi" (reprise; 24) "Edelweiss"; 25) "So Long, Farewell"; 26) "Climb Ev'ry Mountain"

1993

The Sound of Music

Starring Denis Quilley, Liz Robertson, Linda Hibberd; also featuring: The Master Singers
Studio cast recording
Matthew Freeman conductor
Carlton PWKS 4145 (part of *The Show Collection*; also released as *Songs from The Sound of Music* in 2009 on Pickwick)
    1) "The Sound of Music" (Robertson); 2) Morning Hymn/Alleluia (Master Singers); 3) "Maria" (Master Singers); 4) "I Have Confidence" (Robertson); 5) "Sixteen Going on Seventeen" (Elizabeth Simmons, Simon Clarke); 6) "My Favourite Things" (Robertson); 7) "Climb Ev'ry Mountain" (Hibberd); 8) "The Lonely Goatherd" (Robertson); 9) "Do-Re-Mi" (Robertson); 10) "Something Good" (Robertson, Quilley); 11) "Edelweiss" (Quilley); 12) "So Long, Farewell" (Robertson,

Quilley); 13) "Climb Ev'ry Mountain" (reprise) (West End Concert Orchestra)

The 2002 version from Pulse (PLS CD 571) gives Robertson top billing, with Quilley shunted to third place.

The CD's Maria, Robertson, was the widow of lyricist Alan Jay Lerner.

1995

The Hills Are Alive

The Angstones

Canal Records B003M6C3M2

1) Prelude; 2) "Climb Ev'ry Mountain"; 3) "Do-Re-Mi"; 4) "The Lonely Goatherd"; 5) "Something Good"; 6) "My Favourite Things"; 7) "The Sound of Music"; 8) "I Have Confidence"; 9) "Maria"; 10) "Edelweiss"; 11) "Sixteen Going on Seventeen"; 12) "So Long, Farewell"

An off-kilter Ottawa band, whose style it was to give their own unorthodox sound to folk and show music and more, the Angstones released their none-too-serious version of the songs from *The Sound of Music*, including the two from the film. Sometimes they stick close to Oscar Hammerstein II's real lyrics, others, like "Climb Ev'ry Mountain," which goes for a hip hop sound, and "My Favourite Things," which pays tribute to several jazz artists ("great timeless classics from Miles and from Coltrane"), take their own path. As part of their cheeky image, the cover featured three Angstones in lederhosen and one dressed as Maria, complete with swinging guitar case. The lettering of the title also echoed that done for the movie's advertising.

Band member Peter Kiesewalter later founded the Brooklyn Rundfunk Orkestrata, who, in turn, did *their* version of the score in an album of the same name (see 2011).

1999

Forever Sound of Music

"Classics from the musical remodeled for the dance floor"

Lora Munro

Rumour/Almighty CDKOPY 176

Disc 1: "Sound of Music" (Original Mix)/"Lonely Goatherd" (Klubkidz Mash-up Mix by DJ J Saint James; sung with Sound of Music Kids)/"Edelweiss" (Lora Munro & Jason Prince)/"So Long, Farewell" (Munro & Kids)/"Climb Ev'ry Mountain"/"Maria"/"Sixteen Going on Seventeen" (Munro & Prince)/"My Favourite Things"/"Do-Re-Mi"

Disc 2: Klubkidz Mash-up Mix by DJ J Saint James: "Lonely Goatherd" (Munro & Kids)/"So Long, Farewell" (Munro & Kids)/"Edelweiss" (Munro & Prince)/"Sound of Music"/"Climb Ev'ry Mountain"/"Maria"/"Sixteen Going on Seventeen" (Munro & Prince)/"Do-Re-Mi"/"My Favourite Things"

Yes, you can at last dance to "Edelweiss" with a disco beat! There was also a 2007 recording, *The Sound of Lora Munro*, that featured "Do-Re-Mi" and "My Favourite Things," not just straightforward but in a Mountain High Mix for the former and a Crispy Strudel Mix for the latter.

2008

The Sound of Music

Carola & Tommy Körberg
Sony 7411654
Lyrics translated by Lars Sjöberg
1) "The Sound of Music" (Carola); 2) "Det Bästa Jag Vet (My Favorite Things)" (Carola); 3) "Edelweiss" (Tommy); 4) "Do-Re-Mi" (Carola); 5) "Dur Är Sexton (Sixteen Going on Seventeen)" (Carola & Tommy); 6) "Visan Om Vallpojken (The Lonely Goatherd)" (Carola); 7) "Något Gott (Something Good)" (Carola & Tommy); 8) "Jag Tror På Mej (I Have Confidence)" (Carola); 9) "Kärleken Kan Dö (How Can Love Survive)"; 10) "Avskedsviasn (So Long, Farewell)" (Carola & Tommy Körberg); 11) "Sök Dig Till Bergen (Climb Ev'ry Mountain)" (Tommy)
Singer-actor Tommy Körberg, who had played Captain von Trapp in the 1995 Swedish production of *TSOM*, teamed with pop singer Carola (full name Carola Häggkvist) to present most of the songs from the show in their native language. Both movie songs are included, as is "How Can Love Survive," but there is no room for "No Way to Stop It" or "Maria."

2011

The Harry Allen Quintet Plays Music from "The Sound of Music"

Joe Cohn (guitar), Rossano Sportiello (pianist), Joel Forbes (bass), Chuck Riggs (drums); Vocalists: Rebecca Kilgore, Eddie Erickson
Arbors Records ARCD 19410
This jazz CD features the two movie songs as well as the three dropped from the Broadway original, although there is no room for the "Preludium."

The Hills Are Alive

Brooklyn Rundfunk Orkestrata (BRO)
Canal Records B004JP4EUY
Peter Kiesewalter, late of the Angstones (see 1995), returned to *The Sound of Music* with another funky reimagining of the score, this time with his new group, the Brooklyn Rundunk Orkestrata. In addition to featuring the two movie songs, this CD also finds room for "No Way to Stop It." This time the cover features a goat staring directly at you, amid the Austrian mountains.
1) "The Sound of Music"; 2) "Do-Re-Mi" (a mash-up with the Jackson 5's

"ABC" by Alphonzo Mizell, Berry Gordy, Deke Richards, and Freddie Perren); 3) "Something Good"; 4) "Edelweiss on High" (w/Ola Belle Reed); 5) "The Lonely Goatherd"; 6) "Maria"; 7) "Climb Ev'ry Mountain"; 8) "My Favorite Things"; 9) "No Way to Stop It"; 10) "I Have Confidence"; 11) "Sixteen Going on Seventeen"; 12) "So Long, Farewell"

Kiesewalter was featured in a January 6, 2011 article in the *Wall Street Journal* about his extensive collection of *The Sound of Music* memorabilia.

Dates Unknown:
The Best of the Sound of Music & West Side Story

The Scarborough Strings and Orchestra
SuperScope Stereo Reel-to-Reel Tape, 3-A020-N
Program 1: "The Sound of Music"/"My Favorite Things"/"Do-Re-Mi"/"An Ordinary Couple"/"Somewhere" (on the wrong side)
Program 2 is *West Side Story*.
Originally recorded by the Golden Pops Orchestra for Nippon Columbia Co. Japan.

The Sound of Music

Orchestra conducted by Lewis Merritt
Children's Chorus Directed by Michael Hoffmann
Coronet Records CX-102
Side 1: Overture/"The Sound of Music"/"My Favorite Things"/"An Ordinary Couple"/"Do-Re-Mi"
Side 2: "Maria"/"Sixteen Going on Seventeen"/"How Can Love Survive"/"Climb Ev'ry Mountain"/"Farewell" (referring to "So Long, Farewell")

The Sound of Music by Rodgers and Hammerstein

The Peter Pan Orchestra
Vocals by Janet Anderson/Marian Garvey
Peter Pan Records (of Newark, NJ) 8163
Side 1: "The Sound of Music"/"Maria"/"Do-Re-Mi"/"Sixteen Going on Seventeen"/"My Favorite Things"
Side 2: "Climb Ev'ry Mountain"/"The Lonely Goat Herd" [split into two words]/"An Ordinary Couple"
A strong contender for the ickiest cover of a *Sound of Music* album, the drawing by George Peed has Maria surrounded not only by children but by bunnies and squirrels, plus a fairy tale castle in the background!

Words and Music from Rodgers and Hammerstein's The Sound of Music

California Pops Orchestra and Chorus
Custom Records CS-1033
 Side 1: Overture/"The Sound of Music"/"The Lonely Goat-herd"/"My Favorite Things"/"Ordinary People" (another LP bestowing the name of the 1980 Oscar winner on this song)/"16– Going on 17"/"How Can Love Survive"/"Climb Ev'ry Mountain"/"Maria"/"Hello Farewell" (as listed on the LP)/"Do Re Mi"

SELECT RECORDINGS THAT FEATURE INDIVIDUAL *TSOM* SONGS

1959

"Do-Re-Mi"

Anita Bryant
Carlton 523
 "Do" was the "B" side of this 45; "Promise Me a Rose" the "A" side. Before she became notorious in the 1970s for her intolerant views on gays, Bryant had played Maria in touring productions of the show. *Surely* there were no homosexuals in the cast, behind the scenes, or in the audience.
 This was later an "A" side released on London Records (HLL 9353) in the UK in 1961; "An Angel Cried" was on the flip side.

1960

An Enchanted Evening on Broadway

Earl Wrightson
Columbia CL 1519
 Broadway actor-radio singer-television host Earl Wrightson featured "Climb Ev'ry Mountain" on this LP. He would later play Captain von Trapp in productions of *TSOM* opposite Sally Ann Howes and Constance Towers.

Ferrante and Teicher Themes from Broadway Shows

Arthur Ferrante and Louis Teicher
ABC ABCS 336
 Side 1: "The Sound of Music"
 An LP featuring current Broadway songs.

Give My Regards to Broadway

Andre Previn and His Trio; Red Mitchell (bass), Frank Capp (drum)
Columbia CL 1530
    The title song is featured on side one (on the label, Hammerstein is actually billed *before* Rodgers).

"Climb Ev'ry Mountain"

The Harry Simeone Chorale
20th Fox Records 45-174
    The religious connotations of Rodgers and Hammerstein's inspiring song were made clear by Harry Simeone's decision to include this on the album *Sing We Now the Songs of Faith* (Fox 3031). The "A" side is "Onward Christian Soldiers."

Martin Denny's Exotic Sounds Visit Broadway

Liberty LRP-3161
    Revered by lovers of Tiki restaurants everywhere, Martin Denny was famous for his "exotic" lounge music sound, which he applied to the title song from *The Sound of Music* on side one of this album. He also cleared room for his renditions of "Something Wonderful" from *The King and I* and "The Carousel Waltz."

The Village of St. Bernadette

Andy Williams
Cadence CLP 3038
    Side 2 includes "Climb Ev'ry Mountain."
    The LP also features Rodgers and Hammerstein's "You'll Never Walk Alone."

You Don't Have to Be a Millionaire

Russ David
Lammerts Records LALP A-100
    St. Louis bandleader-pianist Russ David featured his easy listening version of "The Sound of Music" on this LP. Rodgers and Hart's "Mountain Greenery" launched the album.

1961

As Long as She Needs Me from the Broadway Hit "Oliver!"

Sammy Davis Jr.
Reprise R-6082

"Climb Ev'ry Mountain" is sung on side one.

This also includes Rodgers and Hart's "Falling in Love with Love" and two other Rodgers and Hammerstein songs, "We Kiss in a Shadow" and "There Is Nothing like a Dame."

"Climb Ev'ry Mountain"

Shirley Bassey
Columbia DB4685

This was considered a double A-side with "Reach for the Stars" on the flip side. "Climb" was #1 in the UK for eighteen weeks.

"Climb Ev'ry Mountain"/"The Sound of Music"

David Whitfield
Decca 45-F 11339

British tenor David Whitfield cut a single of two numbers from the show.

"Edelweiss"/"The Lonely Goatherd"

Ronnie Ranalde
Columbia DB 4644

Because English Musical Hall performer Ronnie Ranalde was noted for his yodeling, it was only fitting that he record "The Lonely Goatherd," although he chose it to be the "B" side of this 45 UK single.

Great Theme Music

Mantovani
London Records PS 224

The conductor concluded this collection with "The Sound of Music," directly after "The Carousel Waltz." (Mantovani returned to *TSOM* in 1968.)

Jane Morgan Sings Big Hits from Broadway

Kapp 1247

Nightclub singer Jane Morgan launched side two of this LP with "The Sound of Music." Side one contained three other Rodgers and Hammerstein's standards, "The Surrey with the Fringe on Top," "Hello, Young Lovers," and "You'll Never walk Alone."

My Favorite Things

John Coltrane
Atlantic Records SD-1361

A thirteen-minute, forty-seven-second jazz version of "My Favorite Things" was featured on side one of this album and soon became one of Coltrane's signature pieces. It would also appear on three more of his LPs during the 1960s: *Newport '63*; *Live at the Half Note: One Down, One Up* (1965), and *Live at the Village Vanguard Again!* (1966).

Overture American Musical Theatre: Vol. 4 1953-1960

Hugo Montenegro and Orchestra
Time Records S/2038
"Do-Re-Mi" (in medley w/"Let Me Entertain You" and "Everything's Coming Up Roses" from *Gypsy*)

"Sixteen Going on Seventeen"

Nick Bennett; with Tony Osborne and his Orchestra
Columbia 45-DB 4656
Nick Bennett played Rolf in the original London production of *TSOM*. "Call Me" is on the flip side.

The Sound Your Eyes Can Follow: Stereo Action Goes Broadway

Dick Schory's Percussion and Brass Ensemble
RCA Victor LSA 2382
Side 2 has "The Sound of Music." The LP also includes renditions of Rodgers and Hammerstein's "Bali Ha'i" and Rodgers's "Slaughter on Tenth Avenue."

The Warmth of Wynter

Mark Wynter
Decca LK4409
This British pop star included "Sixteen Going on Seventeen" (he was eighteen at the time, making him close enough to the lyrics) on this LP. He would eventually hit the Top 10 in his country with songs like "Venus in Blue Jeans" and later, as an actor, toured the UK in *South Pacific*.

After Hours

Sarah Vaughan
Roulette SR52070
The jazz vocalist started off this LP with "My Favorite Things."

1962

By Request

Perry Como
RCA Victor LMP 2567
 Side 2: "My Favorite Things"
 This track was later included on the 2001 CD compilation *A Perry Como Christmas*.
 The LP also features a rendition of Richard Rodgers's "The Sweetest Sounds" from his then-new show *No Strings*.

Coleman Hawkins Plays Make Someone Happy from Do Re Mi

Moodsville MV 31
Side 1: "Climb Every [listed this way on the cover] Mountain"
 This LP also includes "Out of My Dreams" from *Oklahoma!*
 Coleman Hawkins and his Quartet play jazz versions of these songs. Needless to say, the "Do Re Mi" referred to here is not R&H's but the 1961 Broadway musical starring Phil Silvers.

Show Souvenirs No. 3

Harry Secombe (with Willy Stott and his orchestra and chorus)
Philips BBL 7532
 Side B: "Climb Ev'ry Mountain"
 Secombe's LP contains mostly songs by Rodgers and Hammerstein, together or apart, including "The Desert Song," "Falling in Love with Love," and renditions of "Hello, Young Lovers," "This Nearly Was Mine," and "If I Loved You." (The EP version—BBE 12515—does include "Climb Ev'ry Mountain.")

25 Pianos Play Evergreens of Broadway

Tommy Garrett
Liberty SLBY 1069
 This jazz record contains a version on side 1 of "The Sound of Music." Also featured are another Rodgers and Hammerstein selection, "Bali Ha'i," Rodgers's "Carousel Waltz," and Rodgers and Hart's "Manhattan."

1963

Broadway . . . I Love You

Sergio Franchi
RCA Victor Red Seal LSC 2674

This selection of show songs includes "The Sound of Music" on side 2. There is also a recording of Richard Rodgers's "The Sweetest Sounds." (This might have served as an audition, as Franchi wound up starring in Rodgers's next Broadway musical, *Do I Hear a Waltz?*)

An Era Reborn with Helen O'Connell

"Sings Today's Hits with the Big Band Sound"
Music Director: Jack Pleis
Cameo CS1045
    Side 2: "The Sound of Music"

J. J.'s Broadway

J. J. Johnson
Verve Records V608530
    Includes "My Favorite Things." Although the concept seemed to indicate that Johnson was playing selections from *recent* Broadway hits, he snuck in "Nobody's Heart" from *By Jupiter* (1942), by Rodgers and Hart.
    The LP also includes "The Sweetest Sounds" from Rodgers's one solo Broadway effort, *No Strings*.

Joni James Sings My Favorite Things

MGM 4200
    The singer brackets this all-Richard Rodgers LP with two tunes from *TSOM*, "My Favorite Things" and the title song.

Romantically, Johnny Mathis

Columbia CL 2098
    How unexpected of the popular singer to think of romance when he recorded his version of "The Sound of Music" for this collection of love-themed songs. Rodgers and Hammerstein's "Getting to Know You" can be heard here too.

Show Stoppers from O'Keefe Center

Conductor: William McCauley
Capitol T 6040
    Side 2 includes "Climb Ev'ry Mountain."

The Three Sounds Play Jazz on Broadway

The Three Sounds: Gene Harris, Bill Dowdy, Andy Simpkins
Mercury Records MG 20776
    "Climb Ev'ry Mountain" is on side 2. (The LP also includes Rodgers's "The Sweetest Sounds.")

1964

The Jack Jones Christmas Album

Kapp Records KL-1399

Thanks to the lyrics "snowflakes that stay on my nose and eye-lashes," "silver white winters that melt into spring," and, of course, a reference to "sleigh bells," it was decided within the recording world that it was perfectly acceptable to think of "My Favorite Things" as a Christmas song. (Clearly, Oscar Hammerstein was coming up with wintery images because of the Austrian setting, not the holiday.)

Although the Pete King Chorale had released a 1960 single pitching the song as Yule-themed, Jack Jones was among the first popular soloists to include it on a Christmas album, thereby paving the way for several artists to follow suit.

During the decade it could be heard on such LPs as: *Mary Christmas* (Eddie Fisher; Dot Records; 1965), *Merry Christmas* (Diana Ross & the Supremes; Motown; 1965), *Merry Christmas* (Andy Williams; Columbia; 1965), *Have Yourself a Soulful Little Christmas* (Kenny Burrell; Verve Records; 1966), *A Christmas Album* (Barbra Streisand; Columbia; 1967), *Christmas Album* (Herb Alpert and the Tijuana Brass; A&M; 1968), *Snowfall: The Tony Bennett Christmas Album* (Columbia; 1968), *Give Me Your Love for Christmas* (Johnny Mathis; Columbia; 1969).

In fact, it thereafter was seldom included on someone's record *unless* it was a Yuletide one.

Future artists to include it on their Christmas album included: Kenny Rogers (*Christmas,* 1981); The Carpenters (*An Old-Fashioned Christmas,* 1984), Luther Vandross (*This Is Christmas,* 1995), Barry Manilow (*A Christmas Gift of Love,* 2002), Anita Baker (*Christmas Fantasy,* 2002), Dionne Warwick (*My Favorite Time of Year,* 2004), Kenny G (*The Greatest Holiday Classics,* 2005), Rod Stewart (*Sounds of the Season,* 2005), Carole King (*A Holiday Carole,* 2001), Chicago (*Chicago XXXIII: O Christmas Three,* 2011), Kelly Clarkson (*Wrapped in Red,* 2013), and Mary J. Blige (*A Mary Christmas,* 2013)

On the Street Where You Live

Vic Damone; arranged and conducted by Pete King
Capitol ST-2123

Damone sings "The Sound of Music." This Broadway-themed LP also includes Rodgers and Hammerstein's "Younger than Springtime" and Rodgers and Hart's "I Could Write a Book."

With a Smile and a Song

Doris Day, with Jimmy Joyce and His Children's Chorus;
Arranged and Conducted by Allyn Ferguson
Columbia CS 9066

On this album aimed at the children's market, the woman Richard Rodgers assumed would be getting the role of Maria in the movie, Doris Day, includes her rendition of "Do-Re-Mi" as the kick-off of side 2. (To emphasize this song, this LP was reissued in 1967 on Harmony Records in the U.S. and on Hallmark Records in the UK as *Doris Day Sings Do-Re-Mi.*)

1965

The Chipmunks Sing with Children

Alvin and the Chipmunks (Ross Bagdasarian and the Jimmy Joyce Children's Chorus)
Arrangements by Pete King
Liberty LST-7405
Side 1 begins with the Chipmunks' rendition of "Do-Re-Mi."

Curtain Time

Paul Lavalle's Band of America
RCA Victor 3403
The big brass band sound is bestowed upon the overtures to various musicals. Although it did not include such an introduction on Broadway, *The Sound of Music* is one of the tracks, using the opening credit "overture" from the screen version.

Eydie Gorme Sings the Great Songs from The Sound of Music and Other Broadway Hits

Columbia Records CL 2300
Although the title of this album would lead you to believe that *The Sound of Music* will be covered pretty thoroughly, the LP offers only three tracks from the musical, all on side 1 ("My Favorite Things," "The Sound of Music," and "Climb Ev'ry Mountain"). Gorme does, however, offer more Rodgers, with *and* without Hammerstein, on four more cuts.

The Great Songs from the Motion Pictures

Don Baker at the Organ
Kapp KS-3411
Jazz man Don Baker dedicates side 1 to *My Fair Lady*, but presents a kind of homage to the Robert Wise musicals by pairing *The Sound of Music* with *West Side Story* on side 2. *TSOM* is represented by "Climb Ev'ry Mountain," "My Favorite Things," the title song, and "Do-Re-Mi."

Moon over Naples

Billy Vaughn
Dot Records DLP 3654
When you think of Naples, you think of . . . "The Sound of Music"? Actually,

the easy-listening jazz album jumps all over the place for songs ("A Walk in the Black Forest" is here too), not being Italian-specific.

Mr. Stick Man

Pete Fountain
Coral CRL 757473
Clarinetist Pete Fountain uses "The Sound of Music" as the closing tune on his second LP.

My Kind of Broadway

Woody Herman and His Swinging Herd
Columbia CS 9157
This jazz recording includes "My Favorite Things" and "The Sound of Music," and also features Rodgers and Hammerstein's "Hello, Young Lovers" from *The King and I.*

The Robert Shaw Chorale and Orchestra on Broadway

Arrangements: Robert Russell Bennett
RCA Victor LSC-2799
TSOM's title song is among the show tunes performed by Shaw and his forty singers (with lead vocal by Florence Kopleff).

The Nearness of You

John Gary
RCA Victor LSP 3349
Another pop singer uses "The Sound of Music" for the big finale on his album.

Ray Conniff and the Singers Music from Mary Poppins
(and The Sound of Music, My Fair Lady and Other Great Movie Themes)

Columbia CS 9166
Mary Poppins receives the larger "billing" on the front of the album, and therefore the most songs (five). Side 2 features versions of "The Sound of Music," "My Favorite Things," and "Climb Ev'ry Mountain."

You'll Never Walk Alone

The Lettermen
Capitol ST2213
Apart from the title track, the trio represents R&H with "Climb Ev'ry Mountain."

The King Family Show!

Warner Bros. W1601
Although this vast tribe (thirty-five of whom are pictured on the LP cover) used "The Sound of Music" as the theme of their weekly ABC series, it is not among the tracks here, which instead include "Climb Ev'ry Mountain" and "My Favorite Things."

1966

Born Free

Roger Williams
Kapp KS-3501
This LP was notable for including pianist Roger Williams's Top 10 recording of the theme from *Born Free*, but it also contained his rendition of "Edelweiss."

Champagne on Broadway

Lawrence Welk
Dot DLP 25688
The accordion-playing bandleader features two songs from *The Sound of Music* on side 1 of this disc: the title tune and "Maria." Rodgers and Hammerstein are well represented elsewhere with tracks like "I Whistle a Happy Tune" and "If I Loved You." "The Sound of Music" also showed up on the Welk album *You'll Never Walk Alone* (Pickwick/33 Records SPC 3116) the following year.

"Climb Ev'ry Mountain"

Julie Rogers
Mercury Records MF 950
British singer Julie Rogers, who had hit the Top 10 with "The Wedding," released "Climb Ev'ry Mountain" as the "B" side of this religious-themed 45, both songs ("A" was "While the Angelus Was Singing") included on her LP *Songs of Inspiration*.

"Climb Ev'ry Mountain"

The New Silhouettes
Jaime Record Co. 1333
To herald their "comeback," the fifties do-wop group the Silhouettes recorded a single with the Rodgers and Hammerstein standard as the "A" side, backed by "We Belong Together." Both were included the following year on their LP *Get a Job* (named after their biggest hit).

Dance Medley Time

Guy Lombardo and His Royal Canadians
Decca DL74735

The maestro of New Year's Eve opens his LP with a track that combines "The Sound of Music" and "Climb Ev'ry Mountain," with Richard Rodgers's "The Sweetest Sounds" (from *No Strings*) wedged in between them. There are plenty of other Rodgers compositions on the album.

"Edelweiss"

(Tony Keeling and) the Graduates
Pye Records 7N.17201

This Irish show band reached #7 on their country's charts with this recording; the flip side is "Come a Little Closer."

"Edelweiss"

Bill and Boyd
Zodiac AZ/1030

The New Zealand pop duo released a single of "Edelweiss" with Goffin and King's "Don't Ever Change" on the flip side. They had better success cashing in on Broadway with their version of *Fiddler on the Roof*'s "If I Were a Rich Man" the following year.

I've Got a Song for You

Shirley Bassey
Sunset Records SSLP 40773

Having scored a #1 UK hit in 1961 with her version of "Climb Ev'ry Mountain," Bassey returns to the show for her final cut on this album, "The Sound of Music." (This LP was also released on United Artists Records — UAL 3545 — as *Shirley Means Bassey*.)

The Latin American Dance Sound of Cyril Stapleton

Cyril Stapleton Orchestra
Pye Records NSPL18157

The Latin jazz rhythms include the title song from *The Sound of Music* amid more expected themes like "Cielito Lindo" and "Guantanamera."

More I Cannot Wish You

Ed Ames
RCA Victor LSP-3636

Side 2 commences with "Climb Ev'ry Mountain." Ed was back with more *TSOM* material the following year.

My Favorite Things

Tennessee Ernie Ford
Capitol ST 2444
    Insomuch as it is the title of his album, Ford sings "My Favorite Things" on side 2.

My Favorite Things

Dave Brubeck Quartet
Columbia CS9237
    Although this jazz album consists mainly of tunes from Rodgers and Hart's *Jumbo* score, Brubeck launches the LP with "My Favorite Things," hence the title.

The Pipes of Stan

Stan Kann
Norman Records NL 113
    Organist Stan Kann may have concluded side 1 of this LP with "Climb Ev'ry Mountain" and begun the second side with "The Sound of Music," but that hardly earned him nationwide recognition. Instead, the same year of this album's release he began his more famous second career, guesting on *The Tonight Show* and other chat programs where he could show off his prized vacuum cleaner collection!

The Shadow of Your Smile

Arthur Lyman
HiFi Records SL-1033
    A rare opportunity to experience *TSOM* with a jazzy, semi-Polynesian lounge-sound! The Side 1 medley consists of the title song, "My Favorite Things," "Do-Re-Mi," and "Climb Ev'ry Mountain."

Somewhere My Love and Other Great Hits

Ray Conniff and the Singers
Columbia CL 2519
    This *Billboard* chart hit, which reached the #3 position, features easy listening renditions of "Edelweiss" (side 1) and "So Long, Farewell" (side 2), not to mention the title track (from *Doctor Zhivago*) and the immortal "Tie Me Kangaroo Down, Sport."
    Variety: "Another winner from the successful Conniff singers . . . a distinctive sound and blend of voices."

The Stan Getz Quartet in Paris

Verve 2304 044
    The jazz quartet presents their version of "Edelweiss."

The Stone Truth: The Living Sound of the Roy Meriwether Trio

Columbia CL 2584
This jazz trio featured "Climb Ev'ry Mountain" on side 2 of this album.

Triple Winners

The West Indian Tobacco Gay Desperadoes Steel Orchestra
Recording Artists Records RA1002
As if fated to be covered by every possible style of music, *The Sound of Music* gets featured multiple times on this reggae two-disc LP, in a medley, and then in separate renditions of "Maria" and "Edelweiss."

Connie Francis and the Kids Next Door

King Leo LES-903
Targeting this album toward a younger demographic, the pop singer leads off with "Do-Re-Mi."

1967

The Broadway Soundaroundus

Marty Gold and His Orchestra
RCA Victor LSP 3689
Side one of this album is launched with a rendition of "The Sound of Music." Although most of the selections are from hit New York shows, the LP also contains two numbers from the notorious flop version of *Breakfast at Tiffany's*, here called *Holly Golightly*.

"Climb Ev'ry Mountain"

Madeline Bell
Phillips BF 1596
Newark-born soul singer Bell made her career in England, where her singles include this *TSOM* tune backed by "It Makes No Difference Now."

Edelweiss

Vince Hill; with the Eddie Lester Singers
Columbia SCX 6141
The LP opens with "The Sound of Music" and ends with "Edelweiss." The single of the latter became a #2 hit in England and Hill's signature tune.

"Edelweiss"

Udo Jürgens
Ariola 19 650 AU

Proving that not all Germans rejected *TSOM*, pop singer-songwriter Udo Jürgens released "Edelweiss" as the "A" side of this single. The "Maria" on the flip side was not Rodgers and Hammerstein's tune, however, but Leonard Bernstein and Stephen Sondheim's song from *West Side Story*.

Hammonds in Harmony

The Hammond Brothers
Columbia Studio 2 244

The first track on side 2 of this organ orgy consists of a medley of *TSOM* hits: the title song, "Do-Re-Mi," "My Favourite Things," "Edelweiss," and "The Lonely Goatherd." The rest of that side is also a nod to a Julie Andrews musical, consisting of a medley from *Mary Poppins*. (These tracks would later appear on a version of the LP released on Broadway records called *Play Sexy Hammond*.)

More

Billy Vaughn & His Orchestra
Pickwick SPC-3074

Orchestra leader Billy Vaughn featured "Climb Ev'ry Mountain" on side 1 of this LP.

Music from Million Dollar Shows

Boston Pops, with Arthur Fiedler
RCA Victor Red Seal LSC 2965

The conductor selects four Broadway shows to tribute, three with lyrics by Alan Jay Lerner: *On a Clear Day You Can See Forever, My Fair Lady*, and *Camelot*; with Rodgers and Hammerstein's *The Sound of Music* saved for last. A medley from the show consists of the title song, "How Can Love Survive," "The Lonely Goatherd," "My Favorite Things," "Sixteen Going on Seventeen," "So Long, Farewell," "Do-Re-Mi," "Edelweiss," "An Ordinary Couple," "No Way to Stop It," "Maria," and "Climb Ev'ry Mountain."

Two years later, when Fiedler and the Pops offered a nine-LP boxed set, *Pops Varieties*, courtesy of Reader's Digest (RD4-98), the medley took up most of side 5 (with Rodgers's "Slaughter on Tenth Avenue"). This set allowed you to have both Bach's Concert No. 5 in F Minor *and* the theme from *Bonanza* in one package.

Fiedler later dusted off this medley for his 1971 *Fiedler's Favorites for Children* (VCS 7080), a two-LP collection on which side 2 of the first album was dominated by this piece. This meant that *TSOM* was firmly equated in the minds of many with something very wholesome and suitable for children, even the unloved number from the Broadway original, "An Ordinary Couple," which probably wasn't being sung *too* frequently on playgrounds during the previous decade. "The Sound of Music" was also heard on the 1971 release *Fiedler on the Roof*

Fiedler resurrected the medley yet again for his two-LP compilation, *Classics of the American Musical Theatre, Vol 1.* (R233594) in 1971.

My Cup Runneth Over

Ed Ames
RCA Victor LPM 3774
The singer ends this album with his rendition of "Edelweiss."

On Broadway

Four Tops
Motown M 657
The rhythm & blues quartet features "Climb Ev'ry Mountain" on side 1 of this collection of *mostly* Broadway tunes, and "The Sound of Music" as the opening of side 2.

Patricia . . . with Love

Patricia Cahill
Rex LPR 1007
The Irish songstress trills on "The Lonely Goatherd" (which opens the album) and "Climb Ev'ry Mountain," which, as translated in Irish, loses the apostrophe and becomes the more formal "Climb Every Mountain" on the track listing.

A Whiter Shade of Pale

Mellow Fruitfulness
Columbia SX6164
Here's one way *The Sound of Music did* fit into the countercultural psychedelic movement of the late sixties. Presenting instrumentals performed on C3 & M100 Hammond Organs, this LP offers tracks that sound as if they might be providing musical background for a head shop, including a version of "Climb Ev'ry Mountain." According to the liner notes, this album "pours forth its soul in ecstasy" and if that doesn't convince you that it's groovy, some European issues of the album were renamed *Flower Power.*

1968

It Must Be Him

Al Caiola
United Artists UAL 3637
 This includes "The Sound of Music."
 Guitarist Al Caiola was a frequently employed studio musician.

The Mantovani Touch

Mantovani and His Orchestra
London PS 526
 The popular Italian-born, British-raised conductor of easy listening sounds included "Edelweiss" on side 2 of this LP. He had already included his rendition of "The Sound of Music" on an earlier album (see 1961).

Rodgers and Hammerstein Favourites

John Hanson
Phillips SBL 7835
 The Canadian-born British tenor released an entire LP of R&H standards, including "Edelweiss" and "Climb Ev'ry Mountain" on side 2. Hanson had his biggest West End success in a revival of *The Desert Song*.

Sand & Steel

The Rising Sun [Treasure Cove] Steel Band
Trojan Records TRLS 4 (UK)
 This Jamaican steel band allows *TSOM* fans to hear calypso versions of "Do-Re-Mi" and "The Lonely Goatherd."

Sweet & Swinging Hits of the 60s

The Geraldo Singers & Orchestra
Major Minor Records MMLP 24
 Presumably falling into the "sweet" category, "The Sound of Music" is included on British bandleader Geraldo's (Gerald Walcan Bright) salute to the decade.

1969

The Andy Williams Sound of Music

Columbia CS 9752
 This double LP is actually a compilation album of previous recordings. The only new one made especially for the record is the first cut, Andy's version of "The Sound of Music."

Cliff Live at the Talk of the Town

Cliff Richard
Starline SRS 5031

British pop legend Cliff Richard included "Something Good" on this live recording made at London's famed Talk of the Town club.

The Sisters Rosalie & Rosemonde

Casa Maria 805D5385

There was no good reason why The Singing Nun should get all the pop music glory, so other nuns began cutting wax. These sisters (who were in fact, real sisters as well, with the surname Deck) included three *TSOM* numbers on their self-titled LP: the title tune, "The Lonely Goatherd," and "Edelweiss." Just to show that they were aware of Broadway musicals *without* nuns, they also included "Look to the Rainbow" from *Finian's Rainbow*.

The Gospel According to Don Shirley

Columbia CS9723

The Jamaican jazz pianist includes the "magnificent paean to optimism" (per the liner notes) "Climb Ev'ry Mountain."

1971

Climb Ev'ry Mountain

Judith Durham
A&M AMLS2011

The former Seekers singer made the title track the final song on her third solo LP.

1973

Screen Gems

Bill White at the Hammond Organ
NDS (Northern Dance Services) (UK)

Worth a mention because how often can you get a three-song combination of "Do-Re-Mi," "Sixteen Going on Seventeen," and "The Lonely Goatherd" done on an organ to a cha-cha beat?

A Woofer in Tweeter's Clothing

Sparks
Bearsville BR 2110

This rock band included "Do-Re-Mi" as the opening number on side 2.

1978

"The Sound of Music"

Valentine Brothers
Source Records SOR 40971 (45 rpm), SOR-13909 (12" single)
Released at 3:20 and 7:10, this is a disco recording of the song. The flip side was "I'm in Love."

Till We Meet Again

Slim Whitman
Liberty LN-10123
Since he was known for his yodeling abilities, you'd think the country singer would have gone with "The Lonely Goatherd" as *TSOM* song to include on this album, but he instead opts for "Edelweiss."

1983

Buried Treasure

The Fleetwoods
Liberty 10199
The trio's rendition of "Climb Ev'ry Mountain" (recorded in the early 1960s), did not appear on an album until this LP of previously unreleased masters arrived. It was later included on their *Best of the Fleetwoods* 1990 CD.

1992

Empire Brass . . . on Broadway

Empire Brass
Telarc 80303
The brass quintet offers their instrumental rendition of "The Lonely Goatherd" on an album of show themes, which also includes "Bali Ha'i" from *South Pacific*.

1996

Something Wonderful: Bryn Terfel sings Rodgers & Hammerstein

Bryn Terfel
Deutsche Grammophon 449163
The Welsh opera singer Bryn Terfel includes "Edelweiss" among the twenty R&H tracks.

Polka! All Night Long

Jimmy Sturr
Rounder

Just in case you thought they weren't making polka albums in the nineties, this one not only featured the Jordanaires backing up Sturr on "Edelweiss," but won the Grammy Award for Best Polka Album.

1997

Favorite Things

George Shearing
Telarc

Jazz man George Shearing's solo piano tracks on this CD include "My Favorite Things."

The Conquest of You

Kid Creole and the Coconuts
SPV Recordings

Crossing both modern and retro (sometimes campy) dance club sounds, this group (led by August Darnell) includes their own spin on "Edelweiss" on this CD otherwise consisting of their own compositions.

2001

Songs I Heard

Harry Connick Jr.
Columbia C 86077

On this CD aimed at kid-friendly songs, all of the selections come from musicals. There are three from *TSOM*. "The Lonely Goatherd," "Edelweiss," and "Do-Re-Mi."

2002

Bernadette Peters Loves Rodgers & Hammerstein

Bernadette Peters
EMI Angel 34969

Despite having never appeared on Broadway in a Rodgers and Hammerstein show (although she had played Liesl in a regional theatre production of *TSOM* as a teen), Bernadette Peters pays tribute to the songwriters with a CD that concludes with "Something Good."

Elaine Stritch: At Liberty

Broadway Cast Album
DRG 12994

Broadway legend Elaine Stritch concluded her self-examining one-woman stage show with her rendition of "Something Good," which, appropriately, is the finale of the CD recording.

Rodgers & Leonhart

Jay Leonhart
Sons of Sound Productions (SSP)

Jazz bassist Jay Leonhart goes for an all-Rodgers album, featuring "The Sound of Music" (with the American Saxophone Quartet) and concluding with "Edelweiss."

Sacred Songs

Placido Domingo
Deutsche Grammophon

For his CD that includes such traditional pieces as "Kyrie" and "Ave Maria," Domingo finds room for "Climb Ev'ry Mountain." This recording would later be featured on the 2008 CD release *The Three Tenors at Christmas*, turning this particular *TSOM* song into a holiday number for the first time, "My Favorite Things" having been the more obvious selection for most people's Christmas recordings since the 1960s.

2003

Broadway My Way

Linda Eder
Atlantic 83580-2

"Edelweiss" is among the stage songs heard here.

The Von Trapp Children, Vol. I

Rattlesby Records

For their debut CD, the four grandchildren of Werner von Trapp (August, Amanda, Melanie, and Sofia) sing the expected traditional folk songs (not to mention Burl Ives and Paul Simon), but also make room for both "Edelweiss" and "The Lonely Goatherd."

Speakerboxxx/The Love Below

OutKast
La Face/Arista
    The hip-hoppers included their instrumental version of "My Favorite Things" on this double LP.

2004

"Climb Ev'ry Mountain"

Guy Sebastian
    Because he had sung the song on *Australian Idol*, Guy Sebastian made it the B-side of his single of "All I Need Is You."

2006

Essential Musicals

Elaine Paige
W14 Universal Music
    West End star Elaine Page includes three R&H compositions on her CD, "Edelweiss," "I'm Gonna Wash That Man Right Outa My Hair" from *South Pacific*, and, from *Carousel*, "If I Loved You."

2010

Love Songs

Anne Sofie von Otter and Brad Mehldau
Naïve V5241
    Joining together Swedish mezzo-soprano von Otter and jazz pianist Mehldau resulted in a two-disc CD of songs new and old. On disc 2, "Something Good" can be found alongside some tunes sung in French.

2012

Rodgers & Hammerstein at the Movies

The John Wilson Orchestra
Warner Classics
    Despite the title, there is only one song on this collection that was actually written for a motion picture, "I Have Confidence," performed here by Sierra Boggess. The CD also includes Joyce DiDonato's rendition of "Climb Ev'ry Mountain" and the Wilson Orchestra's version of "Main Title/Rex Admirabilis."

2013

Go Back Home

Audra McDonald
Nonesuch Records 517766

The same year she portrayed the Mother Abbess in television's *The Sound of Music Live!*, Broadway singer Audra McDonald concluded this CD with "Edelweiss."

The John Wilson Orchestra at the Movies: The Bonus Tracks

Warner Classics 5099943199327

For their newest cinema-themed album, the Orchestra still cheated by featuring songs written for the stage (e.g., "Oklahoma!"), but did make room for the *other* new song from the movie of *The Sound of Music*, "Something Good," performed by Sierra Boggess and David Pittsinger.

The Award Goes to . . .

Honors and Accolades That Went to *The Sound of Music*

As far as the film industry was concerned, *The Sound of Music* could have *never* received a single honor or award and it would still be looked upon as one of the all-time winners, so rich were its monetary rewards. But in this case, the gleam of success was so bright and so all-encompassing in its reach that the Academy of Motion Picture Arts and Sciences, as well as several other organizations at the time, simply had to take notice.

And the accolades did not end in the sixties. A classic it became, and its lofty stature in motion picture history has kept the honors coming over the passing years.

Here are the major award wins and mentions *The Sound of Music* has received.

ACADEMY AWARDS

The 38th Annual Academy nominations, honoring the year 1965 in film, were announced on February 21, 1966, while the actual ceremony took place on Monday, April 18, 1966 at the Santa Monica Civic Auditorium. (From 1961 through 1967, the Academy of Motion Picture Arts and Sciences used this site for their annual ceremony.) Broadcast on ABC in color for the very first time, this marked the twelfth ceremony to be hosted by Bob Hope.

The Sound of Music entered the race with ten nominations, the same amount garnered by *Doctor Zhivago*, thereby making these the front-runners.

Because it did not receive a nomination for Ernest Lehman's screenplay adaptation, *The Sound of Music* became the first Best Picture Winner since 1952's *The Greatest Show on Earth* to not be a finalist in one of the screenplay categories, although that film received the trophy for Best Story. The last Best Picture winner prior to that to receive no nomination in any of the writing categories was 1948's *Hamlet*. This omission was an even greater slight to Lehman than for his previous Robert Wise musical, *West Side Story* (1961). That time he had been included among the eleven nominations, but ended up being the only person associated with the film *not* to win that evening.

Thanks mainly to *TSOM*, 20th Century-Fox was able to lay claim to earning more nominations from the Academy that year than any other studio: twenty-two total, split among seven films.

To signal the expected dominance of *The Sound of Music*, the Academy orchestra's overture to the festivities was themed "Richard Rodgers in Hollywood."

BEST SOUND RECORDING

Oscar night proper got off to a promising start for *TSOM* when it won the very first award given (by presenters George Hamilton and Patty Duke).

Winner: *The Sound of Music*, **James Corcoran (20th Century-Fox SSD), Fred Hynes (Todd-AO SSD)**
This was won by Todd-AO's sound director Fred Hynes and 20th Century-Fox's James Corcoran. These men were billed in the movie's credits next to "Sound Recording Supervised by," while the men more prominently displayed as "Sound by," Murray Spivack and Bernard Freericks, were not under consideration in this category, no doubt leading the general public to feel even more confused by what constitutes what in the making of a motion picture.

Nominees: *The Agony and the Ecstasy* (20th), James Corcoran; *Doctor Zhivago* (MGM), A. W. Watkins, Franklin Milton; *The Great Race* (WB), George Groves; *Shenandoah* (Universal), Waldon O. Watson

BEST COSTUME DESIGN—COLOR

The trophy was presented by Lana Turner and Julie Andrews's *The Americanization of Emily* co-star James Garner.

Winner: *Doctor Zhivago* (MGM), Phyllis Dalton

Nominees: *The Agony and the Ecstasy* (20th), Vittorio Nino Novarese; *The Greatest Story Ever Told* (UA), Vittorio Nino Novarese, Marjorie Best; *Inside Daisy Clover* (WB), Edith Head, Bill Thomas; *The Sound of Music* **(20th), Dorothy Jeakins**

Although few would ever forget the drapery outfits she concocted for the Trapp children to wear, Jeakins had to go home empty-handed that night for her ninth nomination. She already had three Oscars on her mantle as compensation, including the one she'd just received the year before, for *The Night of the Iguana* (MGM). When she was in the running again the next year for another Julie Andrews feature, *Hawaii*, it was notable insomuch as she herself had worn some of her own designs on screen, having played Julie's mother in the picture.

BEST SUPPORTING ACTRESS

As was usually the custom, the award was presented by the previous year's winner in the supporting male category, in this case Peter Ustinov (who had won for *Topkapi*).

Winner: Shelley Winters, *A Patch of Blue* (MGM)

Nominees: Ruth Gordon, *Inside Daisy Clover* (WB); Joyce Redman, *Othello* (WB); Maggie Smith, *Othello* (WB); **Peggy Wood, *The Sound of Music***

The lady chosen to play the Mother Abbess received a final reward for her gently effective performance by earning an Oscar nomination and might have been the winner had *TSOM* turned into the sort of Academy Award juggernaut that the last Robert Wise musical, *West Side Story*, had, gobbling up nearly every trophy in its path. Instead, she was content to know that her mostly unremarkable motion picture career (which, like fellow nominee Ruth Gordon, actually dated back to silent movies) was capped by the role for which she'd be best known. At seventy-four, she was the oldest of all the evening's acting nominees and was also the only one among them who would never again be seen on a movie screen. *The Sound of Music* was her fourteenth film credit and her last.

Shortly after receiving news of being in the running for the Oscar, Wood, while visiting Buffalo on behalf of the film, remarked cheekily to the press, "It only took 55 years for me to get a nomination!"

BEST FILM EDITING

The film editing award was presented by Jason Robards, the star of one of the evening's Best Picture nominees, *A Thousand Clowns*.

Winner: *The Sound of Music* (20th), William Reynolds

Winning its second Oscar for the evening actually made *TSOM* the most awarded film of the night up to this point, with a mere two. William Reynolds's terrific work was no doubt inspired by the guidance received from director Robert Wise, who had initially made his reputation as one of the best film editors in the business.

Accepting his award, Reynolds flattered the film's star by telling the audience, "When in doubt, cut to Julie Andrews."

Reynolds went on to win again, for *The Sting* (1973), among the seven nominations he would receive.

Nominees: *Cat Ballou* (Columbia), Charles Nelson; *Doctor Zhivago* (MGM), Norman Savage; *The Flight of the Phoenix* (20th), Michael Luciano; *The Great Race* (WB), Ralph E. Winters

BEST ART DIRECTION—SET DECORATION—COLOR

The presenters in both the color and black-and-white categories were Warren Beatty and Debbie Reynolds, who was, at the time, appearing in her own nun's story on screen, *The Singing Nun* (1966).

Winner: *Doctor Zhivago* (MGM), John Box, Terence Marsh, Dario Simoni

Nominees: *The Agony and the Ecstasy* (20th), John DeCuir, Jack Martin Smith, Dario Simoni; *The Greatest Story Ever Told* (UA), Richard Day, William C. Creber, David S. Hall, Ray Moyer, Fred M. MacLean, Norman Rockett; *Inside Daisy Clover* (WB), Robert Clatworthy, George James Hopkins; **The Sound of Music (20th), Boris Leven, Walter M. Scott, Ruby R. Levitt**

The Russian-born Boris Leven saw this Oscar being taken away from him by the mostly British team recreating Russia for *Doctor Zhivago*.

Apart from making Salzburg look vintage late 1930s, Leven and his set decorators were required to create, from scratch, at the Twentieth Century-Fox Studios in Los Angeles, the Nonnberg Abbey interiors—including the "Maria" courtyard and the Mother Abbess's office ("Climb Ev'ry Mountain"); all of the rooms in the Trapp home, most notably the grand foyer with its two staircases ascending in opposite directions, used for the Trapp children's first presentation to Maria and their first rendition of "So Long, Farewell"; the cemetery where the Trapps hid from their pursuers; and perhaps most attractively, the moodily lit gazebo, which paid host to "Sixteen Going on Seventeen" and "Something Good"

Leven had already received an Academy Award, for his production design for *West Side Story* (1961). He followed *TSOM* with Oscar nominations for three more collaborations in a row with Robert Wise, *The Sand Pebbles* (1966), *Star!* (1968), and *The Andromeda Strain* (1971).

As part of the 20th Century-Fox production department, Scott had already claimed four Academy Awards (*The Robe, 1953*; *The King and I, 1956*; *The Diary of Anne Frank, 1959*; and *Cleopatra, 1963*), and would receive another two, for *Fantastic Voyage* (1966) and *Hello, Dolly!* (1969). His collaborator, Ruby Levitt, would not win any of her four nominations.

BEST CINEMATOGRAPHY—COLOR

Presented by then-husband-and-wife team of Richard Johnson and Kim Novak, who were already on the brink of calling it quits, their divorce being finalized in May 1966. They had married in March 1965, which meant that their marriage was outlasted by even the *roadshow* run of *TSOM*.

Winner: *Doctor Zhivago* (MGM) Freddie Young

Nominees: *The Agony and the Ecstasy* (20th) Leon Shamroy; *The Great Race* (WB) Russell Harlan; *The Greatest Story Ever Told* (UA) William C. Mellor, Loyal Griggs; *The Sound of Music* (20th) Ted McCord

This was perhaps the most unexpected loss for *TSOM*, as even its naysayers were awestruck by how beautifully cinematographer Ted McCord had captured Austria, forever making this particular movie many people's defining picture-postcard image of what the country looks like. Among his most arresting visuals were the opening of the "Do-Re-Mi" number with the surrounding Alps taking on an almost living and breathing majesty, and the silhouettes used to emphasize the romantic nature of the "Something Good" sequence.

This was the third of McCord's Oscar nominations, and his first for a color film, the others being *Johnny Belinda* (1948) and Robert Wise's *Two for the Seesaw* (1962).

TSOM was his penultimate credit. Having toiled behind the camera since 1921 (the bulk of his early career had been working on B-westerns), the sixty-five-year-old McCord retired after shooting the Sean Connery comedy *A Fine Madness* (1966).

BEST MUSIC, SCORING OF MUSIC, ADAPTATION OR TREATMENT

The music awards were given out by Italian actress Virna Lisi and one of the co-stars of Julie Andrews's *The Americanization of Emily*, James Coburn.

Winner: *The Sound of Music* **(20th), Irwin Kostal**

There was really no competition in this category; once a musical made as stunning an impact as *TSOM* did, it only made sense for the Academy to honor it in the one category usually set aside for the musical genre. Because Saul Chaplin had relinquished any credit for his musical contributions to the movie, this award went solely to Kostal, who assured Chaplin after the fact that the award should by all means have been shared with him.

Although he'd missed out on the Oscar the previous year, when *Mary Poppins* lost in this category to *My Fair Lady*, Kostal had already won for his previous musical collaboration with both Chaplin and Robert Wise, *West Side Story*.

Nominees: *Cat Ballou* (Columbia), Frank De Vol; *The Pleasure Seekers* (20th), Lionel Newman, Alexander Courage; *A Thousand Clowns* (UA), Don Walker; *The Umbrellas of Cherbourg* (Landau Releasing), Michel Legrand

BEST DIRECTOR

Asking Shirley MacLaine to present this award might have been a sign that the Academy was pretty certain Robert Wise was the front-runner, the actress having been directed by him four years earlier, in *Two for the Seesaw*.

Winner: Robert Wise, *The Sound of Music* **(20th)**

Julie Andrews accepted the award in Wise's absence (he was off in Asia filming *The Sand Pebbles*), thereby allowing her several backstage photo ops holding the Oscar statuette, much as she had the previous year as a genuine winner. Said Andrews in her speech, "It gives me the greatest pleasure in the world to accept this for Robert Wise. I know he's heart-broken not to be here this evening. Unfortunately, he's busy filming in Hong Kong. But on his behalf, thank you very, very much indeed." (After her speech, the camera caught Peggy Wood in the audience, applauding and promptly removing her glasses.)

Andrews, who was, at this time, separated from her husband Tony Walton, attended the ceremonies with *TSOM*'s associate producer Saul Chaplin, and was dressed in a gown created by the film's nominated costume designer, Dorothy Jeakins.

Nominees: David Lean, for *Doctor Zhivago* (MGM); John Schlesinger, for *Darling* (Embassy); Hiroshi Teshigahara, for *Woman in the Dunes* (Pathé Contemporary); William Wyler, for *The Collector* (Columbia)

BEST ACTRESS

This was presented by the year's previous Best Actor winner, Rex Harrison, who had won for *My Fair Lady*. Harrison appeared with nominee Julie Andrews on both the New York and West End stage in the original production of *My Fair Lady*.

Winner: Julie Christie, *Darling* (Embassy)

Nominee: Julie Andrews, *The Sound of Music* (20th)

Singled out for praise by even some of *TSOM*'s most fervid enemies was Julie's captivating performance as Maria, and the picture's gargantuan success meant that she really was being looked upon as the golden girl of the motion picture industry in 1965. Being the previous year's victor for *Mary Poppins*, however, worked against her winning again.

Having just escorted Best Actor Winner Lee Marvin backstage after giving him his award, Andrews was seen on camera waiting in the wings at the moment Harrison read her name among the nominees, not having the time to return to her seat in the auditorium.

Andrews would receive her third Oscar mention, in 1982, for *Victor Victoria*.

Nominees: Samantha Eggar, *The Collector* (Columbia); Elizabeth Hartman, *A Patch of Blue* (MGM); Simone Signoret, *Ship of Fools* (Columbia)

BEST PICTURE

Presented by Jack Lemmon

Winner: *The Sound of Music* (producer: Robert Wise)

Because he was in Hong Kong filming *The Sand Pebbles* at the time of the Oscar ceremony, Wise's associate producer, Saul Chaplin, accepted the award that night. "I'm proud to accept this in behalf of Robert Wise," Chaplin said, at the podium. "I'm sure, if he were here, he would first want to thank the members of the Academy. He would also, I think, want to thank everyone connected with making the film. I can only say as one of those members, I would like to thank *him* for making filmmaking such a rewarding and stimulating experience."

NOMINEES:
***Darling* (Embassy; producer: Joseph Janni)**

One of the key titles of the British New Wave of the 1960s, this film did indeed become the critics' darling of the year, garnering praise for director John Schlesinger's neo-realistic style, its crisp black-and-white portrait of modern-day (or as some called it "Swinging") London, and for star Julie Christie, who became the reigning female representative of British moviemaking during this era.

Doctor Zhivago (MGM; producer: Carlo Ponti)

Just to further emphasize that certain 1965 movies were going to be appreciated for their merits no matter *what* the critics thought, *Zhivago* pretty much repeated *TSOM*'s success story, being dismissed by many reviewers only to be fully embraced by the public. Opening at Christmastime on a reserved-seat basis, it was something audiences wanted to see from the start and kept growing in popularity at a rate nearly as impressive as *Music*, eventually sliding into second place among the top moneymakers of 1965, not to mention becoming MGM's second-highest-grossing release of all time, behind *Gone with the Wind*.

Ship of Fools (Columbia; producer: Stanley Kramer)

Black and white and just as bleak in its own way as *Darling*, Stanley Kramer's 2 ½-hour adaptation of Katherine Anne Porter's epic, multi-character novel was closer to an "art house" hit than something embraced by the mass public.

A Thousand Clowns (United Artists; producer: Fred Coe)

The stage-to-screen transfer of Herb Gardner's 1962 Broadway favorite was a black-and-white valentine to New York City and a successful opening up of a stage-bound property that never lost the bite of the original.

AMERICAN CINEMA EDITORS, USA

The honorary society of the motion picture industry's film editors was founded in 1950, but did not start giving out their own award (referred to as "The Eddie") until 1961. It is worth noting that among the four nominees who lost this award to *TSOM*, only *The Flight of the Phoenix* was in the running for the editing Oscar that year. The previous year's A.C.E. winner had been *Mary Poppins*.

Winner: Best Edited Feature Film: *The Sound of Music*, **William Reynolds**

Nominees: *Dear Brigitte; The Flight of the Phoenix; A Thousand Clowns; Tokyo Olympiad*

BOXOFFICE BLUE RIBBON AWARD

April 1965: *TSOM* was named the Best Picture of the Month for the Whole Family in this monthly poll held by the weekly *Boxoffice* magazine.

It was joining a list that included *A Hard Day's Night* (September 1964), *Kisses for My President* (October 1964), *Mary Poppins* (November 1964), *My Fair Lady* (December 1964), *Father Goose* (January 1965), *A Boy Ten Feet Tall* (February 1965), and *Those Calloways* (March 1965). It was followed in May by *The Truth About Spring*, June by *Mister Moses*, and July by Fox's next big road show, reserved-seat release, *Those Magnificent Men in Their Flying Machines*.

The dubbed print of *The Trapp Family* had won the Blue Ribbon Award for April 1961, and the previous Robert Wise musical, *West Side Story* was the March 1962 winner.

BROADCASTING AND FILM COMMISSION OF THE NATIONAL COUNCIL OF CHURCHES

On February 3, 1966, this organization bestowed its Star Crystal Award on *The Sound of Music* in what it called "Category V," which referred to its "exceptional entertainment value in films for the entire family." (Other winners in other categories included *The Pawnbroker, Nothing but a Man,* and *A Patch of Blue.*)

CUE MAGAZINE

The New York entertainment listings guide (which later folded into *New York* magazine) voted *The Sound of Music* "Best Family Film of the Year"

DAVID Di DONATELLO AWARDS

A nude fellow wearing something resembling a Victorian schoolgirl's hat and leaning on a sword, this statuette was copied after Donatello's famous sculpture. It was given by The Academy of Italian Cinema each year, starting in 1955. The year Julie Andrews won was referred to as awards "covering 1966," although they were announced in July of that year. There were no runners-up or nominees given in addition to Julie's win.

The previous year's winner in this category had been Audrey Hepburn for *My Fair Lady* (1964), while Andrews would receive the award yet again in 1983, for *Victor Victoria* (1982).

Winner: Best Foreign Actress: Julie Andrews, *The Sound of Music*

DIRECTORS GUILD OF AMERICA

The one-time Screen Directors Guild was formed in 1936 and began awarding trophies in 1948, initially on a quarterly basis, then, starting the following year, annually.

The awards were held on February 12, 1966 at the Beverly Hilton Hotel.

Winner: Outstanding Directorial Achievement in Motion Pictures: Robert Wise, *The Sound of Music*

Once all the critical carping about *TSOM* had been silenced by the amount of money it was bringing it, Hollywood began to admire just how inestimable was Robert Wise's achievement in bringing the property to the screen with such skill. Surely, what could have gone very wrong and turned exceedingly schmaltzy had been handled with care and good judgment, making for a superior entertainment of the sort that kept crossing over to all kinds of demographics.

Wise had already been given this same honor for his work on *West Side Story* (shared with his co-director, Jerome Robbins). So esteemed would he be by this organization that down the line he would also be given the DGA Honorary Life Member Award (1983), the Robert B. Aldrich Achievement

Award (1984), the DGA Lifetime Achievement Award (1988), and the DGA President's Award (2001).

Because Wise was off in Asia filming *The Sand Pebbles,* Julie Andrews accepted the award on his behalf from presenter George Sidney.

Of Wise's competitors here, only John Schlesinger would join him on the list of finalists for the Oscar.

Nominees: Sidney J. Furie, *The Ipcress File;* Sidney Lumet, *The Pawnbroker;* John Schlesinger, *Darling;* Elliot Silverstein, *Cat Ballou*

FILM DAILY

In the 43rd annual poll of film critics conducted by *The Film Daily* industry trade paper and announced in April 1966, *TSOM* came away with five honors: **Best Picture; Best Actress (Julie Andrews); Best Director; Best Musical Score; and Best Cinematography.**

TSOM won the top award with 104 votes. The runners-up were *Ship of Fools* (83 votes), *The Pawnbroker* (81 votes), *Darling* (74 votes), *The Collector* (72 votes), *Those Magnificent Men in Their Flying Machines* (69 votes), and *The Spy Who Came in from the Cold* and *Doctor Zhivago* tying at 65 votes each.

GILBERT YOUTH RESEARCH, INC. TEEN POLL

A poll conducted with 1,063 teenagers in early 1966 by Gilbert Youth Research, Inc. showed that *The Sound of Music* was chosen as the best film seen during 1965. This was followed, in order, by *Thunderball, Goldfinger, My Fair Lady, Mary Poppins, The Great Race, The Ipcress File, Help!, Lord Jim,* and *The Sandpiper.*

On the basis of *TSOM* and *Mary Poppins,* Julie Andrews was voted Top Movie Star in the female category, garnering 48 percent of the ballots. Sean Connery was voted male star of the year.

GOLDEN GLOBE AWARDS

The Hollywood Foreign Press Association had been handing out their annual Golden Globe Awards for excellence in film since World War II. One of its benefits was the increased number of categories (starting with the films of 1950), dividing Best Motion Picture, as well as Best Actor and Best Actress, into the fields of drama and comedy/musical, meaning two winners each year.

For 1965, there were Golden Globe spots for four of the movies that would end up as the Best Picture finalists at the Oscars; *The Sound of Music* and *A Thousand Clowns* in the comedy/musical category; *Doctor Zhivago* and *Ship of Fools* among the dramas. Only *Darling* was left out in the cold.

For the Best Motion Picture—Musical/Comedy, *TSOM* was the only one of the five nominees to qualify as the former, and its victory was hardly a surprise.

Best Motion Picture—Musical/Comedy:

Winner: *The Sound of Music*

Nominees: *Cat Ballou; The Great Race; Those Magnificent Men in Their Flying Machines; A Thousand Clowns*

Best Actress—Musical/Comedy:

Winner: Julie Andrews, *The Sound of Music*
   Andrews had already won in this category the previous year, for her performance in *Mary Poppins*. A definite favorite of the Hollywood Foreign Press, she would win Best Actress a third time in 1982 for *Victor Victoria*; twice be given the now-defunct Henrietta Award for World Film Favorite—Female (1966 and 1967); and garner a total of ten Golden Globe nominations as performer, both in film and television.

Nominees: Jane Fonda, *Cat Ballou*; Barbara Harris, *A Thousand Clowns*; Rita Tushingham, *The Knack . . . and How to Get It*; Natalie Wood, *Inside Daisy Clover*

Best Motion Picture Director:

Winner: David Lean, *Doctor Zhivago*

Nominees: Guy Green, *A Patch of Blue*; John Schlesinger, *Darling*; **Robert Wise,** *The Sound of Music*. (This was the one instance in which Wise and Lean competed for a directorial award in 1965 where the latter came out the winner.) William Wyler, *The Collector*

Best Supporting Actress:

Winner: Ruth Gordon, *Inside Daisy Clover*

Nominees: Joan Blondell, *The Cincinnati Kid*; Joyce Redman, *Othello*; Thelma Ritter, *Boeing Boeing*; **Peggy Wood,** *The Sound of Music*

GRAMMY AWARDS

The soundtrack for *The Sound of Music* was one of the five finalists for Album of the Year at the 8th annual Grammy Awards given for the year 1965 and presented on March 15, 1966 at the Beverly Hilton in Los Angeles.
   The other nominees were *Help!* by the Beatles; *My Name Is Barbra* by Barbra Streisand; *My World* by Eddy Arnold; and the winner, *September of My Years*, by Frank Sinatra.
   Rather than an overall "soundtrack" category, film music was covered under the heading "Original Score Written for a Motion Picture or Television Show," which did not qualify the Rodgers and Hammerstein score. That winner was the Robert Armbruster Orchestra for *The Sandpiper*.

LAUREL AWARDS

This award was an offshoot of *Motion Picture Exhibitor* magazine, with Golden Laurel winners chosen by both American and Canadian film buyers. Films and stars were not selected with the calendar year in mind but announced in the fall, therefore resulting in overlapping nominees from two different years.

TSOM was actually included among the films announced on October 19, 1966, which consisted of both 1965 and 1966 titles.

Being given the highest honor of "General Entertainment," this meant that the exhibitors looked at the movie as the industry's crowning achievement. (The previous year this had gone to *Mary Poppins*, while *My Fair Lady* was honored as the top Roadshow achievement, a category not included this year.) It also meant that *TSOM* was not deemed eligible to be placed among the nominees in the separate musical category. The winner there was *The Singing Nun*, which bested the Beatles' second feature, *Help!*, and the rather sorry trio of the barely musical Ann-Margret vehicle *Made in Paris*, Elvis Presley's *Frankie and Johnny*, and the one cold-climate entry in AIP's "Beach Party" series, *Ski Party*.

Winner: General Entertainment: *The Sound of Music*

Winner: Musical Performance, Female: Julie Andrews, *The Sound of Music*

Nominees: Ann-Margret, *Made in Paris*; Patty Duke, *Billie*; Connie Francis, *When the Boys Meet the Girls*; Debbie Reynolds, *The Singing Nun*

Winner: Special Award: Robert Wise "In recognition of his outstanding motion picture achievements that have raised the artistic, entertainment, and boxoffice standards of the industry to towering new levels." This honor was not, therefore, specifically given for his work on *The Sound of Music*, although this clearly was a major factor.

ALSO
Julie Andrews came in second place for Female Star (the winner was Elizabeth Taylor), while Charmian Carr was in fourteenth place for New Faces, Female (*A Patch of Blue* star Elizabeth Hartman won), and Robert Wise was fifth on the list of Producer-Directors (Alfred Hitchcock was the winner).

NATIONAL BOARD OF REVIEW

Established in 1909 as a kind of self-censoring board for the film industry to avoid government intervention on this subject, the National Board of Review began bestowing awards in 1930, as well as including its ten best list for each year. This would consist of their winner at the top of the list, and the nine "next best."

TSOM was included as one of the Year's Ten Best Films:

1. *The Eleanor Roosevelt Story* (Best Film)
2. *The Agony and the Ecstasy*

3. *Doctor Zhivago*
4. *Ship of Fools*
5. *The Spy Who Came in from the Cold*
6. *Darling*
7. *The Greatest Story Ever Told*
8. *A Thousand Clowns*
9. *The Train*
10. **The Sound of Music**

NATIONAL CATHOLIC OFFICE FOR MOTION PICTURES

The National/Catholic Legion of Decency was founded in 1933 as a way for the Roman Catholic Church (not to mention its additional Protestant and Jewish members) to wield power over the motion picture industry, pointing out instances when their sanctimonious members felt something contained "morally" questionable content. By the 1960s, they were losing their clout because of more lenient censorship rules and, in fact, changed their name in 1966 to the National Catholic Office for Motion Pictures. Not surprisingly, since there appeared to be nothing in it to offend them, they launched their First Annual Awards by giving *TSOM* its highest honor:

Best Film for General Audiences: *The Sound of Music*
    Peggy Wood accepted the award, which was presented on February 2, 1966. The organization bestowed other honors that year on *Nobody Waved Goodbye* (Best Film for Youth), *Darling* (Best Film for Mature Audiences), and *Juliet of the Spirits* (Best Foreign Language Film).

NEW YORK FILM CRITICS AWARDS

The circle of New York City movie reviewers handed out their first awards in 1936, covering the previous year's offerings (Best Film being *The Informer*).
    Despite the mostly negative response in Manhattan to *TSOM* itself, Julie Andrews's inclusion here among the finalists for Best Actress is a clear indication that New York reviewers in no way considered her one of its demerits. She had also been in the running the previous year, being second runner-up for *Mary Poppins* (the winner then was Kim Stanley for *Séance on a Wet Afternoon*).

Best Actress:

Winner: Julie Christie, *Darling*

Nominees: Julie Andrews, *The Sound of Music*; Catherine Deneuve, *Repulsion*

PHOTOPLAY AWARDS

Winner: Best Picture of 1965: *The Sound of Music*

Often considered the granddaddy of the movie "fan" magazine genre, *Photoplay* debuted in 1911 but didn't really adapt its celebrity coverage format until 1918. Two years later, it began giving out awards (originally the Photoplay Medal of Honor) to what it considered the year's best movie, with no nominees or finalists announced. After a lapse in which no winners were selected (1940–43), they resumed as the Photoplay Gold Medal Winners, with additional mentions for the year's most popular stars, determined by a Gallup Poll. These awards were no longer given after 1967, while the magazine itself, which had already merged with *Movie Mirror* in 1941, merged again in 1977 with *TV-Radio Mirror*, becoming *Photoplay and TV Mirror*. Three years later, it was no more.

Prior to *The Sound of Music,* only six other Academy Award Winners for Best Picture received the Photoplay top honor as well: *All Quiet on the Western Front* (1930), *Cimarron* (1931), *Gone with the Wind* (1939), *Going My Way* (1944), *From Here to Eternity* (1953), and *Gigi* (1958).

The presentation of the 1965 awards was seen by television viewers on an episode of the New York–based syndicated talk series *The Merv Griffin Show* in March 1966. Peggy Wood was present to accept the Best Picture award for *TSOM.*

SCREEN PRODUCERS' AWARDS

Best-Produced Theatrical Film of 1965 (David O. Selznick Award): Robert Wise for *The Sound of Music.*

Julie Andrews accepted the award for Wise at the March 8, 1966 banquet at the Beverly Hilton Hotel. It was the first time the award was given in the name of the late David O. Selznick, who had died on June 22, 1965.

THEATRE OWNERS STAR OF THE YEAR AWARD

On October 30, 1965, at its 18th annual convention (and 10th anniversary of the award) at the Ambassador Hotel in Los Angeles, Julie Andrews was given this honor on the basis of *Mary Poppins, The Americanization of Emily,* and *The Sound of Music.* Previous recipients included Danny Kaye, William Holden, Doris Day, and Ann-Margret.

TROPHY OF THE FIVE CONTINENTS

In 1966, this curiously named award was bestowed upon *TSOM* by representatives of several international cinema federations at a meeting held in Milan, Italy, in October of that year.

WRITERS GUILD OF AMERICA

Winner: Best Written American Musical: *The Sound of Music*

The WGA Awards were first given out honoring 1948 releases. Ernest Lehman was much luckier with this organization than he was with the Academy, having already won three times previously, for *Sabrina* (1954), *The King and I* (1956), and *West Side Story* (1961). The first and last brought him Oscar nominations with no wins; *King* did not even rate an Academy Award nomination.

Always congratulated by his collaborators on *The Sound of Music* for improving the stage script and making the piece play so effectively on screen, he was constantly overlooked in the awards arena for the most part, notably at the Oscars where he was not even in the running in the adapted screenplay category. This would be his sole award won for *TSOM*. No doubt because of the fairly weak collection of 1965 releases that would qualify as musicals, there were no nominees or finalists announced.

This award was given on March 23, 1966 at the Beverly Hilton Hotel.

Lists and Polls

AMERICAN FILM INSTITUTE

The American Film institute took the opinions of more than 1,500 producers, directors, actors, screenwriters, historians, and other contributors to the world of motion pictures for its much-publicized ranking of the 100 Greatest American Movies of All Time.

1998:

AFI's 100 Years . . . 100 Movies ranked *The Sound of Music* at #55, one notch under *All Quiet on the Western Front* (1930) and one above *MASH* (1970). The #1 movie was *Citizen Kane* (1941).

2007:

The AFI revisited and therefore revised the list for a tenth (*sic*) anniversary, *AFI's 100 Years . . . 100 Movies: 10th Anniversary Edition*. *The Sound of Music* had now risen fifteen places to #40, below *Dr. Strangelove* (1964) and above *King Kong* (1933). Apparently having gotten on someone's bad side, *All Quiet on the Western Front* had dropped off the list altogether. *Citizen Kane* retained its top spot.

Not content to simply keep finding a new top 100, the AFI moved on to other categories. These included:

2002:

AFI's 100 Years . . . 100 Passions (CBS, June 11), which selected the greatest love stories from the cinema.

The Sound of Music came in at #27 (under *The Lady Eve*, 1941; and above *The Shop around the Corner*, 1940). *Casablanca* (1942) topped the list.

2004:

AFI's 100 Years . . . 100 Songs (CBS, June 22) ranked the top songs to be heard in the movies, although it did not draw the line at whether or not these songs were written expressly for the film in question. As a result, *The Sound of Music* made the list three times:

10. "The Sound of Music" as performed by Julie Andrews
64. "My Favorite Things" as performed by Julie Andrews
88. "Do-Re-Mi" as performed by Julie Andrews (and ensemble)

There was one other Rodgers & Hammerstein song that made the cut, "Shall We Dance" (from *The King and I*), at #54; while Hammerstein was also represented by "Ol' Man River" (as performed by Paul Robeson in the 1936 version of *Show Boat*), and Rodgers by "Isn't it Romantic?" from *Love Me Tonight* (1932), ranked at #73.

The top song was "Over the Rainbow" from *The Wizard of Oz* (1939).

2006:

AFI's 100 Years . . . 100 Cheers (CBS, June 14), referring to what they considered the "most inspiring" movies of all time. *The Sound of Music* made it to #41 on the list, after *Mrs. Miniver* (1942) and before *12 Angry Men* (1957). The #1 inspiring movie was *It's a Wonderful Life* (1946).

AFI's Greatest Movie Musicals

In September 2006, AFI announced the Top 25 (*only* 25?) movie musicals (it was not televised), which gave *The Sound of Music* its highest ranking on any of their lists, coming in at #4. This gave director Robert Wise two films in the top five; with *West Side Story* filling the #2 position (*Singin' in the Rain* was #1). Julie Andrews was also represented by *Mary Poppins* (#6), while the other Rodgers and Hammerstein title was *The King and I* at #11. The #24 spot was claimed by the 1936 version of *Show Boat* for which Oscar Hammerstein II wrote the script and lyrics (with music by Jerome Kern).

BRITISH FILM INSTITUTE

In 2004, the BFI, rather than vote by critical or public opinion, came up with the interesting idea of ranking the movies to have the greatest number of admissions or tickets sold in the United Kingdom since the dawn of sound. (A special unveiling of the results of the research, *The Ultimate Film*, aired on Channel 4 in the UK on November 27–28, 2004 with John Cleese as host.)

The Sound of Music came in at #2, with approximately 30 million tickets sold since its release in England in March 1965. The top ten consisted of:

1) *Gone with the Wind*—35 million admissions; 2) **The Sound of Music**—30 million admissions; 3) *Snow White and the 7 Dwarfs*—28 million; 4) *Star Wars*—20.76 million; 5) *Spring in Park Lane* (1948; a UK film starring Michael Wilding and Anna

Neagle)—20.5 million; 6) *The Best Years of Our Lives* (UK: 1947)—20.4 million; 7) *The Jungle Book* (UK: 1968)—19.8 million; 8) *Titanic* (UK: 1998)—18.9 million; 9) *The Wicked Lady* (1945: a UK film starring Margaret Lockwood and James Mason)—18.4 million; 10) *The Seventh Veil* (1945: a UK film starring James Mason and Ann Todd)—17.9 million tickets sold

Another Rodgers and Hammerstein film, *South Pacific*, came in at #13 with 16.5 million tickets sold; while *The King and I* (1956) was found at #92 with estimated attendance of 8.2 million.

100 Greatest Family Films

Another Channel 4 poll had viewers voting on that always debatable category of "family" films. A special airing of the countdown ran in the UK on the nights of December 22 and 23, 2005. This time *The Sound of Music* did not crack the Top 10, instead coming in at #18.

The top three slots were filled by *E.T. The Extra-Terrestrial* (1982), *Shrek* (2001), and *Mary Poppins* (1964).

100 Greatest Musicals

Britain's Channel 4 polled audiences to find out what were their favorite movie musicals, then ranked the results from 1 to 100, announcing the countdown on a two-part special that aired December 26 and 27, 2003 and was hosted by Denise Van Outen. Among those popping in to comment on the selections were *TSOM*'s co-choreographer Marc Breaux.

While *The Sound of Music* had to concede the top spot to the 1978 homage to the fifties, *Grease*, its second place showing was still a mighty testament to its enduring power over audiences.

The top ten were:

1) *Grease* (1978); 2) **The Sound of Music** (1965); 3) *The Wizard of Oz* (1939); 4) *West Side Story* (1961); 5) *Mary Poppins* (1964); 6) *Singin' in the Rain* (1952); 7) *The Rocky Horror Picture Show* (1975); 8) *Chicago* (2002); 9) *Oliver!* (1968); 10) *Moulin Rouge!* (2001).

The Rocky Horror Picture Show and *Oliver!* were the only two titles in the top ten to qualify as actual British productions; while *Moulin Rouge!* hailed from Australia. The rest were U.S. productions.

The full list also found room for four other Rodgers and Hammerstein musicals: *The King and I* (1956) at #23; *Oklahoma!* (1955) #35; *South Pacific* (1958) at #39; and *Carousel* (1956) at #41. Julie Andrews not only had two films in the top five, but was also represented at #51 by *Thoroughly Modern Millie*. Surprisingly, *Victor Victoria* (1982) did not make the cut.

Oscar Hammerstein II was also represented by *Carmen Jones* (1954; #52) and the 1951 version of *Show Boat* (#71).

Any ranking of movie musicals that can't bother to find a spot for Rodgers and Hart's *Love Me Tonight* (1932) is already missing a good deal of credibility.

HOLLYWOOD REPORTER POLL

Proving that the industry that created some of our fondest memories haven't very long memories of their own, *The Hollywood Reporter* conducted a 2014 poll to find out what were the favorite motion pictures of Hollywood insiders (directors, producers, executives, etc.). The compiled list of 100 "Best Loved Movies" went back no further than 1939 (*The Wizard of Oz* and *Gone with the Wind*, of course), and featured all of *three* movies from the 1940s. It *did* at least find a spot for *The Sound of Music*, which came in at #25 (below *Jaws* and above *Singin' in the Rain*). Robert Wise was also represented by *West Side Story*, while *Mary Poppins* gave Julie Andrews two credits on the list. *The Godfather* was #1.

NATIONAL FILM PRESERVATION BOARD

In 1989, the Library of Congress started selecting films that it felt deserved to be preserved for historical and culturally significant reasons.

For its thirteenth year, announced on December 18, 2001, *The Sound of Music* finally made the cut. It shared the list that year with the following commercial features:

Abbott and Costello Meet Frankenstein (1948), *All That Jazz* (1979), *All the King's Men* (1949), *America, America* (1963), *Hoosiers* (1986), *It* (1927), *Jaws* (1975), *Manhattan* (1979), *The Miracle of Morgan's Creek* (1944), *Miss Lulu Bett* (1921), *National Lampoon's Animal House* (1978), *Planet of the Apes* (1968), *Stormy Weather* (1943), and *The Thing from Another World* (1951).

20 TO 1

The Australian series *20 to 1* counted down certain facets of pop culture by compiling "Top 20" lists. On December 4, 2006, they came up with what they called "Magnificent Movies," which found *The Sound of Music* at #4 (*Star Wars* was #1). There were four Australian movies on the list: *Crocodile Dundee* (#5), *Moulin Rouge!* (#7), *The Adventures of Priscilla, Queen of the Desert* (#10), and *Chopper* (#15).

The Sound Lingers On

References or Connections to *The Sound of Music* Featuring Those from the Film and the Original Broadway Production

Y ou can't be a part of something as huge as *The Sound of Music* and not be expected to revisit it every now and then in your career.

Here (chronologically) are several instances when those associated with either the original Broadway production or the motion picture version paid tribute to the work or sang songs from it in the years since *TSOM* first appeared. Also included are some unrelated reunions; as well as documentaries that contained *TSOM* clips and paid tribute to its importance in the careers of its creators or in motion picture history in general.

The Ed Sullivan Show (CBS, November 29, 1959)

Only days after *The Sound of Music* opened on Broadway, Ed Sullivan welcomed one of its cast members to sing a tune from the show. Curiously, Marion Marlowe (who played Elsa) was on hand, not to sing either "No Way to Stop It" or "How Can Love Survive," but the title number. Sullivan, a longtime supporter of Rodgers and Hammerstein—whom, in this episode, he reminds us had dropped by in 1948 for his series' premiere—assures the audience afterwards that *TSOM* is a "perfectly wonderful show."

What's My Line? (CBS, November 29, 1959)

An hour and a half after *The Ed Sullivan Show* signed off for the evening, audiences got another promo for *The Sound of Music* when Richard Rodgers and Oscar Hammerstein II appeared as the mystery guests on *What's My Line?* This marked the second time the duo did this spot on the show together (previously on February 19, 1956), while Hammerstein had shown up solo on January 6, 1952 and Rodgers by himself on May 27, 1951.

On this particular episode, panelist Bennett Cerf disqualifies himself from participating, recognizing the songwriters' disguised voices instantly, having dined with them the previous night. It is up to Dorothy Kilgallen to make the correct guess, rather quickly. She goes on to praise their new musical, "May I just recommend that everybody of all ages and all temperaments and all nationalities go and see it because it's such a wonderful show?" A beaming Rodgers encourages host John Daly to allow her to say just that. Cerf adds good-naturedly, "If Oscar and Dick had heard me singing "Do-Re-Mi" upstairs a few moments ago they'd have both shot themselves."

Also taking guesses on the panel were Martin Gabel and Paulette Goddard.

The Ed Sullivan Show (CBS, December 20, 1959)

For his Christmas show, Sullivan welcomed the "nuns" from the cast of *The Sound of Music* to perform the "Preludium," and Patricia Neway to sing "Climb Ev'ry Mountain." Interestingly, this same episode contains segments featuring the puppetry of Bil Baird, whose marionettes would later be featured in the movie of *TSOM*.

Ford Startime Talent Scouts (NBC, February 23, 1960)

The concept of this episode of the omnibus series is for established celebrities to bring on their protégés; young talents they are "sponsoring" or feel are worth watching. Dave Garroway introduces Richard Rodgers, who explains how Lauri Peters won the role of Liesl in *The Sound of Music*. She then sings "Sixteen Going on Seventeen." Although a young man stands by looking "Rolf-like," Peters dances alone.

Others on hand include Maureen O'Hara (presenting the dance team of Brasica and Tybee), Hugh Downs (subbing for Jack Paar, who was feuding with NBC at the time, presenting Lester James), Ethel Merman (trumpeting Paul Wallace, from the cast of *Gypsy*), Tommy Sands (sponsoring Joanie Sommers), and Joan Crawford (for Colleen Dewhurst). Garroway himself presents the John La Salle Quartet.

Music for a Spring Night: On and Off Broadway Tonight (ABC, March 23, 1960)

This special served as a promotion for several on and off-Broadway shows running during that time, including *My Fair Lady*, *Gypsy*, *Little Mary Sunshine*, *Flower Drum Song*, and *Parade*. Original *TSOM* cast member Brian Davies was on hand to sing "Sixteen Going on Seventeen."

1960 Tony Awards (WCBS-TV, April 24, 1960)

Although no songs are performed at this ceremony, taking place at the ballroom of the Astor Hotel in New York, after Mary Martin receives her Tony (from

Ray Bolger) for her performance as Maria in *The Sound of Music*, she inspires the audience (specifically some students in attendance) by reciting Oscar Hammerstein's lyrics from one of the songs she does *not* sing in the show, "Climb Ev'ry Mountain." She concludes by stating that "I hope, for the rest of my life, I shall have a mountain to climb in the theatre, for the rest of my days."

When *The Sound of Music* won Best Musical that night, Howard Lindsay and Russel Crouse were on hand to pick up their awards, but accepting for Leland Hayward, Richard Halliday, Richard Rodgers and Oscar Hammerstein II (as, curiously, the orchestra played "That's Entertainment") were Mary Rodgers, Larry Hagman, and James Hammerstein.

Among the presenters that evening was Christopher Plummer.

What's My Line? (CBS, July 3, 1960)

Everybody's favorite segment of this quiz show was the "mystery guest," when a famous celebrity would appear on stage and try to fool the blindfolded panelists, who asked questions in hopes of establishing the secret identity. During the Broadway run of *TSOM*, all seven children from the original cast showed up in hopes of fooling Bennett Cerf, Arlene Francis, Tony Randall, and Dorothy Kilgallen. As was the custom, guests were obliged to sign their name on a chalkboard upon entering, usually to a loud applause from the studio audience. Lauri Peters (the company's Liesl) did the honors, signing the seven in as "The Trapp Family Children." Each took turns answering the questions, leading up to Ms. Francis making the correct guess, with the help of Mr. Cerf.

Each of the kids got a chance to introduce themselves by name and give their ages: Lauri Peter (Liesl; seventeen years old, having just turned that age the day before the broadcast); Evanna Lien (Gretl; nine); Mary Susan Locke (Marta; ten); Marilyn Rogers (Brigitta; twelve); Joseph Stewart (Kurt; thirteen); Kathy Dunn (Louisa; twelve); and Billy Snowden (Friedrich; thirteen).

Godfrey Time (CBS radio, July 7, 1960)

Children from the Herald Fresh Air Fund join Arthur Godfrey's guest Mary Martin on "Do-Re-Mi" during her run on Broadway in *The Sound of Music*.

The Garry Moore Show (CBS, May 2, 1961)

The host welcomes Julie Andrews, for her first of four visits to the show. After her song-set, Moore praises her performance in the current New York success, *Camelot*, but worries—presciently, as it turns out—that Hollywood won't give her the role in the film version, as is their habit. (Vanessa Redgrave would get the part, six years down the line.) Speaking of the movie industry's improbable casting trend, he inadvertently goes close to the bone. "Take a show like *Sound of Music*, starring Mary Martin on Broadway," he brings up, as an example. "They buy it and take it to Hollywood and who do they put in the lead? . . . Tuesday Weld!" Andrews giggles politely and innocently, no idea of what was to come her way three years in the future.

For their faux *Camelot* movie casting, Julie comes up with Bobby Darin as Lancelot, Jayne Mansfield as *Guenevere*, and Dean Martin as King Arthur, whom Moore pictures not only at the head of the Round Table but *under* it as well.

(The) *American Musical Theatre* (WCBS-TV)

Described as "an informal workshop" hosting contributors to the musical theatre scene, this half-hour local New York series welcomed theatre-educated youth from the city high schools to hear stories and songs.

"The Musicals of Rodgers and Hammerstein," June 6, 1961

Host: Jim Morske, with Richard Rodgers, Martha Wright, John Reardon.

Rodgers gives some background on his collaboration with Oscar and the difference between working with him and Lorenz Hart. Wright and Reardon duet on one of the songs she would *not* get to sing on stage in *TSOM*, "Climb Ev'ry Mountain." Rodgers also talks about writing lyrics and music for three songs for a new film of *State Fair* and plans for a (never fulfilled) collaboration with Alan Jay Lerner.

"Salute to Richard Rodgers," June 24, 1962

Host: Earl Wrightson Jr., with Martha Wright, Ralph Curtis.

Basically a Rodgers concert performed by the three singers, it climaxes with the trio doing the same *TSOM* song Wright had chimed in on during her previous visit to the show, "Climb Ev'ry Mountain."

Bell Telephone Hour

"The Music of Richard Rodgers" (NBC, November 10, 1961)

Rodgers himself appeared to bracket this program, part of which celebrated the upcoming second anniversary of *The Sound of Music* on Broadway. Martha Wright, who had taken over the role of Maria from Mary Martin, sang the title song, while Elizabeth Howell (then playing Mother Abbess) led a nun's chorus of seventeen in "Dixit Dominus/Alleluia" and "Climb Ev'ry Mountain."

The Bob Newhart Show (NBC, February 7, 1962)

On Bob's weekly New York–based variety show, Martha Wright is joined by the children from the current cast of *The Sound of Music* to perform "Do-Re-Mi," described by Newhart as "the highpoint of the play." The girls are dressed in rather garish costumes instead of their sailor outfits.

The Garry Moore Show (CBS, December 19, 1961)

So, *The Sound of Music* wasn't the *first* time audiences could watch Julie Andrews perform "My Favorite Things." More than three years before she sang it on screen, she was seen chirping it during her third guest appearance on this variety show, surrounded by a chorus of men grinding street organs. Since it was heard on the program's Christmas episode, this meant the song was being offered as a holiday selection, as it came to be considered by many in future years.

Julie & Carol at Carnegie Hall (CBS, June 11, 1962)

In one of the great ironic, prescient moments in show business history, Julie Andrews poked fun at the musical she'd find herself forever linked with, two years before the filming of *The Sound of Music*.

Having clicked so well with Carol Burnett after they appeared together on several episodes of *The Garry Moore Show*, it was decided that they would do their own special, taped (on March 5, 1962) at New York's prestigious Carnegie Hall. It ended up winning Emmy Awards as Outstanding Music Program and Outstanding Performance in a Variety or Music Program or Series for Burnett (shared with her other special that season, *An Evening with Carol Burnett*).

In one of the show's highlights, the two women starred in a sketch called "The Pratt Family Singers" (direct from Switzerland, as the placard board tells us). Julie is "Mama," presiding, with "Papa," over a brood of no less than nineteen lederhosen-clad boys (all with distinctive German names, including the two from the Broadway show that also ended up in the movie, "Friedrich" and "Kurt") and one girl, "Cynthia" (Burnett).

Introducing the company as the "Swiss Family Pratt," Julie informs the audience, "We bring you a happy song that I used to sing when I was a happy nun, back home in Switzerland." This leads to a slap-happy spoof of "My Favorite Things," the troupe singing that "The things we like best are these . . . pig's feet and cheese." For their follow-up number, ribbing "Do-Re-Mi," they dismiss the idea of learning music the standard way, as Burnett sings that "We have found a ghastly sound for every single note." This leads to a cutesy demonstration of sounds like "yum yum," "ho-ho," "ding-dong," and various baby noises, and the offer for the audience to "sing along, if it doesn't make you sick."

The writers were Mike Nichols and Ken Welch; the musical director, Irwin Kostal, who would handle this duty on the film of *The Sound of Music*.

Julie and Carol would team for two later, post-*TSOM* specials, *Julie & Carol at Lincoln Center* (1971) and *Julie & Carol Together Again* (1989). In the former, the two teased each other about what they'd been doing in the 9 1/2-year interim. When Julie mentioned that she went out to Hollywood to do *TSOM*, Carol joked, "Say, did that thing ever come off?"

The Ed Sullivan Show (CBS, November 4, 1962)

A special edition of the series, "A Tribute to Richard Rodgers," was filmed, not at the emcee's usual location, CBS-TV Studio 50 (the former Hammerstein Theatre), but at Carnegie Hall. Broadway's current Maria, Nancy Dussault, was on hand with the seven children from the cast of *TSOM* to perform "Do-Re-Mi." Rodgers took to the stage at the finale to conduct "You'll Never Walk Alone" (sung by Cesare Siepi) from *Carousel*.

The Ed Sullivan Show (CBS, April 18, 1965)

Always on the lookout for the hottest show business acts, Sullivan cashed in on the growing popularity of *The Sound of Music* by inviting all seven of the film's von Trapp children to recreate the "So Long, Farewell" number. Performing on a scaled-down version of Boris Leven's staircase set and wearing their sailor outfits, Charmian Carr and her celluloid siblings went through the same staging of the number as in the movie, to a playback of the soundtrack recording. It is of interest to see a much taller Nicholas Hammond with his real, darker hair color.

Sullivan, in his inimitable way with words, refers to *TSOM* as "the 20th Century Fox flicker." There is no conversation with Sullivan and the kids before or after the segment.

The Julie Andrews Show (NBC, November 28, 1965)

Somehow, between film assignments, the very busy Julie Andrews found time to squeeze in her own NBC special, on which she welcomed guest stars Gene Kelly (who, according to screenwriter Ernest Lehman, had flatly and dismissively turned down his offer to direct *The Sound of Music*) and the New Christy Minstrels. Billed in *TV Guide* as "the Program All America Has Been Waiting For . . . ," there was no doubt Julie was going to give eager audiences a taste of her current blockbuster movie, singing "The Sound of Music" and "My Favorite Things" (paired in the same segment with *My Fair Lady*'s "I Could Have Danced All Night").

It is interesting to note that although Julie rated a *TV Guide* cover on the May 22, 1965 issue in conjunction with a story about the making of this special, the article never mentioned *The Sound of Music*, indicating that the "phenomenon" was still in its early stages.

Mary Martin at Eastertime (NBC, April 3, 1966)

This entire Mary Martin special takes place at Radio City Music Hall in New York, with the star taking part in the movie palace's annual "Glory of Easter" pageant and dancing with their fabled Rockettes. She also finds space to sing the title song from *The Sound of Music.* Other numbers include "There Is Nothing Like a Dame" from *South Pacific.* At the time this program aired, the Music Hall was screening the *other* movie from the era about a warbling sister, *The Singing Nun.*

Star! (20th Century-Fox, October 22, 1968)

This film is worth noting in *TSOM* history because it marked the only other time Julie Andrews collaborated with director-producer Robert Wise. Also along from *TSOM* team were Saul Chaplin (here receiving producer credit); production designer Boris Leven; editor William Reynolds; set decorator Walter M. Scott; assistant director Ridgeway Callow; sound recorders Bernard Freericks and Murray Spivack; special photographic effects men L. B. Abbott and Emil Kosa Jr.; and second-unit supervisor Maurice Zuberano, here listed as "production associate."

While the movie, a lavish biography of West End and Broadway star Gertrude Lawrence, famously did not even begin to duplicate the box office success of *TSOM,* both Andrews and Wise remained very proud of their work, which would rise in critical estimation over the years.

Star! received seven Oscar nominations: supporting actor (Daniel Massey, as Noël Coward); cinematography; art direction-set decoration; costume design; sound; music—score of a musical picture; and song (the title song).

The Julie Andrews Hour (ABC)

(Season 1, Episode 1; September 13, 1972)

On the premiere episode of her variety series Julie sings "Do-Re-Mi" while animated musical notes and lyrics dance across the screen.

(Season 1, Episode 16; January 20, 1973)

Moving to Saturday night in an effort to boost ratings, Julie's weekly variety show was trumpeted in that week's *TV Guide* as a salute to *The Sound of Music,* with an ad using the familiar swirling letters of the movie's logo. In addition to footage from the film, Julie sings the title tune as well as "Do-Re-Mi."

The real treat, however, is the appearance of Maria von Trapp, who banters with her host, who inquires timidly about the real lady's assessment of her movie performance. Maria assures her that she was "absolutely wonderful," but has reservations about her yodeling during "The Lonely Goatherd." This results in a brief lesson in the art of yodeling, with the two women warbling together. Returning from a station break, Julie and Maria chat, with the latter informing fans of the movie what happened to the Trapp Family *after* their (fictitious) mountain crossing. The highlight of the evening is an all-too-brief duet of "Edelweiss" by the two ladies, and the segment is concluded by Maria giving Julie a signed copy of her newest book, *Maria*.

Fred Astaire Salutes the Fox Musicals (ABC, October 24, 1974)

Although he was more readily associated with RKO and MGM, or even Paramount for that matter, Fred Astaire is given the task of hosting this special (aired as part of the late-night *ABC Wide World of Entertainment*) containing highlights of the 20th Century-Fox musical output over the years ("their trademark has always been the word 'variety,'" Astaire informs us, including "the blockbuster of them all, *The Sound of Music*").

The great dancer could lay claim to having been in only one musical made on the Fox lot, *Daddy Long Legs* (1955). In addition to Astaire's "History of the Beat" drum number, the "Sluefoot" dance, and the hit song "Something's Gotta Give" from that picture, there are clips from such movies as *Folies Bergère* (1935), *The Gang's All Here* (1943), *Carmen Jones* (1954), *Call Me Madam* (1953), *Hello, Dolly!* (1969), *Pigskin Parade* (1936), *On the Avenue* (1937), *Stormy Weather* (1943); *Hello Frisco Hello* (1943), *State Fair* (1945), and *Doctor Dolittle* (1967). There's also a brief wartime newsreel glimpse of a reverse sex, Floradora sextet which happens to include *TSOM*'s Peggy Wood among its all-star cast.

TSOM segment includes the Oscar trailer heralding its wins. According to Fred, that same year, 100 film critics and columnists were asked to select the "12 musicals which they felt were the greatest in film history." *TSOM* made the cut. Julie Andrews is seen performing the title number.

As Fred gives a rundown of some of the great dance directors/choreographers in the business, he includes Marc Breaux and "his lovely wife Dee Dee Wood." And so he should, as he points out, the male choreographer of *TSOM* just happened to be the director of this special.

Julie—My Favorite Things (ABC, April 18, 1975)

For this special, Julie Andrews keeps the promise of the show's title and sings (partially in voice-over) "My Favorite Things," as the opening number (the first shot is of "raindrops on roses"). A barrage of images appear, presumably these being some of her favorite things, including Carol Burnett, Jim Henson's Muppets (who are among the program's guests), John F. Kennedy, Richard Burton, Rex Harrison, Fred Astaire, crunchy peanut butter, Charlie Chaplin, her children, and husband Blake Edwards (who directed and co-wrote the special).

When Julie tries to join the rockin' beat of the Muppets' Dr. Teeth and the Electric Mayhem, they halt their number to tell her she simply isn't cutting it.

Tonight
JULIE ANDREWS
sings, dances, and laughs
about some of her favorite things

With guest stars
Peter Sellers
and
The Muppets
"Julie-My Favorite Things"
(abc) SPECIAL 9:00PM (7)

One of *The Sound of Music*'s most famous songs became the subtitle of Julie Andrews's 1975 television special.

"Just a little too much of *The Sound of Music* there, lady," Dr. Teeth opines, which Julie interprets as "square." Seeking advice on her lack of "hep-ness" from unhinged psychiatrist Fritz Fassbender (guest star Peter Sellers, reprising his role from the 1965 film *What's New Pussycat* and tossing in some lines from Mel Brooks's *The Producers*), Julie hopes to convey to him what kind of singer she is, this time by humming "My Favorite Things."

Salute to Sir Lew—The Master Showman (ABC, June 13, 1975)

The Sir Lew in question is impresario Sir Lew Grade (chairman of ATV, Associate Television Corporation Ltd.), who is saluted in this special videotaped on April 18, 1975 at the Grand Ballroom of the Hilton Hotel in New York City. Because his company was behind her weekly television show and several of her specials, Julie Andrews was on hand to sing "The Sound of Music" (as well as "Wouldn't It Be Loverly?," "I Could Have Danced All Night," and "If a Picture Paints a Thousand Words," and, with Tom Jones, "I've Grown Accustomed to His/Her Face" and "You Will Be My Music").

The other talent included Peter Sellers, John Lennon (in what turned out to be his last public performance), Dave Allen, and Dougie Squires's Second Generation.

The Merv Griffin Show (Syndicated, December 19, 1975)

On the eve of the opening of his latest directorial credit, *The Hindenburg*, Robert Wise is toasted by one of that film's stars, Gig Young, as well as by Julie Andrews and Walter Pidgeon, who appeared in Wise's 1954 film *Executive Suite*.

One to One (Syndicated, December 1975)

In this special promoting the children's relief organization World Vision International, Julie Andrews (who explains that she had recently adopted two Vietnamese orphans) teaches members of the Korean Children's Choir to sing

"Do-Re-Mi." But since they use a Pentatonic scale, it comes out as "Do-re-mi-so-la-do-la-so," and so they invite Julie to sing their version, which segues into a medley including "I'd Like to Teach the World to Sing," "Put Your Hand in the Hand," "Day by Day," and "Make Your Own Kind of Music." Julie even ends "Do-Re-Mi" by going for the high note as she ascends some steps, a la the film, but climaxes this version by banging a gong.

She also is joined by the children for a rendition of Rodgers and Hammerstein's "Getting to Know You."

An Evening with Julie Andrews (RCA, 1977)

This album (released in Japan and Australia) was recorded live at Osaka Festival Hall on September 21, 1977. Among the numbers are a medley consisting of "My Favorite Things," "Do-Re-Mi," and Mary Poppins's "Supercalifragilisticexpialidocious," as well as a separate presentation of "The Sound of Music." Other tunes include then-recent titles like Seals and Crofts' "I'll Play for You" and Carole Bayer Sager's "I'd Rather Leave While I'm in Love."

Oscar's Best Movies (ABC, February 13, 1977)

In this two-hour, fifteen-minute special, consisting of clips from all forty-eight movies to have won the Academy Award for Best Picture thus far, Julie Andrews, fittingly, hosted the segment on musicals, which included *her* one Best Picture winner, *TSOM*. The other hosts were Gregory Peck (star of the 1947 Best Picture winner *Gentleman's Agreement*) and Olivia de Havilland (1939's Best Picture, *Gone with the Wind*), as well as three actors who did *not* have any Best Picture winners on their resumes, Goldie Hawn, Walter Matthau, and Katharine Ross (who was the only one on hand to not have an Oscar of her own, having been nominated for *The Graduate* but not winning).

The Billion Dollar Movies (NBC, May 15, 1977)

Producer Lee Mendelsohn presented a special on NBC's *The Big Event* celebrating the fourteen (why not fifteen?) highest-grossing movies of all time. By this point *The Sound of Music* had slipped into fourth position, with *Jaws* (1975) leading the pack. The idea was to get those involved in each of the blockbusters to reminisce, and, surprisingly, it is Christopher Plummer, not Julie Andrews or any of the movie's children, who is called on to represent *TSOM*. Although his own champion moneymaker, *Around the World in Eighty Days* (1956), had slipped below the eligibility list, David Niven served as host.

Apparently having gotten very comfortable with his inseparable association with the mightiest musical of them all, Plummer went one better for the next such special produced by Mendelsohn. For ***Movie Blockbusters: The 15 Greatest Hits of All Time*** (CBS, May 24, 1983), Plummer was promoted to host of the whole affair, which now saw his highest earner at #11, with *E.T. the Extra-Terrestrial* (1982) holding the top spot, and *Grease* (1978), at #7, having dethroned the R&H classic as the top-grossing musical. Seated at a piano, Plummer welcomes Maria von Trapp to the stage, telling her, "I hope you've forgiven me, after this long time, for trying to play your husband." After fluttering his fingers quickly over the keys, Plummer hands the musical portion of the program over to five unidentified youngsters who serenade Maria with "Edelweiss."

America Salutes the Queen (NBC, November 29, 1977)

On the twenty-fifth anniversary of her reign, England's Queen Elizabeth II is given a gala party at the London Palladium (taped on November 1). For her segment, Julie Andrews performed a medley that included: "My Favorite Things" and "The Sound of Music," along with "Camelot" and "I Could Have Danced All Night." (She also sang "I'll Play for You.")

The other guests included Shirley MacLaine, Paul Anka, Harry Belafonte, Alan King, Cleo Laine, Rudolf Nureyev, and the Muppets. London-born Bob Hope was the host.

The Muppet Show (Syndicated; UK airing: December 25, 1977; US airing: February 18, 1978)

For her first number, guest star Julie Andrews performs "The Lonely Goatherd" with not only the requisite goat puppet on hand but the usual diverse Muppet menagerie of chickens, pigs, dogs, etc. These include Kermit the Frog (as "a prince on the bridge of a castle moat") and Miss Piggy (as "one little girl in a pale pink coat"). During the number, Rowlf the Dog tells one of his fellow canines, "You know, I saw the movie twice." Andrews also sings "Whistle a Happy Tune" from Rodgers and Hammerstein's *The King and I.*

The Kennedy Center Honors: A Celebration of the Arts (CBS, December 5, 1978)

Richard Rodgers is rightfully among the very first artists selected to receive this prestigious honor (presented at the Kennedy Center for Performing Arts on December 3, 1978), which would become an annual tradition. Mary Martin serves as the host for his segment, and therefore we hear her rendition of the title song from *The Sound of Music* cast album. The show's road company Maria, Florence Henderson, then appears to sing the song, live. Martin also uses the most famous line of the song to make her point about the enduring nature of Rodgers's music. "And with our dear friend, Oscar Hammerstein's words, when he said 'the hills are alive with the sound of music,' he *knew* what he was talking about." She continues, "Richard Rodgers's music will fill the hills and the valleys of our world for all time to come." There is then a bit of Julie Andrews heard singing "My Favorite Things" over an Al Hirschfeld image of her, one of several caricatures surrounding one of Rodgers. John Raitt and Tony Bennett are also on hand to croon to the honoree.

The other recipients that year were Marian Anderson, Fred Astaire, George Balanchine, and Arthur Rubinstein.

The Parkinson Show (BBC1, March 14, 1981)

During her West End run as Maria in the revival of *TSOM*, Petula Clark made several television appearances to promote the show. This one was of special interest because Michael Parkinson's other guest was the musical's original stage Maria, Mary Martin, who joins Petula in a duet on "My Favorite Things." Petula also performs "Edelweiss."

The Best of Broadway (The Entertainment Channel, 1982)

Taped at the La Mirada Civic Auditorium, this incredible collection of Broadway luminaries reprising some of their most famous numbers initially aired on a short-lived and little-subscribed-to pay cable station, the Entertainment Channel, in 1982 and then was repeated (and therefore more widely seen) on PBS on May 24, 1985. Among those on hand were Ethel Merman, Anthony Perkins, Jerry Orbach, Glynis Johns, and Debbie Reynolds. Mary Martin sang "Do-Re-Mi." The special was retitled *That's Singing: The Best of Broadway* for its transfer to home video, but Martin's sequence was among those not included.

Rodgers & Hammerstein: The Sound of American Music (PBS, March 16, 1985)

Hosted by Mary Martin, this look at the collaboration of the great songwriters is well worthwhile because of the stellar lineup of contributors to their story sharing their memories. They are: Alfred Drake, Gordon MacRae, Joan Roberts, Shirley Jones, Rouben Mamoulian, Agnes de Mille, Dorothy Rodgers, Celeste Holm, John Raitt, James Michener, Joshua Logan, William Hammerstein, Dorothy Hammerstein, Yul Brynner (who would pass away later that same year), Theodore Bikel, Robert Wise, and Mary Rodgers. R&H admirer Andrew Lloyd Webber and later Rodgers collaborator Martin Charnin share their thoughts as well.

The special uses a generous portion of clips (alas, not letterboxed) from the film versions of the shows covered: *Oklahoma!*, *Carousel*, *South Pacific*, *The King and I*, *Flower Drum Song*, and *The Sound of Music*, as well as some television interviews and performances. Although "All Kinds of People" from *Pipe Dream* and "A Fellow Needs a Girl" from *Allegro* are heard over the ending montage, neither of these shows are covered in depth, nor are *Me & Juliet*, *State Fair*, or *Cinderella*.

Mary Martin gives her full endorsement to the woman who landed her role in the film version of *TSOM*, Julie Andrews, stating that "when it came time to cast the movie of *The Sound of Music*, she was at the top of *all* our lists!" Robert Wise talks about the decision to use Andrews in the lead and theorizes on why the movie was so tremendously popular. "I don't have a single answer," he admits. "I think it's a combination of elements . . . the material itself, the marvelous story and the characters and the relationships, the great score of Rodgers and Hammerstein. I think the casting contributed a lot to it, I think the marvelous locations that fed so beautifully into that lovely story." There are clips of the opening number (of course), "Something Good," and "My Favorite Things." Covering the Broadway version, Martin is joined by her stage "captain," Theodore Bikel, for a duet on "Edelweiss" and some fond reminiscing, including Bikel receiving a critical assessment on his whistle-blowing from members of the military.

Hammerstein's older son, William, addresses the R&H naysayers. "Many people have criticized their work as being corny and sentimental and my father's answer was always '*Yes!* That's what they are . . . that's what life is.'"

Julie Andrews . . . the Sound of Christmas (ABC, December 16, 1987)

This Julie Andrews special stands out above all others for fans of *The Sound of Music*, because of its setting, Salzburg, with the star returning twenty-three years after making her most popular movie there. And if the location and the title are not enough to make the connection clear, the show begins with the camera panning over the Alps as the wind blows on the soundtrack, the orchestration rising with a familiar sound as the star comes over a snowcapped hill. The song, however, is not Rodgers and Hammerstein's immortal title tune, but a new one, written especially for this presentation, "The Sound of Christmas" by Larry Grossman and Buz Kohan. There is room later on for one tune from the film, "Edelweiss," a duet performed by Julie and one of her guest stars, John Denver, before a fireplace in an unidentified Austrian lodge.

The hills were alive once again when Julie Andrews returned to Austria for the 1987 special *Julie Andrews . . . the Sound of Christmas*.

Among the familiar movie sights on hand are the Horse Fountain, which Julie and her charges had walked by in the pre-"Do-Re-Mi" montage; the Hohensalzburg Castle, which loomed in the background of many scenes; Schloss Anif, the water castle from the movie's opening aerial views; and Werfen Castle, which sat in the distance behind Julie and the children as they began the hilltop portion of "Do-Re-Mi." It is the last that provides the special with its most haunting moment, as Julie sings "In the Bleak Midwinter," walking through the desolate, mountaintop location.

For an added treat, we get to see the *inside* of Leopoldskron, which was intended to provide the lakefront terrace of the von Trapp villa in the film but ended up being copied nearby. The stand-out site revisited here is, however, the cathedral at Mondsee, where the film's wedding was staged. "You were married here. Am I correct?," guest star Placido Domingo asks his host. To which Julie replies, "Sort of. It was really a marriage made in Hollywood."

This magnificent structure provides the climax of the special, as a Christmas service is attended by Salzburg residents who are treated to the sight of Julie Andrews back on that same altar, sharing the stage with Denver, Domingo, the King's Singers, and a chorus as they sing, among others, "The Wexford Carol," "O Come All Ye Faithful," and "Ave Maria."

The connections to the movie extend even beyond what is presented on screen, as the cast and crew of the new special stayed at Österreichischer Hof during shooting, this being one of the hotels that accommodated members of *TSOM* company back in 1964.

This special won five Emmy awards: Outstanding Achievement in Music Direction; Music and Lyrics (for "The Sound of Christmas"); Editing for a Miniseries or a Special—Multi-Camera Production; Lighting Direction (Electronic) for a Variety/Music or Drama Series, a Miniseries or a Special; Technical Direction/Electronic Camera/Video Control for a Miniseries or Special.

Great Performances: Julie Andrews in Concert (PBS, March 18, 1990)

Julie performs twenty-four songs in this hour-long concert from her tour, taped at Los Angeles' Wiltern Theatre in August of the previous year.

For her intro to "My Favorite Things," she tells a story/joke about a lady spotting her in a hotel lobby and telling her she's seen *The Sound of Music* fifteen times. The reason? She never misses a good Christopher Plummer movie. The song segues into "Supercalifragilisticexpialidocious" (from *Mary Poppins*) and the title tune from *Thoroughly Modern Millie*. Julie caps the show with "The Sound of Music" as her encore.

This program won the Emmy for Outstanding Music Direction (Ian Fraser), with arrangements handled by Chris Boardman, Bill Byers, Bob Florence, J. Hill, and Angela Morley.

The Sound of Music at the Old Courthouse Theatre (1993)

Rolf graduated from louse to hero when Daniel Truhitte was invited to portray Captain von Trapp in a production of *The Sound of Music* at the Old Courthouse Theater in the town where he had moved, Concord, North Carolina. This nostalgic bit of casting prompted a six-minute segment on *Entertainment Tonight*, "A Day in the Life of Daniel Truhitte," which aired on September 10, 1993 (Truhitte's fiftieth birthday). Maria was played by Jenny Cone Carroll.

And it was not Truhitte's last crack at the part (see 2013).

The Sound of Orchestra/The Sound of Julie Andrews (Japanese Broadcasting Corporation, Japan, August 21, 1993)

Julie's second Japanese concert was titled *The Sound of Orchestra* when it aired there on August 21, 1993, while a shorter version was broadcast in the U.S. as *The Sound of Julie Andrews*. Andre Previn (who was the arranger and conductor of the musical numbers for *Thoroughly Modern Millie*) served as conductor of the NHK Symphony Orchestra.

In addition to a Richard Rodgers (whom Julie tells the audience "has had a profound influence on my life") waltz medley, Julie sings "The Sound of Music," "My Favorite Things," and "Do-Re-Mi" (both as part of the "Symphonic Movie Medley," the latter including its Japanese lyrics), and perhaps her most lush rendition ever of "Edelweiss"

Says Andrews in an interview segment: "In a way, that's my mission, now, to keep reminding people that there *were* giants like Rodgers and Hammerstein. I don't want people to *ever* forget . . . They should never be forgotten. And I'm very happy to *try* to help people remember."

The Directors: The Films of Robert Wise (produced by Media Entertainment, Inc. in association with the Directors Company: 1994; distributed as part of a series on Encore Channel and on Fox Lorber DVD, from 1999 on)

This patchy series spotlighting notable directors consists of interviews with the subject and a combination of stills and all-too-brief clips. Some Wise films receive greater scrutiny than others depending on the stories behind them and who wants to talk about them. Therefore there is great attention paid to *Blood on the Moon* and *Two for the Seesaw*, because Robert Mitchum is on hand; *Tribute to a Bad Man*, because Wise tells in detail the story of Spencer Tracy's dismissal from the picture; *West Side Story*, because there are comments by Rita Moreno; and *Star Trek—The Motion Picture*, because Leonard Nimoy offers some insight.

The section on *The Sound of Music* ("It stands as a monument to his directorial talents," says series narrator Dan Stevens) includes on-the-set clips from the *Salzburg Sight and Sound* documentary, and interviews with Julie Andrews (saying they tried to make the movie "as astringent as possible") and Saul Chaplin. Chaplin greatly emphasizes the necessity of having someone like Wise at the helm: "they *need* him," he says, thinking back on the experience, "Because in the hands of the average director it (could) be so sweet and saccharine, but Bob, because he's a reality director . . . it'll take all that out . . . A certain amount of it is necessary but it'll be dampened a lot."

Wise is seen being interviewed at the DGA Theatre, and on the 20th Century-Fox back-lot including Soundstage 14, where the engine room for *The Sand Pebbles* once stood.

The other talking heads are: *TSOM*'s second-unit supervisor Maurice Zuberano; writer Nelson Gidding; *TSOM*'s screenwriter Ernest Lehman; story editor Max Lamb; and producer Charles Maguire.

This series, co-produced with the American Film Institute, covered such other directors as Steven Spielberg, Milos Forman, Clint Eastwood, and Oliver Stone.

Julie Andrews, *Broadway: The Music of Richard Rodgers* (Philips; 1994)

This CD features all new recordings by Julie Andrews of "The Sound of Music" and "Edelweiss." Among the other Rodgers tunes included are "I Have Dreamed" (from *The King and I*), "Where or When" (from *Babes in Arms*), "Nobody Told Me" (from *No Strings*), "Bewitched, Bothered and Bewildered" (from *Pal Joey*), "If I Loved You" (from *Carousel*), and "A Cockeyed Optimist" (from *South Pacific*). Ian Fraser is the arranger and conductor; Angela Morley did the orchestrations for the two *TSOM* songs.

Great Performances: Some Enchanted Evening: Celebrating Oscar Hammerstein II (PBS, March, 1995)

This concert from New York's City Center is hosted by Julie Andrews, who opens the show with "A Cockeyed Optimist" from *South Pacific*. She also narrates a brief bio of the lyricist that includes clips of various movies and TV shows referencing his songs. As part of a Rodgers and Hammerstein medley, cast members from the revivals of *Carousel* and *Show Boat* give us samples from four *Sound of Music* songs: "Do-Re-Mi," "Sixteen Going on Seventeen," "So Long, Farewell," and the title number. Hammerstein's protégé, Stephen Sondheim, reflects on being mentored by Oscar, and Julie offers an expectedly lilting rendition of "Edelweiss." As part of the finale the ensemble sings "A Bell is No Bell," and the New York City Gay Men's Chorus chimes in on a stirring rendition of "Climb Ev'ry Mountain."

Great Performances: Julie Andrews: Back on Broadway (PBS, October 25, 1995)

To promote Julie Andrews's long-overdue return to Broadway for the stage version of *Victor Victoria*, this tie-in documentary looks back on her career with an impressive array of clips, as well as comments from Julie herself and many friends, family, and colleagues.

TSOM segment is introduced with footage from a black-and-white newsreel heralding the making of the movie in Austria. It also includes several scenes from the movie ("Something Good," "Do-Re-Mi," "My Favorite Things," and "The Sound of Music" among them); comments from Robert Wise; Julie's first husband, designer Tony Walton, who mentions seeing the show with his wife and the two of them having reservations about her accepting the role of Maria; Roddy McDowall talking about attending the Los Angeles premiere of the movie with Julie, as footage is seen from the event, and speaking astutely about how overwhelming was the degree of her fame and how well she handled it; praise from Julie for Christopher Plummer "rooting" the film and for Wise teaching her so much about acting in motion pictures.

"It was hard to know then," Julie says, "what I recognize now, which is that it was just the most extraordinary opportunity anybody could have . . . The whole film is *superbly* crafted in every way; the sets, the costumes, the scenery, the way it was shot—it is . . . magical!"

And looking back on it all, she observes, "I hadn't realized . . . that a really major success does kind of bracket you . . . a *huge* success, people remember you *always* for the thing that was the biggest or the most successful."

Rodgers & Hammerstein: The Sound of Movies (A&E, April 7, 1996)

All eight of the movies that contain scores by Richard Rodgers and Oscar Hammerstein II are covered in loving detail in this documentary directed by Kevin Burns and hosted by the star of two of those movies (*Oklahoma!* and *Carousel*), Shirley Jones. Lengthy clips are seen from those two releases as well as both versions of *State Fair* (1945 and 1962), *The King and I, South Pacific, Flower Drum Song*, and *The Sound of Music*. Also shown are a cut portion of Dick Haymes singing "Isn't It Kind of Fun?" from *State Fair*; comparisons of the Todd-AO and CinemaScope versions of *Oklahoma!*, and Frank Sinatra's recording of "If I Loved You" made before he dropped out of *Carousel*. Appearing as co-hosts: Rita Moreno (who played Tuptim) for *The King and I*; Nancy Kwan (Linda Lo) for *Flower Drum Song*; and Charmian Carr (seen in a mock gazebo) for *The Sound of Music*.

TSOM (proclaimed here in the Rodgers and Hammerstein canon as "the crowning achievement of a truly memorable partnership") is covered in the final twenty-five minutes of the special, including snippets of the opening number, "Do-Re-Mi," "I Have Confidence," both "So Long, Farewell" and

"Edelweiss" from the festival sequence, "The Lonely Goatherd," the wedding processional, and "Something Good" as well as a brief glimpse of *Die Trapp-Familie* German movie; TV's *Cinderella*; amusing examples of the foreign, dubbed versions of the title song, "My Favorite Things," and "Maria" ("*The Sound of Music* became Rodgers and Hammerstein's goodwill ambassador to the world," says Jones); and fleeting clips of auditions by Bryan Russell, Tisha Sterling, Danny Lockin, and Kim Darby, among others. Julie Andrews talks about seeing Mary Martin in the original stage production, never dreaming that she'd be taking over her part in the movie. "I think I really thought that probably Mary would do it when the time came for the film," she claims. "But listen, I wouldn't have turned down the role for . . . anything, so . . . I was going to do it come what may, if they asked me."

Despite the proper documentation of the movie's tremendous financial success, Carr sells it short in her narration, stating that it ran in reserved-seat engagements for a year and nothing more, before going into general release, when, in fact, several of its road show bookings went for much longer than that. Only occasionally is it pointed out when certain performers had their vocals dubbed, one such being Deborah Kerr in *The King and I*, with her "ghost," Marni Nixon, interviewed here.

The trailers for all eight movies are included in the extras on the DVD release.

20th Century Fox: The First 50 Years (AMC, January 21, 1997)

For the bulk of this two hours-plus documentary (directed and written by Kevin Burns) on the creation and history of 20th Century-Fox, the viewer is given a pretty good overall look at how Darryl F. Zanuck took the reins in 1935 and merged Fox Studios with 20th Century Pictures. There are clips of the expected Fox stars, including Will Rogers, Shirley Temple, Sonja Henie, Tyrone Power, Henry Fonda, Betty Grable, Gregory Peck, Carmen Miranda, and Marilyn Monroe; highlights from the Oscar winners *Cavalcade* (1933), *How Green Was My Valley* (1941), *Gentleman's Agreement* (1947), and *All about Eve* (1950); a separate section on the Rodgers and Hammerstein musicals of the 1950s (throwing Magna's *Oklahoma!* into the mix); contemporary comments from the likes of Alice Faye, Roddy McDowall, Richard Zanuck, *TSOM* editor William Reynolds, Red Buttons, Don Murray, and Jane Withers, plus narration by James Coburn, who, uncharitably, is not represented in the clips.

Robert Wise is on hand to discuss Zanuck and the development of CinemaScope, and there is a generous amount of time accorded his 1951 sci-fi classic *The Day the Earth Stood Still*. The "climax" of the documentary, so to speak, is actually given over to *TSOM*, looked upon as the studio's rescuer in light of the financial calamities that drove the budget of *Cleopatra* (1963) to the stratosphere. As Coburn puts it, "Fox needed a blockbuster. What they found was . . . *The Sound of Music*." Head of production Richard Zanuck says that because of the musical "We were able to re-establish ourselves as a force in the business, and a force to be reckoned with." Seen are bits of the opening number (what did you expect?), some of "Do-Re-Mi," the Beverly Hills premiere, and footage from on-set filming from *Salzburg Sight and Sound*. Wise and executive David Brown reflect on the movie's impact, as does Julie Andrews, who emphasizes the unprecedented box office phenomenon by saying "It really became its own animal, so to speak. It was almost, sort of, a legend in its own time." The upbeat tone of the documentary is reflected in the narration inaccurately telling us that screenwriter Ernest Lehman was an Academy Award-winner (he would never receive a competitive Oscar—only an honorary one, toward the end of his life), and that *TSOM* reviews were "rapturous" (if only!).

Disappointingly, just when one assumes there will be another hour or so looking at the studio since the mid-sixties, the narrative suddenly speeds through to the present day, mentioning some Fox moneymakers and then leaving it at that. Basically, *TSOM* becomes the studio peak and the harbinger of all good things to come at 20th Century-Fox, at least according to this film.

Victor Victoria (Marquis Theatre, June 8, 1997)

As a way of giving Julie Andrews a memorable send-off to her triumphant return to Broadway in a stage adaptation of her hit movie *Victor Victoria*, the audience at her last performance in the show was asked to join the cast in serenading the star with "Edelweiss." Much to Andrews's and the audience's delighted surprise, Christopher Plummer, who was, at the time, appearing around the corner at the Music Box Theatre in *Barrymore*, showed up on stage to start off the number. The ensemble vocalizing meant that there was little chance of comparing Plummer's rendition of the song to the man who had dubbed him in the movie, Bill Lee.

The American Film Institute Tribute to Robert Wise (NBC, June 7, 1998; later aired in a longer format on A&E)

With Julie Andrews as the host, it is only fitting that the crowning achievement in Robert Wise's output is emphasized here as being *The Sound of Music*. In front of a collage of oversized images from Wise's career that include the much-seen one of Julie atop the hill with her arms outstretched, the gracious hostess tells stories about shooting the classic musical that have become *very* familiar ones over the years: failing to rescue Kym Karath during the boat scene and being knocked over by the helicopter downdraft while trying to shoot the opening. She speaks of her director's gentility and lack of ego, referring to him as "a quiet giant of American film."

In addition to a brief, silent glimpse of Andrews and Christopher Plummer's gazebo kiss, and behind-the-scenes footage of Wise filming "Do-Re-Mi," the evening builds to Andrews reading a verse letter from Plummer (who was on stage in Toronto at the time) that proclaims of Wise, "His list of accomplishments could reach the skies . . ." To demonstrate, Julie then brings on the long-awaited *TSOM* section of the program, referring to it as "the Wise film that *did* touch the skies and fill screens and hearts all over the world." A truncated version of the "Do-Re-Mi" number (starting with the bicycling by the lake) is seen. Soon after, Jack Lemmon (a previous AFI recipient, but one who had never acted in a Wise movie) comes on stage to give Wise his award, but before this happens one more clip is seen from *TSOM*, Julie singing the title song. An instrumental version of the tune is then played as Wise makes his way to the podium.

The full-length two-hour (with commercials) telecast of the evening (which A&E would show after NBC's initial airing of the hour-long version) included appearances at the podium by Peter Fonda (from *Two People*), Rita Moreno (*West Side Story*), Candice Bergen (*The Sand Pebbles*), Richard Crenna (*The Sand Pebbles, Star!*), and James Cameron (admirer, then hot from having helmed *Titanic*), and testimonials from the audience by fellow filmmakers and admirers John Sayles and Martha Coolidge; Patricia Neal (*Three Secrets, The Day the Earth Stood Still, Something for the Birds*); Leonard Nimoy and William Shatner (*Star Trek: The Motion Picture*); George Chakiris (*West Side Story*); Robert Loggia (*Somebody Up There Likes Me*); Broadway's original Captain von Trapp, Theodore Bikel (*I Want to Live!*); Charles Durning (*The Hindenburg*); and Nina Foch (*Executive Suite*).

The actual ceremony had taken place on February 19, 1998 at the ballroom of the Beverly Hilton Hotel in Beverly Hills. Wise was the twenty-sixth recipient of the American Film Institute Life Achievement Award. Also in attendance were Wise's second wife, Millicent; his daughter Pamela; and his granddaughter Alexandra.

Backstage at The Sound of Music (March, 1999)

A behind-the-scenes glimpse (a year into the run, for their 374th performance) at how the 1998 Broadway revival of the musical works, this documentary by director-writer Rick McKay is hosted by executive producer Jamie deRoy, who speaks with many of the technicians and stage crew responsible. As assistant wardrobe supervisor James Nadeaux puts it: "If you can *see* that there are people working backstage, we're doing something wrong. It should look so flawless, and so easy, and just . . . you know, the sound of music flowing over the mountains."

There are visits with Rebecca Luker (Maria) and Dennis Parlato (Captain von Trapp) showing how the actors wear their transmitter mics; and footage (and bits of songs) from the show. Also on hand are Maria-to-be Laura Benanti ("following in the footsteps of Mary Martin, Julie Andrews, and Rebecca Luker," as deRoy points out), and some of the production's current Von Trapp kids: Lou Taylor Pucci (13), Marshall Pailet (11), Andrea Bowen (8), Christianna Ambrey (8), Tracy Walsh (11), and Nora Blackall (13).

The Rosie O'Donnell Show (ABC, January 21, 2000)

For the thirty-fifth anniversary of what host Rosie O'Donnell declares is "the best movie ever made, in my opinion," she is joined by Julie Andrews and Christopher Plummer. O'Donnell boasts that she knows every line in *TSOM* and has to give Andrews some assistance as she's trying to name each of the Trapp children, in order. The two stars giggling while shooting the gazebo scene is brought up; as is the Austrian farmer angrily piercing holes in the fake makeshift brook on whose field they filmed the opening scene; and the need to take some of the saccharine out of the original piece, something Andrews feels was accomplished thanks to Plummer. The actors both claim that they do *not* own copies of the DVD, which is to be distributed to each of that day's audience members.

On Golden Pond (CBS, April 29, 2001)

Sometimes when two actors pair off so memorably on screen, it's best to leave well enough alone and never reunite them, allowing them to be forever linked solely to their great triumph (e.g., Clark Gable and Vivien Leigh were never again co-starred after *Gone with the Wind,* nor did Humphrey Bogart and Ingrid Bergman follow *Casablanca* with a rematch). It was assumed for years that Julie Andrews and Christopher Plummer would keep *The Sound of Music* as their one and only teaming, but then someone came up with the intriguing idea of putting them in a live television broadcast of *On Golden Pond.*

Ernest Thompson's play had already been filmed with tremendous results in 1981, with Katharine Hepburn and Henry Fonda filling the leads and winning Academy Awards in the process. Since Andrews and Plummer knew they were going up against enduring memories of those great actors, the live angle was a smart one. "Together for the first time since *The Sound of Music,*" ran the ad in *TV Guide,* which also referred to them as "two legendary stars."

Playing long-married seniors (Andrews was sixty-five at the time, Plummer seventy-one) facing what will probably be their final summer vacation together, the stars conjured up that same special chemistry that had made them one of the screen's favorite couples thirty-six

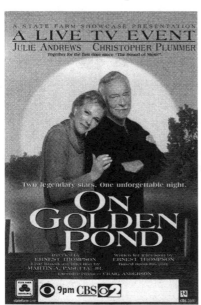

It took Julie Andrews and Christopher Plummer thirty-five years to reteam, which they did for a 2000 television adaptation of the play *On Golden Pond.*

years earlier. Staged at CBS Television City (it was shown on a Sunday evening in a two-hour time slot), under Thompson's direction (he was quoted as saying "I've got two of the most attractive actors imaginable to play these parts"), the production also featured Glenne Headly, Sam Robards, Will Rothhaar, and Brett Cullen.

The Sound of Music Children: After They Were Famous (ITV, March 28, 2001)

This series gave fans of various performers a glimpse into their current lives, years after the property or roles that had sprung them into the spotlight. Occasionally, the show would put aside an entire episode to concentrate on a specific motion picture, with special chapters on such films as *Bugsy Malone, Chitty Chitty Bang Bang,* and *Willy Wonka and the Chocolate Factory.*

Between October 31 and November 7, 2000 the seven cinematic Trapp "children" gathered in Salzburg thirty-six years after filming to relive the experience as the film crew of Tyne Tees Television recorded them traipsing around familiar locations, most specifically those used in the "Do-Re-Mi" sequence, with the older but game Trapps trying to recreate some of Marc Breaux and Dee Dee Wood's unforgettable choreography. Also seen are snippets of the home movies taken during *TSOM* filming.

As the press release for the sixty-minute program stated, "Today, *The Sound of Music* still fills millions of people with enthusiasm and for 70% of the tourists from the USA and the Far East it is the main reason to visit Salzburg."

The 24th Annual Kennedy Center Honors (CBS, December 26, 2001)

Julie Andrews is the recipient of this most prestigious honor hailing the great contributors to the performing arts, taped on December 2, 2001 at the Opera House at the Kennedy Center in Washington D.C. Joining her in the presidential box of honor are fellow recipients Jack Nicholson, Van Cliburn, Luciano Pavarotti, and Quincy Jones. Seen sitting behind Julie is husband Blake Edwards.

Leading off the tribute is Carol Burnett, who jokingly describes her friend and colleague as "An English nanny who became an Austrian nun, who suddenly, miraculously, became the instant mother of 7 yodeling children." She adds that Julie has given us "the greatest mountaintop twirl that was ever seen on the silver screen." Burnett leads the audience through clips from Andrews's career, including that "mountaintop twirl" from *TSOM* and a glimpse of the movie's Wilshire Theatre premiere with Julie and Christopher Plummer in attendance. Burnett reminds us that the film "remains *the* most popular movie musical ever; not so much watched as *absorbed* into our national memory. We all stopped simply to catch our breath."

Those chiming in for the celebration on stage (against a backdrop of Andrews titles, including the familiar swirling one for *TSOM*) are Patrick Wilson, Kristen Chenoweth, Julie's *Camelot* costar Robert Goulet, Audra McDonald (who would later play the Mother Abbess on television's *The Sound of Music Live!*), Jeremy Irons, and Rebecca Luker (Maria in the 1998 Broadway revival of *TSOM*), singing "The Sound of Music," with the others joining in the song for the finale.

As is the custom with these tributes, the honorees make no speeches, but are merely seen appreciating the praise from their seats.

Unconditional Love (New Line Cinema; UK release: August 23, 2002; US premiere on cable television: 2003)

A mild-mannered "homemaker," Grace Beasley (Kathy Bates), impulsively flies off to England to attend the funeral of the singer she worshipped. On the flight over, a terrible thunderstorm causes a frightening degree of turbulence on the plane. Not to worry, because seated next to Grace is Julie Andrews portraying . . . Julie Andrews! Taking charge, and knowing a thing or two about relaxing people during storms, Julie marches into the cockpit, where she is introduced to the passengers by the grateful captain. "Julie Andrews is in the cockpit," says a stunned passenger (Anne Lambton). "Thank God!" her husband (David Darlow) remarks, with a sigh of relief. Although Julie wisely falls back on Rodgers and Hammerstein for her comfort tune, it isn't the song you'd expect, but "Getting to Know You," from *The King and I*. Nevertheless, the parallel to her most famous movie is very clear.

But just to ensure that there *is* something from the score of *The Sound of Music* on hand, Grace is later seen riding with the lover (Rupert Everett) of the deceased singer on a bicycle, zooming downhill, which causes her to sing a few lines from "Climb Ev'ry Mountain."

Perhaps deemed too odd for the paying customers, this comedy by-passed theatres altogether in the U.S.

A Royal Christmas (Touring show: December 3–21, 2002)

At long last Julie Andrews and Christopher Plummer appeared in a live stage performance in this touring show celebrating Christmas. Joining them were soprano Charlotte Church along with some 150 supporting dancers, singers and musicians, from the Royal Ballet Covent Garden, Canada's Royal Winnipeg Ballet, Russia's Bolshoi Ballet, Ukraine's Kyiv Ballet, the Shumka Dancers, London's Royal Philharmonic Concert Orchestra, and the Westminster Concert Choir and Bell Choir. Andrews, who had famously declared in 1997 that a botched operation meant she was no longer able to sing, did manage one number, "I Saw Three Ships." Otherwise, she mainly served as host and recited *A Visit from St. Nicholas* (*The Night before Christmas*). Plummer read poems by

Ogden Nash and Dylan Thomas, and gave his interpretation of Ebenezer Scrooge. Although the program concentrated mostly on holiday music, audiences had every right to expect *something* from *The Sound of Music*, so Julie did join the Bell Choir for a bit of "Do-Re-Mi."

The U.S. and Canadian 2002 schedule was as follows:

Dec. 3 at the USBank Arena in Cincinnati, OH; Dec. 4 at the Van Andel Arena in Grand Rapids, MI; Dec. 6 at the Mellon Arena in Pittsburgh, PA; Dec. 7 at the Joe Louis Arena in Detroit, MI; Dec. 8 at the Nationwide Arena in Columbus, OH; Dec. 10 at the John Labatt Centre in London, ONT; Dec. 11 at the Air Canada Centre in Toronto, ONT; Dec. 12 at the Corel Centre in Ottawa, ONT; Dec. 14 at the Dunkin' Donuts Center in Providence, RI; Dec. 15 at the Fleet Center in Boston, MA; Dec. 16 at the Pepsi Arena in Albany, NY; Dec. 17 at the Giant Center in Hershey, PA; Dec. 18 at the Nassau Coliseum in Uniondale, NY; Dec. 20 at the St. Pete Times Forum in Tampa, FL; Dec. 21 at the Office Depot Forum in Ft. Lauderdale, FL

Good Morning America (ABC, November 11, 2005)

To celebrate the 40th anniversary release of *TSOM* on DVD, ABC's morning news-talk-entertainment show and its hosts, Charles Osgood and Diane Sawyer, welcomed Julie Andrews and the seven actors who played the Trapp children. Julie talks about how ironic it was that she and Carol Burnett made fun of the musical on their 1962 TV special and also points out to Sawyer, that her husband, Mike Nichols, was one of the writers on that sketch. There are familiar stories brought up about Christopher Plummer calling the film "The Sound of Mucus"; the boat flipping over and Kym Karath not being able to swim; and Charmian Carr being 21, not 16, during filming. There is also footage of Plummer talking about the movie at the time, theorizing that it might be a hit judging from the number of columnists on the set. The actors finish the segment by singing an impromptu, shortened version of "Edelweiss."

Shrek the Third (DreamWorks, May 18, 2007)

Julie Andrews reprised the role of ogre Fiona's (Cameron Diaz) regal mum in this third installment of the animated series of films. (She'd first done it in *Shrek 2* in 2004). Although she is given very little to do here, there is a brief but key moment when she comes up with the solution of how to rescue herself, her daughter, and various other storybook princesses from a dungeon—by knocking the wall down with her head. Dizzy from the impact, she is heard humming a teensy bit of "A Spoonful of Sugar" from *Mary Poppins* and an equally small amount of "My Favorite Things." Nothing much to get excited about, except that this marks the one and only time Andrews would musically repeat any of the songs (if only fragmentally) from *TSOM* in another of her movies.

Tooth Fairy (20th Century Fox, January 22, 2010)

While just another throwaway *TSOM* reference line, this fantasy comedy *does* however feature Julie Andrews in the cast and is therefore worth noting as part of her continuing connection to the movie.

The story of a thoughtless hockey star (Dwayne Johnson) who must serve as a tooth fairy for punishment for discouraging belief in dreams, Andrews is cast as the head fairy, if you will. ("Do I not look official enough?" she barks at a skeptical Johnson). During the end credit roll, a fellow fairy (Billy Crystal), joins Andrews in the stands of a hockey game, toting soda and popcorn and handing them to the fairy queen with the line "I got you a few of your favorite things." And that's it, folks.

Oprah and the Sound of Music (ABC, October 28, 2010)

"Who among us has not pictured ourselves spinning around the Austrian Alps singing at the top of our lungs?" asks host Oprah Winfrey for this 45th anniversary reunion. In fact, she treats this *TSOM* get-together with such importance that the usual title *The Oprah Winfrey Show* is dispensed with for this episode in favor of the above one. Much press was made over the fact that this marked the first time *all* of the cinematic Trapps would be together again for an interview, meaning Christopher Plummer was at last coaxed into appearing. (The film's Rolf, Daniel Truhitte, later expressed hurt in not being invited to participate. He was told that it was expressly those who played the Trapp family, *not* all living cast members, they were interested in honoring).

The choicest moment comes near the opening when, after bringing Plummer and Julie Andrews on stage, Winfrey asks the former to summon the seven remaining actors, which he does by whipping out a bosun's whistle, just like in the movie. He then quips that it's "been sterilized in whisky."

Andrews and Plummer get their own time with the host before their cinematic brood rejoins them for the last portion of the show. Charmian Carr admits that Plummer taught her how to drink while on location; Plummer points out how one couldn't help but feeling a bit "irreverent" with all those nuns around and admits to getting fatter because of his excessive alcohol intake; and the children talk about their upcoming project (*The Sound of Music Family Scrapbook*). There are also behind-the-scenes clips; a taped endorsement from performer Rosie O'Donnell, who calls the movie "iconically life altering, for me and *millions* of other people"; and feedback from some fans, including a man who claims to have seen the film 127 times while stationed overseas in the sixties.

As an added bonus, the great-grandchildren of the real Maria and the Captain— Amanda (19), Sofia (22), Melanie (20), and Justin, who would later change his name to August (16)—appear on stage to sing "Edelweiss." The audience is sent home with free copies of the lavish new BluRay edition box set of the movie.

Oprah Winfrey welcomes back the cinematic Trapp family for a fortieth reunion; left to right: Duane Chase, Heather Menzies, Nicholas Hammond, Christopher Plummer, Winfrey, Julie Andrews, Charmian Carr, Angela Cartwright, Kym Karath, and Debbie Turner.

Oscar Hammerstein II: Out of My Dreams (PBS, March 3, 2012)

Rather than a straightforward chronicle of Oscar's career in theatre, this special focuses on how he used his talents as a writer and lyricist to address injustices, his efforts to expand the goals of musical theatre, his liberal politics, and his optimism.

There are many clips from the movie versions of Hammerstein shows (of the Rodgers and Hammerstein musicals on film, *State Fair* and *Flower Drum Song* are passed over), plus comments (archival and current) from Harold Prince, Stephen Sondheim, Oscar Andrew Hammerstein (grandson), Ted Chapin (president, R&H Organization), Susan Blanchard (stepdaughter), Hugh Fordin (biographer), Dorothy Hammerstein, Alice Hammerstein Mathias (daughter), James Hammerstein (son), Shirley Jones, Joe DiPietro (playwright/lyricist, *Memphis*), Mitzi Gaynor, Melinda Walsh (granddaughter), Peter Mathias (grandson), and some archival audio and video interviews with Hammerstein himself.

Hosted by Matthew Morrison (who played Lieutenant Cable in the 2008 *South Pacific* revival), this documentary has the added plus of taking you to Hammerstein's Highland Farm home in Pennsylvania.

The segment on *The Sound of Music* emphasizes the movie more than the stage show, with clips of the opening number (you were expecting Herr Zeller highlights maybe?), "Do-Re-Mi," the captain summoning the children with his whistle, "My Favorite Things," "Edelweiss," and a shot of the marquee of the Rivoli Theatre in New York during the film's run there. "One of the luckiest things that ever happened was that it was made into a movie," says Ted Chapin, "not only made into a movie, but a movie starring Julie Andrews that came out in the mid-1960s and it was a phenomenon in its day and continues to be a phenomenon today." He goes on to explain part of its appeal, "It's the kind of movie people want to see more than once. If you have children, you want to show it to your children. As you children grow up, they want to watch it again. Then they have their own children, they want to show it to their children."

The last clip seen on the program is of the Trapps ascending the mountain at the end of *TSOM*; we then hear an audio of Oscar saying: "In *The Sound of Music*, 'Climb Ev'ry Mountain' is an instance of what I believe: that you should devote your life to finding out what you want to do in life. And then, when you find it, live, live that dream that you find."

The special was written, produced and directed by JoAnn Young.

The Talk (CBS, April 18, 2012)

Charmian Carr and her six celluloid siblings showed up on this syndicated morning talk show to plug their collaborative effort, *The Sound of Music Scrapbook*.

The Sound of Music Concert Presentation(Carnegie Hall, Stern Auditorium/Perelman Stage; New York, NY; April 24, 2012)

A one-night only concert version of the musical was notable for its casting of four members of the movie in miniscule roles, for the sake of nostalgia. Daniel Truhitte (Rolf), showed up at the Trapp party as Baron Elberfeld; while Nicholas Hammond (Friedrich), Heather Menzies (Louisa), and Kym Karath (Gretl) had joke cameos as the Trio of the Saengerbund of Herwegen, who lose the Festival competition to the Trapp Family Singers.

Laura Osnes was Maria and Tony Goldwyn was Captain von Trapp; while Truhitte saw his role played by Nick Spangler; Jake Montagnino was Friedrich, Olivia Knutsen was Louisa, and Charlotte Knutsen was Gretl.

Climbed Every Mountain—The Story Behind the Sound of Music (BBC Two, December 29, 2012)

Despite too much effort on the part of host Sue Perkins to appear cheekily comical, this documentary trying to get to the real story behind *TSOM* has much to recommend it. For one thing Perkins is joined on her trip to Mirabell Gardens by the film's Friedrich von Trapp, Nicholas Hammond (receiving a "Consulting Producer" credit), who relives his role by running with her through the arbor, hitch-kicking around the Pegasus fountain, and hopping on the "Do-Re-Mi" steps, just as one would hope. There are also glimpses of Salzburg's very first stage production of *TSOM* at the Landestheater (snatches of "So Long, Farewell," "Maria," "Do-Re-Mi," "My Favorite Things," and "Edelweiss" are heard in German); footage of Maria von Trapp from the 1980s, including a reunion with the family's music instructor, Father Wasner; the Trapp Family singing on *The Kate Smith Evening Hour* in 1952; a 1942 clip of with the youngest Trapp child, Johannes, singing "Old McDonald" with his mom; Hammond's home movies from the set; and side trips to Ellis Island and the Trapp Lodge in Stowe, Vermont.

Interviewed are the last survivor of the original 7 Trapp children, Maria, who no longer speaks English; two of the three Trapp children born to Maria and the captain, Rosmarie, who speaks openly about having a breakdown following her father's death and being sent to a psychiatrist to receive electric shock therapy; and Johannes, who paints a sober portrait of his mother as a tough and driven woman. Grandchildren Sam, Kristina, and Elisabeth von Trapp (described as the only grandchild to continue the family legacy by having a music career), and Elizabeth Campbell Peters (she says Maria "played up to a myth that was about her"), also offer their feelings about their grandmother.

There are doubts cast regarding the accuracy of the whole story from certain interviewees and displeasure expressed over the dramatic license taken by the musical, none more so than Peter Husty, Salzburg Museum's Head of Exhibitions, who reveals that there is no documentation whatsoever about Maria in the Nonnberg Abbey records. Also heard from are: journalist Caroline Kleibel, who says "people fell in love with Julie Andrews and not the *real* Maria von Trapp, because she was by far not as charming and lovable as she's portrayed by Julie Andrews"; Dr. Barbara Heuberger of the Salzburg Marionette Theatre, who admits they made a mistake in not accepting Fox's offer to participate in the making of the film back in 1964; David Brenner, Minister of Arts and Culture, who credits the movie for boosting tourism, with some 300,000 people visiting Salzburg every year because of it; Karl-Philippe von Maldenghem, Artistic Direct of Landestheater; Uwe Kröger, the actor playing the captain in the stage musical at the Landestheater; journalist Georg Steinitz, who calls Maria a "religious fanatic"; Laurence Maslon, author of *The Sound of Music Companion*; Bert Fink, spokesperson for the Rodgers & Hammerstein Organization; Father Wasner's nephew Franz, who says the Trapp kids hated his uncle for making them rehearse so much; and 98-year-old Marko Feingold, President of the Jewish Community in Salzburg, who insists that many of his fellow Austrians dislike the film for making it seem as if there was a wide acceptance of Nazi domination, which he believes *is* accurate, saying 98 percent of the population *wanted* the Anschluss.

Despite these dark background shadings, there is an overall feeling of the joy the film has brought and continues to bring, suggesting it has far outweighed the reality, or as Perkins concludes, "It's not the facts we care about—the magic in any story lies in the way it is told."

An Evening with Julie Andrews
(Live Performances: May 18—June 5, 2013)

In the spring of 2013, Julie Andrews made it to Australia at last to present a one-woman chat about her career. For an extra added attraction, one of her co-stars from *The Sound of Music*, Nicholas Hammond, who had made the country his home for more than twenty years, agreed to join her, doing the opening introduction. The clip package leading off the event included the entire lead-up to Julie on the hilltop singing the first lines of "The Sound of Music," as well as brief moments from "Something Good" and "I Have Confidence." To cap things off, Andrew and Hammond encouraged the audience to join them in a sing-a-long of "Edelweiss."

The 2013 dates were: May 18: Concert Hall, QPAC, Brisbane; May 21: Riverside Theatre, Perth; May 24: State Theatre, Sydney; May 28: Adelaide Festival Center, Adelaide; May 31: Arts Centre, Melbourne; June 5: The Civic, The Edge, Auckland, New Zealand

Robert Wise: American Filmmaker (Midnight Marquee, 2013)

This shabby hodgepodge has a 2013 copyright date but contains an interview (by Gregory Mank) with Wise done at a Fanex Convention in Hunt Valley, Maryland in 1996. Wise's startlingly good memory, generosity toward stars and colleagues, and easy-going way with a story help to offset some clumsy narration (actually using the term "tinsel town," minus irony); horrid lounge music underscoring; increasingly annoying comments from National Society of Film Critics Chairman David Sterritt; and films clips that consist mainly of scratchy trailers or promos. A good amount of time is given over to *The Curse of the Cat People*, *The Body Snatchers*, *The Day the Earth Stood Still*, *The Haunting*, *The Andromeda Strain*, and *Star Trek—The Motion Picture*, which only makes sense when you realize that the documentary's producer, Midnight Marquee, specializes in films from the horror, sci-fi and fantasy genres.

A questionable introduction to *The Sound of Music* shows the trailer for Elvis's *Wild in the Country* (?!?!?), telling us "While the 1960s ushered in the death of big screen musicals . . ." ignoring the fact that this is the only decade in which four films from that genre won the Oscar for Best Picture. One is not surprised by the curt and ignorant dismissal when there follows bits of the trailer for *TSOM* and nothing else. Therefore the sequence on Wise's greatest success and one of the milestone motion pictures of its era is covered for all of a minute and a half.

Hollywood Auction 56, featuring The Sound of Music collection (July 28-29, 2013)

Profiles in History auction house in Calabasas, California, made *The Sound of Music* their main focus for this two-day event, and no wonder, considering the incredible array of costumes up for grabs.

They were: Julie's signature "Maria" dress from the "Do-Re-Mi" number; the Von Trapp children "drapery' outfits; Julie's yellow return-from-honeymoon outfit and her wool cape from the escape sequence; the Trapp kids' sailor uniforms; Duane Chase's jacket and vest from "So Long, Farewell"; Angela

Cartwright's "Do-Re-Mi" and wedding costumes; and Charmian Carr's outfits from "Edelweiss," "So Long, Farewell," and "Sixteen Going on Seventeen."

TSOM clothing fetched somewhere between $1.3 and $1.56 million, a more impressive figure than the auction house was expecting.

Hollywood Show
fan convention

October 5—6, 2013
Westin Los Angeles Airport
5400 W. Century Boulevard, Los Angeles, CA 90045

The 7 "children" from *TSOM* appeared to greet fans and sign autographs. The group had been scheduled to appear on board the Royal Caribbean's Oasis of the Seas cruise ship that October, sailing from Fort Lauderdale, but that engagement was cancelled.

The captain and Maria's "escape" outfits for the climax of *The Sound of Music* were among the items later sold at auction.

The Sound of Music at the HUB (Hudson Uptown Building) in Hudson, NC (October 10-12, 17-19, 2013)

Twenty years after he had first picked up Captain von Trapp's guitar, Daniel Truhitte once again played the role in this dinner theater production in the state where he had been residing for more than two decades. (This town was about twelve miles north of where the movie of *The Sound of Music* had one of its exclusive engagement runs, in Hickory). Publicity included the actor appearing on the local Charlotte morning show, *Charlotte Today*, on WCNC where he sang "Edelweiss." Jimmy Kurts filled Truhitte's old role of Rolf in this version; Julie McGrath was Maria.

Dream a Little Dream (Heinz Records; March 4, 2014)

A collaborative album between Pink Martini and the Trapps (the grandchildren of Werner von Trapp—the inspiration for Kurt in the musical - and the great-grandchildren of the captain; specifically August, Amanda, Melanie and Sofia) this CD has a special treat for fans of *The Sound of Music* because the track of "Edelweiss" features Charmian Carr performing with the Trapp children. There is also a version of "The Lonely Goatherd" with guests Wayne Newton and Jack Hanna.

This album also included a tie-in tour that ran from March 4, 2014 in Milwaukee to April 18, 2014 in Tacoma, WA.

That Ever-Present Sound of Music

Pop Culture References to the Musical

I n show business you haven't made your mark until you've been parodied, referenced for instant recognition, or flat-out imitated. Although it is common to do so at the moment in time that someone or something makes a splash in the world of pop culture, there's a lot to be said for a motion picture that has held its fascination and grip on the world for a half-century. Such is *The Sound of Music*. Various movies, television shows, plays, and books have referenced many of the familiar song titles, script lines, situations, and names for a quick smile, a broad jab in the ribs, an affectionate salute, or an out-and-out condemnation.

So numerous have been the references that those too swift and blunt aren't worth getting into (these have popped on television shows like *Wings, Parks and Recreation, Being Human, Desperate Housewives, Drop Dead Diva, Nurse Jackie, Mary Tyler Moore,* and *Strike Back,* to name a few). More interesting are those in the sample list compiled here that have elaborated on the mere mention of Maria and company, sometimes with great cheeky affection, sometimes with bile, frequently with lame obviousness, and once in a while sublimely.

AARP "My Favorite Things" Parody (circa 2001)

A send-up of the famous song with new lyrics aimed at senior citizens began circulating (with no credited writer or originator) on the Internet around 2001, and in record time rumors sprang up that Julie Andrews herself had sung this at an AARP-related benefit at Radio City Music Hall. Although this proved unfounded, like most urban legends it has persisted to a certain degree. A sample of the lyrics: "Cadillacs and cataracts and hearing aids and glasses/ Polident and Fixodent and false teeth in glasses/Pacemakers, golf carts and porches with swings/These are a few of my favorite things."

Adam & Steve (TLA Releasing, March 31, 2006)

As a Goth and a club dancer walk over the Brooklyn Bridge before their intended night of sex, the latter boasts that he's up for the role of the captain in the AMDA production of *The Sound of Music* and serenades his pickup with a few bars of "Something Good." Seventeen years after the disastrous results of that particular evening, the same two men come together, now in their true personas of Adam (Craig Chester; also the film's writer and director) and Steve (Malcolm Gets), unaware that they are the ones who hooked up on that fateful night. What tips Steve off is Adam's mention of a guy he once knew who sang him a song from *The Sound of Music*, triggering Steve's dreaded realization of the truth. An unhappy ending seems inevitable until Steve tracks Adam down at Marie's Crisis in Greenwich Village, regrets his mistake in trying to end the relationship, and manages to woo him back into his arms with a sincere rendition of . . . what else? . . . "Something Good."

Addams Family Values (Paramount, November 19, 1993)

In this sequel to the successful 1991 adaptation of Charles Addams's gleefully ghoulish cartoons and their 1964–66 television spin-off, *The Addams Family*, the contentedly morose youngsters of the Addams household, Wednesday (Christina Ricci) and Pugsley (Jimmy Workman), are tricked into being sent away to summer camp. Fed up with the children for not being properly perky, the relentlessly cheerful camp counselors (Peter MacNicol and Christine Baranski) figure they have no alternative but to lock them up, along with another outcast, Joel Glicker (David Krumholtz), in a hut on the camp property and brainwash them. Their technique is to play wholesome videotapes nonstop.

  Although Joel proclaims "It's Disney!," none of the music heard on the soundtrack is, in fact, from that studio. Instead, we get Julie Andrews singing the opening lines of "The Sound of Music"; *The Brady Bunch* theme; and "Tomorrow" from *Annie*. Benumbed by this onslaught of good cheer, Wednesday and her companions leave the hut claiming they are perky enough to participate in the camp production of *Pocahontas*, the dour child going so far as to smile. *Addams* fans know better; it's all a ruse.

Ally McBeal (Fox, Season 1, Episode 9: "The Dirty Joke," November 17, 1997)

This love-it-or hate-it comedy-drama about a quirky Boston lawyer (Calista Flockhart) opened this particular episode with some major Julie Andrews bashing. Upset that her roommate Rene (Lisa Nicole Carson) has interrupted her umpteenth viewing of *What Ever Happened to Baby Jane?*, Ally asks derogatorily what kind of movies Rene watches: "*The Sound of Music?!?*" "What's wrong with *The Sound of Music?*," Rene questions, defensively. "Nothing, if you don't mind Julie Andrews being *alive*," Ally responds snidely. Turns out Ally has decided the actress is "perky," even describing her breasts as such when she revealed them in the movie *S.O.B.* The deeper truth comes out when Ally confesses that her hatred stems from high school when her classmates, convinced she was too prudish, voted her "Most likely to become Julie Andrews." Rene tries to assure her that Andrews isn't like Maria von Trapp or Mary Poppins and "regrets" having done both those films (!!), a strange word choice regarding the two biggest hits of the lady's career, the roles that made her iconic in motion picture history, and the main reasons her name can be dropped so easily into a television script for instant recognition. But, anyway . . .

When Ally declares a joke Rene tells her to be "sick," her roommate is convinced her school designation is accurate, taunting her by singing "My Favorite Things," and later calling work to ask if she wants "to make dresses from drapes." Bar singer Vonda Shepard croons Ally with the opening phrase of "The Sound of Music," as the "perky" lawyer takes the stage to tell her own joke.

American Dad! (Fox, Season 2, Episode 11: "American Dream Factory," January 28, 2007)

Seth McFarlane's very similar follow-up to his successful *Family Guy* offers another lunkhead father, in this instance right-wing CIA operative Stan Smith (voiced by McFarlane), and his dysfunctional family.

When Stan hires several illegal aliens to manufacture his "Cele-*Bear*-tions" stuffed teddies, he runs afoul of the INS. Trying to sneak his underpaid Mexicans out of his house, the subsequent scenes deliberately echo the climax of *TSOM*. Pushing their car out of the driveway, Stan and his employees are stopped by the Herr Zeller stand-in, INS Agent Hopkins (voice of Miguel Ferrer), who shines his headlights on the escaping group, who pretend their car can't start. Once Hopkins's henchman proves them wrong, Stan lies that the Mexicans are "playing the Festival this evening." Skeptical, Hopkins insists on escorting them with the provision that they will be arrested afterwards. After the laborers' rendition of John Denver's "Take Me Home, Country Roads" so moves Stan, he decides he will help them escape by creating a diversion (tossing teddy bears, *not* singing a variation on "So Long, Farewell").

The finale shows Stan leading them over the mountains . . . to West Virginia!

Andy Richter Controls the Universe (Fox, Season 1, Episode 2: "Grief Counselor," March 26, 2002)

Late Night with Conan O'Brien writer-regular Andy Richter starred as a Walter Mitty-ish office worker forever imagining what life *should* be like in this surreal sitcom. Because of a death on the job, one of Andy's fellow employees, Keith (James Patrick Stuart), must back out of taking his girlfriend Wendy (Irene Molloy) to, as he puts it, "this thing where they show *The Sound of Music* and people come dressed up in costumes and sing along and gay-gay-gay-gay-gay-gay-gay." Because he harbors a secret crush on Wendy, Andy is thrilled to fill in for Keith ("Oh, my God!," he tells us in voice-over, "A date with Wendy

AND *The Sound of Music*? These are a few of my favorite things!"). Following their evening together (for which they appear to have passed on the idea of dressing up), Andy and Wendy sing lines from "So Long, Farewell" in her hallway. When Wendy compliments him on his enthusiastic dancing at the screening, he admits to having played Rolf in high school. "It was either that or the drama teacher was going to release some modeling photos that he took of me."

Andy's Fun House/The Andy Kaufman Special (ABC, August 28, 1979)

Off-the-wall comic Andy Kaufman, portraying a clueless talk show host, includes a segment of his special called "The Has-Been Corner," welcoming Gail Slobodkin, who, he tells us, was in *The Sound of Music* when she was ten years old. Ensuring that his guest feels utterly uncomfortable, Andy asks, "What was it like when you first realized that you weren't going to make it in show business?" Since she's here to launch her comeback, Gail sings "The Lonely Goatherd" while Kaufman barely hides his disinterest.

Angel (The WB, Season 3, Episode 2: "That Vision Thing," October 1, 2001)

A spin-off of *Buffy the Vampire Slayer*, this series was full of vampires, demons, and all sorts of supernatural hooey. This time Cordelia (Charisma Carpenter) is so tormented by the visions she is experiencing that aura reader Lorne (Andy Hallett) is summoned to help her out by contacting the Powers That Be . . . or something like that. Rubbing Cordelia's head and trying to get her to relax, Lorne wants her to imagine she's "on a mountain top. And it's warm . . . the sky is blue . . . full of big, fluffy clouds. You're Julie Andrews!" This appears to bring forth a violent reaction, so Lorne apologizes, confessing he just can't help himself. "I just love that movie *so much!*"

As is often the case, *TSOM* allusion does not require the actual mentioning of the movie by name; it's that ingrained in the minds of even this eclectic group of oddballs.

Animaniacs (The WB, Season 3, Episode 13: "The Sound of Warners," November 18, 1995)

Derived from *Tiny Toon Adventures*, this animated series starred three hyperactive cartoon characters, Yakko (voice of Rob Paulsen), Wakko (Jess Harnell), and Dot (Tress MacNeille) running amok on the Warner Bros. back-lot and sending up pop culture icons along the way. This episode bares its teeth at the wholesomeness of *TSOM*.

Opening with the expected helicopter shot, Prunella Flundergust (also voiced by MacNeille) is engulfed by Southern California pollution as she trills "There's no place on Earth that is quite like Burbank . . . ." Coming to the studio to serve as the relentlessly cheerful nanny for the trio of hellions, she lets them know up front that "We're going to have *such* fun together! We'll sing! We'll dance! We'll bicycle wearing clothes made of upholstery fabric!" She takes them on a picnic to sing about poison ivy (the "Edelweiss" parody), during a thunderstorm gives them the rundown of what cheers her up ("Fun Bob Hope specials and Spam on the griddle/Small bouncing babies with long strands of spittle. . ."), and encourages them to eat their oatmeal (a "Climb Ev'ry Mountain" parody?—okay, it's a stretch). The three are temporarily relieved when their friend Slappy sends the happy nanny by rocket to Austria, until her replacement shows up . . . Mary Poppins.

An earlier installment (Season 1, Episode 13, "Hello Nice Warner," Sept. 29, 1993) had waded into Trapp country, when, after a pan over the Austrian countryside, a woman in a novice's outfit was seen singing "The hills are quite full of big rocks and boulders." The destructive stars interrupted her by tearing down her fake Alpine backdrop.

Armistead Maupin's Tales of the City Episode 2 (Channel 4, 1993; US: PBS, January 16, 1994)

In this episode of the miniseries adaptation of Armistead Maupin's popular stories, affable Michael "Mouse" Tolliver (Marcus D'Amico) tries to convince San Francisco newbie Mary Ann Singleton (Laura Linney) to join him at a costume party. Dressed provocatively as Pan, complete with goat pants, horns, and no shirt, Mouse suggests Mary Ann play a shepherdess. "We'll throw in a guitar. You'll be Maria von Trapp and sing 'The Lonely Goatherd.' We'll be the perfect couple." With one of the attendees dressed as half a goat, they certainly would never qualify as "An *Ordinary* Couple." In any event, Mary Ann opts not to attend. Later in the same episode, Michael's visiting dad (Paul Dooley) refers to a group of men roller skating through the streets in nun-wear being "dressed like *The Sound of Music.*"

Away We Go (Focus Features, June 5, 2009)

Expecting a baby, Bert (John Krasinski) and Verona (Maya Rudolph) go in search of a new place to live, based on how they feel about some of the friends and family they visit along the way. A trip to Montreal finds them at the home of their college friends Tom (Chris Messina) and Munch (Melanie Lynskey), who have adopted a diverse brood of four. When we first encounter the kids, they are watching the "So Long, Farewell" scene from *The Sound of Music,* which the two youngest act out for the benefit of the company. Realizing that the youngsters are being treated as if this song marks the climax, Verona inquires, "So, the movie ends when the Von Trapps go to sleep? . . . . You skipped the Nazis?" A sheepish Tom explains, "We kind of figure, what's the point, you know? It's just . . . we think they could live a few more happy years before, you know . . . Juicy Couture and Hitler."

Beautiful Thing (UK: June 21, 1996; US release: Sony Pictures Classics, October 9, 1996)

Set in working-class Thamesmead in South East London, this drama-comedy involves two teenage next-door neighbors, Jamie (Glenn Berry) and Ste (Scott Neal), who are happily able to act on their burgeoning homosexual inclinations when circumstances allow them to share a bed together.

Just as the two boys are getting close to turning a rubdown into something a bit more interesting, Jamie's mum (Linda Henry) knocks on the door, trying to entice them from the bedroom with "Do you want to watch *The Sound of Music?*—it's on Sky!" Disinterested, and anxious to get to what mum later refers to as "doin' the 70 minus one," the boys reject the offer only to be once again interrupted by the old girl, this time inquiring "Who played the baroness?" "Eleanor Parker!" shouts Jamie, showing his gay credentials. As Jamie and Ste are finally able to settle into some physical intimacy, Daniel Truhitte and Charmian Carr's rendition of "Sixteen Going on Seventeen" makes an accurate comment on the situation at hand by playing on the soundtrack.

The Benny Hill Show (BBC 1/ITV, December 17, 1975)

The unapologetically lowbrow British comedian tosses off another one of his anything-goes sketch episodes. In his ongoing segment entitled "Another Host of Your Favourite Stars," Benny shows up in drag as Liza Minnelli; as mentalist the Amazing Kreskin; and finally as Scottish vocalist Moira Anderson (requiring drag yet again), performing her version of "The Sound of Music" while perched on a slowly deflating balloon chair.

The Big Bang Theory (CBS)

Four science nerds try to function in the real world, while still maintaining a very firm foot in their own galaxy. One thing is certain: Raj (Kunal Nayyar) has a "thing" for *The Sound of Music,* as indicated in:

Season 5, Episode 24: "The Countdown Reflection," May 10, 2012

Determined to get married before he takes the Soyuz capsule to spend time on the International Space Station, Howard (Simon Helberg) must come up with an alternate plan when he misses out on getting hitched at city hall. Raj has a suggestion, but Howard quickly shoots this down. "I told you, we are not recreating the wedding from *The Sound of Music*!" Hurt, Raj is well aware that Howard has already made this painfully clear.

Season 6, Episode 24: "The Re-Entry Minimization," October 18, 2012

Back from his trip to space, Howard becomes a tad jealous that his best bud Raj is not only rooming with comic book shop owner Stuart (Kevin Sussman), but planning to go with him to a certain movie. "*Sound of Music* Sing-a-long!" cries Howard, barely hiding his jealousy. "That used to be . . . our thing." Raj suggests he get a scalper's ticket and join them, but Howard doesn't fancy sitting alone. When Raj invites him to swap seats with Stuart after the intermission, Stuart is upset at the prospect. "So, I'd be sitting by myself during 'Edelweiss?'" Howard begs off, leaving the roomies to enjoy the musical by themselves.

Season 7, Episode 21: "The Anything Can Happen Recurrence," April 24, 2014

Appalled by the horror DVD he is watching in order to understand his girlfriend's taste in movies, Raj wonders why he can't be in a relationship with a girl who likes *The Sound of Music*. To which Howard reminds him, "Raj, you *are* the girl in the relationship who likes *The Sound of Music*."

Bill & Ted's Excellent Adventures (CBS, Season 1, Episode 2: "Too Cool for the Womb," September 22, 1990)

An animated spin-off of the 1989 comedy film *Bill & Ted's Excellent Adventure* (with Keanu Reeves and Alex Winter repeating their parts, vocally) sends our bodacious high schoolers through time to visit various notables by way of their transporter phone booth. While the episode leading into this one, "The Birth of Rock and Roll," actually takes place in Salzburg (Bill and Ted visit *Wolfie* Mozart), it is this segment about William Tell that features a *TSOM* gag. Sliding down a Swiss Alp (toward Austria, maybe?), the boys' phone box first nearly wipes out Heidi and then a lady spinning on a field singing "The Alps are replete with the noise of . . . music." She is promptly covered in a pile of snow.

The Black Windmill (Universal, May 16, 1974)

This British thriller about a secret agent, John Tarrant (Michael Caine), whose young son David is kidnapped is unique in the realm of *TSOM* references for actually getting specific about *where* the movie was shown. Because the boy's abduction requires the agency to tape all incoming phone calls to the home of Tarrant's estranged wife, Alex (Janet Suzman), Tarrant finds himself having to come up with a ruse to disguise his identity once he ends up on the run from authorities and needs to call in. His solution is to fake a German accent and tell Alex that he is "Mr. Trapp," looking for "Maria." When she seems puzzled by the inquiry, Tarrant points the receiver toward the pub pianist whose services he has paid for, as the gentleman plunks out "The Sound of Music." He then tells his wife the number he is looking for is "Dominion 8894." Suddenly, she catches on and knows it is Tarrant, passing along a coded message of where they should meet. Sure enough they rendezvous in front of the very London theatre where *The Sound of Music* had its three-year-plus run, the Dominion (for maximum irony, the establishment is shown playing *Battle of Britain*, which starred . . . Michael Caine!).

As they leave the location on a bus, Alex sings the opening of "The Sound of Music" before asking how her husband could have remembered such details. "How can I ever forget it?" John asks, incredulously, "Or the Dominion Theatre? Don't you remember, David dragged us to see that film . . . what? . . . four times?" As the suspense mounts, the audience can't help but wonder, will David live to see *TSOM* a *fifth* time?

The Book of Mormon (Eugene O'Neill Theatre, March 24, 2011)

The 2011 Tony winner for Best Musical poked fun, not at its fellow Tony honoree, the stage version of *TSOM*, but the movie.

The story of two Mormon missionaries sent to a village in Uganda ruled by a brutal warlord gives one of the Elders, Kevin Price (Andrew Rannells), a second-act number, "I Believe," to build up his confidence about his religious faith. Deliberately tossing in some lyrics to draw parallels to Maria's "I Have Confidence," Price sings "Oh, what's the matter with me?" and "What's so scary about that?," although the latter follows the line "A warlord who shoots people in the face."

Bosom Buddies (ABC, Season 1, Episode 19: "Cahoots," April 30, 1981)

Pre-movie stardom, Tom Hanks appeared in this sitcom about two guys cross-dressing in order to secure an apartment in a women-only hotel. In this episode, Kip Wilson's (Hanks) desire to hook up with Sonny, the girl of his dreams across the hall, finds him asking the girl's roommate, Amy (Wendy Jo Sperber) to name Sonny's "favorite things." As Amy deadpans Oscar Hammerstein's lyrics, "raindrops on roses and whiskers on kittens," Kip dutifully writes them down, not catching on to the joke until Amy begins to spin about the office, singing the song. His sardonic reaction is to refer to her as "Julie Andrews von Trapp."

Bridget Jones: The Edge of Reason (Universal, November 12, 2004)

This sequel to the 2001 hit comedy *Bridget Jones's Diary* starts off with its spunky British heroine (Renée Zellweger) blissfully happy over having found her ideal man, Mark D'Arcy (Colin Firth), at the climax of the previous film. To illustrate her joy, she is seen running to a hilltop as an instrumental version of "The Sound of Music" plays and she races into her lover's arms. "You always wonder how it's going to work out at the end of the story," her voice-over narration tells us, before naming some of the great partnerships, "Maria and Captain von Trapp. Snow White and the 7 Dwarfs . . . Bridget Jones and Mark D'Arcy."

The Brittas Empire(BBC 1, Season 5, Episode 7: "UXB," December 12, 1994)

This British sitcom (1991–97) was set in the Whitbury New Town Leisure Center. Those on staff include the emotionally fragile receptionist, Carole (Harriet Thorpe), who has a habit of keeping her three young children inside drawers and cupboards at the reception desk. When a Mr. Trap (Peter Cleall) arrives from Social Services to check on this claustrophobic situation, Carole locks herself in a cabinet with the kids, where they pass the time singing "Edelweiss." Mr. Trap is enchanted by what he hears. "My grandmother used to sing this song to me, when I was a boy, in Salzburg," he tells the center's level-headed deputy, Laura (Julia St. John). "If *my* children could sing like that . . . ," he muses, wistfully.

Given that name, it should come as no surprise that Carole accepts a position as governess to Trap's four children (yes, bringing the total up to seven), dressing them, along with her own offspring, in outfits made from the drapes. Turns out that Trap is a *von* Trap, and has a daughter named Liesl, who is "sixteen going on seventeen." Raising an eyebrow at this overly familiar information, Laura asks, "His family weren't driven out by the Nazis, were they?" "Yes, they were," a naïve Carole replies. "How did you know?"

The Carol Burnett Show (CBS; Season 6, Episode 7: October 25, 1972)

Burnett always had great fun affectionately spoofing famous movies, and this time, during a segment paying tribute to 20th Century-Fox, she ribs "One of the greatest box office successes of all time . . . starring my friend, Julie Andrews . . . ." In the accompanying sketch, the captain (Harvey Korman) informs his brood (of a mere five, including series regular Lyle Waggoner, as hunky "Hans") that Maria, the new nanny (Burnett), has arrived. Telling Maria that the children have "set fire to the baroness, which must be put out immediately," he inquires what she plans to do first. "What else?," she replies, "I'm going to sing," and jumps into a rendition of "Do-Re-Mi" until Hans gets her libido cooking and she switches the tune to "You've Got to Love Your Mama Every Night."

Celebrate The Sound of Music (BBC 1, January 1, 2005)

How much does England love *The Sound of Music*? They came up with an hour-long variety special, hosted by Graham Norton, just to show how much.

Jill Halfpenny, from the long-running UK soap *EastEnders*, takes a crack at the title song; Denise Van Outen, whose roles included playing Roxie Hart in the West End revival of *Chicago*, is joined by a group of children (including future chart-topper Pixie Lott as Louisa) to sing "Do-Re-Mi"; tenor Russell Watson sounds off on "Edelweiss"; Robert Lindsay and Rosemarie Ford (who would later marry) duet on "Something Good"; Clare Buckfield (the sitcom *2point4 Children*) and S Club alumni Jon Lee are "Sixteen Going on Seventeen"; soprano Lesley Garrett soars on "Climb Ev'ry Mountain"; and hip-hoppers Big Brovaz present the song they had sampled for their hit single, "My Favourite Things." Garrett is joined on "Maria" by several "guest" nuns, most of whom would mean nothing to U.S. audiences, including Linda Robson (the sitcom *Birds of a Feather*), TV and radio presenters Gloria Hunniford and Fearne Cotton, June Whitfield (Gran on *Absolutely Fabulous*), Carrie Grant (the competition series *Fame Academy*), Bonnie Langford (Mel Bush on *Doctor Who*), and the team of Dick and Dom (of *in da Bungalow* fame).

Also appearing: Irish singer Brian McFadden, singer Sophie Ellis-Bextor, television presenter Janet Ellis, former London stage "Maria" Petula Clark, and songwriter and future *How Do You Solve a Problem Like Maria?* creator Andrew Lloyd Webber.

The special was a hit, attracting some 6.4 million viewers on its New Year's Day showing.

Cheers (NBC, Season 10, Episode 6: "Unplanned Parenthood," October 24, 1991)

The long-running ensemble comedy about the denizens of the titular Boston watering hole centered principally around its womanizing owner, Sam Malone (Ted Danson), who, as the seasons passed, ended up hooking up with his business manager, Rebecca Howe (Kirstie Alley).

In this episode they agree to babysit the offspring of Sam's acerbic waitress Carla (Rhea Perlman) as a way of testing their parenting skills. All seven children line up in their best Trapp fashion to meet Sam and Rebecca. "Look at you, you look so cute," Rebecca coos. "It's like *The Sound of Music*. Oh, I wish I had a whistle." When one of the boys dutifully provides her with one, she gives it her best shot at playing captain. "Now, when I blow the whistle, you say your name," she instructs them. "Sarafina," the crabby eldest (Leah Remini) replies, before adding "And I'm spending the night with my boyfriend," after which she knocks the offending whistle into Rebecca's mouth to shut her up.

Chicago Fire (NBC, Season 1, Episode 11: "God Has Spoken," January 2, 2013)

Going out to celebrate a business deal fireman Christopher Herrmann (David Eigenberg) doesn't feel very comfortable about, his wife Cindy (Robyn Coffin) tells him the babysitting plans. "It's gonna be *Sound of Music*, but my mom is saying the kids are too young for Nazis." But Cindy admits, "I don't care if they watch *Scarface*—they're occupied and *we're* celebrating." This brings up a good point—just how much does one absorb about the plot of *any* film dependent on one's age? In any case, let's hope more kids have been raised on *TSOM* than *Scarface.*

The Christmas Thief by Mary Higgins Clark and Carol Higgins Clark (Simon & Shuster, November 2004)

Most of the action of this holiday-themed tale of a stolen Christmas tree takes place in Stowe, Vermont, with some of the protagonists staying at the Trapp Family Lodge. According to the storyline, the initial planting of the tree in question, chosen for display at Rockefeller Center, was witnessed by Maria von Trapp. Because of this and the fact that the fortieth anniversary of "the world's most successful musical film" is about to take place, a special reception is planned at which the tree's arrival in Manhattan is to be "greeted by a choir of hundreds of schoolchildren from all over the city who will sing a medley of songs from *The Sound of Music.*"

Following the theft of the tree, Jo-Jo, one of the dim-witted criminals, responds to the idea of disabling someone's car by telling his cohorts, "It's like what the nuns did in *The Sound of Music.* Remember when the nuns said to the mother superior that they had sinned?" In no mood for Trapp-related references, even in Stowe, his boss responds by telling him to shut up.

Chunky Monkey (Head Gear Films, UK: November 2004)

Some things set out to shock and end up making the tiniest squeak in the long run. This cheaply made independent black comedy ran into threats of litigation after invoking the ire of the Rodgers and Hammerstein Organization, Unilever, EMI, and Julie Andrews. And no wonder, since the plot involves a psychotic (David Threlfall) whose fantasy it is to apply Ben & Jerry's Chunky Monkey ice cream while making love to Ms. Andrews as she sings "The Sound of Music".

"The Club Is Alive" by JLS (Epic, July 2, 2010)

For their single "The Club Is Alive," British boy band JLS (Jack the Lad Swing) sampled the Rodgers and Hammerstein title song from *TSOM* for the oft-repeated line "The club is alive/with the sound of music," which is followed by the non-Hammerstein lyrics "Who's that girl in the spotlight/ooh cuz she turns me on." The song (with Andrew Frampton, Savana Kotecha, and Steve Mac sharing the credit with R&H) went to #1 in England and had an accompanying video.

College Road Trip (Disney, March 7, 2008)

Due to complications too formulaic to repeat, uptight and domineering father James Porter (Martin Lawrence) decides to drive his teenage daughter Melanie (Raven-Simoné) from Illinois to her college of choice, Georgetown University. Along the way, due to complications of an even more formulaic nature, they are forced to accept a ride from a relentlessly cheery dad (Donny Osmond) and his equally ebullient daughter (Molly Ephraim). James and Melanie consider it torture that their "hosts" insist on singing songs like Rodgers and Hammerstein's "Getting to Know You" and Paul Vance and Lee Pockriss's "Itsy Bitsy Teeny Weeny Yellow Polka Dot Bikini," and then bid them goodbye as dad and his offspring sing their (mercifully shortened) version of "So Long, Farewell," which apparently proves that they *really, really* are just not hip enough for the room. Melanie gets the opportunity later on, however, to provide her own degree of torture, singing "Double Dutch Bus," accompanied by a busload of Japanese stereotypes.

Donny's sister, Marie Osmond, certainly got to hear "So Long, Farewell" frequently when she toured in *TSOM*, starting in 1993.

Control (Weinstein Company, October 10, 2007; UK: Momentum Pictures, October 5, 2007)

Even the post-punkers can't resist Rodgers and Hammerstein! In this black-and-white bio of the troubled front man for Joy Division, Ian Curtis (Sam Riley), and his early demise, Ian's mistress Annik (Alexandra Maria Lara) tells him she'd like to get to know him better. In response to her query about his favorite movie, he doesn't have to give it much thought, answering, "I really like *The Sound of Music*." Although Annik starts to respond with a chuckle, Ian gives her a look to indicate he's more than serious about his choice. Considering Joy Division's style of music doesn't in any way suggest that of traditional show music, this is quite a testament to the movie's reach.

Not surprisingly, Salzburg's contribution to the worldwide "Cow Parade" included an artistic celebration of the city's most famous movie.

Cow Parade (2000)

This *udder*-ly eccentric worldwide art exhibit consisted of life-size cow statues, each painted individually and displayed throughout select cities, starting in 1999 in Chicago. The following year, Salzburg Land Tourismus and Alpenmilch exhibited more than 150 bovine works of art throughout their city. Panorama Tours very smartly sponsored one featuring images from *The Sound of Music* as decorated by Jutta Krammel.

The centerpiece of one side of the cow was, of course, Julie Andrews in her hilltop pose, while the other was highlighted by Andrews and the children gathered on Winkler's Terrace during the "Do-Re-Mi" number. The statue remains a part of the city, standing in front of the Panorama Tours bus kiosk at Mirabellplatz.

The Critic (Fox) (Season 2, Episode 1: "Sherman, Woman and Child," March 5, 1995); (Season 2, Episode 7: "Sherman of Arabia," April 30, 1995)

This animated series about caustic television movie critic Jay Sherman (voice of Jon Lovitz) was filled with parody clips of real and imaginary movies. The inevitable *Sound of Music* joke had the camera zooming so close to a cartoon version of Julie Andrews that it knocks her right off the mountain and into the valley below. As was his custom, Jay's reaction was "It stinks!"

The Daily Show with Jon Stewart
(Comedy Central; December 9, 2013; December 10, 2013)

Dumbfounded by former Pennsylvania senator Rick Santorum equating apartheid with Obamacare in light of Nelson Mandela's passing, host Jon Stewart stressed that "The systemic subjugation of a race of people is *different* from the establishment of subsidized health care exchanges," and to emphasize the idiocy of this comparison, he asked if he "may shout it from the hilltops . . . ," prompting the famous clip of Julie doing her hill spin, but with Stewart chirping (screeching?) in a high-pitched voice, "Apartheid is not Obamacare!"

Not a day later he was using the same *TSOM* clip to further shout from the hilltops the inanity of Arizona senator John McCain equating Barack Obama shaking hands with Cuban president Raúl Castro with Prime Minister Neville Chamberlain's same gesture toward Adolf Hitler.

Dallas (CBS) (Season 12, Episode 22: "Yellow Brick Road," April 14, 1989); (Season 12, Episode 23: "The Sound of Money," April 28, 1989)

Since its cast included the son of the woman who created the role of Maria in the original Broadway production of *The Sound of Music*, it only made sense that Larry Hagman's career-defining series would make mention of the musical. Rather than take the easy inside-joke route, however, these two episodes of prime-time's soap opera sensation took some of its cast members (Hagman included) off the South Fork ranch and over to Salzburg for some direct and indirect references to the movie version.

In the first episode, the Ewing Brothers, J. R. and Bobby (Hagman and Patrick Duffy) discuss their business reasons for being in Austria as they walk directly past the Pegasus Fountain around which Maria and the children marched in the "Do-Re-Mi" number. They are then seen approaching the famous steps that ended the sequence. Later, Bobby receives an anonymous note asking him to meet someone (his lover, April Stevens, played by Sheree J. Wilson) at the Hohensalzburg, the famous castle spotted throughout *TSOM* in the background. Most interestingly, when the brothers arrive at the house of Rolf Brundin (Gunnar Hellström), he is first seen standing directly in front of the famous horse gates used as the back of the Trapp villa in the film, on Lake Leopoldskron.

When the follow-up episode begins, the references are more direct, although the name of the movie is never spoken. (The episode title is the tip-off.) Bobby and April go horseback riding in the hills, allowing the latter to stop and dismount at a locale that looks appropriately *SOM*-ish, spinning around and declaring how much she wants to sing and has waited years to be able to do this. "Julie Andrews, watch out!" she warns, breathlessly, "April Stevens is staking claim on your mountain!" Bobby decides she'd make a great Maria, and then makes some "babysitter" jokes (apparently the details of the plot have slipped his mind) in a German accent. When this elicits a groan from April, he vows to "keep my von Trapp shut from now on."

Dancer in the Dark (Denmark: Angel Films, September 8, 2000; U.S. release: Fine Line Features, September 23, 2000)

Here's an outstanding example of how a film that couldn't be further apart in tone and intention uses *TSOM* as a point of reference. Danish director Lars von Trier, a founder of the Dogme 95 movement that opts for the "realism" of handheld cameras and a minimum of artificial trappings, presents a dour story of a simple factory worker, Selma (played by Icelandic singer Björk), who tries to save money to pay for the operation to prevent her son's inevitable degenerative eye condition. Because Selma loves musicals to the extent that she escapes from her dead-end life by dreaming of song and dance numbers, the movie is filled with some poorly staged musical fantasy sequences that only go to prove how much work it takes to pull off the real thing. Actually, things aren't much better executed in the dramatic scenes; the effort to present a less Hollywood-ized glimpse into the lives of these hapless people by falling back on shaky camera work and improvisational dialogue comes off sounding more stilted and phonier than any single moment in any traditional Hollywood songfest.

As a relief from her life as a working stiff, Selma, along with her co-worker Cathy (Catherine Deneuve), participates in a threadbare local production of *The Sound of Music*, which appears to have a plotline that, like *Dancer*'s dialogue, is being made up on the spot. Although Selma is cast as "Maria," her main number seems to require that she tap dance in the middle of "So Long, Farewell," while her rendition of "My Favorite Things" requires Cathy to bring the items in question (a bright copper kettle, brown paper packages tied up with string) to Selma on stage. There are only five visible Trapp kids, the two boys being a bit long in the tooth for the correct ages, and the show's director (Vincent Peterson) assures Selma that should she opt for playing a nun, he'll give her a tap number there as well (!). Although the story takes place in Washington State in 1964, one year before the film's release, there is also a reference to a scene in the show where "you come to the convent gate to say goodbye to Maria," which sounds suspiciously like the one in the movie where the Trapp kids drop by Nonnberg in hopes of speaking to their former governess.

Do Not Adjust Your Set (ITV, Premiere: December 26, 1967)

This British sketch-comedy series was notable for featuring three future members of Monty Python in its cast, Eric Idle, Terry Jones, and Michael Palin. In a segment not involving any of these fellows, the Bonzo Dog Do-Dah Band's front man Vivian Stanshall introduces his next song by explaining to the audience how he escaped an onslaught of fans and admirers. "Wildly I sought for sanctuary and I found myself in the darkness of a cinema . . . that day I saw something rather special, something that really moved me," he tells us in earnest. "I want to share this experience with you, which was *The Sound of Music*." He then proceeds to perform a deliberately high-pitched, discordant rendition of the title song, backed up by his cacophonic bandmates.

The 85th Annual Academy Awards (ABC, February 24, 2013)

About to introduce the previous year's winner for Best Supporting Actor, Christopher Plummer (for *Beginners*), Oscar host Seth MacFarlane gave him a dramatic buildup by insisting he was still best known for playing Captain Georg von Trapp in *The Sound of Music*. He then parodied the musical festival sequence from the film, dramatically gesturing toward a door to announce "The Family Von Trapp" as a spotlight hit it, only to have nothing happen until an actor in Nazi garb ran into the auditorium to proclaim "They're gone!"

Everybody Loves Raymond (CBS, Season 4, Episode 6: "The Sister," October 25, 1999)

This sitcom starred stand-up comic Ray Romano as a sportswriter who has the misfortune to live across the street from his bickering parents.

Here is another example of how *TSOM* is so ingrained in the public consciousness that the title needn't be mentioned in order for viewers to get the joke.

In this episode, Ray is dreading a visit from his sister-in-law (Ashley Crow), who, much to everyone's surprise, announces her intention to become a nun. After spending a couple of hours with her watching a film (unseen by us), Ray tell his wife Debra (Patricia Heaton), "You should have stayed up. What a great, great movie." Debra assures him, "Oh, I've seen it a thousand times," to which Ray muses dreamily, "It's almost like the hills really *are* alive." He then proceeds to tell her his favorite part is when Julie Andrews does her spin, which he then demonstrates, to ample audience laughter.

Fade to Black(American Cinema Releasing, October 16, 1980)

A film centered on nutty movie fanatic Eric Binford (Dennis Christopher) has got to find room for at least one offhand reference to *TSOM*, among the many titles that pop up throughout the script, and indeed it does. Trying to impress the Marilyn Monroe lookalike (Linda Kerridge) he's just met that he once saw three movies every day for a year, she assures him he is "lucky." Where she grew up, in the Australian outback, they had no wider choice than the same two movies that were transported by truck into their area and shown "over and over again," *Mary Poppins* and *The Sound of Music*. Considering some of the stiffs Eric no doubt had to sit through, frequent doses of those two films sounds like the better deal. "You're a big Julie Andrews fan?," he asks his prospective "date." She looks at her experience as "The only overdose of Julie."

Family Guy

Fox's sarcastic, button-pushing cartoon series (created by Seth MacFarlane) was famous for throwing in musical numbers or nods to the genre, and, not surprisingly, *The Sound of Music* (which MacFarlane has called a favorite) ended up being referenced on several occasions. Indeed, how would MacFarlane sustain the series for so many seasons without other people's material to fall back on for jokes and parodies?

The Griffin Family of Quahog, Rhode Island, consisted of toy company employee Peter; his wife Lois; their three children, awkward teens Meg and Chris, and baby Stewie, who craved power and spoke with a drily sophisticated British accent; and the family dog, Brian.

Season 1, Episode 1: "Death Has a Shadow," January 31, 1999

Out of a job and desperate for money, Peter thinks he might be able to pick up some cash by winning a talent show. When the emcee announces, from a stage backed by a design of arches, "And the grand prize goes to . . . the Von Trapp Family Singers," Peter, seen holding a tuba, lets his feelings about the decision be heard with an expletive that is drowned out by the applause.

Season 1, Episode 7: "Brian: Portrait of a Dog," May 16, 1999

When Brian refuses to participate in a dog show he finds demeaning, he storms out of the house, but Peter has already disabled the car, a la the Nonnberg Abbey nuns, revealing the engine parts he has removed.

Season 3, Episode 9: "Mr. Saturday Knight," September 5, 2001

When the Griffins ask their children to say goodnight to their dinner guest, Mr. Weed, they respond by performing "So Long, Farewell." Although introducing himself as "Liesl," Stewie, in fact, takes Gretl's role, sitting at the bottom of the stairs and singing "The sun has gone to bed and so must I."

Season 4, Episode 14: "PTV," November 6, 2005

Spoofing the openings of *The Naked Gun* movies (in which a point-of-view police car careens carelessly into the most inappropriate events), Stewie rides his tricycle into the chariot race from *Ben-Hur,* onto the yellow brick road from *The Wizard of Oz,* throughout the Overlook hotel from *The Shining,* and over the Alps to knock Maria over as she's about to sing "The Sound of Music."

Season 4, Episode 25: "You May Now Kiss the . . . Uh . . . Guy Who Receives," April 30, 2006

Brian's cousin Jasper comes to stay with the Griffins in anticipation of his planned nuptials to his Filipino boyfriend Ricardo. At one point the two dogs and baby Stewie are perched in front of the television set watching the finale of *The Sound of Music*. After the Trapps flee and the Nazis have their engine trouble, Sister Berthe lets the Mother Abbess know she has sinned, holding forth the expected car parts. Sister Margaretta has sinned too, but not as we remember; instead, she produces the decapitated head of Rolf. Mother Abbess and Berthe are appalled, but Margaretta is quick to explain "Hey, I didn't start this war—but it's on!"

Apparently not wanting to spend the additional money drawing the full seven, a mere three Trapp children are seen sitting in the caretaker's car.

Season 4, Episode 28: "Stewie Be Goode," May 20, 2006

Dressed in Maria's post-abbey clothing, Stewie swings a bag and a guitar case while singing "I Have Confidence."

Season 5, Episode 10: "Peter's Two Dads," February 11, 2007

Daughter Meg wants a birthday party, but neither of her parents can recall how old she is. "Don't you remember me fakin' my way through her *last* birthday?" Lois asks Peter. We then see a flashback of mom at the piano singing "You are *huh-huh* going on *huh-huh*/fellas will fall in line" to the tune of "Sixteen Going on Seventeen."

Season 5, Episode 11: "The Tan Aquatic with Steve Zissou," February 18, 2007

Taking bad advice, Peter begins behaving like a bully, which includes forcing his friend Joe to act like a marionette and yodel "The Lonely Goatherd."

Season 9, Episode 10: "Friends of Peter G," February 13, 2011

Having sneaked liquor into a showing of *The Sound of Music*, Peter Griffin and his dog Brian end up causing havoc at the Quahog Theatre. Dazed and confused, the inebriated Peter tries to prevent Liesl from being drawn into Rolf's clutches, "Liesl, get away from him—he's a Nazi!" Peter cries at the movie, punching a hole in the screen. He and his pet are arrested and sentenced to thirty days in Alcoholics Anonymous.

What is unusual about this use of *TSOM* is that rather than fall back on an animated re-creation of the movie, actual clips are used of Rolf and Liesl in their "faux" telegram scene and of Gretl telling Max about her sore finger. The only songs heard in the episode, however, are from other sources, "Mr. Booze" (from *Robin and the 7 Hoods*) and "Hushabye Mountain" (from *Chitty Chitty Bang Bang*).

Season 12, Episode 2: "Vestigial Peter," October 6, 2013

Peter develops a vestigial head whom he names Chip. Once Chip is surgically detached, he starts usurping Peter's position in the household. This includes making clothing from the drapes for the children, whom Peter finds in their newly made lake in the backyard, rowing a boat until they fall out because they have stood up to gleefully wave at their dad. He's not impressed.

"Favourite Things" performed by Big Brovaz (Epic Records, March 24, 2003)

For the third version of their debut album, *Nu-Flow*, to be released on the market, the R&B/hip hop group Big Brovaz added a recording called "Favourite Things," which sampled the Rodgers and Hammerstein classic but with new lyrics for the former's melody. "Buy me diamonds and rubies/I'm crazy 'bout Bentleys/Gucci dresses and drop top compressors/Wine me and dine me/Bring those platinum rings/Those are a few of our favourite things."

The song became the group's biggest hit single, climbing to #2 on the UK singles chart.

The 59th Annual Academy Awards (ABC, March 30, 1987)

Before presenting the award for Sound Effects Editing, co-host Chevy Chase paid tribute to the craft by showing a humorous montage of clips from famous movies that might have been less effective had they not featured the correct sound. These include the chariot race from *Ben-Hur*, punctuated by car crash noises and sirens; Dooley Wilson playing "The Woody Woodpecker March" instead of "As Time Goes By" for a dismayed Humphrey Bogart in *Casablanca*; George C. Scott's opening speech in *Patton* interrupted by a discourteous cougher in the audience; and, saving the funniest for last, poor Julie Andrews being besieged by machine gun fire from a descending bomber plane as she runs back for her wimple on her hilltop in *The Sound of Music*.

The opening speech for that evening's ceremony was delivered by the Academy of Motion Picture Arts and Sciences' president, Robert Wise.

The 5 Mrs. Buchanans (CBS, January 7, 1995)

Four diverse women are all married to the Buchanan brothers in a family presided over by the *fifth* Mrs. B, acerbic Emma (Eileen Heckart). One episode revolves entirely around a community theatre production of *The Sound of Music*, directed by the pretentious Vivian Buchanan (Harriet Sansom Harris). "No more of that sappy, sentimental, audience-pleasing slosh," she declares, "We're going to dare to be raw, risky, cutting edge." A puzzled Alex Buchanan (Judith Ivey) needs clarification. "We *are* talking about the show where the nun dances on the hill, right?"

Although former stripper Delilah Buchanan (Beth Broderick) longs to fulfill her dream of starring in her favorite musical, her in-law, Bree Buchanan (Charlotte Ross), goes back on her promise to Alex to blow the audition, doing a wow rendition of the title song and landing the lead. "You chose to make Julie Andrews look like a two-bit lounge singer," a disappointed Alex scolds Bree.

Making it a true family affair, Emma comes on board as the Mother Abbess, only under the condition that she get to sing "Edelweiss." She also has no qualms about taunting Hubert Lombard (Edward Hibbert), the actor she hates who was chosen to portray the captain. "When the gestapo asks the Mother Superior where Captain von Trapp is hiding," Lombard complains to Vivian during rehearsal, "could she *not* point in my direction and say 'He's all yours'?"

Generously, Bree fakes a leg injury to allow Delilah (whose Southern accent causes Alex to joke that they should tell the audience she's from "Southern Austria") to go on in her place, and just to make sure that Alex is not left out of the mix, she does a jazzy version of "My Favorite Things" as the tag scene of the show.

Hibbert would get his chance to do *TSOM* on stage for real, but in the role of Max.

Frasier (NBC)

This *Cheers* spin-off about neurotic radio call-in therapist Frasier Crane (Kelsey Grammer) sharing his Seattle apartment with his crusty old dad (John Mahoney) gave its star a combined twenty-year run as the same character.

Season 1, Episode 12: "Miracle on Third or Fourth Street," December 16, 1993

Hoping to spend Christmas with his son Frederick, Frasier is thwarted by his ex-wife's plans to take the boy to Austria, where they will be renting "the same house they filmed *The Sound of Music* in," which is quite a coup—it's the boy's favorite movie. To add to the prize vacation, Julie Andrews will be singing with the Salzburg Chorale and then joining Frasier's ex and her group for dinner! Figuring the only way to conquer his blues over the matter is to work on Christmas Day, Frasier endures an onslaught of depressing phone calls from saddened listeners. At last one upbeat caller offers his surefire way to beat the holiday blues. "I pop my favorite movie, *The Sound of Music*, into the VCR," he declares, spiritedly. "Watching Julie Andrews lead those adorable tykes through the streets of Salzburg—nobody could be depressed. I mean *nobody*!" Needless to say, somebody is—Frasier.

Season 8, Episode 21: "Semi-Decent Proposal," May 15, 2001

When Martin (John Mahoney) fails in his efforts to hook up the new DVD player, Roz (Peri Gilpin) decides to keep the movie-night gathering moving along by having each of the parties confess something deeply personal about themselves. After some coercing, Martin admits to crying every time he watches *The Sound of Music*. "And I don't mean a single manly tear," he elaborates, "I mean real blubbering, girl-style . . . the nuns . . . those kids . . . that lonely goatherd."

Freakazoid! (The WB, Season 1, Episode 7: "Freakazoid Is History," November 11, 1995)

While saving *Air Force One*, Freakazoid (voice of Paul Rugg), the star of this animated spoof, is sucked into both a time warp vortex *and* a TV show parody, specifically, *Quantum Leap*, in which its protagonist jumped through time and thereby played different people. Here, the clueless superhero ("Quantum Freak") is seen participating in the chariot race from *Ben-Hur*; smashing a bone like the ape in *2001: A Space Odyssey*; strutting on the disco floor in the white suit from *Saturday Night Fever*; hanging off Mount Rushmore a la *North by Northwest*; watching *The Graduate*'s Mrs. Robinson pull her stockings on; facing a shark from *Jaws* (well, the show *was* presented by Steven Spielberg, after all); escaping guard dogs while chained to a fellow prisoner in *The Defiant Ones* fashion; being celebrated at Harmonia Gardens in *Hello, Dolly!*; and—you saw it coming, didn't you?—spinning on a hilltop in novice garb in *The Sound of Music*. When you can simply toss in movie images and have them be immediately recognized by your audience, those images can rightfully claim to have reached iconic status.

French and Saunders (BBC 2, Season 3, Episode 1; UK Airdate: March 15, 1990)

This sketch-comedy series (which ran for seven seasons off and on between 1987 and 2007), starring Dawn French and Jennifer Saunders, often depended on movie spoofs for laughs. In the opening episode of their third season, Saunders portrayed Mother Abbess, attempting to sing "Climb Ev'ry Mountain," but being interrupted by French as an enthusiastic Maria. The latter then breaks into "I Have Confidence," striding right off the set and out the studio doors, swinging her bag and guitar case through the Eastbourne Town Center, until receiving a clout on the chin from the fed-up Abbess.

The end of the episode includes the ladies doing a spoof of "Sixteen Going on Seventeen" in a gazebo, with the lyrics changed to "I am French and you are Saunders."

Friends (NBC)

Putting six twenty-something friends together in New York resulted in one of the major sitcom hits of the '90s.

Season 1, Episode 1: "The One Where Monica Gets a Roommate," September 22, 1994

Having just fled from her wedding, Rachel (Jennifer Aniston) is in need of some comfort, so Phoebe (Lisa Kudrow) starts singing her version of "My Favorite Things," with such lyrical interpretations as "door bells and sleigh bells and *something* with mittens . . . la-la-la . . . *something* and noodles with strings." To get her to stop, Rachel assures her she's fine.

Season 1, Episode 22: "The One with the Ick Factor," May 4, 1995

After Phoebe fills in as Chandler's (Mathew Perry) assistant at work, she informs him that his co-workers like to make fun of his habit of emphasizing certain words for dramatic effect. Agreeing, Ross (David Schwimmer) gives him an example with "The hills are alive with the sound OF music."

Season 10, Episode 19: "The Last One, Part 1," May 6, 2004

After seeing Erica's newborn twins, Mike (Paul Rudd) tells Phoebe he'd like it if they made a child of their own. Phoebe wonders why they shouldn't have several. "We could teach them to sing, and we can be like the Von Trapp family! Only without the Nazis." Her enthusiasm wanes, as she considers this scenario, without the menace, duller than she thought.

Friends and Family (Regent Entertainment, May 16, 2003)

Stephen's (Greg Lauren) parents are perfectly at ease knowing he's gay, but since dad is in the FBI, the last thing he needs to be aware of is that his son and his lover, Danny (Christopher Gartin), are Mafia hit men and *not* New York caterers. Reluctantly, some of their most thuggish "soldiers" are recruited to camp it up and pass themselves off as gay stereotypes in order to fake out Stephen's visiting folks. Flamboyant Richard Grayson (Edward Hibbert) is assigned the seemingly impossible task of putting these "wiseguys" in touch with some benchmarks of gay culture. These include Liberace, J. Edgar Hoover, TV pooch Wishbone (*Wishbone*!?!), Shirley Booth as *Hazel*, Cher, Elizabeth Taylor's various married names, and *The Sound of Music*. The last is presented in a rendition of "Do-Re-Mi" by the awkward Mafioso (Frank Minucci, Richard Petrocelli, Michael Squicciarini, Garry Pastore, and Victor Colicchio), with Grayson leading them in song.

The Sound of Music has been embraced by many demographics, and this film reminds us that the gay community is chief among them. It's also worth noting that Hibbert actually went on to play Max in different productions of *TSOM*.

Full House (ABC, Season 4, Episode 10: "Terror in Tanner Town," November 23, 1990)

In this sitcom about a house inhabited by three men and three kids, Danny Tanner (Bob Saget), the father of those kids, wants to impress a new date, so he lines up his brood (including their dog, Comet) in height order. "What is this? A Julie Andrews movie?" asks Uncle Jesse (John Stamos), prompting Joey (David Coulier) to lead the group in a rendition of "Do-Re-Mi." Danny reminds them that "This is really important to me," making the fatal mistake of ending his sentence with a "me," which brings on the line "Me, a name I call myself." He's way ahead of them, however, when he tells them "this has gone too far," beating them to the punch by singing "Fa, a long, long way to run."

The Full Monty (Eugene O'Neill Theatre, October 26, 2000)

In this musical stage adaptation of the 1997 British movie, Terrence McNally once again adds a reference to *The Sound of Music* (having already done so in *The Ritz* and *Frankie and Johnnie in the Claire de Lune*). As the ragtag group of would-be strippers commence with their dance rehearsal, Harold (Marcus Neville) quite innocently opens with, "Let's start at the very beginning," thereby prompting Malcolm (Jason Danieley) and Ethan (Romaine Frugé) to chime in unison, "A very good place to start." Startled and delighted at their shared interest, Ethan asks "*The Sound of Music?*" "It's my favorite movie," Malcolm informs him. Ethan concurs, claiming to have seen it 200 times. "Try three" is Malcolm's response. Not only do the two men bond, but this becomes one of many instances when a shared love of musicals demonstrates, to quote Lorenz Hart, "how to make two lovers of friends."

Gilmore Girls (The WB)

Somebody behind the scenes of this comedy-drama about single mom Lorelai (Lauren Graham), her teenage offspring Rory (Alexis Bledel), and the quirky inhabitants of the town of Stars Hollow was *clearly* stuck on *The Sound of Music*. Consider these:

Season 2, Episode 6: "Presenting Lorelai Gilmore," November 6, 2001

Dropping by the home of Lorelai's stuffy parents, she and Rory are greeted by the new maid, whose name happens to be Liesl (Jen Dede). "Okay, Liesl," Lorelai replies, cheekily. "I'm Brigitta. This is Gretl." The joke seems to fly over the domestic's head.

Season 5, Episode 11: "Women of Questionable Morals," January 25, 2005

Just to show you the religious order is not a pushover when it comes to the musical, Reverend Skinner (Jim Jansen) responds to Taylor's (Michael Winters) surprise over the man of the cloth watching *Farewell, My Concubine* by asking "What? You picture me watching *Sound of Music* every night, Taylor? Gag me!"

Season 6, Episode 15: "A Vineyard Valentine," February 14, 2006

During a weekend at her daughter's boyfriend's family home on Martha's Vineyard, Lorelai is stunned to see Rory in an apron. "You've not worn an apron since you saw *The Sound of Music* and you put one on so you'd look like Sister Maria," she recalls, accidentally promoting the novice to nun-hood, and then adds, "and you made a big Crucifix out of popsicle sticks."

Season 7, Episode 20: "Lorelai? Lorelai?," May 1, 2007

Dance instructor Patty (Liz Torres) and neighbor Babette (Sally Struthers) are saving their voices for karaoke night but chirp in on a few notes of "So Long, Farewell."

Glee (Fox)

Leave it to *Glee* to equate an interest in *The Sound of Music* with cross-dressing. William McKinley High School's gay glee club member, Kurt (Chris Colfer), first brings up his passion for the *TSOM* sing-along in Season 1, Episode 3, "Accafellas," (September 16, 2009), asking Mercedes (Amber Riley) while washing cars if she brought a change of clothing for the event. We realize this is a ritual when it arises again in Season 2, Episode 3, "Grilled Cheesus," (October 5, 2010), after Kurt's dad (Mike O'Malley) reminds his son about their traditional Friday night dinner. "I can't do this Friday," Kurt awkwardly tells the old man. "It's *Sing-along Sound of Music* at the El Royale Theater. It's a once-a-year event." Kurt will not abide his father making him feel guilty about choosing Julie Andrews over family time. "The whole point of having something sacred is that it takes precedence over anything else you got going on," Kurt explains. "*Sing-a-long Sound of Music* is sacred to me." How does dad realize this is so? Because he reminds his son that he bought him a "Maria bonnet" when he was six years old! And how does the old man finally manage to pull focus from *TSOM*? By having a strategically timed heart attack.

A later *TSOM* reference (Season 5, Episode 4; "A Katy or a Gaga," November 7, 2013) leaves Kurt and the "sing-a-long" out of the mix. Instead, Marley (Melissa Benoist) tries to entice boyfriend Jake (Jacob Artist) to a Julie Andrews triple bill at the Lima Limelight. (Clearly this town has a firm appreciation of Julie's movie legacy.) The lineup consists of *Mary Poppins, The Sound of Music,* and . . . *The Princess Diaries* (*The Princess Diaries?!?*). When Jake complains that this sounds like the same old thing they do every week, Marley suggests other safe things like an orchid show or a mobile cat adoption. Jake is now convinced that his girlfriend can never pull off the glee club assignment of behaving like pop singer Lady Gaga. "Why?" she asks, incredulously, "Because I like cats and flowers and Julie Andrews? That doesn't mean I can't rock a bra made out of gloved leather hands."

Missed opportunity department: wouldn't it have been cleverer to have Marley specifically say she likes roses and kittens?

The God of Animals by Aryn Kyle (Scribner, March 2007)

The story of an eleven-year-old girl living on a run-down horse farm, this novel includes among its characters a rich girl, Sheila Altman, whose family has indulged her ambitions for horseback riding. The narrator, Alice Winston, tells us "Sheila Altman had auditioned for the community production of *The Sound of Music* and was cast as Louisa—the bratty one . . . ." While Louisa may have tried to pull the wool over Maria's eyes about just who was "Brigitta" and was known to climb up the side of house with (alternately, depending on the source) a toad/jar full of spiders, does she really qualify as "bratty"?

The God of Small Things by Arundhati Roy (Random House, April 1997)

Growing up in India means *multiple* trips to see *TSOM* for twins Rahel and Estha. As the former says, "Oh come on, the whole world goes to see *The Sound of Music*. It's a world hit." One particular incident in the narrative involves the siblings being taken to their umpteenth viewing at the Abhilash Talkies in Kerala, which boasts of being the first such venue with a "70mm CinemaScope screen." This is not a satisfying outing, however, as they are late, coming in *after* the famous opening, with Estha having to leave twice, first because he is causing too much of a nuisance singing the lyrics to "Maria" and later because of illness, forcing the theatre party to retreat after the Trapp children have sung the title song for the baroness's sake.

The film appears to be appreciated for its cleanliness above all, its look and tone equated with peppermint, as evident in this description: "Baron von Trapp's seven peppermint children had had their peppermint baths, and were standing in a peppermint line with their hair slicked down, singing in obedient peppermint voices to the woman the Baron nearly married." In contrast, the Kerala cinema itself is said to smell of "breathing people and hair oil," not to mention old carpets. This is, however, cherished as "A magical *Sound of Music* smell that Rahel remembered and treasured."

God, the Devil and Bob (Cartoon Network, Season 1, Episode 9: "Bob Gets Greedy," February 26, 2011)

Auto-plant worker Bob Allman (French Stewart) was given advice by both the Almighty and Lucifer (Alan Cummings) in this short-lived animated series from 2000. This particular episode did not see the light of day for eleven years, when the Cartoon Network took it upon themselves to show the unaired installments.

Certain that the Devil isn't telling him the truth about the need for charities to cure the ills of the world, Bob says he's seen evidence on television. The Prince of Darkness tells the naïve Bob that "Everything on TV is fake!" This includes the Apollo moon landing ("Done on a soundstage in Culver City"). Bob is devastated that Neil Armstrong was a mere actor. "Rent *The Sound of Music* sometime and look closely at Rolf," the Devil advises him. After the Lord of Hell leaves for a Henry Kissinger book party, the clueless Bob, not quite getting it, murmurs to himself "So, that was an actor playin' Rolf."

The Golden Girls NBC, (Season 3, Episode 17: "My Brother, My Father," February 6, 1988)

This sitcom about four elderly ladies sharing a house in Florida was yet another to take some liberties with the plotline of *TSOM*. Blanche (Rue McClanahan) and Rose (Betty White) have landed nun roles in a local production of the musical and, due to plot complications, are obliged to stay in character (and in costume) when they encounter a priest. Their earlier rehearsal of "Scene 3" (certainly not the one in the Mother Abbess's office, from the sound of things) has them listening to artillery shells at the Trapp house (apparently the cloistering rules at Nonnberg Abbey have slackened a bit) and Rose screaming "The Nazis are coming!" Alas, the plotline of the episode does not allow us a glimpse of this, um . . . action-filled production.

Good in Bed by Jennifer Weiner (Washington Square Press, May 2001)

Connie Shapiro takes stock of her romantic life and job as an entertainment journalist on the *Philadelphia Examiner*. In one scene of the novel, she is caught by her mother, once again, drinking tequila and watching *The Sound of Music*. As Connie explains to the reader, "What can I say? I like musicals." Her favorite *TSOM* moment is "the scene where Maria gathers the motherless von Trapp brood onto her bed during the thunderstorm and sings "My Favorite Things." She describes it as seeming "so cozy, so safe—the way my own family had been, for a minute, once upon a time, a long time ago." In these few lines Weiner hits a bull's-eye in describing just one reason for the movie's appeal.

The Good Life (BBC, Season 1, Episode 6: "The Pagan Rite," May 9, 1975; Season 2, Episode 3: "Mr. Fix-It," December 19, 1975; Season 2, Episode 4: "The Day Peace Broke Out," January 2, 1976; Season 2, Episode 5: "Mutiny," January 9, 1976)

This British sitcom about a draughtsman, Tom Good (Richard Briers), who quits the work world to run a farm with his wife Barbara (Felicity Huffman), ran on BBC for four seasons (1975–78).

In four episodes, a plotline involved social-climbing neighbor Margo Leadbetter (Penelope Keith) landing the role of Maria in the local, town hall production of what her fed-up husband Jerry (Paul Eddington) comes to call *The Sound of "Bloody" Music.* "Julie Andrews played my role in the film," the self-involved Margo tells a visiting reporter. As each episode unfolds, it becomes clear that Margo is woefully out of her element, Jerry confessing to the Goods that his wife is miscast and making too much of the whole thing. ("You don't know what it's like being married to Julie Andrews!" he wails.) During the episode "Mutiny," Margo is shown struggling to remember her lines for the "rainstorm" scene, which she attempts to rehearse with Barbara's help. Clearly the movie is the inspiration for the entire premise, as Margo refers to singing "My Favorite Things" during this moment, *not* "The Lonely Goatherd." She then proceeds to mess up the lyrics, coming up with "raindrops on noses" and "when the shark bites," the latter prompting her to lament, "Oh, my God! I've strayed into *The Threepenny Opera.*"

Complaining that one of the Trapp boys has a runny nose, that the captain's lederhosen squeaks, and the flowers she's using on stage *aren't* edelweiss, an anxiety-ridden Margo proceeds to make a shambles of the production (unseen by us). Her biggest mistake? Singing the wrong, "Maria," opting for the song of the same name from *West Side Story.*

When this series was shown in America on PBS in the 1980s, it went under the name *Good Neighbors.*

Goodbye Lover (Warner Bros., April 16, 1999)

In this none-too-serious Los Angeles-set noir, realtor Sandra Dunmore (Patricia Arquette) has no qualms about using the houses she's showing perspective buyers for her sexual assignations with her lover Ben (Don Johnson), who happens to be her husband Jake's (Dermot Mulroney) brother. Of course it all leads to murder, double crosses, and more murder.

Sandra has a thing for *The Sound of Music,* listening to a cassette tape of the soundtrack, which turns out to be a clue that later ties her into one of her crimes. Heard from the film are "Maria," "My Favorite Things," "So Long, Farewell" (as Sandra is trying to drive her husband and *his* lover off a mountain road), and "I Have Confidence." There is not just the film version of "Climb Ev'ry Mountain," but a choral rendition at a party, which prompts Ben to declare "I hate this song!" Jake tosses off a line from "Something Good," and even John Ottman's scoring sounds suspiciously like a portion of "My Favorite Things."

Gossip Girl (Fox, Season 4, Episode 14: "Panic Roommate," February 7, 2011)

Life among the privileged young adults of Manhattan's Upper East Side featured a cast of impossibly good-looking actors going through the customary relationship woes—in more fashionable attire than most of us—while hopping from bed to bed. In this episode, Blair Waldorf (Leighton Meester) needs Nate Archibald (Chase Crawford) to help her salvage a posh party where the 600+ gift bags have failed to be delivered. To ensure his cooperation, she threatens to tell everyone what his favorite movie is. "Hey, do *not* mock *The Sound of Music*," he snaps back, "It's got nuns and Nazis. Julie Andrews is hot!" It's nice to know that someone who makes it his mission to appear so cool is capable of such good taste.

The Happy Hooker Goes Hollywood (Cannon, June 4, 1980)

Desperate for a hit, studio head WB Warkoff (Phil Silvers) decides they should woo best-selling and body-selling madam and author Xaviera Hollander (Martine Beswick) into allowing them to turn her book *The Happy Hooker* into a movie. "What I want is a boffo, socko, kiss my grosses movie," Warkoff barks at his staff, "I want it to be bigger than *The Sound of Music!*" His son-in-law, Joseph Rottman (Richard Deacon), perks up, "Oh, it's going to be a musical?" If only. Later, Rottman imagines Xaviera's childhood in Holland, and his fantasy puts her and her classmates in costumes akin to a bad touring production of *TSOM*.

Interesting to note that fifteen years down the line, *TSOM* was still being used as the gold standard of a box office success.

Home Improvement (ABC)

Stand-up comedian Tim Allen portrayed Tim Taylor, host of *Tool Time* and dad to three rambunctious boys.

In "For Whom the Belch Tolls" (Season 1, Episode 14, January 14, 1992), it's family movie night, and mom Jill (Patricia Richardson) vetoes suggestions of such violent (and fictional) titles as *Bury Me Again* and *Bayonet Hell* in favor of *The Sound of Music*. The men in her family not only scream in horror at the idea but end up having their way—watching *Bayonet Hell*.

Season 6, Episode 23: "The Feminine Mistake," May 6, 1997

Tim is excited that they are going to show an episode of *Tool Time* in 3D, but his co-host, Al (Richard Karn) can't work up the same level of enthusiasm, being no fan of the stereoptic gimmick. As a kid his favorite movie was . . . *The Sound of Music*. "Now there's a movie that would have been better in 3D," Tim theorizes. "Can you imagine 50 nuns comin' at ya like ping pong balls? Like a bad habit!"

Season 8, Episode 8, November 10, 1998

In "Tim's First Car" our hero stumbles upon said vehicle at the local junkyard and hopes to repair it. Circumstances cause Jill to buy him a replacement Corvair, in which they sit to relive the past. Tim remembers them seeing *The Omen* and *The Exorcist* at a drive-in double bill and insists it was Jill who was freaked out. As Jill recalls, Tim buried his head in her chest all night. True, but it hardly had to do with fear since "You did the same thing when we saw *The Sound of Music*," Jill remarks. "The hills were alive," Tim quips in double entendre fashion. "I don't know about alive," Jill responds, looking downward, "but they were a lot higher then."

How Do You Solve a Problem Like Maria? (BBC One, July 29–September 16, 2006; US airing: BBC America: June 7–July 19, 2009)

An unsuccessful attempt by producers Andrew Lloyd Webber and David Ian to cast Scarlett Johansson in a West End revival of *The Sound of Music* led to this reality series, which turned into a ratings smash when it aired in Great Britain during the summer of 2006. Figuring they could generate untold reams of publicity for their proposed stage show, Lloyd Webber (in collaboration with executive producer Gigi Eligoloff and Bea Ballard) came up with the idea of a competitive weekly audition television series to fill the role of Maria.

Following initial open auditions in the spring, 200 women were chosen before whittling the number down to 50. These hopefuls were then subjected to what was referred to as "Maria School," receiving training from a panel of chosen experts, consisting of Lloyd Webber and Ian; West End performer John Barrowman; and vocal coach Zoe Tyler. The 50 were narrowed down to 20, who auditioned before an elite group of show business professionals at Lloyd Webber's estate. From that came the ten finalists who would be spotlighted on the series.

The ten, ranging in age from twenty to twenty-eight, were: Leanne Dobinson, Siobhan Dillon, Helena Blackman, Abi Finley, Connie Fisher, Meliz Serman, Laura Sicurello, Simona Armstrong, Belinda Evans, and Aoife Mulholland.

The Rodgers and Hammerstein score was used for the opening group performances that started the episodes, sometimes with faux Maria competitors being knocked about or comically bashed for entertainment purposes. Therefore audiences heard "Maria" and "I Have Confidence" (show 1), "My Favorite Things" (show 2), "The Lonely Goatherd" (show 3), "Do-Re-Mi" (show 4), "I Have Confidence" (show 5), and, again, "Maria" (show 6). The three finalists, Siobhan, Helena, and Connie, did get their chance to go solo on, respectively, "My Favorite Things," "Do-Re-Mi," and "The Lonely Goatherd." Once Siobhan was bumped, the two remaining women paired off on "The Sound of Music," while all the eliminated Marias piped in on "Edelweiss."

When Connie Fisher won the competition, she wrapped the whole thing up with her version of "The Sound of Music."

Of interest was an episode in which Lloyd Webber and his three finalists took a trip to Salzburg, where they were seen visiting familiar locations from the film, including Nonnberg Abbey and Leopoldskron.

Despite initial criticism of Lloyd Webber for stepping outside professional show business for his casting, the series led to further television competitions of this ilk covering such other shows as Lloyd Webber's own *Joseph and the Amazing Technicolor Dreamcoat,* as well as Lionel Bart's *Oliver!* and a stage adaptation of Harold Arlen and E. Y. Harburg's *The Wizard of Oz.*

There was also a Canadian version of *How Do You Solve . . . ?* (CBC Television, 2008), in order to cast Lloyd Webber's Toronto revival of *The Sound of Music,* and a Belgian version, that aired (VTM, March 25—June 3, 2009) under the name *Op zoek naar Maria (Looking for Maria).* The latter was directly responsible for one of the most notable and viewed of all YouTube videos.

In a genius stroke of promotion, a seemingly random group of commuters gathered at the Antwerpen-Centraal (Antwerp Central) railway station in

Contestants vying for the coveted leading role in a West End revival of *The Sound of Music* turned *How Do You Solve a Problem Like Maria?* into a UK television hit.

Antwerp, Belgium, on March 23, 2009 at approximately 8:00 a.m. Suddenly, over the loudspeakers, Julie Andrews's version of "Do-Re-Mi" began playing, causing members of the crowd to erupt into a choreographed series of movements, much to the startled pleasure of those who were genuinely innocent bystanders. This mass choreography (or "flash mob") became such a hit that similar numbers were staged by amateurs throughout the world.

The Canadian *How Do You Solve . . . ?* winner was Elicia MacKenzie (Princess of Wales Theatre in Toronto, October 15, 2008–January 10, 2010; at more than 500 performances this entered the record books as the longest-running revival in Toronto history); the Belgian champion was Deborah de Ridder, who appeared in *TSOM* at the Efteling Theatre (November 2009–January 2010).

The BBC's *How Do You Solve . . . ?* would eventually make its way to the U.S., three years after the fact. Those in the know were already fully aware that Fisher was the champ.

Hyundai ad (Premiered on ABC, March 7, 2010)

This thirty-second ad featured Daniel Truhitte's rendition of "Sixteen Going on Seventeen" playing on the soundtrack while the camera panned around a cluttered disaster area of a room belonging to a teenager. Intoned narrator Jeff Bridges, "Thankfully, most of us don't have to share a room with sixteen year olds. But we *do* have to share the road with them." This was an invitation to buy a safe car, the Sonata from Hyundai. Charmian Carr's voice was not heard.

I'm Over All That: And Other Confessions by Shirley MacLaine (Atria Books, April 2011)

Proving that *The Sound of Music* is an ideal "go-to" title to grab attention, even if the facts are sketchy at best, Shirley MacLaine (in her thirteenth book) refers to it while talking about her relationship with Canadian Prime Minister Pierre Trudeau. According to MacLaine, she complied with Trudeau's request to see a Hollywood studio up close by taking him to Fox. Although the two were recognized at the front gate, they were denied permission to set foot on the 20th Century-Fox lot. "I'll never forget Pierre looking longingly at the New York street set from *Hello, Dolly!*, the house from *The Sound of Music* visible in the background," she relates, "as he was told he wasn't allowed in."

Although the New York set from *Dolly* did indeed remain a part of the entrance to the Fox studios for years, there were no exterior sets for *TSOM* sitting on the lot, the Trapp house being constructed there expressly on soundstages. But it did help to embellish the tale.

The Jacksons: An American Dream (ABC, November 15 and 18, 1992)

This two-part biopic of the rise of the Jackson 5 accurately depicts the group's breakout member, Michael Jackson (Alex Burrall), winning over the audience at Garnett Elementary School (in Gary, Indiana) with his a cappella rendition of "Climb Ev'ry Mountain." So thrilled is his mother (Angela Bassett) that she declares, "I guess the Jackson 4 just became the Jackson 5!" (Considering the location, points to Michael for not taking the obvious route and singing a certain song from *The Music Man* . . . .)

This performance took place in 1963 (Jackson would have been five years old), which meant the song was then associated expressly with the Broadway show. Michael, however, did become a tremendous fan of the movie, one of the reasons he was eager to have his Encino home decorated by Charmian Carr.

Johnny Bravo (Cartoon Network, Season 1, Episode 13: "Johnny Bravo Meets Donny Osmond," December 15, 1997)

Slow on the uptake, narcissist Johnny Bravo (voice of Jeff Bennett) is informed by his mama that he needs a nanny, so the old lady hires none other than pop singer Donny Osmond (voiced by himself) to do the job. Donny's ultra-perky efforts to educate his new charge include taking the reluctant slouch to a hilltop to play the guitar and show him "a fun way to remember musical notes." Before you can say "Do-Re-Mi," he's singing a version requiring serious television trivia credentials to interpret: "Ay, like Nick from *Family Ties* . . . Bee, the bug you try to dodge . . . See, the thing your eyes do best . . . Dee, and Rerun, Dwayne and Raj." Johnny responds by tossing Donny's guitar into the nearby Alps, only to have his "nanny" break out his bagpipes. Although the *Sound of Music* references may be over, there's still room for one more Julie Andrews–related gag as Donny, feeling his job is done, flies away on an umbrella, Mary Poppins-style. This episode being written by Seth MacFarlane, he's promptly hit by lightning.

Just Shoot Me! (NBC, Season 7, Episode 19: "Son of a Preacher Man," August 9, 2003

This sitcom was set in the offices of a tawdry women's fashion magazine called *Blush*.

Proving that even rock stars are up on all the plot details of *TSOM*, this episode finds dim-witted musician Simon Leeds (Simon Templeman) briefing his fiancée on the backstory he's made up about her to his conservative parents. Not only was she convent raised, but she served as "a nanny for some adorable Austrian children . . . you taught them how to sing . . . you hid them from the Nazis . . . ." But Nina (Wendie Malick) will have none of this fabrication, "My life is not something out of *The Sound of Music!*" she snaps. Unfazed, Simon suggests *Erin Brockovich* instead.

The King Family Show (ABC, 1965–66)

They weren't just a wholesome singing family with a *lot* of members; they even used "The Sound of Music" as their weekly theme song. This brood of thirty-six (or thereabouts) were prescient enough to include not only that tune but "Do-Re-Mi" and "Climb Ev'ry Mountain" on their March 6, 1965 episode, aired only four days after *TSOM* premiered in theatres.

Kiss Me, Guido (Paramount, July 18, 1997)

Italian stereotype meets homosexual stereotype as Frankie (Nick Scotti), a clueless aspiring actor, ends up sharing an apartment in Manhattan's Little Italy with the openly gay Warren (Anthony Barrile) in this broad comedy.

In one scene, Warren has curled up on the couch to watch *The Sound of Music*, as we hear dialogue from the pre-"Laendler" scene and then clips of "So Long, Farewell." Curious as to what is holding his roommate's attention, Frankie has to ask not only what the film is but who's in it. "Julie Andrews," Warren answers only to receive the query, "She did that before *Pretty Woman?*," Frankie confusing her with Julia Roberts. When Warren decides to forfeit viewing the rest of the movie for a night at the bar with some friends, Frankie ends up watching it. Queried later on about his reaction, Frankie proves that this sort of thing has its limitations when it comes to impressing certain straight guys, admitting it was "Good . . . good. A little too much singing."

It does, however, have its lasting impact on him, when Frankie has a nightmare of his Italian family clad in lederhosen performing their version of the Trapp children's famous number.

The Last Blind Date by Linda Yellin (Gallery Books, October, 2011)

In this memoir, the author vents her feelings about some of the more unpleasant stepmothers throughout fiction. In addition to those of Cinderella and Snow White, she tosses in her personal favorite, "the Baroness in *The Sound of Music.* I mean, really, twenty minutes after she got that rock on her finger she was booking reservations to ship those singing little Von Trapps off to boarding school."

This is just one of many instances in which those referencing the musical, in their effort to make a point, get some of the details a bit off, as the baroness never got as far as receiving a "rock" from Captain von Trapp, the two going their separate ways before anyone went shopping for jewelry.

The Late, Late Show with Craig Ferguson (CBS, January 29, 2009)

Scottish late-night talk show host Craig Ferguson basked in the silly, which included tossed-off musical numbers, sometimes performed by his troupe of animal hand puppets. A gay unicorn takes the lead as he mimes to the movie soundtrack's recording of "The Lonely Goatherd," joined by various other creatures including a shark and a lion.

Late Show with David Letterman (CBS, May 4, 2000)

Plugging her appearance as the Blue Fairy in an upcoming television musical of *Pinocchio* called *Geppetto,* Julia Louis-Dreyfus takes center stage to show off her vocal prowess, singing "Sixteen Going on Seventeen." The big surprise is when her "Rolf" shows up, with Jerry Seinfeld making an unexpected appearance and proving that, unlike his former *Seinfeld* co-star, when it comes to hitting notes, he'd best not quit his day job.

Mad (Issue #108, January 1967)

A favorite feature of this satirical magazine is the movie parody, with the *Mad* artists drawing pretty accurate caricatures of the stars and the writers providing their own irreverent interpretations of the plot. What is most surprising about the *TSOM* satire is that it took so long to show up, not appearing in the magazine until nearly two years after the movie's opening.

Retitled *The Sound of Money*, with illustrations by Mort Drucker and text by Stan Hart, the seven-page send-up features a novice named Mitzia who goes to work for Captain von Tripe, after leaving an abbey presided over by the Mother Obsess. There are song parodies of the title tune ("I'm not singing now; I am pre-recorded/I'm just mouthing words I have sung before"), "Maria," which shows Mr. Hart has done his homework making offhand references to several other cinematic nuns including Audrey Hepburn, Donna Reed, and Loretta Young; "My Favorite Things" ("See how the children all love one another/You know that's nonsense if you have a brother!"); "Do-Re-Mi" ("It will bring us back much dough . . . dough . . . dough . . . dough"); and "Climb Ev'ry Mountain" ("With all these profits, Things will be fine!/When

Not surprisingly, *Mad* magazine kidded the lederhosen off of *The Sound of Music*; more surprisingly, the spoof did not show up until nearly two years after the movie had debuted. *From: MAD #108 © E.C. Publications*

we top *Fair Lady,* Vengeance . . . will . . . be . . . mine!"). There is the expected inclusion of Mary Poppins, and more unexpected appearances from TV's *The Fugitive,* David Janssen; *Peanuts'* Linus; and Rex Harrison.

For maximum lunacy, closer inspection of Drucker's depiction of the final escape over the mountains shows the captain carrying on his back, not his youngest girl, Gretl, but his oldest boy, Friedrich!

On *Mad*'s animated TV series spin-off, called, appropriately, *Mad* (Season 1, Episode 1: "Class of the Titans/Zeke and Lex Luthor," November 8, 2010,), an insert segment presents the concept of "Mad-inization—a revolutionary way to make movies less boring." This includes providing actual wind for Rhett Butler in *Gone with the Wind* and adding a dinosaur to *Julie & Julia.* For *TSOM* spoof, a cartoon novice spins on a hilltop singing "The chills make me thrive . . ." before an alien invasion interrupts the moment.

Mad About You (NBC, Season 1, Episode 6: "I'm Just So Happy for You," October 28, 1992)

This sitcom about high-strung documentary filmmaker Paul Buchman (Paul Reiser) and his relationship with wife Jamie (Helen Hunt) featured an episode in which the couple question how much the other pays attention and cares about what the other does for a living. (Jamie is in public relations.) As Paul is rambling on about a documentary he's made about a longtime Yankee Stadium peanut vendor named Vacky, he mentions with amazement that Vacky actually went to see *The Sound of Music* in 1960 with legendary Yankee Yogi Berra. Although he is clearly referring to the Broadway musical, Jamie's response seems to lean more toward the movie adaptation. Quizzed by her exasperated husband as to what he's just said, Jamie has only caught pieces of his monologue (which included references to Gary Cooper playing Lou Gehrig in *Pride of the Yankees*), assuming he was talking "about some Gary Cooper movie and how it was nuts to compare it to *The Sound of Music.*"

Could she be making an ironic point when she tries to make it up to him by buying an autographed program from Yankee Stadium? It is, after all, signed by the lady Mary Martin beat out for the Tony the year she won for *TSOM*, Ethel Merman!

Mad Men (AMC)

Set in the 1960s, this series about the personal and professional world of Manhattan advertisers would slip in an occasional pop cultural reference to give it some credibility and resonance of the time. Since Season 4 brings the action up to fall of 1965, it is plausible that *The Sound of Music* would be very much in the air and its protagonist would be known by Don Draper (Jon Hamm).

In Episode 13 ("Tomorrowland," October 17, 2010), Don is badly in need of someone to accompany him to California in order to look after his three children, turning to his secretary, Megan (Jessica Paré), for help. When he returns to find her at the hotel teaching them a song in French, he is impressed by her child-friendly manner. "You said you didn't have any experience, and you're like Maria von Trapp," Don says, extolling her skills.

Season 5, Episode 3, "Tea Leaves" (April 1, 2012) concludes with Daniel Truhitte's portion of "Sixteen Going on Seventeen" from *TSOM* soundtrack.

Madtv (Fox, Episode 7, Season 12: November 25, 2006)

This sketch-comedy series satirizes *TSOM*'s 40th Anniversary DVD, hosted by a very gushing and chin-heavy Julie Andrews (as played by series regular Nicole Parker). On hand are three "alternate endings" of the cemetery scene. In the first, Rolf reacts to Captain von Trapp's insistence that he'll "*never* be one of them" by promptly mowing down the family with a machine gun. In ending #2, Maria assures Rolf that they *too* have become Nazis and proceeds to prove it by singing an anti-Semitic number of all the "things she hates." Finally, the Trapps unleash their superpowers with Liesl fighting the Third Reich with her laser eyes, Gretl turning to metal, and Brigitta teleporting the family to safety, a la *Star Trek.*

Maile Flanagan's One-Woman *Sound of Music* (1995)

Principally a voice actor, Maile Flanagan wrote, produced, and starred in a fifty-minute stage act in which she poked fun at *The Sound of Music* with more vitriol than good-natured affection. In her version, the captain is a drunk, Liesl has an insatiable libido, an effete Kurt longs to be a designer, and there are suggestions of fun in the showers at the abbey. The act played in Minneapolis, Chicago, and West Hollywood. The reviews for the piece weren't much better than the negative ones for *TSOM*.

Martian Child (New Line Cinema; November 2, 2007)

In this sentimental drama-comedy, David, a widowed sci-fi writer (John Cusack), adopts an odd little boy who believes he's from Mars. David's friend Marlee (Amanda Peet) believes he should embrace the child's curious behavior, as if "a little Martian chose you to teach him about being human." David isn't convinced, so Marlee tries to draw a parallel to her own eccentricities as a child. "Listen, when I was 11 years old I saw *The Sound of Music* and from that moment on I was convinced I was the lost Von Trapp sister." "Yeah, but did you go to school in lederhosen?" David inquires, failing to see the similarity. Yes, she tells him, as a matter of fact she did. "That's a good look for you," David admits.

The Michael J. Fox Show (NBC, Season 1, Episode 14: "Couples," January 16, 2014)

During dinner preparations, Eve (Juliette Goglia) and her aunt Leigh (Katie Finneran) are having great fun singing "Sixteen Going on Seventeen." Eve's mom (Betsy Brandt) is so impressed that she thinks her daughter should try out for the school musical, which the teen dismisses as "cheesy." She'd rather spend literary night at a downtown bar. No mention is made of where the song is from, but it's presented as a given that two different generations would know it, or at least two generations of females. Alas, Eve's younger brother, Graham (Jack Gore), isn't interested in joining in the tune.

Modern Family (ABC, Season 5, Episode 3: "Larry's Wife," October 2, 2013)

This award-winning comedy focuses on three different couples within the same family, including patriarch Jay (Ed O'Neill), his much younger second wife, Gloria, and Gloria's teen son from a previous marriage, Manny (Rico Rodriguez).

Only in the alternate world of show business can people in 2013 get a chance to see either *The Sound of Music* or *Death Wish* at their local theatre.

Although Jay would prefer his stepson see something more aggressive like the Charles Bronson vigilante actioner, they end up at the beloved musical ("a relaxing trip to Nazi-occupied Austria"), where Jay's temper explodes at some kid for being rude, giving the lad a wedgie and causing his stepson to express his embarrassment at his stepdad's short fuse. "Judgmental, hot-tempered, loud; these are a few of my *least* favorite things," Manny scolds him. But there is worse to come. Jay ticks off another patron prior to the film for telling Manny he got him Sno-Caps, "'cause you know, at the end, they escape across the Alps," thereby spoiling the climax.

Meanwhile, another young punk talks loudly on his phone telling his friend, "My parents dragged me into this stupid movie," once again causing Jay to fume, not so much at the disparaging assessment but at the lack of etiquette. Manny is trying to tell him to let it roll off his back, until the same teen explains that *TSOM* features "that chick from that crapfest, *Mary Poppins*." Manny won't stand for this and reacts with his stepdad's same degree of anger, getting them ejected from the screening. Not surprisingly, they end up at the Bronson movie instead.

Monty Python

Of course Britain's sextet of gleefully subversive, off-the-wall comedians would have a go at *TSOM*, most notably:

Monty Python's Flying Circus

Season 1, Episode 8: "Full Frontal Nudity," UK airdate: December 7, 1969

A group of senior citizens, or "Hell's Grannies," terrorize a city with their delinquent antics. As a frightened cinema manager (Terry Jones) explains it: "They come here for the two o'clock matinee, all the old bags . . . especially if it's something like *The Sound of Music*. We get seats ripped up, hearing aids broken; all that sort of thing."

Season 4, Episode 42: "Light Entertainment War," UK airdate: November 14, 1974

As part of the entertainment on "telly," two rat-bags (Jones and Graham Chapman) watch championship horse jumping, in which the principal obstacle for rider Mrs. M. Mould and her mount, Ocean, is the cast of *The Sound of Music*, with a human wall of nuns, Trapp kids, and Maria lined up on the track. To add to the "challenge," Maria lets go with the opening lines of "The Sound of Music," with Julie Andrews's recording heard quickly on the soundtrack. Thanks to editing, Ocean makes the jump.

The Meaning of Life (Universal, March 31, 1983; UK opening: April 22, 1983)

In one of the last segments of their episodic feature film, the Pythons take us to their version of heaven, which resembles a gaudy Las Vegas showroom, with a singer (Chapman) promising residents in the afterlife that "It's Christmas in heaven/There's great films on TV/*The Sound of Music* twice an hour/And *Jaws 1 & 2 & 3* . . . ."

Moulin Rouge! (20th Century-Fox, May 18, 2001)

Director Baz Lurhmann's berserk musical mash-up set in turn-of-the-century Paris features extensive flash cuts, hyperactive visuals, and a busy soundtrack to tell the story of a writer named Christian (Ewan McGregor) who is drawn into the decadent world of Montmartre and falls in love with a famed courtesan.

Shortly after he has taken up lodgings, Christian is interrupted by the upstairs residents, who are attempting to create a revolutionary musical they call "Spectacular Spectacular." When one of their company, a narcoleptic Argentinean (Jacek Koman), proves indisposed, Christian steps in to lend a hand. Their efforts to come up with the correct lyrics for their story of a young, sensitive Swiss goatherd produces such curious efforts as "The hills are vital in toning the descant" and "The hills are incarnate with symphonic melodies" until Christian belts out the opening lines of "The Sound of Music," thereby impressing them all and solving their quandary. Toulouse-Lautrec (John Leguizamo) is now certain they "can write the truly bohemian revolutionary show that we've always dreamt of." This is followed by a mash-up of the Rodgers and Hammerstein tune with Marc Bolan's "Children of the Revolution" (interpreted by Ozzy Osbourne through the image of Kylie Minogue as a green fairy).

Moving Violations (20th Century-Fox, April 19, 1985)

A group of reckless drivers is sentenced to traffic school in this ensemble comedy. Just as Scott Geeber (Brian Backer) is about to "get it on" with classmate Stephanie McCarty (Nadine Van der Velde), they are interrupted by the arrival of her teamster father. Dispensing with her tough girl cover, Stephanie admits to being only fifteen and proceeds to strip her room of posters of the British punk group the Clash. Turning one such display around reveals the poster for *The Sound of Music*, which is supposed to show that Stephanie is the "nice" girl her father believes her to be.

Stephanie has not gone all out to get the original one sheet, however, but that of the 1973 reissue. In any event, negotiations for using the art work must have been relatively easy, since the studio releasing this "B" entry was the same one that distributed *TSOM*, 20th Century-Fox.

Mrs. Miracle (Hallmark Channel, December 5, 2009)

Leaning more toward *Mary Poppins* territory, this Christmas-themed TV movie has a new nanny show up seemingly out of the blue to take charge of widower Seth's rambunctious twin boys. Although the clever lady does everything but jump into chalk paintings to draw obvious parallels to the Disney film, it is not in this nanny-heavy storyline but the subplot about a former actress who becomes Seth's love interest where the reference to *TSOM* appears.

Reba (Erin Karpluk) has left behind her acting career to run a travel agency, but her friend Kate (Chelah Horsdahl) chides her for having given up something she was so clearly suited to. "You're smart and you're gorgeous and you're talented," Kate tells her. "Your Maria in *The Sound of Music* made everyone say 'Julie who?'"

Not "Mary who?'

The Muppets

The Muppet Show (Syndicated)

For Episode #217, Kermit and the gang got the real deal when Julie Andrews guest starred (see page 314). Although she was not on hand to chime in on "Do-Re-Mi," the song was featured on two occasions: on #205 (US: January 28, 1978), being performed in serious fashion by Judy Collins and Rowlf (playing separate pianos); and on #310 (US: December 16, 1978), where Kermit was joined by a chorus of Muppets (including Fozzie and Scooter), who get a bit mixed up on their cues and proceed to massacre the tune.

There was also a passing joke in #319 (US: January 27, 1979) referring to the title song of *TSOM*. After a "Pigs in Space" sketch in which the landscape of the distant planet Koosbane actually speaks, acerbic senior Waldorf cracks, "The hills are alive!" Not unexpectedly, his partner Statler, and Statler's infant grandson, pipe right back at him "with the sound of music!"

For their 1998 calendar parodying famous movies, the Muppets sent Miss Piggy to the hills for her interpretation of *The Sound of Music*. © Disney

Muppet Magazine (Winter 1985)

The Muppets took their ribbing of *The Sound of Music* to the pages of their short-lived quarterly magazine. In the comic *The Swine of Music* (by Jay Itzkowitz, illustrated by Manhar Chauhan), the editors extend their apologies to Julie Andrews "for the role played by Fräulein Piggy in our movie spoof."

Miss Piggy comes to work for Count von Trippe (Kermit the Frog) and his brood of five rats (they resemble their late mother). Unlike Ms. Andrews, Piggy is pretty atrocious in the singing department as she chimes in on such lyrics as "Dough, to cook a loaf of bread/Ray, who owns the grocery store/Moi, a name I call myself . . ." and "Down in the swill/stood a lonely pigherd." "She's not even good enough for hog calling," remarks a critical goat. Having had their fill of this caterwauling, the Alpine villagers decide it is time for the burgomaster (Sam the Eagle) to arrest the culprits, forcing the von Trippes to escape . . . to Hollywood.

Muppets Tonight (ABC, Season 1, Episode 1: March 8, 1996)

Incensed that Michelle Pfeiffer is the evening's special guest star instead of her, Miss Piggy's competitive urges arise. When Pfeiffer explains to the short-tempered sow that *she* will be playing Maria von Trapp in the show's big musical number, rationalizing that "You can't play Maria von Trapp, you're a pig!," the gloves are off. Clad in appropriate Austrian garb, Pfeiffer attempts to sing "Do-Re-Mi" to four Muppets passing themselves off as the Von Trapp kids (two are Miss Piggy's dim-witted nephews, one is the mustachioed Lew Zealand), but is constantly interrupted by the hissy Miss, who jumps in with her rendition of "My Favorite Things." It all ends with Piggy firing a cannon at Pfeiffer.

Muppet Movie Parodies Calendar (for 1998, Dream Day Publishing)

The third in a line of calendars in which the Muppets sent up famous images from movies, March 1998 featured Miss Piggy standing atop a hill in a copy of Julie Andrews's famous dress, wearing a pair of headphones. The name? *The Sow of Music.*

Muppets Most Wanted (Disney, March 21, 2014)

Miss Piggy's march up the church aisle to wed Kermit look-alike Constantine ("Evilen Froggen") looks suspiciously like Maria's famous walk to marry Captain von Trapp, as filmed from a high angle.

My Favorite Fangs: The Story of the Trapp Family Vampires by Alan Goldsher (Thomas Dunne Books, August 2012)

Something akin to a gaggle of sniggering schoolboys trying to top each other with gross-out gags, this send-up of *TSOM* , taking place in "Salzburg, Austria: The Last Revolting Days of the Thirties," sets out to be as deliberately vile and offensive as possible. Following the structure of the movie, not the stage play, song lyrics are turned into dialogue, sometimes in a straightforward manner, other times not ("my heart wants to sigh like the green stench of undeath that flies from a coffin in the breeze . . ."), and Oscar Hammerstein's name is often referenced irreverently, as part of the winking, *meta* tone.

Maria is a lusty vampire prone to shedding her clothes (she also likes singing arias by Haydn—a nod perhaps to the film's Richard Haydn?); the abbey is populated by zombies; when the alcoholic captain and his new governess first meet, they both end up vomiting in the ballroom; the Mother Zombie beheads her charges by tossing a meat cleaver; Maria speaks to the spirit of John Coltrane about his seminal recording of "My Favorite Things"; Rolf is an effete member of the Nazi Undeath Squad of vampire hunters; Elsa is a succubus; Maria lusts after the frequently aroused Friedrich; and Liesl and the fanged governess indulge in lesbian sex. It's *that* kind of book.

The eye-catching cover takes the famous movie poster and places a moon behind Julie Andrews, puts blood in her mouth, and has her carrying a dismembered Nazi arm and a document in place of her traveling bag and guitar.

My Girlfriend's Boyfriend (Opus Films, October 22, 2010)

Café waitress Jesse Young (Alyssa Milano) appears to have found the ideal guy when she starts dating aspiring writer Ethan Reed (Christopher Gorham). So what's she doing seeing a fellow named Troy Parker on the side?

Taking Ethan to a piano bar where the customers enjoy singing show songs, she is shocked to hear him complain that "It's all musicals!" as well as adding the customary insult from those who don't appreciate the genre, "They don't make any sense." Jesse assures him that they do and can't believe he doesn't care for her favorite, *West Side Story*. "So, next you're going to tell me you hate *Sound of Music*," she suggests, anticipating the worst. "Oh, please, you lost me at singing nuns" is Ethan's snarky reply. He then goes on to dismiss *Grease* (not to mention *Grease 2!*) but gives a listen when a bar patron gets up to sing "Fifty Percent" from the Broadway musical *Ballroom*, indicating that perhaps he's willing to find the pleasures if he'll just pay attention to the songs.

Although this sequence suggests that Jesse might be better off dumping someone who can't get into *TSOM*, Ethan's good traits ultimately outweigh his bad, and it isn't outrageous to assume he'll get into those singing nuns, eventually.

The Nanny (CBS)

Unlike other television series, *The Nanny* had a better reason than most to turn to *TSOM* for some cheeky jokes; its premise, after all, involved an outsider coming to take care of the young charges of a wealthy widower, only to win his heart, against all odds. The outsider in this case, however, was hardly a novice in a nunnery but the proudly lowbrow Fran Fine (Fran Drescher), a former Queens beautician, while the object of her affections and the man writing her paychecks was Broadway producer Maxwell Sheffield (Charles Shaughnessy), erudite father of three.

Season 1, Pilot: "The Nanny," November 3, 1993

During Fran's job interview, Maxwell's son Brighton (Benjamin Salisbury) declares that he hates the new applicant, but his dad tells him not to be too hasty in his judgment. "Yeah," Fran agrees. "I haven't even sung 'Climb Ev'ry Mountain' yet."

Season 1, Episode 10: "The Nanny in Law," January 12, 1994

Maxwell's former Nanny Mueller (Cloris Leachman with a German accent) visits and tries to enforce discipline on the household by dressing the three kids in matching sailor outfits, to their humiliation. Nanny Fine says, "Wow, if it isn't the von Sapp family."

Season 3, Episode 12: "The Kibbutz," December 4, 1995

Worried that daughter Maggie (Nicholle Tom) will be hanging out too much with boys during the coming holidays, Maxwell decides it might be best to send her to a convent in Switzerland instead. Naturally, Maggie balks at the prospect, but Fran tries to convince her otherwise. "I got two words for you," she proclaims, "*Sounda Music.*" As she goes on to explain, "I mean in two hours, Maria managed to ditch the nuns, marry a gorgeous captain, sell the movie rights, and never have to schlep up another mountain again." Hopefully the aborted running time she chooses doesn't mean Fran grew up seeing an edited print (!) of the film.

Season 3, Episode 21: "Where's the Pearls?," February 26, 1996

A bump on the head in a cab (while running an errand with guest star Elizabeth Taylor's pearls) puts Fran in the hospital with a case of amnesia. When the three kids introduce themselves in hopes of getting their nanny to remember, Fran seems on the brink of bouncing back to normal. "You know, this seems familiar to me," she opines, "Say, did I ever sing on some Austrian hillside with a really butch haircut?"

Season 3, Episode 22: "The Hockey Show," March 4, 1996

When Fran agrees to date a handsome hockey player from the NY Rangers, her friend Val (Rachel Chagall) asks about her previous vow to refrain from dates. "What happened to living like a nun? I pictured you climbing ev'ry mountain, fording ev'ry stream." To which Fran responds, "Well, I followed ev'ry Ranger, 'til I found my dream."

A further extension of *The Nanny* premise mixed with *The Sound of Music* was Fran Drescher's one big screen vehicle, *The Beautician and the Beast* (Paramount, February 7, 1997), which had no direct mention of the R&H musical, but clearly played as a homage to the story. As beauty school instructor Joy Miller, who mistakenly ends up in an Eastern European country teaching the offspring of a distant dad (and dictator), played by Timothy Dalton, she wins her way into everyone's heart, not with her singing (thank goodness) but with her down-to-earth manner. The most obvious nod to *TSOM* is Joy coming up with a makeshift outfit for one of the girls, not made from the drapes but from some Ralph Lauren sheets. Ironically, it's another Robert Wise musical, *West Side Story*, that rates a direct discussion.

National Lampoon's European Vacation (Warner Bros., July 26, 1985)

The second traveling adventures of the Griswold family (following *National Lampoon's Vacation*, in 1983) finds patriarch Clark (Chevy Chase) dreaming on the plane to Europe. As the camera swoops over trees toward a hilltop field, most audiences know just what to expect. Spinning around while clad in lederhosen, Clark sings "The hills are alive with the sound of Griswold . . ." followed by a tossed in four-letter word and a romp with the rest of his family (Beverly D'Angelo, Jason Lively, Dana Hill), also dressed in Tyrolean garb.

Nearest and Dearest (ITV)

This British comedy (1968–73) about the bickering Pledge siblings (Jimmy Jewell as Eli and Hylda Baker as Nellie) often depended on swapped insults between the two or the latter's malapropisms for laughs.

In "Take a Letter" (Season 1, Episode 4, September 5, 1968), Eli is delighted that a voluptuous lady named Nemone (Margaret Nolan) has answered his ad for a secretary. Nemone later tells Nellie that she thinks her brother is at the age where he'd like to settle down, judging from the look in his eyes. "Sometimes his eyes remind me of Christopher Plummer's when he was proposin' to Julie Andrews in *The Sound of Music*," she remarks, dreamily. "Funny," Nellie replies, "They look more to me like the hound in *The Hound of the Baskervilles*."

In "The Birds and the Bees" (Season 3, Episode 2, October 16, 1969), Nellie is excited to be paying host to a young teen, whom she mistakenly thinks is an innocent and wholesome sort. "He reminds me of that little lad in *The Sound of Music*," she tells Eli, "You know, what have those beautiful songs sung to him by that lovely girl who worked at the nunnery . . . ah . . . what's her name? Eamonn Andrews!" Eli sets her straight by coming up with the correct Andrews, Julie. "That's him!" Nellie cheerfully agrees.

For those on this side of the pond, Eamonn Andrews was an Irish television and radio host/commentator known in the UK for headlining the British versions of such series as *What's My Line?* and *This Is Your Life.*

NewsRadio (NBC; Season 3, Episode 15: "Rose Bowl," February 5, 1997)

Among those loonies on the staff of WNYX all-news radio in New York were station owner Jimmy James (Stephen Root), who, in this episode, proudly shows off his recently purchased, questionably "authentic" movie memorabilia to station director Dave Nelson (Dave Foley). In addition to unmatched stone tablets from *The Ten Commandments* and a sled marked "Rose Bowl" from *Citizen Kane*, he's got another surprise prop. "Maybe you've heard of a little movie called *Sound of Music?*," he asks Dave to build anticipation. "Well, who could forget it?," Dave responds without a good deal of enthusiasm. And what item does Jimmy produce? A sword! "I don't recall a sword in *The Sound of Music*," says a skeptical Dave, so Jimmy proceeds to demonstrate the title as sung to the "Hallelujah Chorus" with some fancy sword moves thrown in.

The Nixon Interviews (PBS, May 4–25, 1977)

During David Frost's legendary interviews with ex-president Richard Nixon, the idea that the chief executive may have ordered the invasion of Cambodia on April 30, 1970 because of his ecstatic reaction to 20th Century-Fox's recently released biopic of World War II general George Patton was raised. Because Nixon's previous April 20th optimism about the conflict had changed over the ten-day interval, Frost suggested from what his researchers had uncovered "that you'd seen *Patton* twice, so they thought that movie might be the reason." Nixon scoffed at the idea, replying "Well, I've seen *The Sound of Music* twice, and it hasn't made me a writer either." Why exactly Nixon chose the job of "writer" to draw a parallel to viewing the Julie Andrews musical isn't clear, but it was nice to know that one of the U.S. presidents thought highly enough of the film to see it a second time.

The O.C. (Fox, Season 3, Episode 13: "The Pot Stirrer," January 26, 2006)

That's "Orange County" for the uninitiated. In this episode about the lives of affluent California teens, Kaitlin (Willa Holland) thinks longingly of her birthday celebrations of the past. She tells Johnny (Ryan Donowho), "We'd stay up late and eat cake and watch *The Sound of Music* . . . sing along," meaning, specifically, to "Sixteen Going on Seventeen." As Kaitlin explains, "However old I was turning, we'd always put in the ages."

The bus company Albus was the first to cash in on tourists' fascination with the Salzburg locations seen in *The Sound of Music.*

The Original *Sound of Music* Tour (Officially launched in June 1967)

Salzburg now offers a wide variety of bus tours taking fans to several of the locations used in *The Sound of Music*, but Bus Company Albus (Albus Salzkraft) not only got there first but can lay claim to having a role in the movie. It is one of their buses, after all, that Julie Andrews rides on her way to the Trapp villa. Despite the country's initial disinterest in the movie, this company figured they were missing out on a good deal when so many tourists began asking about *TSOM* during its initial run in theatres. After conducting unofficial trips in 1966, the official tour was launched in June 1967.

Currently, the coach takes sightseers to Mirabell Gardens, Leopoldskron, Nonnberg Abbey, Lakes Fuschl and Wolfgang (from the opening montage), the wedding church at Mondsee, and the gazebo (now situated at Hellbrunn Palace).

Out of It (UA, December 1969)

Although this comedy purports to take place on Long Island in "the early 1960s," it very clearly is happening later in the decade. Not only is a marquee visible showing *The Deadly Affair* (1967) and *Fahrenheit 451* (1966), but it was not until the latter half of the sixties that *TSOM*'s box office grosses surpassed all others, became legendary, and would rate the mention they get here.

When the film's protagonist, lovestruck intellectual high schooler Paul (Barry Gordon) reads a letter he'd written to his sister, it details his fantastical dreams of becoming a successful screenwriter. His second fictitious effort, *The*

Man Who Killed Men, is not just a smash, in Paul's mind, but "sweeps the globe. Even bigger than *The Sound of Music.*" For added R&H impact, he later quotes lyrics from "Some Enchanted Evening," while the supporting cast includes the replacement Rolf from the original Broadway run of *TSOM,* Jon Voight.

The Pacifier (Walt Disney Pictures; March 5, 2005)

Hollywood Formula #15: Take a macho action star and place him in an unlikely situation, forcing him to play nursemaid to unruly children, and watch the money roll in. Vin Diesel is Navy SEAL Shane Wolfe, assigned to guard the children of a slain security expert whose coveted secret formula is hidden somewhere in the family domicile.

When oldest son Seth (Max Thieriot) fails repeatedly to show up for wrestling practice, juvenile delinquency is assumed. When he dyes his hair an Aryan shade of blond and an armband with a swastika is found in his locker, Wolfe fears the worst. Tracking the teen down to a gathering that at first appears to be a white supremacy meeting, Wolfe instead discovers that the lad is playing Rolf in a cheesy local production of *The Sound of Music,* croaking his way through "Sixteen Going on Seventeen" while trying not to fall flat on his face dancing with a long-in-the-tooth Liesl (Anne Fletcher). To appease Seth's worry that he'll be made fun of for preferring *TSOM* to sports, the proud SEAL tells him "The idea of a nun ditchin' her habit for a guy in the military . . . nothin' wrong with that!"

Not only does Wolfe end up directing the play, but *TSOM* fever envelops the rest of the family, who greet their mother's (Faith Ford) return home by standing in a straight line as the soundtrack recording of the Trapp children singing "The Sound of Music" plays. The movie climaxes with the cast of the tatty stage production singing "Climb Ev'ry Mountain," which, for reasons best left unquestioned, features Rolf raising his arms majestically and the vice principal (Brad Garrett), who had previously taunted the lad and had nothing whatsoever to do with the show, playing the Mother Abbess (!).

Naming the family Plummer (and mom "Julie Plummer," at that) shows a knowing touch; misspelling Liesl (as "Liesel") in the closing credits does not.

Passion of Mind (Paramount Classics; May 26, 2000)

A widow (Demi Moore) is so lost in her dreams that she isn't sure which is real: a life as book reviewer and mother Martha Marie in France or a completely different existence as single literary agent Marty Talridge in New York. *The Sound of Music* is actually used as one of the links between the two worlds.

In France, Martha's younger daughter Sarah (Chaya Cuénot) is heard singing "My Favorite Things" to impress her mom. In New York, Marty's lover, Aaron (William Fitchner), stumbles upon a tape recorder playing a cassette of the *TSOM* soundtrack with Julie Andrews's rendition of the same song. Aaron is a tad uncharitable about the discovery, figuring it must belong to an "older housekeeper," but Marty assures him that "I'm very identified with Julie Andrews . . . We're practically the same person on the inside." Aaron is probably more excited over Marty's choice of music than he cares to admit, because after this playful bantering, the two wind up making love.

People Are Unappealing: Even Me; True Stories of Our Collective Capacity to Irritate and Annoy by Sara Barron (Three Rivers Press, March 2009)

The author's comical chronicle of her upbringing and her efforts to make it in show business feature observations on the various men she dated/slept with. Speaking of a fellow called Elijah, she conjures up images from her two favorite "sex scenes" in American cinema. The first involves *Pretty Woman*, while the second—surprise! surprise!—comes from *The Sound of Music*. Not one involving the captain and Maria but Liesl and Rolf. Barron extolls the scene when "Lisle (her spelling) and her Nazi lover, Rolf, kiss in her father's garden gazebo." She adds, "I've never been much of a Nazi supporter, personally, but I do *love* gazebos. They're so romantic!" Her dream is to experience a blend of both movie moments. "We'd share a desirous outdoor kiss (albeit in the urban jungle in lieu of my father's Austrian estate) . . . ." Alas, it turns out Elijah is more interested in getting wet, and not because of an unexpected rainstorm, as happened to our Austrian lovers.

The Pervert's Guide to Ideology (US: Zeitgeist, November 1, 2013, UK: BFI/Film 4, October 4, 2013)

Yugoslav philosopher Slavoj Zizek presents a cinematic lecture on subtexts and underlying meanings within such motion pictures as *Jaws, Brief Encounter, Seconds, They Live, Titanic, Triumph of the Will, Taxi Driver*, and *Full Metal Jacket*; in doing so he is often seen on re-creations of sets from the movies in question and wearing costumes corresponding to key scenes.

Early in the documentary, for a six-minute segment, Zizek examines what he refers to as "the great, classical Hollywood film" (or rather "*fee-lum*" per his heavy accent) *The Sound of Music* (he is seen standing in an approximate re-creation of the Mother Abbess's office), and the hidden message behind the Mother Abbess's advice to Maria regarding her feelings for Captain von Trapp. Clips are shown from *TSOM* of the Preludium, the Laendler, and most importantly, "Climb Ev'ry Mountain."

"We all know it's the story of a nun who is *too* alive with too much energy—ultimately sexual energy—to be constrained to the role of a nun," Zizek theorizes in his narration. According to him, the Mother Abbess's advice can be summed up as "Go back, seduce the guy, follow this path, do not betray this desire." This is then further stressed by the song "Climb Ev'ry Mountain," about which Zizek insists, "It is this hidden, obscene permission that you get 'You are covered by the Divine Big Other; you can do whatever you want. Enjoy!'" He then startles us by stating that because of its message, this song was excised from the movie when it ran in Yugoslavia during its initial run.

Despite a rather heavy premise, some of Zizek's theories are worth pondering, if not the final word of just what these filmmakers were trying to say.

The Pink Panther Strikes Again
(United Artists, December 17, 1976)

Between the 1964 release of the first *Pink Panther* film and this fourth installment of the slapstick-laden Inspector Clouseau comedies, the movies' director-writer, Blake Edwards, had married Julie Andrews, so he was in a very privileged position to affectionately rib his wife's most celebrated film.

During the opening credits, the wily Pink Panther is pursued by an animated version of Clouseau into a movie theatre. There, on the big screen, the evasive feline keeps popping up in re-creations of some famous movie moments, including King Kong atop the Empire State building, Gene Kelly's jaunty dance to "Singin' in the Rain," and, funniest of all, Andrews's hilltop spin. As the camera zooms in and the familiar strains of "The Sound of Music" are heard, the Panther's novice outfit walks off by itself, revealing the cat in spotted underwear.

The Postman (Warner Bros., December 25, 1997)

This three-hour adventure about a post-apocalypse America being taken over by a fanatical demagogue (Will Patton), who is thereby challenged by a drifter (Kevin Costner) pretending to be a representative of the newly established postal system, was one of the "mustn't see" movie events of its year.

Shortly after Costner is captured by Patton and his army, he is knocked out cold. He awakens to what appears to be a dream image of the scene from *The Sound of Music* when Julie Andrews returns from Nonnberg Abbey, much to the delight of the Trapp children, asking Gretl about her injured finger. It is not a dream, however, as those in the military compound spend their evenings watching movies on a large screen suspended from a cliff over a lake, in the center of which sits the projection booth. When the hapless projectionist tries to get the audience interested in the 1992 sci-fi actioner *Universal Soldier*, they protest loudly, demanding *TSOM* instead. He complies, and the cliffside moviegoers settle back with contentment as Julie sings the opening song on her hilltop. Costner, on the other hand, reacts negatively. Later, a print of John Ford's *She Wore a Yellow Ribbon* gets a good response from the crowd as well.

Just what exactly was being said here is up for grabs. Were the violent aggressors none too pleased to see bone-crunching entertainment that reminded them of their own deplorable behavior? Or were we simply being reassured that sixteen years in the future (the story takes place in 2013), despite the partial destruction of the world, *The Sound of Music* would still be making people feel good?

Pride (UK: BBC-Pathé, September 12, 2014; US: CBS Films, September 25, 2014)

The true story of how, in 1984, a group of gay London activists gave their support to the striking miners in a small Welsh town, this film once again draws attention to *TSOM*'s place in gay culture. The approaching holidays finds lesbian Stef (Faye Marsay) joking about how she and closeted Joe (George MacKay) should pass themselves off as a couple to put the relatives at ease. She could be his "alibi," Stef theorizes, "and I can watch *The Sound of Music*."

Pushing Daisies (ABC, Season 2, Episode 2: "Bzzzzzzzzz!," October 1, 2008)

An ultra-strange series about a pie maker with a knack for raising people from the dead (albeit with consequences), this episode found pie shop employee Olive Snook (Kristen Chenoweth) quitting her job and then being banished to a nunnery to ensure that she not tell the resurrected "Chuck" Charles that her Aunt Lily (Swoosie Kurtz) is, in fact, her actual mother. We discover Olive's whereabouts through the familiar sweeping shot taken from the opening of *The Sound of Music*, with Olive computer-inserted into Julie Andrews's place, swirling around and showing off her vocal prowess until some nuns shush her up. Later, Olive informs Lily that she doesn't feel the nuns she's forced to spend time with are her kind of people, "unless you're telling me 'flibbertigibbet' is a title of respect."

Queer as Folk (Showtime, Season 4, Episode 1: April 18, 2004)

This U.S. adaptation of the groundbreaking British series featured the largest number of gay characters on a weekly series to date. In this episode, lesbian couple Melanie (Michelle Clunie) and Lindsay (Thea Gill) arrive at the home of Debbie Novotny (Sharon Gless), dressed in nun's garb and lederhosen, respectively. "I can only dream of what perversions go on in *your* house," quips Debbie's brother Vic (Jack Wetherall) at their curious choice of attire. Ben (Robert Gant) guesses they are on their way to the sing-along *Sound of Music*. The women are quick to explain that they are passing themselves off as the Mother Superior and Friedrich for a masquerade benefit for pediatric AIDS. Following the requisite song reference ("Bet you worked up an appetite climbing all those mountains"), the plot resumes.

The Ritz (Stage: Longacre Theatre, January 20, 1975; Screen: Warner Bros., August 12, 1976)

Terrence McNally's romp set in a gay bathhouse made direct reference not to the film of *The Sound of Music*, but to the original play. Rita Moreno, as the establishment's self-aggrandizing but hopelessly second-rate, manic Latina entertainer,

Googie Gomez, assumes she's bonding with Gaetano Proclo (Jack Weston), a patron on the run from his murderous brother-in-law, whom she mistakes for a noted stage producer. Asked if he's been on the stage himself, Proclo admits to doing a walk-on in the Cleveland Little Theatre Masque and Mummers production of *The Sound of Music*. Turns out, Googie was *nearly* in the same show on Broadway. "The original cast?," asks an awed Proclo. "I was more original than anyone in it," Googie responds. She admits to having been fired before opening night, being somewhat ill-suited for the role, which she describes as "One of those f—g Trapp kids." Undaunted, she tells Proclo she picketed the show nightly.

McNally's farce was transported to the screen with both Moreno and Weston repeating their roles and the scene retained.

[*Note: Moreno did a variation on the Googie character for her unaired 1976* The Rita Moreno Show *pilot, at one point donning a typewriter cover and wailing "Climb Ev'ry Mountain."*]

Romantics Anonymous (U.S. release: Tribeca Films, November 25, 2011, French Release: December 22, 2010, as *Les* émotifs *anonymes*)

This French comedy gets right to *The Sound of Music* reference during the opening credits with leading lady Isabelle Carré singing "I Have Confidence," in French. The translation (credited to Lemarchand, no first name) is not direct, with such lyrics as "With each step I feel more sure/Everything will be fine/I am sure the world is mine/They'll see me shine/For I truly believe in me."

The plot involves Angélique Delange (Carré) a hopelessly shy woman who is a wizard at making chocolates but cannot cope with being the public face of her product. The movie momentarily becomes a musical when, in celebration for finally making a sale, she reprises "I Have Confidence," this time striding through a shopping gallery, swinging her sample case like it is Julie Andrews's guitar.

Romeo Is Bleeding (Gramercy, February 4, 1994)

Corrupt cop Jack Grimaldi (Gary Oldman) juggles affairs with two women as well as his wife Natalie (Annabella Sciorra), who reminisces with him at one point about their courtship. "Do you remember on our second date," she asks him, "when we went to the Rialto and saw *The Sound of Music* and you cried?" Jack insists it was she who did the weeping.

"Rialto" is a generic, go-to name for a cinema for scriptwriters, but since the movie is set in the New York area, one can imagine the Rialto in question is the one in Pathogue, Long Island, where *TSOM* had two separate post-road show runs; unless of course Jack and his future wife were traveling through Louisville, Kentucky, to see that area's roadshow engagement at the time. In any case, they were awfully young to be going on dates back in the late 1960s.

The Sarah Jane Adventures (CBBC, Series 1, Episode 3: "Eye of the Gorgon, Part 1," October 1, 2007)

Don't trust the nuns! They're hiding the mythical Gorgon in this episode of a spin-off of BBC's immortal *Doctor Who*. When investigative journalist Sarah Jane Smith won't hand over the talisman needed for the nun's diabolic plot, they get hold of Sarah's teenage neighbor, Maria (Yasmin Paige). When Maria mouths off, the most sinister of the sisters, Helena (Beth Goddard), can't resist. "I'd shut up if I were you," she warns. "Or the Abbess might show you *her* idea of solving a problem like Maria."

Saturday Night Live (NBC)

Television's never-ending late-night sketch-comedy show took a swing at *TSOM* on several occasions, including:

Season 4, Episode 1: October 7, 1978

Nerdy Lisa Loopner (Gilda Radner) and Todd DiLaMuca (Bill Murray) arrive at Lisa's house singing the title song from *TSOM*, or at least Todd's version, which changes a word, "With songs they have sung for *ONE* thousand years." Leave it to nerds to get the lyrics wrong.

Season 16, Episode 2: October 6, 1990

"You've seen him in videos," cries the announcer, "Now see him on Broadway! MC Hammer IS *The Sound of Music*." Chris Rock sends up the then-hot rapper by performing his versions of the Rodgers and Hammerstein score to the constant, unchanging beat of Hammer's hit single "Can't Touch This." "These are some of the things I like," Rock sings "mittens . . . with kittens." Reviews pop up on the screen, such as "So bad I walked out twice."

Season 19, Episode 20: May 14, 1994

To bid goodbye to Phil Hartman after eight seasons with the show, the other cast members do their version of "So Long, Farewell," most of them in the guise of characters they'd become famous for. For example, in response to the lyrics "So long, goodbye/It's time to say farewell," Mike Myers, as gossipy Linda Richman, sings "I feel verklempt/So talk among yourselves." And so on. Each performer dances away after finishing his or her portion of the song.

Season 21, Episode 19: May 11, 1996

On "The Courtney Love Show," guest Julie Andrews (Christine Baranski) coaxes her host (Molly Shannon) to join her on what she refers to as "Doe, A Dear." But

Courtney just isn't cutting it and decides the whole thing is making her dizzy. Of course Julie suggests "A Spoonful of Sugar," but Courtney prefers vodka.

Season 25, Episode 8: December 11, 1999

On this parody of *NBC's Nightly News*, anchor Tom Brokaw (Chris Parnell) asks actor Arnold Schwarzenegger (Darrell Hammond) whether people are being silly anticipating some great upheaval in the world because of the approaching millennium. Arnold assures him that everything will be the same. "It's all back?," Brokaw asks. "Liv Tyler? The unmeetable demand for organ transplants? Snapple?" "Now you're getting the hang of it," Arnold commends him, which prompts Brokaw to wonder about "Raindrops on roses," leading to a few lines of *TSOM* song between the two men before they announce "Live! From New York . . ."

Season 32, Episode 3: October 21, 2006

During guest star John C. Reilly's monologue, Will Ferrell shows up doing his impression of interviewer James Lipton, praising Reilly for his performances in movies he's not in, including *Pulp Fiction* and *The Sound of Music.*

Season 32, Episode 11: January 20, 2007

In the series' *TV Funhouse* segment, *Frontline's Year in Review* reveals that President Bush has tried desperately to improve his image with the public by "farting in a shallow pool." This technique quickly catches on among several prominent newscasters and, we are told, "By year's end even the most uplifting classics could not resist the technology," so we get to see Julie Andrews and Peggy Wood, in actual footage from *TSOM*, surrounded by CGI water making . . . um, gaseous bubbles, as Wood sings "Climb Ev'ry Mountain."

Season 35, Episode 5: November 7, 2009

Representatives from the "Scared Straight" program (including guest star Taylor Swift) reprimand three lads who stole their parents' car for some joy riding and loud music because they were bored. MacIntosh (Kenan Thompson) admonishes them, "What? You don't think I like music? Back in the day I was a nun who couldn't stop singin'. So then the other nuns sent me to be a governess for the von Trapp Family! Pretty soon I was runnin' through the mountains teachin' 7 children how to sing. Is *that* what you want? Hmmn? You're runnin' away from Germans and you wonder how do you solve a problem like Maria? 'cause this here is real!" One boy (Bobby Moynihan) is not impressed by this backstory, struck by the pop culture familiarity, as is the customary humor in these sketches. "Okay. That's just *The Sound of Music*," he complains. This is followed by a bad Trapp pun and a parody of "Do-Re-Mi" involving prison assault, which is about as strained as it sounds.

Season 36; Episode 7: November 20, 2010

Spoofing Turner Classic Movies, excised scenes are shown from *The Wizard of Oz*, featuring an actor named Lon Donson (Fred Armisen), who was supposedly cut from *many* classic films. These include *The Sound of Music*, where he played "a neighbor who asked the von Trapps to 'please keep it down.'" Donson is superimposed into the photo image of Maria and the children on Winkler's Terrace during the "Do-Re-Mi" number, covering his ears.

Season 39; Episode 8: December 7, 2013

In the wake of *The Sound of Music Live!* broadcast two days earlier, *SNL* presented *The Sound of Music Live and Condensed.* A perky Maria (Kate McKinnon) arrives to tend to the children of Captain von Trapp (Taran Killiam), who refers to her as being "so beautiful in that terra cotta disaster of a dress." His brood of six is missing Marta and Brigitta, but includes a freakish recurring character, Dooneese (Kristen Wiig), late of a sister act on *SNL*'s spoof of *The Lawrence Welk Show*. Shortened versions of "Do-Re-Mi" (e.g., Dooneese's response to "sew" is "a chicken to the wall"), "Edelweiss," and "Climb Ev'ry Mountain" are interrupted by the uninhibited Dooneese . . . as the routine peters out.

Scooby Goes Hollywood (ABC, December 13, 1979)

One more trip to the mountaintop.

In this prime-time special derived from the surprisingly enduring Saturday morning cartoon *Scooby-Doo, Where Are You!*, cast regulars Shaggy and Scooby decide they are tired of appearing on their mystery series and feel it's time they became movie stars. This presents a chance to parody various films and television shows, from *Laverne and Shirley* to *Superman*. When Scooby, clad in a dress, begins twirling on a mountain with the intention of singing, it's not long before the inevitable gag cuts him short, as he falls off a cliff and into a stream.

The Simpsons (Fox)

The long-running animated series satirizing life in the small town of Springfield centered on dim-witted Homer Simpson and his family, which also included his high-haired and sensible wife Marge; his bratty scamp of a son, Bart; and his daughter, Lisa, a junior crusader for fairness and decency.

Season 5, Episode 17: "Bart Gets an Elephant," March 31, 1994

When Bart wins a radio call-in contest, he insists on the gag prize—a real live African elephant. After his pet pachyderm ends up at the Springfield Tar Pits ("The Best in Tar Entertainment" says an endorsement from *Time* magazine), the Simpson family arrive by car, with Homer crashing into a deer statue. As he reacts with his trademark expression, "D'oh!," one can only hope the family will follow through with the gag, as they do, with Lisa adding "a deer!" and Marge capping it off with "A female deer!"

Season 18, Episode 14: "Yokel Chords," March 4, 2007

When Lisa sees Principal Skinner and Superintendent Chalmers denying education to some town yokels, she threatens to take action and expose the unconstitutionality of their act, prompting some musical interludes that bear a very close resemblance to the score from *TSOM*. In best "Maria" style, Skinner and Chalmers sing "How do we gag a blabber mouth like Lisa?/How do we crush her First Amendment rights?" Their solution—to have Lisa serve as tutor to the seven hillbillies in question—sits with her just fine. "The hillbilly tykes will become my tutees," she trills while spinning on a hilltop, before landing in the family's pig sty. The tutoring of the Spuckler children (whose names included

For the umpteenth time, *Saturday Night Live* pokes fun at *The Sound of Music*, taking aim at the 2013 live television presentation. Kristen Wiig is front and center as "Dooneese."

"Crystal Meth" and "Incest") involves taking her charges downtown to experience the treasure trove of "cultural and multi-cultural" activities, or as Lisa sings, echoing "My Favorite Things," "Pretentious laughs at Buñuel retrospectives/ Outsider art made by mental defectives," concluding "We've finally experienced cultural things/And now they don't seem so lame." (This includes watching Principal Skinner's wife play the starring role in a production of *Auntie Mame*). Crusty the Clown is so impressed by the children's musical talents that he gives them a spot on his television show, and better yet, engages them for their own prime-time special with music by none other than Stephen Sondheim!! ("I know you hear this all the time," Sondheim tells Crusty, "but I think you're great.")

Less pointedly, in the series' Mary Poppins spoof, "Simpsonscali-fragilisticexpiala-D'uoh-cious" (1997), nanny Shary Bobbins mutters "Do-Re-Mi-Fa-So . . ." under her breath when Homer can't wait on himself, and in "Guess Who's Coming to Criticize Dinner?" (1999), a *TSOM* poster can barely be glimpsed in the background among the decorations in a Planet Hollywood–type restaurant.

Sister Act (Touchstone, May 29, 1992)

Nuns and singing? Of course there has to be a *Sound of Music* reference, but not in the context you'd expect.

The plotline has second-rate Reno lounge singer Deloris Van Cartier (Whoopi Goldberg) having to hide out in a San Francisco convent after witnessing a mod rub-out. She takes over the establishment's shaky choir and turns it into a hip attraction that puts "butts in the seats."

TSOM is mentioned even before the choir storyline commences. Anxious to step out of her cloistered existence, Deloris, now going under the name of Sister Mary Clarence, drops by at a biker bar across the street. "Hey, sister," a sassy patron (Mike Jolly) calls out to her, "this juke box got anything on it from *Sound of Music?*" Give the biker credit for being familiar with the Rodgers and Hammerstein musical at all. Deloris, however, chooses to play Etta James's rendition of "Roll with Me, Henry," instead.

Six Feet Under (HBO, Season 3, Episode 4: "Nobody Sleeps," March 23, 2003)

Revolving a weekly series around a family in the funeral business meant that each episode was launched by an unfortunate death. This time, an AIDS sufferer expires during a viewing of *The Bad Seed*, the 1956 melodrama being mercilessly skewered by a group of gay men. At the man's funeral, his partner (Dennis Christopher) eulogizes him with gratitude for all their relationship gave him. Not certain what he did to deserve such happiness, he says, "To quote Julie Andrews, as Maria von Trapp, 'it must have been something good.'" Okay, so to nitpick, Maria wasn't exactly a von Trapp at the time she sang the song, but the point is taken, nonetheless.

The Six Million Dollar Man (ABC, Season 2, Episode 12: "The Cross-Country Kidnap," January 10, 1975)

Astronaut-turned-cyborg Steve Austin was the superhero star of this sci-fi favorite of the mid-seventies. This installment involves a computer program designer, Liza Leitman (Donna Mills), who finds herself the target of possible kidnappers/assassins. When Austin's boss Oscar (Richard Anderson) tells Liza that she should not be competing in a three-day equestrian trial for fear of being abducted, she scoffs at the possibility, assuring him that "The hills will be alive with the sound of . . ." "Music?" Oscar suggests, facetiously. No, what she meant to say was "contestants, stewards, trainers, other people." This is little more than an early example of a typical "hills arc alive" joke, but what gives this one an almost self-referential edge is the fact that Liza's trainer is played by none other than *TSOM*'s Herr Zeller, Ben Wright.

The Sixth Sense (Hollywood Pictures, August 6, 1999)

There's a *Sound of Music* reference in *The Sixth Sense*? Yes, indeed, although the title is never spoken.

Child psychologist Malcolm Crowe (Bruce Willis) stumbles upon the video from his wedding playing on the television set, just as a bridesmaid (Lisa Summerour) is drunkenly speaking to the camera about how she expects Malcolm to make her friend Anna happy. "And I'm not talkin' about no—mmm—this tastes like real butter kind of happy," she explains, "I'm talkin' about . . . Julie Andrews . . . uh-huh . . . twirlin' around like a mental patient on a mountaintop kind of happy . . . !"

Those who've seen *Sixth Sense* know Malcolm wasn't quite able to keep that happiness going, for reasons beyond his control.

The Sound of Edna (Charisma Records, June 1978)

Actor Barry Humphries's cross-dressing alter ego, Dame Edna Everage, a seemingly genteel old biddy with ghastly taste in clothing and a scalding tongue, presents an album of comical songs ranging from "The Night We Burnt My Mother's Things" to "Every Mother Wants a Boy like Elton." The LP cover is a direct parody of the famous poster art for *The Sound of Music*, with Edna prancing on the hilltop with guitar case and bag. Rather than being followed by the Trapp children, her charges are played by fellow-Australian stars Olivia Newton-John, the Bee Gees, Andy Gibb, Rolf Harris . . . and a kangaroo. The disapproving stand-in for Captain von Trapp is none other than Humphries himself, out of drag.

The Sound of Mumbai: A Musical (HBO, November 23, 2011)

The transformative nature of singing and the wide reach of *The Sound of Music* are the focus of this enlightening, inspiring, and sometimes heartbreaking

Before she really caught on in America, Dame Edna Everage, the cross-dressing alter ego of Australian performer Barry Humphries, released this LP very clearly spoofing "you-know-what" on its cover,

documentary directed by Sarah McCarthy. A group of children from the slums of Mumbai get a chance to perform songs from the Rodgers and Hammerstein musical with the Bombay Chamber Orchestra at a concert to be held at the National Centre of the Performing Arts (on August 30, 2009). Conductor Johannes Steinwender gives the project a link to the musical's origins, being from Austria. The kids are seen rehearsing such tunes as "The Lonely Goatherd" and "So Long, Farewell," with an eleven-year-old named Ashish stealing the show and becoming the center of the film as he is given a solo spot on the title song, evoking some jealousy from his fellow choir members.

The youngsters' incredible excitement over the experience of singing in a posh venue (just their enthusiasm over the flushing toilets in the concert building speaks volumes) is contrasted with the startling poverty of their everyday lives and their surprising optimism in the face of an uncertain future. Ashish psyches himself up by looking in the mirror and declaring, "I'm not a self-conscious boy. I have confidence in me. I can do it—everything."

Scoring from *TSOM* is heard throughout, along with soprano Lucy Crowe singing the title song, "Something Good," and "I Have Confidence."

Spice World (UK release: PolyGram, December 15, 1997, U.S. release: Columbia, January 23, 1998)

The Spice Girls, a quintet of pop singers calling themselves Scary, Baby, Sporty, Ginger, and Posh Spice, send up their moment in the spotlight as they prepare for their first live concert at the Royal Albert Hall. Sent by their ever-nervous manager to "Dance Camp" to learn some moves for the show, they are put under the tutelage of the flamboyant martinet Mr. Step (Michael Barrymore), who barks at the girls, "Don't give me any of that Julie Andrews, high on a hill type claptrap. Chop, chop. I'm your mother now, and I don't mean superior!" This is followed by a drill/dance routine to the tunes "Never Give Up on the Good Times" and "Sound Off." One can only assume that the choice of the word "claptrap" was meant to have a double meaning, as in "Clap-Trapp."

Spotswood/The Efficiency Expert (Australia: Hoyts, January 23, 1992, U.S.: Miramax, November 6, 1992)

This charming Australian comedy about a moccasin factory in the Melbourne suburb of Spotswood under scrutiny by a by-the-book efficiency expert takes place in an unspecified year in the late 1960s. Carey (Ben Mendelsohn), a shy and guileless worker hopelessly smitten with the factory owner's daughter Cheryl (Rebecca Rigg), tries to woo her at first by asking if she'd like to join him at the cinema to see *Doctor Zhivago*. Later, he changes his tactic to another 1965 blockbuster, asking, "What do you think of Julie Andrews? . . . She's supposed to be good in *The Sound of Music* . . . It's on at the Grand on Monday night." Having secured his movie date, Carey is then approached by the girl (Toni Collette), who has a crush on *him* with the same film in mind. He tries to placate her by assuring her he'd be willing to see it a second time. When at last Carey and Cheryl make it to the theatre, she decides she'd rather see the show with a more loutishly aggressive factory employee (Russell Crowe). As the distraught Carey exits, we see a placard in the lobby with the familiar *TSOM* title font.

Assuming the Spotswood folks were traveling into Melbourne for their moviegoing, there was indeed a Grand Theatre there, although depending upon the exact date the action was taking place, *TSOM* had its initial showing in that city, for nearly three years, not at the Grand but at the Paris, starting in April 1965.

Taxi (ABC, Season 2, Episode 8: "The Great Race," November 6, 1979)

While trying to win a contest between himself and his obnoxious dispatcher, cabbie Alex Reiger (Judd Hirsch) is slowed down by a pair of nuns who get into his vehicle and then can't decide which movie they want to attend. One nun (Julie Payne) wants to see *The Muppet Movie*, while the other (Kres Mersky) prefers a "revival" of *The Sound of Music*. The other nun reminds her that "we've seen it twelve times," but an anxious Alex assures them "you can't see *that* one too many times!" Despite the fact that the pro-*TSOM* nun "can't stand that little frog," it is the Muppets who win out in the end. Perhaps this is because the sisters stood a better chance of seeing *The Muppet Movie*, which *was* released to theatres the year this episode aired, than a 1979 NYC revival of *TSOM*.

Ten Circles upon the Pond: Reflections of a Prodigal Mother by Virginia Tranel (Alfred A. Knopf, April 2003)

Through a series of essays covering more than twenty years, the author tells the story of the ten children she and her husband raised. While claiming that she "knew nothing of *The Sound of Music* when I took down the curtains in our apartment as we prepared to leave Pullman, Washington," Virginia ends up using them to make herself some maternity clothes, a la the Trapp children's play clothing. This is clearly a reference to the stage version, as the author explains "the musical had been presented for the first time in New York a few months before," admitting she may have been "operating in the aura of Maria, the nun-turned-nanny who fashions curtains into children's outfits."

The Tetherballs of Bougainville by Mark Leyner (Harmony, September 1997)

Here's an odd bit of speculation on the legacy of *TSOM*. In his idiosyncratic novel, Leyner presents himself as a thirteen-year-old awaiting his father's execution in a New Jersey prison. According to the teen, he can see outside a prison window a "wrought-iron gazebo completely swathed in concertina wire." This, he tells us, is "the original gazebo used in *The Sound of Music*," presented by singer Michael Jackson to then-governor Christine Todd Whitman, "the only proviso being that the gazebo be used for the delectation of the state's penal population." To this end, it is used for "conjugal visits and punitive confinement."

While Leyner mentions its importance as being the site of the "Sixteen Going on Seventeen" scene in the picture, he's another writer who opts for an eccentric spelling of Liesl, specifically "Liselle."

That Girl (ABC, Season 3, Episode 19: "My Sister's Keeper," February 6, 1969)

This one gets points for being the rare sitcom of the time to actually mention *TSOM* while it was still circulating in theatres. Worried that her audition for a commercial requires her to sing, Anne Marie (Marlo Thomas) decides she can't possibly concentrate on the movie she and her boyfriend Donald (Ted

Bessell) were planning to see that night. Insisting she go to the film to take her mind off the fact that she's not much of a singer, Donald taunts Anne with potential titles they could see . . . "*Singin' in the Rain* . . . *The Sound of Music* . . . *Song of Norway* . . . *With a Song in My Heart* . . . *The Singing Fool.* . . *20,000 Years in Sing Sing.*" This might be the only instance of Al Jolson's forgotten 1928 box office hit *The Singing Fool* getting mentioned *anywhere* in the sixties.

3rd Rock from the Sun (NBC; Season 3, Episode 22: "Just Your Average Dick," April 28, 1998)

The Solomons were space aliens posing as a not-so-average American family, so they ran into their share of complications when it came to hiding the truth from the Earthlings they encountered. Here, the teen of the quartet, Tommy (Joseph Gordon-Levitt), tries to invent a fake family history for girlfriend August (Shay Astar). "My great grandfather escaped from the Nazis through the Alps," he lies, "with his family and their singing nanny." August is quick to catch on, admonishing him for stealing the premise of *The Sound of Music.* "Yeah . . . I know," Tommy assures her to cover his tall tale. "And don't think that we're not suing!!"

30 Rock

(NBC; Season 6, Episode 9: "Leap Day," February 23, 2012)

This weekly sitcom that skewered the world of television and its often cluelessly self-involved stars and executives often dropped in a "flashback" gag, visualized for maximum laughs after the character had spoken of the situation in the present, sometimes inaccurately to what actually happened.

In this episode, head writer Liz Lemon (Tina Fey) encounters a rather nerdy fellow named Thad (Steve Little) from her college days who brings up her "starring" role in a school production of *The Sound of Music.* Liz shrugs off being called the "star" since she was merely playing "the young Nazi boy." In the flashback, we see Liz, complete with mustache and swastika arm band, singing "You are one age, going on another age . . . ." As she informs Thad, "A lot of people didn't realize that was the free, unlicensed version."

Thriller Night (DreamWorks short; September 13, 2011)

The cast of the *Shrek* films (minus Julie Andrews's role of Fiona's mother and minus the original well-known voice actors) show up to give *TSOM* a kick in the lederhosen. Taken to the movies (Admission prices: Adults: 10, Children: 3, Dwarves: 7) to see *The Music of Sound*, Shrek comes screaming from the theatre unable to bear it anymore. Donkey and Puss-in-Boots, however, are more than delighted to sing a bit of "The Lonely Goatherd." "What kind of person screams when they see singing nuns?," Donkey asks with disbelief. It's Halloween, Shrek reminds his friends, and he would much prefer to see something scary, leading to an extended parody of Michael Jackson's famous *Thriller* video from the 1980s. When Shrek awakens from what turns out to be merely a dream, he's back in the movie theatre as *The Music of Sound* starts to play on the screen, with a lady resembling the pre-Ogre Fiona spinning on a hilltop. "For the next three hours," Donkey assures Shrek, "you're looking at nothing but children, and puppets and nuns," prompting another scream.

Thumbelina (Golden Films direct-to-video release; June 8, 1992)

This unremarkable Japanese-made, forty-nine-minute update on the Hans Christian Andersen story is notable for actually working a *Sound of Music* song into its storyline. (Most of the background scoring uses classical music.) On her way to the meadow to warn the creatures that the dam is in danger of breaking, teeny little Thumbelina ends up moving in with Mona the Mouse. While doing house chores, Thumbelina sings the opening of "Edelweiss" and later reprises it for Mona's guest, Mr. Mole, who is so enchanted that he wants to marry the girl. The interspecies nuptials, however, do not take place.

Tiny Toon Adventures (Fox, Episode 57: "Pollution Solution," February 14, 1991)

Executive produced by Steven Spielberg, this Saturday morning cartoon series centered around the offspring of some of the famous Looney Tunes characters. At the start of this episode, the camera pans across a mountainous landscape until it finds Babs Bunny (voice of Tress MacNeille) spinning joyfully on a bluff before welcoming viewers to Acme Acres. She does *not* sing the expected song.

The Tonight Show with Jay Leno (NBC, February 6, 2014)

When it came time for Jay Leno to wrap up his twenty-two-year-run as the host of the *Tonight Show* (handing the reins over to Jimmy Fallon), Billy Crystal, backed by a chorus of seven in lederhosen, gave the comedian a musical send-off with a revamped version of "So Long, Farewell" ("And all the executives who run NBC are popping in to say 'You're through!'"). There followed a celebrity lineup of well-wishers joining in the tune: Jack Black ("So, long, farewell, auf wiedersehen, my dear/if Fallon tanks, you'll be back here next year"), famous-for-being-famous Kim Kardashian, Chris Paul from the Los Angeles Clippers, singer Sheryl Crow, *The Big Bang Theory*'s Jim Parsons, Carol Burnett, and Oprah Winfrey.

Two Lovers (Magnolia, February 14, 2009)

Troubled Leonard Kraditor (Joaquin Phoenix) suddenly has two possible women in his life, the equally messed-up Michelle and a more stable prospect, Sandra (Vinessa Shaw). While being shown samples of Leonard's photography, Vinessa is impressed by the number of DVDs in his room, leading to a discussion on movies. Asked to name her favorite, Vinessa gives one of those apologetic explanations. "Well, my favorite movie's probably . . . *Sound of Music.*" Quickly she adds, "Not because of the film, really, but because—ya know—whenever it's on my family always watches it. It's that kind of thing." But Leonard is not so eager to dismiss it. "No. That's a good movie," he assures her. "Very underrated." Although we don't hear Michelle's opinion on the musical, it seems a wise decision when Leonard chooses Vinessa at the finale.

Ugly Betty (ABC, Season 1, Episode 9: "Lose the Boss?," November 23, 2006)

This American version of a Colombian telenovela soap opera placed naïve, goodhearted Betty Suarez in a personal assistant's job at a high-stakes New York fashion magazine run mostly by self-involved snobs. One of those snobs, Marc St. James (Michael Urie), dares to spend Thanksgiving with another staffer goofing off and trying on dresses in the office of Marc's dragon-lady boss, Wilhelmina (Vanessa Williams), a definite no-no. When Wilhelmina becomes all too aware that *someone* has been disturbing her space, Marc tries to cover up, pretending to be equally appalled that someone would spend the holiday in such a manner. "Wouldn't they be satisfied with watching the parade and *The Sound of Music* for, like, the 80th time?" Wilhelmina wonders if that's exactly how her minion celebrated. Covering, but no doubt revealing aspects of actual holidays gone by, he tells her he spent the time in Schenectady with his family, but that he left to return to New York "right before the von Trapps escape the Nazis. If I leave before 'Edelweiss' I can be home and in bed by midnight."

Under Wraps (Disney Channel; October 25, 1997)

A mummy comes to life in this comedy aimed at kids. Marshall (Mario Yedidia) is exasperated after his friend Gilbert (Adam Wylie), once again walks out of a horror movie. Gilbert confesses he prefers "nice, happy movies like, uh . . . *The Sound of Music.*" A typical adolescent boy, Marshall simply can't believe it, but Gilbert insists, "It's a great movie! It's got singing . . . dancing . . . Nazis. Well, the Nazis don't sing and dance, which would be really cool, but it's still a great movie." As for his assessment of Liesl? "What a babe!"

Unlikely Angel (CBS, December 17, 1996)

This Christmas-themed TV movie wades deep into *TSOM* territory (with a touch of *Mary Poppins, Here Comes Mr. Jordan/Heaven Can Wait,* and *It's a Wonderful Life* thrown in as well).

Dolly Parton plays recently deceased roadhouse singer Ruby Diamond, sent back to Earth by Saint Peter (Roddy McDowall) to help a family in need and thereby earn her wings. The dad (Brian Kerwin) is widowed and as distant from his two kids as a certain captain; Ruby encourages eight-year-old Matthew (Eli Marienthal) to resume his former interest in learning the piano, and even accompanies him on guitar, singing "Jingle Bells"; and although it seems like Ruby is developing romantic feelings for her employer, her no-longer-mortal state forces her to step aside so that his work colleague (incidentally not a baroness) can have him.

When Ruby first arrives on Earth, Peter jokingly sends her there dressed in a dirndl, dropping her and her carrying bag on the lawn of her assigned family. Sizing up the situation Ruby quips, "All I need is a guitar, and I'll be ready for *The Sound of Music.*" Quick to comply, Peter sends that very instrument plummeting to Earth to land by her side.

Up in the Cellar (AIP, August 12, 1970)

An antiestablishment comedy from Hollywood's most youth-oriented independent company of the day, American International Pictures, *Up in the Cellar* stars Wes Stern as a poet dismayed to learn that a computer error has taken his college scholarship away. When his subsequent suicide attempt is thwarted by the opportunistic college president Camber (Larry Hagman), he decides to take revenge on his savior by bedding the man's wife, mistress, and daughter Tracy (Nira Barab, later known as Catlin Adams). The last involves filming the teen in a state of undress, footage she gleefully consents to have surreptitiously shown at her dad's Free-But-Decent Speech Society meeting in place of the eagerly anticipated main feature, *The Sound of Music.*

As Camber explains to his prospective voters, "If saving your country is not enough inducement to come to the meeting, I have also arranged for a free screening of that great, American, clean, film classic, *The Sound of Music.*" *Cellar* is an ideal example of how certain "antiestablishment" types of the era looked upon Robert Wise's movie as the antithesis of the sort of edgy entertainment they were seeking. Worse, to some, it represented conservatism and backward thinking. According to the young conspirators here, *TSOM* being screened means, "Every up-tight voter in the county will be there." Those voters, in turn, are heard joining Camber's rant against objectionably immoral entertainment by singing "Censor, Censor, Hallelujah." Needless to say, they are appalled when they get Tracy's bosoms up there on the screen rather than the Trapp Family's puppet show.

Thrown in for those in the know is a little in-joke, with Hagman asking if the busloads of supporters have arrived yet from Wetherford, that being the real-life hometown of his mother and *TSOM*'s original Maria, Mary Martin.

Insomuch as the porn footage is shown on a tiny square screen unsuitable for Todd-AO, it is just as well that *TSOM* was not subjected to such an inferior form of exhibition.

The Vicar of Dibley (BBC 1, Episode 4: "The Wind and the Weather," December 1, 1994)

This British sitcom, created by writer Richard Curtis, featured Dawn French as Geraldine Granger, the first female vicar to preside over St. Barnabas' Church in the conservative Oxfordshire village of Dibley.

In this episode, as a storm rages outside, Geraldine is visited by the church's ditsy verger, Alice (Emma Chambers), seeking company in the inclement weather. "Do you remember in *The Sound of Music* when Julie Andrews was scared, she sang about her favorite things?," Alice asks the deeply disinterested vicar. After claiming to have an expert memory for lyrics, Alice then proceeds to butcher the number, singing "Snow drops on roses and noses on kittens . . . da-da-dee-da-da dee-da-da-da . . . mittens." When Hugo Norton (James Fleet) shows up in the middle of this performance, Geraldine is quick to explain that "We were just singing a chirpy Julie Andrews tune to stop us from getting scared . . . ."

Von Trapped! (ITV, September 4, 2004)

This special, about a peripatetic hairdresser obsessed with *The Sound of Music*, tops them all when it comes to pop cultural references to the Oscar-winning musical. Written by Jonathan Harvey, this comedy-drama was part of a UK trilogy that was paired up with "Beauty" and "King of Fridges."

Set in the town of Oldham (home of the tubular bandage), the program begins with our heroine, Maria Moogan (Caroline Oldham), rushing across town in nun's garb while lighting a cigarette, anxious to get to the *Sing-a-long-a Sound of Music* only to be told she's arrived on the wrong week.

There's nothing Maria doesn't like to share with others about her love of *TSOM*, telling one customer (of her door-to-door hairdressing service, Do Re Mi Hair Fashion), "Christopher Plummer's a very mixed-up individual, Myra. He called it 'The Sound of Mucus.' I've three words to say to that . . . section the bugger." Maria wears her own hair closely modeled after Julie Andrews's "do" in the film; has a daughter she originally named Liesl (although the transgendered girl prefers to be called Lee in anticipation of her hoped-for sex change); tells a market researcher her occupation is "nun-turned-governess"; and possesses a musical key chain that turns off her car to the notes of "the hills are alive . . . ."

Eight years after the incident, Maria still carries a torch for the Manchester newscaster, Larry Lavelle (Jim Carter), who left her waiting at the altar (where Maria was to tie the knot in a copy of Julie's wedding gown from the film) and obliged to bring up Lee on her own. A key reason for loving Larry? "You were the only bloke I knew loved *Sound of Music* as much as I did that was straight," Maria tells him.

"What's so special about that *blessed* film?," Maria's wheelchair-bound friend Connie (Lynda Rooke) demands to know. Answers Maria, "It's magical. It's beautiful. And it's a true story." But Connie has her own theory about the obsession. "You saw it that night. The night he stood you up," she reminds her. "You went to that picture house and it made you feel better. And, you've kept using it like an anesthetic ever since." But Connie is a good enough friend that when she wins the lottery she gives over a portion (£10,000) of her winnings to Maria, for providing her with one of the lucky numbers, 7 (as in "7 children"), allowing Maria to realize her long-cherished dream of going to Salzburg. ("I could buy flipping Salzburg with this much . . . .") Connie is hopeful that a holiday together with her daughter means Maria can put her torment over her non-wedding behind her. "See the sights, *drown* in *The Sound of Music* if you have to," she advises her friend, "then put it to bed, shut up about it, and move on!"

Arriving in Salzburg, Maria insists on dressing Lee, as well as Maria's mum (Una Stubbs), in drapery-like matching outfits as they join a bus tour that relinquishes being Mozart-themed to concentrating on *Sound of Music* locations, by popular demand of the mostly-Asian participants. Says the incredulous, sarcastic guide (Philip Jackson) when asked about Julie Andrews, "She was evil! She completely misrepresented my people!" We are treated to glimpses of the hallowed gazebo, which the guide properly reminds his group was actually recreated in Los Angeles; the church at Mondsee, where Maria drifts into a wedding fantasy clad in that copied dress; a bicycle ride through the Mirabell hedge canopy and around the Pegasus fountain; a spin on a hilltop; and an attempt to recreate the final moments of "Do-Re-Mi" on the Mirabell steps. By coincidence, Larry is in town covering the urinals of Salzburg for his new investigative television show, prompting a date with Maria to a *TSOM* dinner show, and some startling revelations about what *really* happened eighteen years ago.

The coach passengers sing a bit of "My Favorite Things," some overage singers present their version of "Sixteen Going on Seventeen," the Wedding Processional version of "Maria" is used, and Big Brovaz's hit recording of "Favourite Things" is heard on the soundtrack.

A must for all *TSOM* fans.

The War at Home (Fox, Season 2, Episode 17: "Kenny Doesn't Live Here Anymore," February 15, 2007)

Tossed from his own home for being gay, Kenny (Rami Malek) takes up residence with the dysfunctional Golds. When the uptight principal finds out, he threatens to send Social Services, so the Golds consider sneaking Kenny out and putting him up in a motel, which is compared to the climax of *The Sound of Music,* "when they sneak out of the amphitheater when no one's looking and hide from the Nazis in the convent." This prompts wearied dad (Michael Rapaport) to snap at his son Larry (Kyle Sullivan), "If you start singing, I swear to God, I'm gonna knock your head right off your shoulders." Sorry, dad. He gets to hear a few lines from "So Long, Farewell," regardless.

Welcome to Woop Woop (Australia: August 13, 1998; US Release: Samuel Goldwyn Films, November 13, 1998)

This grotesque Australian comedy is awash in not only *TSOM* references (the U.S. poster contained the ad line "The hills are alive . . ."), but Rodgers and Hammerstein musicals in general. In director Stephan Elliott's follow-up to his 1994 hit *The Adventures of Priscilla, Queen of the Desert*, an American con artist (Jonathan Schaech) facing extermination high-tails it to Australia, where he is shanghaied by a hitchhiker (Susie Porter), who takes him home to her off-the-radar, lowbrow town of Woop Woop, where he is basically held prisoner by the few but eccentric inhabitants, chief among them the girl's loutish father (Rod Taylor).

Woop Woop's total population of fifty is obsessed with all-things R&H, or, as they mistakenly call them, Rodgerson Hammerstein. Selections play on the film's soundtrack or on the town's audio systems throughout the storyline, including "Chop Suey" (*Flower Drum Song*), "Happy Talk" (*South Pacific*), "Getting to Know You" (*The King and I*), and, more unexpectedly, the title song from *Allegro* and the Christmas Seals tune the team wrote in 1952, "Happy Christmas, Little Friend."

The scruffy citizens are seen gathering for an outdoor showing of *The Sound of Music*, allowing us to glimpse Julie Andrews's opening number and a bit of "Do-Re-Mi." There is also a rude joke that comes from the locals misinterpreting Peggy Wood's question to Andrews in the sequence leading up to "Climb Ev'ry Mountain," when she asks, "What is it you can't face?"

The '65 soundtrack versions of "Climb Ev'ry Mountain" and "The Lonely Goatherd" are used, as is the film's "overture," and the final credits commence with the dedication "To Richard and Oscar . . . ." (The *Woop Woop* soundtrack concludes with the Junior Vasquez remix of "Climb Ev'ry Mountain" with Peggy Wood, not Margery McKay, listed as his collaborator.)

One assumes Rodgers and Hammerstein would have preferred to be tributed by better movies than this.

What's Up, Tiger Lily? (American International Pictures, November 2, 1966)

Comedian Woody Allen took an obscure 1964 Japanese espionage thriller called *Kagi no Kagi* and added his own irreverent voice track to it, for what qualified as his first "directorial" effort.

Following the opening credits, some men are seen watching an exotic dancer undulate in an adult club, prompting one of them to remark, "She was even better in *The Sound of Music*," making this the earliest known movie reference to take place while the blockbuster musical was still circulating in theatres. The line did not survive on the subsequent videocassette release of *Tiger Lily*, however, being replaced by "Hold on, she's just getting warmed up." Both versions would later be available on the 2003 DVD release.

When I Was a Loser: True Stories of (Barely) Surviving High School edited by John McNally (Free Press, March 2007)

This collection of essays about the traumas of surviving high school includes "Do Not Wear Green on Wednesdays" by Quinn Dalton. Among the brighter incidents in Quinn's life are "scoring the role of your heart's desire in the spring musical, *The Sound of Music*. You are Liesl," she gushes to herself. "You are sixteen going on seventeen in life and on stage." She then describes her co-star's efforts to accomplish their big number. "Your Rolf is a lanky boy with mile-long arms and legs and huge feet. In his enthusiasm during dance routines he sometimes forgets his own strength, and you've both very nearly broken bones."

Will & Grace (NBC, Season 8, Episode 10: "Von Trapped," January 5, 2006)

"What is it about *The Sound of Music* that makes otherwise reasonable people dress up and act like lunatics?" So asks one of the characters in this episode of the sitcom's final season, its twenty-two minutes focusing entirely on "*Sing-a-Long Sound of Music.*"

An excited Grace (Debra Messing) makes sure she doesn't miss the latest participatory screening of the movie in New York, dressing in Maria's "I Have Confidence" outfit (with bag, but minus guitar) and expecting Will (Eric McCormick) to join her, clad in Captain von Trapp's whistle-tooting attire. Jack (Sean Hayes) chooses curtain-made lederhosen, while Karen (Megan Mullally) is simply along to drink and toss her flask from the balcony, getting everyone into deep trouble with the theatre management.

There are sung snatches of "Do-Re-Mi," "My Favorite Things," and "So Long, Farewell," and the plot playfully parodies the movie by having Grace get stuck looking after seven kids in the lobby and the four principals re-enacting the cemetery scene, hiding from authorities in a utility closet as the candy counter attendant (named *Ralph*; played by Steven Petrarca) Jack has been hitting on comes looking for them with a flashlight.

The most telling moment finds Will flirting with a young man (Taye Diggs) he's met when he arrives at the wrong theatre, pretending to find *TSOM* "sentimental," only to immediately renege on his assessment and admit his love for the film when his prospective boyfriend says without embarrassment how much he likes it.

No footage from the movie is actually shown.

TSOM was referenced in passing on several other episodes of the series as well.

Season 1, Episode 20: "Saving Grace," April 29, 1999

Jack informs Will that he's in love with a guy from the Dominican Republic, but Will isn't in the mood to hear about another one of Jack's on-again, off-again affairs. Jack decides his friend is jealous because he's "Stuck inside the nunnery while all the other girls run around in their miniskirts and take the pill." Or, as he adds, "How do you solve a problem like Will Truman?"

Season 3, Episode 24: "Sons and Lovers," May 17, 2001

Knowing Will doesn't like her boorish neighbor, Nathan, Grace doesn't tell Will she's still dating the fellow. "So, the whole time you've been dating this guy, sneaking around behind my back?" an incensed Will gripes, "God! I feel like Captain von Trapp and you're Liesl making out with that Nazi in the gazebo."

Season 6, Episode 8: "Swimming from Cambodia," November 20, 2003

Anticipating their big *TSOM*-themed episode in Season 8, Will shows off a gold blazer he bought as part of his costume for the upcoming *Sound of Music* sing-along, the idea being that he'll be "re, a drop of golden sun." "Wow, I'm impressed," Grace tells him. "Somehow you managed to gay up the *Sound of Music* sing-along." Worried that she intends to return to Cambodia where she has moved, Will asks her to stay, or at least attend the sing-along. Grace is tempted. "You know how much I love *The Sound of Music*," she admits. "And now I've got an excuse to get the blonde braids back from Jack."

Season 6, Episode 15: "Flip-Flop, Part 1," February 26, 2004

Karen's latest lover (and eventual fourth husband), Lyle Finster (John Cleese), has moved in to her penthouse. So tickled by her affections for him, Karen asks what she ever did to deserve him. "I guess, somewhere in my wicked, miserable past," she begins, reading the lyrics like straightforward dialogue, "there must have been a moment of truth." Soon, she is singing "Something Good" with Lyle joining in. "Promise me it will always be this way," Karen coos, "That we'll always spend our mornings over coffee and enjoying an impromptu song!"

Season 8, Episode 8: "Swish Out of Water," November 24, 2005

As a representative for the Coalition for Justice, Will is appalled to discover that a hated slumlord turns out to be Karen. As her punishment, she's dragged by the police into one of the run-down apartments in Spanish Harlem, where she is forced to spend some time. Terrified of her predicament and needing some comfort, she starts to sing "Raindrops on roses and whiskers on kittens . . . ."

"Wind It Up," performed by Gwen Stefani (written by Stefani and Pharrell Williams) (2006)

Stefani's music video takes many of its visuals (*not* the singer chained to a gate in flowing gown) from what she declared was her favorite movie, *The Sound of Music.*

The song samples "The Lonely Goatherd" (taken from a mash-up originally created by DJ Jeremy Healy) and, in fact, actually opens with this, before seguing into the "Wind It Up" tune proper. For maximum irreverence, Stefani wears a groovy nun's outfit in parts of the video, cut short, like baby doll pajamas. Sitting on a bed in an image mirroring the "My Favorite Things" sequence, she tells her attentive "Trapp Children-like" dancers, "You've got to let the beat get under your skin . . . you've got to open up and let it all in." She also comes up with the idea of making outfits for her dancers out of the drapes.

The song was introduced, minus the Rodgers and Hammerstein addition, in 2005. The mash-up single was released on October 31, 2006, in advance of the album on which it appeared, *The Sweet Escape,* which debuted in December of that year. It peaked at #5 on the U.S. Hot Dance Club charts.

Wombling Free (Rank Film Distributors Ltd., 1977)

Derived from the stop-motion British children's series (1973–75), this feature film (written and directed by actor Lionel Jeffries) has the environmentally conscious creatures called the Wombles ("4 foot, fat and furry") played by dwarves in costumes. A staging of one of their hit tunes, "Wombling White Tie and Tails" ("sing, sing, sing like a Womble . . . dance, dance, dance, like a Womble . . .") features references to Fred Astaire and Ginger Rogers, *Singin' in the Rain, On the Town,* and . . . a Womble on a hilltop in a novice outfit holding a guitar case while singing "the world is alive with the sound of Womble."

World's Greatest Dad (Magnolia Films, August 21, 2009)

In director-writer Bobcat Goldthwait's jet-black comedy, hapless teacher Lance Clayton (Robin Williams) tries to make the best of his strained relationship with his blatantly rude and loathsome offspring Kyle (Daryl Sabara). Trying to get the teen to bond with his girlfriend Claire (Alexie Gilmore), Lance takes them out to dinner and suggests they watch a movie together when they get home. Claire rejects his offer of a zombie movie, telling him she prefers musicals. Trying to find a shared interest, Lance opines that Bob Fosse was a great director of musicals, specifically mentioning *Sweet Charity* and *All That Jazz.* Claire enthusiastically tosses *Cabaret* onto the list. "One of the great Nazi musicals of all time," Lance remarks cheekily. "Besides *The Sound of Music.*" Bringing the two most famous "Nazi musicals" together in the same reference makes this one worth noting.

Yellow Submarine (United Artists, UK release: July 17, 1968; U.S. release: November 13, 1968)

With the soundtrack for *TSOM* being one of the Beatles' chief competitors for LP chart domination in the 1960s, it was only to be expected that they'd take a poke at the Rodgers and Hammerstein sensation.

In this animated feature, the enslaved inhabitants of the undersea world of Pepperland are at last freed by the music of Sgt. Pepper's Lonely Hearts Club Band, much to the displeasure of their captor, the Chief Blue Meanie. As the Beatles' "With a Little Help from My Friends" starts to play, the film cuts to the chief remarking, "Ahh . . . the hills are alive," thereby prompting his henchman, Max, to pipe in by singing "with the sound of music." His boss responds by punching him.

Young @ Heart (Fox Searchlight, April 9, 2008)

A documentary about a group of seniors who defy expectations by giving concerts where they perform songs from such unlikely sources as the Clash (or "Crash" as one member calls them) and Sonic Youth. For most of them, their taste in music leans elsewhere, as in classical or opera. Eileen Hall tells the interviewer, "I like *My Fair Lady* and *The King and I* and . . . um, what's the very popular one with Julie Andrews—Climb Ev'ry Mountain?" Okay, so she forgets the name of one of her favorite musicals, but when the interviewer reminds her that it is *The Sound of Music*, the fond smile on her face and exclamation of "yes" speaks volumes.

A Different Way of Looking at Maria

Four Notable *Sound of Music* One-Offs

ore than mere references or homages to *The Sound of Music*, there are four works that require separate consideration of their own.

The Trapp Family Story (*Torappu ikka monogatari*)

A 40-episode Japanese animated series shown on Fuji Television Network
A Live-evil presentation; Nippon Animation Co., Ltd.
    January 13, 1991–December 28, 1991
    This weekly series retelling of the Trapp Family Story was a part of *World Masterpiece Theatre*, a long-running series of anime adaptations of classic stories done by Nippon Animation. Others in this series included *Tom Sawyer, Swiss Family Robinson,* and *Little Women,* the only three to be later broadcast in the United States.
    The idea of stretching out the familiar story of Maria arriving at the Trapp villa, teaching the children to sing, marrying the baron/captain, and escaping from the Anchluss was not to the advantage of the series, which, in its need to fill forty half-hour episodes, fell all over itself to create drama over such trivial things as dirty clothing, a teddy bear in need of washing, and baking a cake. In soap opera fashion, plot points were emphasized over and over again until they wore out their welcome, while turning the housekeeper, Matilda, into a bossy snob whose actions bordered on villainy made this character simply insufferable rather than dramatically compelling.
    Unlike the musical, this series did use the correct names of the children, although they were not accurately presented chronologically (e.g., in real life, Agathe was the name of the oldest Trapp daughter; here she was the youngest). Maria's age was lowered a bit, making her a mere eighteen when she arrived at the Trapp villa.

Executive Producer: Motohashi Kouichi. Translation: Gumbaloom. Planning Support: Johannes von Trapp, Hans Wilhelm. Editing: Tylnnec, Vashsensei. Screenplay: Shiroya Ayo. Music: Kazato Shinsuke. Character Design: Seki Shuuichi. Animation Director: Irie Atsushi. Producers: Tachikawa Yoshihisa (Fuji TV), Matsudo Takaji. Director: Kusuba Kouzou.

Theme Songs: "Doremi no Uta (Doremi Song)" a Japanese version of Richard Rodgers and Oscar Hammerstein II's "Do-Re-Mi" featured vocals by Eri Etoh and Children's Choir of the Forest; this was replaced on DVD and video by "Hohoemi no Mahou (Smile Magic)"; Lyrics: Ishii Megumi. Composition: Kishi Masayuki. Vocals: Itou Eri.

"Ryoute o Hirogete (Spread Both Hands)"; Lyrics: Ishii Megumi. Composition/Arrangement: Kazato Shinsuke. Vocals: Itou Eri.

VOICE ACTORS: Katsuki Masako (Maria), Hori Katsunosuke (Captain Trapp), Fujita Toshiko (Frau Matilda), Shiratori Yuri (Mädchen Maria), Adachi Shinobu (Rupert), Kawamura Maria (Hedwig), Matsuokaya Youko (Werner), Ishikawa Hiromi (Johanna), Suzuki Saori (Marta), Irokayawa Kyokayo (Agathe), Ohyama Takao (Franz), Yamaguchi Nana (Mother Abbess), Fuji Natsuko (Mistress of Novices), Aya Hisakawa (Rafaela), Hirano Masato (Hans), Etoh Haru (Rosy), Irokawa Kyoko (Clarine), Mari Nakamura (Mimi), Eiko Yamada (Yvonne)

Episode 1: "My Aspiration to Be a Catholic Nun"

Maria's unorthodox behavior at Nonnberg Abbey leads the Mistress of Novices to believe the girl might belong elsewhere.

Episode 2: "My Future as a Sister"

The Mother Abbess decides that Maria should be the one to fill the governess position for widowed Captain von Trapp, who needs someone to tutor his sickly child.

The Japanese turned the Trapp saga into a forty-episode television series, *Torappu ikka monogatari*, minus the glorious Rodgers and Hammerstein score.

Episode 3: "The Captain and His 7 Children"

Maria meets the captain and six of his children: Rupert, Hedwig, Werner, Johanna, Martina, and Agathe. Hedwig tells her siblings they must work together to drive the new governess away. When Maria insists that the sickly child, *mädchen* Maria, join them at the dinner table, she invokes the ire of the family's stern housekeeper, Matilda.

Episode 4: "The 26th Governess"

Matilda is certain Maria is a bad influence on *mädchen* Maria, but the captain is convinced that only good will come from the new governess being here.

Episode 5: "Maria Is the Cause of Drama"

With the captain traveling to Linz, he has made the decision that Maria is to stay on for her intended nine-month period, much to the displeasure of Matilda and Hedwig. When *mädchen* Maria overhears that Maria was an orphan, she feels a bond with her, still agonizing over having lost *her* mother.

Episode 6: "The Missing Children and the Hunger Rebellion"

Johanna goes missing on her way home from school; after she is found by Maria, Werner suddenly disappears until found suffering from a stomach ache from having eaten too many blueberries. Johanna is grateful over Maria's concern for her safety and now prefers she stay on.

Episode 7: "I Can Not Trust Adults"

The captain has decided that he would like Johanna to be tutored by Maria as well. Hedwig explodes at the idea of keeping Maria around until the governess convinces the girl not to close her heart to others because of previous unhappy experiences.

Episode 8: "Courtesy Is Important?!"

Realizing the children are forbidden to indulge in much physical activity, Maria teaches them a song and is impressed by their vocal abilities. Hedwig is distraught by her father's plans to marry the Earl of Belvedere's daughter Yvonne, a union that would benefit the family financially.

Episode 9: "Baron von Trapp's Fiancée?"

Yvonne visits and barely hides her disinterest in spending time with the children. Hedwig lets it be known how disgusted she is at the thought of Yvonne becoming their mother, while the lady herself admits to the captain that she's only interested in him and not playing nursemaid to his seven offspring.

Episode 10: "Sewing Machine and Violin"

Finding a violin and sewing machine in the house, Maria decides they can be made useful, making clothing for the children and encouraging *mädchen* Maria to learn the instrument. The captain is initially upset because both these items belonged to his late wife, but Maria convinces him that it would be a way for *mädchen* Maria to remember her mother.

Episode 11: "Playing in the Mud Is Supreme!"

Worried that her poor health is the reason the other children are discouraged from playing outside, *mädchen* Maria comes up with the idea of an athletics meet for the family. The captain is delighted that his children end up cutting loose and having so much fun.

Episode 12: "Chocolate Cake: Maria Style"

When Matilda leaves to visit her ailing sister, Maria feels free to take the children on a picnic, after which she engages them to help her bake a cake.

Episode 13: "Don Quixote's First Love"

When the girl on whom Rupert harbors a secret crush, Nastassja, announces that her family is moving to Russia, the Trapps host a farewell party. Rupert carves her a wooden statue of Don Quixote as a going-away gift, but worries that a rival boy, Anton, has upstaged him by giving Nastassja a music box with a ballerina figurine, which ends up broken.

Episode 14: "The Music Box's Secret"

Although Rupert insists he did not break the ballerina figurine, Anton taunts him, leading the boys to settle their differences in a fencing match. Anton wins, but Nastassja, disgusted by his behavior, slaps him. As she leaves she finds out it was Anton who accidentally broke the figurine, and gladly accepts Rupert's Don Quixote statue at the train station.

Episode 15: "Martina and the Bear, Nikola"

During a picnic, Martina accidentally drops her teddy bear in the river and falls in after it. Although Maria rescues the girl in time, she is wracked with guilt over the incident and decides to return to the abbey.

Episode 16: "The House Without Fräulein Maria"

Devastated that Maria has returned to Nonnberg, Johanna and Martina sneak out of the house to visit her but are told that they are not allowed to enter the abbey. Martina asks if she can leave her teddy bear for the governess. Back at the house, as the children perform a song for Matilda's birthday, they are surprised and delighted when Maria returns.

Episode 17: "The Wounded Fawn"

Werner is made to feel bad about his undignified behavior and runs off to the woods where he discovers a wounded fawn. Maria finds the boy and agrees to help him nurse the animal back to health.

Episode 18: "All God's Creatures, Great and Small"

When Maria brings the other children to see the fawn, Werner feels betrayed and locks himself in the barn. Maria bonds again with the boy by sneaking his lunch to him, against Matilda's orders. When the captain explains to his son that the deer will not always show the boy affection, Werner agrees to let the now-heeled animal be released back into the mountains.

Episode 19: "Lady Yvonne's Gifts"

Yvonne returns bearing gifts, in hopes of winning the children's favor. She is unmoved when Maria tells her she must take control if she plans on being their mother. When Yvonne trips on the carpet, she accidentally tumbles down the stairs, injuring herself and Maria in the process.

Episode 20: "Each Person's Life"

Maria suffers a concussion, and Yvonne has sprained her ankle from the fall. The children are clearly more concerned over the former when they are taken to the hospital to visit. Yvonne admits to the captain that she only wants to be married to him, that it's best to leave the children to Maria.

Episode 21: "Baron von Trapp's Decision"

Returning from the hospital, Maria is worried that the children are more excited to see her recovered than Yvonne and pretends to be cold to them. Yvonne informs her that this performance is not necessary—she will win the children over herself. When Matilda informs her employer that she will be leaving in the near future to take a job in Vienna, the captain impulsively announces that he *will* marry Yvonne. The news so upsets *mädchen* Maria that she faints.

Episode 22: "Can You Live Alone?"

Taking off for the train station in hopes of somehow stopping her father's planned engagement, Hedwig is robbed and then injured. A milk boy nurses her back to health at his home, but the girl insists he send for Maria when she realizes she is having other problems. Maria brings her back to the Trapp villa.

Episode 23: "Letters to the Angel"

Maria helps the children prepare for the Christmas holiday but is worried by the intimate glances that have passed between her and the captain. When Martina declares that the family doesn't need Yvonne since Maria is here, Matilda insists the governess must return to the abbey, but the children protest loudly at the possibility of losing her.

Episode 24: "Christmas Carol"

Despite Matilda's insistence that the children are spending too much time together, Maria defiantly teaches them to sing "Hark! The Herald Angels Sing," which they perform for their delighted father. Knowing that the family is happy for Christmas, Maria leaves for mass at the abbey, during which she cannot stop thinking of the captain and his children.

Episode 25: "In the Snow of the Alps"

The captain and his family are invited to spend the New Year at the Earl of Belvedere's vacation house in the Alps. Yvonne even encourages the captain to bring Maria. Werner is injured while skiing, and Rupert is worried because he is uncertain of what he wants to study in school. His father tells him it is his decision as long as the profession he chooses will be useful to others.

Episode 26: "Oranges and Flower Seedlings"

Maria returns from the family vacation with flower seedlings she hopes that the gardener, Franz, will plant on the Trapp property. When the captain goes to visit the ailing Yvonne, Maria gives him a seedling to bring to her, telling her it is from the children. Yvonne knows better. Returning home, the captain brings everyone oranges, feeling far happier to be with his family than his betrothed.

Episode 27: "Yesterday, Today, and Tomorrow"

Maria hopes the family will join her in giving up something meaningful for the weeks leading up to Easter. The captain decides he will stop smoking for forty days and give the money saved to Nonnberg Abbey. Maria tells the story of how she ran away from home when she was young and got a job judging tennis matches at a posh resort, allowing her to save money to go to Teacher's College.

Episode 28: "Naughty Agathe"

Little Agathe's unruly behavior includes getting hold of a pair of scissors, forcing Maria to scold her. In contrast, Yvonne appears to have very little instinct for how to deal with the child.

Episode 29: "A Wife, a Mother"

Worried that she is a barrier between Yvonne and the children, Maria plans to return to the abbey earlier than planned. The captain will not hear of it, finding it thoughtless where the children are concerned. Yvonne is now certain he loves Maria, which the captain finally admits. Yvonne tells Maria that *she* should be the next mother to the children.

Episode 30: "Would You Marry Me?"

Yvonne effectively ends any possibility of marriage by accepting a proposal from someone else. While waiting for Johanna to pass the coin she has swallowed, the children come to the conclusion that the only way to keep Maria around is for their father to propose to her, which he does.

Episode 31: "God's Decree"

Uncertain how to answer the captain's proposal of marriage, Maria returns to the abbey for advice. The Mistress of Novices assures her that God meant for her to be a part of the Trapp family, causing Maria to rush back to the captain's waiting arms.

Episode 32: "A Bride in July"

Contrary to Matilda's prediction, the captain's in-laws *do* approve of him marrying Maria and send her a dress for the wedding. The captain and Maria marry at Nonnberg, and Matilda decides it is now time for her to move on.

Episode 33: "A True Family"

Returning from their honeymoon, the Trapps are greeted with the good news that Rupert has passed his exams for medical school, along with the bad news that the bank has failed and they are now bankrupt. As a solution, Maria suggests they take in boarders from the Catholic University.

Episode 34: "The Trapp Family Singers"

One of the Trapps' boarders, Father Wasner, gives the children instruction in singing. When opera singer Lotte Lehmann visits, she is so impressed by what she hears that she suggests the Trapp family participate in the choir competition at the Salzburg Festival, where they prove a great success.

Episode 35: "Singing in the Wind"

Despite protestations from the captain that he doesn't want his family singing for money, the Trapps sing on the radio and are so successful that the President of Austria invites them to sing at a lavish dinner in Vienna. This allows the children to visit their ailing grandmother.

Episode 36: "The Nazi Invasion"

Months after the Trapps have sung at the president's request at Kleinen Hall in Vienna, they are devastated by the news that the Germans have invaded and taken over Austria.

Episode 37: "The New Salute"

At school the new instructors insist that the children all learn to greet one another with the new "Heil Hitler!" salute. The captain is disgusted by this turn of events, refusing to give in or to remove the Austrian flag from his home. The children manage to subvert the new rule by saying "Tail Hitler" so that none of the teachers are any the wiser.

Episode 38: "Hans' Secret"

The Secret Police want the captain to hang the Nazi flag on his house in time for Hitler's visit to Salzburg, but he refuses. When Maria falls ill and Georg is informed that Dr. Vortman has been taken away by the Nazis, they travel to Munich, where she discovers she is pregnant. Back home the Trapps' butler, Hans, has put up the flag in hopes that the captain will not get in trouble, revealing to his employer that he is a member of the Nazi party.

Episode 39: "Pride and Belief"

The captain wants to dismiss Hans, but the servant insists that his being there will keep them protected from the Nazis for the time being. The captain is asked by the new regime to take command of a submarine, but he knows he must refuse. When the family is invited to sing at Hitler's birthday, they realize they must flee the country.

Episode 40: "Farewell to My Country"

Under the pretense of going hiking, the Trapp Family leave their home and journey to Tyrol where their former employee, Mimi, and her husband, Karl, help them cross the border into Italy. From there, they journey to Switzerland and escape the Nazi threat. With the money and tickets an American agent has sent them, they are able to take a ship to the United States, where they will continue their singing careers.

Sing-a-Long-A Sound of Music/Sing-a-Long Sound of Music

For those moviegoers who spent years resenting fellow patrons and theatre staff deriding their rude efforts to interrupt films, a breakthrough of sorts came their way in the late seventies, with midnight showings of the 20th Century-Fox musical *The Rocky Horror Picture Show* (1975). This strange and irresistible bit of self-proclaimed camp went from West End and Broadway stage flop to a film that initially very few wanted to see to pop cultural phenomenon. Thanks to screenings in New York in which audiences were encouraged to talk back to the movie and dress up as any of the flock of weirdos on screen, *Rocky Horror* entered the consciousness as the ultimate cult/midnight/audience participation

movie. Because of it, it seemed inconceivable to many that you would watch the movie any *other* way, or perhaps actually keep quiet as it unspooled. Jump ahead nearly twenty-five years, and another 20th Century-Fox release was about to get a similar treatment.

Supposedly inspired by hearing that a senior citizen center (in either Glasgow or Inverness, depending on the source) passed around the lyrics to its occupants so that they could enjoy a showing of MGM's 1954 musical *Seven Brides for Seven Brothers* all the more, an event organizer for the 1998 London Gay and Lesbian Film Festival hit upon the idea of applying this audience participation approach to their one-time showing of *The Sound of Music*. The tremendous response to the screening caught the attention of theater producer David Johnson, who arranged for a London repertory house, Prince Charles Cinema (located at 7 Leicester Place), to present the movie with subtitles (by Martin Wagner of London's National Film Theatre) for a few performances starting on August 13, 1999.

The audience participation version of *The Sound of Music* makes the transatlantic crossing to America, this showing taking place in Wisconsin.

Nuns o' fun. Wimpled audience members strut their stuff to the *Sing-along-a Sound of Music.*

The Prince Charles, which had begun life as a live theatre when it opened in 1962, failed in this department and went over to cinema exhibition in 1965. After a complete overhauling, it reopened for movies in 1969 with an increase of 631 seats. It thereafter concentrated on showing current titles, foreign films, revivals, porn (*Emmanuelle*), pseudo-porn (*Caligula* ran for some time), and cult items. A subtitled *TSOM* would fit the bill.

Despite what writer Anthony Lane would describe as "a scuzzy print" with "alarming color shifts as the reels change," this all-new way of experiencing a title that was beloved by many, and just as derided and ripe for irreverent exhibition by others, became a hit attraction, with twice-a-week showings, on Friday evenings and Sunday afternoons. Like *Rocky Horror,* audiences didn't simply come casual to chime in on "Climb Ev'ry Mountain," but took the whole thing to another level of kitschy celebration, not only dressing as nuns and curtain-clad Trapp kids, but reaching for surreal levels of the outrageous. There was a costume competition, after all, with winners voted during the movie's intermission.

Among those seen over the years were people passing themselves off as Brown Paper Packages Tied Up with String; Girls in White Dresses with Blue Satin Sashes; Ray, a Drop of Golden Sun (a fellow in a Lycra yellow body suit); Alps; and Goats (with and without lonely goatherds). An emcee presided over the event, which attracted not just the expected gay contingent ("Don't worry if you can't sing," an emcee was quoted as saying to the crowd, "the gay men in the audience will carry you"), but families and the after-work crowd as well. For those looking for a little something extra to pump up their participation, the theatre sold a gift pack consisting of such items as fake edelweiss; cough drops; a head scarf; and a small foam rubber nun to stick on your finger. (Other venues would add such choice paraphernalia as an invitation to the Trapp ball and a party popper to snap when the captain and Maria first kiss.)

By the winter of the following year the *Sing A-Long-A* (as it was known) had grown so big that it was decided that further subtitled prints of *TSOM* would have to start traveling to cinemas in other parts of Great Britain. And of course, it would travel to the U.S. as well.

The film managed to snag Manhattan's best movie theatre, the Ziegfeld, for multiple showings, beginning on September 7, 2000. A press release informed audiences that they could "Sing along with Julie! Wave your edelweiss! Cheer the Von Trapp kids! Bark at Rolf! Boo the Nazis! Hiss the Baroness! Join in earnest choruses of 'Climb Ev'ry Mountain.'" The faux goats and nuns showed up for a period, until the venue had to clear the way for current movies. The print ended up elsewhere in the city, including the Loews State Theatre 4, under the Virgin Megastore in Times Square.

Over on the West Coast, the movie capital figured they could show up all the other venues by booking the film at no less than the Hollywood Bowl, for a June 30, 2001 screening. This proved another success, and so the hallowed venue made it an annual tradition, with special appearances by various combinations of the actors who played the Trapp children in the movie. (Charmian Carr devoted an entire chapter to these events in her 2000 book *Forever Liesl*, describing the fun she has had attending them.)

The *Sing-a-long* (or *Sing A-Long-A*, depending on where it played) continued to circulate at various theatres throughout the world, sometimes bringing the movie back to some of the same places it had screened during its initial, reserved-seat run (the 5th Avenue Theatre in Seattle, which had hosted the road show run of *TSOM* starting in March 1965, for example, first ran the *Sing-a-long* in January 2009 and then brought it back several times afterwards).

While most theatres booked the movie for a few performances and then moved on, the Prince Charles made it a staple of its schedule, even after the theatre was twinned in 2008. It paved the way for similar showings there of subtitled sing-a-long-a versions of *Moulin Rouge!, Hairspray, Dirty Dancing, The Muppet Christmas Carol, Joseph and the Amazing Technicolor Dreamcoat*, and *Grease*.

The Salzburg Marionette Theatre's (Salzburger Marionettentheater) presentation of *The Sound of Music*

It was only fitting that Salzburg's venerable institution present a puppet version of *The Sound of Music*, since their stringed creations had served as the inspiration for "The Lonely Goatherd" sequence in the movie. Despite initial requests for the theatre to participate in the movie back in 1964, they passed, allowing Bil Baird and his team to take over.

The Salzburg marionettes date back to 1913, when Professor Anton Aicher presented a version of Mozart's *Bastien und Bastienne* and met with enough

Salzburg's fabled Marionette Theatre got into the act when they created an acclaimed puppet version of the Rodgers and Hammerstein musical.

success that he expanded the repertoire over the years, his shows becoming a favorite attraction of the city, as well as other countries where he toured. At the time *TSOM* company arrived to film in the city, the marionettes were staging their shows at the Kapitelsaal in Salzburg, where they had moved in 1962. They remained in this location until July 1971, when they took up residence at their current location, the Salzburger Marionettentheater at Schwarzstraße 24 between the Landestheater and the Mozarteum, adjacent to the Mirabell Gardens made famous in *TSOM*.

In 2007, under the direction of Richard Hamburger, the Rodgers and Hammerstein musical became a part of the company's repertoire, although it did not debut in Austria but first toured the United States as a sort of "out of country" tryout for the show. (The marionettes, approximately three-feet high, required multiple versions dependent on the character's costume changes, as they were not able to be redressed during the show.)

Opening at the Dallas Theatre Center on November 2, 2007 for three evenings, *The Sound of Music* (marionette-style) then toured for five weeks. The rest of the schedule was as follows:

Laurie Auditorium at Trinity University in San Antonio, TX (November 5); Philadelphia's Kimmel Center for the Performing Arts (November 8–10); Princeton's McCarter Theatre (November 12); Fulton Opera House in Lancaster, PA (November 13–16)—as the Fulton Theatre this was the very same venue where the movie of *TSOM* had its local reserved-seat engagement back in 1966; Shriver Hall in Baltimore, MD (November 17–18); the Phillips Center Black Box Theatre, University of Florida in Gainesville, FL (November 21 and 23); the Flynn Center for the Performing Arts in Burlington, VT (November 27); New Jersey Performing Arts Center's Victoria Theatre in Newark, NJ (November 30 and Dec. 1–2); the Auditorium in Roberts Hall at

Rhode Island College, Providence, RI (December 3); and finally New York's Metropolitan Museum of Art, where it was staged at the Grace Rainey Rogers Auditorium (December 7–9).

The recorded voices for the marionettes were provided mostly by Broadway regulars, with Christiane Noll as Maria and Martin Vidnovic as Captain von Trapp. The supporting vocal cast consisted of: Kelsey Fowler (Marta), Joy Franz (Sister Berthe/Frau Schmidt), Jenn Gambatese (Louisa), Kylie Goldstein (Gretl), Jonathan Groff (Rolf/Friedrich), Matthew Gumley (Kurt), Betsy Hogg (Brigitta), Jeanne Lehman (Mother Abbess), Michael McCarty (Franz/Baron Elberfeld/ Admiral von Schreiber), Crista Moore (Elsa/Sister Margaretta), Jennifer Hope Wills (Sister Sophia/Liesl), and Bill Youmans (Max Detweiler/Herr Zeller).

Among the puppeteers were Philippe Brunner, Pierre Droin, Vladimir Fediakov, Heide Hölzl, Gerda Michel, Michaela Obermayr, Emanuel Paulus, Pavel Tikhonov, Vladimir Tikhonov, Eva Wiener, and Ursula Winzer.

The design team included Chris Barreca (scenic designer), Anita Yavich (costume and puppet designer), David Budries (sound), and David Rosenmeyer (musical direction). Pierre Monnerat was the marionette sculptor, while Vladimir Fediakov and Pavel Tikhonov were the puppet makers. Larry Blank conducted the Istropolis Philharmonic Orchestra for the recorded score.

Encouraged by rave reviews, the show (running approximately 1 hour and 45 minutes and therefore requiring edits to the piece) finally opened in Salzburg on May 9, 2008 and became a staple of the Marionettentheater.

The production also traveled to Athens in 2008, while a French version played in Paris for four weeks during Christmastime 2010.

The Sound of Music Live!

Airdate: NBC; Thursday, December 5, 2013; 8–11:00 p.m. EST
Storyline Entertainment, Sony Pictures Television, Universal Television.

Directed by Beth McCarthy-Miller. Theatrical Direction by Rob Ashford. "The Sound of Music" Adapted for Television by Austin Winsberg. Choreography by Rob Ashford. Executive Producers, Craig Zadan & Neil Meron. Suggested by "The Story of the Trapp Family Singers." Music by Richard Rodgers. Lyrics by Oscar Hammerstein II. Book by Howard Lindsay and Russel Crouse. Produced by Priscilla Taussig. Music Director, David Chase. Production Designer, Derek McLane. Lighting Designer, Robert Dickinson. Costume Designer, Catherine Zuber. Casting by Bernard Telsey, CSA, Abbie Brady-Dalton, CSA. Assistant Directors, Stefani Cohen, Susan Kopensky. Production Supervisor, Lesley Jill Nathan. Supervising Technical Director, Bob Muller. Music Produced by David Chase, Doug Besterman, Frank Wolf. Orchestrations by Doug Besterman. Original Broadway Orchestrations by Robert Russell Bennett. Original Choral and Incidental Music Arrangements by Trude Rittmann. Music Coordinator: Janet Weber. Head Hair and Wig Design, David Bryan Brown. Make-Up Design, Joseph A. Campayno.

CAST: Carrie Underwood (Maria Rainer), Stephen Moyer (Captain von Trapp), Laura Benanti (Elsa Schraeder), Christian Borle (Max Detweiler), Audra McDonald (Mother Abbess), Ariane Rinehart (Liesl von Trapp), Michael Campayno (Rolf Gruber), Sophia Caruso (Brigitta), Peyton Ella (Gretl), Michael Nigro (Friedrich), Grace Rundhaug (Marta), Ella Watts (Louisa), Joe West (Kurt), Jessica Molaskey (Sister Berthe), Christiane Noll (Sister Margaretta), Elena Shaddow (Sister Sophia), Kristine Nielsen (Frau Schmidt), C.J. Wilson (Herr Zeller), Sean Cullen (Franz), John Bolger (Admiral von Scrieber), Michael Park (Baron Elberfeld), Stowe Brown (Postulant/Nun), Catherine Brunell (Frau Zeller), Paula Leggett Chase (Baroness Elberfeld), Brandon Henschel (Lieutenant),Ward Billeisen,

NBC's heavily promoted presentation of *The Sound of Music Live!*

Jason Boyd, Ashley Brown, Nikki Renée Daniels, Adrienne Danrich, Margot de La Barre, Gina Ferrall, Jennie Ford, Bob Gaynor, Rayanne Gonzales, Joy Hermalyn, Leah Horowitz, David Hull, Autumn Hurlbert, Andrea Jones-Sojola, Jordan Lage, Marty Lawson, Shannon Lewis, Dyney Morton, Linda Mugleston, Laura Shooper, Megan Sikora, Georgia Stitt, Alex Michael Stott, Matt Wall, Karl Warden, Rema Webb, Charlie Williams, Samantha Zack (Dancers/Chorus), Cameron Adams, Wendi Bergamini (Nuns)

Executive producers Craig Zadan and Neil Meron had a habit of dusting off previously filmed properties like *The Music Man, Brian's Song,* and *A Raisin in the Sun* and doing television remakes that didn't exactly wipe away memories of their superior predecessors. Therefore, it might have seemed equally superfluous when it was announced that they would be presenting a new version of *The Sound of Music* for the small screen. This near-sacrilegious suggestion was somewhat abated by the fact that this was not going to be so much a "remake" of the movie as a direct adaptation of the Broadway show. What's more—and this was the real selling point—it would be done live. Suddenly, what seemed rather wrong-headed became highly intriguing.

Carrie Underwood (as Maria) leads the children through "Do-Re-Mi" in this scene from *The Sound of Music Live!*

Although television used to do this sort of thing on a regular basis in its earlier days, live musical productions had pretty much become a thing of the past. Chief among the notable live presentations were the March 7, 1955 (NBC) adaptation of Broadway's *Peter Pan* (for *Producers' Showcase*), with Mary Martin recreating her stage role (she would do it a second time, live, on January 9, 1956), and Rodgers and Hammerstein's one and only original work written for the medium, *Cinderella* (CBS, March 31, 1957), with Julie Andrews in the lead.

Making sure that there would be tremendous interest in the new version of *TSOM* from the word "go," the producers chose Carrie Underwood to fill the role of Maria. Since winning the fourth season of *American Idol*, Underwood had turned into a country music superstar, with six Grammy Awards and such hit singles as "Before He Cheats," "Jesus, Take the Wheel," and "Blown Away" to her name. She'd already tested the waters as an actress, playing a pharmaceutical sales rep on an episode of the CBS sitcom *How I Met Your Mother*, and a church leader helping a maimed surfer regain confidence, in the theatrical feature *Soul Surfer*. While neither of these suggested untapped depths, all were certain that Underwood could pull off a full-scale lead, and her casting was announced in late November 2012, more than a year before the show was broadcast.

Wisely, the staging of the piece was given over to someone with experience in musical theatre. This job landed on Rob Ashford, who had received Tony Awards for choreographing *Thoroughly Modern Millie* (2002) and *Cry-Baby* (2008), and had made the leap to director-choreographer with the revivals of *Promises, Promises* (2010) and *How to Succeed in Business Without Really Trying* (2011). The woman responsible for directing the piece for television was Beth McCarthy-Miller, a veteran of such series as *Saturday Night Live* and *30 Rock*.

While the production followed Howard Lindsay and Russel Crouse's book for the most part (the adaptation was credited to *Gossip Girl* producer-writer Austin

Winsberg), there were compromises. Insomuch as "Something Good" had become the sanctioned replacement number for "An Ordinary Couple," the former was heard on the telecast, although a separate mention in the credits of Richard Rodgers being both composer and lyricist of this particular song was nowhere to be found. Cross-over scenes that had been included in the original in order to cover up scene changes (the frightened girls in the hallway with their candles, et al.) were no longer needed. Rather than use a Manhattan space, the show would be broadcast from the Grumman Studios in Bethpage on Long Island, about thirty miles from New York City. Cost of the production came in close to $9 million.

Additional casting included one of the stars of HBO's popular vampire series *True Blood*, U.K.-born Stephen Moyer (at forty-four he was closer in age to the real Captain von Trapp than thirty-four-year-old Christopher Plummer and thirty-five-year-old Theodore Bikel had been); four-time Tony-winner Audra McDonald as the Mother Abbess, a bit of color-blind casting that made the Nazis seem implausibly tolerant, although her vocal abilities made her a sublime choice; Laura Benanti as Elsa, a clever choice for those in the know, since she had played Maria in the 1998–99 Broadway revival of *The Sound of Music*; and Christian Borle, Tony Award winner for *Peter and the Star Catcher*, as Max. Not surprisingly, relative unknowns were chosen for the Trapp children.

The amount of advance advertising on the production was extreme to say the least; NBC had a great deal riding on this "experiment" and wasn't about to let it slip by unheralded. There was even an hour-long, behind-the-scenes promotional special aired on Thanksgiving Eve, *The Making of "The Sound of Music Live!"* (NBC; November 27, 2013). This included glimpses of the casting process, rehearsals, set building, and cast recording. Underwood summed up the anticipated program: "It's like you went to a Broadway show, except we're going to be in your living room."

The telecast was going forward with several disadvantages. Modern audiences, for one, weren't accustomed to seeing something on television so clearly stage-bound with no audible reaction from an audience for applause or laughter, giving the show a very muted, rather lifeless feel. There was also the problem of utilizing a book that had pretty much been declared lacking compared to the improvements Ernest Lehman had made in the movie script; viewers who were only familiar with the motion picture would now see a good deal of the flaws that had been smoothed over in the transfer. Most unfortunate of all the presentation's drawbacks turned out to be its leading lady, as Underwood simply was not a good actress, to put it mildly. Her stiff and hesitant emoting came under a barrage of criticism and hostile comments from both reviewers and the even less charitable bloggers throughout the Internet. (Among those weighing in were the movie's original Gretl, Kym Karath, who mentioned watching the event with cinematic siblings Charmian Carr and Angela Cartwright and being extremely disappointed in the results.)

As far as on-camera glitches were concerned, Underwood looked about to trip on the hillside for a millisecond while performing the title tune; Benanti had the train of her dress walked upon at the Trapp party; and John Bolger (as Admiral von Schreiber) became tongue-tied during his one scene with Captain von Trapp. Otherwise, there was nothing too glaring or embarrassing going out before millions of viewers. These minor glitches were later omitted for the DVD release and replaced by corrected footage.

If it was clear that Underwood was the biggest detriment, she might also have been its greatest draw, as the show won its night in the ratings, with an estimated viewership of 18.5 million. NBC was thrilled enough to eagerly request another such presentation of a live (and audience-familiar) musical for the future, ultimately settling on another Mary Martin title, *Peter Pan*. A second "encore" airing of *TSOM Live!* took place on Saturday, December 14th; a soundtrack (*Music from the NBC Television Event*) was made available two days before the broadcast on Sony Masterworks; and the DVD was in stores by December 17th, in time for maximum Christmas sales. On Sunday, December 22nd, ABC aired the real thing, *The Sound of Music* film, and earned their best ratings for the movie in years.

The Sound of Music Live!

Music from the NBC Television Event
Soundtrack; Sony Masterworks B00FGGN7LW; Release date: December 3, 2013

1. Preludium (McDonald, Noll, Molaskey, Shaddow) (2:56)
2. The Sound of Music (Underwood) (3:06)
3. Maria (McDonald, Noll, Molaskey, Shaddow) (3:15)
4. My Favorite Things (McDonald, Underwood) (3:02)
5. Do-Re-Mi (Underwood, Rinehart, Nigro, Watts, West, Caruso, Rundhaug, Ella) (5:01)
6. Sixteen Going on Seventeen (Rinehart, Campayno) (5:11)
7. The Lonely Goatherd (Underwood, Rinehart, Nigro, Watts, West, Caruso, Rundhaug, Ella) (3:28)
8. How Can Love Survive? (Benanti, Borle) (3:06)
9. Reprise: The Sound of Music (Moyer, Rinehart, Nigro, Watts, West, Caruso, Rundhaug, Ella) (2:07)
10. The Grand Waltz (David Chase) (1:29)
11. Ländler (David Chase) (2:00)
12. So Long, Farewell (Rinehart, Nigro, Watts, West, Caruso, Rundhaug, Ella) (2:54)
13. Climb Ev'ry Mountain (McDonald) (2:46)
14. No Way to Stop It (Borle, Benanti, Moyer) (3:08)
15. Something Good (Underwood, Moyer) (2:54)
16. Processional & Maria (The Wedding) (McDonald, Noll, Molaskey, Shaddow) (2:48)
17. Reprise: Sixteen Going on Seventeen (Underwood, Rinehart) (2:12)
18. Reprise: Do-Re-Mi (The Concert) (Underwood, Moyer, Rinehart, Nigro, Watts, West, Caruso, Rundhaug,Ella) (1:18)

19. Edelweiss (The Concert) (Moyer, Underwood, Rinehart, Nigro, Watts, West, Caruso, Rundhaug, Ella) (2:09)
20. Reprise: So Long, Farewell (The Concert) (Underwood, Moyer, Rinehart, Nigro, Watts, West, Caruso, Rundhaug, Ella) (1:59)
21. Finale Ultimo: Climb Ev'ry Mountain (McDonald, Noll, Molaskey, Shaddow) (1:37)
22. End Credits (David Chase) (2:56)

The Sound of Music on Television

The Long Prime-Time Run of the Film

*T*he *Sound of Music* would take eleven years to make it from the big screen to television, and when it arrived, while not breaking any Nielsen records, as one might have presumed, it certainly was a ratings hit. As a result, it became a staple not only on television but in prime-time broadcasts, a most unusual achievement in the age of cable, home video, and other choices for viewing.

Here are the prime-time airings it received (so far).

Prime-Time Broadcast #1:
ABC, February 29, 1976

An area-specific New York City television publication announcing the small screen debut of *The Sound of Music*.

Nearly eleven years to the day after its theatrical debut, *The Sound of Music* made it to prime-time television amid great fanfare, with ABC paying $15 million for a package deal with Fox that included a one-time airing of the musical. The deal, which was announced in December 1974, gave ABC air rights to eleven other, more recent Fox titles including *Cinderella Liberty, The Paper Chase,* and *Claudine.*

Allowing the film to dominate its Sunday night schedule, ABC placed the movie in a three-hour, twenty-five-minute time slot between 7:00 and 10:25 p.m. EST. While normally holding aside 9:00–11:00 p.m. for its *ABC Sunday Night Movie,* this showing required the preempting of the soon-to-be-cancelled *The Swiss Family Robinson* and the Top 10 hit *The Six Million Dollar Man.* Following the broadcast, and therefore receiving a very desirable lead-in audience, was the preview episode of Carl Reiner's new sitcom, *Good Heavens,* to commence at 10:25, time approximate. As competition, NBC was offering *The Wonderful World of Disney*'s premiere of "The Survival of Sam the Pelican"; *Ellery Queen* (the guest cast of which, ironically, included Broadway's Captain von Trapp, Theodore Bikel); and a *Columbo* episode featuring Jack Cassidy. On CBS was *60 Minutes*; *The Sonny and Cher Comedy Hour* (with guests Don Knotts and Chastity Bono); a rerun of *Kojak*; and the unaired pilot of a foundering detective series, *Bronk*. In the New York syndication market, WOR was offering another classic musical, Judy Garland's 1954 version of *A Star Is Born*. Because of having to compete with *TSOM*, both *Kojak* and *Columbo* posted their lowest Nielsen numbers all season.

TV Guide heralded the broadcast with a close-up (a badge of honor for all programs considered important) and a two-page essay by Maria von Trapp giving her impressions on the movie and featuring a picture of herself at thirty-five years of age. Maria's hearty and enthusiastic endorsement of the movie helped to compensate for *TV Guide* critic-in-residence Judith Crist's highly negative condemnation of *TSOM* in her weekly column.

When *The Sound of Music* made its television debut in 1976, it was treated as a very big event.

Audiences were just as quick to dismiss Crist's assessment as they had been a decade earlier, and *TSOM* was, not surprisingly, a winner, drawing a total-household rating of 33.6 and a 49 share of the television audience, making it the top-ranking program to air that week. It also gave ABC the best ratings for any night all that season. (This made it ABC's second most-watched theatrical movie shown that season; *Jeremiah Johnson*, starring Robert Redford, making the top of the list.)

Prime-Time Broadcast #2:

NBC, February 25, 1979

Three years lapsed before *TSOM* would have its second telecast and thereby begin its twenty-one-year run on the NBC prime-time schedule. To ensure it held exclusive rights to the movie over this period, the network shelled out a staggering $21.5 million to 20th Century-Fox.

Once again the film was given a Sunday night, 7:00 p.m. EST starting point, running for three and a half hours, thereby qualifying it as a presentation of NBC's omnibus series *The Big Event* (which commonly held the 8 to 10 p.m. slot). Preempted was *The Wonderful World of Disney*, while an abbreviated edition of the customarily hour-long *Weekend* followed the film's showing. Strongest opposition was ABC's final installment of *Roots: The Next Generations*, this particular episode boasting Marlon Brando's first acting role on television in thirty years. CBS went less high-falutin' with a presentation of *Celebrity Battle of the Sexes*, which included a bicycle race between Gary Coleman and Quinn Cummings.

TSOM was again given a close-up by *TV Guide*, as well as a three-fourths-page ad calling it "The world's favorite movie" and listing among the cast "seven beautiful children." As fate would have it, *A Star Is Born* once again found itself scheduled against the mighty musical in the New York market, this time on WNEW Channel 5.

Nielsen reported a 21.6 rating and a 30 share to rank *TSOM* 20th of all programs aired that week. It was ranked the 22nd most-watched theatrical movie (out of 199 titles) to air on prime time during the 1978–79 season (*Rocky* was #1).

In June 1978, it was announced that the BBC paid $4 million for the rights to show *TSOM* over a nine-year period.

- Note: At this point, *The Sound of Music* was now available to be purchased for home viewing on video cassette, which would forever reflect upon its television ratings. A title this heavily purchased by consumers would never again rank so high on the Nielsen charts.

Prime-Time Broadcast #3:

NBC, December 2, 1979

Giving *TSOM* its second prime-time showing within the same calendar year, NBC ran a half-page ad in *TV Guide* to promote the third broadcast but angered fans when they chose to cut nearly a half-hour from the print, coming in around 145 minutes for this showing, with 30-minutes plus for commercials and bumpers. Unfortunately, this was the version that would air for years to come. Among the missing footage were the nuns singing in the chapel near the beginning, the captain talking about going to Vienna at the dinner table, and the captain questioning his children about the berries.

Again starting at 7:00 p.m. EST on a Sunday night, this airing went under the network's *Big Event* banner and ended at 10:00 p.m. *The Wonderful World of Disney* was preempted during the 7–8:00 p.m. slot.

Ranked 32nd for the week's programs with a 28 share.

Prime-Time Broadcast #4:

NBC, November 27, 1980

TSOM left Sunday behind to make its only appearance (to date) as a Thanksgiving presentation, taking up the 8–11:00 p.m. slot. Thursday was now an NBC movie night, so the only program being preempted from the regular schedule was the short-lived sports omnibus *Games People Play*. Among the competition was ABC's premiere of the Tom Hanks sitcom *Bosom Buddies*. This time *TV Guide*'s half-page *TSOM* ad spoke of "a love that survives every obstacle in its path!"

With a 16.0 rating, 29 share, *TSOM* came in 70th on the list of 185 theatrical motion pictures to run in prime time during the 1980–81 season (*Hooper* was first).

Prime-Time Broadcast #5:

NBC, January 24, 1982

Back to Sunday evening at 7:00 p.m. EST, the three-hour *TSOM* airs for the first time without a special ad in *TV Guide*. *CHiPs* is preempted, while the final hour of the telecast fills what is commonly the first hour of *NBC Sunday Night at the Movies*. ABC competes with the premiere telecast of the 1979 disaster epic *Meteor*, while over at CBS the 16th Super Bowl overlaps with the beginning of *TSOM*.

Nielsen reported a 14.4 rating, 20 share for this fifth broadcast of the movie. *TSOM* was ranked 95th among 177 theatrical movie airings that season (the two-part broadcast of *Superman* took the first and second spots).

Prime-Time Broadcast #6:

NBC, May 27, 1983

Making its latest appearance yet in the television season, *TSOM* found itself on the Friday leading into Memorial Day weekend, airing from 8–11:00 p.m. EST. It also marked the first time it was not officially part of an already established time slot for movies. Since rerun season was in full swing, ABC's movie *The Sins of Dorian Gray* (starring Anthony Perkins) was about the only notable new addition on the competing networks. Preempted on NBC were the already cancelled *Powers of Matthew Star*, the popular *Knight Rider*, and an hour reserved for specials.

Thanks to a 16.5 rating and a 30 share, *TSOM* led the night in all programming. It also made a considerable jump back up the list of 181 theatrical features shown during the prime-time season, ranking #49. (Top-rated movie was *9 to 5*.)

Prime-Time Broadcast #7:

NBC, December 23, 1984

After having skipped the 1983–84 season, *TSOM* is scheduled for the first time as a Christmas season event, taking over the 8–11:00 p.m. period on Sunday, directly opposite a rerun broadcast of the 1978 blockbuster movie *Superman*. As this week's *NBC Sunday Night at the Movies*, *TSOM* was required to preempt (for the second time in a row) *Knight Rider*.

It's third place for *TSOM* with a 14.1 rating, 23 share, following both *Superman* and the CBS lineup that includes repeats of *Murder, She Wrote* and *Trapper John M.D.* The film was #40 for the 1984–85 season among 123 theatrical movies aired. Another Julie Andrews musical, *Victor Victoria*, was #1.

Prime-Time Broadcast #8:

NBC, March 28, 1986

Having covered Thanksgiving and Christmas, *TSOM* is now scheduled for the Easter holidays, airing on Good Friday from 8 to 10:00 p.m. EST and receiving a half-page ad ("One of America's favorite things!") in *TV Guide* for the first time in years. As if chasing it around the schedule, *Knight Rider* is preempted by the movie for the third time; others on hiatus for the night are *Riptide* and *Miami Vice*. Competition includes the premieres of two short-lived ABC comedies, *Mr. Sunshine* and *Joe Bash*.

Although the 15.4 rating and 27 share were impressive, *TSOM* actually came in second place for the night, bested by a CBS rerun of the 1983 Chevy Chase comedy *National Lampoon's Vacation*. This rating put *TSOM* at #23 for the season among 120 theatrical movies on prime time. *Mr. Mom* was in the top spot.

Prime-Time Broadcast #9:
NBC, December 28, 1986

Wedged into the customarily low-rated week between Christmas and New Year's, *TSOM* once again takes the Sunday, 8–11:00 p.m. EST slot, up against mostly reruns and CBS's preview of the western series *Outlaws*.

It is worth noting that *TV Guide*'s Judith Crist was softening in her assessment of the film, her weekly column assuring us that despite the half-hour of missing footage, the movie's "prime pleasures remain." Two sitcoms, *Valerie* and *Easy Street*, were bumped from the schedule for the film's first hour, while the second and third hours filled the regular NBC movie position.

Nielsen rating was 16.7, which put it below CBS's *Murder, She Wrote* rerun and *Outlaws*, but above the NBC lineup of Disney and a repeat of the James Bond movie *For Your Eyes Only*. *TSOM* was the 16th most-watched theatrical movie for the season; with *Raiders of the Lost Ark* the highest rated of the batch of 116 titles.

Prime-Time Broadcast #10:
NBC, December 18, 1987

This week television viewers get a double dose of Julie Andrews in Salzburg, as ABC aired the special *Julie Andrews . . . the Sound of Christmas* two days before NBC's *TSOM* Friday, 8–11:00 p.m. broadcast. Julie's variety special found her revisiting some of the sites used in the movie and even opened with the familiar strains of "The Sound of Music" building to her appearance on a snowcapped hilltop.

The 13.9 rating, 24 share means the broadcast was topped that night by both CBS's *Dallas* and ABC's *20/20*. *TSOM* was #21 for the season on the list of 103 theatrical features aired in prime time. *Beverly Hills Cop* topped the list.

Prime-Time Broadcast #11:
NBC, December 30, 1988

Now listed in the *TV Guide* as a "holiday perennial" and erroneously identified by them as the "8th network" broadcast (instead of the 11th), *TSOM* is in its Friday, 8–11:00 p.m. EST slot for the second year in a row. The first two hours take over a hiatus between regular programming, while hour three preempts *Miami Vice*.

The 13 Nielsen rating (23 share) means that *TSOM* was, for the most part, lagging behind the ABC lineup of reruns. It is #30 for the season on the list of 133 theatrical movie airings. The first position belongs to *Top Gun*.

Prime-Time Broadcast #12:
NBC, December 25, 1989

After hovering around the actual holiday for previous broadcasts, *TSOM* gets its first airing on Christmas Day (Monday, 8–11:00 p.m. EST). Bumped for the first hour were the sitcoms *ALF* and *The Hogan Family*; the remaining hours were the regularly scheduled movie time.

With an 11 Nielsen rating, 20 share, *TSOM* was no competition for ABC's *Monday Night Football*. Theatrical movie ranking (among 89 titles) for the season, #32 (#1: *Lethal Weapon*).

Prime-Time Broadcast #13:
NBC, March 29, 1991

It's back to Easter for the 1990–91 season broadcast, again at 8–11:00 p.m. EST. The preempted series are *Open Time* and *Hunter*, while the final hour was a hiatus period following the cancellation of the revision of *Dark Shadows*.

Nielsen: 10.4 rating, 19 share; this is trumped by the ABC lineup (*Full House, Family Matters, Perfect Strangers, Baby Talk, 20/20*) of both new episodes and repeats. Theatrical movie ranking (among 120 titles) for the season, #58 (#1: *Three Men and a Baby*).

Prime-Time Broadcast #14:
NBC, December 23, 1991

For another 8–11:00 p.m. showing, *The Fresh Prince of Bel Air* and *Blossom* stepped aside for *TSOM*'s first hour; the rest of the musical takes up the customary Monday night movie time.

One of its less successful airings, the 10.6 rating places it after both the CBS lineup of reruns and ABC's *Monday Night Football*. Theatrical movie ranking (on a list of 122 possible titles) for the season, #50 (#1: *Kindergarten Cop*).

Prime-Time Broadcast #15:
NBC, April 11, 1993

Another Easter Sunday showing, 8–11:00 p.m., bumping *I Witness Video* before leading into the regular movie time slot.

The 10.5 Nielsen rating places it below both ABC's broadcast of 1989's *Next of Kin* and CBS's premiere of 1989's *Steel Magnolias*.

Prime-Time Broadcast #16:

NBC, April 24, 1994

For the first time in more than a decade, *TSOM* is aired without linking it to any sort of holiday celebration. *SeaQuest DVS* is preempted for the first hour of the 8–11:00 p.m. Sunday night broadcast of *TSOM*.

A 10.8 Nielsen is topped by ABC's repeat of the 1985 Clint Eastwood western *Pale Rider* and on CBS a repeat of *Murder, She Wrote* and a new version of *The Yearling*.

Prime-Time Broadcast #17:

NBC, April 9, 1995

As a way of celebrating the film's thirtieth anniversary, NBC finally decides to reinstate the edited footage (although the entr'acte is still not included), thereby stretching the time slot from three hours to four, starting at 7:00 p.m. on this Palm Sunday airing. For the first time in years the movie receives both an ad and a close-up in *TV Guide*, but the big attraction is having Julie Andrews actually serve as host for the broadcast. This night *TSOM* goes up against one of ABC's movie perennials, Cecil B. DeMille's 1956 epic *The Ten Commandments*. Off the schedule for the night are two of NBC's sci-fi series, *Earth 2* and *SeaQuest DVS*.

TSOM comes in third in the competition (with an 11.5 rating), with *Commandments* on top and CBS's repeat of 1991's *Robin Hood: Prince of Thieves* in second place.

Prime-Time Broadcast #18:

NBC, December 22, 1995

After the hopeful sign back in April of showing *TSOM* intact, NBC once again reverts to the edited print in a three-hour, 8-11 p.m. EST time slot for this Friday showing. *TV Guide* does run an ad, however, heralding it as "America's Most Beloved Musical!" *Unsolved Mysteries*, *Dateline NBC*, and *Homicide: Life on the Street* are preempted.

With only an 8.8 rating, *TSOM* is below a repeat of ABC's *Family Matters* and *20/20* that evening.

Prime-Time Broadcast #19:

NBC, Dec. 20, 1996

Another Friday night, pre-Christmas, 8–11:00 p.m. airing. The very same series from the previous season (*Unsolved Mysteries*, *Dateline*, and *Homicide*) are preempted.

ABC is definitely the winner this time out, with repeats of *Family Matters, Boy Meets World, Sabrina—the Teenage Witch, Clueless,* and *20/20* all doing better than *TSOM*'s 7.8 rating.

[*After this broadcast,* TSOM *will disappear from the next three prime-time season schedules.*]

Prime-Time Broadcast #20:

NBC, December 17, 2000

Sunday, four-hour broadcast, the latter half in the scheduled NBC movie slot, *TSOM* is featured in an "Editor's Choice" box in *TV Guide,* letting viewers know it was being shown "without cuts." Preempted for hours one and two of the movie are *World's Most Amazing Videos* and *Dateline NBC.* This wraps up the movie's twenty-one-year run on NBC.

For its final NBC run, the Nielsen rating is 8.9 with a 14 share and some 14.3 million viewers.

Prime-Time Broadcast #21:

Fox Network, November 30, 2001

With the NBC agreement finally having come to a close, Fox picks up *TSOM* for this one-time airing, taking place on a Friday, 8–11:00 p.m., which means it has opted to show the edited version. *Dark Angel* has been preempted for the first hour, the second hour is in flux before becoming the latest spot for *24,* and 10–11:00 p.m. is the customary news time.

Nielsen reports a 4.7 rating, 8 share, and 6.9 viewers. ABC, CBS, and NBC are able to report better ratings on nearly all of their shows.

Prime-Time Broadcast #22:

ABC, December 29, 2002

TSOM is now back where it first began on network television, on ABC. Happily, they choose to screen it in the longer version, the four-hour broadcast running from 7 to 11:00 p.m. EST on Sunday night. *The Wonderful World of Disney, Alias,* and *The Practice* clear the way this evening.

The 6.7 rating, 11 share, and viewership of 11.5 million make this a formidable competitor that night. This broadcast marks the start of the film's unbroken (to date) run of airings on ABC expressly as a year-end holiday season staple.

Prime-Time Broadcast #23:

ABC, December 27, 2003 (episode 9, season 6 of The Wonderful World of Disney)

This ABC airing of *TSOM* is an oddity, insomuch as rather than simply preempting *The Wonderful World of Disney*, it is treated as an episode of that omnibus series, airing Saturday, 8–11:00 p.m. Although the Disney series more often than not showed either new programming or theatrical features exclusively produced by Walt Disney Productions, there were exceptions. *TSOM* has now taken on such a status as a "family" entertainment that this *Wonderful World* airing might lead some to believe that the fabled Mouse House was behind it.

Two other movies on the Disney show's schedule that same season are *Eloise at Christmas* and *The Princess Diaries*, both of which include Julie Andrews in the cast.

This *TSOM* showing earned a 4.9 rating and a 9 share, which meant it came out ahead of CBS's repeat of the 1999 movie *Wild Wild West* and NBC's marathon of *Boomtown*.

Prime-Time Broadcast #24:

ABC, December 25, 2004 (episode 6, season 7 of The Wonderful World of Disney)

While it has become a holiday season standard, this marks only the second time *TSOM* has aired on Christmas Day. It is also the second and last time it will be treated as a presentation of *The Wonderful World of Disney*. It again airs in the 8–11:00 p.m. time slot, on Saturday.

Nielsen reports a 4 rating, 8 share, with 6.9 million viewers.

Prime-Time Broadcast #25:

ABC, December 17, 2005

A Saturday airing, once again in the four-hour length, shown at 7–11:00 p.m. EST. This time slot is customarily put aside for a movie and sometimes *America's Funniest Home Videos*, or whatever other programming can compensate for the shorter films.

Prime-Time Broadcast #26:

ABC, December 23, 2006

The third Saturday 7 to 11 p.m. EST, four-hour broadcast in a row. Perhaps because the alternatives elsewhere on the dial include episodes of *Cops* and an edition of *Dateline NBC* called "To Catch a Predator," *TV Guide* spotlights *TSOM* as "For the Family." *Saturday Night College Football* is the preempted show. ABC Family is also airing Julie Andrews that night, in a rerun of the 2003 TV movie *Eloise at Christmastime*.

With a 5.4 rating, 10 share, and viewership of 8.3 million, *TSOM* tops the CBS, Fox, and NBC lineups.

Prime-Time Broadcast #27:
ABC Family, April 6, 2007

This family-friendly cable network purchased the rights to *TSOM* for $3 million, thereby sharing it with its sister broadcast network, ABC, over a three-year period. The contract stipulated that ABC Family could show the movie up to seven times each year, but only between January and September. The October through December period was reserved for ABC.

ABC Family first showed the film in a four-hour time slot on Friday, April 6, 2007 with encore showings that weekend on April 7 and 8, also in the 7–11:00 p.m. EST slot.

ABC, December 30, 2007

In a period customarily made up of reruns (between Christmas and New Year's Day), the network airs the four-hour *TSOM* on Sunday, 7–11 p.m. EST. Cleared off the schedule for the night are *America's Funniest Home Videos*, *Extreme Makeover: Home Edition*, *Desperate Housewives*, and *Brothers & Sisters*.

This showing brings *TSOM* a rating of 4.6, an 8 share, and 7.7 million viewers.

ABC, December 28, 2008

What might have been just another post-Christmas *TSOM* airing is notable for being the first HD resolution broadcast. Once again the full version is shown in a four-hour slot, on a Sunday evening, 7–11:00 p.m. Off the schedule for the night, the very same shows from the previous season: *America's Funniest Home Videos*, *Extreme Makeover: Home Edition*, *Desperate Housewives*, and *Brothers & Sisters*.

A 6.5 Nielsen rating, beaten by CBS's *60 Minutes*, *Million Dollar Password*, and a repeat of *Cold Case*.

ABC, December 27, 2009

Taking over yet another Sunday night on ABC, *TSOM* goes up against football on NBC, a two-part finale for FOX's short-lived *Brothers*, and a rerun of one of Tom Selleck's *Jesse Stone* movies, *Thin Ice*.

This time the 18–49 rating was 1.5 with a 4 share, with 6.43 million viewers.

ABC, December 26, 2010

Once again a four-hour Sunday slot presentation, preempting the very same shows it's bumped for four years running. Nielsen reported 4.52 million viewers. (0.9 rating/3 share for adults 18-49).

ABC, December 24, 2011

Having been seen all around the holiday season for years, *TSOM* finally gets a showing on Christmas Eve, slotted into the Saturday night lineup for another four-hour period, thereby giving audiences a break from the usual college football telecasts. Over on NBC, another classic movie that has become a prime-time perennial, *It's a Wonderful Life*, is taking up the entire evening's schedule. While the 174-minute *TSOM* filling up 4 hours is enough of a stretch, this means the 129-minute Frank Capra favorite is required to come up with 1 hour, 51 minutes of extra material to fill the time!

Nielsen ratings posted 3.7 million viewers, with 0.9 rating (adults 18–49)/3 share.

ABC, December 23, 2012

Another Sunday, four-hour airing, 7–11:00 p.m. EST, this one preempting *America's Funniest Home Videos, Once Upon a Time, Revenge,* and *666 Park Avenue.*

This represented an increase from the previous year's telecast, with 5.2 million viewers, a 1.1 rating for adults 18–49, and a 3 share. The film, not surprisingly, couldn't compete with NBC's *Sunday Night Football* but trumped the CBS schedule.

ABC, December 22, 2013

This telecast of *TSOM* had the distinction of coming only seventeen days after NBC presented their much-heralded live version of the Rodgers & Hammerstein musical. This gave prime-time audiences two Maria von Trapps in the same month!

Once again, *TSOM* filled ABC's entire Sunday night schedule, preempting three of the same programs from the previous year, *America's Funniest Home Videos, Once Upon a Time,* and *Revenge,* as well as *Betrayal.*

The 1.3 rating/4 share was an 18 percent increase from the previous year's showing.

ABC, December 21, 2014

It's the eighth Sunday-Before-Christmas broadcast in a row for the network in the 7-11 p.m. slot, as the movie's 50th Anniversary year approaches. The very next evening, the network presented its first airing of the "Sing-A-Long' version of the movie.

The All-Time Highest-Rated Prime-Time Broadcasts of Theatrical Films

In the days before cable and home video/DVD formats, prime-time airings of theatrical features made for blockbuster ratings, with select titles ranking among the most watched programming of all time. The heyday for this was the 1970s. By the 1980s, viewers were looking elsewhere for ways to watch movies.

		Network/Airdate	Rating	Share
1.	*Gone with the Wind* Part 1	NBC, Nov. 7, 1976	47.7	65
2.	*Gone with the Wind* Part 2	NBC, Nov. 8, 1976	47.4	64
3.	*Airport*	ABC, Nov. 11, 1973	42.3	63
4.	*Love Story*	ABC, Oct. 1, 1972	42.3	62
5.	*The Godfather* (Part 2)	NBC, Nov. 18, 1974	39.4	57
6.	*Jaws*	ABC, Nov. 4, 1979	39.1	57
7.	*The Poseidon Adventure*	ABC, Oct. 27, 1974	39.0	62
8.	*True Grit*	ABC, Nov. 12, 1972	38.9	63
9.	*The Birds*	NBC, Jan. 8, 1968	38.9	59
10.	*Patton*	ABC, Nov. 19, 1972	38.5	65
11.	*The Bridge on the River Kwai*	ABC, Sept. 25, 1966	38.3	61
12.	*Jeremiah Johnson*	ABC, Jan. 18, 1976	37.5	56
13.	*Ben-Hur*	CBS, Feb. 14, 1971	37.1	56
14.	*Rocky*	CBS, Feb. 4, 1979	37.1	53
15.	*The Godfather* (Part 1)	NBC, Nov. 16, 1974	37.0	61
16.	*The Wizard of Oz*	CBS, Dec. 13, 1959	36.5	58
17.	*The Wizard of Oz*	CBS, Jan. 26, 1964	35.9	59
18.	*Planet of the Apes*	CBS, Sept. 14, 1973	35.2	60
19.	*The Wizard of Oz*	CBS, Jan. 17, 1965	34.7	49
20.	*Born Free*	CBS, Feb. 22, 1970	34.2	53
21.	*The Wizard of Oz*	CBS, Nov. 3, 1956	33.9	53
22.	**The Sound of Music**	**ABC, Feb. 29, 1976**	**33.6**	**52**
23.	*Bonnie and Clyde*	CBS, Sept. 20, 1973	33.4	38
24.	*The Ten Commandments*	ABC, Feb. 18, 1973	33.2	54
25.	*The Longest Yard*	ABC, Sept. 25, 1977	33.1	53

18

Bringing Home
The Sound of Music

Video, Laserdisc, DVD, and Blu-ray

With the late 1970s advent of home video, a whole new way of movie watching was born, allowing film lovers a chance to not just see films that might have been hard to catch elsewhere, but for the really dedicated ones to *own* a copy. Not surprisingly, *The Sound of Music* phenomenon continued when it came time to transfer it to the home viewing format, and it has never been too far away ever since, making its presence felt through VHS tape, laserdisc, DVD, and Blu-ray. It has conquered them all, racking up further millions for 20th Century-Fox.

Here is a brief history of its various home entertainment releases throughout the years.

March 1979

A two-part pan-and-scan tape (available in Beta or VHS) debuted on Magnetic Video; this marked the first time *TSOM* was made available to buy in a home entertainment format. Retail price, according to *Billboard*, was $79.95. The film was split awkwardly between the tapes, following the "berry picking" scene, after Brigitta suggests the children sing "My Favorite Things" and Liesl jumps in with an agreed "yes," going to black before Brigitta even gets in her last line before the tune.

Magnetic had made a deal with 20th Century-Fox to launch the first batch of studio films on the VHS tape format. Although it has been erroneously stated in several sources that *The Sound of Music* was one of the very first titles made available, it was not yet among the initial batch of fifty that were offered in November 1977. (These included *MASH, The French Connection, Doctor Dolittle, The Longest Day, The King and I,* etc.)

TSOM hit the Billboard Top 40 video sales chart shortly after its debut and still holds the chart's longevity record, of more than 300 weeks and counting.

The first week of *Billboard* tallying the sales on videocassettes, November 17, 1979, found *The Sound of Music* (Magnetic Video, CL-1051) at #3, under two other 20th Century-Fox titles, *Butch Cassidy and the Sundance Kid* (at #1) and *MASH* (#2).

(On the back of the video boxes for the Magnetic releases, *TSOM* was listed first among the titles available.)

Cassettes of the film were first made available in the UK in September 1979, selling at £39.95.

In March 1980, *Billboard* reported that *TSOM* home video was one of the cassettes to be certified gold, meaning it had unit sales of a least 25,000 with a retail list value of $1 million. Others joining it on the "golden" list were three other Magnetic (Fox) features: *MASH*, *Patton*, and *The French Connection*.

The very first home video version of *The Sound of Music* as it appeared in 1979.

1981

TSOM made its laserdisc (pan-and-scan) debut as part of a two-disc set from Magnetic Video. Along with *Patton*, *TSOM* was one of the two priciest titles, at $49.95 (others retailed for $29.95). The botched song list on back (e.g., "Hodcla—Puppet Show" for "The Lonely Goatherd") led one to believe that nobody was paying much attention to facts.

1982

When the studios began to realize the goldmine that could result from the release of their titles for home consumption, Fox very quickly made sure that they took charge, buying out Magnetic Video (for $7.5 million) and becoming 20th Century-Fox Video at the start of 1982 (this, in turn, would become CBS/Fox Video; this partnership lasted until 1991).

Under this label, *The Sound of Music* was reissued on VHS (again on two tapes).

At its very first trade meeting in August 1982, the Video Software Dealers Association polled hundreds of video retailers for most popular releases in several categories. *The Sound of Music* was named "Most Popular Classic Movie, Musical." Other films winning included *Casablanca* (Most Popular Classic Movie, Drama), *Airplane!* (Most Popular Classic Movie, Comedy), and *Jane Fonda's Workout* (Most Popular Instructional Program).

1983

In June 1983, *TSOM* home video was now certified platinum in sales. Other Fox titles making this list at the same time included *All That Jazz*, *Patton*, *The Verdict*, and *Porky's*.

The two-disc CED VideoDisc version of *The Sound of Music* required the actual packaging of the film to be inserted into the player, which would then retrieve the disc and play it.

1985

For its twentieth anniversary, *TSOM* received a third issue on VHS and a second on laserdisc.

April 1986

Another two-set VHS on the CBS Fox label (in Hi-Fi Stereo) was released in 1986 and quickly charted at #28. By June of that year it was ranked #2 on *Billboard*'s list of the best-selling home videos.

It was issued as part of CBS/Fox's Five Star Collection. One of thirty movies for sale at $29.98 (other titles included *West Side Story, Patton,* and *Alien*).

Billboard reported that in home video sales *TSOM* was the #5 best seller of 1986 and #6 in 1987.

August 1989

Fans could at last rejoice: *TSOM* was finally made available on laserdisc in a wide-screen format, approximating the correct ratio of the original theatrical look; price $69.98. For the cover, the familiar image of Julie on her hill was seen under a gray matte banner that had a "Special Widescreen Edition" logo over the title.

September 13, 1990

For the twenty-fifth (Silver) anniversary, only days after the film was screened in 70mm prints in select New York and LA theatres, *TSOM* was finally being treated with *some* degree of prestige on VHS, this CBS/Fox edition including an intro-duction by director Robert Wise and clips from the 1964 documentary *Salzburg: Sight and Sound.* In order to fit on one tape, however, the entr'acte was removed.

It was released as part of a Fox collection of Rodgers and Hammerstein titles, along with *State Fair, Oklahoma!, Carousel, The King and I,* and *South Pacific.* To once again show how much *TSOM* stood higher than these other titles, it is priced at $24.98, as opposed to the other five being $19.98. The two-disc laser set was priced at $69.98.

1992, 1994, and 1996

There were further VHS and laserdisc releases on Fox Video during this period. The 1994 edition is listed as part of "The Rodgers and Hammerstein Collection," while the 1996 edition included the description of "Family Feature" on the box. It was letterboxed and offered in THX sound.

The 30th Anniversary laserdisc, released on December 21, 1994, was the most elaborately packaged to date and contained the most fascinating extras yet.

Side 4 included:

- "Salzburg Sight and Sound," the original fourteen-minute 1964 documentary that circulated in theatres to build anticipation for the movie, was included in its entirety. Charmian Carr hosts and narrates her tour around "the enchanting fairy tale town of music" taking us to Mozart's house, inside Mirabell Palace, Salzburg's glockenspiel, the Hohensalzburg Castle, and the Marionette Theatre. There are clips of filming on Winkler Terrace, at the Rock Riding amphitheater, and Saul Chaplin and choreographers Marc Breaux and Dee Dee Wood working on the timing of the "Do-Re-Mi" number. (A Visual Projects Films, Ltd. production, written and produced by Newton E. Melzer; directed and edited by F.-J. Spieker.)
- Previews and Trailers.
- *The Sound of Music: From Fact to Phenomenon.* This eighty-six-minute documentary is narrated by Claire Bloom and features new appearances by Julie Andrews, Christopher Plummer (who sums up his hesitation about playing the captain as written on the stage with "I knew the Baroness—she could *not* have married a dull man!"), Nicholas Hammond, Charmian Carr, Anna Lee, Portia Nelson, Marni Nixon, Members of the Trapp Family, Oscar's son James Hammerstein, Rodgers & Hammerstein Organization president Theodore S. Chapin, Saul Chaplin, second-unit director Maurice Zuberano, Fox executive Richard D. Zanuck, and Robert Wise. This very comprehensive look at the film and its origins includes background on Maria von Trapp; storyboard and sketches for the film; footage of musical director Bobby Tucker going over songs with the cast; dubbed clips from *The Trapp Family*; stills from Broadway; and more.
- A 24-karat gold CD of the soundtrack made from a new seventy-five-minute master and including previously unreleased music.
- A booklet, "The Saga of the Ernest Lehman Screenplay," detailing the adaptation from stage to screen.
- Interactive archives that chart the pre-production, filming, and post-production of the movie.
- Audio interviews with Ernest Lehman and Daniel Truhitte.
- An eight-page booklet of color images from the film and behind-the-scenes.

August 29, 2000

To commemorate the 35th Anniversary of the movie's release, Fox offered a two-disc DVD (the first time in this format) for $29.98 and a VHS tape for $14.98. Referred to as a hi-def video transfer from the original 65mm film source, with the soundtrack restored and presented in discrete 4.1 Dolby Digital.

The DVD featured commentary by Robert Wise and a DVD-ROM link to *TSOM* websites and events on disc one. The supplemental material on disc two consisted of:

- *Salzburg Sight and Sound*
- *The Sound of Music: From Fact to Phenomenon*
- Audio supplement by Ernest Lehman
- Audio interviews with Julie Andrews and Robert Wise
- DVD-ROM games and links to fan site
- Storyboards, sketches, production stills
- Theatrical trailers, radio and TV spots

40th Anniversary release: November 15, 2005

The extras on this DVD consisted of:

My Favorite Things: Julie Andrews Remembers (63:16)

Deceptively titled, this documentary does not restrict itself to Andrews's memories, but includes interviews with Christopher Plummer; Robert Wise (who died two months before this edition hit the stores); the youngest von Trapp child, Johannes; President of the Rodgers & Hammerstein Organization, Ted Chapin; Andrew Lloyd Webber (explaining the deceptively simple nature of "Do-Re-Mi"); choreographer Dee Dee Wood; Anna Crouse, widow of the show's co-writer Russel Crouse; and Charmian Carr. Plummer offers the very accurate assessment that with this one film his co-star managed to "seduce the world."

One of many different versions of *The Sound of Music* as it continued to be a highly desirable moneymaker on various home viewing formats.

Julie Andrews and Christopher Plummer: A Reminiscence (19:22)

Unencumbered by a moderator, the two stars chat in spontaneous fashion with good humor about making the movie Plummer describes as "It's always there . . . sort of banging on our door."

On Location with The Sound of Music (22:33)

Charmian Carr is the host for this tour of Salzburg, pointing out in detail some of the locations from the film, while others are seen and then compared to the scene from the movie without any explanation of what they are. A highlight has her joining a busload of fans for the Panorama Tour of the locations.

The 2010 Blu-ray release of *The Sound of Music* gave fans a feast of extras, including a music box that played "My Favorite Things."

From Liesl to Gretl: A 40th Anniversary Reunion (33:31)

The seven actors who played the Trapp children are brought together once again, each agreeing that their involvement with *TSOM* breaks down barriers between them and strangers, the need people have to connect to someone from the film. It is, in a sense, they conclude, *their* "home movie."

The set also contains: Restoration information; Mia Farrow's screen test; trailers & TV spots; storyboard gallery; behind the scenes gallery; lobby cards and one sheets gallery.

45th Anniversary release, November 2, 2010

The Sound of Music arrived in the new Blu-ray format with a lavish packaging to not only outdo previous issues of the film, but to rival pretty much *any* movie as far as their presentation for the home viewing trade.

Remastered in hi-def with 7.1. DTS-HD sound, this three-disc set contained both the Blu-ray and regular version of the film; various interactive features including a "back-lot" tour of locations and virtual map of Salzburg; a sing-a-long; audio commentary by Julie Andrews and Christopher Plummer, as well as an archival Robert Wise commentary; the newest CD release of the soundtrack; a reproduction of the original 1965 souvenir program; Salzburg postcards; a hardcover book, *The Sound of Music: A Few of Our Favorite Things*; and a music box that plays "My Favorite Things."

19

The Sound on the Page

Books Connected to *The Sound of Music*

I n addition to the many Trapp Family accounts published by Maria von Trapp, there have been several books on or by those involved in the film of *The Sound of Music*, be they autobiographical or full-out accounts of the making of the work.

The Story of the Trapp Family Singers

Maria Augusta Trapp. Lippincott, Philadelphia, 1949, 309 pages. (See Chapter 2 for details.)

The Trapp Family Book of Christmas Songs

Selected and Arranged by Franz Wasner; Illustrations by Agathe Trapp; Introduction by Maria Augusta Trapp. Pantheon Books, 1950, 128 pages.

This songbook breaks down its selections by categories: Latin and Macaronic (incl. "Carol of the Nuns of Saint Mary's, Chester"), English ("The First Noel," "Deck the Hall," "What Child Is This," etc.), American (incl. "It Came Upon the Midnight Clear," "We Three Kings"), German (incl. "O Tannenbaum!" and the intriguingly titled "Maria on the Mountain"), Austrian, of course ("Silent Night"), French ("Angels We Have Heard on High"), Italian ("Carol of the Bagpipes"), Spanish ("Fum, Fum, Fum"), Swedish ("Mary the Virgin to Bethlehem Went"), Czech ("Come All Ye Shepherds"), and Polish ("Jesus Christ Is Born"), In addition to offering the music to these numbers, the book is informative (chances are that many weren't even aware which traditional Christmas songs derived from which countries), with Father Wasner giving some background on the tunes at the end of the book.

The later edition of the book (from 1973) was sold with the image from the movie of Julie Andrews playing her guitar at the picnic amid the Alps. This version had the line "The famous Trapp family portrayed in the 20th Century-Fox motion picture *The Sound of Music*" printed along the top of the cover.

Yesterday, Today and Forever: The Religious Life of a Remarkable Family

Maria Augusta Trapp. Lippincott, 1952, 220 pages.

This is the Trapp family story from the spiritual point of view and is therefore of interest only to those who absorb *The Sound of Music* in this manner. Maria speaks of teaching the children about the importance of Jesus as they became famous through their lives as concert performers. Because of the success of the movie, this book received several later printings as well.

Around the Year with the Trapp Family

Maria Augusta Trapp. Pantheon, 1955, 251 pages.

Like the previous book, this emphasizes the Trapp family from a religious point of view. Broken down into two sections, *Celebrating with the Family in Heaven* and *Celebrating with the Family on Earth*, which are, in turn broken down by Christmas Season, Carnival, Easter Cycle, The Green Meadow, and The Land Without a Sunday, the book details how they celebrate the various religious holiday throughout the year including Advent, Lent, Ash Wednesday, and, of course, Christmas. There are songs (arranged for voice by Father Wasner ranging from "Drop Your Dew, Ye Clouds of Heaven" to "Turkey in the Straw"), poems, illustrations by Rosemary (formerly Rosmarie) Trapp and Nikolaus E. Wolff, and recipes.

A Family on Wheels: Further Adventures of the Trapp Family Singers

Maria Augusta Trapp and Ruth T. Murdoch. Lippincott, 1959, 222 pages.

This time, Maria picks up the story where she left off with her first book, telling tales of the family's travels all over the world for their concert tours, the last one taking place in 1955. Related are stops in South America, Australia, their triumphant return to Austria after a twelve-year absence, and a visit to the Father Damien Molokai leper colony in Hawaii.

The Sound of Music

Howard Lindsay and Russel Crouse. Random House, 1960, 141 pages.

The playscript was first published in hardcover format within a year of the show opening on Broadway. There are a handful of photos and no introduction; just the up-front credits and then the dialogue and lyrics. The familiar image from the back of the LP and the playbill of Mary Martin playing guitar for the stooped-over children is on the cover.

Later editions included an introduction by Timothy Crouse, Russel's son.

Maria

Maria von Trapp. Creation House, 1972, 203 pages.

Although one would assume that by this point Maria von Trapp had said everything that needed to be told about her story, she published yet another book on the topic, following the success of *The Sound of Music* on stage and screen.

Pretty much covering a lot of the same background of her early life, her days at Nonnberg Abbey and how working for the Trapp family brought her marriage and a musical career, Maria does have a few surprising revelations on hand. In Chapter 14 ("Interesting Friends"), for example, she talks about her close friendship with Dolores Hope and, subsequently, Dolores's very famous husband, Bob, whom Maria wasn't even aware of when the former stayed at the Trapp family lodge. In time, Maria would often stay at the Hope home when she was on the West Coast, often sleeping in Bob's bed . . . when he was away, that is.

The title of Chapter 18 points out one of Maria's quirks about the title of the musical that made her world famous: she persistently leaves off the word "The." Here, she talks about how she was contacted throughout her world travels by Mary Martin's husband in an effort to sell the rights to allow her story to become a stage musical, written by the team of (according to her spelling) "Lindsey and Kraus"; how the German film company pretty much shafted her when purchasing the rights to her story, for which she ended up with a paltry $9,000; and her admiration for Mary Martin and the show itself.

She is less thrilled by Hollywood's treatment of her, insisting that the producer of the film version (presumably Robert Wise, although his name is never stated) told her, "We are not concerned about persons and facts. I haven't read your book, and I don't intend to read it. We are more or less going to make our own version of your story." This was followed by the person hanging up, which sounds a lot more ruthless and rude than any other description of Wise. She also talks about not being invited to the premiere in New York (she was in attendance at the Boston opening a few weeks later—one can assume someone figured Boston was closer to Stowe, Vermont), and that she was overall pleased with the finished product. "I was so relieved by what I saw . . . ," she states. "I really like it very much, especially the beginning where you can see beautiful Austria photographed from the helicopter."

Making it quite clear that she and her family did not exactly end up rolling in cash because of the movie's tremendous success, she nevertheless is grateful for the outpouring of love that came her way as a result. "There is the uncountable number of letters from all countries of the world, telling me that looking at the film *Sound of Music* has strengthened their trust in God . . . Letters like this make me fold my hands and say from the bottom of my heart, 'Dear Lord, thank You for the *Sound of Music*.'"

The Sound of Music: Sing 'N' Color Fun!/
Lyrics & Coloring Book Crayons/Cassette

Hal Leonard Corporation, 1993.

Not surprisingly, there was a coloring book published of *TSOM* complete with crayons and cassette. There were also paper dolls issued in Sweden.

The Sound of Music: The Making of America's Favorite Movie

Julia Antopol Hirsch. McGraw-Hill Books, 1993, 240 pages.

Twenty-eight years after its release, *TSOM* received a long-overdue book paying tribute to its enduring impact and telling, in tremendously informative detail, the story of its making. Lavishly illustrated and including interviews with Robert Wise, Julie Andrews, Charmian Carr, and many other involved in the production, Hirsch's wonderful documentation cannot be underestimated. An absolute *must* for any *TSOM* fan, although it would be hard to imagine that any of them did not make sure they had tracked it down and purchased it by this point.

Fans were thrilled at the arrival of Julia Antopol Hirsch's 1993 book, the first to document the making of the movie.

Rodgers and Hammerstein's My Favorite Things

Lyrics by Oscar Hammerstein II; Music by Richard Rodgers; Illustrations by James Warhola. Simon & Shuster Books for Young Readers, 1994, 14 pages.

Oscar Hammerstein's memorable lyrics to "My Favorite Things" (referred to on the book flap as "one of everyone's favorite songs") are accompanied by rather cutesy animal illustrations by James Warhola. These include a chicken holding a parasol trying to block said raindrops from landing on those roses; the menagerie tucked inside "bright copper kettles"; "crisp apple strudel" being served by a pig in an apron; and a bear eating a plate full of "schnitzel with noodles." Because this is meant to entertain the very young, there are no scenes of dogs biting or bees stinging, however. To justify Richard Rodgers's credit on the jacket, the endpapers contain the sheet music score of the song.

This was a follow-up to a 1993 book from the same publisher and the same artist, *Rodgers and Hammerstein's The Surrey with the Fringe on Top.*

The Golden Age of the Hollywood Musical and Me

Saul Chaplin. University of Oklahoma Press, 1994, 262 pages.

TSOM's associate producer and uncredited music director Saul Chaplin published an autobiography that is not so much about his personal life as his dealings with some of the top names in the musical field during his many years behind the scenes. Chaplin is, in fact, so much more interested in throwing the spotlight to others that the cover photo on the book favors Bing Crosby and Grace Kelly, with Chaplin, seated at the piano turned away from the camera.

Chaplin's approach works, skipping most of the pre-show business backstory that can often be a drag in such bios and getting right to the career stories, first as lyricist Sammy Cahn's collaborator, then laboring under tyrannical mogul Harry Cohn at Columbia, his opportunity to contribute to some of MGM's best musicals, and working with Robert Wise on *West Side Story, The Sound of Music,* and *Star!*

Chapter 20 is devoted entirely to *The Sound of Music.* Chaplin admits, like so many others who ended up attached to the property, that he was not a big fan of the show when he saw it on Broadway ("too sweet for me"). It was Ernest Lehman's screenplay that won him over, and what, he claims, he used to coerce a reluctant Robert Wise to come aboard. He was, however, always fond of Rodgers and Hammerstein's songs and was thrilled to have Julie Andrews sing them (he describes her vocalizing as being "near-perfect" every time). Despite the overall experience being a positive one, not to mention bringing him a second wife, when he fell in love with the film's script supervisor, Betty Levin, Chaplin does not mince words when he takes Christopher Plummer to task for his aloof manner on the set and his need to continually apologize over the years for having been part of something so popular. Chaplin won't even cut him slack where his musicality is concerned, claiming he could "carry a tune in a modestly pleasant manner" at best, and was too florid a pianist for his taste when the actor would entertain others in the lobby of his Salzburg hotel during the shoot.

There are the now-familiar stories of trying to rehearse the numbers in the busy streets of Salzburg with choreographer Marc Breaux; how Chaplin and Ernest Lehman devised the first section of "I Have Confidence" because Richard Rodgers couldn't quite grasp what they were looking for in that part of the song; the decision to dub both the dialogue *and* the songs for select foreign countries; and being overwhelmed by the tumultuous fan response to Julie Andrews when he escorted her to the Academy Awards that year.

He has nothing but high praise for Robert Wise, calling him "the most accessible director I've ever worked with."

Robert Wise on His Films: From Editing Room to Director's Chair
Sergio Leemann. Silman-James Press, 1995, 226 pages.

Leemann states up front that the main reason behind writing this book was to rectify the fact that there hadn't been any books about Robert Wise written until this one. Although sufficient background is given on the filmmaker, as well as chronicling his career, the book basically serves as a chance to have Wise comment on each of his movies. In this respect it is the closest thing we have to the autobiography he never wrote. In addition to reflections on his years spent at RKO as an editor (which basically covers, as one would expect, his interactions with Orson Welles), each of his thirty-nine directorial credits is covered per chapter, with credits, a synopsis, and then recollections by Wise on certain aspects of the movie. Some are more detailed than others, depending on the importance of the project.

The Sound of Music gets one of the longer reminiscences, with Wise giving his thoughts on the efforts on everyone's part to remove the sugary content of the original show; the casting he had counted on and achieved with Julie Andrews and Christopher Plummer; the replacements for the three missing songs from the show; the dubbing of the film for different countries; the decision to go ahead with an aerial opening similar to the one that had given *West Side Story* such a memorable starting point; the importance of production designer Boris Leven; and the ambivalent feelings he has about how the tremendous success of the movie has caused so many people to overlook his other achievements of which he is equally proud.

The World of the Trapp Family: The Life Story of the Legendary Family That Inspired "The Sound of Music,"
William Anderson; Photography by David Wade.
Anderson Publications, 1998, 168 pages.

Visually, this lavishly illustrated biography is certainly the handsomest book published about the Trapp family. Spun off from a Japanese equivalent published there in 1995 by Rutaro Adachi, this American version was produced with the full cooperation of the Trapp family lodge and features comments from the surviving Trapp children: Agathe, young Maria, Rosmarie, Eleonore, Werner, and Johannes. Because of this, the book is full of rare and unique photos from the family collection, as well as such interesting visuals as the passenger list from the ship that brought them to the U.S. in 1938, the *S.S. American Farmer*, playbills of various concert engagements throughout the years; tour photos; and lovely pictures (by David Wade) from both Salzburg and Stowe, Vermont.

Chapter 14: *A New Song: The Sound of Music* talks about Mary Martin's determination to track down Maria in order to secure the rights to the story for

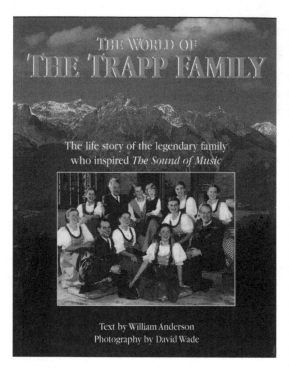

The life story of the legendary family who inspired *The Sound of Music*

Text by William Anderson
Photography by David Wade

A colorful examination of all things Trapp and *Sound of Music*, this book was distributed by the Trapp family lodge.

Broadway; the Trapps' own recording of the Rodgers & Hammerstein score; and, of course, the movie. A skeptical Maria is quoted as worrying, "For heaven's sake, what am I going to do if they have me twice divorced in this film?" Her reaction seems more generous than those of some of her children, including Rupert, who claimed he had to buy his own ticket for the premiere (!) and considered what he saw on screen "all wet"; Agathe, who chose not to bother to see it at all; and Rosmarie, who seemed surprised that the movie was supposed to be depicting her life, although it did not, of course, include a character based on her. All agreed that both the stage and screen versions did their father a grave injustice with its uptight and stern portrayal. There is no denying, however, on anyone's part how the movie brought them undreamed-of fame and booming business to their lodge in Vermont. The book includes a list of the Trapp family recordings.

Overture and Finale: Rodgers & Hammerstein and the Creation of Their Greatest Hits.

Watson-Guptill Publications, 1999, 192 pages.

The Making of "The Sound of Music."

Routledge/Taylor & Frances Group, 2007, 111 pages. Both by Max Wilk.

Wilk originally wrote a book about the collaboration between Richard Rodgers and Oscar Hammerstein II by concentrating on their first and last shows together, *Oklahoma!* and *The Sound of Music*. Figuring there was more money to be made from the fans of both popular musicals, he later published their stories separately, as *OK! The Story of Oklahoma! A Celebration of America's Most Beloved Musical* (2002), and *The Making of "The Sound of Music"* (2007).

Despite Wilk's insider credit of having worked for one of the show's producers, Leland Hayward, fans of the beloved 1959 Rodgers & Hammerstein musical had best beware; Wilk informs us in the introduction how much he dislikes it. That said, he presents a fast and straightforward account of putting the show together and how it triumphed and continued to triumph over all the naysayers, for generations to come.

A good portion of the book is devoted to the movie, starting in Chapter 6, with the subheading "Lehman and Lazar," referring to screenwriter Ernest and agent Irving "Swifty." The following three chapters (7, "The Filmmakers"; 8, "Verdant and Over Budget"; 9, "Triumph Again") encompass familiar stories about the efforts to get people to participate in a property many found too sweet, casting, filming in the rains of Austria, and the tumultuous worldwide response.

Strangest comment in the book comes from Anna Crouse, widow of the show's book writer, Russel Crouse, when she insists the original London production wasn't allowed to employ actual children for the Trapp family and had to depend on hiring midgets!!!

Forever Liesl: A Memoir of The Sound of Music

Charmian Carr, with Jean A. S. Strauss. Viking. 2000, 246 pages.

This is essential reading for any *TSOM* aficionado, as it is the only time someone directly involved in the film wrote an autobiography based almost entirely around the movie. Although Carr tells her own life story, she weaves it throughout with tales of not only the making of the musical for which she will be forever linked, but the aftermath, the enduring nature of it, and how it has shaped her life.

What is most fascinating is the fact that she did not really pursue the role, show business having not been her fervid goal, despite coming from a family (albeit a broken one) that dwelled in it. Unhappy stories about her absent father and her alcoholic mother are contrasted with her close relationship with sisters Sharon (later Shannon) Farnon and Darleen Carr, and, even more importantly, the six actors who went from being her celluloid siblings to a surrogate family of their own. There are comments and reflections a-plenty from these people as well as Christopher Plummer and screenwriter Ernest Lehman, but nothing from Julie Andrews, who receives her own chapter about her professionalism and her decision not to remain as closely linked to the seven "children." Carr also has loving praise for Saul Chaplin and his inestimable contribution to the movie.

One of the most satisfying aspects of the book is the inclusion, at the end of each chapter, of correspondence and letters from fans of the movie Carr has received over the years, testament to its power and lasting effect on so many. This would play a part in Carr's follow-up book, *Letters to Liesl.*

[*Note: The UK paperback released in November 2000 has a cover photo of Carr dancing with Daniel Truhitte, while the book's interior images are moved from the front of the chapters to a center insert.*]

Rodgers & Hammerstein's My Favorite Things

Illustrated by Renée Graef. HarperCollins Publishers, 2001, 32 pages.

Curiously, there was a *second* preschoolers' book that followed the same format as James Warhola's 1994 release, with artist Renée Graef creating her own illustrations to accompany Hammerstein's lyrics for "My Favorite Things." This time children are used to enact the images; for example, a little girl awaiting some tea from a "bright copper kettle" being poured by a little boy wearing "warm woolen mittens."

Graef dedicates the book "For stepparents who guide and nurture their children with love, especially Maria von Trapp and my own mother Louise."

Letters to Liesl

Charmian Carr and Jean Strauss. Areté Publishing, 2001, 192 pages.

Among the highlights of Charmian Carr's memoir *Forever Liesl* were the letters from fans that opened each chapter. Taking this concept one step further, Carr and co-author Jean Strauss structure the entire, less-known follow-up book around more of these letters. These in turn are interwoven with the story of Carr and her fellow movie "siblings" (including Nicholas Hammond, for whom she holds particularly deep affection) flying off to Salzburg together for the first time since filming there in 1964 in order to appear in a British-made documentary (*The Sound of Music Children: After They Were Famous*). The letters (not credited directly to the authors) are presented under such topics as "family," "bachelor dandies" (mainly those who developed a crush on Liesl/Charmian after seeing the film), "friends around the world," and "Singalonga" (Carr explains the extra "a" for Americans).

To say that this book further emphasizes the unprecedented impact the movie continues to have and the tremendous outpouring of love people throughout the world have for it is an understatement. Perhaps most moving is a letter from a blind person (whose sex is made unclear) who grew up knowing the movie and its characters by sound only.

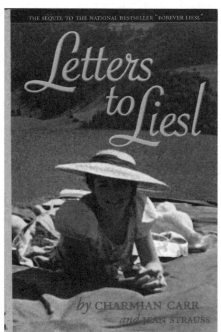

Charmian Carr followed her best seller, *Forever Liesl,* with this less well-known book, *Letters to Liesl.*

Maria von Trapp: Beyond the Sound of Music

Candice F. Ransom. Carolrhoda Books, 2002, 112 pages.

Aimed at juvenile readers, this biography of Maria von Trapp (whom author Candice Ransom sums up as "a woman whose life is as enchanting as any movie . . . and much more") is, in fact, quite informative and a good read for anyone of *any* age wanting a quick overview of her life.

Chapter 10, "Farewell Song," talks about the first German film, *Die Trapp-Familie* and how it led to the idea for the musical. According to the author, Mary Martin spent ten days at the Trapp lodge studying her subject's physical mannerisms and behavior, and thanked her by sending her a dress to wear on the Broadway opening night, a pale green gown with matching shoes. Whatever her reservations about the dramatization of her life, it was Maria who led the standing ovation that evening. "When Maria finally saw the movie," according to the book, "she felt that Julie Andrews made her sweeter than she really was," but was thrilled with how beautiful the film made her homeland look.

From *The Sound of Music*, there are photos of the real Maria on set with director Robert Wise and her fictional husband, Christopher Plummer, as well as the familiar shot of Julie Andrews on the hilltop.

This was part of the publisher's "Trailblazers Biographies Series," which also celebrated such other people as Albert Einstein, Mary Cassatt, Thomas Jefferson, and Ernie Pyle.

Memories Before and After the Sound of Music

Agathe von Trapp. Publish America (self-published), 2004 (republished by Harper Paperback in 2010), 256 pages.

Although Maria von Trapp's first book, *The Story of the Trapp Family Singers*, is important for bringing her story into the public eye, the eldest Trapp daughter's autobiography is well worth reading because it fills in so many missing details from her stepmother's writings. We get much more backstory on her father's life before his children were born; the details of their various homes and which children were born where; a dash of Austrian history; the fact that Maria was referred to by Agathe as "Gustl Kutschera," something never mentioned by Maria; the musical evenings of singing and instrument playing that took place *before* Maria showed up; and the far more contentious relationship between Maria and housekeeper Baroness Mandelsloh than was portrayed in Maria's book. Indeed, Agathe's book is clearly the more valuable one in terms of picking up pertinent information about the Trapps and their lives.

Chapter 17 is entitled "Oh! *The Sound of Music*" and Agathe admits, up front, to her mixed feelings about the highly fictional musicalization of her family's lives. She theorizes that the reason for its popularity "lies in the fact that it does

AGATHE VON TRAPP

MEMORIES BEFORE *and* AFTER

THE SOUND of MUSIC

An Autobiography with Sketches by the Author

The eldest Trapp daughter, Agathe, got her chance to tell the tale her stepmother had made famous in her own self-published autobiography.

not matter to people whether or not the story is true, but that it is a beautiful wholesome story that appeals to the emotions of the viewers." Her main bone to pick is the stern depiction of her father, whom she praises for his love and devotion to his children. There is also the matter of royalties. Although she is grateful to Mary Martin, Richard Halliday, and Leland Hayward for signing a small percentage of the royalties over to her stepmother, Agathe makes it clear that her financial gain is hardly plentiful, but the goodwill directed her way as a result of the musical has made up for it.

She also speaks of the surviving Trapps being invited to receive the Golden Decoration of Honor from the state of Salzburg for their Austrian Relief efforts following the war. Also on hand, to pick up the Mozart Medal for their connection with *The Sound of Music*, were the seven actors who had portrayed the Trapp children, marking the first time since the movie had been released that they were meeting their true-life counterparts (or some of them) face to face. She concludes, "I finally came to terms with *The Sound of Music*. . . Who am I, then, to criticize this movie? After a long inner struggle, I finally learned to separate the memories of my life from the screenplay."

The 2010 reprint arrived in stores only three months before Agathe passed away at the age of ninety-seven.

I Could Have Sung All Night: My Story

Marni Nixon, with Stephen Cole. Billboard Books, 2006, 306 pages.

Hollywood's most famous ghost singer tells her story, putting aside Chapter 9 ("Getting into the Habit") to talk about her on-camera appearance in *The Sound of Music*. Nixon says she was terrified of meeting Julie Andrews, because of having dubbed the vocals for Audrey Hepburn on *My Fair Lady*, the movie of which Andrews had been passed over for, after having caused such a sensation in the original Broadway production. Not surprisingly, there was no animosity, the star greeting Nixon with a gracious "I'm such a fan of yours!" In addition to giving some familiar background on the origins of *TSOM* on stage and the making of the film, the singer talks about being asked by Saul Chaplin to record "I Have Confidence," with the revisions he had added, so that the demo could be heard and, hopefully, approved by Richard Rodgers. This made her the first person to record the song.

The Fox music department had originally recommended her to play one of the nuns, with vocal coaching from Bobby Tucker and Saul Chaplin. Despite only being seen singing "Maria," Nixon was also asked to contribute to the "Preludium" vocals as well. Her hopes of getting at least one close-up in the movie were dashed, she theorizes, because she had gone against orders ("the makeup department had forbidden us to wear mascara") and put it on in order to keep her eyes from looking washed out. This caused her to constantly blink, ruining takes. Not being required to journey overseas to Salzburg, her entire role was shot during the first two weeks of April 1964 at the Fox Studios in Los Angeles.

Anna Lee: Memoirs of a Career on General Hospital and in Film
Anna Lee, with Barbara Roisman Cooper. McFarland, 2007, 322 pages.

Although Anna Lee was not able to complete her autobiography before her death in 2004, Barbara Roisman Cooper (who had helped director Ronald Neame on *his* autobiography, *Straight from the Horse's Mouth*) was able to take over the manuscript and finish the job. Lee (and/or her collaborator) gives a very thorough account of her career in both British and Hollywood movies, her first two troubled marriages (to future *Mary Poppins* director Robert Stevenson and on-again off-again business-man George Stafford), and her later, happy one to writer Robert Nathan (author of *Portrait of Jennie*); her late career renaissance as a favorite on the daytime serial *General Hospital*; and the illness that rendered her wheelchair bound.

In Chapter 21, "Back to Work with a Vengeance," she talks about how, in the midst of putting an end to her crumbling marriage to husband #2, she gladly took the role of Sister Margaretta in *TSOM* (although she had her sights set on playing the baroness). She cites this as one of three times she played a nun, the other two instances being on television, on episodes of *Peter Gunn* (a series created by Julie Andrews's future husband, Blake Edwards) and *Combat!* She chooses to let the reader believe that she did *all* of her own singing, writing that "I finally got to sing a Rodgers and Hammerstein song, even a few solo bars," making no mention whatsoever of having a handful of notes dubbed over by Marie Greene.

Lee discusses both the New York and Los Angeles premieres of the movie (noting that her former son-in-law, Russ Tamblyn, who was briefly married to her daughter, Venetia Stevenson, was in attendance); and correctly points out that she says but a single line to star Julie Andrews ("You may go in now, Maria").

While *TSOM* was a positive experience, Lee's life in 1964 was less rosy. As she writes, "After such a happy time, I reached a point in my life where I decided I had to divorce George." And so they did, that same year.

The Sound of Music Companion

Laurence Maslon. Fireside Books, 2007, 192 pages.

This beautifully illustrated book explores all facets of *The Sound of Music* story and phenomenon, giving background on the Trapp family, the creation of the Broadway show, the making of the film, and the subsequent revivals. A real bonus are reproductions of some of Hammerstein's first draft lyrics, showing, for example, how the famous "A Bell Is No Bell" verse to the reprise of "Sixteen Going on Seventeen" was originally intended to open "Climb Ev'ry Mountain." Another fascinating bit of ephemera is the tentative rundown of songs, before they were actually created, with such "dummy titles" as "Yodeling Song" (to drown out thunder), "Face Life" (which became "Climb Ev'ry Mountain"), "Why Buck the Tide?" (which turned into "No Way to Stop It"), and "I've Been in Love Before—So I Know What I'm Saying" (a precursor to "An Ordinary Couple").

Andrew Lloyd Webber provides the foreword to the book; lyrics to all songs that appeared in the movie are inserted throughout the text.

In Spite of Myself: A Memoir

Christopher Plummer. Alfred A. Knopf, 2008, 648 pages.

Christopher Plummer charts his long and colorful life as an actor, filling chapter after chapter with stories of some of the great roles he's played and some of the outstanding thespians with whom he has shared stage, screen, tube, and sometimes a beverage. Knowing damn well that it has played an instrumental part in his fame and that he'd never be forgiven for brushing off *The Sound of Music* in a sentence or two, Plummer devotes all of Chapter 25 to the making of the musical and its impact. Calling the chapter "S&M," he is quick to explain that it is his "perverse name for the musical epic."

The opening section is a warm recollection of the hotel where some of the other cast members stayed during filming, the Bristol, and its larger-than-life staff, notably owner Gretl Hübner. Just when it appears that he's going to talk about this aspect of the shoot and nothing else, Plummer writes bluntly of his feelings about the assignment, admitting that he "was not a happy camper. It did not promise to be one of 'my favourite things.'" He also admits that he was somewhat spoiled by his run of great stage parts, was a bit arrogant, and behaved badly.

Plummer gives nothing but high marks to the creative team, however, crediting writer Ernest Lehman for making the captain more fully dimensional, saluting Robert Wise for his patient and gentlemanly demeanor, and looking back fondly on his drinking sessions with cast member Gil Stuart (who played the Trapp Butler, Franz). He saves highest praise "first and foremost in importance" to his leading lady, "Eliza Doolittle and Queen Guinevere wrapped into one magical rosy-cheeked bundle of British pluck, my friend forever, the once-in-a-Blue-Moon Julie Andrews! . . . There was a radiance in her she couldn't suppress even if she'd tried." As far as he is concerned, *TSOM* was and is Julie's triumph, through and through.

Having softened over the years, he now concludes how proud he is to have been a part of something so beloved and famous; certain that it has enhanced and enriched the Austrian economy and really put Salzburg on the map for so many. More surprising is his comment, while stating that "Edelweiss" was the easiest song in the piece, that it was also "my favourite," it being well documented that Plummer wrote to director Robert Wise in advance of filming hoping there might be a chance of cutting the number, calling it "boring and schmaltzy."

My Favorite Songs: Maria von Trapp's Childhood Folk Songs (w/CD)
Maria von Trapp. Veritas Press, 2009, 69 pages.

These selections are, in fact, chosen by Captain von Trapp's second-eldest daughter, Maria, and not *the* Maria as the billing might suggest. Maria translates notable Austrian folk songs she and her siblings sang while telling stories of her life. There is also an accompanying disc of most of these songs being performed by the current-day von Trapp children (the grandchildren of Werner von Trapp). Among the titles offered are "Blue Jeans," "The Cuckoo and the Donkey," "Little Chickadee" (no relation to W. C. Fields, one assumes), "When Our Pug a Puppy Was," "Fox, You Stole My Goose," "Hop, Hop, Hop" (which is, in fact, featured in the German film *Die Trapp-Familie*), "O, Christmas Tree" (a rare recognizable title for the uninitiated), "Johnny Stay Home," and "Yodel of the Bells."

The Sound of Music: A Classic Collectible Pop-Up
Richard Rodgers & Oscar Hammerstein II; Howard Lindsay & Russel Crouse; Adapted by Bert Fink; Illustrated by Dan Andreasen. Paper Engineering by Brue Foster. Little Simon, 2009, 14 pages.

Everyone loves pop-up books, something proven by just how mangled most of them are when you open them in bookstores or public libraries. This version of *The Sound of Music*, adapted by the Rodgers & Hammerstein Organization's senior vice president Bert Fink, goes back to the playscript, telling the story with six major pop-up set pieces, with mini-pop-ups (the goatherd and his goat, a cuckoo clock, et al.) located within the text written in inserted mini-pages. The three-dimensional centerpieces show Maria on her mountain (she even spins, for maximum Julie Andrews–like impact); the interior of the Trapp family villa, complete with the children on the grand staircase; Maria's bedroom, with the children joining her for song ("The Lonely Goatherd," *not* "My Favorite Things"); the church interior for the wedding of the captain and Maria; the

Riding Rock concert stage—perhaps the most imaginatively designed of all Dan Andreasen and Bruce Foster's visuals, with assorted Nazis seen through the arches; and the family ascending the Alps for the finale.

Although Max, Elsa, Rolf, and Herr Zeller have been eliminated, there is still plenty of material here to make youngsters feel like they are experiencing the pivotal moments from the musical, with the lyrics to eight of the songs included. There are even clever references to lyrics within the text, "The fiery colors of autumn gave way to silver white winter . . ." or, pertaining to the wedding, "Maria always said that 'girls in white dresses' were among her favorite things, but she never thought she would be one of them!"

V Is for Von Trapp: A Musical Family Alphabet.

"Story of the legendary family who inspired *The Sound of Music*, for children grades 1- 4." Written by William Anderson and illustrated by Linda Dockey Graves. Sleeping Bear Press, 2010, 32 pages.

Author William Anderson teaches the alphabet by structuring the true story of the Trapp Family Singers around it. While he tells the straightforward tale on the side panels, each page offers a new letter with an example corresponding directly (or *indirectly*) to the Trapps. "A is for Austria . . . B is for Brothers and sisters, seven siblings in all. Each of them came running when they heard Papa's whistle call . . . I is for Invasion . . . M is for Maria von Trapp, mother, storyteller, and musician. With her strong determination she told of her family's tradition . . . T is for the Trapp Family Lodge" . . . , and so forth.

"S" is saved for the inclusion of the stage musical and the movie. "S is for *The Sound of Music*, a movie and a play with songs we love like 'Do-Re-Mi.' A favorite story . . . forever it will be." The side panel text also mentions the two German movies, Julie Andrews and Christopher Plummer, how filming took place in Austria, that people have watched it in as many as forty languages and dialects, and that it is "the most successful movie musical ever made." It also justifiably states that the Trapp family became *very* famous because of it (would they have an alphabet book written about them otherwise?).

The Sound of Music Family Scrapbook

Fred Bronson. Applause Books, 2012, 96 pages.

After Julia Antopol Hirsch and Laurence Maslon's thorough and essential books about the creation of *The Sound of Music*, one would have thought there was no need to cover similar ground, until this particular book came along. The real selling point here is the fact that it "contains never-before-seen personal photos and collectables from Charmian Carr, Nicholas Hammond, Heather Menzies, Duane Chase, Angela Cartwright, Debbie Turner, and Kym Karath." And they're not kidding. In addition to great on-set photos and familiar official stills from the movie, there are pictures taken by various parents and relatives during the shoot, and reproductions of such oddities from these young actors' careers as a sketch of Mirabell Gardens by the five-year-old Karath; an ad for pancake batter featuring Chase; and Cartwright's LP, recorded when she was a cast member of *The Danny Thomas Show.*

For an added treat, there are also "pockets" containing reproductions of such curios as a portion of Hammond's copy of the script; a costume sketch by Dorothy Jeakins, a thank-you note to the cast from Robert Wise, Cartwright's Beatles diary, and Turner's Pan Am plane ticket overseas.

20

Life After
The Sound of Music

What the Cast Principals Did
After the Movie

Impossible as it may seem to those focused expressly on *The Sound of Music*, there was life *after* the film for its principal cast members, although this Mount Olympus of screen credits would be hard to surpass for so many of them. Here is a look at just what these actors accomplished in the years since the monumental musical triumph.

Julie Andrews

By the time she received her second consecutive Oscar nomination, for playing Maria in *The Sound of Music*, Julie Andrews had become arguably the most famous motion picture star in the world. It was ridiculous to even imagine that anyone could top the impact of starring in the decade's biggest financial success, not to mention Walt Disney Studio's crowning achievement of *Mary Poppins*. Indeed, even though there were good box office returns on her next two films (the Hitchcock thriller *Torn Curtain* and the costume epic *Hawaii*, both released in 1966) and excellent ones on Universal's 1920s musical send-up, *Thoroughly Modern Millie* (1967), all of them arrived in theatres, made the rounds, and were gone from circulation while *TSOM* continued to play off and on.

As if desperate to knock her down a peg for becoming one of the most significant and instantly recognizable names in the entertainment field, the media seemed to take great delight when her follow-up project with director Robert Wise, the Gertrude Lawrence biography *Star!* (1968), resulted in tepid reviews and meager box office returns. Despite the poor response tarnishing the movie's reputation, her true admirers looked beyond the baggage and championed it for containing some of Julie's finest work on screen. While a second big-budgeted musical, *Darling Lili* (1970), made even less money, it did bring Andrews a new husband, the film's director-writer Blake Edwards. (They married on November 12, 1969 in Hollywood.)

If Hollywood's idea of what kind of entertainment it wanted to present to reflect the newer freedom of the late 1960s was changing rapidly, nobody with taste was ready to count the actress out just yet. Even after a variety series, *The Julie Andrews Hour* (ABC, 1972–73), couldn't attract enough viewers, it still won a batch of Emmys and made some people very glad to know Andrews was still going to make the effort to be around, one way or another. It was on television that she was mostly seen during the 1970s, in various specials, including *Julie on Sesame Street* (1973), *Julie and Dick* (Van Dyke) *at Covent Garden* (1974), *One Step into Spring* (1978), and a reunion with Carol Burnett (*Julie and Carol at Lincoln Center* in 1971). Another cinematic collaboration with her husband, the romantic thriller *The Tamarind Seed* (1974), disappeared rather quickly.

It was not until the end of the decade that Andrews began to bounce back, cinematically, once again working with Edwards, first on the box office hit *"10"* (1979), although she was required to take a backseat to star Dudley Moore and pinup sensation Bo Derek; and then in the strident Hollywood satire *S.O.B.* (1981), which received much press because the plot required Julie to thoroughly throttle her wholesome image by exposing her breasts. These were warm-ups to her most satisfying Edwards credit, the comedic musical *Victor Victoria* (1982; for the second time playing opposite James Garner), as a down-on-her-luck singer who pretends to be a cross-dressing cabaret performer and becomes the toast of Paris. Andrews earned a third Oscar nomination; the film became one of her defining credits and one of the most highly regarded comedies of the 1980s. Amid these she could be seen in a secondary role in the remake of *Little Miss Marker* (1980).

Having reestablished herself as a viable motion picture attraction, she chose two further Edwards assignments where she was cast yet again in supporting roles to the leading men: Burt Reynolds in *The Man Who Loved Women* (1983) and Jack Lemmon in *That's Life!* (1986), the latter another one of her "A" credits, and an underrated one at that, with Andrews pretty much playing a version of herself, the devoted wife of a neurotic man having trouble facing his advancing years. Working outside the Edwards universe, she accepted another image-shattering part, as a violinist stricken with multiple sclerosis in *Duet for One* (1986).

From this point on her movie career was spotty at best. When she sought large audiences, she turned to performing in concert and, after a long absence, the New York stage, first in the off-Broadway Stephen Sondheim revue *Putting It Together* (1993) and, even more profitably, a live version of *Victor Victoria* (1995), under Edwards's supervision. There was very little doubt by this point that she was nothing less than a show business legend, proven by the tremendous outcry when it was announced that a botched surgery had destroyed her vocal abilities. One of the world's great instruments was no more.

On television she did a third variety special with Burnett, *Julie and Carol . . . Together Again* (1989); a barely seen sitcom, *Julie* (1992), which went straight to the summer schedule; two dramatic television movies, *Our Sons* (1991), as Hugh Grant's mother, and *One Special Night* (1999), reuniting with James Garner; and a live broadcast of *On Golden Pond* (2000), which rated headlines because it

To coincide with *The Sound of Music's* 1973 reissue, the cast came together for what would turn out to be the first of *many* reunions over the years. From right to left are slightly older versions of Charmian Carr, Duane Chase, Heather Menzies, Nicholas Hammond, Julie Andrews, Angela Cartwright (partially blocked), Kym Karath, and Debbie Turner.

brought her back together with Christopher Plummer. For Disney, she returned to nanny country for two movies (both 2003): *Eloise at the Plaza* and *Eloise at Christmastime;* and, most curiously, a short subject, *The Cat That Looked at a King* (2004), based on a P. L. Travers story, which had her popping back into chalk paintings and reprising her famous silhouette as Mary Poppins.

At cinemas there were minor playdates for *A Fine Romance* (1992), a comedy with Marcello Mastroianni; and none in the U.S. for *Relative Values* (2000), her first and only actual British film, derived from Noël Coward, and *Unconditional Love* (2002), in which she showed up in two scenes to poke fun at herself. Those that did find big audiences barely made any demands of her: *The Princess Diaries* (2001), very much in support but fittingly cast as a queen; *Shrek 2* (2004), providing the voice of an ogre's mother; and the fairy tale send-up *Enchanted* (2007), as the unseen narrator. In between, there appeared *The Princess Diaries 2: Royal Engagement* (2004); *Shrek the Third* (2007); *Tooth Fairy* (2010), in support of "The Rock"; *Shrek Forever After* (2010); and *Despicable Me* (2010), as the voice of Steve Carell's mom; all of which couldn't help but appear like slumming for a regal lady who once lit up the world of stage and film musicals.

In addition to appearing on various sit-down interviews for the many home video issues of *The Sound of Music,* she was present front and center for various reunions honoring the film with other members of the cast. In 2001, she was one of the recipients of the Kennedy Center Honors.

Her albums include *A Christmas Treasure* (1967); *A Little Bit in Love* (1970); *A Little Bit of Broadway* (1977); *Love Me Tender* (1982); *Love Julie* (1987); a studio recording of *The King and I* (1992), with Ben Kingsley; *Broadway: The Music of Richard Rodgers* (1994), on which she offered new renditions of "The Sound of Music" and "Edelweiss"; *Here I'll Stay: The Words of Alan Jay Lerner* (1996); and *Thoroughly Modern Julie: The Best of Julie Andrews* (1996).

Billing herself as "Julie Edwards," she published her first two children's books, *Mandy* (1971) and *The Last of the Really Great Whangdoodles* (1974). It was not until the new millennium that she returned to this field with a vengeance, making a second career out of writing books for young readers, mostly in collaboration with her daughter, Emma Walton Hamilton. These include *Simeon's Gift* (2003); *Dragon: Hound of Honor* (2005); *The Great American Mousical* (2006); the *Little Bo* series; the *Very Fairy Princess* series; the *Dumpy the Dump Truck* series; *Thanks to You: Wisdom from Mother and Child* (2007); and *Julie Andrews' Collection of Poems, Songs and Lullabies* (2009). The first portion of her autobiography, entitled *Home*, was published in 2008.

Christopher Plummer

It is curious that so much sarcasm was sent in the direction of *The Sound of Music* by Christopher Plummer, considering how much poorer were the follow-up movies he appeared in during the late 1960s. In demand, he went from project to project for a five-year stretch, playing a possessive movie mogul in *Inside Daisy Clover* (1965); a real-life World War II spy in *Triple Cross* (1967); Field Marshal Rommel (an extended cameo) in the mystery *The Night of the Generals* (1967); the lead in a very specialized presentation of *Oedipus the King* (1968); a politician wanted for murder in *The High Commissioner* (1968); a grotesque royal in *Lock Up Your Daughters* (1969); an Incan ruler in *The Royal Hunt of the Sun* (1969), having played the other lead role, Francisco Pizarro, in the original stage production; and a World War II pilot in the all-star epic *Battle of Britain* (1969). All of these were non-starters at the box office and quickly wiped away the high status he had achieved with *The Sound of Music*, making it quite clear that his reputation would have to rest on his stage work.

Fortunately, he was never far from the boards, appearing in New York in *The Royal Hunt* (1965) while *TSOM* was still raking in cash in movie theatres, and returning to the Bard for *Antony and Cleopatra* (1967) at the Stratford Shakespeare Festival. On Broadway, he fulfilled a long-cherished dream of actually doing his own singing in a musical, in *Cyrano* (1973), which, despite its poor showing at the box office, brought Plummer his very first Tony Award. More popular was an adaptation of Chekhov, *The Good Doctor* (1973), because it had the unlikely name of Neil Simon on its credits; while Plummer received some of his best notices, playing Iago to James Earl Jones's Othello (1982) and returning to *Macbeth* (1988), earning a Drama Desk Award and a Tony nomination for the former. Over in London he did *Danton's Death*

(1971), *Henry V* (1981) for the American Shakespeare Festival, and *Drinks Before Dinner* (1978) off-Broadway.

Much as he liked to dismiss them as jobs strictly for the money, he did keep movies on his "to do" list. Some of them would quickly fall off the radar, like the uncalled-for remake of *The Spiral Staircase* (1975), in the George Brent part; *The Day That Shook the World* (U.S.: 1977), as the assassinated Archduke Ferdinand; the aptly named *The Disappearance* (1977), a Canadian thriller that took a full four years to reach U.S. shores; and *Aces High* (1976), as a World War I flyer, in this remake of *Journey's End.* He fared better playing Lord Wellington in a gargantuan, costly multi-national production of *Waterloo* (1970); reprising David Niven's old role in *The Return of the Pink Panther* (1975), his first movie since *TSOM* to actually make money; embodying Rudyard Kipling for a colorful cameo in *The Man Who Would Be King* (1975); playing a vengeful bank robber in *The Silent Partner* (1979); and taking his place as one of the screen's best Sherlock Holmeses, in *Murder by Decree* (1979).

Around to provide classy support, he was an Israeli diplomat in *Eyewitness* (1981); a cuckolded secret service agent in the old-fashioned *Hanover Street* (1979); Jane Seymour's domineering manager in another one that tapped into a bygone era, *Somewhere in Time* (1980); a Czech intelligence agent in *The Amateur* (1982); yet one more unpleasant government official, in the fantasy *Dreamscape* (1984); a shifty priest, playing for comical effect, in *Dragnet* (1987); and a filthy derelict with a rude nickname in a comedy, *Where the Heart Is* (1990). On television, he added his name to the starry casts of some major mini-series: *The Moneychangers* (1976), as a nasty banker, a perfect example of how Plummer could think little of a role and yet make a strong impression, in this instance winning himself an Emmy Award; *Little Gloria . . . Happy at Last* (1982), as Reginald Vanderbilt, her father, who quickly expired after her birth; *The Scarlet and the Black* (1983), as a Gestapo officer opposing heroic priest Gregory Peck; and *The Thorn Birds* (1983), as a papal ambassador, which earned him another Emmy nomination. There was also a much-heralded live presentation of *On Golden Pond* (2001), the press making much of the fact that this was Plummer's long-overdue reteaming with his *TSOM* co-star, Julie Andrews.

It was clear he was held in high regard, a name that added prestige to a product, although there seemed to be very little discretion in what he did, as Plummer's name popped up in all kinds of things simply for the desire to work, sometimes for a quick paycheck, and once in a while landing in something that stood out from the pack. Films in the plus category were: *Star Trek IV: The Undiscovered Country* (1991), under a ton of makeup as the power-crazy alien villain; *Malcolm X* (1992), a worthy epic biography, as a chaplain; a superior Stephen King adaptation, *Dolores Claiborne* (1995), as the investigating detective; the freaky *Twelve Monkeys* (1995), as a scientist conducting unorthodox experiments; *The Insider* (1999), one of his career peaks, as imperious newsman Mike Wallace; *A Beautiful Mind* (2001), as a doctor whom paranoid Russell Crowe is certain is a foreign agent, in Plummer's second credit to win the Academy Award for Best Picture; *Nicholas Nickleby* (2001), as the deeply unpleasant Uncle Ralph; *Inside Man* (2006), as the founder whose bank is being robbed; *The Imaginarium of Dr. Parnassus* (2009), as a withered street entertainer; and Pixar's *Up*, as the voice of the bad guy.

Meanwhile, he remain a vibrant stage presence, on Broadway in *No Man's Land* (1994), a last hurrah opposite longtime colleague and friend Jason Robards; *Barrymore* (1997), as the famed actor on his downslide, a piece he would later tape for posterity; *King Lear* (2004); and *Inherit the Wind* (2007), as Henry Drummond. Each performance earned him a Tony nomination, with *Barrymore* winning him his second trophy.

Surprisingly, Hollywood had pretty much taken Plummer for granted where awards were concerned until he captured their fancy as a very lively Leo Tolstoy, engaging in affectionate battle with lover Helen Mirren at the end of his life in *The Last Station* (2009), earning an Oscar nomination in the supporting category. Two years later he delivered a real gem, as a senior citizen who finally decides to come to grips with his homosexuality and make up for lost time, in *Beginners* (2011). Plummer began scooping up every award in the book for this one, the triumph finally capped off by his Academy Award, making him, at eighty-three, the oldest acting winner, ever.

Rather than rest on his laurels, he continued to accept film roles (*The Girl with the Dragon Tattoo*, 2011; *Hector and the Search for Happiness*, 2014; *Elsa & Fred*, 2014; *Danny Collins*, 2015, et al.), and even did a one-man stage show (*A Word or Two*), doing readings of some of his favorite works.

His second marriage, in 1970, to actress Elaine Taylor, was a happy and enduring one. In 2008, he published his memoirs, *In Spite of Myself*, which turned out to be one of the better sellers among celebrity biographies of the day.

Peggy Wood

For Peggy Wood, *The Sound of Music* was something of a "last hurrah." She would never again appear in a motion picture, although she did participate in her share of projects elsewhere. During the long run in theatres for *TSOM*, she could be seen in the taped version of her off-Broadway playlet *Opening Night*, which premiered as an episode of WNET's *New York Theatre Playhouse* (January 24, 1966). In September 1969, she did an extended guest role on a few episodes of the ABC soap *One Life to Live*, playing a doctor.

Otherwise, she stuck to her first love, theatre. Apart from founding the American College Theatre Festival, which selected university plays to present in competition in Washington, D.C., in the spring of 1969; she appeared in *A Madrigal of Shakespeare*, at Lucille Lortel's White Barn Theatre in Norwalk/ Westport, Connecticut, in the summer of 1967; toured with Arthur O'Connell in a production of *I Never Sang for My Father*; joined the cast (which included Blanche Yurka and Jacqueline Susann) of a revival of *The Madwoman of Chaillot* at Sokol Hall in New York in 1970; and in 1973 supported Barry Nelson and Robert

Alda in *Detective Story*, at Playhouse on the Mall in Paramus, NJ, during the run of which her second husband, businessman William Walling, passed away.

Wood served on the board of trustees of the Goodspeed Opera House, received the Straw Hat Achievement Award from the Council of Stock Theatres in 1972, and was presented with a Distinguished Service Award from the American Theatre Association in August 1974. She was living in a retirement home in Stamford, Connecticut, when she died from a cerebral hemorrhage on March 18, 1978 at the age of eighty-six.

Richard Haydn

You would think that after playing it straight in the biggest box office success of the sixties, Hollywood would be interested in tapping into a different side of Richard Haydn. Instead, he appeared in only three more theatrical features, in each one playing variations on his Edwin Carp character, adenoidal ninnies each of them. He was an instructor, around to freak out at the appearance of the title character in *Clarence, the Cross-Eyed Lion* (1965), and a pompous Shakespearean actor out West in Disney's *The Adventures of Bullwhip Griffin* (1967), both intended for young audiences. Most popular was the Mel Brooks comedy *Young Frankenstein* (1974), in which he appeared at the outset to tell Gene Wilder of his family legacy.

Beyond these it was television guest roles, playing a schoolmaster lost in the West on *Laredo* (1966); a very unconvincing Japanese businessman on *Bewitched* (1968); a cockney magician on *Bonanza* (1969); a retired spy on *It Takes a Thief* (1969); a cellist on *McCloud* (1972); and a suspect, a writer, on a pilot that not only didn't sell but sat on the shelf for six years, *The Return of Charlie Chan* (1979). He was last heard doing a reprise of sorts of his Caterpillar from *Alice in Wonderland*, this time as a worm, in a children's special, *The Hugga Bunch*, which was shown the same year he was found dead of a heart attack at his home in Pacific Palisades, California, on April 25, 1985.

Eleanor Parker

Eleanor Parker was fortunate to have the golden glow of *The Sound of Music* to wipe away her two follow-up movie credits. Strictly part of the ensemble, she was a Hollywood talent scout who subjects the moviegoing public to egomaniacal Stephen Boyd in *The Oscar* and was Stuart Whitman's shrewish wife who takes a plunge from their apartment near the start of *An American Dream*. Both were among the trashier 1966 releases. She was still an ensemble player but in better hands in the cop thriller *Warning Shot* (1967), as the boozy widow of a slain doctor. Over in Italy, she tolerated husband Vittorio Gassman's dalliance with Ann-Margret in *The Tiger and the Pussycat* (1967), then took to bed as an invalided, wealthy feline-fancier whose nephew tries to relieve her of her fortune, in *Eye of the Cat* (1969). It was not surprising that she turned at this point to television, taking a role on an NBC series set behind the scenes of a fictional movie studio (20th Century-Fox, actually), *Bracken's World* (1969–70), but she was so unhappy with the experience that she exited before it went into its second season.

Nevertheless, she remained on the small screen for the next decade: for a poorly received musical version of *Hans Brinker* (1969), in this instance being asked to sing, as the skater's mom; *Vanished* (1971), which made the record books as the first two-part television film; two movies with Sally Field: *Maybe I'll Come Home in the Spring* (1971) and *Home for the Holidays* (1972), as her mother and sister, respectively; *The Great American Beauty Contest* (1973), a return to top billing, as a one-time contestant turned coordinator; a failed attempt to turn *Guess Who's Coming to Dinner* into a sitcom (1975), in a variation on Katharine Hepburn's role; and a period mini-series that did well in the ratings, *The Bastard* (1978), as a titled lady refusing to acknowledge Andrew Stevens as her heir.

She ventured into live theatre, replacing Alexis Smith in a production of *Applause* at the State Fair Music Hall in Dallas (1973); *Finishing Touches* (1974), at the Pheasant Run Playhouse in St. Charles, Illinois; and *The Night of the Iguana* (1976), in Los Angeles, in the role Bette Davis had created on Broadway. When the production went to New York, she vacated the part, and the more appropriately cast Sylvia Miles played it. Around this same time she might have made her long-overdue Broadway debut on another project, playing Vera Simpson, in a Circle in the Square revival of *Pal Joey*, but left before opening due to "artistic differences" with the director (she was replaced by Joan Copeland).

Out of the blue, after a ten-year lapse, she showed up, unheralded, in her last theatrical release, *Sunburn* (1979), as the wife of a slain tycoon, and therefore one of the suspects. Returning to television, she was mostly seen in the sort of programs that welcomed a phalanx of old-time guest stars each week, *The Love Boat, Fantasy Island, Hotel, Finder of Lost Loves,* and *Murder, She Wrote.* After playing John Glover's mother in a TNT soap movie, *Dead on the Money* (1991), and still looking quite chic and lovely at sixty-nine, she retired to Palm Springs, where she had made her home for several years.

When she died there of complications of pneumonia on December 9, 2013, there was hardly a newspaper that didn't emphasize Parker having played the baroness in *The Sound of Music*, so major did the film's impact continue to be. "Eleanor Parker was and is one of the most beautiful ladies I have ever known," Christopher Plummer was quoted as saying. "I hardly believe the sad news for I was sure she was enchanted and would live forever."

Charmian Carr

Even though Charmian Carr would rack up all of *two* professional show business credits, she managed to hit the bull's-eye each time. While *The Sound of Music* was circulating and making her one of the most famous newcomers in film, she was selected to appear opposite Anthony Perkins in an episode of the ambitious, one-season anthology series *ABC Stage 67*. The program in question was "Evening

Primrose," and its score was provided by none other than Stephen Sondheim. This quirky and ultimately disturbing story (which originally aired on November 16, 1966) about a group of misfits who escape from the world by hiding out in a Manhattan department store didn't cause much of a stir at the time, but once Sondheim became the most revered Broadway songwriter of the latter half of the twentieth century, *Primrose* rose in status to become one of the most sought-after "cult" items. Carr soloed on "I Remember Sky" and dueted with Perkins on "When" and "Take Me to the World."

Rather than find suitable roles in films and television, Carr's contract with Fox basically used her as a "good-will ambassador," sending her throughout America and eventually around the world to attend premieres of *TSOM*. It hardly mattered as Carr was more interested in marrying and starting a family, wedding a dentist in May 1967 and making the decision to leave show business behind. When she did return to work, it was in the field of interior design, starting her own company, Charmian Carr Designs, and including some of her cinematic "sisters," Heather Menzies and Angela Cartwright, among her clients. Her most noteworthy assignment, however, was helping to design singer Michael Jackson's home in Encino.

Carr published her memoir, *Forever Liesl*, in 2000, and the success of the book led to a follow-up, *Letters to Liesl* (2001).

Nicholas Hammond

Of the seven cinematic Trapp siblings, it was Nicholas Hammond who stayed at the acting profession the longest and had the most successful career. Although he wasn't usually called upon to carry the load, he became the definition of a "working actor," sometimes popping up ever so briefly, in other instances getting parts of size and substance, and for one moment in the spotlight landing a role that gave him elite status in the fantasy/sci-fi world.

His first post-*TSOM* role found him as an ancestor of Winston Churchill, perishing from smallpox, in the *Hallmark Hall of Fame* drama *Soldier in Love* (1967), in support of Jean Simmons. Returning to Broadway (*and* to the very same theatre he'd acted in before, the Ethel Barrymore), he had a minor role as a British soldier stationed in India in *Conduct Unbecoming* (1970; when the play was turned into a movie five years later, Christopher Plummer took one of the leads). At the Mark Taper Forum in Los Angeles he was seen in productions of *Juno and the Paycock* (1974), and, in repertory, *Travesties* (1977), and *The Importance of Being Earnest* (1977). Years down the line (1983), he was back in Los Angeles, this time at the Ahmanson, to play Celeste Holm's devoted fan in a production of Noël Coward's *Hay Fever*.

Bouncing between cinema and television, he was a straitlaced frat boy Barry Primus assumes is gay in *Been Down So Long It Looks Like Up to Me* (1971); Walter Pidgeon's son, who has his eye on fellow passenger Susan Dey, in MGM's disaster melodrama *Skyjacked* (1972); the self-involved football hero who rejects

Maureen McCormick after her nose is injured on an episode of *The Brady Bunch* (1973); one of the thugs tormenting Robert Culp in *Outrage* (1973); a pretentious student, dancing briefly with Susan Blakeley, in a widely-seen mini-series, *Rich Man, Poor Man* (1976); a pompous law student Bob Crane wants his daughter to marry instead of the more down-to-earth Kurt Russell in a Disney flop, *Superdad* (1973); Season Hubley's nemesis in a battle for child custody on ABC's acclaimed series *Family* (1976); Susan Richardson's last-minute Christmas Eve date on *Eight Is Enough* (1977); a "runner" trying to trap Gregory Harrison in the TV spin-off of *Logan's Run* (1977), which gave him a chance to share the screen once again with Trapp "sister" Heather Menzies; a frustrated groom taken hostage by Barry Gordon in the last-aired installment of one of network TV's most notorious failures, *Supertrain* (1979); a waiter pretending to be a banker to impress Hayley Mills on a segment of *The Love Boat* (1980); and an astronaut returning to a fabricated version of his hometown in another heavily publicized mini-series, *The Martian Chronicles* (1980).

He landed his most famous post–*Sound of Music* role when he was chosen to embody comic book hero Peter Parker in CBS's live-action attempt at bringing *The Amazing Spider-Man* to the masses. Although the show ran ever so briefly as a weekly series (April–May 1978) and then as random specials (1978–79), it cultivated enough faithful followers in the sci-fi genre to give Hammond a second signature role.

Getting a chance to flex his muscles with Shakespeare, he was hired to appear in two adaptations made direct for the video market, *Richard II* (1982), as Hotspur, and *The Tempest* (1983), as Ferdinand; then went to Australia for a pair of 1986 mini-series, *Cyclone Tracy*, a multi-character recreation of a real-life disaster, and *The Challenge*, as U.S. yachtsman and America's Cup winner Dennis Conner. These assignments would prove to be life-changing as Hammond was so completely taken with Australia that he decided to move there.

Down Under he was a treacherous Englishman out to sell a member of the royal family to the highest bidder in the time-tripping mini-series *Mirror, Mirror* (1995); the Cunard rep who hires Patrick Dempsey to investigate the destruction of their ships in the remake of *20,000 Leagues Under the Sea* (1997); the U.S. president (a character not seen in the original movie) in a new version of the 1959 end-of-the-world drama *On the Beach* (2000); a time-traveling tourist facing dinosaurs on an episode of *The Lost World* (2000); sported a waxed moustache to play Adolphe Menjou in *Child Star: The Shirley Temple Story* (2001); popped up as a variety of characters on the satirical sketch series *BackBerner* (2000-2); and was TV producer Aaron Spelling (whom he physically resembled about as much as he did Adolphe Menjou) in *Dynasty: The Making of a Guilty Pleasure* (2005).

Behind the scenes he co-wrote (with Steve Vidler) a four-hour mini-series, *A Difficult Woman* (1998), and a TV movie, *Secret Men's Business* (1999), in collaboration with Christopher Lee (*not* the actor). In 1987, he was seen in Alan Ayckborn's *Woman in Mind* with the Sydney Theatre Company. Also for the stage, he and Australian magician James Galea penned *Lying Cheating Bastard*

(2009), which marked Hammond's directorial debut (at the Old Fitzroy Theatre, Woolloomooloo, New South Wales) as well. That same year Hammond acted under Bruce Beresford's direction in *Moonlight and Magnolias* for the Melbourne Theatre Company. Hammond returned to directing in 2010 for a production of *Girl Crazy* at Sydney's Darlinghurst Theatre.

Heather Menzies

Menzies had the distinction of being the only one among the movie's Trapp kids to act again with Julie Andrews; almost immediately at that. While *TSOM* was first circulating in cinemas, she joined the cast of the epic *Hawaii*, in a small role as Andrews's sister, her scenes confined to the New England prologue of the story and not the fiftieth state. Only days after *Hawaii*'s gala premiere in New York, Heather was seen in her sole Broadway credit, the short-lived *We Have Always Lived in the Castle* (1966), as an unbalanced young woman. Taking a big step away from her *TSOM* role, she was a teen doped up on LSD on the premiere of the new *Dragnet* (1967). Not only was she called back by that particular show to play four more entirely different characters, but after this she pretty much became a staple of the guest star circuit. She was a pioneer reluctant to help Michael Landon save his dad on *Bonanza* (1970); a runaway riding the rails on *Alias Smith and Jones* (1971); Bill Daly's pampered sister on *The Bob Newhart Show* (1973); an environmental activist on *The Six Million Dollar Man* (1977); and a doctor in a *Captain America* (1979) pilot. On the TV movie front she was a fellow acting student (with a honeyed southern accent) in a *James Dean* (1976) biopic and a reporter out to get the facts on the late Joe McCarthy in *Tail Gunner Joe* (1977). Amid these she was seen on the big screen in the horror films *Sssssss* (1973), as the daughter of mad scientist Strother Martin, and one that was *supposed* to be tongue in cheek, *Piranha* (1978), as an insurance investigator who discovers that a group of missing teenagers ended up as fish food.

Certainly the most newsworthy events in her life during the seventies had nothing to do with her acting credits. She caused a stir in the press when she went *au naturel* in the August 1973 issue of *Playboy*, in a spread that coyly paid tribute to her most famous role, headlining it "The Tender Trapp." The following year, a commercial for Libby's corned beef hash put her in contact with up-and-coming actor Robert Urich, whom she married in 1975.

Menzies did at last score a starring role on a television series of her own, the adaptation of *Logan's Run* (1977–78), running from annihilation with Gregory Harrison in the twenty-third century, in the part Jenny Agutter had played in the movie. The show lasted a mere fourteen episodes, but one of them, "Judas Goat," gave her the opportunity to reunite with her older Trapp "brother," Nicholas Hammond; while another, "The Collectors," featured younger Trapp "sister" "Brigitta," Angela Cartwright, in the cast.

Her husband shortly afterwards would headline a more popular series, *Vega$*, on which Menzies guested on several occasions, each time as a new character.

Heather joined Urich again on another of his series, *Spenser: For Hire*, and in his failed effort to make the transition to the big screen, *Endangered Species* (1982), although not as Urich's leading lady. On stage they teamed for Neil Simon's *Barefoot in the Park* (1981) at the Kenley Players in Ohio; for a revival of *The Hasty Heart* (1983), which played the Burt Reynolds Dinner Theatre in Florida and the Kennedy Center in Washington; and *Love Letters* (1994), performed in Park City, Utah, near their home in Deer Valley. Apart from this last appearance, a fund-raiser, she quietly allowed her acting career to peter out by the late 1980s.

After Urich's death from cancer in 2002, Menzies founded the Urich Fund for Sarcoma Research at the University of Michigan Comprehensive Cancer Center.

Duane Chase

Staying in "family friendly" entertainment, Chase's immediate follow-up to *TSOM* was a role in Disney's *Follow Me, Boys!* (1966). As a member of Fred MacMurray's first Boy Scout troop, he pretty much blended into the ensemble, his one moment in the spotlight showing him firing a miniature cannon. He also turned up in an episode of *The Big Valley* (1966), where his outburst of violence causes Richard Long's amnesia, and in an early commercial for Pringle's potato chips. When the acting work stopped coming, Chase accepted the fact that his future lay elsewhere. At the University of California in Santa Barbara he studied geology, eventually working at the Geological Survey of Alabama. Shifting his interest to the computer side of things, he ended up in Seattle in the late 1980s, working for Sierra Geophysics Corp., a geological software company.

Angela Cartwright

Shortly after *The Sound of Music* wrapped, Angela Cartwright was back reprising the role that had made her a recognizable television face, Linda Williams on *The Danny Thomas Show*, for a reunion special that aired on Valentine's Day, 1965, only a few weeks before the launch of *TSOM*. Angela soon found herself back on the Fox lot when producer Irwin Allen selected her to play the younger of the two Robinson daughters, Penny, on his sci-fi adventure series *Lost in Space*. This colorful and eventually campy concoction became a children's favorite, ran for three seasons (1965–68), and continued to air in syndication for decades to come, giving Cartwright yet another guaranteed slot at fan conventions for the rest of her life.

Not a week after *Lost in Space* took off (September 15, 1965), she was seen on an episode of *The John Forsythe Show*, playing a student with a genius I.Q. *My Three Sons* invited her to guest on two separate occasions in a three-year span (1965, 1968), in both instances playing different girls on whom cast regular Stanley Livingston develops a crush. While *Lost in Space* was still airing, there was yet another Danny Thomas reunion, this once entitled *Make More Room for Daddy* (November 11, 1967), which paved the way for an official restart. Two seasons after *Space*'s cancellation, Cartwright was again portraying Linda Williams for

Make Room for Granddaddy (1970–71), but nostalgia didn't win over enough viewers, and it lasted a single season.

Back in guest roles, she was a blood donor pinned down by sniper fire on *Adam-12* (1971) and caused a stir as a cheerleader who opted not to wear a bra in *Room 222* (1972). Staying in the world of cheerleading, she was an instructor for the TV movie *High School USA* (1981), which had the gimmick of casting television stars from the past as the adults. Fellow *TSOM* alumnus Heather Menzies welcomed her on the second episode of *Logan's Run* ("The Collectors," September 23, 1977) , as a "runner" who brings the principals to a temporary sanctuary; she was back with her TV mom, Marjorie Lord, for a production of *40 Carats* on the regional theatre circuit (she had also starred in a dinner theatre presentation of *Butterflies Are Free* in 1975); played a surrogate mom on a subplot of *The Love Boat* (1982); reunited with some of the *Lost in Space* team for a week of the game show *Family Feud* (1983); and was roped into the ship salvage sequel *Beyond the Poseidon Adventure* (1979) by her old boss, Irwin Allen, who paired Angela off with Mark Harmon. When a big-budget update of *Lost in Space* was created for the big screen (1998), she and a few other original cast members made cameo appearances.

By the 1980s, she was more interested in a life outside show business and decided to focus on her store, Rubber Boots, which she opened in Toluca Lake, California, in 1977 and ran for over twenty years. Her interest in photography and art resulted in the books *Mixed Emulsions, In This House,* and *In This Garden,* and even spun off into clothing design using her artwork.

Drawn back to the studio where she made her most famous film, Cartwright co-authored *Styling the Stars: Lost Treasures from the Twentieth Century Fox Archive,* with Tom McLaren, in 2014.

Debbie Turner

For Debbie Turner *The Sound of Music* was not only the summit as far as her acting career was concerned but the end of the line. Despite efforts to find other roles, Turner faced a disinterested industry and would never again appear in a movie, or land work on stage or television either. Moving on, she became a skiing enthusiast, winning the West Coast National Championship while in high school. She went on to study photography and real estate at Orange Coast College and then attended the Interior Designer's Guild of Newport Beach and Beverly Hills. She married in 1980 and eventually opened her own floral arrangement business, DTO (Debbie Turner Originals).

Kym Karath

Kym had the right kind of "cute" that Hollywood was looking for in girls her age, so, although she would never again appear on the big screen, there was a good run of television guest roles for the year or so after *The Sound of*

Music premiered. On Fox's *Peyton Place* (1965) she was a disagreeable child taunting series regular Kimberly Beck on the playground; *My Three Sons* (1965) allowed her to interact with Fred MacMurray while he was dressed in a tin robot costume; *Dr. Kildare* (1966) found her as the offspring of a nurse facing a potentially dangerous operation in a special two-part episode; she was traumatized over being separated from her beloved doll on *Lassie* (1966); and was a space princess awakened by Billy Mumy's kiss on *Lost in Space* (1966), a storyline that allowed her no interaction with her *TSOM* co-star, Angela Cartwright.

No doubt having gotten over her own need for a plaything, the older Kym tried to guilt Anissa Jones into giving up *her* doll on *Family Affair* (1971); had very little to do playing one of Judy Norton's classmates on *The Waltons* (1973), which, if nothing else, gave the show a connection to its source material, *Spencer's Mountain*, in which Karath had played one of the children; and was the new girl in school whom Christopher Knight tries to woo in Cyrano de Bergerac fashion on *The Brady Bunch* (1972). She was seen fleetingly as a second-rate cheerleader hexed by school witch Melissa Sue Anderson in the TV movie *Midnight Offerings* (1981), but put her career behind her to raise her son, who had developed brain damage. This ultimately led Karath to create the Aurelia Foundation offering programs for the mentally disabled.

Daniel Truhitte

The same year Truhitte finished shooting his role in *TSOM*, he made the decision to put show business on hold and join the Marines, which meant that there was no chance of fulfilling the seven-year contract he had signed with 20th Century-Fox. In addition to everlasting film fame, he got a wife out of his one movie experience, marrying Charmian Carr's stand-in. Following his release from the service, Truhitte joined Juliette Prowse as a member of her nightclub act and worked extensively in regional theatre, including productions of *Bye Bye Birdie* (in support of Tab Hunter); *No, No, Nanette* (as Tom Trainor; with Ken Berry); and *Once Upon a Mattress* (as the Minstrel; with JoAnne Worley and Henry Gibson). In 1977, he was hired to portray Gene Kelly in the MGM Grand Las Vegas extravaganza *Hallelujah Hollywood*. Remarried, he eventually moved to North Carolina, where he continued his sideline career of teaching voice and twice ended up appearing as Captain von Trapp in productions of *The Sound of Music*, twenty-years apart (1993 and 2003).

Anna Lee

Filmed after her appearance in *The Sound of Music*, but airing two months before it premiered, was yet another assignment in which Anna Lee was found in a wimple, in this instance playing a French nun in a town that has been mined with explosives by Robert Duvall in ABC's *Combat!* (1965).

By this point in her career, Lee was working but hardly wealthy and took employment where she could find it, be it on Listerine mouthwash commercials or toiling as a saleslady at David Orgell's silver shop in Beverly Hills. Doing what she was *supposed* to be doing, she was seen as a lonely widow who captures Fred MacMurray's fancy on *My Three Sons* (1966), an episode that happened to feature *TSOM*'s Herr Zeller, Ben Wright; a missionary in her final role for dear friend John Ford in his last feature, *7 Women* (1966); one of the women planning world domination via brainwashing hairdryers in the loopy spy spoof *In Like Flint* (1967); Sebastian Cabot's former flame on *Family Affair* (1967); Sheriff Ralph Bellamy's loyal wife on *Gunsmoke* (1967); a dinner party hostess shocked by Julie Andrews's vulgar manners in Robert Wise's *Star!* (1968), seen so briefly that she wasn't even given billing; Tommy Kirk's protective mom on *The Streets of San Francisco* (1973); and FDR's cousin Laura Delano, her personal favorite of all her television roles, in two movies: *Eleanor and Franklin* (1976) and *Eleanor and Franklin: The White House Years* (1977). During this period she married for a third time (John Ford gave her away at the ceremony), to Robert Nathan, author of *Portrait of Jennie* and *The Bishop's Wife* (she was Nathan's seventh wife!). They remained happily wed until he passed away in 1985.

Just when she was about to consider retirement, she was invited to portray the gentle, albeit somewhat scatterbrained family matriarch Lila Quatermain on a daytime serial, *General Hospital*, in 1978. The show soon became the most watched of all programs of this genre, and Lee had herself a steady job for the next twenty-five years. Due to back trouble caused by a car accident, as well as a past horse riding incident, she developed acute osteoarthritis of the hips and knees, which took its toll on her physical state, requiring her to play Lila from a wheelchair. When the producers of *GH* decided to develop a spin-off, *Port Charles*, in 1997, this allowed Lee to segue between two series.

She ceased playing the part the year before she died of pneumonia at the age of ninety-one at her Beverly Hills Home on May 14, 2004, only a few weeks before she was scheduled to receive a Lifetime Achievement Award from the Daytime Emmy Awards.

Portia Nelson

Following her "habit wearing" turns in both *The Trouble with Angels* (1966), as an uptight art teacher, and on an episode of *The Big Valley* (1967), lending "sisterly" advice to Ellen Burstyn, fans got to see Portia Nelson in somewhat less pious roles, although she was, in fact, around to express moral disapproval toward the Hardy Boys in a failed pilot, *The Mystery of the Chinese Junk* (1967), as their spinster aunt, and *Doctor Dolittle* (1967), as Rex Harrison's embarrassed, spinster sister. Her subsequent acting roles, however, were sporadic. She was driven to a heart attack by the demonic twins in the horror movie *The Other* (1972), was suspected of being a witch in the *ABC Weekend Special* "The Ghost of Thomas Kempe," and was seen fleetingly as a beleaguered receptionist in the Village

People musical *Can't Stop the Music* (1980). Starting in the 1980s, she made a handful of appearances on the daytime serial *All My Children*, as a nanny.

On Dunhill Records, she recorded *Piccadilly Pickle* (1968), billed as "Lady Nelson & the Lords," but restricting her contribution to playing the organ. The following year she was a producer and writer for a Debbie Reynolds special, *The Sound of Children*, composing the song "Make a Rainbow," which would later be sung at President Bill Clinton's inauguration by Marilyn Horne. She joined the cast of the Stephen Schwartz musical *The Baker's Wife* (1976), again playing a spinster, but the show closed before it reached Broadway.

It was in the New York cabaret world that she was most revered, however, and she became a staple of the scene, singing at such venues as Ted Hook's On Stage and Freddy's Supper Club. In 1996, she released a recording, *This Life*, that featured both solos as well as duets with other cabaret artists.

One of her most lasting contributions came neither through singing nor acting. In 1977, she published a book of writings, *There's a Hole in My Sidewalk: The Romance of Self-Discovery*, which featured a poem, "Autobiography in Five Short Chapters," which took on an inspirational life of its own, referred to by 12-step groups and therapists.

She died of cancer on March 6, 2001 at her Manhattan home, at the age of eighty.

Ben Wright

Ben Wright was the only *TSOM* cast principal to also show up in director Robert Wise's follow-up film, *The Sand Pebbles*. He appeared early in the lengthy tale as an English passenger arguing Chinese politics with missionary Larry Gates aboard a steamer. Oddly, despite his prominence in *TSOM* and having an adequate share of dialogue in *Pebbles*, he did not even rate billing up front or in the end credits.

And so continued a very busy career of supporting roles of varying sizes and no certainty of whether the part would rate any mention. He was a KAOS agent infiltrating a spy school on *Get Smart* (1965); a pub owner running bets in the theatrical spin-off *Munster, Go Home!* (1966); another nasty Nazi, this one hoping to trade prisoners, on an episode of *The Rat Patrol* (1966); one of the specialists testing to see if Jack Lemmon is faking his back injury in *The Fortune Cookie* (1966); a British colonel trying to seize the emperor's throne in an installment of *The Wild, Wild West* (1966); the voice of Mowgli's adopted "father" in Disney's *The Jungle Book* (1967); various Nazis on different episodes of *Hogan's Heroes* (1967–70); a French general in Hitchcock's *Topaz* (1969); the caretaker who ends up burying most of the cast in the black comedy *Arnold* (1973); a coast guard who comes to Desi Arnaz Jr.'s rescue in *The Voyage of the Yes* (1973); an art forger on *Ellery Queen* (1976); and the voice of Prince Eric's valet in Disney's *The Little Mermaid* (1989). The last was released after his death of complications of heart bypass surgery, on July 2, 1989 in Burbank, California.

Norma Varden

Varden would show up in another costly 20th Century-Fox roadshow musical later in the decade, *Doctor Dolittle* (1967), sharing the screen at one point with another *TSOM* alumnus, Portia Nelson. Her big comical moment had her freaking out when her hat is overrun with mice. She was also Dick Shawn's mama in *A Very Special Favor* (1966), served on the college school board in the generation-gap comedy *The Impossible Years* (1968), and showed up as a snooty member of Mrs. Drysdale's bridge club on an episode of *The Beverly Hillbillies* (1969). A few years later she officially retired from acting and settled down in Santa Barbara, where she passed away of heart failure on January 19, 1989, at the age of ninety.

Marni Nixon

Thanks to extensive publicity about who was *really* doing the singing in *My Fair Lady*, Marni Nixon was a voice everyone suddenly wanted to hire. It certainly didn't hurt having contributed not only to that movie but to three other beloved musicals (*The King and I, West Side Story,* and *The Sound of Music*). In the same year of *TSOM*'s release, she was soloist for three New York Philharmonic concerts; performed in nightclub engagements (where her set included a version of her then-husband Ernest Gold's *Theme from "Exodus"*); sang in Israel with the Haifa Symphony Orchestra; and had the lead in a musical, *The Genius Farm*, which never made it to Broadway after an unsuccessful out-of-town tryout. Liberace engaged her to be part of his act, and the two appeared together on an episode of *Hollywood Palace* (1966), with Nixon performing songs from *My Fair Lady*. (Later she joined Victor Borge as part of *his* act.) She was the voice of the magical harp in Gene Kelly's part live–part animated version of *Jack and the Beanstalk* (1967) and by this point had added "The Sound of Music" to her nightclub repertoire.

She sang *Mignon* with the San Francisco Opera (1966); starred in *Lady in the Dark* for Pasadena Playhouse (1967); was heard on an LP of Charles Ives's music on Nonesuch Records (1967); was considered enough of a "name" that she got to present the Musical Score award (with Henry Mancini) on the 1968 Academy Awards, where she was introduced as "the voice of the stars" and *sang* the nominees; was introduced under her married name, "Marni Gold," on an episode of *The Mothers-in-Law* (1969), which included *TSOM*'s touring company Captain von Trapp, John Myhers, in the cast; was part of the company of *Musical Theatre Cavalcade* for the LA Civic Light Opera Company (1970); and became Director of Voice at the California Institute of the Arts in 1970.

Moving to the Seattle area, she sang for their opera company and hosted her own children's show, *Boomerang*, which brought her a local Emmy in 1976. At Seattle's Palace Theatre, she appeared opposite Ron Husmann in *I Do! I Do!*, and, for the Spokane Opera House, was allowed to move up from supporting nun to the lead in their production of *The Sound of Music* (1978). Returning to

New York, she acted off-Broadway at the Entermedia Theatre in a musical, *Taking My Turn* (1983), which had a successful enough run (345 performances) that it was taped for PBS and shown in 1985. Nixon earned a Drama Desk nomination for her performance. She was back in New York in 1992 for *Opal* and then a long-overdue return to Broadway for a musical interpretation of *James Joyce's The Dead* (2000), where one of her co-stars was another lady who had strummed a guitar playing Maria von Trapp on stage, Sally Ann Howes. She also joined the casts of the Broadway revivals of *Follies* (2001; singing "One More Kiss") and *Nine* (2003; as Guido's mother).

Never too far from her hallowed earlier works, she was the Mother Abbess to Christine Andreas's Maria in the Muny opera production of *The Sound of Music* (1993); returned to the part opposite Melissa Erico at the Hollywood Bowl for three performances in July 2006; and then had the non-singing role of Higgins's mother in a 2007 NY Philharmonic concert staging and a 2008 national tour of *My Fair Lady* (2008; replacing Sally Ann Howes). Between these she put together a cabaret celebrating her contributions to the musical genre, *Marni Nixon—The Voice of Hollywood*; played Frau Schneider in the Barrington Stage production of *Cabaret* (1997); was finally seen on movie screens again, as Lauren Velez's straight-talking aunt in an independent feature, *I Think I Do* (1997); sang "Honor to Us All" in a Disney cartoon, *Mulan*, as the title heroine's mother (1998); and was a dog-loving neighbor of the murder victim on an episode of *Law & Order: Special Victims Unit* (2001), a rare instance of Nixon being hired expressly for her acting. In 2012, she was back at the Hollywood Bowl to reprise the Mother Abbess.

Her autobiography, *I Could Have Sung All Night: My Story* (written with Stephen Cole), was published by Billboard Books in 2006. In 2011, she received the George Peabody Medal for Outstanding Contributions to Music in America.

BIBLIOGRAPHY

Anderson, William. *The World of the Trapp Family: The Life Story of the Legendary Family That Inspired "The Sound of Music."* Davidson, MI: Anderson Publications, 1998.

Barthel, Joan, "Biggest Money-Making Movie of All Time—How Come?," *New York Times Magazine*, November 20, 1966.

_____, "The Sweet Smell of Ernie's Success," *New York Times*, November 24, 1968.

Bronson, Fred. *The Sound of Music Family Scrapbook*. Montclair, NJ: Applause Books, 2012.

Cahill, Tim, "Poppins Picks Up the Pieces," *New York Daily News*, August 21, 1977.

Canby, Vincent, *"Sound of Music"* to Leave Rivoli," *New York Times*, October 19, 1966.

_____, *"Sound of Music"* Flat in Germany," *New York Times*, April 7, 1967.

_____,

"Sound of Profits Resounds at Fox," *New York Times*, May 17, 1967.

Chaplin, Saul. *The Golden Age of the Hollywood Musical and Me*. Norman: University of Oklahoma Press, 1994.

Charmian, Carr, with Jean A. S. Strauss. *Forever Liesl: A Memoir of The Sound of Music*. New York: Viking, 2000.

_____. *Letters to Liesl*. New York: Arete Publishing, 2001.

Crist, Judith, "This Week's Movies," *TV Guide*, February 28, 1976.

Hirsch, Julia. *The Sound of Music: The Making of America's Favorite Movie*. New York: McGraw-Hill, 1993.

Itzkowitz, Jay, "The Swine of Music," *Muppet Magazine*, Winter 1985.

Jankiewivz, Pat, "Her Favorite Things," *Starlog*, May 2005.

Lane, Anthony, "The Maria Problem—Going Wild for *The Sound of Music*," *New Yorker*, February 14, 2000.

Lane, Harriet, "Ray, A Drop of Golden Nun," *Observer*, October 3, 1999.

Lee, Anna. *Anna Lee: Memoirs of a Career on General Hospital and in Film*. Jefferson, NC: McFarland, 2007.

Leemann, Sergio. *Robert Wise on His Films: From Editing Room to Director's Chair*. Los Angeles: Silman-James Press, 1995.

Ley, Alan, "Where 'Music' Sounded," *New York Times*, June 1, 1975.

Lindsay, Howard, and Crouse, Russel. *The Sound of Music.* New York: Random House, 1960.

Mackin, Tom, "How to Sell a TV Musical," *Newark Sunday News,* November 2, 1969.

Maslon, Laurence. *The Sound of Music Companion.* New York: Fireside Books, 2007.

McClelland, Douglas, "Eleanor Parker," *Films in Review,* March 1962.

Motion Picture Exhibitor January 1965–December 1965.

Motion Picture Herald, January 1965–December 1967.

Nixon, Marni, with Stephen Cole. *I Could Have Sung All Night: My Story.* New York: Billboard Books, 2006.

Plummer, Chistopher. *In Spite of Myself: A Memoir.* Toronto/New York: Alfred A. Knopf. 2008.

Rodgers, Richard, "Sounds of (Movie) Music," *New York World Telegraph & Sun,* March 13, 1965.

TV Guide, "She Has Plenty of Reason to Sing," July 29, 1955

Variety, "Cutting of 20th's *Sound of Music* to Appease Neo-Nazis Costs Wolf His Job," June 22, 1966.

————, *"Sound of Music" Track,* February 24, 1965.

————, "'*Music*' Nears Recouping Negative Cost as U.S.-Canada Rentals Hit $7,500,000," August 11, 1965.

————. "*Sound of Music* May Top 'Wind' as All-Time Grosser," September 21, 1966.

————. "'*Sound of Music*' to BBC," June 14, 1978.

Von Trapp, Agathe. *Memories Before and After The Sound of Music.* Maryland: PublishAmerica, 2004.

Von Trapp, Maria. *Story of the Trapp Family Singers, The.* Philadelphia: Lippincott, 1949.

————. *Maria.* Carol Stream, IL: Creation House, 1972.

————. "*The Sound of Music,*" *TV Guide,* February 28, 1976.

Walter, Danton, "Broadway," *Daily News,* April 2, 1959.

Wilk, Max. *The Making of "The Sound of Music."* New York: Routledge/Taylor & Frances Group, 2007.

Index